Reforming The World Trading System

Legitimacy, Efficiency, and Democratic Governance

Edited by

ERNST-ULRICH PETERSMANN

With the assistance of

JAMES HARRISON

OXFORD

UNIVERSITY PRESS

OXFORD

UNIVERSITY PRESS

Great Clarendon Street, Oxford OX2 6DP

Oxford University Press is a department of the University of Oxford.
It furthers the University's objective of excellence in research, scholarship,
and education by publishing worldwide in

Oxford New York

Auckland Cape Town Dar es Salaam Hong Kong Karachi
Kuala Lumpur Madrid Melbourne Mexico City Nairobi
New Delhi Shanghai Taipei Toronto

With offices in

Argentina Austria Brazil Chile Czech Republic France Greece
Guatemala Hungary Italy Japan Poland Portugal Singapore
South Korea Switzerland Thailand Turkey Ukraine Vietnam

Oxford is a registered trade mark of Oxford University Press
in the UK and in certain other countries

Published in the United States
by Oxford University Press Inc., New York

© E.-U. Petersmann, 2005

British Library Cataloguing in Publication Data

Data available

Library of Congress Cataloging in Publication Data

Data available

Typeset by Newgen Imaging Systems (P) Ltd., Chennai, India
Printed in Great Britain
on acid-free paper by
Biddles Ltd., King's Lynn

ISBN 0–19–928262–5 (hbk.)
ISBN 0–19–928263–3 (pbk.)

1 3 5 7 9 10 8 6 4 2

General Editor's Preface

The Oxford University Press series of books on International Economic Law is once again honoured to present a distinguished work in the general subject-matter indicated. The goal of this OUP series is to present works that probe deeply problems inherent in the 'globalized' and 'interdependent' world in which we now live. As General Editor, I am delighted to introduce the latest volume in the International Economic Law Series, a volume of essays about reforming the world trading system, resulting from three exceedingly interesting international conferences organized at the European University Institute in Florence, under the direction of Professor Ernst-Ulrich Petersmann. This book is a second book in this OUP series deriving from the interesting activity of the European University Institute in relation to transatlantic and international law institutions. The previous book, *Trans-Atlantic Economic Disputes*, also resulting from a series of conferences, was published in 2003.

This book takes a somewhat different approach, examining some of the defects and needs for reform in the current world trading system, which focuses on the World Trade Organization (WTO). The subtitle of the book—*Legitimacy, Efficiency, and Democratic Governance*—is very descriptive of the intent of the author and director, Professor Petersmann, and his view of the endeavour. An examination of the book reveals that it is one of the most thorough and probing scholarly works on the subject, based on scholarship from major practitioners and officials that have been deeply engaged in WTO negotiating and other activity. The book could not be more timely, since the subject-matter is under intense discussion, both in international institutions and in academia. Indeed, some of this discussion in the WTO context has resulted in the appointment by the WTO Director-General of a 'Consultative Board', which has been charged with reporting to the Director-General, and through him, to the Membership, about important institutional problems of the WTO, and what might be some of the options for reform.

This book probes virtually all of the important reform needs, including substantive subjects (e.g. agriculture and services) of international trade norm directions of the Doha Round of negotiation which is currently ongoing. This volume also examines some important institutional questions, such as the 'political legitimacy' of the WTO system, with references to subjects such as parliamentary oversight, transparency, and decision-making procedures (including consensus norms). In addition, this volume looks particularly at the degree to which the system protects consumer welfare, and how that goal of the system could be evaluated.

This book is an outstanding contribution both to the general theoretical literature regarding International Economic Law, and also to the very current practical policy debates that will continue over the next several years, some of it in the context of the major ongoing negotiating round. It is my pleasure again to welcome this book that will enhance public and expert understanding of these complex topics.

JOHN H. JACKSON[1]

[1] *University Professor of Law*, Georgetown University Law Center (GULC), Washington, DC; *Director*, Institute of International Economic Law, GULC; *General Editor*, International Economic Law Series, Oxford University Press; *Editor in Chief*, *Journal of International Economic Law*, Oxford University Press.

Foreword

In the three years since the launch of the Doha Development Round (DDA) we have observed many ups and downs in the World Trade Organization (WTO) negotiating process. On the downside there was obviously the collective failure of the 5th Ministerial Conference in Cancún. On the upside was the collective success of the July package agreed last summer in Geneva.

WTO negotiators have drawn lessons from those ups and downs. The conferences in Florence were more than a meeting place of leading academics and trade negotiators. They offered a unique opportunity to analyse in a somewhat more detached way both the process and the content of the negotiations. The discussions were refreshing and stimulating and very much to the point as well. They certainly have contributed, as far as the trade negotiators are concerned, to a better understanding of the complexities of the negotiations and the conflicting concerns of the various stakeholders. This cross-fertilization of academic knowledge, diplomatic wisdom, and practical experience on the ground was a positive one and on behalf of my WTO colleagues I wish to express our gratitude to the organizers for offering us this opportunity.

Much has been said and written on the reasons why the Cancún Conference broke down. It has also inspired more thorough reflections on the functioning of the WTO, its legitimacy, and its efficiency.

In my Foreword to last year's conference report I concluded that 'one of the lessons of Cancún is that the present organization of the WTO is not sufficiently equipped to meet the new challenges and pressures that the multilateral trading system now faces'. I stand by that conclusion whilst acknowledging that even in the present system progress can be achieved. Last summer's July package is the very proof of it.

The simple answer to what went wrong in Cancún is that the Membership at large was not sufficiently prepared. That was particularly the case for a large number of developing countries. But there are also a number of lessons to be drawn from Cancún.

The first one is that, while European Union (EU)/United States (US) leadership remains indispensable, it is by no means sufficient any more. The second one is the increasing need for well-defined negotiating objectives for a large group of developing countries. The third one is that enormous Ministerial Conferences—even better-prepared and managed ones than was the case in Cancún—are not conducive to effective decision-making in the WTO.

Developments since Cancún have demonstrated the EU/US leadership can still make the difference, provided it is part of a wider process. It has to embrace such developing countries' representatives as Brazil and India as was the case in the run-up to the July package (with the so-called Five Interested Parties (FIP) process in agriculture). It has to reach out to others too, including the weaker and more vulnerable developing countries and least-developed countries (LDCs).

Since Cancún new alliances have emerged in which developing countries have actively participated. This is by all means a positive development. These alliances include groupings among developing countries and groupings that transcend the notional developed/developing country divide. Regional groups (e.g. Africa) and interest groupings cooperating across all issues of the agenda (e.g. the African, Caribbean, Pacific group (ACP), LDC, G90), as well as subject-specific groupings (e.g. G20 and G33 in agriculture) have made an active and constructive contribution to the negotiating process. Developing countries have also collaborated with developed ones on issues of common interest such as agriculture (G10) and geographical indications.

What emerged as well after Cancún is that active ministerial involvement can also be organized in the context of General Council meetings in Geneva without the full panoply of a set-piece Ministerial and, let it also be said, without the same media attention or temptation for WTO Members to play to the broadcasting gallery. Much depends on the inclusiveness of the process, on outreach and reporting back to groups, and the personal involvement of Ministers.

It is no secret that the personal involvement of such personalities as Messrs Lamy, Fischler, Zoellick, Amorim, Nath, and others made all the difference to the successful conclusion of the July package.

We have to build on all these experiences in the run-up to the 6th Ministerial Conference in Hong Kong in December 2005. We may also build on the Sutherland Report on the functioning of the WTO, which is due to come out early in 2005 and may well provide a lot of important food for thought as the WTO marks its 10th birthday.

The July Framework Agreement puts the DDA back on track. It gives a clear signal that the multilateral trading system—after a period of doubt—can still deliver on the needs of all its members, in particular of developing countries. We could not have afforded yet another failure. The July package sets out the parameters for further negotiations in five key areas—agriculture, market access for non-agricultural products, trade facilitation, development, and services—and sets a date for the 6th Ministerial Conference in Hong Kong, which now becomes the next important staging-post in the negotiations. With the July package we now have reasonable prospects for concluding the DDA no later than 2006. This obviously implies comprehensive progress across all areas under negotiation within the Single Undertaking. The framework on agriculture was the most detailed part of the July package and the most heavily negotiated in the preceding discussions. In the run-up to Hong Kong, we need to catch up on the non-agricultural issues: non-agricultural market access, services, and trade facilitation. But work must also intensify in areas not covered in detail by the July package such as rules (anti-dumping, subsidies, regional trade agreements (RTAs)), geographical indications, Trade-Related Aspects of Intellectual Property Rights (TRIPS), and the environment.

The development dimension continues to run like a red thread through all aspects of the negotiations, both in market access and rules related areas. There is, however, a growing recognition that one size does not fit all developing countries and that the more advanced developing countries should take on their share of responsibilities in the world trading system, particularly as far as South–South trade is concerned.

While we have a solid negotiating basis, many hard decisions remain to be taken, both in agriculture and elsewhere. Hong Kong is just around the corner and we cannot expect the circumstances that led to the success at the end of July to repeat themselves automatically.

Concluding the Round will still require strong commitment and hard work. The 'heavy lifting' starts now.

Carlo Trojan
Ambassador, Permanent Representative of the
European Commission to the World Trade Organization

Acknowledgements

The editor acknowledges with gratitude the financial support of the BP Chair in Transatlantic Relations which was established, thanks to a generous grant by BP, in the Robert Schuman Centre for Advanced Studies of the European University Institute at Florence in September 2001, and made possible the organization of the three international conferences out of which this book grew. The editor also expresses his appreciation to his doctoral student James Harrison for his assistance in the preparation of this volume and in the organization of the conferences on *Preparing the Doha Development Round: WTO Negotiators Meet the Academics* at the European University Institute in 2003 and 2004.

Contents

Notes on Contributors

Abbott, Frederick M.	Edward Ball Eminent Scholar Professor of International Law, Florida State University College of Law.
Bacchus, James	Professor of Law, Vanderbilt University Law School; former Member and Chairman of the Appellate Body of the World Trade Organization; former member of the US Congress; former Special Assistant to the US Trade Representative.
Blackhurst, Richard	Adjunct Professor, The Fletcher School, Tufts University, and former Editor of the *World Trade Review* (2001–04) .
Bora, Bijit	Counsellor in the Economic Research and Statistics Division, World Trade Organization, Geneva.
Charnovitz, Steve	Associate Professor, George Washington University Law School.
Dam, Kenneth W.	Max Pam Professor Emeritus of American and Foreign Law and Senior Lecturer, The University of Chicago; Senior Fellow, The Brookings Institution.
Ehlermann, Claus-Dieter	Senior Counsel with Wilmer, Cutler, Pickering; former Member, and in 2001 Chairman, of the Appellate Body of the World Trade Organization; former Director-General of Competition and of the Legal Service at the European Commission.
Ehring, Lothar	Directorate-General for Trade of the European Commission, formerly with the Legal Affairs Division of the World Trade Organization Secretariat and the Appellate Body Secretariat.
Graham, Edward M.	Senior Fellow, Institute for International Economics, Washington, DC.
Harbinson, Stuart	Director, Office of the Director-General of the World Trade Organization; former Permanent Representative of Hong Kong, China to the WTO.

Hartridge, David	Senior Director of White & Case (Geneva), Geneva; former director in the World Trade Organization.
Hilf, Meinhard	Professor of Law, University of Hamburg.
Hoekman, Bernard	World Bank, Groupe d'Economie Mondiale, Sciences Po and Centre for Economic Policy Research, London.
Ismail, Faizel	Head of the South African Delegation to the World Trade Organization; formerly Head of South Africa's trade negotiations with the European Union, the Southern African Development Community, the Southern African Customs Union, and with other trading partners.
Lacarte, Julio A.	Former Chairman of the World Trade Organization Appellate Body and Ambassador of Uruguay to the WTO.
Mann, Erika	Member of the European Parliament.
Mavroidis, Petros C.	Edwin B. Parker Professor of Foreign and Comparative Law at Columbia Law School, New York; Professor of Law at the University of Neuchâtel, Switzerland and Centre for Economic Policy Research, London.
Messerlin, Patrick A.	Professor of Economics, Institut d'Études Politiques, Paris.
Odell, John S.	Professor, School of International Relations, University of Southern California.
Petersmann, Ernst-Ulrich	Joint Chair Professor of Public Law and Policy, Robert Schuman Centre for Advanced Studies and European University Institute, Florence; former legal advisor in the General Agreement on Tariffs and Trade and the World Trade Organization.
Sampson, Gary P.	Senior Counsellor, World Trade Organization; Professor of International Economic Relations, Institute of Advanced Studies, United Nations University, Tokyo.

Shaffer, Gregory	Professor, University of Wisconsin Law School; Director, University of Wisconsin European Union Center; Co-Director and Senior Fellow, University of Wisconsin Center on World Affairs and the Global Economy.
Skaggs, David E.	Executive Director, Center for Democracy and Citizenship, Council for Excellence in Government, Washington, DC; Counsel, Hogan & Hartson LLP, Washington, DC; former US Congressman.
Souty, François	Counsel for Multilateral Affairs, Conseil de la Concurrence, Paris; Associate Professor, University of La Rochelle, France; Organisation for Economic Co-operation and Development countries coordinator at the United Nations Conference on Trade and Development Intergovernmental Group of Experts IGE on Competition Law and Policy.
Sutherland, Peter	Chairman of BP; former Director-General of the General Agreement on Tariffs and Trade and the World Trade Organization; former European Union Commissioner.
Tangermann, Stefan	Director for Food, Agriculture and Fisheries, Organization for Economic Co-operation and Development, Paris; formerly Professor of Economics, University of Göttingen, Germany.
Trachtman, Joel P.	Professor of International Law, The Fletcher School of Law and Diplomacy, Massachusetts.
Trojan, Carlo	Ambassador, Head of European Commission Delegation to the World Trade Organization, Geneva.
VanDuzer, J. Anthony	Associate Professor at the University of Ottawa, Faculty of Law; Adjunct Research Professor at Carleton University's Norman Paterson School of International Affairs, Ottawa, Canada.
Winters, L. Alan	Director, Development Research Group, The World Bank; formerly Professor of Economics, University of Sussex.

List of Abbreviations

AB	Appellate Body
AGP	Agreement on Government Procurement
AoA	Agreement on Agriculture
ACP	African, Caribbean, Pacific Group
AMS	Aggregate Measurement of Support
ASCM	Agreement on Subsidies and Countervailing Measures
ASEAN	Association of Southeast Asian Nations
BISD	Basic Instruments and Selected Documents
BIT	bilateral investment treaty
CAP	Common Agricultural Policy
CBD	Convention on Biological Diversity
CG.18	Consultative Group of Eighteen
CITES	Convention on International Trade in Endangered Species of Wild Fauna and Flora
COG	Congressional Oversight Group
CTD	Committee on Trade and Development
CTE	Committee on Trade and Environment
CTS	Council for Trade in Services
DDA	Doha Development Agenda
DSB	Dispute Settlement Body
DSU	Dispute Settlement Understanding
EC	European Community
ECJ	European Court of Justice
ECHR	European Convention on Human Rights
EEA	European Economic Area
ESM	emergency safeguard measure
EU	European Union
EUI	European University Institute
FAO	Food and Agriculture Organization
FDI	foreign direct investment
FSC	Foreign Sales Corporations
FTA	free trade agreement
GATS	General Agreement on Trade in Services
GATT	General Agreement on Tariffs and Trade
GC	General Council
GDP	gross domestic product
GG	*Grundgesetz*
GMO	genetically modified organism

GSP	General System of Preferences
ICCPR	International Covenant for Civil and Political Rights
ICESCR	UN Covenant on Economic, Social and Cultural Human Rights
ICPO	International Competition Policy Office
IFF	International Finance Facility
ILO	International Labour Organization
IMF	International Monetary Fund
IPR	intellectual property right
IPU	Inter-Parliamentary Union
ITC	International Trade Centre
ITO	International Trade Organization
JITAP	Joint Integrated Technical Assistance Programme
LDC	least developed country
MAI	Multilateral Agreement on Investment
MEA	Multilateral Environmental Agreement
MFA	Multi-Fibre Arrangement
MFI	Multilateral Framework on Investments
MFN	most favoured nation
MTO	Multilateral Trade Organization
NAFTA	North American Free Trade Agreement
NAMA	non-agricultural market access
NATO	North Atlantic Treaty Organization
NG5	non-group of five
NGO	non-governmental organization
N/I	nullification/impairment
NT	national treatment
NTTB	non-tariff trade barrier
OAS	Organization of American States
OAU	Organization of African Unity
ODA	official development assistance
OECD	Organisation for Economic Co-operation and Development
PRSP	Poverty Reduction Strategy Paper
PSE	Producer Support Estimate
RTA	regional trade agreement
SDT	Special and Differential Treatment
SNT	single negotiating text
SPS	Sanitary and Phytosanitary Standards
TBT	technical barriers to trade
TEU	Treaty on European Union
TPA	Trade Promotion Authority
TNC	Trade Negotiations Committee
TRIMS	Trade-Related Investment Measures
TRIPS	Trade-Related Aspects of Intellectual Property Rights

UDHR	Universal Declaration of Human Rights
UK	United Kingdom
UN	United Nations
UNCTAD	United Nations Conference on Trade and Development
UNDP	United Nations Development Programme
UNEP	United Nations Environment Programme
UNCESCR	UN Committee on Economic, Social and Cultural Human Rights
UNESCO	United Nations Educational, Scientific and Cultural Organization
UNHCHR	United Nations High Commissioner for Human Rights
US	United States
USTR	United States Trade Representative
VER	voluntary export restraint
WGTCP	Working Group on the Interaction between Trade and Competition Policy
WHO	World Health Organization
WIPO	World Intellectual Property Organization
WTO	World Trade Organization

PART I

INTRODUCTION AND SUMMARY OF THE BOOK

WTO Negotiators and Academics Analyse the Doha Development Round of the WTO: Overview and Summary of the Book

ERNST-ULRICH PETERSMANN

Justice is the end of government.
It is the end of civil society.
It ever has been and will be pursued
until it is obtained, or until liberty be lost in the pursuit.

James Madison, *The Federalist* (51)

This book is the result of three international conferences on *Preparing the Doha Development Round: WTO Negotiators Meet the Academics* which I had the pleasure to convene, in my role as academic director of the Transatlantic Programme of the Robert Schuman Centre for Advanced Studies, at the European University Institute (EUI) in Florence, Italy. In each of these conferences, leading academics presented papers on the various subjects of the Doha Development Round of the World Trade Organization (WTO), and WTO negotiators commented on these reports, entailing stimulating discussions among WTO ambassadors, other practitioners from developed and less-developed WTO member countries, economists, political scientists, and legal academics.

The world trading system has promoted half a century of historically unprecedented economic growth and welfare in the majority of the 148 WTO member countries. Even though all economics has become global, politics remains local. The democratic legitimacy, economic efficiency, and social justice of WTO rules and WTO negotiations are increasingly challenged by national parliaments and civil society. For example, the Doha Round negotiations—like the preceding Uruguay Round negotiations—are criticized for being too much driven by powerful producer lobbies, and for neglecting general citizen interests (e.g. consumer welfare), including the basic needs of the more than 1 billion poor people in less-developed countries living on 1 dollar per day or less. The numerous questions raised by the ongoing Doha Round negotiations call for answers that may be best found through transparent, interdisciplinary discussions among practitioners, academics, and civil society representatives from rich and poor, industrialized and less-developed countries. Florence, which had already flourished as a city republic during the Renaissance thanks to its trade in goods and services (such as art and financial services) until—in the words of Dante—'all the cities of Italy became full of tyrants',[1] and the cosmopolitan European University Institute located in monasteries and Renaissance villas in the hills overlooking Florence, offered an attractive venue for convening such discussions on the future of the world trading system.

I. WTO NEGOTIATORS MEET ACADEMICS: PREPARING THE DOHA ROUND OF WORLDWIDE TRADE NEGOTIATIONS

Notwithstanding their high level of expertise for each of the more than 20 subjects of the Doha Round, the conference participants at Florence shared the view that academic knowledge and diplomatic wisdom are not enough to secure a successful conclusion of the negotiations if, as warned by James Madison, 'liberty and justice' are lost in the pursuit—as appeared to have happened at the WTO Ministerial Conference at Cancún, Mexico, in September 2003. Freedom of trade and non-discriminatory conditions of competition for producers, investors, traders, and consumers, with due respect for the regulatory powers of each WTO Member to correct market failures and supply public goods, remain the primary objective of the WTO Agreement. This WTO objective of protecting liberty across discriminatory, welfare-reducing border barriers fits well with the 'first principle of justice' proposed by modern theories of justice, according to which rational citizens would give priority to maximum equal freedom, protected by rule-of-law and effective judicial remedies.[2] Yet, even though the necessary 'secondary principles of justice'—such as 'social justice' and empowerment of poor people by means of satisfaction of their basic needs and fulfilment of their human rights—are reflected in the WTO objective of 'sustainable development' as well as in the Doha Round objective of a 'Development Round', WTO negotiators—and also most academics—fail to agree on how the intergovernmental structures of WTO law and policies can be

---

[1] Dante Alighieri, 'Purgatorio' in *La Commedia* (G. Petrocchi ed.) (1967) at 100 ('Ché le città d'Italia tutte piene son di tiranni').

[2] Cf. E. U. Petersmann, 'Theories of Justice, Human Rights and the Constitution of International Markets' in Symposium: The Emerging Transnational Constitution, *Loyola Law Review* (2003) 407–460.

reconciled with the human rights obligations of every WTO Member to respect, protect, and fulfil human rights, especially of poor and vulnerable people. This book differs from many other books on the world trading system by the efforts, in many of the following 29 chapters, to combine economic, legal, and political analyses with due regard to the need to promote a Development Round and social justice.

A. The WTO legal and dispute settlement system: improving the legal foundation for a mutually beneficial worldwide division of labour

From the perspective of theories of justice, it was rational to begin the first conference, in September 2002, with analyses of the WTO negotiations on *Improvements and Clarifications of the WTO Dispute Settlement Understanding* (DSU). The conference results were published in a separate book early in 2004, together with additional academic analyses of both the WTO dispute settlement practice as well as the WTO negotiations on reforms of the DSU.[3] The intense discussions among trade negotiators and academic experts demonstrated, in the words of Ambassador Peter Balas (then Chairman of the WTO negotiations on improvements of the DSU) and Julio A. Lacarte (former Chairman of the WTO Appellate Body and former Ambassador of Uruguay), 'an object lesson of how two apparently different worlds can approach issues of interest to the international community, and can discuss them frankly, constructively, and in an atmosphere of mutual respect'.[4] The post-war trading system based on the 1947 General Agreement on Tariffs and Trade (GATT 1947) had been dominated by power politics, such as (neo)colonial trade preferences for (former) colonial countries, and the exemption from GATT disciplines—in response to protectionist pressures in the United States (US) and Europe—of large areas of cotton trade, textiles, agricultural trade, and steel products to the detriment of competing exports from developing countries. The GATT 'pragmatism' was reflected in an 'anti-legal culture' which prided itself, up until 1983, in *not* having a GATT Office of Legal Affairs.[5] The 1994 WTO Agreement established, for the first time in history, a worldwide rule-of-law system for international trade, protected by compulsory WTO dispute settlement procedures and by

---

[3] Cf. F. Ortino and E. U. Petersmann (eds), *The WTO Dispute Settlement System 1995–2003* (2004).

[4] Cf. 'Introduction' by Ambassador Balas, and the 'Policy Conclusions' by Ambassador Lacarte in the conference report by E. U. Petersmann, *Preparing the Doha Development Round: Improvements and Clarifications of the WTO Dispute Settlement Understanding* (2002) at 139.

[5] On my personal experience as first legal officer ever employed by GATT in 1981, see E. U. Petersmann, *The GATT/WTO Dispute Settlement System* (1997), Introduction.

their successful invocation for the settlement of so far (October 2004) 317 international trade disputes.[6] The more than 50 proposals, on behalf of more than 100 WTO Members, for further clarifications and improvements of the WTO dispute settlement rules and procedures bear witness to the fact that, today, WTO governments value rule of law in international trade as no less important for welfare-increasing, peaceful cooperation across frontiers than the liberalization of welfare-reducing market access barriers, which remains the primary economic function of WTO rules. The WTO guarantees of individual freedom, non-discrimination, rule of law, and social safeguard measures have proven to be of particular importance for the more than 100 less-developed WTO member countries:[7] the latter have successfully used the WTO dispute settlement system for challenging foreign market access barriers and market distortions (e.g. EC import restrictions on bananas, EC sugar subsidies, US import restrictions on cotton, US cotton subsidies). The example of China also illustrates that the domestic implementation of WTO rules, even if it requires far-reaching legal reforms (e.g. the establishment of independent courts protecting private rights and rule of law), is crucial for attracting foreign investment flows and for increasing the national gains from trade. The engaged discussions among WTO negotiators and academics revealed their often different perspectives, for instance regarding the proposal by lawyers to decentralize, depoliticize, and prevent intergovernmental WTO disputes over private rights (e.g. intellectual property rights) by enabling such disputes to be decided by domestic courts with due regard to applicable WTO rules.[8]

---

[6] See Chapter 26 and Annex I in: Ortino and Petersmann, *supra* n. 3. As of 22 October 2004, there had been 317 requests for consultations under the DSU; 90 WTO panel reports covering more than 100 disputes; 63 adopted Appellate Body reports; 26 compliance panel reports; 18 arbitration awards pursuant to Art. 21.3; and 16 arbitration decisions pursuant to Art. 22.6 of the DSU. One systemic problem of the WTO dispute settlement system is that hardly any of the *ad hoc*, part-time members of WTO dispute settlement bodies has the time to read and understand this ever more comprehensive WTO jurisprudence.

[7] Cf. E. U. Petersmann, *Constitutional Functions and Constitutional Problems of International Economic Law* (1991). The publication of a Chinese translation of this book in 2004 illustrates the increasing insight, also outside constitutional democracies, into the advantages of a 'constitution of liberty' for investment security and an extended, welfare-increasing division of labour. This function of liberal trade rules to promote not only economic welfare but also individual freedom, was strongly emphasized by my former economics teacher F. von Hayek, *The Constitution of Liberty* (1960).

[8] On the need for differentiating the various kinds of WTO disputes according to their underlying conflicts of interests, and on the advantages of depoliticizing and decentralizing WTO disputes over private rights, see E. U. Petersmann, 'Prevention and Settlement of Transatlantic Economic Disputes' in E. U. Petersmann and M.Pollack (eds), *Transatlantic Economic Disputes: The EU, the US, and the WTO* (2003), ch. 1.

B. Challenges to the legitimacy and efficiency of the WTO system

According to the theory of justice of the leading American philosopher John Rawls, rational citizens would give priority to maximum equal liberty as the 'first principle of justice', but would also recognize the 'principle of fair equality of opportunity' and a 'difference principle' favouring the least well-off within a system of equal basic rights.[9] These social concerns inspired the second and third conferences on *WTO Negotiators Meet the Academics*, which examined *Challenges to the Legitimacy and Efficiency of the World Trading System* (June 2003) and, more specifically, the role of *Developing Countries in the Doha Round: WTO Decision-Making and WTO Negotiations on Trade in Agricultural Goods and Services* (July 2004). The lack of any reference in WTO law to the traditional safeguards of input-legitimacy (e.g. respect for human rights, democratic procedures) and output-legitimacy (such as consumer welfare) impedes public understanding and political support of the WTO by national parliaments and civil society. Transparency, publicity, and also legitimacy of WTO rule-making are indispensable for winning public confidence and for responding to the widespread distrust vis-à-vis producer-driven, secretive WTO negotiations and one-sided reliance on market solutions without adequate regard to social adjustment problems. Just as the European concept of a 'social market economy' takes into account that lack of social solidarity may reduce economic efficiency and weaken public support for market competition, the Doha Development Round can realize reciprocal trade liberalization only if it is complemented by social adjustment assistance for the losers in international trade competition and by credible poverty-reduction strategies.

Diplomatic and academic arguments and perspectives often differed in the conference discussion at Florence. Economists and human rights supporters increasingly emphasize that the WTO objective of 'sustainable development' should be defined—as suggested by Nobel Prize economist A. Sen—not only in macro-economic terms but also as

---

[9] Cf. J. Rawls, *A Theory of Justice* (revised edn 1999) at 220: 'Each person is to have an equal right to the most extensive total system of equal basic liberties compatible with a similar system of liberty for all.' Such equal liberties must be protected before 'social and economic inequalities are to be arranged so that they are both (a) to the greatest benefit of the least advantaged and (b) attached to offices and positions open to all under conditions of fair equality of opportunity' (*ibid.* at 72). This 'difference principle' is rationally chosen by individuals in order to limit social and economic inequalities (which inevitably result e.g. from the unequal distribution of human capacities) and provide a 'social minimum' of resources for the least well-off group through what Rawls calls the 'transfer branch' of government. For a criticism of Rawls' theory of international justice (cf. J. Rawls, *The Law of Peoples* (1999)), notably its inconsistency with UN and European human rights law, see Petersmann, *supra* n. 2.

positive freedom and human capacity for personal self-development.[10] Former WTO Director-General Peter Sutherland, in his 'cosmopolitan perspective' on the 'political challenges to the world trading system' (Chapter 1), endorses the increasing WTO initiatives to involve parliamentarians and open up to civil society groups, and welcomes the fact that the WTO has so far steered around the controversial issues of labour rights and other human rights.[11] Faizel Ismail, South Africa's WTO Ambassador (Chapter 2), agrees with defining the 'Development Round' objectives in the light of A. Sen's human self-development objectives, without taking a position on the view of human rights supporters that development and 'justice' must be defined, today, by the universal recognition of human rights.[12] His contribution reflects the difficulty of reconciling the fact that most WTO diplomats oppose references to human rights in WTO discussions, with the need for legitimacy, a development focus, and civil society support of the Doha Round negotiations.

The controversies over the 'Singapore issues' (trade-related competition rules, investment rules, trade facilitation, transparency in government procurement), and over how to make the Doha Round a 'Development Round', reveal profound disagreements among WTO Members over the appropriate goals and priorities of the WTO. As described by former US Deputy Secretary of State Kenneth Dam in Chapter 3, the US Congress perceives the WTO as essentially a framework for bureaucratic bargaining over reciprocal trade liberalization. The EC has offered most less-developed countries a 'Round for free' and has called for trade-related competition rules, investment rules, and more transparent government procurement rules in order to strengthen the 'WTO system' for the benefit of developing countries. The more than 100 less-developed WTO member countries are divided among those (notably in the 'Group of 20') who give priority to market liberalization commitments and the phasing-out of agricultural export subsidies by developed countries; and others (notably in the 'Group of 90') who appear more intent on using the consensus-based WTO negotiations as a means for extracting development assistance commitments from industrialized countries (such as trade preferences, technical and financial capacity-building assistance).

---

[10] On defining economic development not only in terms of *Pareto efficient* satisfaction of consumer preferences within the existing distribution of income, but also in terms of individual autonomy, individual 'immunity from encroachment', and substantive individual 'opportunity to achieve', see A. Sen, *Rationality and Freedom* (2002) (e.g. ch. 17 on 'markets and freedoms'); *idem, Development as Freedom* (1999).

[11] On involvement of parliamentarians see also the WTO publications *WTO Policy Issues for Parliamentarians* (2001) and *Regional Workshops for Parliamentarians on the Multilateral Trading System* (2003).   [12] Cf. Petersmann, *supra* n. 2.

Just as democracy and democratic 'opinion markets' are sustainable over time only as 'constitutional democracy', the proper functioning of economic markets and of the world trading system requires constitutional safeguards protecting non-discriminatory competition and open markets against their inherent tendencies of destroying themselves ('paradox of freedom'), for instance through abuses of economic power (e.g. cartel agreements) and unjust distribution of the gains from trade.[13] The UN High Commissioner for Human Rights has emphasized the legal relevance of human rights for the interpretation and application of WTO rules in a number of recent reports on the human-rights dimensions of the WTO Agreements on Trade-Related Intellectual Property Rights (TRIPS), the Agreement on Agriculture, the General Agreement on Trade in Services (GATS), international investment agreements, non-discrimination in the context of globalization, and on the impact of trade rules on the right of everyone to the enjoyment of the highest attainable standard of physical and mental health. As discussed in Chapter 17, the UN High Commissioner's appeal in favour of a 'human rights approach to trade policy' has remained without any official response by the WTO so far. The discussions among WTO diplomats and academics in Florence confirmed that—just as UN human rights covenants do not refer to the importance of economic liberties, property rights, and open markets for creating the economic resources necessary for enjoying and fulfilling human rights—trade diplomats also prefer to avoid complicating worldwide trade negotiations by references to the often controversial human rights obligations of WTO Members.[14]

C. Structure and objectives of this book

This first part offers an introductory overview and brief summary of the main conclusions of the 29 chapters of this book. Part II begins with political and strategic proposals for a successful conclusion of the Doha Round negotiations by former WTO Director-General Peter Sutherland (Chapter 1), by South Africa's WTO Ambassador Faizel Ismail (Chapter 2), and by Kenneth Dam, one of the leading international

---

[13] Cf. E. U. Petersmann, 'Constitutional Economics, Human Rights, and the Future of the WTO' in *Swiss Review of International Economic Relations (Aussenwirtschaft)* (2003) 49–91. For an historical explanation of what makes markets work see also J. McMillan, *Reinventing the Bazaar: A Natural History of Markets* (2002).

[14] For a refutation of the often authoritarian and *dirigiste* misconceptions of human rights lawyers vis-à-vis a liberal trading system and rights-based trade law see E. U. Petersmann, 'Taking Human Dignity, Poverty and Empowerment of Individuals More Seriously: Rejoinder to Alston' in *European Journal of International Law* (2002) 845–851.

economic law and policy experts in the US (Chapter 3). Parts III to V publish the papers on three central issues of the Doha Round negotiations which were discussed at the third conference in Florence in July 2004:

- the reduction of subsidies for agricultural products, and other building-blocks for concluding the Doha Round negotiations on agriculture (Chapters 4–6);
- the liberalization of trade in services in a way that developing countries can more actively participate in the international services economy, and liberalization of public health, education, and social services under the GATS that does not unduly restrain the domestic regulatory powers and social responsibilities of WTO member countries (Chapters 7–9);
- a 'more just' differentiation of WTO obligations and WTO rights meeting the 'Doha Development Round' objective of helping less-developed WTO member countries to benefit more from the worldwide division of labour through international trade and investments (Chapters 10–11).

The failure of the 5th WTO Ministerial Conference in September 2003 at Cancún to respond more convincingly to justice-related claims of less-developed WTO member countries illustrated not only—in the words of the WTO Representative of the EU, Ambassador Carlo Trojan—that 'some of the issues identified in Florence as being core problems of the WTO as an organization turned out to be stumbling blocks which contributed to the failure of the Ministerial Conference'. Another lesson of Cancún was also that 'the present organization of the WTO is not sufficiently equipped to meet the new challenges and pressures that the multilateral trading system now faces'.[15] Some of these legitimacy and governance problems are discussed in the revised conference papers published in Parts VI to VIII of this book:

- the need for better protection by WTO rules of consumer welfare, non-discriminatory conditions of competition, and investment security (Chapters 12–16);
- more regard for democratic legitimacy, parliamentary control, and civil society support of WTO agreements and of 'member-driven' WTO decision-making processes (Chapters 17–24);
- the needed improvements in the institutional capacity, consensus-based decision-making processes, and collaboration of the WTO with UN institutions (Chapters 25–29).

---

[15] C. Trojan, 'WTO Negotiators Meet the Academics', Foreword to the second conference report by E. U. Petersmann, *Preparing the Doha Development Round: Challenges to the Legitimacy and Efficiency of the World Trading System*, (2004) at ix.

Even though the Doha Ministerial Declaration of November 2001 does not refer to these legitimacy and governance problems of the WTO, the Doha Round risks foundering on its—in the words of EU trade commissioner Pascal Lamy—'medieval' negotiation and governance methods,[16] with unpredictable dangers for worldwide welfare and international cooperation. The Doha Ministerial Declaration emphasizes that 'with the exception of the improvements and clarifications of the Dispute Settlement Understanding, the conduct, conclusion and entry into force of the outcome of the negotiations shall be treated as parts of a single undertaking'.[17] As only 30 WTO Members account for about 90 per cent of world trade, consensus-based negotiations among 148 WTO Members may be neither necessary nor effective if all liberalization were to be extended, without reciprocity, to the more than 100 small developing countries. As discussed in Part VIII of this book, the 'member-driven' consensus practices in WTO negotiations, the lack of powers of the WTO Director-General to initiate proposals defending the collective interests of all WTO Members, the numerous other legal and institutional deficiencies of the WTO system, and the diversity of interests among less-developed 'trading countries' and other developing countries which sometimes appear to regard the WTO as just another development agency offering rights without obligations, make a successful conclusion of the Doha Round negotiations exceedingly difficult. As discussed in the contribution by Ambassador Faizel Ismail from South Africa (Chapter 2), the Doha Round negotiations have not yet delivered the promise of a 'Development Round', and it remains controversial how the development dimension of the Doha Round should be defined[18]—not only for the benefit of consumers with real purchasing power, but also for the about 2 billion poor people living on less than 2 dollars per day. The paradoxical fact that so many

---

[16] Cf. P. Lamy, 'Europe and the Future of Economic Governance' in *Journal of Common Market Studies* (2004) 5–21.

[17] WT/MIN(01)/DEC/W/1 of 14 November 2001, para. 47.

[18] The definition of the development dimension of the Doha Round remains controversial also among developing countries. See, e.g., the contributions by J. Bhagwati who argues that the development dimension requires poor countries to liberalize their own trade and open up their own economies, and by T. Ademola Oyeijde, who believes that poor countries should not liberalize too hastily and should not be subject to the same trade rules as developed countries, in M. Moore (ed.), *Doha and Beyond: The Future of the Multilateral Trading System* (2004) chs. 5 and 7. Whereas estimates by the World Bank and others suggest that developing countries could receive bigger gains from their own trade liberalization than from the trade liberalization by developed countries, a recent study by the Commonwealth Secretariat (J. Stiglitz and A. Charlton, *The Development Round of Trade Negotiations in the Aftermath of Cancún* (2004)) focuses on 'unilateral concessions by the developed countries, both to redress the imbalances of the past and to further the development of the poorest countries of the world'.

less-developed WTO member countries celebrated as a victory the WTO decision, in the Doha Work Programme of 1 August 2004, to abandon the negotiation of WTO competition, investment and government procurement rules limiting the widespread abuses of international cartels and the enormous outflows of needed capital from less-developed countries,[19] illustrated once again that diplomatic and academic perspectives on intergovernmental WTO negotiations often clash.

By combining economic, political, and legal studies of the world trading system, and academic as well as 'diplomatic' analyses of the Doha Round negotiations, this book offers broader insights than purely economic or legal books on the WTO. Most contributors to this book support not only the economic view that 'the world needs more globalization, not less',[20] and the legal arguments for an international rule-of-law system, but also the political concern that the Doha Round negotiations must deliver substantive benefits for less-developed countries.

D. Florentine visions of politics: lessons from Machiavelli for WTO reforms?

The city–republics in Italy during the Renaissance, notably Florence, gave rise to debates of lasting historical significance about liberty and republican self-government, and the rival merits of princely rule. No wonder, therefore, that several WTO negotiators—given the Florentine setting of the conference discussions—referred to Machiavelli (1469–1527), for example in order to justify the political necessity that trading countries should not allow protectionist governments of WTO member countries to block welfare-increasing trade liberalization in the WTO. Yet is Machiavelli's hypothesis—described in his book *Il Principe* (1513), and illustrated by the book's infamous hero Cesare Borgia— correct that necessity (*necessità*), occasion (*occasione*), fortune (*fortuna*), and virtue (*virtù*) require statesmen to disregard morality and justice in order to advance the 'interests of the state'?[21] Is the long-standing alternative political claim—dating from Plato, Aristotle and Cicero continued through James Madison (see the quotation above) to modern

---

[19] See World Bank, *World Development Report 2005: A Better Investment Climate for Everyone* (2004) which calls for improving investment climates and reducing corruption and misgovernment in many developing countries.

[20] For thorough explanations of this economic insight see M. Wolf, *Why Globalization Works* (2004) at 320; J. Bhagwati, *In Defense of Globalization* (2004).

[21] See the recent edition of *Il Principe*, with annotations by Napoleon, edited by Italian Prime Minister Silvio Berlusconi: *Il Principe di Niccolò Machiavelli, annotato da Napoleone Buonaparte* (1993).

theories of justice—wrong that 'justice is the first virtue of social institutions, as truth is of systems of thought' (John Rawls)?[22]

The modern universal recognition of human rights has rendered the two premises underlying Machiavellian power politics even more suspect. First, contrary to Machiavelli's assumption that, in relations between the individual and the state, the state interest must always prevail, human rights and democracy are based on recognition of inalienable human rights as primary values and constitutional restraints on all government powers. The rational self-interest of citizens in maximum equal liberty as the 'first principle of justice'[23] offers, also in the trade policy area, a more convincing definition of the 'state interest' than power-oriented government discretion to restrict mutually beneficial trade. The WTO Agreement qualifies its guarantees of freedom and non-discrimination in international trade by so many 'public interest exceptions' that every WTO Member remains sovereign to regulate and restrict trade if it is necessary for protecting other, more important public policy objectives.

Second, the Machiavellian premise that the 'national interest' has primacy over international law is inconsistent with the 'golden rule' that equal treatment under the rule of law, in international relations no less than inside states, is of crucial importance for peaceful cooperation. In order to transform aggressive nationalism, trade protectionism, and other forms of Machiavellian power politics into a mutually beneficial division of labour based on the rule of law, trade negotiators may learn more from other Florentine political philosophers than from 'murderous Nick' (as Niccolò Machiavelli was nicknamed by Shakespeare). Donato Gianotti's book on the Republic of Florence (1534),[24] for example, written in exile (after the overthrow of the Third Florentine Republic (1527–30) by the Medici dynasty) with the intention of helping to avoid a repetition of the political and constitutional failures of earlier republics, offers inspiring suggestions for constitutional 'checks and balances' on abuses of foreign policy powers in order to protect freedom, self-government, the rule of law and international trade as the major sources of the wealth of the Florentine city–republics.

Though Machiavelli's writings offer little inspiration for discussions on how to safeguard transnational freedom (e.g. of trade) and the rule of law, they remain important for understanding policy-making processes. Yves Mény, President of the EUI, referred in his welcome remarks to the conference participants to Machiavelli's insight that political resistance to change tends to be better organized than political

---

[22] Rawls, *A Theory of Justice, supra* n. 9 at 3.   [23] Cf. *ibid.* Ch. II.
[24] Donato Gianotti, *Della Republica Fiorentina* (G. Silvano ed.) (1990).

support for change. The beneficiaries from future changes (e.g. from competition) tend to be dispersed and less well informed than those likely to suffer from the adjustment costs. Professor Quentin Skinner, one of the world's leading historians of the gradual decline of Italy's city–republics, has drawn attention to another political insight in Machiavelli's *Discorsi* (1522): due to their rational egoism and limited altruism, self-interested people are prone to be self-deceived 'by a false image of the good' and 'very often will their own ruin'.[25] In order to convert private vices (like selfish 'rent-seeking') into public benefits (like mutually beneficial trade), individual and collective freedom must be protected by constitutional restraints on abuses of power. How can the public good of a liberal (i.e. liberty-based) international division of labour be protected more effectively through WTO law and the Doha Round of multilateral trade negotiations?

II. THE DOHA DEVELOPMENT ROUND AND THE FUTURE OF THE WTO: POLICY PROPOSALS

Part II of this book is composed of three Chapters: *Peter Sutherland*, in Chapter 1 on *The Doha Development Agenda: Political Challenges to the World Trading System—A Cosmopolitan Perspective*, notes that the WTO *has* delivered on dispute settlement and on helping developing countries, but has yet to show its potential as a negotiating machine. Frustration with slow progress in the negotiations at Geneva and a failed mid-term review were characteristic also of the Uruguay Round negotiations (1986–94). The Doha Work Programme—finally adopted by the WTO General Council on 1 August 2004—justifies hopes for a successful conclusion of the Doha Round negotiations, presumably only in 2006/2007. The objective of a 'Development Round' might entail that least-developed countries may undertake few market-access commitments. However, the idea that more advanced developing countries could avoid meaningful market-opening commitments in exchange for market-access commitments by developed countries, has proven to be unrealistic. Sutherland calls on developing countries to exploit more actively the opportunities which the WTO offers for promoting economic welfare through trade liberalization and legal reforms. The undermining of the most-favoured-nation (MFN) requirements of WTO law through the proliferation of preferential trade arrangements, and the increasing recourse to WTO dispute settlement

---

[25] Machiavelli, quoted from Q. Skinner, *Visions of Politics, Vol. II: Renaissance Virtues* (2002) at 164.

procedures for realizing what could not be achieved in WTO negotiations, are noted as potentially dangerous developments. The decisions to phase out export subsidies and to move forward with negotiations on trade facilitations rules are welcomed. More detailed modalities for concluding the agricultural negotiations need to be agreed no later than by the end of 2005 when the next WTO Ministerial Conference will take place in Hong Kong. Sutherland notes that the WTO panel and Appellate Body decisions on EC sugar subsidies and US cotton subsidies are likely to influence the Doha agreements on trade in agriculture.

Sutherland acknowledges that meeting the 'development agenda' of the Doha Round through a better-defined differentiation of WTO obligations, and through additional technical assistance and capacity-building efforts, poses political and conceptual challenges. Additional commitments by advanced developing countries may enable the bargain on the basis of which industrial countries will have the political space to remove some of their most testing—and for developing countries most damaging—market-access restrictions. Sutherland finds it difficult to see the Doha Round conclude successfully were there to be any new attempt to push labour rights or additional environmental criteria on the agenda. China must be kept constructively engaged in the Doha Round so as to ensure it has an interest, and a willingness to contribute significantly, to a worthwhile outcome. Civil society and non-governmental organizations (NGOs) must be encouraged to support the Doha Round and to better understand its political significance for peaceful cooperation across frontiers. Sutherland proposes a number of institutional reforms as part of the Doha Round agreements so as to give the WTO the tools to do its job better. A successful outcome is needed, for 'there are too many countries and too many people with an interest in advances in the WTO to support economic growth and the assimilation of poor countries into the global economy for failure to be an option'.

Faizel Ismail discusses, in Chapter 2, *A Development Perspective on the WTO July 2004 General Council Decision*, starting from the premise of Amartya Sen's definition of 'development' as the expansion of substantive human freedom and personal self-development. He derives from this approach four development dimensions for the Doha Development Round negotiations: fair trade, capacity-building for the poorest countries, balanced rules, and good governance. Ismail emphasizes that Special and Differential Treatment (SDT) is only one aspect of the broader development dimension of the trading system and no substitute for it. Each of the five critical issues negotiated in the WTO July General Council (GC) Meeting—i.e. agriculture, cotton, non-agricultural market access (NAMA), Singapore issues, and the development issues—are then explained and evaluated. The cotton issues, for example, are viewed as an illustration of 'the unfairness of WTO rules' and of the need for a 'more inclusive and transparent negotiating process in the WTO' for the benefit of African cotton producing countries and their poor farmers. With regard to NAMA negotiations, Ismail draws attention to 'the enormous imbalances in the global trading system reflected in the inequitable distribution of the gains from globalization and the continued protection in the developed countries of products competing with like products of poor people from developing countries'. Ismail concludes that the outcome of the July GC Decision justifies cautious optimism, and calls on all WTO members to build on this platform.

Chapter 3 by *Kenneth W. Dam* on *Cordell Hull, the Reciprocal Trade Agreement Act, and the WTO* recalls that the year 2004 was the 70th anniversary of the US Reciprocal Trade Agreements Act of 1934 which fundamentally changed trade policy-making in the US and furnished the template for Congressional advance authorization for Executive Branch negotiations for reciprocal trade liberalization agreements based on unconditional most-favoured-nation treatment. Dam describes how Secretary of State Cordell Hull designed this Act as a means of breaking 'the logrolling dynamics' of the protectionist Smoot–Hawley tariff legislation of 1930 by giving export industries an equal voice with import-competing industries in trade policy-making. Dam explains why the Hull principles of reciprocity and non-discrimination are harder to apply to sectoral services negotiations than to cross-sectoral tariff liberalization commitments. Following the Congressional refusal to implement some of the Kennedy Round agreements in the 1960s, the introduction—since 1974—of Congressional 'fast track legislation', with Congressional demands in the negotiation authorizing legislation as to what should be in the final trade agreements, has so far ensured that no international trade agreement negotiated by the United States Trade Representative (USTR) has failed to win Congressional fast track approval after the completion of negotiations.

Yet the 'Cordell Hull principles' of advance authorization, international trade negotiations out of the public eye, reciprocal international trade agreements, and their more or less automatic approval and domestic implementation by Congress have been changed by the provisions in the 2002 authorizing legislation: the current trade negotiating authority of the USTR expires on 1 June 2005 and will be extended up to 1 June 2007 only under specific conditions (i.e. a request by the President, a report by the International Trade Commission on the economic impact of the Doha Round agreements, no 'resolution of disapproval' by either the House of Representatives or the Senate). Giving export interests a strong voice in the political struggle against discriminatory market access barriers in order to offset protectionist pressures from import-competing producers will be politically more necessary than ever before. The rollback of the ever more protectionist anti-import procedures does not appear to be a politically viable strategy. However, there are powerful transparency and fairness arguments for balancing the 'rights to protection' of import-competing producers by 'rights to import' of those who benefit from trade liberalization. The WTO Agreement includes only a few provisions giving exporters procedural rights and judicial remedies in an importing country. The lack of WTO provisions protecting importers and exporters in their own country reflects the 'mercantilist bias' of WTO rules and policies. As long as the few import-competing producers threatened by trade competition can influence domestic trade policy-making so much more strongly (e.g. by election campaign financing) than the many consumers and exporters benefiting from trade liberalization, Cordell Hull's insights on the 'constitutional failures' of trade policy-making and on the need for offsetting the political influence of import-competing firms remain of crucial importance for promoting consumer welfare, rule of law, and peaceful international cooperation through liberal trade.

III. BUILDING-BLOCKS FOR CONCLUDING THE DOHA ROUND NEGOTIATIONS ON AGRICULTURE

The Uruguay Round Agreement on Agriculture was the first comprehensive attempt at reducing the systemic distortions of international trade in agricultural products which have undermined the effective application of GATT rules to agricultural trade ever since, in March 1955, the US extracted a 'GATT waiver' without time limit, in exchange for withdrawing its threat of leaving the GATT, for its restrictions on agricultural imports under the US Agricultural Adjustment Act. Just as the Uruguay Round of trade negotiations remained on the brink of failure until an agreement was reached on the liberalization of trade in agricultural goods, a successful conclusion of the Doha Round negotiations is widely seen as impossible without substantial market-access commitments and subsidy-reduction commitments for agriculture. In the Doha Work Programme of 1 August 2004,[26] WTO Members agreed for the first time to eliminate all forms of agricultural export subsidies by a date to be determined through negotiations, including also export credits, export credit guarantees or insurance programmes which are

---

[26] WTO document WT/L/579: Decision adopted by the General Council on 1 August 2004.

not in conformity with new disciplines to be established, trade-distorting practices of exporting state trading enterprises as well as of food aid. They have also taken on commitments to substantially reduce and otherwise discipline trade-distorting domestic support in agriculture, and to undertake substantial improvements in market access for all agricultural products. Special and differential treatment for developing countries will include not only longer time-frames and lower reduction commitments but also the ability to designate some products as 'special products' which will be eligible for more flexible treatment and a new Special Safeguard Mechanism for developing countries.

The WTO Decision of 1 August 2004 also confirms that the trade-related aspects of cotton, which had become a 'deal-breaker' at the insistence of least-developed countries in Africa during the Cancún ministerial conference, will be addressed 'ambitiously, expeditiously and specifically' within the agricultural negotiations and that work to be undertaken will encompass all three pillars of market access, domestic support, and export competition. A Sub-Committee on Cotton will be established, which will report periodically to the main Agriculture Negotiating Group. Work will also continue on the development assistance aspects of cotton. Part III of the book includes three chapters analysing building-blocks for concluding the Doha Round negotiations on agriculture.

Stefan Tangermann, in Chapter 4 on *How to Forge a Compromise in the Agriculture Negotiations*, explains why the Uruguay Round Agreement on Agriculture had not resulted in a fundamental liberalization of agriculture in the Organisation for Economic Co-operation and Development (OECD) area, and why the Doha Work Programme of 1 August 2004 is still far away from the full modalities with numerical reduction commitments that WTO Members had originally hoped they could have already agreed by March 2003. He recalls the OECD statistics indicating that, since the entry into force of the Uruguay Round Agreements in 1995, overall trade protection decreased more than overall financial farm support in the 30 OECD member countries. Negotiating proposals tabled so far in the Doha Round appear to suggest that cuts in border protection and output payments may be deeper in the Doha Round Agreements than in the Uruguay Round Agreements. Price and output support behind border protection remains not only an inefficient means of supporting farm incomes because only a small share of the money transferred to agriculture through such policies ends up in the farmer's pocket; such trade-distorting support also fails to deal effectively with market failures like positive or negative externalities (e.g. in terms of the effects of agricultural production on biodiversity and the environment) and public goods (e.g. maintenance of a pleasing landscape, provision of food security). Moving from border protection and output-related farm payments to support decoupled from production is necessary for improving domestic agricultural policies. In terms of WTO categories of domestic support, this means shifting support out of the 'amber' and 'blue boxes' into the 'green box' of domestic support measures, even if such 'box shifting'—as allowed by the Agreement on Agriculture—is unlikely to eliminate all trade-distorting effects.

As regards stricter rules and disciplines on the interrelated, diverse forms of import protection, domestic support and export subsidies, Tangermann recalls that a watertight distinction between domestic support and export support is difficult to strike in exporting countries, as confirmed in the WTO dispute settlement findings on *Canada—Dairy* and *EC—Sugar*. Hence, the export competition disciplines must be complemented by appropriate disciplines on domestic support in order to avoid domestic cross-subsidization of exports, just as domestic support disciplines must be complemented by disciplines on import protection so as to limit the scope for lifting domestic market prices above the level of world market prices. According to Tangermann, the most significant achievement of the WTO Decision of 1 August 2004 is the agreement 'to establish detailed modalities ensuring the parallel elimination of all forms of export subsidies and disciplines on all export measures with equivalent effect by a credible end date', which will finally remove the biggest difference in treatment of agriculture compared with WTO rules for non-agricultural goods. It remains to be seen how equivalence between all export support measures can be defined in practical and legally justiciable terms. The agreement to establish a new overall limit on all trade-distorting domestic support, and to negotiate reductions in *de minimis* support, will limit the scope for 'box shifting'. In contrast to the quantitative parameters for domestic support and export support commitments, the market access provisions of the framework agreement of 1 August 2004 remain less precise. Yet agricultural policy reform through the Doha Round agreements offers the potential of a win–win situation rendering national policies as well as trade policies more effective.

Chapter 5 with the contribution by *Stuart Harbinson*, who chaired the Doha Round negotiations on agriculture until 2003, sets out various proposals for *How to Keep the Agriculture Negotiations on a Positive Track*. The WTO Ministerial conference at Cancún had already enabled significant progress in the search for consensus on a framework for 'modalities' for reduction commitments in market-access protection, internal support, and export subsidies. The 'July package', approved on 1 August 2004, includes an 'historic' agreement to negotiate a credible end date for the parallel elimination of all forms of export subsidies and to further harmonize domestic support measures, combined with an overall cut and a down-payment regarding internal support. Tensions and possible inconsistencies remain most evident in the area of market-access commitments. The interrelationships among all three pillars, and the need for some equivalence of their treatment, are stressed by many negotiators. Harbinson suggests four elements for keeping the negotiations on the present positive track. First, the 'end game' cannot be started before more detailed options for achieving the objectives of the negotiations in all three pillars have been elaborated. Second, detailed time-frames and benchmarks should be agreed by the next WTO Ministerial Conference at Hong Kong in December 2005. Third, while the Round cannot be completed until the agriculture negotiations are ripe for conclusion, such agreement to conclude the agriculture negotiations will depend on roughly equivalent progress in other areas such as NAMA, trade in services, and WTO rules on trade remedies. Fourth, in order to maintain the procedural dynamism in the agriculture negotiations, participants must continue to search for creative ways in finalizing detailed modalities for further reforms of the increasingly unsustainable *status quo* in agricultural trade policies.

Ernst-Ulrich Petersmann, in Chapter 6 on *Strategic Use of WTO Dispute Settlement Proceedings for Advancing WTO Negotiations on Agriculture*, notes that, up to the end of GATT's Kennedy Round (1964–7), the large number of GATT disputes over agricultural restrictions and subsidies seemed to have influenced GATT negotiations on agriculture only marginally. The 'GATT 1947 bicycle' rolled and, through periodic intergovernmental trade liberalization commitments, created the necessary political momentum for liberalizing domestic market-access barriers. Petersmann gives detailed evidence how, during the Tokyo Round (1973–9) as well as during the Uruguay Round (1986–94), the large number of agricultural dispute settlement proceedings influenced the bargaining power, negotiating positions, the final contents, and progressive development of the 1979 and 1994 Agreements on Subsidies as well as the Uruguay Round Agreement on Agriculture. The 'peace clause' in Article 13 of the Agreement on Agriculture did not prevent that, out of more than 317 complaints under the DSU from 1995 up to October 2004, more than 140 related to agricultural, fishery, and forestry products. More than 46 dispute settlement panels were established in order to examine the alleged WTO-inconsistency of agricultural market-access restrictions (e.g. for imports of salmon, desiccated coconut, bananas, hormone-fed beef, poultry products, apples, milk and dairy products, beef, wheat gluten, lamb, vegetable oils, sardines, peaches), domestic subsidies (e.g. for dairy, cotton, sugar), and export subsidies (e.g. for dairy products, cotton, sugar). A large number of dispute settlement findings established violations of export subsidy reduction commitments under the Agreement on Agriculture (e.g. for Canadian dairy, US cotton, EC sugar), or of the subsidy disciplines in the Agreement on Subsidies (e.g. as regards US Foreign Sales Corporations, US cotton), and clarified the contested meaning of certain WTO rules (such as GATT Article XVII on 'state trading enterprises', Article 6 of the Subsidy Agreement relating to 'serious prejudice', the classification of 'green box subsidies' pursuant to the Agreement on Agriculture). According to Petersmann, two major policy conclusions emerge from this WTO dispute settlement practice:

- There is clear evidence for GATT/WTO dispute settlement proceedings influencing GATT/WTO Rounds of multilateral trade negotiations, and vice versa. The fact that litigation strategies (e.g. Brazil's successful 2003 complaints against US subsidies for cotton and EC subsidies for sugar) can change the bargaining power and bargaining positions in WTO negotiations illustrates that the 'GATT 1947 bicycle' has been transformed into a 'WTO tricycle': intergovernmental negotiations and domestic implementing rules by WTO Members are increasingly influenced by WTO jurisprudence.
- The unstable and slowly moving 'WTO tricycle' needs to be transformed into a four-wheel vehicle by empowering the WTO Director-General to defend the collective interests of WTO Members vis-à-vis producer-driven intergovernmental bargaining, nationalist agricultural legislation, and single-interest NGOs. Improving the institutional capacity of the WTO could enhance the quality and culture of WTO negotiations by promoting better 'deliberative politics' and more 'principled' rather than merely 'positional bargaining'. This could also strengthen political support and public understanding of WTO rules by democratic legislatures and civil society. Without such support, the intergovernmental and domestic 'two-level negotiations' on the reduction of the numerous trade distortions in agricultural trade are bound to be much more difficult.

IV. THE DOHA ROUND NEGOTIATIONS ON SERVICES TRADE

The Doha Work Programme of 1 August 2004 sets out agreed guidelines for making progress in the services negotiations, and urges WTO Members who have not yet submitted their initial offers to do so as soon as possible. By October 2004, only 48 initial offers on behalf of more than 70 WTO Members had been tabled. Many initial offers had been criticized for their lack of ambition. The WTO Working Parties on

Domestic Regulation (e.g. administrative measures relating to visas and entry measures) and on GATS rules (e.g. emergency safeguard measures, government procurement, subsidies) had also reported only slow progress. Part IV of this book includes three chapters analysing the Doha Round negotiations on services trade.

Alan Winters, in Chapter 7 on *Developing Country Proposals for the Liberalization of Movements of Natural Service Suppliers*, criticizes the mercantilist rhetoric of some of these initial proposals because they request other countries to liberalize their imports without offering reciprocal and equivalent market-opening commitments. Winters also notes the extreme caution of developed country offers and concludes that—even though 'Mode 4' (i.e. temporary cross-border movements of natural service suppliers) appears to be the principal way in which developing countries might expect to reap market access benefits in services—there may not be much liberalization of 'Mode 4 services' during the Doha Round in view of, *inter alia*, the xenophobic European fears of permanent migration. Developing countries likewise continue to be restrictive on opening their labour markets for professional services of foreign workers, in contrast to their more liberal attitude vis-à-vis 'commercial presence' (Mode 3) of foreign services suppliers. In order to separate temporary service providers under the GATS from permanent labour and immigration flows, India, for example, proposes a special GATS visa for temporary Mode 4 services outside normal immigration procedures. The United Kingdom (UK) has already used such 'GATS visas' for liberalizing a limited number of services sectors. Overall, however, liberalization of market access for foreign lower-skilled workers (e.g. by abolishing economic needs tests, professional qualifications, social security requirements) appears to be often resisted by local interest groups and to make little progress in view of the spectre of cultural and social strife (e.g. adverse labour market effects for local less-skilled workers), even though the potential economic gains from increased labour mobility could be huge. An important counteracting force are firms that wish to use foreign labour and push for increased mobility. But many of the existing temporary labour schemes are administered bilaterally (e.g. access of Indian medical doctors to the UK) rather than multilaterally, for instance in view of the most-favoured-nation requirements in GATS Article II and the comparatively lesser flexibility of GATS provisions. Winters warns against dropping demands for the liberalization of lower-skilled mobility and suggests that GATS should rather ignore bilateral deals outside GATS than legalize departures from GATS' non-discrimination requirements.

Anthony VanDuzer, in Chapter 8 on *Navigating between the Poles: Unpacking the Debate on the Implications for Development of GATS Obligations Relating to Health and Education Services*, recalls the different opinions regarding the implications of GATS for public services like health and education in developing countries: while some believe that GATS may enhance the effective delivery and regulation of essential services, others view GATS liberalization commitments as a significant threat to the effectiveness and viability of national health and education systems. Before deciding on what GATS commitments to undertake in health and education, developing countries should make prior policy choices regarding how much private sector participation to permit in the delivery of these services which are often extensively regulated, funded, or even delivered by governments. Apart from determining the net benefits from permitting foreign supplies of health and education services, developing countries also have to examine whether they might prefer to liberalize their health and educational services regimes without making GATS commitments limiting their future policy options. VanDuzer provides an overview of the so far limited GATS commitments in these sectors and suggests possible strategies for making the GATS more relevant for improving the regulation and delivery of health and education services in developing countries. As equitable access to a basic level of health and education is widely considered to be a human right and fundamental responsibility of the state with far-reaching macro-economic effects, GATS commitments and GATS obligations for health and education policies raise numerous legal and political questions. Both health and education services are characterized by market failures, and large segments of health and education services are therefore delivered or funded by the state in all countries. In most developing countries, private and public health and education systems are closely intertwined and are increasingly traded—mainly through consumption abroad (GATS Mode 2), but also through commercial presence (GATS Mode 3), health and educational professionals from developing countries providing their services abroad (GATS Mode 4) as well as cross-border supply (GATS Mode 1). VanDuzer analyses the specific GATS commitments undertaken by WTO Members for health and education services, identifies obstacles to—and benefits from—liberalization of trade in this area, and explains why most developing countries continue to be reluctant to make commitments that restrict their policy options.

Chapter 9 by *Joel P. Trachtman* on *Negotiations on Domestic Regulation and Trade in Services (GATS Article VI): A Legal Analysis of Selected Current Issues* argues that it may be difficult for developing countries to insist on policy flexibility for their own domestic prudential regulation of services and request greater, asymmetric disciplines on regulatory barriers in developed countries (e.g. immigration controls) if such barriers impede services exports from developing countries. Trachtman distinguishes horizontal disciplines (e.g. under GATS Article II), sectoral disciplines (e.g. under GATS Article VI:4) and specifically negotiated disciplines (e.g. under GATS Article XVIII), and examines related legal problems (such as discrimination against foreign 'like services' and 'like service providers' inconsistent with Articles II, XVII GATS, 'nullification or impairment' of specific commitments inconsistent with Article VI:5, measures 'not more burdensome than necessary to ensure the quality of the service' in the sense of Article VI:4). The *Disciplines on Domestic Regulation in the Accountancy Sector*, adopted by the WTO Council on Trade in Services in 1998, and the Article VI:4 Work Programme are discussed.

V. LESS-DEVELOPED WTO MEMBERS IN THE DOHA ROUND NEGOTIATIONS

Part V of this book includes two chapters elaborating upon some of the specific developing country concerns in the Doha Round negotiations. Chapter 10 by *Bernard Hoekman* on *Operationalizing the Concept of Policy Space in the WTO: Beyond Special and Differential Treatment* recalls that efforts to realize the Doha Round objective of strengthening WTO provisions on special and differential treatment of developing countries by making such SDT provisions 'more precise, effective and operational'[27] have so far failed. The 'adjustment burden' of new WTO rules will fall on developing countries to the extent that such rules reflect 'best practices' already applied in developed countries. If the Doha Round is to become a Development Round, the resource capacity constraints and lesser ability of developing countries to implement new rules will need to be addressed more effectively. The 'old approach' to SDT (based on preferences, opt-outs, arbitrary transition periods) has not effectively promoted development because, *inter alia*, trade preferences are increasingly being eroded, and most SDT provisions were exhortatory or disadvantageous since exempting less-developed countries from WTO disciplines excluded them from the major source of gains from trade liberalisation—namely the reform of their own policies. A possible new approach should provide for acceptance of the core rules by all WTO Members and greater reliance on explicit

[27] Doha Ministerial Declaration, *supra* n. 17, para. 44.

cost–benefit analyses so as to identify the net implementation benefits and implementation costs of WTO rules with due regard to different circumstances in individual developing countries. Through a cooperative, country-specific 'enabling mechanism', based on credible commitments by high-income countries to assist developing countries in implementing 'resource-intensive' WTO rules and benefiting from trade opportunities, a new 'multilateral trade and development body' should offer country-specific technical and financial assistance for implementing WTO rules ('aid for trade'), for instance by helping to enhance the 'supply capacity' of exporting countries and financing trade adjustment costs.

Gregory Shaffer, in Chapter 11, examines the question: *Can WTO Technical Assistance and Capacity-Building Serve Developing Countries?* After describing the multiple capacity constraints which less-developed countries face in advancing their interests in WTO meetings, WTO negotiations, rule-implementation, and WTO dispute settlement proceedings, he examines competing rationales for trade-related capacity-building and technical assistance by the WTO, such as promoting internal trade-related capacity in governments rather than in the private sector. Shaffer describes the evolution of WTO capacity-building programmes (e.g. the Integrated Framework for Trade-Related Technical Assistance to Least-Developed Countries carried out by WTO, the United Nations Conference on Trade and Development (UNCTAD), International Trade Centre (ITC), United Nations Development Programme (UNDP), the International Monetary Fund (IMF), and the World Bank since 1997, the Doha Development Agenda Global Trust Fund created in 2001) and discusses their various difficulties and uncertain future after the end of the Doha Round. The much more active engagement of developing countries in the Doha Round than in previous GATT negotiations reflects their 'much greater "ownership" of the technical assistance provided'. As developing countries will need to work more closely with their private sectors in order to take advantage of WTO rules, Shaffer suggests making WTO trade-related capacity-building more effective by involving broader-based constituencies in developing countries and promoting regional cooperation among developing countries.

VI. ARE WTO RULES ADEQUATELY PROTECTING CONSUMER WELFARE?

Part VI of the book includes five chapters examining, from diverse perspectives, whether WTO rules offer adequate protection of consumer welfare. Chapter 12 by *Petros C. Mavroidis* on *Producer Welfare*,

Consumer Welfare, and WTO Rules explains why, even though the basic WTO rules do not take a stance on the issue of whether producer interests, consumer interests, or a balancing of both should guide trade liberalization, the dynamic of WTO negotiations tends to lead to progressive liberalization of market-access barriers promoting consumer welfare. As all agreements tend to be 'incomplete', it is a legitimate task of WTO judges to clarify progressively the WTO requirements of non-discriminatory treatment of like goods and of like services. The additional requirements, in the WTO Agreements on Technical Barriers to Trade (TBT) and on Sanitary and Phytosanitary Standards (SPS), to base restrictive measures on the 'necessity principle' and on 'scientific evidence', offer useful 'double checks' for judicial identification of protectionist measures. While the WTO rules on non-discriminatory market access offer weak safeguards for consumer welfare, the WTO's contingent protection instruments protect import-competing producers from 'injurious competition' without regard to consumer welfare. Because of the importance of the overlapping safeguard, anti-dumping and countervailing duty instruments, Mavroidis concludes that 'the WTO rules are producer-oriented' and need to be changed by governments committed to promotion of consumer welfare.

Chapter 13 by *Patrick A. Messerlin* on *Non-Discrimination, Welfare Balances, and WTO Rules: An Historical Perspective* offers historical and economic explanations for why WTO rules (including those on 'special and differential treatment', GATS provisions permitting 'economic needs tests', and quantitative restrictions rather than price-based instruments) fail to take into account cost–benefit analyses based on welfare balances. In view of the difficulties of such cost–benefit analyses, as illustrated by the occasionally conflicting assessments of transatlantic competition restraints by European Community (EC) and US competition authorities, Messerlin concludes that 'it is hard to see the benefits of introducing a strong competition culture directly into the WTO system (other than through improved market access)'. His economic recommendation is to shift away from anti-dumping and anti-subsidy protection towards safeguard measures and to subject such safeguard measures to reciprocal liberalization commitments. The Doha Round negotiations and WTO practices offer, however, little hope for putting such academic proposals into trade practice. The protection of *foreign consumer interests* by trade negotiators demanding access to foreign markets remains indirect and driven by producer interests (export industries).

Chapter 14 by *François Souty* gives an overview of past academic proposals, as well as of the recommendations of the WTO Working Group on the Interaction between Trade and Competition Policy (WGTCP), for negotiating international competition rules in the context of the WTO. Souty also points to the increasing empirical evidence of the very considerable costs imposed by international cartels on less-developed countries, often dwarfing the administrative costs of introducing a competition law and setting up an antitrust authority. According to Souty, WTO competition rules should focus on prohibiting hard-core cartels, providing technical assistance for less-developed countries, instituting a WTO Competition Committee for peer reviews of trade-related national competition rules and policies, and continuing the clarification of trade-related competition problems in the WTO. The Decision adopted by the WTO General Council on 1 August 2004 provides, however, that—among the four 'Singapore issues' (trade-related competition rules, investment rules, transparency in government procurement, trade facilitation)— only negotiations on trade facilitation would commence in 2004 and negotiations on the other three issues, including trade-related competition rules, will not take place within the Doha Round.

Chapter 15 by *Frederick M. Abbott* examines the question: *Are the Competition Rules in the WTO Agreement on Trade-Related Intellectual Property Rights Adequate?* The competition rules in the TRIPS Agreement (notably Articles 6,8:2,40) leave each WTO Member substantial discretion in the development and application of competition law to intellectual property rights (IPRs), including the right to forestall anti-competitive abuses of IPRs (e.g. undue restrictions on transfer of technology and other anti-competitive practices in contractual licences). He concludes that there are no compelling grounds for changing these TRIPS rules (e.g. in the context of a WTO framework agreement on trade-related competition rules). Both IPRs and competition rules aim at promoting innovation and general consumer welfare and should be applied in a mutually compatible manner. The lack of competition laws and of effective competition authorities in many less-developed countries could, however, entail that anti-competitive abuses of IPRs are not effectively constrained in those countries. There is inadequate evidence on whether, and how, the 'positive comity' obligations in Article 40:3 of the TRIPS Agreement had been used so as to prevent anti-competitive practices in contractual licences. The WTO Working Group on the Interaction between Trade and Competition Policies could assist the TRIPS Council in clarifying the need for better cooperation among competition authorities and IPR authorities in controlling anti-competitive abuses of IPRs which adversely affect international trade. As a 'down-payment' in the Doha Development Agenda, developed WTO Members should agree to reform their competition laws such that anti-competitive conduct undertaken by their enterprises in foreign markets is no longer exempted, tolerated, or encouraged. The Doha Declaration on the TRIPS Agreement and Public Health, as well as the

WTO Decision of 30 August 2003 on *Implementation of Paragraph 6 of the Doha Declaration on the TRIPS Agreement and Public Health* which solved the potential difficulties of WTO Members with insufficient or no manufacturing capacities in the pharmaceutical sector by granting a waiver from Article 31(f) of the TRIPS Agreement enabling exporting Members to grant a compulsory licence for producing and exporting certain pharmaceutical products to certain eligible importing Members, confirm the legal flexibility of WTO law in order to respond to particular development needs.

Chapter 16 by *Bijit Bora and Edward M. Graham* on *Investment and the Doha Development Agenda* examines the progress made since 2001 in the WTO Working Group on Trade and Investment. They conclude that the Working Group's current mandate was so broad that the outcome of slow progress towards a Multilateral Framework on Investments (MFI) was to be expected. Further progress could only be determined in the context of negotiations where true 'bottom-line' positions would be exposed. Any future mandate for the Working Group should be more precise and exclude certain issues (such as investor–state dispute settlement procedures). The discussions about the feasibility and architecture of an MFI should not delay current commitments and disciplines on investment-related issues such as in the Agreement on Trade-Related Investment Measures (TRIMS), the Agreement on Subsidies, and 'Mode 3 commitments' in the context of GATS. For example, the needed disciplines on investment incentives should be negotiated in the context of the Subsidies Agreement or TRIMS Agreement. And the needed extension of the TRIMS Agreement to additional trade-related investment measures should be negotiated in the context of the TRIMS Agreement rather than in the context of a future MFI. Following the Decision adopted by the WTO General Council on 1 August 2004 that—among the four 'Singapore issues'—only negotiations on trade facilitation would commence in 2004, negotiations on trade-related investment rules can take place within the Doha Round, if at all, only in the context of negotiations on reforms of the TRIMS Agreement and on additional GATS commitments.

VII. CHALLENGES TO THE POLITICAL LEGITIMACY OF THE WTO SYSTEM

Part VII includes nine chapters discussing the challenges to the democratic legitimacy of the WTO system. Chapter 17 by *Ernst-Ulrich Petersmann* examines *The 'Human Rights Approach' to International*

Trade Advocated by UN Human Rights Bodies and by the ILO: Is it Relevant for WTO Law and Policy? Petersmann claims that the contemporary worldwide recognition of human rights requires taking the 'external challenges'—by citizens, parliaments, and NGOs—to the legitimacy and efficiency of WTO rules and WTO negotiations more seriously than this is done in intergovernmental WTO bargaining among trade experts on the more than 20 'technical' agenda items of the Doha Development Round. As the traditional safeguards of 'input legitimacy' (like human rights protection, democratic procedures) and 'output-legitimacy' (like promotion of general consumer welfare) are not mentioned in WTO law, parliamentarians and public opinion rightly question the legitimacy of producer-driven WTO negotiations, for example if they legalize welfare-reducing trade protection and one-sided domestic trade regulation. In contrast to the anti-market bias of an earlier report by the UN Commission on Human Rights that had discredited the WTO as 'a veritable nightmare' for developing countries and women, more recent reports by the UN High Commissioner for Human Rights on the human rights dimensions of various WTO agreements call for making trade liberalization and realization of human rights more complementary. As every WTO Member has accepted one or more UN human rights treaties as well as other human rights obligations requiring *government by the people* (input legitimacy) and *government for the people* (output legitimacy), a positive WTO response to the UN proposals for a 'human rights approach to trade' is desirable. The flexibility of WTO rules renders conflicts with human rights most unlikely. Similar to the 1996 Singapore Ministerial Declaration on core labour standards (which affirmed the support by WTO Members for the International Labour Organization's (ILO) agreed standards and work in this field, and rejected protectionist abuses of such standards), a WTO Declaration to respect universal human rights could—without creating new legal obligations or new WTO competences, and without prejudice to the diverse human rights traditions in WTO member countries—promote synergies between WTO activities and the work of UN human rights bodies. The WTO should remain an economic organization and leave 'human rights assessments', and the interpretation and monitoring of human rights, to specialized human rights bodies and national governments. Greater openness of the WTO to NGOs could help to reduce existing 'information asymmetries' in democratic 'opinion markets' and in trade policy-making. Just as parliamentary meetings and most UN meetings are public and observed by NGOs, so public access to WTO meetings would not prevent legitimate confidentiality of intergovernmental negotiations.

Chapter 18 by *Gregory Shaffer* on *Parliamentary Oversight of WTO Rule-Making: The Political, Normative, and Practical Contexts* explains that, since the US Congress strongly influences US trade policy, US Congressmen focus on the *national* level of parliamentary authorization, control, and implementation of WTO negotiations and rule-making. Inter-parliamentary meetings at the international level (e.g. in the Inter-Parliamentary Union and WTO) are sometimes considered as diminishing, rather than enhancing US power and US 'sovereignty', for instance if foreign representatives in such meetings lack democratic legitimacy and do not effectively control trade policy-making. US congressmen fear that, because they are held accountable through national elections, they have to respond to protectionist constituencies and risk not being re-elected if they devote too much attention to distant intergovernmental negotiations. Shaffer suggests that proposals to create a WTO parliamentary body should be judged also in terms of their ability to enhance participation of the majority of less-developed WTO Members and their constituents. Parliamentarians from less-developed WTO Members fear that inter-parliamentary bodies would reinforce the power of developed over less-developed WTO Members in WTO negotiations, for instance because NGOs from developed countries are in a stronger position to lobby and influence parliamentary bodies. Many parliaments in less-developed countries lack the expertise and resources necessary for effectively influencing WTO negotiations.

Chapter 19 by former US Congressman *David Skaggs* offers a US Congressional perspective on the question of *How Can Parliamentary Participation in WTO Rule-Making and Democratic Control Be Made More Effective in the WTO?* Skaggs welcomes inter-parliamentary WTO meetings as a means for rendering 'closed trade politics' more transparent and accountable, for building public support for non-discriminatory trade liberalisation (e.g. vis-à-vis one-sided 'civil society' critics, protectionist pressures from industry and from local constituencies), and for more effective parliamentary oversight at the national level.

Chapter 20 by *Meinhard Hilf* offers a European perspective on the same question of *How Can Parliamentary Participation in WTO Rule-Making and Democratic Control Be Made More Effective in the WTO?* Hilf criticizes the inadequate parliamentary control of trade policy-making in Europe, compared with the US, and emphasizes the constitutional requirements (e.g. in Article 23 of the German Basic Law) of democratic control of foreign-policy powers. He explains the different context of parliamentary control of trade policy-making in Europe and the US because, in the EU, trade policy is an executive power assigned to the EU Commission (cf. EU Treaty Article 133) rather than to parliament (as in the US); the European Parliament has only limited 'approving power'. In the European view, legitimacy of decision-making derives not only from popularly elected bodies or democratic votes, but also from other 'accountability mechanisms' holding decision-making processes accountable to those affected by them, notably consumers who benefit from trade liberalization but often remain 'rationally ignorant' vis-à-vis complex WTO negotiations. Inter-parliamentary cooperation in the WTO could offer additional information (e.g. on the impact of WTO rules abroad) and political control (e.g. of WTO bodies) that national parliamentarians lack.

Chapter 21 by *Erika Mann*, Member of the European Parliament, explains the different views in the US Congress and the European Parliament regarding parliamentary oversight of rule-making in the WTO, and why *A Parliamentary Dimension to the WTO is More than Just a Vision*. She draws attention to the new parliamentary powers in the trade policy area if the 2004 Treaty establishing a Constitution for Europe enters into force. Parliamentary involvement could balance the influence by NGOs that represent much smaller 'constituencies'. According to Mann, inter-parliamentary cooperation and control at the international level offer better first-hand information. The positive experiences with supra-national governance mechanisms in Europe prompt European parliamentarians to support inter-parliamentary meetings at the WTO level as a means of complementing and strengthening their much weaker parliamentary control of trade policy-making (compared with the US Congress) at national and EU levels. Mann offers a positive evaluation of the inter-parliamentary meetings at the WTO Ministerial Conferences in Seattle (1999), Doha (2001), and Cancún (2003). The limited participation or absence of US Congressmen in the Doha and Cancún conferences seemed to reflect their view that little may be gained from talking to foreign parliamentarians for advancing US negotiation positions in the WTO.

The US view of the WTO as a 'bureaucratic bargaining system' which does not need additional democratic legitimization at the international level is further explained by *James Bacchus* in his *Few Thoughts on Legitimacy, Democracy, and the WTO* (Chapter 22). Bacchus, a former Congressman and former Chairman of the WTO Appellate Body, perceives the WTO as a collective effort of WTO Members to increase their welfare through trade. The WTO's legitimacy derives 'from the individual legitimacy of each of the individual "nation–states" that, together, comprise "the WTO" '. Bacchus emphasizes 'bottom–up democracy' since democratic input and output legitimacy depend on *domestic* rather than international decision-making. NGOs representing special citizen interests may have no more legitimacy than special producer interests. Multilevel legal restraints (e.g. through WTO adjudication) and 'transnational deliberative democracy' in distant intergovernmental organizations, far away from local stakeholders, can offer only little 'top–down legitimacy' (e.g. by limiting abuses of multilevel trade policy-making).

Steve Charnovitz, in his contribution on *The WTO and Cosmopolitics* (Chapter 23), comments on the proposals by EU Commissioner Pascal Lamy to promote 'cosmopolitan constituencies' supporting welfare-increasing trade liberalization and transnational market regulation through WTO negotiations. Charnovitz makes a number of proposals for improving external WTO transparency and mainstreaming inter-governmental organizations, parliamentarians, and NGOs into the work of the WTO's functional committees and bodies. WTO decision-making would benefit from better connection to national democratic processes inside WTO member countries. WTO cooperation with NGOs needs to be regulated so as to limit 'single-interest pressures', hold NGOs more accountable, and protect the effectiveness of WTO decision-making processes. Even though the narrow mandate and limited institutional capacity of the WTO currently limit its cooperation with NGOs, Charnovitz points out that the additional administrative burdens resulting from consultations with NGOs could be outweighed by the political advantages of more inclusive WTO discussions and more inclusive WTO constituencies.

Chapter 24 by former WTO ambassador and chairman of the WTO Appellate Body *Julio A. Lacarte* supports proposals to make the formerly secretive negotiation culture inherited by the WTO more trans-parent, for example by setting up an advisory WTO Economic and Social Committee enabling more representative civil society participa-tion and closer WTO contacts with 'the real world'. Governmental prerogatives have to be respected but should be subjected to stronger 'checks and balances', notably regarding the sometimes one-sided influ-ence of producer interests on WTO decision-shaping.

VIII. WTO DECISION-MAKING PROCEDURES, 'MEMBER-DRIVEN' RULE-MAKING, AND WTO CONSENSUS PRACTICES: ARE THEY ADEQUATE?

Part VIII concludes the book with five chapters examining proposals for improving WTO decision-making rules and practices. *Richard Blackhurst* and *David Hartridge*, in Chapter 25, call for *Improving the Capacity of WTO Institutions to Fulfil their Mandate*. They start from the widely accepted premise that the WTO's 'rule-making' bodies are working poorly, if at all. The weaknesses of 'Green Room debates and negotiations' relying on 'inner-circle meetings' of some WTO Members, preparing draft texts for subsequent consensus-decisions by all 148 WTO Members, are explained. As large and influential developing countries are regular participants in Green Room meetings, the needed reform of the WTO's decision-making process is *not* a North–South issue but rather an insider–outsider issue, with the industrial countries and 'important' developing countries on the inside, and the other 110 or so WTO Members on the outside. Blackhurst and Hartridge conclude that, if Green Room meetings cannot accommodate all WTO Members wishing to participate, the WTO should have recourse to a new WTO Consultative Board which would need to be composed in a transparent and legitimate manner for the purpose of discussing and negotiating draft decisions that can be put to the entire membership for adoption. Whereas the largest trading countries would have permanent seats, the remaining WTO Members would be divided into groups, each with one seat to be shared among the members of the group on a rotating basis. The transparency, consultative character, and accessibility of such a Board to all WTO Members would facilitate its political acceptability and consensus-building efforts. The so-far 'disenfranchised outside WTO Members' should insist on establishing such a WTO Consultative Board, since the 'insiders' might not take such an initiative limiting their own privileges.

Depending on the subject (e.g. agriculture), the current Doha Development Round negotiations involve far more negotiators (e.g. 80–100) compared with the preceding Uruguay Round negotiations (usually no more than up to 40 negotiators), which renders trade-offs more difficult. Chapter 26 by *John S. Odell* on *Chairing a WTO Negotiation* explains why efforts by WTO Members to negotiate multilateral decisions have been less efficient and less legitimate than many would like. Two of the three most recent WTO Ministerial Conferences have ended in frustrating impasses and contributed to increased recourse to WTO dispute settlement challenges (e.g. of agricultural subsidies). As long as WTO Members fail to agree on formal changes to WTO negotiation and decision-making procedures, it remains important to enhance the limited but significant capacity of WTO chairs to influence the efficiency of consensus-building, the resulting distribution of gains and losses, and its legitimacy. Odell explains the various reasons why rational governments delegate influence to a mediator and consensus-builder, and why developing WTO Members show today greater willingness to stand firm and block consensus in order to increase their gains and reduce their losses from negotiations. He criticizes the lack of explicit authority of the WTO Director-General to advance original proposals, as well as the absence of a representative

WTO Executive Body that could function as a site for more efficient consensus-building. Also chairpersons lack authority to originate substantive proposals or to make policy decisions for any other WTO Member. Odell describes WTO mediation tactics (including observation, diagnosis, communication tactics), formulation tactics (e.g. use of a single negotiating text, compromise packages, 'reservation values') as well as manipulation tactics (e.g. threats by the chair to abandon mediation efforts as a means of stimulating further concessions). Odell concludes that deadlocks in multilateral WTO negotiations are more difficult to resolve today than under GATT 1947. By diagnosing impasses, separating bluffs from true reservation values, imagining integrative multi-issue deals, deciding when to offer a single negotiating text and how to weight the demands of diverse members, by pushing particular members in certain directions or wait before ending a stalemate, a WTO chair–mediator has limited but significant influence on the efficiency and legitimacy of negotiations. As long as WTO Members cannot agree on formal changes of WTO procedures and WTO institutions, they will continue to depend in part on their chairpersons to mediate and build consensus.

Chapter 27 by *Claus-Dieter Ehlermann* and *Lothar Ehring* examines the question: *Are WTO Decision-Making Procedures Adequate for Making, Revising, and Implementing Worldwide and 'Plurilateral' Rules?* The authors recall that, at a time when global governance is more necessary than ever before, the WTO offers an important forum for worldwide rule making and rule enforcement. Yet signs of inefficient decision-making have appeared regularly in WTO negotiations on new WTO rules and on applying or revising existing WTO rules. Effectiveness and efficiency are not the sole benchmarks for evaluating WTO decision-making because transparency, participation, accountability, and other aspects of democratic legitimacy cannot be discounted. As formal changes of WTO decision-making rules are difficult to achieve, Ehlermann and Ehring explore, first, the scope for improving WTO decision-making practices within the framework of existing WTO rules. With regard to procedures for implementing WTO rules, the WTO Dispute Settlement Body (DSB) decides by consensus or 'qualified consensus' (e.g. for the establishment of panels, the adoption of dispute settlement reports, authorization of retaliation), and other WTO bodies 'shall continue the practice of decision-making by consensus followed under GATT 1947' subject to the proviso that, 'where a decision cannot be arrived at by consensus, the matter at issue shall be decided by voting' (Article IX:1 of the WTO Agreement). According to Ehlermann and Ehring, the possibility of adopting authoritative interpretations of WTO rules by a three-quarters majority of WTO Members (cf. Article IX:2) constitutes a necessary instrument of checks and balances vis-à-vis the WTO's quasi-judiciary. The WTO consensus practice has so far prevented authoritative interpretations and creates a trade-off between the ability of easily objecting and the difficulty of achieving desired decisions. Ehlermann and Ehring criticize the political paralysis and imbalance resulting from the burdensome consensus practice: legislative responses to judicial developments have been prevented, and the WTO's (quasi-)judiciary eludes effective control and loses legitimacy. The authors suggest abolishing the taboo of resorting to majority decision-making and increasing the costs of blocking a consensus, for example by actively using the existing procedural requirement of referring a matter to the General Council if subordinate WTO bodies are unable to reach a decision by consensus. WTO Members should also use the existing possibilities of adopting authoritative interpretations by a three-quarters majority (cf. Article IX:2) and of concluding agreements among interested WTO Members (cf. Article X). The creation of a representative, high-level Steering Group with rotating membership could further promote more effective decision-making in the WTO.

Chapter 28 by *Gary P. Sampson* examines the question: *Is There a Need for Restructuring the Collaboration among the WTO and UN Specialized Agencies so as to Harness their Complementarities?* Sampson shows that the WTO and United Nations (UN) agencies pursue common goals, like 'sustainable development', and could mutually benefit from closer cooperation among the WTO and UN bodies. Sampson identifies specific areas (such as protection of intellectual property rights, traditional knowledge, genetic resources, the environment, public health, labour standards, human rights, the rule of law) in which a 'bottom–up' approach to collaboration should be pursued complementing the numerous 'top–down' political commitments to mutual cooperation among WTO and UN agencies. As Article V of the WTO Agreement requires the WTO Council to make appropriate arrangements for effective cooperation with other intergovernmental organizations and NGOs that have responsibilities related to those of the WTO, Sampson recommends more specific cooperation arrangements between the WTO, UN agencies, and NGOs, similar to the successful WTO cooperation with intergovernmental and non-governmental environmental organizations. The need for deviations from WTO rules for non-economic policy reasons should be clarified by WTO Members collectively (e.g. as done in the WTO Decisions on the TRIPS Agreement and Public Health) rather than through WTO litigation. A WTO Group on the Functioning of the WTO System should be set up to make recommendations on how to bring greater coherence to policy-making at the global level and improve collaboration among the

WTO and UN agencies. The focus of the Doha Round on development needs should help to promote positive synergies in the capacity-building assistance of WTO and UN agencies. The recent 'summit conferences' (e.g. in Monterrey, Johannesburg, and Doha) have, however, not yet succeeded in transforming the objective of 'sustainable development' into reality.

The last chapter (Chapter 29) by *Claus-Dieter Ehlermann* and *Lothar Ehring* examines whether WTO dispute settlement bodies can effectively deal with competition disputes. The authors describe how WTO rules (e.g. on national treatment) and the DSU are already applicable to trade-related competition rules of WTO Members and to individual decisions on their application by competition authorities. The proposals to extend the application of the DSU to a future WTO framework agreement on trade-related competition policies would, therefore, not lead to a *qualitative* innovation. The discussions in the WTO Working Group on the Interaction of Trade and Competition Policy have, however, revealed reservations against application of the DSU, notably against review by WTO dispute settlement bodies of individual decisions applying future WTO competition rules. According to Ehlermann and Ehring, only some of these reservations are justified in view of certain weaknesses of WTO dispute settlement procedures (e.g. inadequate panel procedures for access to and protection of confidential business information, limited fact-finding capacities of *ad hoc* panellists). The standard of review set out in Article 11 of the DSU could also be appropriate for trade related competition rules. Even though the full application of the DSU to future WTO competition rules should not present major problems, and some problems could be dealt with in the current negotiations on reforms of the DSU, restriction of dispute settlement provisions in a future competition agreement to review of laws as such might be a necessary price to pay for reaching political consensus on such an agreement. The adoption, in June 2004, of the WTO Panel Report on *Mexico—Measures Affecting Telecommunications Services*,[28] which found that Mexico had failed to maintain 'appropriate measures' to prevent 'anti-competitive practices' by Mexican telecommunications operators in violation of the competition safeguards in Mexico's GATS commitments, appears to confirm the view of Ehlermann and Ehring that WTO dispute settlement panels can effectively apply trade-related competition rules, such as those in the 'Reference Paper' included into the commitments of many WTO Members under the 1997 GATS Protocol on Basic Telecommunications.

[28] WT/DS204/R (2 April 2004).

PART II

THE DOHA DEVELOPMENT ROUND AND THE FUTURE OF THE WTO: POLICY PROPOSALS

1

The Doha Development Agenda: Political Challenges to the World Trading System—A Cosmopolitan Perspective

PETER SUTHERLAND

I. INTRODUCTION

The Doha Development Agenda (DDA) negotiations in the World Trade Organization (WTO) have reached a point where the shape of a worthwhile agreement can be envisaged even if its final delivery is far from guaranteed. This is, therefore, an appropriate time to look closely at what has been achieved and what has been lost and to seek to reach some conclusions that may brighten the prospects of eventual success.

One way of looking at the challenges to the system posed by and around the DDA is to consider first what has gone wrong and what has gone right since the Round was launched in 2001. In some senses the exercise has been problematic since its inception. If there is to be something worthwhile at its conclusion we need to understand why progress has been so troubled.

There is also a need to explore why the difficulties encountered in the DDA are, in part, systemic. The WTO is 10 years old. It has surely had its successes; it has equally suffered some disappointments. Those of us who believe in multilateralism as ultimately the safest and surest means of global governance need the WTO to deliver as intended. It *has* delivered on dispute settlement; it *has* made significant advances in helping developing countries draw advantage from the system, but it has yet to show its potential as a negotiating machine. That is the test posed by the DDA.

II. RECOGNIZING THE FAULT LINES IN THE DOHA AGENDA

This is not the first time that political enthusiasm to launch a multilateral trade round has overwhelmed political willingness subsequently to negotiate in substance and make concessions. In the case of the Tokyo Round of the General Agreement on Tariffs and Trade (GATT), launched in 1973, little happened for more than three years. In the period after the Punta del Este ministerial meeting, in 1986, the Uruguay Round was very slow moving until after the crisis of the Brussels ministerial conference in 1990. However, it is important to note that in the latter case there was a huge job to be done in exploring new areas for trade rules—like services and intellectual property—as well as seeking new approaches on agriculture and dispute settlement before serious practical negotiation was possible.

So frustration with slow progress in Geneva is the rule not the exception. From that perspective we should not be overly concerned that the Doha Round has not concluded on time and will take at least another two years to reach an outcome. It is true that the time-frame originally imposed was unrealistic: there was never any reason to suppose that this time around a relatively ambitious trade negotiation would be treated with a greater sense of urgency than any other. To imagine a conclusion at the end of a year in which the European Commission was to change and with major elections in the United States (US) and India—to name just three key WTO members—was optimistic.

A greater problem had its roots in the sense of balance and ambition within the Doha agenda. The Europe-driven aspiration to drive forward the 'Singapore issues' has been a source of internal conflict in the WTO and has held back meaningful progress in other aspects of the Doha negotiations. That is not to say the aspirations were misplaced. It is clear that multilateral agreements on investment, competition policies, and government procurement transparency, as well as trade facilitation, could all make good sense from a development perspective. Many poor WTO members recognize the fact. It is equally the case that a broader agenda that held out the hope of valuable new disciplines in areas of importance to developed-country investors might have made prospective concessions in agriculture easier.

However, in pressing the Singapore agenda, some industrial countries failed to appreciate the difficulties that a number of developing nations were having in implementing existing WTO disciplines from the Uruguay Round. Understandably, and notwithstanding the potential advantages, poorer WTO members shied away from the prospect of new obligations that they could not afford to implement but which might in part be enforceable through the dispute settlement procedure. Moreover, there has always been some scepticism that the substantial levels of technical assistance needed for the implementation of existing as well as potential future WTO obligations would be forthcoming.

In short, coming so soon after the Uruguay Round, the original Doha agenda was just too demanding on too many members to be sustainable and meaningful within a short time-frame.

But there were other fundamental faults in the design of the new trade round. The price of inclusion of the Singapore issues was a lack of balance in the contributions to be made in the mainstream negotiations—notably, market access. A traditional multilateral trade round was reinvented as a 'Development Agenda'. The lack of reciprocity implicit in the Doha bargain was an illusion. While it has always been the case that least-developed countries contributed little in trade rounds—which may or may not have been in their true interests—the idea that more advanced developing nations could avoid meaningful market-opening commitments while industrial members made politically difficult decisions to further open theirs was unreal. From a political perspective, all trade negotiations must provide for a mutual exchange of commercially credible concessions among the key players. Perfect symmetry is never possible, but all sides must return from the negotiating table with something of value for their exporters.

Of course, a major reason for the adoption of the development agenda device was the impact of the anti-globalization, anti-WTO movements in the late 1990s and thereafter. The idea that developing countries had been 'losers' from the global trading system gained so much currency that political leaders of industrial countries and even the WTO itself embraced it. Yet the notion was always a gross exaggeration, certainly an oversimplification. That too many poor countries have remained poor despite being members of the WTO is hardly in question. That it is a fundamental fault of the institution—or of the treatment of those poor nations within the institution—surely is.

While we can point to elements of the WTO's rules and practices that are sometimes a challenge for developing countries, the essential principles of the system are unchallenged as a framework for economic progress. Developing countries that maintain highly protected markets, that offer no security or predictability to investors or, indeed, to their own domestic firms, that fail to put in place the institutional structures and practices that encourage rather than hold back trade-led development have been and will be failures. Whether they are members of the WTO or not will make little difference. The WTO provides a framework for reform and secure access to markets; opportunities that are there to be exploited, but which do not guarantee success.

Somehow the Doha agenda lost contact with these realities. Political leaders have tended to repeat mantras about the shortcomings of the system while failing publicly to defend the institution as an essential support for trade, investment and development. Playing to the gallery of critics is not a responsible position when the critics have no alternative to present as a coherent replacement for the system.

This drift has led to disappointments—the system seems unable to deliver what is needed. There is a need to get back to the essentials and understand clearly what is within the capacity of the WTO to achieve and what lies outside.

Two other trends have made progress within the Doha Round difficult. One is the proliferation of trade agendas outside the multilateral system. The most active of those is the new enthusiasm for regional trade agreements. Together with the spread of preferential arrangements, the energy being put into essentially politically motivated free trade agreements (FTAs) is detracting from the motivation and capacity of negotiators to secure multilateral agreements. That is not to say there is no value in regional arrangements—it may well be, for instance, that those that are opening up some Asian markets may be beneficial globally. But the reality is that one of the central pillars of the WTO—most-favoured nation (MFN) treatment—has been undermined to the point that it may become meaningless.

A second tendency that has undercut the will to negotiate is, perversely, the success of the WTO's dispute settlement system. So efficient—and, for the most part, respected—is the system that the belief has grown that most trade issues can be resolved through WTO litigation. It may well be that many outstanding differences among WTO members can, indeed, be resolved this way. But it is a dangerous assumption that dispute resolution procedures can indefinitely take all the strain that should be shouldered by collective negotiation among the full WTO membership. That would rightly be criticized as a negation of democratic legitimacy.

III. WHAT THEN HAS GONE RIGHT WITH THE DOHA ROUND?

The agreement reached by the WTO General Council in July 2004 went some way in correcting the shortcomings and illusions of the original mandate or, at least, the suppositions that underlay the declaration in 2001. In essence, negotiators now have a more confined agenda and an undefined time-frame. All the same, the Doha Round can still provide valuable results for the WTO and its members.

Two elements of the July agreement stand out as offering hope for a very substantial outcome. The decision to eliminate export subsidies and other trade-distorting forms of export support was welcome and impressive. Farmers in many nations who can market their produce competitively, in the absence of these grossly unfair practices, have much to gain if the decision in principle can be translated into a final settlement. It would not be the end of the story of reform in agriculture, but a very important step that, even a year ago, seemed unlikely.

The other outstanding agreement in July 2004 was the decision to move forward with negotiations on trade facilitation rules. It is difficult to underestimate how much could be achieved by such disciplines in easing the difficulties of moving goods across borders in an efficient, secure, and non-corrupt manner. This should be a development-friendly negotiation. It should also be an ambitious negotiation, going further than minor clarifications of GATT provisions. However, negotiators are going to need to tackle early on the very high potential cost that will be entailed. Introducing information technology, streamlining administrative arrangements, and, above all, reforming customs services to ensure personnel do not need bribes to support even an elementary standard of living, require substantial financial outlays. If the governments of poor nations are prepared to go down these challenging paths then they must have the necessary financial backing as well as technical support to do so.

Apart from these two key dossiers, much was left open in the framework agreements under which negotiators are now operating. In particular, the relative ambition for market-access talks—in agriculture, industrial goods, and services—is largely undefined. This does not, of course, exclude a high level of commitment at the end of the round. It is to be hoped that a result of significant commercial value can be achieved. However, that will require some of the advanced developing countries making a substantial contribution alongside those of the industrial nations. On this, the 2004 agreement is vague, yet the conclusion is inescapable if there is to be balance and some shared pain in the final outcome.

Even on this sensitive point, however, there is reason for some optimism. After the failure of the ministerial conference in Cancún in 2003, it took a major political effort to get the Doha Round back on track. For all the concerns about multiple trade agendas it was important to see the US and the European Union (EU) leading that political effort. Their respective trade representatives travelled the world and pursued consensus with an energy probably not seen since the end of the Uruguay Round. They were quickly joined by the representatives of key developing WTO members like India, Brazil, and South Africa and then by trade ministers from every continent as the potential for an accord became a realistic expectation.

In the final analysis, governments almost everywhere recognized that they had much more to lose than to gain from a further failure that would not merely have ended any hopes for the Doha Round but severely undermined the WTO itself. In a sense it was a crisis to which the membership rose. Not for the first time, or the last, the system needed to be on the point of cracking for good sense to prevail.

At the very least, the WTO found within itself the capacity to find consensus among almost 150 sovereign nations. It is to be hoped that the lessons learned will be remembered. The agreements were far from perfect, far from precise, and far less in content than was supposed to be achieved at that stage. Yet it was a step forward. The next steps may be no easier.

IV. WHERE DO WE GO FROM HERE?

Any trade round can only be viewed within a broad political framework. Negotiations never were entirely self-contained or impermeable to domestic interests: but that is less the case now than ever. I will return to the institutional issues that may affect the proceedings: the Director-General's Consultative Board, of which I am chairman, has reviewed these in some depth. But irrespective of what happens within the Organization, any conclusion of the Doha Round will be highly dependent on a collection of interlinked external events and decisions that will be taken by governments largely on the basis of domestic political imperatives.

The focus will continue to be on agriculture, even if it is now vital that the other negotiating dossiers catch up with the relatively advanced state of the farm trade talks. The process should, with some luck and much energy and commitment, reach the point of deciding detailed modalities for agricultural negotiations by the end of 2005 when the next ministerial conference is due to take place in Hong Kong.

However, not even this should be taken for granted. The hiatus in meaningful negotiations caused by the US presidential election campaign and the changeover of the EU Commission will end at some point in the first half of 2005. By then, regardless of the progress made within the Doha Round, both Washington and Brussels will have before them definitive judgments on two key dispute settlement cases. For the US, it will be the findings of the panel and Appellate Body concerning a range of support policies in the cotton sector. For the EU it will be the case brought against its sugar regime. The decisions taken by governments on these two sets of WTO findings will inevitably have some impact on the potential reform targets and negotiating modalities to be adopted in the Doha Round.

For the EU, willingness and ability to implement a negative panel finding on sugar will be related to ongoing changes in the Common Agricultural Policy (CAP) and perhaps to budgetary pressures. These factors will largely determine the stance taken in Geneva and the shape of commitments that may be possible.

Similarly, for the US at least some of the response to a successful challenge to its cotton policies will lie in the sustainability of the current budget deficit. Clearly, if budget adjustments require a cutback in farm spending, it might be advisable for the new administration to look at programmes that have been found to be inconsistent with international obligations. A little further down the road, in any event, there must be negotiations with Congress on a new Farm Bill to replace the spending limits and programmes contained in the 2002 legislation. Again, these are the developments that will ultimately determine what the US can sign on to in Geneva.

Of course, domestic political judgements on reform of the farm trade environment—both market access and domestic support programmes— will have to be made in many countries, developed and developing. Yet the willingness of the two biggest players in the WTO to move significantly will be the determining factor in the contributions that others will make and the political discomfort they will be prepared to bear.

Agriculture is just one example of the political complexity faced by WTO Members in pursuing Doha negotiations. Other external changes will also have an impact. So I will now turn to the various trade agendas that intersect, to some degree at least, with the DDA.

V. THE DEVELOPMENT CHALLENGE

The 'development agenda' facet of the Doha Round has to be met, of that there is no doubt. While there is no case in their own interests for sheltering developing countries from all the obligations of the WTO whilst offering them all the benefits, it is clear that a better-defined differentiation of obligations may help. The framework agreements on agriculture and non-agricultural market access set out copious arrangements—or potential arrangements—to secure special and differential treatment. The remains of the pre-Seattle 'implementation' agenda may still render some modest results. Additionally, members should be able to go further on the Special and Differential Treatment (SDT) mandate itself. At every point in the agenda there will be continued and increased need for well-focused, efficiently delivered, and properly coordinated technical assistance.

It would be a mistake to imagine much of this will assist the integration of poor countries into the global economy; rather, such efforts will provide breathing-space for the implementation of WTO obligations where it is most needed. As always, the least-developed countries will be faced with few binding requirements to implement anything of substance generated by the Doha Round.

It is probably best that the world's poorest countries are left to decide when, how quickly, and to what extent they wish to make use of the WTO framework to guide their own reforms. It has been well demonstrated that the WTO can have little impact on poverty alleviation in the absence of other more fundamental policy reform. Open markets in the least developed countries are of no value while supply-side restraints are extreme and while no credible and stable governmental and institutional structures exist to underpin business development, investment, and external trade.

However, other developing countries are not in that situation. Many are successful exporters and are moving fast to dominate global markets in a variety of farm products, industrial goods, and even services. Thus, in one form or another—explicitly or implicitly—some differentiation in the treatment of developing countries (outside the least-developed countries (LDC) group) is going to have to be faced in the Doha Round. Whether we call it 'differentiation' or the more formal, and feared, 'graduation', a WTO that is global and inclusive must now fully recognize the class of successful exporters, with increasingly high gross domestic product (GDP) per capita levels, within its ranks. And those members themselves owe it to the rest of the developing-country membership to be so recognized and to take the consequences in terms of higher levels of obligations and commitments.

We should also keep in mind that concessions made by many developing countries may serve merely to bring a higher proportion of WTO bindings within the national tariff or to contract the often large differences between applied and bound rates. In terms of immediate impact on import competition, the results, if any, are likely to be minimal. That is not to say, of course, that investors would not welcome such increased predictability; clearly they would.

Whatever its nature, there will have to be some movement by advanced developing countries. That seems to me to be the bargain on the basis of which industrial countries will have the political space to consider moving on some of the most testing—and to developing countries, damaging—policies of market protection that remain in place. It is on these foundations that an ambitious outcome to the Doha Round can still be secured, particularly with respect to market access.

VI. THE CHALLENGE OF REGIONAL
AND BILATERAL TRADE DEALS

That the Doha Round is deeply affected by the recent explosion of regional, bilateral, and preferential trade arrangements is clear. Whether the increased energy directed towards regionalism is, itself, a reflection of the lack of meaningful outcomes from multilateral activity is probably arguable. Yet all WTO Members continue to insist that multilateral trade benefits are the most valuable. This divergence between the pursuit of the optimal and the parallel enthusiasm for the more easily attainable needs resolution if we are to see a conclusion to the DDA within some acceptable period.

Certainly it would be difficult to pretend that proliferating negotiations on regional and preferential trade do other than draw negotiating capacity and attention away from Geneva and the WTO. Few countries have a sufficiently large number of trained and capable negotiators to engage on several fronts at the same time and with the same intensity. The reality is that governments are programming their attention to fit a variety of negotiating schedules. For poorer nations, with the least capacity, that is a serious loss of focus.

There is a natural tendency among trade ministers—whose terms in office are limited—to wish to be seen delivering new trade initiatives. Further, there is now an additional tendency to link bilateral trade agreements as much to urgent foreign-policy objectives as to commercial interests. The picking off of 'helpful' countries for beneficial trade treatment is only adding to the decline of multilateralism. It is something of a reversion to an era of friendship, commerce, and navigation treaties of nearly two centuries ago. The practical trade impact is often minimal but the practice exacerbates the undermining of the MFN principle—which is fundamental to the multilateral trading system. (It is worth noting, however, that the nineteenth-century equivalents, if inspired by foreign policy interests, were founded on full reciprocal MFN treatment.)

The tendency is doubly concerning since the WTO appears incapable of policing—or even monitoring—such agreements. Do they meet the criteria of Article XXIV of the GATT or the 'Enabling Clause'? As things are, we shall never know. The issue of making Article XXIV properly and adequately operational is part of the Doha mandate. Yet there is so far not even a consensus on how and when agreements should be notified to the WTO. As the arrangements spread, there are fewer and fewer WTO Members with an open mind or an interest in seeing a resolution. Yet the issue is vital to the future credibility of the institution.

No less worrisome is the treatment of preferences in the WTO. There are a large number of members for whom almost the sole objective in the Doha Round appears to be the safeguarding of their preferences in the major markets. Yet, while local political interests may continue to encourage such a position, the evidence continues to grow that preferences are far from being universally beneficial to those that receive them. As the WTO Secretariat's *2004 World Trade Report* pointed out, the absolute value of preferences is falling as MFN tariff levels fall. At the same time, dependence on preferences can sometimes drive developing economies into product segments where they have little or no comparative advantage. In other words, investment is taking place, on the basis of preferences, which may have no long-term likelihood of viability.

The EU has begun to take this problem seriously with the start of a negotiating process that should lead to an end, by 2008, of the non-reciprocal preferences of the present Cotonou Treaty with the large African, Caribbean, Pacific (ACP) Group. These will be replaced by a series of reciprocal trading arrangements—the 'economic partnership agreements'—with various regional groups within the ACP. The political challenge for the EU will be to support the change with adequate financial and other aid to help agricultural producers and other current preference targets to diversify out of products in which they will no longer be able to compete.

That will begin to provide a degree of fairness in access for poor countries. Too many have been left out under current arrangements providing preferential access to the major markets.

That there should be open access for the least-developed countries seems not to be in dispute—after all, it is an objective of the Doha Round and one which the EU has gone a long way towards providing. It is to be hoped that all industrial nations and advanced developing markets will offer undiluted tariff-free, quota-free access to these nations in the very near future. The amount of international trade so covered is not—and cannot—be more than a tiny fraction of the total. Yet the value of providing a few practical opportunities to export—so long as they are not negated by non-tariff restrictions—can be significant in providing a foothold into the global economy.

VII. THE CHALLENGE OF NON-TRADE AGENDAS

The temptation to bring non-trade agendas into the GATT and the WTO is long-standing. Provisions in both treaties allow for policies relating to national security, conservation of natural resources, and slave labour, among others, to cut across normal obligations. That is understood, and accepted. More recently, we have seen efforts to bring the WTO to bear on the furtherance of a number of admirable causes. The improvement of observance of international labour standards and other aspects of human rights have been among such causes. On the other hand, equally energetic attempts have been made to keep the WTO away from having any locus in certain policy areas, like the protection of animal species or aspects of certain food-safety regulations.

Happily the WTO has so far steered itself around these difficult and publicly controversial issues. The membership has wisely held out against initiatives that owed more to protectionist interests than, for instance, to serious concern for the rights of foreign workers. Furthermore, the dispute settlement system has generated a series of wise and sensitive findings that have encouraged successful resolutions of differences over animal safety and conservation policies.

It is to be hoped that any further temptation at the political level to seek to reopen these questions—and to pursue new ones, like outsourcing—will be resisted. While domestic debate may be necessary to quell disquiet over the loss of jobs and investment to foreign competition, it is for national governments to respond in a positive manner—notably through policies providing adjustment assistance—not to seek to pass the burden back to poorer nations. Certainly, it is difficult to see the Doha Round concluding successfully were there to be any new attempt to push labour rights or additional environmental criteria on to the agenda.

VIII. THE CHALLENGE AND OPPORTUNITY OF CHINA

Another intersection of conflicting interests by which the Doha Round may be affected is that concerning China. There is no question that the entry of China into the WTO was a significant success—perhaps the institution's biggest success since it was established. Equally, there is no question that the extraordinary vitality and growth of the Chinese economy will be of benefit to every other WTO member in the years ahead.

Yet the growing dominance of China as a trader and as a magnet for investment will need to be managed by governments at home and by the WTO, in particular, in the international arena. Presently, the ending of quota restraints under the Agreement on Textiles and Clothing is putting particular pressure on rich and poor nations alike. We will undoubtedly see efforts to dampen the force of Chinese competition in this and other sectors.

Clearly, the instruments exist to provide some short-term relief for embattled industries. The Chinese WTO accession agreement provides special safeguard provisions for some years ahead. At the same time, these and other mainstream trade contingency instruments will need to be used correctly and probably sparingly. The global economic stimulus that China can provide—is already providing—is too great to risk being undermined by ill-conceived protectionist reactions. That too would damage the Doha Round. China is a full participant already. As we move towards a conclusion, in some years time, it will be important for China to make a significant new contribution in terms of commitments on market access. China is already a gigantic market for the rest of the WTO—and that means for poor nations no less than rich—and will develop progressively towards one of the largest markets of all. There is, therefore, much to be gained in keeping China constructively engaged in the Doha Round and ensuring it has an interest, and a willingness to contribute significantly, to a worthwhile outcome.

IX. ENCOURAGING CIVIL SOCIETY TO SUPPORT DOHA ROUND GOALS

There is no doubting the increased activity and influence of non-governmental organizations (NGOs) in the trade policy field. Let us leave aside the irresponsible groups at the margin who seek only to destroy any international economic arrangement that stimulates trade and investment. More serious development and environmental NGOs—as well as some trade union groups—seem to have understood that even if the WTO may not be their most popular international institution it provides a vehicle for supporting their objectives.

It is regrettable that even some of these groups still tend to misrepresent the nature of the WTO. Yet some of their more targeted work has been exemplary. The campaigns and studies of Oxfam on the sugar and cotton sectors stand out. Indeed, it has long been apparent that if and when powerful NGOs could focus on narrowly targeted trade issues—particularly those relating to poverty alleviation—they could make a big contribution in pushing the WTO towards appropriate advances. In the case of these two agricultural sectors, a combination of NGO campaigning, WTO dispute settlement rulings, and some concerted action by WTO members themselves looks likely to make a practical, even dramatic, difference.

Clearly, if even the NGOs have an interest in a successful conclusion to the Doha Round that can only be positive. If they can accept the WTO as part—though a small part—of the answer to the many desperately difficult issues they seek to treat, rather than part of the problem, then we have the basis for a constructive, mutually reinforcing relationship.

My years leading the GATT and WTO Secretariat taught me one thing: the people in the institution are motivated not by any desire to reinforce corporate interests; they do their jobs to ensure fair rules of trade and support development and wealth creation among ordinary people, especially the poorest. Thus, in progressively opening up to responsible NGOs—even if that will always stop short of any direct non-governmental involvement—the WTO Secretariat is seeking to establish a degree of partnership. The days when the WTO was a rather opaque institution are long gone. Negotiations are now easy to follow externally and documents are available freely on the internet, often within hours of them circulating to delegations. It may be that further measures in transparency will be necessary. Some limited access to observe dispute settlement proceedings may be worth pursuing. Additional measures to involve parliamentarians could also be valuable.

NGOs have the tools to do their work in influencing governments in capitals on trade policy issues. But if the WTO is opening up to civil society groups, then those groups must take care to understand the institution. They need to recognize that, even if it has shortcomings, it still represents the lessons learned from a century of war, strife, and economic hardship born partly of foolish trade policies.

X. GIVING THE WTO THE TOOLS TO DO ITS JOB BETTER

We should not exaggerate the extent to which institutional reform will facilitate negotiations. For the most part, if there are difficulties in moving forward it is because substantive differences exist between the participants or that domestic political realities prevent governments from moving constructively towards consensus.

That said, the mechanics of decision-making in the WTO are not necessarily the most efficient. The nexus between ministers, senior officials, the Geneva representatives, and the Secretariat is not necessarily the most comfortable or the most effective possible. The method of selection of Directors-General has been incompetent and unfair to the recent incumbents. The overall management of the institution's work ought probably to be in the hands of tighter management structures than the General Council. The consensus rule serves the credibility of the WTO well and lends weight to its decisions when governments are required to change or adjust their policies. Yet, it is cumbersome and sometimes unnecessarily time-consuming. There may be circumstances in which it could be adjusted.

These are all issues that need to be considered seriously. The Director-General's Consultative Board has done so and it is for WTO Members to reach their own conclusions. However, it would be a mistake to insist they can all await the conclusion of the Doha Round. The difficulties in pursuing multilateral negotiations have been glaringly obvious since the launch of the Round in 2001. We still have a very long way to go before the talks can be rounded out. There is nothing to prevent a serious discussion on institutional reform from taking place in parallel. Some changes could well be implemented in a short time-frame; short enough to provide a boost to the Doha process.

XI. CONCLUSION

The political and institutional environment in which the next phase of the Doha Round will be conducted is extraordinarily complex and will remain so. There is absolutely no guarantee of ultimate success. Indeed, the challenges are sufficiently great for there to be real doubt that a commercially meaningful package can be secured.

Yet such an outcome is needed. There are too many countries and too many people with an interest in advances in the WTO to support economic growth and the assimilation of poor nations into the global economy for failure to be an option. Political spin can, of course, create victories out of thin air. That cannot work in the WTO. We need a large and balanced outcome that all WTO Members can justifiably regard as valuable and pertinent to their own national circumstances. As in every other trade round, that means a lot of energy, much commitment and an understanding, by every participant, of the common good.

2

A Development Perspective on the WTO July 2004 General Council Decision

FAIZEL ISMAIL[1]

I. INTRODUCTION

Amartya Sen has defined development as 'the removal of unfreedom'.[2] Development, in the view of Sen, is the process of expanding human freedoms. These substantive freedoms include elementary capabilities like being able to avoid such deprivations as starvation, and enjoy political participation. Human freedom is seen as the pre-eminent objective of development. It is also seen as the means of achieving development. The focus on rights, opportunities, and entitlements, he argues, contributes to the expansion of human freedom and the promotion of development. Thus, for Sen, development is understood as the process of removing these unfreedoms.

We have identified four types of unfreedom or deprivation in Sen's work that are relevant to our discussion in this chapter of development and the multilateral trading system. First, Sen argues that deprivations can result when people are denied the economic opportunities and favourable consequences that markets offer and support. Second, Sen argues that poverty should be understood not so much as low incomes but as a deprivation of basic capabilities. Third, whilst Sen argues for government regulation to enable markets to work more effectively, he states that a system of ethics is required to build vision and trust for the successful use of the market mechanism. Sen urges policy makers to

[1] Head of the South African Delegation to the World Trade Organization. He joined the new democratic government of South Africa in 1994 as it began its transition to reintegrate with the world economy and led South Africa's trade negotiations with the European Union, the Southern African Development Community, the Southern African Customs Union, with a number of bilateral trading partners, and with the WTO. He joined South Africa's Mission to Geneva in May 2002. This chapter is written in his personal capacity. [2] A. Sen, *Development as Freedom* (1999) at 3.

base this ethical system on social justice as the foundation and objective of public policy. Sen recognizes that individuals would assert their 'prudent and material concerns' but argues that policy-makers can balance these concerns with the values of social justice through public discussion. Fourth, Sen argues against the view that the denial of political liberty and basic civil rights is 'good' for rapid economic development and states that the deprivation of the opportunity to participate in crucial decisions regarding public affairs is to deny people the right to develop and strengthen a democratic system. The latter is seen as an essential part of the process of development.

In applying the above definition of development to the trading system, it could be argued that a fair trading system would remove the obstacles that developing countries experience in exporting their products to developed country markets and create opportunities for them to advance their development. Secondly, increasing the capacity of developing countries to develop their comparative advantage to produce and export would provide the necessary institutional, productive, and export capabilities needed by these countries to level the playing field in the trading system. Thirdly, establishing rules that ensure that there is a fair balance between (a) the costs and the benefits of new agreements, (b) the values and interests of developed and developing countries, (c) appropriate flexibility for developing countries to implement development policies, and, (d) the need for a strengthened rules-based system would contribute to the legitimacy and sustainability of these rules. Fourthly, by building a transparent and inclusive system of decision-making in the World Trade Organization (WTO), members will be contributing to the capacity of developing countries to participate effectively in the making of decisions that are democratic and consistent with the above dimensions of development. Thus in terms of this definition, four elements of the development dimension of the multilateral trading system can be unpacked: fair trade, capacity building, balanced rules, and good governance.

The concept of Special and Differential Treatment (SDT), which has emerged since the earliest days of the formation of the General Agreement on Tariffs and Trade (GATT), has called for the interests of developing countries to be given special consideration.[3] This concept remains essential to ensure that there is proportionality in the commitments undertaken between developed and developing countries, reflecting their different levels of development and gains from the trading system.[4] However,

---

[3] P. Low and A. Keck, *Special and Differential Treatment in the WTO: Why, When and How?* WTO Staff Working Paper, (2004).

[4] B. Hoekman, 'Operationalizing the Concept of Policy Space in the WTO: Beyond Special and Differential Treatment' in this volume.

this chapter argues that SDT should not be confused with the broader development dimension of the trading system nor become a substitute for it. SDT is only an aspect of the broader development dimension.

However, both the concept of development and of SDT have tended to be marginalized in the debate and negotiations in the WTO and treated as an 'optional extra' or a 'nice thing to do'. It is argued that in order to address effectively the development dimension of the multilateral trading system one needs to focus on the core issues of the WTO and how it functions: viz. fair trade, capacity-building for the poorest countries, balanced rules, and good governance.

This paper evaluates the recent WTO July 2004 General Council (GC) decisions using the above definition of the development dimension of the multilateral trading system. The chapter is structured as follows: section II provides a brief background to the July GC Meeting. Each of the five critical issues negotiated in the WTO July GC Meeting—i.e. agriculture (section III), cotton (section IV), non-agricultural market access (NAMA) (section V), Singapore issues (section VI), and the development issues (section VII)—are then discussed. Some background is provided on each of the issues. The outcome of the July GC Decision is then evaluated drawing on the perspective developed above. The Conclusion is cautiously optimistic and calls on all WTO members to build on the advances of the WTO July GC Decision.

II. BACKGROUND TO THE JULY PACKAGE

The July GC Meeting was scheduled by the WTO in an attempt to complete the work and make decisions that Ministers failed to achieve at the collapsed Cancún Ministerial Meeting. The Chair of the Meeting, Minister Derbez, announced before closing the meeting that the negotiations would move back to Geneva.

The Doha Ministerial Conference, in November 2001, launched a broad-based round of multilateral trade negotiations that included agriculture; services; intellectual property rights (TRIPS); industrial tariffs; rules (anti-dumping, subsidies); and environment. In addition, four further areas were to be included in the negotiations, if WTO Members agreed at the 5th Ministerial Conference (10–14 September 2003): investment; competition; transparency in government procurement; and trade facilitation. All negotiations were to be concluded by December 2004.

A significant part of the overall balance that Ministers agreed to in Doha involved the balance in the *negotiating process* as expressed in the deliberate staging of a series of interim deadlines. These milestones contained a logic that aimed, in the first phase, to build confidence amongst developing countries by resolving, upfront, outstanding issues of critical concern to them, namely, implementation issues, SDT, TRIPS and public health. The date set to agree to modalities in agriculture—the end of March 2003—was also deliberate as it was intended to unlock political will, and create the basis for all Members to engage meaningfully in preparations for a decision in Cancún on launching negotiations on the Singapore issues.

Three key issues of great interest to developing countries—i.e. public health and TRIPS, SDT, and other problems with existing agreements, the so-called 'implementation issues—had interim deadlines in December 2002. These were missed. Consensus was finally reached on TRIPS and public health—on establishing a mechanism that would allow countries with no or insufficient manufacturing capacity to import medicines for public health reasons under compulsory licenses—in August 2003. Second, there was agreement in Doha that a range of provisions on SDT in favour of developing countries would need to be made operational and effective by December 2002. This deadline also passed. Third, developing countries confront a range of problems with existing WTO agreements (implementation issues), and these were to be resolved by December 2002. Again, no progress was made on these issues. In failing to meet these deadlines, the balance in the process was disrupted.

The Cancún Ministerial Meeting was intended to be a review of progress made in the Doha Development Agenda. However, as we moved closer to Cancún the WTO had made little progress on meeting its deadlines. Other than an agreement on TRIPS and public health which was outside the single undertaking, little progress was made on the development issues (implementation and SDT) or modalities on agriculture and NAMA. In addition the Joint Text agreed by the European Union (EU) and the United States (US) on agriculture took the negotiating process further back by agreeing to a mere 'Framework' for the agriculture negotiations just a few weeks (13 August 2003) from the Cancún Ministerial Meeting that was held in September 2003. The Doha Mandate envisaged agreement on 'modalities' for the agriculture negotiations by March 2003. The WTO then also regressed the process in the NAMA negotiations, which had made greater progress on developing modalities,[5] by drawing up a 'framework' for negotiations for decision at Cancún.

---

[5] In the NAMA negotiations the Chair had proposed a formula for market access reductions (the Girard Formula) with the majority of members willing to engage on this formula.

The Cancún Package included a list of 28 issues to be agreed on, including 'framework agreements' on agriculture and NAMA and 'modalities' for the launching of negotiations on transparency in government procurement and trade facilitation.[6] This was clearly an awesome task for the Ministers. The breakdown of the negotiations and the shifting of these issues back to the Geneva process meant that this package had to be reviewed. In the period after Cancún, the Chairman of the GC, Carlos Castillo, decided to focus on the issues that were critical to put the Doha negotiations back on track. These included: agriculture, cotton, NAMA, the Singapore issues, and the 'development issues'. He had hoped to conclude this process by mid December 2003. However, there was little substantive movement by the major countries in this period—the EU participated in a protracted internal process of reflection on Cancún and the US waited for the EU to revive the process. However, as we got to the end of the year, the EU (Pascal Lamy) under pressure from its member states to revive the talks agreed to meet with G20 Ministers in Brasília in the second week of December. This provided a much-needed shot in the arm for the WTO to revive the talks. The US (Bob Zoellick), not to be outdone, sent a letter to all WTO Ministers in the first week of January 2004—changing its tone from rebuke and criticism to constructive dialogue.

Thus began the 'Pascal and Bob' roadshows, with both Pascal Lamy and Bob Zoellick travelling to several capitals to discuss the relaunch of the negotiations.[7] With the election of the new chair of the GC and new chairs of the various negotiating groups (11 February), the negotiations began in earnest again. The Chair of the GC focused on the five core issues: agriculture, cotton, NAMA, Singapore issues, and development. The EU and the US began negotiating meetings with the G20. It became clear early in the process that agriculture was the fulcrum of the negotiations and movement on all other issues was linked to it. Thus the US initiated (in the third week of March 2004) an agriculture negotiating group of five countries comprising the US, EU, Australia, India, and Brazil, which began to meet regularly (seven or eight such meetings were held) in the next few months until the end of July 2004. In addition, the group began to meet at ministerial level to stimulate the process. Mini-Ministerial Meetings (mainly between these five countries) were held in London (1 May 2004), in Paris, on the margins of the Organization for Economics Co-operation and Development (OECD) Ministerial Meetings, in São Paolo, on the margins of the United Nations Conference

---

[6] See Draft Ministerial Text, 2nd Revision, JOB(03)/150/Rev.2 (13 September 2003).

[7] Zoellick travelled to nine countries in ten days, including India, China, Indonesia (ASEAN), Pakistan, South Africa, and Kenya (18 February). He also attended the Cairns Group meeting in Costa Rica (23 February).

on Trade and Development (UNCTAD) XI Ministerial Conference, again in Paris, before the Mauritius G90 Ministerial Meeting, and then finally in Geneva in the week before the July GC Meeting.

The Chair of the GC succeeded in maintaining the focus of the July GC meeting on the five key issues (see above) in his initial draft (16 July) although there were some other issues (viz. services) that were highlighted in the first revision (30 July), the second revision (31 July), and final decision (2 August). We will thus focus our analyses on these five issues: agriculture, cotton, NAMA, trade facilitation, and development issues.

III. AGRICULTURE

A. Background

Two-thirds of all poor people in developing countries live and work in the agricultural sector, depending on agriculture for their livelihoods. In contrast agriculture accounts for less than 5 per cent of output and employment in the EU and the US. In 2003 the 30 members of the OECD transferred US$257 billion to their farmers. This amount represents a substantial amount in the share of farmers' total revenue and accounted for up to 32 per cent in 2003.[8] The Uruguay Round brought these agricultural policies and trade in agriculture under GATT/WTO disciplines for the first time. However, the Uruguay Round Agreement on Agriculture failed to ensure that developed countries and, in particular, the main subsidizers (the EU, US, and other OECD subsidizers) reduced the extremely high existing levels of subsidies. Farm subsidies in the main subsidizers did not decrease substantially even after the Agreement on Agriculture came into force in 1995. Ironically, farm support actually increased in some countries.

Almost two-thirds of OECD farm support is still in the form of the most trade-distorting type—market price support and output payments. Policy changes in the main subsidizers has reduced this support somewhat in the EU (by decoupling of support in its Common Agricultural Policy (CAP) reforms) whilst for the US the move has been backwards with its 2002 Farm Bill locking in the high levels of support provided in preceding years through *ad hoc* payments.[9] Similarly, with regard to market access, agricultural tariffs of OECD countries remain extremely

---

[8] S. Tangermann, 'How to Forge a Compromise in the Agriculture Negotiations' in this volume. Out of each dollar of revenue for the average farmer in the OECD 32 cents resulted from government policies and only 68 cents came from the market.

[9] Tangermann, *supra* n. 8.

high. A substantial percentage of tariffs of several OECD countries contain mega-tariffs, i.e. tariffs above 100 per cent—almost 70 per cent in Norway and Iceland, 40 per cent for Japan, over 30 per cent for the EU, and about 12 per cent in the US. These tariffs are in many cases simply prohibitive, and minimal reduction commitments have simply 'squeezed the economic water out of the tariffs' without affecting price levels and trade flows. Export subsidies, which are the most notorious form of farm support, have declined significantly, according to the OECD, although current levels still remain at over US$10 billion.

Some observers have argued that part of the reason for the Uruguay Round disciplines not being effective has been that the new rules on agriculture have been deficient and left too many loopholes, and secondly, that the reduction commitments have been too generous, thus allowing too much scope for the continuation of high levels of protection and support. Thus, in the current negotiations, negotiators have been concerned to refine the rules and ensure real and deeper cuts in support levels.[10] There is indeed a linkage between all three types of support (tariff protection, domestic subsidies, and export subsidies)—all acting in concert to increase levels of protection. Thus some writers have argued that the distinction between domestic support and export support becomes blurred as export support is essentially 'the tip of the iceberg' of domestic support.[11] In addition a domestically administered higher price, created through the use of domestic price support, that is significantly above world market levels can only be sustained behind high tariff protection. In turn the increased supply created by higher domestic prices can only be exported with the use of export subsidies.

These policies of the developed countries in agriculture have been criticized for: (a) preventing access for the exports of developing countries, which in many cases is their main comparative advantage; (b) distorting world markets and thus stifling the exports of agriculturally competitive countries; (c) and destroying the livelihoods of poor farmers in the South by dumping subsidized products in their local markets. These inequities in agricultural trade thus became the critical issue for the launch of the Doha Round of negotiations.

The Doha Ministerial Conference was largely regarded as being successful for the ambitious mandate it succeeded in obtaining from developed countries to liberalize agricultural trade. The Doha Mandate called for 'substantial reductions in trade distorting domestic support', and 'substantial improvements in market access', and in export competition it called for reductions 'with a view to eliminating all forms of

---

[10] Some observers (for instance, Tangermann, in this volume) point out that there was too much 'water' in both the domestic support commitments and tariff commitments.

[11] See for example Tangermann, *supra* n. 8.

export subsidies'.[12] In the negotiating process, since Doha, the WTO failed to reach agreement on modalities by the agreed date of the end of March 2003. There are several reasons for this, including that of the failure of the EU to produce a proposal that was in line with its Doha commitments.[13] In addition, the EU CAP reforms announced by the Agriculture Ministers at Luxembourg in June 2003 were criticized widely for agreeing to reforms that were 'too little, too late'.[14] Furthermore these reforms did not make an offer to reduce the EU's prohibitively high tariffs or phase out its export subsidies as the Doha mandate had agreed.

There followed a series of intense bilateral meetings between the EU and the US before Cancún leading to the EU–US Joint Text on Agriculture.[15] This Framework Agreement of the EU and US was widely criticized as falling far short of the Doha mandate and accommodating the agricultural protections interests of both the EU and the US.[16] In response developing countries led by Brazil and India created a formidable developing-countries alliance to ensure that this deviation from the Doha mandate did not prevail at the Cancún Ministerial Meeting. Although several meaningful negotiating engagements did take place between the EU/US and the G20 at Cancún, this process had not succeeded in reaching any consensus. The collapse of the Cancún Conference meant that this issue had to be deferred back to Geneva.

The process of negotiations began in earnest again with the G20–EU Ministerial Meeting in Brasília, on the 12 December 2003. After January 2004, the Agriculture negotiations began to take place in various forms: meetings between the EU/US and the G20 and other negotiating groups such as the G33, G10 and Africa Group/ACP/LDCs known as the G90. In addition, the new chair of the agricultural negotiations, Ambassador Tim Groser, appointed in February, began to hold intense 'Agriculture Weeks' every month which brought capital-based negotiators to Geneva. However, the most intense negotiations began to take place in the non-group of five (NG5) process—a small group of countries comprising the US, EU, Brazil, India, and Australia. The group began to meet regularly from April 2004 at senior capital-based negotiators level and held several negotiating meetings at ministerial level (see above).

---

[12] WTO Doha Ministerial Declaration adopted on 14 November 2001, para. 13.

[13] Faizel Ismail, 'On the Road to Cancun: A Development Perspective on EU Trade Policies and Implications for Central and East European Countries' in 4 *Journal of World Investment*.

[14] See Statement by Australian Minister Mark Vaile of the Cairns Group.

[15] See *Joint EC–US Paper*, WTO, JOB(03)/157 (13 August 2003).

[16] Ismail, *supra* n. 13.

B. The July package on agriculture

1. *The Groser Text*

This assessment of the July GC decision on agriculture is preliminary and does not seek to be comprehensive. We focus on the key issues for the purpose of the analyses. At a general level the G20 was of the view that the initial Groser Text of July 16 was skewed in favour of the subsidizing and protectionist countries. The Groser Text did integrate the G20 principles of progressivity (deeper cuts in higher tariffs), and proportionality (lesser reduction commitments from developing countries) in the market access section of the text and that of an 'overall reduction', 'strengthened disciplines', and 'transparency and monitoring' in the domestic support pillar; whilst in the section on export competition, the principle of 'equivalence' was applied to all forms of export subsidies in 'parallel' with the phasing out of the subsidy element in export credits, food aid, and the activities of exporting state trading enterprises.[17] However, the Groser Text was criticized for allowing the EU wide discretion in excluding its sensitive products from any significant tariff reductions and in allowing the US the use of a 'new' blue box, without any additional disciplines, thus enabling the US to commit to almost no real reductions in domestic support in the Doha Round. In addition, there was inadequate specificity for SDT for developing countries in contrast with the more detailed specification of the treatment and protection of 'sensitive products' for developed countries.

There was a period of intense negotiations in the NG5 and with other groups in the WTO before the tabling of the text by the Chairman of the GC, henceforth referred to as the Oshima Text, of 30 July 2004. In response to some significant concerns by the G20, Cairns Group and other groups, the second revision that was decided on the 31 July made further changes to the original Groser Text (see 2 August Text for final decisions). Thus, the G20 and Cairns Group, supported by a large number of developing countries, succeeded in ensuring that the July Agriculture Framework Agreement was broadly in line with the Doha mandate.

2. *The Oshima Text*

(a) On market access

The 'Blended Formula' as initially proposed by the EU–US Joint Text was abandoned in favour of a 'Banded Formula' (tiered with different bands). This approach took into account that developed and developing

---

[17] See G20 paper on Market Access and on Domestic Support and Export Competition.

country tariff structures were mostly different and that the tariff-cutting formula would need to take this into account. Whilst the EU and other developed countries were allowed to designate an appropriate number of products as sensitive, it was agreed that there would be substantial improvement in market access for each product. In addition, the principle of progressivity, requiring the highest tariffs to have the highest cuts, was accepted, thus laying the basis for significant market access.

SDT was recognized and would be applied through a range of measures, including the number of sensitive products and longer implementation periods. This treatment thus recognized the application of the concept of 'proportionality' that the G20 proposed.

In addition, the framework agreed to allow developing country members to designate an appropriate number of products as 'special products', based on the criteria of food security, livelihood security, and rural development needs. The criteria and treatment of these are to be decided later in the negotiations. The issue of preference erosion was recognized and sought to be addressed in the negotiations.

(b) On domestic support

The G20 principle of higher levels of support receiving higher cuts was agreed to in the Agriculture Framework. It was agreed that the overall level of support will be reduced and to ensure goodwill there will be an upfront 20 per cent cut in bound levels in the first year of the implementation process. There will also be product specific cuts and 'capping' at levels to be agreed. In addition, whilst there was a recognition that a new blue box could be created to allow for reform in agricultural support, there was agreement that this will be subject to additional criteria to be negotiated.

It was agreed that SDT will be an integral component of domestic support, and thus could include lower reductions and longer implementation periods.

In addition, whilst the above would ordinarily apply to reductions in *de minimis* support levels, some countries argued strongly for and succeeded in obtaining agreement that 'developing countries that allocate almost all *de minimis* support for subsistence and resource-poor farmers will be exempt'.

(c) Export competition

Here it was agreed that export subsidies will be eliminated by an end date to be agreed. The principle of equivalence was applied to the phasing out of the subsidy element in export credits, state trading enterprises, and food aid. The principle of SDT was applied to developing countries for the phasing out of all forms of export subsidies.

In addition, it was agreed that export subsidies for developing countries could be maintained for a longer period to be negotiated, and state trading enterprises in developing countries that preserved 'domestic price stability and food security will receive special consideration'.

(d) Transparency and monitoring

The Framework also provided for the transparency and monitoring of the commitments on all three pillars of the agriculture agreement to be enhanced.

C. An evaluation of the agriculture text

We apply the four elements of the Development Dimension proposed above—Fair Trade, Capacity Building, Balanced Rules, and Good Governance—to the Agriculture Text (Annex A of the July Text) in this section.

Whilst the July Agriculture Text raises the level of generality to avoid an impasse at this stage of the negotiations, it is vague in many cases and postpones the debate on many issues, it has however succeeded in providing hope that the Doha Mandate can still be implemented fully, and fulfil its promise of fair trade and development in agriculture. Thus an evaluation of the outcome of the agreement may be too early. However, for the purposes of the analysis we can apply each of the elements of the development dimension proposed above.

1. Fair trade

The commitment to the elimination of export subsidies and substantial reductions in domestic support, together with the promise of substantial market opening, even for sensitive products, has built the foundations for an ambitious result for the removal of protection and distortions in agricultural markets. Developing countries could at last be assured of developing their comparative advantage and expanding their exports into developed countries' markets. Developing countries were successful in ensuring that the principles of 'proportionality' and of 'lesser reductions' were applied to their commitments. The recognition that developed and developing country tariff structures are different and would need to be taken into account was important for adherence to the principle of proportionality and SDT. This took into account the fact that most developing countries which are largely agricultural economies would bear the largest adjustment costs (economic and social impact) in liberalizing their markets.

The Text had a number of provisions that went beyond the traditional SDT provisions. The market-access section agreed to allow developing country members to designate an appropriate number of products as 'special products', based on the criteria of food security, livelihood security and rural development needs.

The above issue can be seen as additional to the normal special and differential treatment applied to developing countries. In applying the above criteria for special products (which is over and above the number of sensitive products of developing countries) the levels of development of these countries and vulnerability will need to be taken into account.

2. Capacity-building

The issue of preference erosion was recognized and will be addressed in the negotiations. The issue of preference erosion poses complex development challenges for several developing countries. A range of measures may need to be applied to assist these countries to manage their adjustment and diversification strategies. These could include funding from the Bretton Woods institutions, but without immersing these countries into more unsustainable debt. Thus, additional finance to fund supply-side and diversification strategies may be required. New and creative ways of raising these additional funds is called for. The recent initiative by the Chancellor of the Exchequer of the UK, to create an International Finance Facility (IFF) to raise an additional US$50 billion to fund the Millenium Development Goals, including trade policy capacity-building, is worth pursuing.[18]

In applying these strategies the WTO would need to implement fully the concept of coherence in multilateral decision-making. Decisions made in the WTO would need to be coordinated with the other Bretton Woods institutions and vice versa. In addition, the WTO would need to build formal relationships with the institutions that have expertise to assist with building supply-side capabilities for the countries most in need. An appropriate mechanism in the WTO to advance these new approaches should be developed.

3. Balanced rules

In the section on domestic support, it was agreed that 'developing countries that allocate almost all *de minimis* support for subsistence and resource-poor farmers will be exempt'. In the section on export competition, it was agreed that export subsidies for developing countries could be maintained for a longer period to be negotiated and that state

---

[18] See speeches by Gordon Brown to the Conference on *Making Globalization Work for All—The Challenge of Delivering the Monterrey Consensus* (16 February 2004) and at the Seminar on *Poverty and Globalization: Financing for Development* (9 July 2004): http://www.hm-treasury.gov.uk/documents/international_issues/internation.

trading enterprises in developing countries that preserved 'domestic price stability and food security will receive special consideration'.

In applying the above criteria for these additional special and differential treatment measures, the WTO would need to take account of the levels of development and vulnerability of these developing countries. Interestingly, it was India and China who argued most strongly for the above provisions. These are large agrarian economies with a considerable number of people whose livelihoods depend on agriculture (650 million and 850 million) and whose populations have the largest number of people (300 million and 350 million) who live on incomes below US$1 a day.

In applying these rules in a flexible manner to facilitate the development of those countries most in need, the WTO would need to ensure that damage to other countries, especially the poor developing countries, is minimized and that the rules based system is not weakened. Thus the application of such flexibilities would need to be monitored by a mechanism to be established in the WTO.[19] Such a mechanism would assist in extending such flexibilities to those countries that need it, and review the application of such measures and their continuation, based on criteria to be agreed.

4. *Good governance*

The issue of transparency and monitoring of the implementation of WTO agreements has been agreed and will go a long way in building confidence in the WTO. Developed country notifications in agriculture were criticized for being too late and lacking in transparency. This will improve the good governance of the WTO.

The agriculture negotiations, despite being largely successful in the final week of the July GC meeting in building a compromise, were criticized for not being conducted in a transparent manner. The most intense part of the negotiations was conducted amongst a small group of five countries. Although Brazil and India represented the G20, the detail and complexity of the negotiations and the differences in interest amongst the members of the G20 required greater transparency and inclusiveness. However, other major groups were largely left out of these negotiations. These included the Africa Group, ACP and LDCs, and the G10 (including countries such as Japan and Switzerland) which had more protectionist interests in agriculture. The latter expressed their dissatisfaction with the process. A more inclusive process would need to be found for the continuation of the negotiations post-July.

---

[19] S. Prowse, 'The Role of International and National Agencies in Trade-Related Capacity Building' in 25 (9) *World Economy* (2002) 1235–1261.

IV. COTTON

A. Background

The issue of cotton subsidies and their devastating impact on cotton farmers and over 10 million people in West Africa was tabled in the WTO as a formal submission.[20] It was argued that cotton plays an essential role in the economic development of West and Central African countries (WCA), accounting for 5 to 10 per cent of the gross domestic product (GDP) in Benin, Burkina Faso, Chad, Mali, and Togo and around 30 per cent of total export earnings and over 60 per cent of earnings from agricultural exports.

A WTO meeting in Cotonou, Benin, on 23–24 March 2004, focused attention on the issue and was attended by WTO Members and several multilateral institutions (the World Bank, the International Monetary Fund (IMF), the Food and Agriculture Organization (FAO), and UNCTAD). Technical presentations concluded that West African cotton producers are the most competitive in the world (least-cost producers with highest quality).[21] The cause of the decline in their cotton sector is a direct result of high levels of subsidies in the US and EU which have depressed world cotton prices, amongst other factors.

The development challenges that also impact on the cotton sector include: efficiency of production, distribution and marketing; improved infrastructure, cotton production methods and increasing yield with new varieties; commodity risk management; quality control and standards; and diversification and value addition in textiles and clothing.

The West African countries called for the phasing out of trade-distorting cotton subsidies, with a view to their elimination as a separate issue in the negotiations, and financial and technical support to address a range of supply-side and infrastructure challenges that faced these poverty-stricken countries. In Cancún, the second revision of the Text called for these countries 'to direct existing programmes and resources toward diversification of the economies where cotton accounts for the major share of their GDP',[22] and was criticized for diverting attention from the high levels of trade-distorting subsidies of developed countries—mainly the USA—in the cotton sector.

[20] WTO TN/AG/GEN/4 (16 May 2003).
[21] See Presentation on Cotton by International Cotton Advisory Council to the WTO Cotonou, Benin Workshop (23–25 March 2004).
[22] WTO JOB(03)/150/Rev.2 (13 September 2003).

B. The July package

The July GC Decision recognized the 'complementarity between the trade and development' aspects of the cotton issue. The Secretariat was urged to work with the 'development community', i.e. multilateral and bilateral agencies. With a promise to ensure that the issue of cotton would be dealt with 'ambitiously, expeditiously and specifically',[23] the July GC decided to negotiate the cotton issue within the context of the agriculture negotiations and not as a stand-alone issue that would be fast-tracked as the West African countries had initially demanded.

C. An evaluation

The cotton issue illustrated for many observers of the WTO that trade-distorting subsidies can and do impact negatively on the livelihoods and development prospects of the poorest developing countries. By refusing to deal with this issue separately, the US underlined the inextricable link between fair trade and development. The cotton countries could not obtain relief from the trade-distorting subsidies that were depressing world prices and undermining their opportunity to expand their exports of the 'highest-quality cotton produced at lowest cost' without fighting for a fair deal in the agriculture negotiations for all developing countries.[24] Thus the fate of the West African cotton producers is now inextricably linked to an ambitious and successful outcome of the Doha agriculture negotiations. Success in achieving the high ambition of increased market access, domestic support, and export competition thus remains critical.

In addition, subsidized export credits also assist US exporters to compete unfairly in global markets. Indian government officials explain that their importers of cotton are attracted by the US exporters who are able to supply them with concessional credit facilities. Governments of West African farmers are too poor to support their exporters with the equivalent export credit facilities. This issue is part of the agriculture negotiations on export competition.

The WTO did make an important advance in boldly recognizing the complementarity between the trade and development aspects of the cotton issue.[25] Furthermore it recognized that it would need to work

---

[23] WTO WT/L/579 (2 August 2004).

[24] A number of other countries also produce cotton and are negatively affected by developed country cotton producers. These include another 26 African countries, in addition to the four West African countries, and Brazil (initiated a dispute against the US cotton subsidies), India, Pakistan, and China.

[25] See 1b and Annex A 4 and 5 of WTO WT/L/579 (2 August 2004).

closely with the development community, including multilateral and bilateral agencies. Thus the WTO has recognized that it has a role in the building of institutional, productive, and export capabilities. In addition, the WTO has recognized some responsibility for these development impacts of trade and that it needs to play a role in building coherence between the various levels and bodies responsible.

The cotton issue is another good illustration of the unfairness of WTO rules: developing countries are not allowed to use subsidies in their nascent industrial sectors whilst developed countries such as the US are allowed to use trade-distorting subsidies which destroy the livelihoods of poor West African farmers.

On the issue of transparency and inclusiveness of the decision-making process, it was apparent that the West African countries' campaign to seek relief for the plight of their farmers did not yield any significant short-term gains. The negotiating process in the run-up to the July GC saw a somewhat fragmented and non-transparent negotiating process with the NG5 leading the agriculture negotiations and the West African countries negotiating bilaterally with the US on cotton. The bargaining power and negotiating capacity of the West African cotton countries could be more effectively enhanced by the more powerful G20 group of countries, whose members also have an interest in the elimination of trade-distorting cotton subsidies. A more inclusive and transparent negotiating process in the WTO would thus benefit the development prospects of the poor West African farmers.

V. NON-AGRICULTURAL MARKET ACCESS

A. Background

In the area of industrial products or non-agricultural market access the Doha mandate agreed to 'reduce or as appropriate eliminate tariffs . . . in particular of export interest to developing countries'. This mandate thus recognized the many criticisms of the results of the Uruguay Round by developing countries.

Developing countries have argued that whilst developed countries achieved significant gains from the Uruguay Round including increased access to the services sector of developing countries and new rules on anti-dumping and TRIPS, most developing countries did not secure benefits through access to developed country markets in products of interest to them, and they have continued to labour under implementation problems. In addition, global trends in trade over the past decade have seen more rapid growth in the exports of some countries, particularly in sectors that embody high value-added and high-skilled products. However, the bulk of developing countries' exports, made up of agricultural products and labour-intensive manufacturing, has remained static, and their share of global markets has declined.[26]

The WTO agreed that the deadline for modalities for NAMA should be at the end of May 2003, after the modalities on Agriculture that was agreed in the Doha mandate to be the end of March 2004. Thus the chair of the NAMA negotiating group, prior to Cancún, Ambassador Girard, began work on developing these modalities. A number of countries put forward proposals for tariff-cutting formulae. The chair modified these and proposed his own compromise formula and proposal—'Elements of Modalities for Negotiations on Non-Agricultural Products'[27]—the Girard Proposal. The Girard Proposal contained a number of elements including: a formula for tariff reductions, a sectoral approach, SDT provisions, recognition of the particular situation of newly acceded countries, a supplementary approach that included zero-for-zero sectoral harmonization and request-and-offer approaches, negotiations to reduce non-tariff barriers, and the provision of technical assistance to developing countries during the negotiations.

This approach was broad enough to include an ambitious outcome to the negotiations and to allow for flexibilities for developing countries' needs and interests. The Girard Proposal, whilst it was roundly criticized by developed and developing countries, succeeded in providing a basis for the negotiations on modalities for NAMA. However, as the process of developing modalities was diverted both by the failure to reach agreement on agricultural modalities at the end of May 2003 and the EU–US Joint Text agreed on 13 August 2003, the WTO decided to also produce a 'Framework Agreement' for the Cancún Ministerial Meeting to be in line with the agriculture negotiations.

Annex B of the Cancún Text ('Framework for Establishing Modalities in Market Access for Non-Agricultural Products'[28]) was criticized by developing countries before and at Cancún for being biased in favour of developed countries and not paying sufficient attention to the principle of 'less than full reciprocity' called for by the Doha mandate. In particular the Cancún Text was criticized by developing countries for calling for a 'non-linear formula'[29] and mandatory

---

[26] World Bank, *Global Economic Prospects and the Developing Countries* (2002); UNCTAD, *Trade and Development Report* (2002).

[27] WTO TN/MA/W/35 (16 May 2003).

[28] WTO JOB(03)/150/Rev.2 (13 September 2003).

[29] See Annex B para. 3. Some developing countries argued that when this is applied to their own tariff reductions, it would create relatively significant adjustment burdens compared to that of developed countries whose tariffs were relatively low already.

sectoral tariff reductions.[30] The Cancún Text was not adopted due to these criticisms and the collapse of the meeting.

In the period up to the July 2004 Ministerial Meeting some of the major delegations began to display flexibility in their approach to the NAMA framework. Bob Zoellick, in his conciliatory letter to WTO Ministers in January 2004, called for both ambition and flexibility.[31] Indeed the letter appeared creative in the manner it dealt with less-developed developing countries. Instead of the non-linear formula, he was prepared to explore a 'blended' concept for these countries. Thus the letter stated that 'for less competitive developing economies, a blended methodology could give flexibility for sensitive items while enabling the WTO to proceed with an ambitious formula that significantly narrows the larger gaps'. On the issue of mandatory or voluntary sectoral negotiations the letter argued that we need to find a balance and provide 'flexibility for developing countries, especially the poorer and less developed'. However, in the negotiations in the months before the July GC Meeting developed countries began to insist that the Cancún Text or the Derbez Text as it is referred to,[32] should not be amended but accepted as it was, in spite of the criticisms and objections of developing countries to this Text.

B. The July package

The current chair of the NAMA negotiation, Ambassador Stephan Johannesson, was thus constrained to make changes to this text to accommodate developing countries' concerns. In addition, the strong linkage many developing countries made between the NAMA negotiations and the outcome of the agriculture negotiations slowed down the process of negotiations on NAMA. In the event the NAMA negotiations continued until the very last moments of the July GC negotiations. At this stage the only possibility that remained for developing countries was to ensure that the Derbez Text remained open to negotiation and that the views and perspectives of developing countries could be included in the post-July negotiations for the development of modalities. Thus Annex B of the July package on NAMA called for additional negotiations on the elements of the Derbez Text. These issues would relate to

[30] Some developing countries were willing to entertain the possibility of sectoral negotiations but only if this was decided on a voluntary basis. They feared that the burden of adjustment for them would be relatively large especially if the most sensitive of their sectors were targeted for sectoral tariff reductions.

[31] See letter by Bob Zoellick to WTO Ministers (11 January 2004).

[32] Developed countries created an informal negotiating group to support the Derbez Text called 'Friends of Ambition'.

the treatment of unbound tariffs, flexibilities for developing countries, participation in sectoral negotiations, and the issue of preferences.[33]

C. An evaluation

Developing countries thus succeeded in ensuring that the Derbez Text, which was perceived to be biased in favour of developed countries, was not imposed on them. The July Framework agreement on NAMA has made it possible for the elements of the Derbez Text to be further negotiated and to ensure that the outcome of the negotiations on modalities would be more balanced and take into account the interests of developing countries. The debate on the substance of the framework has thus been postponed.

The negotiations on modalities post-July would probably focus on the Girard Proposal for modalities once again. The debate on the approach to the different elements of the Girard Proposal (see above) would need to be negotiated. A developmental outcome would need to take into account the four elements of the development dimension proposed in this paper.

In addressing the issue of fair trade the WTO negotiator will need to ensure that due recognition is given to the enormous imbalances in the global trading system reflected in the inequitable distribution of the gains from globalization and the continued protection in the developed countries of products competing with like products of poor people from developing countries. Thus, the modalities for liberalization in NAMA must accomplish two things simultaneously: (a) address the issues of tariff peaks, tariff escalation, and the remaining high tariffs that prevent developing country exports from entering into developed country markets; and (b) ensure sufficient flexibility that accommodates the diversity in levels of development of developing countries.

Whilst the sectoral approach provides Members with the opportunity to enhance market access, this should be used as a supplementary approach and entered into on a voluntary basis. In addition, where developing countries choose to use this approach, it should include the principle of asymmetry by allowing for limited exclusions, longer phase-in periods, and the possibility for a tariff end-rate above zero for developing countries. In addition, developing countries need more time to adjust given the significantly larger impact of tariff adjustments on output, employment, and revenue loss. The principle of 'less than full reciprocity' would need to be applied in a manner that recognized the need

---

[33] See Annex B para. 1 WT/L/579 (2 August 2004).

for proportionality in the adjustment process between developed and developing countries. However, developing countries are at different levels of industrial and economic development and thus those less-developed countries who are new entrants to the global economy would need a different coefficient in the formula to allow for a relatively slower adjustment process.[34]

In addition, some developing countries would suffer some additional burdens of adjustment due to their peculiar development situation including through the loss of preferences. Appropriate adjustment support will need to be explored for these countries in the modalities. The burden of these adjustments should not be borne by poor developing countries. For many of these countries, including the new entrants, the larger challenge to market access remains that of addressing their capacity constraints that would include measures to build their institutional, productive, and export capabilities.

The NAMA framework proposal has recognized that 'Non-tariff barriers are an integral and important part of the negotiations'.[35] Reducing tariff barriers alone will not succeed in providing genuine market access for developing countries. Non-tariff barriers such as anti-dumping, technical barriers to trade, and import licensing in developed countries often pose significant barriers to developed country exports. Some issues, such as anti-dumping, are currently under discussion in other negotiating groups. Real progress in these areas must be achieved as part of a single undertaking. Other issues, such as technical barriers to trade and import licensing, are being addressed by WTO subsidiary bodies. However, these negotiations must be supervised strongly by the NAMA negotiating group to ensure that the outcome of the NAMA negotiations also includes more balanced rules that support the effort made in the market-access negotiations and do not continue to impede the exports of developing countries in an unfair manner.

The outcome of the NAMA negotiations in the WTO reflects the increasing assertiveness of developing countries to ensure that an unfair agreement is not imposed on them. The US had earlier called for a 'blended approach' to the tariff formula to take into account

---

[34] South Africa made a proposal to differentiate between the small group of industrial economies and more advanced developing countries (the 'leaders') that have been able to make the necessary adjustments in their economies to compete effectively in the global economy and have achieved gains from increased global trade, others (the 'adjusters') that have begun to make significant but painful adjustments in their domestic economies and are beginning to compete more effectively in the global economy and those economies that are 'new entrants' to the trading system, accounting for a small share of global trade and are still making the necessary adjustments to participate effectively in the world trading system. See WTO TN/MA/W/42 (13 August 2003).

[35] Annex B para. 14.

developing country concerns and 'a middle ground' to the debate on mandatory or voluntary sectoral negotiations that would take into account that need for a 'critical mass'.[36] However, the attempts by the developed countries, including the US, not to change the Derbez Text later in the negotiations, whilst recognizing that it does not adequately reflect the needs of developing countries, underlines the need for a more inclusive and transparent negotiating process, which is essential to ensure a balanced and fair outcome.

VI. SINGAPORE ISSUES: TRADE FACILITATION

A. Background

The first Ministerial Conference of the WTO held in Singapore in 1996 decided to establish a work process to study and clarify the issues that could be included in possible agreements on the four Singapore issues. Whilst the study process continued no agreement could be reached on the launching of negotiations on these issues at subsequent WTO conferences. The Singapore issues were included by the Ministers in Doha as part of the comprehensive Doha Development Agenda (DDA).

The Doha Declaration provides identical mandates for investment, competition, trade facilitation, and transparency in government procurement. It instructs the various bodies to clarify core issues that may form subjects for inclusion in the various agreements should there be 'explicit consensus' to launch negotiations on them. The mandates also stress the need for enhanced technical assistance and capacity-building in these areas and specifically adds that assistance provided to developing and least-developed countries should include policy analysis to enable them to better evaluate the implications of closer multilateral cooperation for their development policies and objectives, and human and institutional development.

At Cancún, the chair's draft ministerial text[37] was criticized for misrepresenting the debate on the Singapore issues—competition, investment, transparency in government procurement and trade facilitation. The text called for the immediate launch of negotiations on two of the four issues and the launch of negotiations on the most controversial issue—investment—in a few months' time. One issue—competition—was postponed for further study. The vast majority of developing countries were unwilling to launch negotiations on these new issues and provided several reasons for this stance. Most countries argued that the

---

[36] Zoellick, *supra* n. 31.   [37] WTO JOB(03)/150/Rev.2. (13 September 2003).

Singapore issues had been wrongfully imposed on them in Doha, and were overburdening an already complex negotiating agenda. Some countries felt that insufficient progress had been made in Geneva on the discussions to establish a balanced and consensual basis for negotiations. Moreover, other countries believed that it was premature to discuss the Singapore issues when the EU (and Japan) as principal *demandeurs* had failed thus far to indicate adequate willingness to reform their agricultural policies.

Since Cancún, there has been much debate on the Singapore issues in Geneva. Bob Zoellick in his January 2004 letter to WTO Ministers clearly stated the preference of the US to include only one issue: trade facilitation in the DDA negotiations. He was indifferent about how the other three issues were to be treated—'either drop them or develop a plan of study'. The EU returned in January 2004, after its prolonged internal discussions amongst the member states, with an ambivalent mandate, but finally agreed to include only one of the Singapore issues in the Doha Round.[38] There were some intense negotiations prior to the July GC on the possible modalities for negotiations on trade facilitation, coordinated by the Deputy Director-General of the WTO, Rufus Yerxa, on behalf of the Chair of the GC.

B. The July package

The July package decided to commence negotiations 'by explicit consensus' on trade facilitation on the basis of the modalities set out in Annex D of the GC Decision.[39] On the other three issues—investment, competition and transparency in government procurement—the text stated that 'no work towards negotiations' will take place 'within the WTO during the Doha Round'.

C. An evaluation

The modalities agreed in Annex D make a strong effort to build more balanced rules in the WTO by stating that 'the extent and timing of entering into commitments shall be related to the implementation capacities of developing and least developed countries'.[40] This makes an explicit linkage between the implementation commitments of developing countries and their capacity.

---

[38] Pascal Lamy agreed to this in the Paris OECD Meetings of 12–14 May 2004.
[39] See 1g and Annex D of Text, WTO WT/L/579 (2 August 2004).
[40] Annex D para. 2 WTO WT/L/579 (2 August 2004).

The modalities in Annex D were at pains to provide assurances to developing countries that the cost implications of their needs and priorities, technical assistance and support for capacity-building, including infrastructure development will be addressed by developed country members, failing which implementation obligations will be waived.[41] In addition, the modalities provide that 'LDCs will only be required to undertake commitments to the extent consistent with their individual development, financial and trade needs or their administrative and institutional capabilities'.[42] The commitment of the WTO to build coherence with other multilateral agencies, especially the World Customs Organization, is made in paragraphs 8 and 9 of the Annex. These provisions have laid the basis for the possibility of new rules that would be balanced and provide for the building of capabilities in developing countries, particularly the least developed, so that they can also benefit from international trade and the multilateral trading system.

Developing countries, particularly the less-developed and least-developed countries, were very concerned about the development impact of these new rules and negotiated for more balanced rules. In the period after Cancún and especially in the months before the July GC meeting a large number of developing countries formed a strong alliance and negotiated collectively on these issues,[43] with some groups—the LDCs, Africa Group and ACP Group—being instructed by strong ministerial mandates in preparation for the July GC meeting. The negotiations on trade facilitation were relatively more transparent and inclusive in the period before July. Learning the lessons of Cancún, the developed countries did not underestimate the strong views of developing countries again, and were more willing to take into account their concerns in the drafting of modalities.

The Doha Mandate had sequenced the negotiations in a manner that called for modalities to be agreed and negotiations to be launched on the bases of explicit consensus *after* agreement on modalities on agriculture and the WTO decided to set a deadline for modalities on NAMA by the end of May 2003.[44] The modalities for the Singapore issues were only to be decided 'by explicit consensus' at the Cancún Ministerial Meeting, set for September 2003. The fact that the modalities for one of the Singapore issues were being decided *before* those of agriculture and NAMA could also have been a consideration by

---

[41] *Ibid.* paras. 4, 5, and 6.   [42] *Ibid.* para. 3.
[43] See Ministerial Mandates of LDCs, African Union, and ACP groups.
[44] Modalities for agriculture were to be agreed at the end of March 2003 and the WTO decided on a deadline of end of May 2003 for agreement on modalities for NAMA.

developed countries for a more balanced and development friendly
outcome on trade facilitation.

VII. DEVELOPMENT ISSUES

A. Background

The 'development issues' in the July text had their genesis in the discussions post-Cancún about which critical issues needed to be addressed to revive the DDA after the failure of the Cancún Ministerial Meeting. The then chair of the GC, Carlos Castillo, suggested the inclusion of the development issues, together with agriculture, cotton, NAMA and the Singapore issues. In the months before July, the new Chair of the GC included the development issues as part of the package for July. However, he did not clarify which issues would be included as part of the development package—other than the issue of SDT which was the focus of the work of the Committee on Trade and Development Special Session. It was also clear that the implementation issues—which were managed by the Director General as chair of the Trade Negotiations Commitee—would need to be added to the development package.

As the July GC preparations proceeded some developing countries argued for the inclusion of a range of other development issues in the July package including LDCs, small economies, preferences, commodities, capacity-building, trade debt and finance, and trade and technology transfer.[45] However, as work on these issues had not advanced substantially in the period since Cancún, the Chair of the GC was reluctant to include substantial language on these issues except to refer to these issues in the ongoing WTO work programme.[46]

B. An evaluation of the July GC outcomes

The July package thus focused on five issues in the Development section of the Decision: SDT, technical assistance, implementation, other development issues, and least-developed countries. The outcomes of the WTO July GC Decision on each of these issues are discussed and evaluated below.

1. Special and Differential Treatment (SDT)

The work on SDT advanced slowly in the negotiations after Doha. In the period before Cancún, the Chair of the GC, Carlos Castillo,

---

[45] See Statement by Ambassador of Mauritius on behalf of the Africa Group to July 2004 Informal General Council.

[46] See I(h) of July GC Decision: 'Other Elements of the Work Programme'.

categorized the 88 proposals that were submitted by developing countries to review the SDT provisions with a view 'to strengthening them and making them more precise, effective and operational',[47] into three groups. Category One included 38 proposals that he viewed as having a good chance of succeeding, Category Two included 38 proposals that were referred to the relevant negotiating groups and WTO bodies for their consideration and recommendations for decision by the General Council, and Category Three included proposals concerning 12 issues on which he observed that wide divergences of opinion existed. In the period before Cancún and at Cancún, WTO members were able to reach agreement on 28 of these proposals. These were not adopted at Cancún because of the closure of the Meeting.

In the period before the July GC Meeting, the new chair of the Committee on Trade and Development (CTD) Special Session called for a review of the approach to the negotiations so as to enable greater convergence on the underlying issues raised by the 88 proposals.[48] Developing countries insisted on prioritizing the negotiation of specific proposals, before discussing the so-called 'cross-cutting issues'. Developed countries on the other hand expressed the view that they had made great efforts to reach agreement on the 28 SDT proposals and that they were unlikely to make further progress on the rest of the proposals unless there was a change of approach to the issues. Developing countries also were of the view that they should not adopt or harvest the 28 proposals in the July package as they felt that these agreements were of little 'economic value' and that adopting them now might prejudice the negotiations on the rest of the proposals.

The July package thus simply recognized that some progress had been made in the negotiations on SDT without adopting the 28 proposals. The CTD was instructed to complete the review of the outstanding proposals and work on the cross-cutting issues, monitoring mechanism and incorporation of SDT into the architecture of WTO rules,[49] and report to the GC by July 2005. In addition, the negotiating groups and the bodies to which the Category Two proposals above were referred were instructed to report back with clear recommendations to the GC by July 2005.

Thus, the July GC Meeting did not advance the negotiations on SDT much further than the period before Cancún.

---

[47] Doha Declaration, para. 44.

[48] The author of this paper was appointed to the Chair of the Committee on Trade and Development Special Session on 11 February 2004.

[49] This work programme of the CTD was agreed at a previous GC meeting as reported in TN/CTD/7.

2. *Implementation issues*

The implementation issues were scheduled by the Doha mandated work programme to be decided as a matter of priority by December 2002.[50] Differences of views and interests of a significant number of countries, such as on the issue of extension of geographical indications, has created a stalemate in the negotiating process. The mandate agreed that negotiations on all outstanding implementation issues shall be an integral part of the work programme.

Paragraph 12 of the Doha Ministerial Declaration called for those issues for which a negotiating mandate exists (12a) to be referred to such working groups and for the other issues (12b) to be addressed by WTO bodies as a matter of priority. Some members felt that the issue of extension of geographical indications should not be regarded as a negotiating issue unless agreement is reached on this issue in the Council for TRIPS. Other members argued that all the implementation issues should be regarded as negotiating issues and treated in the same manner. Thus the process of the negotiations on the implementation issues has been held hostage by the debate on the extension of geographical indications. The Cancún Text on implementation issues recognized the impasse in the negotiations and renewed the determination of members to find a solution, requesting the Director-General to continue his efforts in this regard.

The July Decision could not take this process much further, as no significant progress was made between the Cancún Ministerial Meeting and the July GC. The July Decision once again requested the DG to continue with his consultation process and to report to the Trade Negotiating Committee by May 2005 and the Council to review progress on these issues and make appropriate decisions by July 2005.

3. *Technical assistance*

The Doha Declaration confirmed that 'technical co-operation and capacity building are core elements of the development dimension of the multilateral trading system', and recognized that 'sustainably financed technical assistance and capacity building programmes have important roles to play'.[51] The WTO has made considerable advances on providing technical assistance, particularly in support of information and training for the Doha Round. The Cancún Text acknowledged the role of the DDA Global Trust Fund in providing funding for these efforts. The Cancún Text also recognized the significant cooperation begun by the WTO with some agencies (viz. World Bank, IMF, UNCTAD, International Trade Center (ITC)) in joint projects such as the Integrated

---

[50] Doha Mandate, para. 12.   [51] *Ibid.* paras. 38 and 2.

Framework (IF) and the Joint Integrated Trade Programme (JITAP) in implementing these programmes.

The July text whilst recognizing these efforts calls for 'developing countries and in particular least developed countries to be provided with enhanced Trade Related and Technical Assistance (TRTA) and capacity-building to increase their effective participation in the negotiations, to facilitate their implementation of WTO rules and to enable them to adjust and diversify their economies'. In addition the section on other development issues commits the WTO to ensure that 'special attention shall be given to the specific trade and development related needs and concerns of developing countries, including capacity constraints'.

Thus the July text by recognizing the need for the WTO to address the implementation and supply side needs of developing countries, in addition to its capacity-building role in building developing country negotiation skills, has advanced the development dimension of the WTO.

4. *Other development issues*

In a letter to the Ministers of the G90 and then to all WTO Ministers, Pascal Lamy called on WTO Members to take into account the special needs of small, 'weak, and vulnerable countries'. He argued that these economies should be treated in a similar manner as LDCs in the negotiations to determine their reduction commitments and their obligations to implement trade rules. Essentially, he argued that they should enjoy the 'round for free'. Lamy's letter was partly a response to the views of many smaller developing countries that they should be allowed similar status to that of LDCs in the negotiations as they were relatively weak economies and surrounded by LDCs who enjoyed better preferences in developed-country markets. Some developing countries who enjoyed significant preferences in developed-country markets argued that the erosion of their preferences would entail significant adjustment costs for which they wanted to be compensated.

The issue of preferences has been contentious in the WTO and has led to several disputes initiated by those developing countries who have argued that they have been prejudiced by the discriminatory application of these preferences.[52] In addition, the attempt by some countries to create a category that would enjoy similar status to LDCs (i.e. small and vulnerable economies) has been resisted by other developing countries that have feared that this could lead to further discrimination between developing countries and prejudice their interests.[53] More recently, some

---

[52] Report of the Panel, *European Communities—Conditions for the Granting of Tariff Preferences to Developing Countries*, WTO WT/DS246/R (1 December 2003).
[53] See speech by Celso Amorim at the Meeting of some G90 Ministers in Guyana.

of the larger developing countries have criticized developed countries for attempting to 'graduate' them out of the normal provisions of SDT and thus Lamy's proposal was also perceived as another attempt to achieve this objective.

In the weeks before the July GC Meeting, the Ambassador of the EU, Carlo Trojan, decided to table a proposal in the WTO that called for these small, weak and vulnerable countries (including landlocked and commodity-dependent countries) to be given special consideration in the negotiations—to address their particular concerns, in particular from the impact of the erosion of non-reciprocal trade preferences. This proposal created a vigorous debate amongst developing countries. Countries from the ACP group and a few Latin American countries (Bolivia and Paraguay) supported the EU approach whilst almost all other developing countries, particularly from Latin America and Asia, were cautious and critical of such a proposal. The Chair of the CTD Special Session was requested by the Chairman of the GC to find a solution and build an acceptable compromise between these countries.

The July GC Decision finally did agree to a text in the section on 'Other Development Issues'.[54] The compromise text contains three sentences which, firstly, refer to both the fundamental principles of the WTO (including the concept of most-favoured nation (MFN)) and the flexibilities contained in the various agreements and provisions of GATT 1994 which address the specific trade and development related needs and concerns of developing countries; secondly, recognize that the particular concerns of developing countries, including those relating to food security, rural development, livelihood, preferences, commodities, and net food imports, as well as unilateral liberalization, should be taken into consideration in the negotiations; and thirdly, agree that the concerns of small, vulnerable economies should be addressed without creating a sub-category of members.

This formulation was a compromise negotiated by developing countries which attempts to balance their different interests. It created a debate which, whilst being vigorous, built a greater appreciation and understanding amongst the different groups about the concerns, interests, and fears of each group. There was greater appreciation amongst the groups that particular concerns, e.g. of rural development, livelihood, and food security, were not restricted to the smaller countries only, as some of the larger developing countries, such as India and China, had large rural populations, the majority of whom lived on less than US$1 a day. The debate and compromise amongst these developing countries may have contributed to the strengthening of the common alliance built

[54] WT/L/579 (2 August 2004).

amongst developing countries for a fairer trade deal on agriculture and NAMA in the July GC meeting.

5. *Least developed countries (LDCs)*

In the weeks before the July GC the LDC Group recalled the language from the Cancún Text and argued for this language to be included in the July package. The Cancún Text which was not adopted at Cancún called for duty-free and quota-free market access for products originating from LDCs; for rules of origin that facilitate exports from LDCs; and for the prioritization of LDCs' service suppliers by importing countries, particularly in Mode 4.[55]

The July package on LDCs merely reaffirmed the commitments made in Doha to address the concerns of LDCs. In addition, in view of the concerns by some LDC members that the possible extension of LDC type treatment to some developing countries might erode their preferential access in global markets, the July decision provided some reassurance that 'nothing in this decision shall detract in any way from the special provisions agreed by members in respect of these countries'. The July decision did not, however, make any significant advances for the special interests of LDCs on duty-free, quota-free market access, relaxation of the rules of origin, and increased access for their Mode 4 service providers.

VIII. CONCLUSIONS

This chapter has argued that on each of the critical issues negotiated in the July package (agriculture, cotton, NAMA, trade facilitation, and the development issues) the development dimension and its four elements— fair trade, capacity-building for the poorest countries, balanced rules, and good governance—has been generally advanced. Whilst the wording in the text is vague in many cases, and the negotiations on some more detailed and controversial issues have been postponed for the modalities stage, developing countries have succeeded in ensuring that the July GC Decision is broadly in line with the hopes and ambitions of the DDA and still capable of delivering on its promise of increasing growth and development for all. The July GC Decision is thus an advance for all of humanity. In addition, by succeeding in saving the WTO from another collapse and ensuring that the WTO is still on track, albeit much delayed, to achieve the objectives of the DDA, WTO members have made a significant contribution to the development dimensions of the multilateral rules based system.

[55] WTO JOB(03)/150/Rev.2 (13 September 2003).

The July Decision of the WTO has extended the DDA to the 6th Ministerial Meeting to be held in Hong Kong in December 2005. Whilst Pascal Lamy expressed an optimistic view that the DDA could be concluded by this date, WTO members will still need to develop a work programme and set new deadlines in the post-July phase to advance the DDA. These would include the deadlines for modalities in agriculture and NAMA. In addition, a new work programme would need to be developed to ensure that some of the other areas of the DDA that were not negotiated as part of the July package—rules, environment, and TRIPS—also gain some momentum. The progress and successful conclusion of the Doha Round will also depend on the elections in the US and the ability of the new US Administration to obtain fast-track authority for the WTO negotiations in the second quarter of 2005. In addition, the EU, with the election of a new President and new Commissioners, and with an enlarged number of member states (from 15 to 25), will need to develop the political will and mandate to negotiate an ambitious agreement in agriculture in line with its commitments in the Doha mandate.

Developing countries too will need to maintain the momentum of their negotiating efforts, and strengthen their delicately knit alliances on different issues. The success of the G20 in the agriculture negotiations will need to be built on, strengthening its alliance with the Cairns Group and the G33 and G90 group of countries, and thus creating greater and more equal bargaining power between developed and developing countries in the WTO. Vigorous debate within these groups should result in balancing both the interests of developing countries for a more open trading system, including between themselves, and accommodating the need for greater flexibility for less developed members. The active participation of civil society groups, including the private sector, in developed and developing countries, to ensure that the voice of those seeking a fairer, more balanced and strengthened multilateral trading system prevails over protectionist lobbies, will be crucial for the successful outcome of the Doha Round.

3

Cordell Hull, the Reciprocal Trade Agreements Act, and the WTO[1]

KENNETH W. DAM

The significance of the Reciprocal Trade Agreements Act of 1934 for the present General Agreement on Tariffs and Trade/World Trade Organization (GATT/WTO) system lies in a very few central ideas. They are all principles espoused by Cordell Hull. It is therefore worth understanding how these ideas came to dominate the thinking of Cordell Hull and how they led directly, under his leadership, to the Reciprocal Trade Agreements Act of 1934. Against that background we can investigate how those ideas came to be central concepts in the second half of the twentieth century in the GATT system. The final question addressed in this paper is whether those concepts retain validity in the Doha Round and the post-Doha world.

Cordell Hull was a Democrat from Tennessee. He was therefore from his first adult years a low-tariff proponent as fitted the pattern for Democrats not just in those days but from the earliest days of the Republic. It was after all the North that had sought protection for manufactured goods and the South that was more interested in exports, primarily agricultural products. Indeed, this difference goes all the way back to the Constitution itself, when it was the Southerners who backed the prohibition on export taxes.[2] In Hull's days the economic truth that a country that taxes imports will find it harder to export was instinctively understood in the South.

I. EVOLUTION OF CORDELL HULL'S THINKING

In his instructive *Memoirs*, Hull explained that before he came to Washington he had 'breathed in the fire of great tariff battles—but they

[1] The first draft of this essay was presented at a round-table meeting, *Pause for Reflection on the WTO System*, convened by the Cordell Hull Institute in Washington, DC, on 16 June 2004, to mark the 70th anniversary of the Reciprocal Trade Agreements Act of 1934. The author would like to thank Hugh Corbet, Richard Gardner, Douglas Irwin, and Ernst-Ulrich Petersmann for their comments and suggestions.

[2] Kenneth W. Dam, 'The American Fiscal Constitution' in 44 *University of Chicago Law Review* (1977) 271.

were battles fought on the home grounds that high tariffs or low tariffs were good or bad for the United Sates as a purely domestic matter. There was little or no thought of their effect on other countries.'[3]

Only later, during World War I, did Hull change his perspective. What distinguished Hull from most of his colleagues in the United States (US) Congress at that time was that he came to see the tariff issue as an international issue. In 1916 he made a speech in the House of Representatives calling for a post-war international trade conference (remember this was World War I, not II). The conference would reach agreements not just on tariffs but on 'trade methods, practices, and policies which in their effects are calculated to create destructive international controversies . . .'[4] The conference never took place, but in 1925 he introduced a resolution in the House calling for a trade conference. His addition to the draft resolution of a call for immediate unilateral reduction in US tariffs 'of course doomed it', as he later admitted.[5] Evidently he had even in 1925 not fully appreciated the reciprocity principle that was later to become obvious to him as Secretary of State.

Even before his 1916 House speech proposing a trade conference, Hull in 1914 wrote to Secretary of State Lansing urging the adoption of an unconditional most-favoured-nation clause. In doing so, he had three evils in mind. The first was boycotting of countries (we would call it 'trade sanctions' today). The second was subsidizing exports that had the effect of destroying particular foreign industries. And the third was Imperial Preference, under which Britain, its colonies, and the Commonwealth countries gave one another more favorable trade treatment than they gave others, which he considered patently unfair.[6] Here we see the birth of his passion for non-discrimination in trade matters.

When I first became interested in trade matters, I read a bit about Cordell Hull. But I did not spend much time exploring his ideas because, frankly, I thought they were a bit silly. I thought the great emphasis he repeatedly put on tariffs as a threat to world peace was rather too idealistic. How could lowering tariffs help avoid war? Such talk was just political hyperbole, I thought.

I still hold that view of the early Hull, but two later events have changed my mind on the substance of the issue. The first grew from an interest I developed as a visiting professor in Germany when I learned how Adolf Hitler had ruthlessly used bilateral trade agreements and exchange controls to subjugate Balkan countries as a prelude to sending in his panzer divisions. The most-favoured-nation (MFN) clause of the GATT and the work of the International Monetary Fund (IMF) on

---

[3] Cordell Hull, *The Memoirs of Cordell Hull, Vol. I* (1948) at 83.   [4] *Ibid.* at 82.
[5] *Ibid.* at 126.   [6] *Ibid.* at 84–85.

exchange controls makes it hard today to grasp fully the Europe of the 1930s.

The second event is much more recent. With the growth of terrorism we have come to understand that the higher incomes that economic development can bring will have to be part of any long-run solution to terrorism in the Middle East and elsewhere. We now know from extensive cross-country economic studies that growth rates in the Third World are directly related to a country's openness to trade.[7] Even in this light, Hull's fixation on tariffs as a threat to peace may seem a bit shallow. But we should remember that tariffs were the only important trade barriers that he knew as a young legislator. The technology of trade protection, with its anti-dumping duties and the like, had not yet taken hold. And under the gold standard, exchange restrictions were rare.

So we can conclude that Hull was ahead of his time in thinking about the non-economic effects of rampant protectionism and especially of trade discrimination. His appointment as Secretary of State by President Roosevelt in 1933 and his experiences that year with the London Economic and Montevideo conferences caused Hull to turn from advocacy to action. He saw the shortcomings of multilateralism of the London and Montevideo kind and became interested in bilateral solutions.[8] He came to realize that mere persuasion does not carry one very far, either in Washington or in the world at large. And he was appalled by the results of the Smoot–Hawley tariff legislation of 1930. Logrolling in the Congress on individual tariff items had led to such a great general increase in US tariffs in that 1930 legislation that Hull felt it had been a cause of the Great Depression. And when he got to the State Department he quickly realized that Smoot–Hawley had produced indignation throughout the world, had caused many countries to retaliate by raising their own tariffs on US exports, and had caused the British Commonwealth in the Ottawa agreements of 1932 to formalize Imperial Preference in a way that badly hurt US exports.[9]

II. INSPIRATION FOR A MULTILATERAL REGIME

Hull had many accomplishments. But the reason Hull is remembered today is not that he was an original author of the US income and estate tax laws. Nor is he is given the credit he deserves for his role as Secretary of State in World War II, helping to thwart Treasury Secretary

---

[7] E.g. J. Sachs and A. Warner, 'Economic Reform and Global Integration' in 1 *Brookings Papers on Economic Activity* (1995). See also J. Bhagwati, *In Defense of Globalizaton* (2004) at 60–64. [8] Hull, *supra* n. 3 at 356.
[9] *Ibid.* at 355.

Morgenthau's post-war plans for returning Germany to an agrarian society. Nor is he primarily remembered because—as Secretary of State in charge of post-war planning—he merited President Roosevelt's view of him as 'the Father of the United Nations'.[10]

Rather remarkably, in an era when war and peace rank higher in public attention than international trade policy, he is best known today for the key strategic concepts that underlay the Reciprocal Trade Agreements Act of 1934 and that became the motive forces behind the GATT and WTO. Today we can see all of the benefits that trade liberalization has brought in worldwide prosperity in the last half of the twentieth century. It is true that the 1934 Act provided only for bilateral agreements, but it furnished the template for Congressional advance authorization for Executive Branch negotiation of trade agreements that has been so important for those post-war accomplishments and for the trade issues that the world is dealing with today.

Hull's key insight was that *unilateral* tariff reduction was not in the political cards in most countries and certainly not in the US Congress. One could not expect to get something for nothing. Only the prospect of expanding markets for exports through foreign tariff reduction could lead to a reduction of domestic tariffs. Hence reciprocity was the key, and trade agreements were the mechanism.[11] To be sure, reciprocity has been called mercantilism, and indeed it is based on the primitive premise that exports are good and that imports are bad. But practical trade politics is based on just such a premise. The readers of this essay do not need to be told how limited that premise is. And not just in economic theory! The fact is that in the US 270 million people vote with their feet, or perhaps one should say with their wheels, for cheap imports when they drive to their local shopping malls. Still, individual behaviour is one thing, and politics—especially trade politics—is another.

The 1934 Act had, from Hull's point of view, two other advantages. The first was that it involved getting advance authority from the US Congress.[12] I would add that implicit in Hull's thinking, especially in the light of the then recent Smoot–Hawley experience, was that it gave exporting industries an equal voice, at least potentially, with

[10] Julius Pratt, *Cordell Hull* (1964) at xiii.

[11] In recent decades some countries have unilaterally reduced tariffs. See J. Bhagwati (ed.), *Going Alone: The Case for Relaxed Reciprocity in Freeing Trade* (2002). Australia is a leading developed-country example. And of course the US and most developed countries have done so for the poorer developing countries as part of a worldwide movement in the Generalized System of Preferences. Some developing countries have also reduced tariffs unilaterally, notably China throughout the 1990s. See W. Martin, B. Dimanrana, T. W. Hertel, and E. Ianchovichina, 'Trade Policy, Structural Change, and China's Trade Growth' in N. C. Hope, D. T. Yang and M. Y. Li (eds), *How Far Across the River? Chinese Policy Reform at the Millennium* (2003) at 153, 159 (Table 6.1).

[12] Hull, *supra* n. 3 at 359.

import-competing industries. Moreover, the Act broke the logrolling dynamics of Smoot–Hawley, when any day a new product might come up for a vote on a higher tariff without anyone having the occasion to consider the overall effects of dozens of such protectionist votes.

Another important aspect of the Hull approach was the inclusion in the bilateral agreements of the unconditional MFN clause. Although unconditional MFN had been widely used prior to World War I, conditional MFN had been followed for a time by the US. The idea behind the conditional version was that the US would not have to give away something for nothing by making concessions available to all countries just because it made concessions to one country. Concessions would be generalized, but only at a price of reciprocal concessions. Conditional MFN sounds good in a political speech, but the short of it is that it did not work. The complications in trying to apply it to dozens of countries on thousands of products were mind-boggling. The result was that discrimination was becoming the rule, not the exception. The US therefore moved to unconditional MFN in the 1922 Trade Act, getting it through the Congress perhaps only because that act increased average tariff rates greatly. And because the 1922 Act was so protectionist, little good came of the transition to unconditional MFN; if there are no concessions, there is nothing to generalize to third countries.

In the context of tariff reductions, however, unconditional MFN acted as a trade accelerator, lowering tariffs in the world generally. To be sure, in any one bilateral agreement, the 'giving away something for nothing' objection had greater rhetorical appeal than it would have later in a post-World War II GATT context. In that later multilateral context, negotiations were carried on with the principal supplier of a product and hence uncompensated spill-overs were minimized. And in the multilateral context, the end-of-round settling up process was an opportunity to deal with political objections back home by extracting last-minute concessions from otherwise uncompensated MFN beneficiaries.

Though the 1934 Act provided only for bilateral agreements, Hull intended to negotiate with a great many countries, and he did not intend to let third country principal suppliers get a windfall. He could reduce that MFN-related problem by agreeing to a US concession on any given product first with that product's principal supplier in order to obtain the maximum reciprocal concessions. I have not been able to verify that that was Hull's strategy, but clearly the political vulnerabilities from applying unconditional MFN in the bilateral context was a motive for moving after World War II to a multilateral forum. In the meantime, Hull achieved his objective of avoiding discrimination. He was perhaps fortunate that the gradual recovery of the world economy in the last half of the 1930s helped to win negotiating reauthorization in 1937, 1940, and 1943, and to validate the notion that reciprocal negotiations and non-discrimination were in the national interest.

After World War II the Hull approach was incorporated in the Havana Charter of 1948, which created the International Trade Organization (ITO). Ill health had increasingly forced Hull to reduce his activities as Secretary of State and he finally resigned in late 1944. So Hull was unable to participate in the formulation of the US 1946 proposal for an ITO, and he does not mention the subject in his memoirs. Nonetheless, the trade portion of the ITO charter was built on the principles that I have just reviewed.

The ITO went beyond trade. The Havana Charter was an ambitious effort to create an international institution comparable to the IMF and the World Bank. Indeed, it went well beyond trade negotiations to include a full range of economic chapters ranging from commodity agreements to economic development and even to employment. When one considers the socialist thinking, nationalizations, and central planning that were so much the vogue in the late 1940s in Paris and London and other major capitals, we are perhaps fortunate that it failed and thus those ideas did not become part of official international trade doctrine through the ITO. But a caveat is worth considering. One reason it failed was the trade provisions: organized opposition by protectionist forces was among the factors that persuaded President Truman to draw back from asking the Senate to ratify.[13]

That's the bad news. The good news is that the first round of trade negotiations envisaged in the Havana Charter had already been concluded in Geneva in 1947 in the course of the successive diplomatic meetings leading to the Havana Charter the following year. In an example of inspired pragmatic innovation, trade officials rescued the trade portions of the Havana Charter. The 1947 agreement was called the General Agreement on Tariffs and Trade. It was primarily a list of tariff concessions by various countries, but in order to prevent backsliding most of the text of the trade ITO 'Commercial Policy' chapter had been included as general terms. With the ITO gone, those general terms became the core of a broad international agreement.[14]

The General Agreement on Tariffs and Trade thus rather incongruously became a *de facto* international organization, the GATT. Trade officials found a small chateau near the edge of Lake Geneva to house what became known as the Secretariat and also found a way to finance staff activities. With strong leadership by the US State Department and by

---

[13] R. N. Gardner, *Sterling-Dollar Diplomacy in Current Perspective* (new expanded edn 1980) at 373–378.

[14] K. W. Dam, *The GATT: Law and International Economic Organization* (1970) at 10–16.

GATT's outstanding Director-General, Eric Wyndham White, a number of successive trade rounds were organized and successfully concluded. The GATT did not have as august a name as the IMF or the World Bank, but the pragmatic innovation flourished.[15]

III. CHANGES IN THE WORLD TRADING SYSTEM

Today, of course, we have the World Trade Organization. Views may vary on whether it is a better organization than the old GATT. Aside from the greater capacity to handle more meetings and more countries and publish more reports, the biggest difference is the Dispute Settlement Understanding (DSU). Lawyers tend to believe it to be a great step forward. A cynic might say that that fact merely shows the power of self-interest in motivating people to take trade issues seriously. But the DSU is a big change, and its full significance is only now becoming appreciated. Cases have already been brought for the tactical advantages their outcomes will have in the Doha Round negotiations. And over the longer term it is likely that Chinese accession to the WTO will lead to extensive legalistic disputes about Chinese compliance, with unpredictable effects for the world trading system.

The real question is not the GATT versus the WTO, but rather what has been happening outside of their meeting rooms. A second change is the steady movement away from tariffs and toward a multitude of indirect protectionist devices, especially barriers embedded in domestic national legislation. It is harder to apply the Hull principles of reciprocity and non-discrimination in that context.

The third change is the growing importance of trade in services. Here the protectionist mechanism does not lie in trade law at all, but rather in domestic regulation of the particular service industry. Service industries are mostly subjected to comprehensive economic regulation, best known not to trade lawyers but to specialized lawyers and bureaucrats involved in that regulation. But perhaps a more serious problem is that services negotiations fail to meet one of the conditions that were so important to Hull that he did not draw specific attention to it. What happens in a conventional tariff round is that countries make trade-offs, seeking concessions in goods of interest to their exporters and reluctantly making concessions on goods of import-competing industries. In other words, reciprocity works. But such reciprocity is unlikely to be present in purely sectoral negotiations.

[15] *Ibid.* at 335–341.

In the Doha Round financial services negotiations, for example, developing nations have little or no interest in trying to compete in developed-country financial markets because they know it would be a money-losing proposition. The reciprocity principle that served the world so well in the industrial tariff world where cross-sectoral trade-offs were the *modus vivendi* has little to offer in making sectoral negotiations in services a success. Sweet reason (as opposed to hard bargaining) may bring an opening of financial services markets, but reason did not play a decisive role in opening industrial markets. It is true that at the end of the financial services negotiations some cross-sectoral trade-offs may occur even though the structure of the services negotiations is sector by sector. But the Doha Round is so complex that the opportunity for last-minute trade-offs is limited. To make trade in services negotiations productive, we have to rethink the whole basis of negotiations. In doing so, we shall probably be led to try to find a way to utilize Hull's concept of reciprocal concessions.[16]

The fourth big change is the proliferation of regional and bilateral free trade areas. The US Trade Representative Robert Zoellick makes a powerful case for competitive liberalization. It is true that in the early going in the Uruguay Round, the US would probably not have arrived at the bargaining table at all if the Europeans had not been convinced that the US was going to push regional arrangements. But on the other hand, these free trade agreements are a major challenge to Hull's non-discrimination principle. It is not just that the Article XXIV criteria for the exception to MFN are a dead letter—indeed, a dead article. Rather it is that too many bilateral agreements are simply an extension of the area of protection rather than a move toward true trade liberalization. They turn trade theory on its head. And of course the practical effect of the proliferation of such agreements is what Jagdish Bhagwati accurately describes as a spaghetti bowl. Not only does the result make a mockery of what Hull admired as a single-column tariff—the same rate for every country. Today countries have many columns—occasionally more than a dozen—and increasingly complex rules of origin, all carefully drafted by trade lawyers and lobbyists. Though Cordell Hull would be gratified by the success in bringing down average tariff rates around the world, he would not be entirely satisfied with the role of free trade areas in that process.

In any event, the current US push for new bilateral and regional agreements has produced only modest results, judged by amounts of increased trade. And Zoellick is right in stressing that the US is late to the game of seeking advantages by discriminatory provisions. The EU

---

[16] For more on services negotiations, see K. W. Dam, *The Rules of the Global Game: A New Look at US International Economic Policymaking* (2001) at 113–130.

has some kind of discriminatory arrangement with the vast majority of all countries in the world, taking into account special provisions for developing countries and for aspirants for future membership as well as its various free-trade-area agreements. Even Japan has started to explore special trading arrangements. The sum of all of this activity raises the question of the current force of Hull's non-discrimination principle.

IV. GROWTH OF CONGRESSIONAL MEDDLING

Perhaps the greatest current problem in the Doha Round is a result of the continuing effort of the US Congress to undercut a further import-ant principle of Cordell Hull's Reciprocal Trade Agreements Act. Under that Act and well into the period of successive GATT negotiating rounds, it was fully accepted that so long as the results of the negoti-ations were within the scope of the authorizing legislation, those results went into effect as soon as the round was over. All that the President had to do was to proclaim that the negotiating results had become effective.

Once GATT negotiations began to go beyond tariffs and other border barriers, implementation no longer consisted of anything so simple as, for example, simply changing the duty rate for a particular product in a customs schedule. Internal law had to be changed. But since the whole point under the Hull principles for a President in obtaining advance nego-tiating authority was to avoid having at that early point to identify what particular concessions he would make, it would not be prudent—indeed, before the round commenced it would often be impossible—to identify the particular internal statute that might need amendment as a result of negotiations stretching over several years. The substantive committees of the Congress, which had not had an opportunity to participate in the ini-tial authorizing legislation (traditionally within the scope of the House Ways and Means and the Senate Finance Committees) would want an opportunity to hold hearings and pass on the changes to 'their' statute.

This potential problem became a reality in the 1960s when Congress refused to enact several important legislative changes that the Executive Branch negotiators had agreed to as concessions in response to negoti-ating demands from GATT partner countries. 'The refusal of Congress to pass the required bills (one on an "American selling price" customs valuation for certain products and the other a change in the antidump-ing statute) created a challenge for the Executive Branch because the US negotiators' commitment to change the legislation had been part of the US quid for other countries' quo on other trade measures.'[17]

---

[17] *Ibid.* at 44.

This imbroglio, even though embarrassing to the US negotiators, raised the inter-branch stakes substantially in the struggle to obtain Congressional authorization for a further round of GATT trade negotiators, since it was clear (in view of the great progress in bringing down tariff barriers among developed countries) that the new round would necessarily cut much deeper into internal non-tariff trade barriers. The upshot, enacted for the first time in the Trade Act of 1974, was what became known as 'fast track'. Congress would commit in advance, as part of the authorization legislation, to vote up or down the entire package of concessions. It would be all or nothing.

Even in the 1974 Act, Congress imposed a number of procedural safeguards to assure that it would not be surprised by what happened in the Geneva negotiations. It would be kept informed and be in a position to bring political pressures on the negotiators if it saw fit to do so. The safeguards became progressively more stringent in later trade acts.[18] In addition, Congress began to seek to include certain demands in the negotiation authorizing legislation as to what should be in the final package and as to what should not be negotiated. Although fast track had originally reduced the power of interest groups to engage in logrolling because it would be too late once the negotiations were completed, these new wrinkles on the authorizing process brought interest-group logrolling into the equation at a much earlier time in the process. Demands by powerful interest groups and consequently important Congressional leaders that future trade agreements include provisions on labour and environmental standards led to sharp divisions in the Congress; the Clinton Administration was consequently without negotiating authority for most of its period in office.

By the time the Bush Administration was able to obtain in 2002 what was now called Trade Promotion Authority (so named in part to attempt to avoid the 'fast track' nomenclature that proved anathema to various Congressional leaders and import-competing industries and their unions), the Congress had coalesced around a number of procedural provisions that would allow Congressional leaders to influence the negotiations as they progressed.[19] Although the steadily encroaching role of the Congress frustrated US negotiators and infuriated some

---

[18] H. H. Koh, 'The Fast Track and United States Trade Policy', 18 *Brooklyn Journal of International Law* (1992) 143; L. L. Wright, 'Trade Promotion Authority: Fast Track for the Twenty-First Century' in 13 *William & Mary Bills of Rights Journal* (2004) 979.

[19] A review can be found in H. Shapiro and L. Brainard, 'Trade Promotion Authority Formerly Known as Fast Track: Building Common Ground on Trade Demands More Than a Name Change' in 35 *George Washington International Law Review* (2003) 1, and G. Shaffer, 'Parliamentary Oversight of WTO Rule-Making: The Political, Normative, and Practical Contexts' in 7 *Journal of International Economic Law* (2004) 629, 637.

foreign negotiators who felt that they never knew whether US negotiators would be able to follow through on proposed compromises, the fast-track process has actually worked quite well since its original passage in 1974, leading to unparalleled low tariff rates and to substantial inroads on non-tariff barriers. No trade agreement has yet failed to win Congressional fast-track approval after the completion of negotiations.

V. UNDERMINING OF TRADE NEGOTIATIONS

The question that remains in many minds, especially outside the US, is whether the Congress will eventually undermine entirely the traditional GATT/WTO process of negotiations by professional trade officials meeting out of the view of the public in order to achieve breakthroughs in the struggle for freer international trade. The fear is that the Congress may eventually reject the results of a multi-year negotiation or—more likely—that the US interest group process, operating through the Congressionally retained right to be currently informed on all US proposals even before they are tabled in Geneva, may result in no major agreements being reached in the first place. Congressional objections to US negotiators' proposals have to be taken seriously because Congress has the power to terminate its advance authorization at any time. In fact, the current authorizing legislation explicitly provides that either house of the Congress can repeal the authorization outright at any time.[20]

Perhaps more alarming for free trade proponents, particularly in view of the slow progress of the Doha Round, is the 'drop-dead date' of 1 June 2005. Congress gave itself an opportunity to stop the Doha Round in its tracks as of that date. The legislative technique used was to provide, in the 2002 authorizing statute, negotiating authority only through to 1 June 2005. True, the statute provides for an automatic extension of negotiating authority through to 1 June 2007, but only under specific conditions. In addition to the procedural requirement that the President must seek the extension, providing prescribed information about the agreements he expects to achieve, along with a report on economic impact from the International Trade Commission (a body that by no means is controlled by the President), an ominous provision is that any individual member of either the House of Representatives or the

---

[20] See discussion of 19 U.S.C. 2903(d), in Shapiro and Brainard, *supra* n. 19 at 19. In any event, one should remember the 'oft-overlooked fact that, as a legal matter, the Fast Track "emperor" has no clothes: the statutory Fast Track procedures that modify internal house rules in no way legally "bind" Congress [because] the Constitution specifically authorizes "[e]ach House [to] determine the Rules of its Procedures".' Koh, *supra* n. 18 at 151–152.

Senate may introduce a 'resolution of disapproval', which is to be considered on a 'fast track' basis by the House in question.[21] This provision opens the possibility that one House of the US Congress may abort the Doha Round in 2005 under a procedure affording a veil of Congressional deliberative process to cover what could prove to be simply a surrender to protectionist forces. Such a resolution would require a majority vote of disapproval, but only in one of the houses of Congress. This extension-disapproval arrangement is potentially a threat to the Doha Round, depending on the state of the US economy and the constellation of political power in the Presidency and the Congress after the 2004 elections.

VI. INHIBITING US ABILITY TO LEAD

Perhaps more ominous than this June 2005 Congressional opt-out date, however, is the continuing departure from the simple Cordell Hull principles of reciprocity, advance authorization, professional negotiations out of the public eye, and more or less automatic adoption of the results of the negotiations. It has been said that the essence of the Hull approach was that Congress agreed, in authorizing negotiations, to tie its hands thereafter. The hands of Congress have been largely untied and are increasingly meddling in the negotiations themselves. Moreover, the very right of Congress to be fully informed in advance of forthcoming US proposals means that the concept of professional negotiations out of the public eye is increasingly at risk.

One can, of course, make an argument that transparency is a democratic value. But it is also true that the original idea of advance authorization was that it would be difficult to know at that early point exactly what domestic ox was likely to be gored. Moreover, at that early point both exporter industries and import-competing industries would have equal access to the Congressional process. But when Congress—most likely a single individual, but politically powerful, member of Congress—uses the right to be informed to attempt to pre-empt a US concession on behalf of a constituent protectionist interest, exporting interests are unlikely even to know what is happening, much less be able to organize to oppose. After all, normal principles of collective action tell us that the costs to individual exporting companies from the opportunities indirectly foregone through the failure of the negotiators in the face of Congressional opposition to make an additional concession are likely to be quite small, while the transaction costs of bringing about

[21] 19 U.S.C. 3803(c).

united countervailing influence from exporters as a class are likely to be large. That is the very type of collective action problem that Hull's Reciprocal Trade Agreements Act, especially as complemented by the fast-track procedure, was designed to overcome.

What can be done to arrest the resulting gradual erosion of the US ability to lead—indeed, to continue to support—the long-term fight for freer trade? Probably very little. But returning to first principles, it would be interesting to see what could be done to strengthen the role of those economic interests that seek lower barriers. Bringing exporters into the process that import-competing firms dominated in Smoot–Hawley was the Hull-inspired form of statecraft to overcome the influence of protectionist forces.[22] The question today is how exporting interests can find renewed influence in the domestic US struggle between the forces of freer trade and protection in view of the gradual erosion of the original fast track rules.[23]

One way to achieve some balance would be to give importers who benefit from trade concessions rights balancing those that import-competing firms have in domestic law to protect themselves from imports through anti-dumping and countervailing duty cases and Section 201 escape-clause proceedings. Since the persistent trend is to make such anti-import procedures ever more protectionist and stringent, the rollback of those anti-import procedures is almost surely not a politically viable strategy. Attempting to accord domestic interests favouring imports procedural rights in the foregoing protectionist-friendly proceedings may be equally problematic, though there are powerful transparency and fairness arguments to be made for allowing everyone with an interest to be heard.

How can exporters be given a greater voice to offset protectionism? There are few precedents in US domestic law for exporter rights. The principal one, Section 301, even if regarded as generally a positive provision, addresses foreign protectionism, not domestic protectionism. One international precedent is the provision in the Trade-Related Intellectual Property agreement requiring WTO countries to provide a domestic remedy in intellectual property infringement situations.[24] Another international precedent is to be found in the 1996 plurilateral

---

[22] See Dam, *supra* n. 16 at 36–72.

[23] An alternative approach would, in effect, attempt to co-opt the US Congress through inter-parliamentary participation in some form of WTO parliamentary oversight. See Ernst-Ulrich Petersmann, 'Challenges to the Legitimacy and Efficiency of the World Trading System: Democratic Governance and Competition Culture in the WTO' Introduction and Summary, 7 *Journal of International Economic Law* (2004) 585, 590–592. This idea does not seem likely to lead to fruition at this time, but domestic political changes in the US could make it a more promising idea in the future.

[24] Agreement on Trade-Related Aspects of Intellectual Property Rights, Part III.

Agreement on Government Procurement. Article XX of that Agreement requires governments to allow suppliers to challenge breaches of the Agreement.[25]

These two international precedents involve giving exporters procedural rights in an importing country, but they do not address exporters' rights in their own country. Still, they are perhaps a first step in internationalizing the understanding that international trade liberalization is often less about the international negotiating process than about providing a domestic mechanism by which exporters can be given opportunities and means to offset the political influence of import-competing firms. In the fast track (now the Trade Promotion Authority) initial authorizing process the influence of exporters and importers is reasonably balanced. But as David Skaggs, a former Congressman, observed, members of Congress most often hear from constituents about trade when they are angry,[26] which in practical terms means that those who lose from trade are more likely to gain the ear of Congress than those who hope to gain.

Hopes for continued trade liberalization therefore depend, at least in the US, on institutional arrangements assuring that exporting interests can be provided opportunities and means to offset the political influence of import-competing firms threatened by such liberalization. That idea first reached fruition in Hull's Reciprocal Trade Agreements Act. It flourished with the GATT and with fast track, but it is always exposed to domestic backsliding.

---

[25] See discussion in B. M. Hoekman, 'Introduction and Overview' in B. M. Hoekman and P. C. Mavoidis (eds), *Law and Policy in Public Purchasing* (1997) at 20–22.

[26] D. E. Skaggs, 'How Can Parliamentary Participation in WTO Rule-Making and Democratic Control Be Made More Effective in the WTO?' in 7 *Journal of International Economic Law* (2004) 655.

PART III

BUILDING-BLOCKS FOR CONCLUDING THE DOHA ROUND NEGOTIATIONS ON AGRICULTURE

4

How to Forge a Compromise in the Agriculture Negotiations

STEFAN TANGERMANN[1]

I. INTRODUCTION

The Uruguay Round Agreement on Agriculture (AoA) was the first serious attempt at overcoming the large distortions that have plagued international trade in agricultural products for a long time. It changed the treatment of agriculture in the international trading order fundamentally. For the first time in the history of the General Agreement on Tariffs and Trade (GATT) it brought agricultural policies and trade under operationally effective disciplines and established quantitative commitments for all World Trade Organization (WTO) Members. This progress was not easily achieved. The negotiations on agriculture were controversial, complex, and strenuous. At a number of junctions, the whole Uruguay Round was on the brink of failure because of agriculture, and it was not before a settlement was found for the agricultural issues that the overall round came to a conclusion.

However, any hopes that the Uruguay Round might have put agricultural issues in the WTO to rest were soon to prove futile. In the ongoing Doha Development Agenda (DDA) negotiations, agriculture is again at the forefront, and progress or hold-ups in the talks on farm trade once more impact decisively on the fate of the negotiations overall. It was only after agreement on the agricultural elements was reached, after serious tensions and protracted negotiations, repeatedly on the brink of collapse, that the WTO General Council could decide, on 1 August 2004 in Geneva, how to complete the Doha work programme, clearing the way to a continuation of the DDA negotiations. The framework agreed for further talks on agriculture is a significant and welcome step forward and contains a number of promising elements, in particular the pledge to eliminate, by a date to be agreed, export subsidies and certain

[1] Helpful comments on an earlier draft from Carmel Cahill and Dimitris Diakosavvas are gratefully acknowledged. The views expressed are those of the author and do not necessarily reflect those of the OECD and its member countries.

other export competition measures. However, even this hard-fought accord obviously is still far away from the full modalities with numerical reduction commitments that WTO Members had originally hoped they could have already agreed by March 2003.

Why is it that agriculture is again so difficult in this round of negotiations? Has the Uruguay Round, in spite of all its success, left too much unfinished business in agriculture? Have the new rules not worked well? Or were reduction commitments a problem? Where are the priorities for this round of negotiations, and is there a chance that progress will be made? In discussing such questions, this chapter will first take a look at what the Uruguay Round has achieved, in terms of how agricultural policies in the Organisation for Economic Co-operation and Development (OECD) area have developed after the new AoA was agreed. Finding that progress was limited, the paper will then address the question of whether this was due to the rules agreed in the Uruguay Round, or to the quantitative parameters in the reduction commitments. Focusing on the reduction commitments, the chapter will then argue that priority should be on reducing border measures and output payments. Regarding the future of the rules, some observations will also be offered on the economics of the relationship between export competition and domestic support. After commenting, against this background, briefly on the framework for agriculture agreed in August 2004, the chapter ends on some concluding remarks.

II. AGRICULTURAL POLICIES IN THE OECD AREA AFTER THE URUGUAY ROUND

The preamble of the Uruguay Round AoA identifies the long-term objective of establishing 'a fair and market-oriented agricultural trading system and . . . a reform process' providing 'for substantial progressive reductions in agricultural support and protection'. Have agricultural policies of the industrialized countries achieved these objectives? Indicators of farm support as calculated regularly by the OECD should provide some insight.

OECD summarizes the policy-induced transfers directly affecting the revenue of individual farmers in the Producer Support Estimate (PSE), the most prominent indicator in the family of OECD's agricultural support statistics. The PSE can be expressed as an absolute sum of money, showing that in 2003 the 30 member countries of the OECD transferred US$257 billion to their farmers.[2] More telling than this absolute amount is the share

---

[2] Out of the 30 member countries of the OECD, 15 are member states of the European Union. In measuring agricultural support, the EU is treated as one aggregate, because all EU countries are covered by the Common Agricultural Policy.

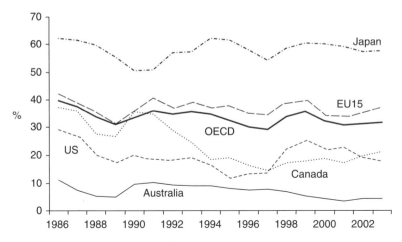

FIGURE 4.1 Farm support (%PSE) in the OECD area and Selected Member Countries

Source: OECD, PSE/CSE database, Paris (2004).

in farmers' revenues that it represents, the %PSE. In 2003, this indicator stood at 32%. In other words, out of each dollar of revenue for the average farmer in the OECD area, 32 cents resulted from government policies, while only the remaining 68 cents came from the market. This is only a marginal decline compared to the situation at the beginning of the Uruguay Round (1986–88), when the PSE in the OECD area stood at 37%.

A closer look at support developments over time actually shows that most of this slight decline in the %PSE for the aggregate of OECD countries was achieved during the first half of Uruguay Round negotiations, from 1986 to 1989. Since that time, the support level has fluctuated somewhat, but not shown any obvious downward trend (Figure 4.1). However, there were significant differences among countries. In some cases, support has declined substantially over the last 15 years. In other countries, though, a declining support level in earlier years was later followed by a rise in support. Overall, after the reduction commitments of the Uruguay Round AoA entered into force, i.e. after 1995, farm support in the OECD area has not decreased. As a matter of fact, it is precisely during this period that support noticeably increased in some OECD countries. The commodity composition of support has also not changed much after the Uruguay Round (Figure 4.2). The three products receiving the highest support levels remain rice (around 80% PSE), sugar and milk (the two latter around 50% PSE).

What about the Uruguay Round's objective of a reduction in the level of agricultural protection? The relevant indicator here is the Producer Nominal Protection Coefficient (NPCp), measuring the ratio between

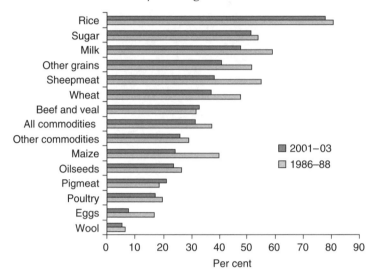

FIGURE 4.2 Producer support estimate by commodity (OECD average as percentage of value of gross farm receipts)
Source: OECD, PSE/CSE database, Paris (2004).

the average price received by producers (at farm gate), including payments per tonne of current output, and the border price (measured at the farm gate). As portrayed in Figure 4.3, more progress has been made on this count for the OECD area overall. While in 1986 domestic producer prices in OECD countries were on average 63 per cent above world market prices, by 2003 that gap had halved, to 31 per cent. Again, a good part of this decline occurred while the Uruguay Round negotiations were still going on. But before the implementation period started, in 1994, OECD domestic producer prices were still 43 per cent above the international market level, and thus further progress was indeed made during the implementation period. As in the case of support levels, there are obvious differences in market protection among individual OECD countries, and also the development over time has differed significantly among countries. However, overall, there has been notable progress in the OECD area towards less market protection.

The decline in the level of market protection for OECD agriculture, with significantly less decrease in support levels, indicates that some re-instrumentation of policies must have occurred over time. This change in policy structure is also apparent in the evolution of the composition of the various measures that provide transfers directly to individual farmers, as captured in the Producer Support Estimate (Figure 4.4).

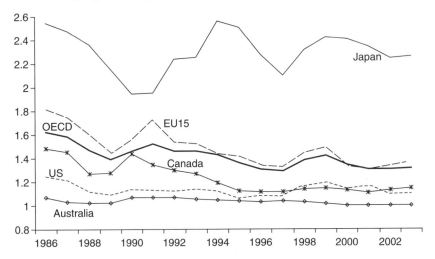

FIGURE 4.3 Producer price protection in selected OECD countries (Producer Nominal Protection Coefficient), average over all products
Source: OECD, PSE/CSE database, Paris (2004).

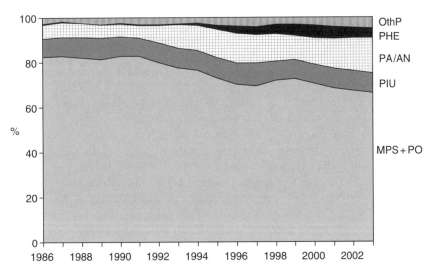

FIGURE 4.4 Composition of Producer Support Estimate, OECD aggregate (share of individual policy instruments in overall PSE)
Note: For an explanation of acronyms, see text.
Source: OECD, PSE/CSE database, Paris (2004).

In particular, the share of overall OECD producer support that comes in the form of market price support (MPS) and payments per tonne of output (PO) has declined significantly over time, from 83 per cent in 1986 to 66 per cent in 2003, and mirrors the reduction in market protection. This decline is an important development, as market price support and output payments are among the most production- and trade-distorting instruments of agricultural policy.[3] However, for the same reason, it is also noteworthy that two-thirds of OECD producer support still comes in this form.

Payments based on input use (PIU), also strongly market-distorting, have exhibited a roughly constant share of aggregate producer support, at 9 per cent in 2003.[4] The share of payments based on area planted and animal numbers (PA/AN) in aggregate producer support has expanded, mainly since the early 1990s. In 2003, such area and livestock payments accounted for a share of 16 per cent in aggregate OECD producer support. These types of payment, while somewhat decoupled from production, can still have significant effects on markets and trade, but are less distorting than market price and output support.[5] Still more decoupled and less distorting are payments based on historical entitlements (PHE), another category of measures whose share in producer support expanded at the expense of market and output support and in 2003 stood at 4 per cent of producer support.

Overall, since the early 1990s, a noticeable shift in OECD agricultural policy composition has taken place, with some movement away from strongly distorting price and output support, towards more decoupled, and hence less production- and trade-distorting measures. The extent to which this happened has differed markedly among countries. For example, in Japan, 97 per cent of all producer support still comes in the form of price support, output and input payments, unchanged from the mid-1980s. On the other hand, in the United States (US), the share of these distorting forms of support in the PSE has declined somewhat (from 70 per cent in 1986–88 to 65 per cent in 2001–03), and in the European Union (EU) it was reduced significantly (from 96 per cent to 68 per cent). Policy changes continue, but not all countries go in the same direction. For example, the US Farm Bill, passed in 2002, locked in the higher levels of support provided in preceding years through *ad hoc* payments, and was a step backwards from the decoupling of support.[6] Conversely, the reform of the EU's Common Agricultural Policy (CAP), decided in 2003, while maintaining a higher

---

[3] OECD, *The Market Effects of Crop Support Measures* (2001) at 19f.   [4] *Ibid.*
[5] *Ibid.*
[6] OECD, *Agricultural Policies in OECD Countries: Monitoring and Evaluation* (2003).

level of support than in the US, made a further significant step towards decoupling support from production.[7]

In summary, the record is mixed regarding the extent to which the objectives of the Uruguay Round AoA have been achieved among OECD countries, if seen from the perspective of the support indicators as used in OECD's work on monitoring and evaluation of agricultural policies. Overall, the level of agricultural support has declined somewhat since the beginning of the Uruguay Round negotiations. Progress was more pronounced regarding the nature of policy instruments used. The most production- and trade-distorting policies, i.e. market price support and output payments, have declined noticeably, and have given place to forms of support that are more decoupled from production decisions. On the other hand, price and output support, as well as payments based on input use, still account for by far the largest share of all agricultural support in the OECD area, jointly making up for three-quarters of producer support. Within these overall trends in the OECD area, there are obvious differences among individual countries. In particular, producer support has significantly decreased in some countries, while in other countries it has remained at high levels, and progress towards decoupling support from production has been uneven across countries.

III. RULES OR REDUCTION COMMITMENTS— WHERE IS THE PROBLEM?

In spite of some progress, and notwithstanding more recent reform decisions such as those taken in the EU, one cannot say that the AoA has resulted in a fundamental liberalization of agriculture in the OECD area. This lack of deep change has caused some disappointment, not least among developing countries, and such frustration has added to the tensions about agriculture that have plagued a good part of the DDA negotiations, most noticeably at Cancún. Why is it that the significant progress made on agriculture in the Uruguay Round has not yielded more in terms of actual policy change and liberalization? There are several conceivable reasons.

One possibility is that countries have simply disregarded the new disciplines in agriculture established in the Uruguay Round. However, that does not appear to have been the case, as shown, for example, by the fact that discussions in the WTO Committee on Agriculture regarding implementation of the AoA have gone reasonably smoothly. Also, there

---

[7] OECD, *Analysis of the 2003 CAP Reform* (2004).

have been only a limited number of formal disputes regarding central provisions of the AoA. Some of these disputes may have an important bearing on future dealings with agriculture in the WTO, and we shall have to come back to this below. But overall there is no reason to suggest that the AoA did not have much effect because many governments have ignored its provisions.

This leaves us with two alternative potential explanations. First, the new rules on agriculture agreed in the Uruguay Round might have been deficient and left too many loopholes. Second, the quantitative reduction commitments for tariffs and subsidies established under the AoA may have been too generous and allowed too much scope for continuing to provide high levels of protection and support. Depending on which of these two potential explanations is considered dominant, the priorities of those parties who want to make more progress in the current round of negotiations would have to focus on either refining the rules or agreeing deeper cuts. Let us therefore explore these two potential explanations, in reverse order.

Did the quantitative commitments agreed in the Uruguay Round contain so much 'water' that even the reductions agreed in the Uruguay Round did not yet effectively constrain policies? This was obviously true in many cases, as shown in a number of analyses.[8] Let us consider just a few indicators.

Regarding market access, many tariffs in agriculture are still very high indeed. In the schedules of several OECD countries, a substantial share of all agricultural tariff lines exhibit mega-tariffs with rates above 100 per cent (Figure 4.5). Indeed, many of these tariffs are simply prohibitive, and hence reducing them, in a given range, does no more than squeeze some of the economic water out of these tariffs, without affecting domestic price levels and trade flows. This was a major reason why exporting countries were keen to have minimum access commitments agreed in the Uruguay Round. However, it has turned out that many of these newly established tariff rate quotas, even where within-quota tariffs were significantly below 'normal' tariffs, have not so far been fully utilized.[9] There is much speculation and political argument about the reasons for such low fill rates, and a lot of research remains to be done in this regard.

---

[8] For example, OECD, *The Uruguay Round Agreement on Agriculture: An Evaluation of its Implementation in OECD Countries* (2001); OECD, *Agriculture and Trade Liberalisation: Extending the Uruguay Round Agreement* (2002); OECD, *Agricultural Policies in OECD Countries: Monitoring and Evaluation* (2002); D. Diakosavvas, 'The Uruguay Round Agreement on Agriculture in Practice: How Open Are OECD Markets?' in M. Ingco and A. Winters (eds), *Agriculture and the New Trade Agenda* (2004).

[9] OECD, *Agriculture and Trade Liberalisation: Extending the Uruguay Round Agreement* (2002) at 20–27.

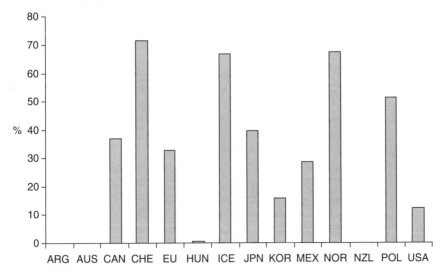

FIGURE 4.5 Mega-tariffs (defined as a tariff equal or greater to 100 per cent) in selected countries, percentage of agricultural tariff lines in 2000

Source: OECD calculations based on 3,152 tariff lines from the AMAD database.

In the case of domestic support, the situation is simply that commitment levels were set at such high levels that in many cases both their original and the reduced final levels provided more room for manoeuvre than actual policies required. This is shown by the large percentage of all country/year observations in which only rather small shares of the domestic support commitments were actually utilized. On aggregate, in the OECD area, the level of Current Total Aggregate Measure of Support (AMS) was no higher than 56 per cent of the AMS commitments on average in the years 1995 to 1999, and only 45 per cent in 2000 (Figure 4.6). It is, though, interesting to note that, even though the domestic support commitments agreed in the WTO were not binding in many countries, the actual level of accountable domestic support as defined under WTO rules still declined during the implementation period, and substantially more than the level of economic support as measured by OECD. Of course, when interpreting this finding one has to keep in mind that market price support, an important element in the Current Total AMS, is, for WTO purposes, measured between administered prices and fixed external reference prices. Another interesting finding is that the total level of green box support in the OECD area has remained roughly constant since the beginning of the AoA implementation period. In other words, for the OECD aggregate, one does not find a significant shift of support into the WTO green box. This holds true

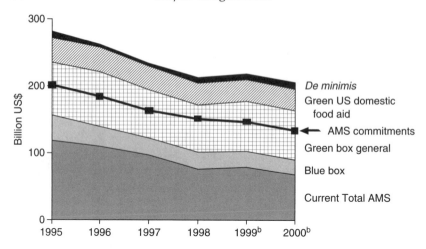

FIGURE 4.6 Domestic support[a] and WTO commitments, OECD aggregate

[a] Domestic support levels notified by the individual OECD countries, as well as their AMS commitments, have been converted into US$ using current exchange rates for the years concerned.

[b] Notifications for 1999 and 2000 do not include Mexico and Switzerland; 2000 notifications do not include Canada.

Source: WTO notifications.

even if one disregards for a moment domestic food aid in the US, a significant share of all green box notifications. Usage of the *de minimis* provisions, though, has increased somewhat recently for the OECD aggregate. Of course, these developments of OECD aggregates hide significant differences in the usage of the domestic support commitments across individual countries. For example, in the US, Current Total AMS has risen from 27 per cent of the domestic support commitment to 88 per cent in 2000 and 75 per cent in 2001.

The commitments on export subsidization are generally considered to have been the most binding of all the new quantitative disciplines agreed in the Uruguay Round. A look at the aggregate usage of export subsidy outlays as notified by all WTO Members, in comparison with aggregate commitments, does not appear to confirm this view (Figure 4.7). It is evident, though, that the EU had the lion's share in all notified export subsidies. And for the EU, the export subsidy commitments have indeed constrained the room for manoeuvre in several commodity sectors, as shown by the high degree to which quantity commitments were used for a number of products (Figure 4.8). On the other hand, there are also product sectors in the EU where the export subsidy commitments have been far less than fully utilized in recent years. Generally, use of

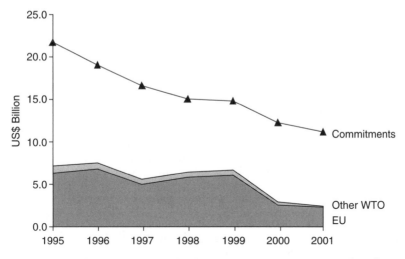

FIGURE 4.7 Outlays on export subsidies: aggregate commitments for all WTO
Members

Note: 1999, 2000, and 2001 notifications do not include Cyprus and Venezuela, 2000 and 2001
notifications do not include Australia.

Source: WTO notifications.

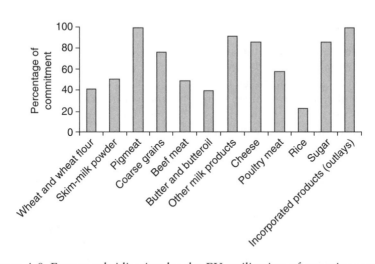

FIGURE 4.8 Export subsidization by the EU: utilization of quantity commitments, average 2000–02, selected products

Source: WTO notifications of the EU.

export subsidies by the EU, and hence in the WTO overall, has declined noticeably in recent years. In addition to international market developments, reforms in the EU's CAP have contributed to this decline. The WTO was a factor that contributed to these reforms[10] and to policy changes in other countries, and in that sense the Uruguay Round did have an effect on the actual development of agricultural policies.

Overall, many of the new quantitative commitments on agriculture that were agreed in the Uruguay Round did not constrain policies, and this appears to be the primary reason why the AoA has not yet resulted in more significant changes in agricultural policies in the OECD area. The non-binding character of the new commitments may have been the price that had to be paid during the Uruguay Round for the acceptance of a wholly new legal framework in the WTO for agricultural trade and policies. But further progress on reduction commitments can be made in the current round of negotiations, and a few comments on that subject will be made in the following section.

While many of the quantitative reduction commitments agreed in the Uruguay Round obviously contained much water, it cannot be said that the rules embodied in the AoA exhibited many loopholes. It appears that overall they have worked reasonably well, although some issues did indeed become apparent. For example, the rules on domestic support make it possible to reduce notified support by changing commodity programmes such that an administered price is eliminated without much effect on actual producer prices received. This possibility was used in some cases, and contributed to the decline in Current Total AMS shown in Figure 4.6. Also, certain issues regarding the interpretation of the rules on export subsidies have become apparent in dispute cases. Moreover, after overt export subsidies were subjected to disciplines in the AoA, an equivalent coverage of other forms of export competition has become an issue in the current round of negotiations. These issues regarding rules on export competition will be discussed in a later section.

IV. REDUCTION COMMITMENTS: FOCUS ON BORDER MEASURES AND OUTPUT PAYMENTS

Given that existing quantitative commitments still contain substantial amounts of water, it is reassuring that there appears to be essentially universal acceptance in the current round of negotiations of the need to agree on further substantial reductions. Indeed, proposals tabled so far

---

[10] W. Moyer and T. Josling, *Agricultural Policy Reform: Politics and Process in the EU and US in the 1990s* (2002).

appear to suggest that cuts this time may eventually be deeper than in the Uruguay Round. Moreover, in the framework accord of July 2004, agreement has now been reached that export subsidies and other forms of export competition will finally be eliminated. Though full-blown negotiations on numerical reduction parameters still have to start, growing attention has been paid in recent months to market-access issues, in particular the formulae for tariff cuts. This is a positive development in the sense that there is a great deal of merit in giving priority to the reduction of border measures in agriculture.

OECD research, and the policy conclusions drawn from it—agreed among all OECD member countries—suggest that price support provided to domestic producers, maintained behind border protection and export subsidies, is ineffective and inefficient in achieving the objectives of agricultural policies. Hence, from a purely domestic perspective, the reduction of border measures is a priority in agricultural policy reform. The same holds true for government payments per tonne of output or per unit of input. It is easy to see why.[11]

The most important objectives pursued by governments in agriculture fall into one of two categories, support to farm income and correction of market failures. Regarding farm income, price and output support is unnecessary, inefficient, and inequitable. It is unnecessary because there is not a general farm income problem in the OECD area. In many OECD countries, incomes of farm households are in line with, or above, incomes in the rest of the economy, and where incomes of farm households lag behind, the margin is not big. Price and output support is an inefficient means of supporting farm incomes because only a small share of the money transferred to agriculture through these policies ends up in the farmer's pocket. In a typical situation, one extra dollar transferred to agriculture through price support adds no more than 25 cents to the income of farm operators. The remaining 75 cents end up in the hands of landlords and in the input industry, or evaporate through extra resource costs.[12] The reason is that price and output support provides an incentive for farmers to expand output, and in order to do so farmers demand more land and intermediary inputs. This also drives up prices of all these inputs. Hence, a significant share of the extra receipts farmers receive when their selling prices are supported ends up as higher expenditure on inputs. The net result is that no more than a quarter of

---

[11] The following paragraphs provide a brief overview of some of the major points made in the report by OECD, *Agricultural Policies in OECD Countries: A Positive Reform Agenda* (2002). That report also provides quantitative information that underpins the arguments advanced here, and makes reference to other OECD reports dealing with these issues in more detail.

[12] OECD, *Farm Household Income: Issues and Policy Responses* (2003) at 67.

the extra transfer to farmers from consumers and taxpayers through price support actually results in extra income for the farm operator and his or her family. Finally, farm income policy through price and output support is inequitable as this support is distributed across farms in essentially the same way as production volume, rather than in accordance with needs. The largest farms receive the largest sums of support, and those are not typically the farms owned by the poorest farmers most in need of income support. The 25 per cent largest farms in the EU receive 70 per cent of all government support, and in the US the 25 per cent largest farms even get 90 per cent of support.[13] The irony is that a policy arguably pursuing equity objectives has rather inequitable results.

As far as the correction of market failures is concerned, agricultural policies pursue objectives related to positive and negative externalities (e.g. the effects of agricultural production on biodiversity and the environment) and public goods (e.g. maintenance of a pleasing landscape or providing food security). However, price and output support is not really doing a good job when dealing with such market failures.[14] Negative externalities, such as those resulting from an expansion and intensification of agricultural production, are often actually made worse through such policies. Positive externalities and any public goods that agriculture can provide usually do not come in anything like a fixed proportion with agricultural output, and hence output raising policies such as price and output support often make little, if any, contribution to attaining such objectives, and are in most cases less efficient than payments made directly dependent on the delivery of such services. In only very specific and probably rare cases may the transaction costs involved in making such targeted payments be so high that output support is the preferable approach. In other words, border policies, implemented to provide price support, and output-related domestic payments rarely do a good job in pursuing objectives related to the multifunctional characteristics of agriculture.

What is the alternative to price and output support, in dealing with agricultural issues that cannot be left to the market? Decoupling support from production is a first, very useful step in improving the domestic functioning of agricultural policy. As far as farm incomes are concerned, decoupled payments have at least the advantage that their transfer efficiency is better. For example, compared with price or output support, payments based on historical entitlements can get double the amount across to farm operators per dollar spent by consumers and taxpayers.

---

[13] OECD, *Farm Household Income: Issues and Policy Responses* (2003) at 22.
[14] OECD, *Multifunctionality: The Policy Implications* (2003) at 76–77.

Targeting payments directly to the objectives pursued is another very helpful step, because in nearly all cases this is significantly more efficient than supporting farm prices and output.

Hence, for purely domestic reasons, it is promising to move from border measures and output-related payments to payments decoupled from production and targeted to specific objectives. In the context of international trade, a second big advantage of such policy reform is that distortions of production, markets, and trade are reduced. This is why the reduction of border measures, i.e. tariffs and export subsidies in all forms, as well as the reduction of payments per unit of output or input, merits priority. As far as the WTO categories of domestic support are concerned, policy reform in this direction also means moving support out of the amber (and possibly the blue) box and into the green box. In this context, concern is often voiced, in particular from the perspective of developing countries, regarding the phenomenon of 'box shifting'.[15] In its simplest form, this criticism suggests that it doesn't matter in which form the governments of rich countries subsidize their farmers—all forms of support distort trade. Shifting support from the amber or blue box into the green box, as allowed by the AoA, doesn't improve the conditions on international markets, the criticism goes, and should therefore not be allowed. There is a grain of truth in this view. It is certainly the case, as confirmed by OECD research, that any payment made to a farmer is likely to have some effect on production. In that sense, a policy change that moves support from the amber to the green box is unlikely to eliminate, in a strict quantitative sense, all production and market effects. But OECD research has also shown that the production impacts of strongly decoupled policies, such as payments based on historical entitlements, and not related to current prices, are orders of magnitude below those of typical amber box measures, such as administered market prices and output payments.[16] From that perspective, any 'box shifting' of this nature is beneficial for international markets as well as for the domestic economy. Such policy reform should, therefore, be encouraged. At the same time, along with policy reform in this direction, support can also be reduced because, as argued above, decoupled and targeted payments are more effective regarding both farm incomes and dealing with market failures.

---

[15] See, for example, M. S. Jank and M. de Queiroz Monteiro Jales, 'On Product-, Box-, and Blame-Shifting: An Assessment of the Cancun Frameworks for WTO Negotiations on Agriculture', paper presented at the Second IDB–CEPII Conference on *Economic Implications of the Doha Development Agenda for Latin America and the Caribbean*, Washington, DC, 6–7 October 2003.   [16] OECD, *supra* n. 3 at 19f.

V. RULES: THE SUPPORT JUNGLE

As far as refinement of the rules in the AoA is concerned, it appears that the spotlight is on those regarding export competition. How can rules be formulated that extend beyond overt export subsidies and establish equivalent disciplines for other policies with potentially similar effects, such as export credits, food aid, and state trading enterprises? In addition, there is also the more fundamental issue of the definition of export subsidization, or more specifically of what the relationship is between domestic support and export competition. This issue figured in the disputes on Canada's dairy policies and US cotton programmes, and from the media news on the as yet unavailable interim report of the panel dealing with the EU sugar regime, it appears that this issue played a role in that case, too. Negotiators in the Uruguay Round aimed at a comprehensive set of rules and agreed separate disciplines for the three areas of market access, domestic support, and export competition. Given the mechanics of economic relationships, it was clear from the beginning that there are overlaps between these three areas. For example, a domestic administered price above the world market level (covered under the AoA rules on domestic support) can be sustained only behind tariff protection (covered under rules on market access). If this price support results in surplus supplies on the domestic market, exports can only take place with export subsidies (covered under the rules on export competition). In such cases, a given economic phenomenon, resulting in a trade distortion, is disciplined, in the AoA, by more than one rule. The advantage may well be that this creates multiple security.

On the other hand, there are alternative policies with rather similar effects that the AoA covers in different parts of its rules, with the result that different reduction rates and degrees of stringency may apply. For example, a government payment per tonne of output has the same effect on domestic supply (though not on domestic demand) as an equivalent level of price support. However, while in an exporting country with domestic price support the exported share of domestic production is subject to the (product-specific) commitments on export subsidies, an output payment, including that on exported output, is submerged into the sector-wide commitment on domestic support. It would be difficult to argue that this is equivalent treatment of alternative forms of policies with essentially the same effects.

In the same context, it is clear that a watertight distinction between domestic support and export support is difficult to strike in exporting countries. Essentially, export support is the tip of the iceberg of domestic support. What makes a policy have an effect on exports is the incentive it provides, at the margin, to domestic producers (and/or any disincentive to domestic consumers). The implication for rule design is obvious: the tighter the disciplines are on domestic support, and in particular on domestic support for exported output, the less there is a need to rely on rules regarding export competition. In principle, appropriate disciplines on domestic support could substitute for export competition disciplines.

The same logic can also be extended to the relative effects of alternative forms of export competition. What counts here is the extra amount of output that is shipped abroad, over and above of what would be the case in the absence of the policy measure concerned.[17] In the final analysis, this depends on any extra incentives to produce that domestic farmers receive as a result of the policy measure concerned. Even though the measure is implemented at the point of export (as opposed to a payment to domestic farmers), any incentive to domestic producers, and hence any additional exports, can only originate from an increase in the price these producers receive. In other words, a policy that does no more than make it easier for the importing country to buy the produce concerned, without raising the producer price in the exporting country, will not result in an expansion of exports from the country pursuing that policy.[18] From this perspective, too, it can be said that a tight discipline on domestic support (the 'iceberg') might well capture the export competition phenomenon (the 'tip of the iceberg'). Hence, sufficiently stringent and demanding rules on domestic support could well bring about equivalent discipline for all forms of export competition, without the need for specific provision regarding the individual export competition measures. Moreover, the link with tariffs, emphasized above, is relevant here too. In the absence of tariffs, domestic market prices cannot be lifted up by any policies. This adds further weight to the priority focus on market access.

VI. THE FRAMEWORK AGREEMENT OF 1 AUGUST 2004

Against this background, the Decision Adopted by the WTO General Council on 1 August 2004,[19] and the Framework for Establishing Modalities in Agriculture annexed to it, constitute an important step

---

[17] In addition, there are also issues such as market displacement, which are not discussed here.

[18] As a matter of fact, this policy may allow the importing country to import more than it might otherwise have done, thereby raising global import demand. This would allow all exporters to ship more, including the exporting country pursuing the policy concerned.

[19] WTO, *Doha Work Programme—Decision Adopted by the General Council on 1 August 2004*, WT/L/579.

forward, though many questions are still left wide open. The agreement reached in Geneva is a significant achievement far beyond signalling progress in the agricultural talks. It has also saved the WTO, and the multilateral regime of economic relations among nations overall, from the depression that could have resulted from a failure to agree on at least a rough outline for further negotiations in the DDA round. WTO Members have, through this agreement, shown their political determination to make progress in these talks and, quite irrespective of the concrete content of the Decision, the symbolic value of the fact that countries could agree on some form of accord was very important at that moment. The Framework for agriculture has a number of elements that provide more precision, at this stage, than some observers might have considered achievable, but in other parts it remains rather vague.

The most significant achievement of the Framework is the accord 'to establish detailed modalities ensuring the parallel elimination of all forms of export subsidies and disciplines on all export measures with equivalent effect by a credible end date'. What that end date will be is still to be negotiated. Some participants have already indicated that they think more in terms of 10 to 15 years, rather than in orders of magnitude similar to the duration of the implementation period for the Uruguay Round AoA (six years for developed countries). In any case, the eventual elimination of export subsidies and equivalent measures, generally seen as the most unacceptable forms of agricultural support, will be a major accomplishment, removing what so far remains the biggest difference in the treatment of agriculture compared with the rules for manufactured trade where export subsidies were prohibited a long time ago. It is also in line with the priority focus on border measures advocated above. Negotiators will, though, still have to work hard in search of appropriate approaches to establish 'parallelism' across the various forms of export competition measures. One pragmatic step in this direction has already been taken through the agreement to eliminate, by an end date to be agreed, export credits, export credit guarantees, or insurance programmes with repayment periods beyond 180 days. However, what 'parallelism' with the treatment of overt export subsidies will mean when it comes to shorter-term export credit measures, exporting state trading enterprises, and food aid will still have to be determined. It will be interesting to see whether equivalence between all these measures will be defined based on an economic analysis of their respective effects on markets and trade, as briefly discussed in the preceding section of this paper, or whether more mechanical approaches will be adopted.

Regarding domestic support, the Framework has opened the door somewhat towards more specific disciplines that could in future potentially cover the economic relationships between domestic subsidies and export competition, as also briefly discussed in the preceding section. It has done so, in particular, through providing that product-specific domestic support will be capped, according to a methodology still to be agreed. The agreement to harmonize levels of domestic support across countries will eliminate (some of) the base-period effects that allowed countries with high levels of support before the Uruguay Round to continue providing larger rates of support than countries whose support levels were already lower during the Uruguay Round base period. The agreement to establish a new overall limit on all trade-distorting domestic support (sum of aggregate measurement of support, redefined blue box, and *de minimis*) guards against some forms of 'box shifting', as does the understanding to establish a new ceiling on the blue box, and to negotiate reductions in *de minimis* support. The resolve to make a down-payment in the form of a 20 per cent reduction in all trade-distorting domestic support in the first year of the implementation period will take some of the water out of current domestic support commitments. At the same time, the blue box has been opened up more widely so as to provide a home also for payments that do not, as required in the Uruguay Round AoA, come under production-limiting programmes, though only as long as such payments do not require production. The new requirement for blue box payments, that their base must not be changed, should guard against updating of the production base for these payments, and hence against the production-stimulating effects that can result if farmers are given reason to expect that they can inflate their base for future payments by expanding production. Regarding the green box, it is not fully clear how the agreement to review its criteria will be put into practice in further negotiations. It is reassuring that in the text on the three pillars of the AoA (market access, domestic support, and export competition) non-trade concerns are mentioned only in relation to the green box.

The area where the Framework is least precise is market access. In addition, while the texts on both domestic support and export competition contain at least some quantitative parameters, the section on market access does not. Agreement was reached to make deeper cuts in higher tariffs, through a tiered approach. However, what that will mean remains unclear as the number and definition of bands remained open, as did the nature of the reduction formulae to be applied in each band. This may uphold the option of not only making deeper cuts in the bands with higher tariffs, but also to apply a progressive reduction formula within each band. However, whether any of these options will become embodied in the final agreement remains to be seen. The biggest open question is what precisely the scope will be for countries to treat 'sensitive products' more leniently. The Framework does not provide guidance regarding the number of products that can be assigned to that category, nor does it indicate the degree to which markets for these products will be opened up. There is the expectation that 'substantial improvement' of market access for such products will be achieved as well, essentially through expansion of tariff rate quotas. However, in the absence of more concrete parameters in the Framework, much remains to be negotiated in this most important area. It remains to be seen whether these still open-ended Framework provisions for market access will be followed by negotiations and final results that reflect a priority for the reduction of border measures as advocated above.

The Framework aims at responding to the concerns of developing countries by providing for several elements of special and differential treatment. These provisions will not be discussed here as the focus of this chapter is on OECD country policies.

VII. CONCLUSIONS

The AoA concluded in the Uruguay Round was a big step forward. Almost half a century after the formation of the GATT, it brought to an end the era in which agriculture had escaped most international disciplines. The price paid for this leap forward was a relatively generous set of quantitative reduction commitments that have often not yet constrained actual policies. In spite of this generosity, the existence of the new rules and commitments has already triggered some important policy reforms. And more reforms will follow if further reductions are agreed in the current round of negotiations. In this round, agriculture is again one of the most difficult items on the negotiating agenda. Does that say the Uruguay Round has failed on agriculture? Quite the contrary. The AoA has laid the foundations that allow negotiators in this round to focus on the rates of reduction to be agreed. In the Uruguay Round, agriculture was difficult because it was not clear how the rules should be formulated. In the DDA round, agriculture is difficult because the serious reduction business is about to begin. In that sense it can also be read as a reassuring sign that agriculture is generally considered to be one of the most challenging elements of the DDA negotiations: governments are aware of the fact that only a big step forward towards reducing protection and trade-distorting support will be considered sufficient progress, and they are concerned about the political implications. This may help to understand why it was so difficult to find agreement on the way forward for the agriculture negotiations in the

DDA round, and why negotiators had a hard time to reach consensus, at the last minute, on the Framework for further agricultural talks that was eventually agreed on 1 August 2004 in Geneva. This Framework features a number of promising elements, in particular the envisaged elimination of export subsidies and equivalent disciplines on other forms of export competition. However, it still leaves much to be achieved in the coming negotiations. In particular, most of the approach to be adopted to improve market access—a priority for this round of negotiations—needs still to be agreed.

At the same time, the current difficulties should not cloud the historical perspective: the process of reform has much advanced. Anyone who in the mid-1980s, in the run-up to the Uruguay Round, would have predicted that 20 years into the future the issue would not be whether there should be any effective disciplines on agriculture, but whether tariffs on farm products, all meanwhile bound, should be reduced according to the Swiss formula or by a flat rate of possibly 36 per cent, or by some combination of these and other elements, would most certainly have been considered a naive optimist.

It is appropriate that focus in the negotiations should turn to market access. Price support behind border protection and export subsidies, as well as other forms of directly output-related support, are neither effective nor efficient in reaching the objectives of agricultural policies. It is in the domestic interest of countries in the OECD area to reform these policies, and to move in the direction of decoupled and targeted payments, while at the same time achieving their policy objectives in agriculture with lower levels of support. It is good to know that such policy reforms, in the best domestic interest, also have the extra benefit of greatly reducing distortions of production, markets, and trade. Agricultural policy reform, therefore, has the potential of generating a win–win situation in the DDA negotiations: national policies become more effective, and in the WTO they allow progress to be made, both in agriculture and in other sectors.

As far as WTO rules on agriculture are concerned, the situation is not static, either. An extension of rules on export competition is envisaged, to create equivalence between disciplines for export subsidies and those for export credits, food aid, and exporting state trading enterprises, including the pledge to finally eliminate all such forms of government influence on export competition. At the same time, some findings in recent dispute cases have thrown new light on the relationships between domestic support and export competition. Conceptual thinking may be required on how the various support policies affect markets, and how these market effects can be disciplined in an equivalent way.

5

The Agriculture Negotiations: The Road from Doha and How to Keep the Negotiations on a Positive Track

STUART HARBINSON

The World Trade Organization (WTO) negotiations on agriculture are at the core of the Doha Round of multilateral trade negotiations. Their economic and political significance is such that the pace of the agriculture negotiations determines the pace of the negotiations overall. The Round as a whole will not be concluded unless and until the agriculture negotiations are ready for conclusion. Where do we stand in these pivotal negotiations and what are the prospects for successful completion?

The November 2001 Doha Declaration envisaged conclusion of the Round in little over three years, by 1 January 2005. Detailed 'modalities' for further commitments—effectively the template for scheduling reduction commitments in border protection, internal support, and export subsidies and for drawing up the associated new multilateral rules—were to be established in little over a year, by March 2003. The objectives of the negotiations were set out in paragraph 13 of the Doha Declaration. This paragraph needs to be read in its entirety as every phrase has coded significance and there is a delicate overall balance. The main elements of the outcome envisaged were: substantial improvements in market access; reduction of, with a view to phasing out, all forms of export subsidies; and substantial reductions in trade-distorting domestic support. Special and Differential Treatment for developing countries was to be an integral part of all elements of the negotiations and so-called 'non-trade concerns' were to be taken into account.

Many observers have come to regard the Doha timetable as unrealistically brief given the recent history of multilateral trade negotiations (for example the seven to eight years taken by the Uruguay Round), the complexity of the agenda, the greater complexity and diversity of the WTO as an institution compared with the General Agreement on Tariffs and Trade, the fact that the boundaries of the 'single undertaking' were not well defined and the political sensitivity of much of the subject matter. However, many of those Members in favour of launching a Round at Doha preferred a short duration with clear benchmarks, in order to keep the pressure on negotiators and to prevent the negotiations from drifting. 'No repeat of the Uruguay Round' was a phrase often heard. It is true that the intermediate benchmarks contained in the Declaration, including that for the agriculture negotiations, were not well debated or thoroughly considered by participants for the simple reason that the all-consuming focus to the very end of the Doha Ministerial Conference was on whether or not there was going to be a Round at all. But the thinking in some quarters was that the date of March 2003 for the establishment of modalities in agriculture was feasible given that negotiations had already been under way for two years under the built-in agenda of the Uruguay Round. The timing would also tie in with the European Union (EU) timetable for reform of the Common Agricultural Policy (an estimate which in the event proved to be over-optimistic).

Against this background, serious negotiations got under way with considerable enthusiasm on all sides once the Trade Negotiations Committee, on 1 February 2002, decided on various organizational formalities. The agricultural negotiations were making a fresh start, but not a standing start.

The Special Session of the Committee on Agriculture, as the negotiating group was known, had by March 2002 drawn up and agreed an ambitious work programme providing for the technical elaboration of detailed possible modalities in the three pillars of market access, domestic support and export competition during the course of the year. The Chairperson was to prepare an overview paper by the end of the year and provide a first draft of modalities for further commitments in February 2003, to be finalized and established by the end of March 2003.

While no one could fault the enthusiasm and diligence of the negotiators, the 2002–03 work programme transferred the burden of drafting the modalities to the Chairperson rather than having them emerge as the product of a direct negotiation between the participants. Despite constant appeals from the WTO's Director-General (and from the Chairperson himself), negotiators largely confined themselves to restatement of starting positions from then on. The Chairperson had a range of options in the circumstances pertaining in early 2003. He decided, rightly or wrongly but at any rate in line with the agreed work programme, to try to kick-start the negotiations with a detailed draft of modalities for further commitments. Described somewhat kindly at a mini-ministerial meeting in Tokyo in February 2003 as a 'catalyst', the detailed draft was roundly criticized from all sides.

The EU and the United States (US) in particular began to feel at this stage that the achievement of detailed modalities was too ambitious a target for 2003. They advocated an intermediate 'framework', to be agreed at the Fifth Ministerial Conference in Cancún later that year, as a stepping-stone to the full modalities. In July 2003, at a mini-ministerial meeting in Montreal, they were asked by a number of other major participants to provide leadership to the negotiations by agreeing between themselves such a framework. After intensive bilateral exchanges, and with not inconsiderable difficulty, a paper was produced and circulated the following month.

This further catalysed the negotiations. Scenting the danger of being presented with a *fait accompli*, other Members, including a large number of developing countries, were galvanized into forming new groupings in order to counter the EU–US alliance which was seen as focused mainly on reconciling the views of the two parties concerned. The most prominent of these new groupings was the so-called G20, which submitted its own version of a possible framework in advance of the September 2003 Cancún meeting. As compared with the EU–US paper, the G20 raised the level of ambition with respect to reductions in domestic support and the elimination of all forms of export subsidies, and lowered the level of ambition with respect to improvements in access to the markets of developing countries.

Strenuous, if not heroic, efforts were made at the Cancún Ministerial Conference to reach agreement on a framework for modalities in agriculture, not least by the ministerial 'facilitator', George Yeo of Singapore. A commonly heard view shortly after the Conference was that a deal could have been reached had not the negotiations at Cancún broken down in other areas. We shall never know. Undeniably consensus was still not within immediate reach in many areas, including agriculture, when the Conference was brought to an end. In retrospect it seems clear that Cancún came at a time when the negotiations were undergoing a period of dynamic change, principally through the emergence of the G20, and that finding a static point of equilibrium across a range of complex subjects during the Conference itself was a virtually impossible task. Even so, the prevailing feeling among the negotiators in agriculture was that progress had been made. In agriculture at least, Cancún was not a 'breakdown' as portrayed in the media but another significant step in the search for consensus.

As the weeks and months ticked by after Cancún it became clear that the status quo in agriculture was not an option favoured by many Members. Letters circulated to Ministers by Ambassador Zoellick of the US and Commissioners Lamy and Fischler of the EU in January and May 2004 respectively re-energized the negotiations. For the first time, a viable cross-cutting forum for direct negotiations between major groups (though not all groups) of participants was formed in the so-called 'Five Interested Parties' (FIPs)—the US, the EU, Brazil and India representing the G20, and Australia representing the Cairns Group. Through intensive meetings and a process of reaching out to others, and with the expert management of a seasoned negotiator with a cool head as Chairperson, a Framework for Establishing Modalities in Agriculture was forged and agreed by consensus in the very early hours of 1 August 2004, part of what became known as the 'July package'.

A striking feature of the recent history of this negotiation has been the highly dynamic interaction between participants. In the 18 months from February 2003 to July 2004 we have seen the main driving force move from the multilateral level to the Chairperson, to the EU/US, to the G20, to the Five Interested Parties, and finally back to the multilateral level in, by WTO standards, rapid succession and in what might almost be characterized as a series of chemical reactions.

What did the Framework agreement accomplish? Some saw it as an exercise to paper over the cracks and present a rosy picture to the outside world. Others saw it as a major achievement pointing the way to complete consensus on the detailed modalities. This is not the time and place for a full analysis and it is in any case for the participants themselves to judge. Taking a broad view, there seem to be elements of both tendencies.

A framework agreement by definition should leave many issues open and numerical targets undefined. However, underlying tensions, even inconsistencies, are perhaps most evident in the area of market access where the goal of substantial improvement is hedged around with concepts which have the potential to undermine it. The possible expansion of the blue box has been seen by some critics as inconsistent with the objective of substantial reductions in trade-distorting domestic support. On the other hand, the Director-General of the WTO has rightly described the agreement to negotiate a credible end date for the parallel elimination of all forms of export subsidies as historic. The general direction is also clear in domestic support where the concepts of harmonization, an overall cut and a down-payment are accepted. Substantial improvements in market access are now to be achieved for all agricultural products.

Overall, the Framework appears to build on the Doha mandate in many key areas and sets a course for the remainder of the negotiations. The achievement of a consensus at the midpoint of the negotiations was in itself remarkable. It was essential for the future health of the Round that WTO Members should reach an agreement in July 2004 which captured the progress made to date and which set the scene for the continuation and eventual conclusion of the negotiations. To have failed to achieve this would have sent a message of uncertainty and deep malaise.

Where do we go from here and how can we reach that elusive consensus on detailed modalities for further commitments which will bring the end of the Round within sight? There are reasons for overall optimism. The Doha Mandate itself was based on an increasingly common appreciation that price support behind high border protection, export subsidies, and other forms of output-related support, are an inefficient means of achieving domestic policy objectives as well as being harmful internationally. While there are still some voices in favour of the status quo, the weight of opinion is for change. The argument essentially is about the pace of change.

It is not possible, certainly at this stage, to identify any precise formula which will provide a magic solution. No such solution presently exists—it can only be worked out painstakingly by the participants. Market access may be the key element. It is a sensitive area for almost all participants whether they are on the 'offensive' or 'defensive' side; it is the area in the Framework which contains the most innate tension; and border protection has knock-on effects for the other pillars. Yet politically there has to be some equivalence of treatment of all three pillars. The interlinkages have been continually stressed by many participants.

Four elements are suggested here as a means of keeping the negotiations on the present positive track.

First, there is a requirement for detailed technical analysis of options in the short-term. The July Framework agreement sets out the general directions to be pursued but there is a need under all three pillars, and perhaps especially under market access, to explore the various detailed avenues for achieving the objectives of the negotiations. Only when the participants have an adequate grasp in this area will they be equipped to start the end game.

Second, it will be important at some stage to set out time-frames. Targets and benchmarks are often a rod for the WTO's back, given the complexity of the processes and the diversity of the Membership. On the other hand, for the same reasons of complexity and diversity, targets and benchmarks appear to be necessary to create pressures to move forward at all. An obvious milestone is the 6th Ministerial Conference which will take place in Hong Kong in December 2005. Experience tends to show that it is a recipe for failure to go into a high profile and politically complex event such as a Ministerial Conference with too many issues open. For the Doha Round to maintain credibility, a relatively high level of ambition to be achieved at, or preferably by, Hong Kong would seem to be key.

Third, from now on it will be more important politically to ensure that progress is made across the board in the Doha negotiations. While it is true that the Round will not be completed until the agriculture negotiations are ripe for conclusion, it is also true that some important participants will be unable for political reasons to foresee the conclusion of the agriculture negotiations, in which they are on the defensive, until they can see the real prospect of compensatory gains in areas such as non-agricultural market access, trade in services, or the WTO rules relating to trade remedies. The Sixth Ministerial Conference will need to be able to note roughly equivalent progress across the board. In this sense the future of the agriculture negotiations is now also in the hands of the negotiators in other areas.

Fourth, it would be beneficial if the procedural dynamism exhibited in the agriculture negotiations from March 2003 onwards can be maintained. The Five Interested Parties configuration was vital for success at the Framework stage. However, it may be less appropriate for the current stage, at least in the short-term when technical options are being analysed. This is not to say that current groupings have outlived their usefulness—far from it. No particular alternatives are proposed. The essential point is that the negotiations should not get bogged down in sterile repetition. Participants must constantly search for creative ways to engage each other in a variety of productive formats.

In conclusion, the status quo in agricultural trade policy is increasingly unsustainable for a variety of reasons. There is therefore every reason to be confident that the current WTO agriculture negotiations will succeed. No magic formula exists that will provide the key to success. The Framework agreement achieved in July 2004 is an important milestone which provides impetus and a sense of direction. The elements of the final, detailed modalities for further reform of agricultural trade policy must be painstakingly negotiated by the participants. Participants are approaching this task realistically but positively. After a period of detailed technical analysis, they should use the coming months to reach as high a level of progress and ambition as they can by the next Ministerial Conference in Hong Kong in December 2005.

6

Strategic Use of WTO Dispute Settlement Proceedings for Advancing WTO Negotiations on Agriculture

ERNST-ULRICH PETERSMANN[1]

1. INTRODUCTION: THE GATT 1947 BICYCLE, THE WTO TRICYCLE, AND THE NEED FOR A FOUR-WHEEL VEHICLE FOR THE WTO

According to the 'bicycle theory', the multilateral trading system risks toppling down unless periodic 'rounds' of intergovernmental negotiations lead to progressive, *reciprocal* liberalization of national and foreign trade barriers. Trade negotiators often warn that such 'bi-level negotiations' at home (over national trade barriers) and abroad (over foreign trade barriers) risk being damaged by World Trade Organization (WTO) dispute settlement proceedings aimed at *unilateral* liberalization of trade barriers or trade-distorting subsidies. This chapter shows how much General Agreement on Tariffs and Trade (GATT) and WTO dispute settlement proceedings have already become part of GATT and WTO negotiation strategies and have transformed the 'GATT bicycle' into a 'WTO tricycle'. Several recent WTO disputes (e.g. on United States (US) cotton and European Community (EC) sugar subsidies, EC approval procedures for genetically modified organisms, EC application of geographical indications) pursue not only the settlement of bilateral disputes, but also the clarification of existing WTO obligations in order to improve bargaining positions (e.g. of Brazil, the US) in the Doha Round of multilateral trade negotiations. Well-designed litigation strategies and judicial clarification of the often-contested meaning of WTO

[1] The author wishes to thank Thomas Friedheim and Paul Shanahan from the WTO Secretariat for helpful criticism.

rules can enhance the bargaining power of WTO Members and facilitate welfare-increasing trade liberalization, especially at times and in areas where WTO Members are not (yet) ready for consensus-based rule-making. In view of the slow and imbalanced momentum of the member-driven 'WTO tricycle', the WTO needs a more powerful four-wheel vehicle based on empowering the WTO Director-General to defend the collective WTO interests more strongly vis-à-vis bi-level bargaining, quasi-judicial dispute settlement proceedings, and one-sided interest group pressures. Modern negotiation theories confirm that granting the WTO Director-General the right to act as 'guardian of the collective interest', by initiating independent reform proposals, could improve the quality and 'deliberative culture' of 'principled bargaining' in the WTO.

II. ALL INTERNATIONAL AGREEMENTS ARE INCOMPLETE: THE JUDICIAL FUNCTION TO CLARIFY THE MEANING OF WTO RULES

The 1994 Agreement establishing the WTO serves 'constitutional functions' in the sense of constituting worldwide rules and institutions that legally limit national and intergovernmental trade policy discretion and lay down procedures for international rule-making, decision-making, and peaceful settlement of disputes. The WTO Agreement explicitly recognizes that, in many regards, WTO rules remain incomplete for achieving the agreed objectives of e.g. 'substantial reduction of tariffs and other barriers to trade and elimination of discriminatory treatment in international trade relations' (WTO Preamble). Hence, the 'WTO shall provide the forum for negotiations among its Members concerning their multilateral trade relations' and a 'framework for the implementation of the results of such negotiations' as well as for the peaceful settlement of disputes (Article III:2,3). The WTO Dispute Settlement Understanding (DSU) explicitly 'serves to preserve the rights and obligations of Members under the covered agreements, and to clarify the existing provisions of those agreements in accordance with customary rules of interpretation of international law' (Article 3:2 DSU).

Modern negotiation theories demonstrate that multilateral trade negotiations in the WTO are shaped mainly by national and international legal, political, and economic constraints, intergovernmental bargaining, and by the beliefs and skills of negotiators in 'two-level bargaining' at home and abroad.[2] GATT and WTO negotiators often resorted, and still resort, to 'constructive ambiguity' as a consensus-building technique

---

[2] Cf. J. S. Odell, *Negotiating the World Economy* (2000).

so as to enable agreement on international trade rules even if there is no agreement on the precise meaning of the agreed rules.[3] As the 'WTO shall continue the practice of decision-making by consensus followed under GATT 1947',[4] the consensus practice prevailing in WTO decision-making has so far prevented the adoption of authoritative interpretations by a three-quarters majority of WTO Members pursuant to Article IX:2 of the WTO Agreement. The main thesis of this paper is that many of the more than 45 WTO dispute settlement panels involving agricultural, fishery, or forestry products have been established over the preceding years not only in order to settle bilateral trade disputes, but also for clarifying the contested meaning of WTO obligations with the view to improving one's bargaining power in WTO negotiations and progressively developing WTO rules through agreed WTO dispute settlement rulings (e.g. regarding the legal relevance of the use of domestic subsidies for cross-subsidizing exports for the interpretation of the subsidy disciplines in Articles 9 and 10 of the WTO Agreement on Agriculture).

The same political reasons—such as the prisoner dilemma in the collective supply of international public goods (including liberal trade and rule of law)—which induce rational governments to limit their policy discretion by reciprocal international legal obligations, also justify international rules on the peaceful settlement of disputes and on the delegation of the 'clarification' of international rules to independent judges as a means of protecting, and progressively developing, the rule of law. The DSU emphasizes the legal limits of legitimate adjudication. For instance, the mandate of WTO dispute settlement bodies is limited (e.g. by Articles 2, 3, 7, 11, 17, 19), and '(r)ecommendations and rulings of the DSB cannot add to or diminish the rights and obligations provided in the covered agreements' (Articles 3:2, 19:2). The 1994 Ministerial Decision inviting the WTO 'to complete a full review of dispute settlement rules and procedures under the WTO within four years after the entry into force' of the WTO Agreement[5] illustrates another problem of international rule-making: governments learn from experience and recognize the need for periodic review and improvements of newly agreed rules that, in practice, may turn out to be suboptimal, incomplete, and needing adjustments to additional exigencies.

The increasing imbalance between, on the one side, the large number of so far (October 2004) 317 formal consultations under the DSU since

---

[3] Cf. M. Moore, *A World Without Walls: Freedom, Development, Free Trade and Global Governance* (2003) at 111.   [4] Art. IX:1 of the WTO Agreement.
[5] WTO, *WTO Dispute Settlement Procedures*, (1995) at 42.

1995 (leading to more than 90 panel reports, 26 compliance panel reports, almost 60 appellate reports, and more than 30 arbitration awards) and, on the other side, the continuing inability of WTO Members to meet their self-imposed deadlines for new rule-making (e.g. on DSU reforms) is widely criticized.[6] The obvious lack of adequate political rule-making mechanisms for clarifying and complementing WTO rules has also contributed to the large number of more than 105 pending consultations under the DSU, as well as to the frequent resolution of WTO disputes outside the quasi-judicial panel and appellate procedures, i.e. by means of mutually agreed solutions (in 45 cases by October 2004) and other dispute settlements (in 26 cases up to October 2004).[7] These statistics confirm the insight, increasingly emphasized also by WTO negotiators, that 'dispute resolution, the management of trade relations, and trade negotiations need to be clearly seen as part of a coherent integrated process'.[8] As can be seen from the evidence described below, governments have often resorted to GATT and WTO dispute settlement proceedings as a means of improving their negotiating position 'in the shadow of the law'[9] even if, for political reasons, the government may prefer, in the end, to negotiate a bilaterally agreed settlement of a dispute rather than to litigate its contested legal claims through (quasi-)judicial panel and appellate proceedings. Modern dispute settlement theories explain why, and on the basis of which criteria, international trade disputes can be subdivided, according to their underlying intergovernmental or domestic conflicts of interests, into various categories that lend themselves to different kinds of optimal dispute prevention and dispute settlement methods at national and international levels.[10]

---

[6] See e.g. C. D. Ehlermann and L. Ehring, 'Are WTO Decision-Making Procedures Adequate for Making, Revising, and Implementing Worldwide and "Plurilateral" Rules?' in this volume; C. Trojan, 'Foreword' in E. U. Petersmann (ed.), *Preparing the Doha Development Round: Challenges to the Legitimacy and Efficiency of the World Trading System* (2004) at x–xi. On the WTO jurisprudence and the WTO negotiations on reforms of the DSU, see F. Ortino and E. U. Petersmann (eds), *The WTO Dispute Settlement System 1995–2003* (2004).

[7] These figures are taken from *Update of WTO Dispute Settlement Cases*, WT/DS/OV/22 (14 October 2004) at ii.

[8] J. M. Weekes, former WTO Ambassador of Canada, 'The external dynamics of the Dispute Settlement Understanding: an initial analysis of its impact on trade relations and trade negotiations' in J. Lacarte and J. Granados (eds), *Intergovernmental Trade Dispute Settlement: Multilateral and Regional Approaches* (2004) at 75.

[9] On the influence of legal rules on political negotiations, mediation and conciliation, see e.g. Y. Dezalay and B. G. Garth, *Dealing in Virtue: International Commercial Arbitration and the Construction of a Transnational Legal Order* (1996).

[10] Cf. E. U. Petersmann, 'Prevention and Settlement of Transatlantic Economic Disputes' in E. U. Petersmann and M. Pollack (eds), *Transatlantic Economic Disputes: The EU, the US and the WTO* (2003) ch. 1.

III. AGRICULTURAL DISPUTES DURING THE TOKYO ROUND AND THE URUGUAY ROUND: LESSONS FROM GATT DISPUTES INVOLVING THE EC AND THE US

Since the entry into force of the GATT in 1948, the GATT provisions on market access and subsidies for agricultural goods have been progressively clarified and strengthened by treaty amendments (e.g. of GATT Article XVI), supplementary agreements (e.g. the 1979 and 1994 Agreements on Subsidies and Countervailing Measures), additional market access commitments, domestic support commitments as well as export subsidy commitments (e.g. pursuant to the 1994 Agreement on Agriculture).[11] Even though trade in agriculture accounts today for less than 10 per cent of world merchandise trade, almost half of the 115 dispute settlement reports issued up to 1995 under Article XXIII of GATT 1947 and under the 1979 Tokyo Round Agreements related to agricultural goods.[12] This dispute settlement practice contributed to the progressive clarification of GATT rules (e.g. as regards minimum import prices, variable import levies, domestic support prices, export subsidies) and to the negotiation of ever more specific, additional legal disciplines (e.g. in the context of the 1994 Uruguay Round Agreements on Agriculture and Subsidies). The current section illustrates how some of the GATT disputes relating to production and export subsidies for agricultural products in the EC and the US—i.e. the two most important producers, traders, and 'subsidizers' of agricultural goods—have influenced the Tokyo Round and Uruguay Round negotiations in the GATT. The following section discusses some of the recent WTO disputes whose legal findings are likely to influence the ongoing WTO negotiations on trade in agriculture.

Up to the end of GATT's Kennedy Round (1964–67), the large number of GATT disputes over agricultural restrictions and subsidies seemed to have influenced GATT negotiations on agriculture only marginally. The 'GATT 1947 bicycle' rolled and, through six major GATT Rounds of reciprocal trade liberalization commitments, created the necessary political momentum for liberalizing domestic market access barriers. During the Tokyo Round (1973–79), the US successfully challenged various EC import restrictions for agricultural products through GATT

---

[11] Cf. M. D. Ingco and J. D. Nash (eds), *Agriculture and the WTO* (2004) e.g. chs. 2 and 11.

[12] See the lists of dispute settlement reports in Annexes A and B to E. U. Petersmann, *The GATT/WTO Dispute Settlement System* (1997). For a list of 196 disputes under GATT Art. XXIII up to 1995 (including disputes that did not lead to a dispute settlement report) see WTO, *Guide to GATT Law and Practice, Vol. II* (1995) at 771–787.

dispute settlement proceedings.[13] The GATT panel reports on the 1978 complaints by Australia and Brazil against EC refunds on exports of sugar led to findings that the EC system of export refunds for sugar constituted a threat of prejudice in terms of GATT Article XVI:1.[14] Yet no violation of the vaguely drafted GATT prohibitions of export subsidies (Article XVI:3) was established. The discussions—in two subsequently established GATT Working Parties—of the possibility of limiting EC subsidies of sugar exports ended without formal agreement on the settlement of the dispute.[15] The large number of agricultural disputes influenced the final Tokyo Round Agreements in several ways:

- the evidence that import restrictions could be successfully challenged through GATT dispute settlement proceedings offered support for additional market access commitments;
- the threat of GATT disputes (e.g. against EC import restrictions and export support for beef) facilitated political dispute settlement arrangements (e.g. the setting-up of the International Meat Consultative Group, the conclusion of the 'International Bovine Meat Arrangement' as part of the Tokyo Round Agreements);
- the ineffective GATT disciplines on agricultural export subsidies, and the disappointing outcomes of GATT dispute settlement challenges of the GATT consistency of such export subsidies (e.g. US tax refunds on the exportation of agricultural products, EC refunds on exports of sugar), contributed to the conclusion of the 1979 Tokyo Round Agreement on Subsidies;
- the threat of 'too much GATT litigation' prompted the EC to oppose the establishment of a GATT Legal Office until 1983, notwithstanding the previous codification of GATT dispute settlement practices in the Tokyo Round 'Understanding Regarding Notification, Consultation, Dispute Settlement and Surveillance'.

Following the Tokyo Round up to the beginning of the Uruguay Round (1986–94), a similar pattern of clear GATT dispute settlement findings on import restrictions—yet only vague dispute settlement findings regarding subsidies for agricultural goods—prevailed: GATT dispute settlement proceedings challenging EC market access restrictions led to Panel findings that, for instance, EC restrictions on imports of apples from Chile were inconsistent with GATT Article XIII,[16] and EC

---

[13] The 1978 Panel Report on *EEC—Measures on Animal Feed Proteins* found various measures in violation of GATT Art. III, cf. GATT *Basic Instruments and Selected Documents (BISD)* 25S/49. Another 1978 Panel Report on *EEC—Programme of Minimum Import Prices, Licenses and Surety Deposits for Processed Fruits and Vegetables* established various violations of GATT Art. XI (*BISD* 25S/68).
[14] *BISD* 26S/290 (1979); 27S/69 (1980).   [15] *BISD* 28S/80; 29S/82.
[16] *BISD* 27S/98.

restrictions on imports of beef from Canada violated Articles I and II of GATT.[17] Yet the 1981 US complaint—under the 1979 Tokyo Round Agreement on Subsidies—against EC subsidies on exports of wheat flour led only to a vague Panel finding that the export refunds had caused undue disturbance of the normal commercial interests of the US in the sense of GATT Article XVI:2; the Panel was unable to find that the EC export refunds on wheat flour had resulted in the EC having more than an 'equitable share of world export trade', or had caused 'market displacement', in the sense of Article 10 of the Subsidies Agreement.[18] The 1982 US complaint against EC subsidies on exports of pasta products led to a legal finding by the majority of the Panel that the EC subsidies violated Article 9 of the Subsidies Agreement. Yet this Panel report also was not adopted due to opposition by the US.[19] There were, however, two new developments in agricultural disputes during this period. First, the 1982 US complaint against EC production aids granted on canned fruit led to a GATT Panel finding that the EC production aids had nullified US benefits under EC tariff concessions legally bound under GATT Article II.[20] Second, a number of complaints (e.g. by the EC, US, Canada, Brazil) challenging the legal consistency of countervailing duties led to various Panel findings clarifying and enforcing the legal disciplines of the Subsidies Agreement for the application of countervailing duties on subsidized imports.[21]

During the Uruguay Round, GATT dispute settlement challenges of import protection and subsidies for agricultural goods remained frequent. GATT dispute settlement practice confirmed that import restrictions, domestic subsidies, and countervailing duties could be challenged more effectively through GATT dispute settlement proceedings than export subsidies for agricultural goods. Several GATT Panels found, for example, that:

- EC import restrictions for apples and bananas were inconsistent with GATT Articles XI and XIII;[22]
- US import restrictions on sugar violated Articles II and XI of GATT;[23]
- US import restrictions on tobacco were inconsistent with GATT Article III.[24]

The 1990 Panel report on the US complaint against EC subsidies for producers and processors of oilseeds established a violation of GATT

[17] *BISD* 28S/92.   [18] SCM/42 (not adopted).   [19] SCM/43.

[20] The Panel report (L/5778) was not adopted after the parties agreed on a settlement of their dispute.

[21] See e.g. the 1986 Panel report on the EC complaint against the US definition of industry concerning wine and grape products (*BISD* 39S/436).

[22] *BISD* 36S/93; 135; DS32/R (1993—not adopted); DS38/R (1994—not adopted).

[23] *BISD* 36S/331.   [24] DS44/R.

Article III:4 as well as the impairment of tariff bindings under GATT Article II.[25] Some of these disputes illustrated the various shortcomings of GATT dispute settlement procedures and legal remedies, for instance if adoption of panel reports was blocked for political reasons (e.g. in the banana disputes), or when illegal safeguard measures were reintroduced on an annual basis necessitating repeated complaints (e.g. against seasonal EC restrictions on imports of apples). Interrelationships between GATT negotiations and dispute settlement practice were obvious in various ways:

- The successful dispute settlement challenges of import restrictions, domestic subsidies and countervailing duties demonstrated that many agricultural non-tariff trade barriers appeared to be inconsistent with GATT (e.g. Article XI:2,c). One major objective of the Uruguay Round Agreements was to avoid such disputes by means of reciprocal market access commitments, 'tariffication' of non-tariff trade barriers, 'minimum access' for agricultural imports, and a 'peace clause' (Article 13 of the Agreement on Agriculture) limiting access to WTO dispute settlement proceedings.
- As export subsidies for agricultural goods had eluded effective GATT disciplines, the Uruguay Round negotiations led to additional export subsidy reduction commitments and stricter disciplines on subsidies (e.g. in the Agreements on Agriculture and on Subsidies).
- The frequent 'blocking' of consensus on the adoption of panel reports for political reasons (e.g. in the case of the dispute settlement findings on the EC's import restrictions on bananas), and the annual reintroduction of safeguard measures that had been previously found to be in violation of GATT (e.g. in the case of the EC's import restrictions on apples), demonstrated that GATT dispute settlement procedures needed further reforms (as finally agreed in the DSU).
- Mutual agreements on the settlement of agricultural disputes (e.g. the EC–US oilseed dispute from 1988 to 1992) were of crucial importance for reaching political agreement on stricter rules for trade in agricultural goods (e.g. the 1992 Blair House Agreement clearing the way for the Uruguay Round Agreement on Agriculture).

This admittedly incomplete survey of GATT dispute settlement proceedings over agricultural market access restrictions, domestic subsidies, and export subsidies confirms that political GATT negotiations (e.g. on market access commitments and new rules) and quasi-judicial dispute settlement proceedings have been closely interrelated in GATT practice for a long time. For example, consultations in the EC–US dispute over subsidies for wheat flour began during the Tokyo Round in 1977; formal Panel proceedings challenging the EC's subsidies, as well as the US's

---

[25] *BISD* 37S/86; 39S/91.

countermeasures, started, however, only in the 1980s after the entry into force of the Tokyo Round Agreement on Subsidies. Recourse to GATT dispute settlement proceedings could depoliticize a dispute by transforming it into a technical legal exercise, which could help to fend off domestic political pressures and mitigate international disparities in power (e.g. in the case of the various complaints by Latin American agricultural exporters against EC import restrictions). Many disputes 'were settled bilaterally, some reached the panel report stage but the report was never adopted, and others were subsumed in broader ongoing trade negotiations. In a few cases, a subsidy war replaced diplomacy and resulted in an *ad hoc* accommodation'.[26] The disputes helped all GATT contracting parties to better understand the scope of their GATT obligations. The oilseed dispute settlement proceedings, and the parallel Uruguay Round negotiations on new rules for agriculture, facilitated not only a resolution of the oilseed conflict, but also the 1992 Blair House Agreement clearing the way for the 1994 Uruguay Round Agreement on Agriculture: 'The existence of the talks had facilitated the conclusion of the GATT dispute, but the need to resolve the dispute had provided an opportunity for a 'package deal' that might not have been possible if each element would have been considered in isolation.'[27] GATT disputes over the legal disciplines for *domestic subsidies* and countervailing duties have led to rather precise legal findings. GATT disciplines on agricultural *export subsidies* were no longer effectively enforced through GATT dispute settlement proceedings, notwithstanding the rather strict GATT Panel report back in 1958 which had found French export subsidies for wheat and wheat flour to violate GATT Article XVI.[28] This negative dispute settlement experience reinforced the Uruguay Round negotiations on more precise legal disciplines for export subsidies and more effective legal and judicial remedies, as provided under the Uruguay Round Agreements on Agriculture and on Subsidies.

IV. AGRICULTURAL DISPUTES IN THE WTO: INTERRELATIONSHIPS BETWEEN NEGOTIATIONS, CONSULTATIONS, PREVENTION, AND SETTLEMENT OF DISPUTES IN THE WTO

The 1994 Uruguay Round Agreements on Agriculture (AoA), Subsidies, and Countervailing Measures changed radically the rules for market

---

[26] T. Josling and S. Tangermann, 'Production and Export Subsidies in Agriculture: Lessons from GATT and WTO Disputes Involving the US and EC' in Petersmann and Pollack, *supra* n. 10 at 208.   [27] *Ibid.* at 214.
[28] *BISD* 7S/46, 22.

access commitments and subsidies in agricultural trade. They increase the transparency and legal precision of market access and subsidy commitments; offer additional political procedures for the multilateral surveillance (e.g. by the Committee on Agriculture) of compliance with the agreement; and conditionally shelter certain export subsidies (e.g. by the allowable subsidy limits specified in the schedules of commitments), 'green box' subsidies (for non-trade-distorting payments that are not related to output or prices), and other subsidy practices for a nine-year 'implementation period' (as defined in Article 1,f) from legal challenges (cf. Article 13). The declining use of export subsidies in agriculture is one of the reasons why pressures from competing interest groups— which are the starting-point for many GATT and WTO dispute settlement proceedings—also appear to have declined, at least until the expiry of the peace clause in Article 13 of the Agreement on Agriculture.

Even though the 'peace clause' limited recourse to WTO dispute settlement procedures until its expiry in 2003–04,[29] the improved accessibility, enhanced procedures, and quasi-automatic decision-making in the WTO dispute settlement system contributed to a large number of WTO disputes over the consistency of agricultural market access restrictions and subsidies with WTO legal disciplines. The timing and legal targets of some of the various agricultural disputes suggest that WTO complaints, panel, and appellate proceedings were used not only for the settlement of bilateral disputes, but also for clarifying existing WTO obligations, identifying the need for additional WTO rules, improving the bargaining position of countries in multilateral WTO negotiations, and putting pressure on other WTO Members to engage in WTO negotiations on additional rules and commitments to reduce agricultural support and subsidy levels. WTO negotiators confirmed that 'the impact on negotiations of the dispute settlement system of the WTO and its predecessor the GATT is substantial'.[30]

A large number of requests for DSU consultations in the field of agriculture continue to be pending and focus on market access restrictions (e.g. Korean measures concerning the testing and inspection of agricultural products, Japanese restrictions on imports of pork, US measures affecting imports of poultry products, EC import duties on rice and corn

---

[29] The precise date (end of 2003 or end of the marketing year in 2004) depends on the contested interpretation of Arts. 1,f and 13 AA. The WTO Panel report on *United States—Subsidies on Upland Cotton*, WT/DS267/R (8 September 2004) did not have to clarify this issue because Brazil and the US agreed that Brazil's Panel request was within the nine-year implementation period. The Panel report clarified, however, that Art. 13 is not in the nature of an affirmative defence and does not preclude dispute settlement based on GATT 1994 and the Subsidies Agreement.

[30] Cf. Weekes, *supra* n. 8.

gluten feed) rather than subsidy practices (e.g. alleged EC subsidies on processed cheese).[31] Most of the completed WTO Panel reports relating to agricultural products concern market access restrictions (e.g. for imports of salmon, desiccated coconut, bananas, hormone-fed beef, poultry products, apples, milk and other dairy products, beef, wheat gluten, lamb, vegetable oils, sardines, peaches). The 1999 Panel and Appellate Body reports on *Canada—Measures Affecting the Importation of Milk and the Exportation of Dairy Products* led to the first WTO dispute settlement ruling that export subsidies for certain dairy products exceeded the quantity commitment levels specified in Canada's Schedule in violation of Articles 3.3 and 8 of the Agreement on Agriculture.[32] The 1999 Panel report and 2000 Appellate Body report on *US—Tax Treatment for Foreign Sales Corporations* (FSC) led to a dispute settlement ruling that the US acted inconsistently with its obligations under Articles 10.1 and 8 of the AoA by applying export subsidies, through the FSC measure, in a manner which results in, or threatens to lead to, circumvention of its export subsidy commitments with respect to agricultural products; however, the Appellate Body reversed the Panel's finding that the FSC measure involved 'the provision of subsidies to reduce the costs of marketing exports' of agricultural products in violation of Articles 3.3 and 9.1(d) of the Agriculture Agreement.[33] The findings, in the Panel report on *Measures Affecting Imports of Beef*, that Korea's domestic support for beef exceeded Korea's commitment levels in violation of Articles 3:2 and 7:2(a) of the AoA, were reversed by the Appellate Body.[34]

The 2004 Panel report on *Canada—Measures Relating to Exports of Wheat and Treatment of Imported Grain* found that certain Canadian import restrictions were inconsistent with GATT Article III:4 but that the US had failed to establish its claim that the Canadian Wheat Board export regime was inconsistent with the rules for state-trading in GATT Article XVII:1.[35] In the dispute over *United States—Subsidies on Upland Cotton*, the Panel report of 8 September 2004 found that several US

[31] Cf. *Update of WTO Dispute Settlement Cases, supra* n. 7 at 1–34.

[32] The Panel findings (WT/DS103/R, WT/DS113/R (17 May 1999)) were partly upheld, partly reversed by the Appellate Body and adopted in October 1999; cf. *Update of WTO Dispute Settlement Cases, supra* n. 7.

[33] The Appellate Body report (WT/DS108/AB/R) and the Panel report, as modified by the Appellate Body, were adopted in March 2000, cf. *Update of WTO Dispute Settlement Cases, supra* n. 7.

[34] Cf. WT/DS161/R, WT/DS169/R, and WT/DS161,169/AB/R and *supra* n. 7. The Appellate Body was unable, in view of the insufficient factual findings made by the Panel, to complete the legal analysis of the alleged violations of the Agreement on Agriculture.

[35] WT/DS276/R (6 April 2004). These findings were essentially confirmed by the Appellate Body, see WT/DS276/AB/R (September 2004).

support measures for upland cotton violate the WTO Agreements on Agriculture and Subsidies and do not fall under the peace clause (Article 13 AoA). The Panel found, *inter alia*, that:

- US export credit guarantee programmes offered export subsidies that are inconsistent with Articles 8 and 10.1 AoA and Articles 3, 5 and 6 of the Subsidies Agreement;
- US user marketing payments to domestic users of upland cotton constituted an import substitution subsidy prohibited by Article 3 of the Subsidy Agreement;
- US domestic support measures had caused serious prejudice, within the meaning of Article 5,c of the Subsidy Agreement, to the interests of Brazilian producers by suppressing cotton prices.[36]

The cotton dispute is also the first dispute challenging a WTO Member's classification of domestic subsidies as 'green box subsidies' exempted from WTO subsidy reduction commitments. Press reports quoted Brazil's trade minister as commenting that the ruling would be very important for the future of the Doha Round as Members might find negotiations a better way to achieve their subsidy reduction ambitions than dispute settlement where the implementation of WTO rulings can drag on for several years.[37]

The complaints by Australia, Brazil, and Thailand against *EC—Export Subsidies on Sugar* have given rise to three Panel reports which found, *inter alia*, that the EC sugar regime had provided export subsidies within the meaning of Article 9.1 (a) and (c) AoA in violation of the EC's obligations under Articles 3.3 and 8 of the Agreement on Agriculture.[38] The participation of 25 WTO members as third parties, intervening either for the three complainants or for the defendant, in this sugar dispute—similar to the intervention of 13 WTO Members (counting the EC as one Member) in the cotton dispute—illustrates the systemic importance attached to these disputes by WTO Members. Other currently pending WTO Panel proceedings—e.g. challenging an alleged lack of protection of trademarks and geographical indications for agricultural products in the EC[39]—are likewise linked to contentious issues in the Doha Round negotiations (e.g. on the extension of geographical indications).

---

[36] WT/DS267/R (8 September 2004). The Panel findings were mostly confirmed by the Appellate Body (WT/DS267/AB/R, 3 March 2005).
[37] *Bridges*, ICTSD May 2004, at 7.
[38] WT/DS265/R, 266/R, and 283/R (15 October 2004), currently under appeal before the WTO Appellate Body.
[39] WT/DS174 (complaint by the US), 290 (complaint by Australia).

V. FIRST CONCLUSION: WTO DISPUTE SETTLEMENT PROCEEDINGS CAN HELP TO ADVANCE WTO NEGOTIATIONS ON AGRICULTURE

According to the case-studies by Josling and Tangermann, 'experience in the Kennedy, Tokyo and Uruguay Rounds suggests that subsidy disputes can be used as a lever in GATT/WTO negotiations'.[40] This chapter offers additional evidence that, also in the Doha Development Round, WTO Members resort to WTO dispute settlement proceedings not only as a means for settling bilateral disputes over market access restrictions or trade-distorting agricultural subsidies. The timing and legal targets of WTO dispute settlement proceedings suggest that WTO complaints, panel, and appellate proceedings are also used for clarifying existing WTO obligations, identifying the need for additional WTO rules, improving the bargaining position of countries, or putting pressure on other WTO Members to engage in negotiations on additional rules and commitments. The terms and temporary nature of the 'peace clause' confirm that WTO Members perceived such interrelationships between recourse to dispute settlement proceedings and trade negotiations, after the expiry of the peace clause, as legitimate tools for reaching agreement on new rules and reciprocal liberalization commitments. According to Article 20 of the AoA, the mandated negotiations on agriculture, now folded into the Doha Round, were to begin 'one year before the end of the implementation period', i.e. at the beginning of 2000. The peace clause afforded, at a minimum, an additional four years of conditional protection as from 2000 while the negotiations were under way. One could hypothesize that these time-frames were likewise motivated by the insight that, while a temporary assurance of peace on the dispute settlement front could be conducive to negotiated trade liberalization in agriculture, the potential leverage of dispute settlement findings was perceived to be important for the final conclusion of the negotiations.

Trade negotiators sometimes react to adverse dispute settlement findings by claiming that, e.g. 'developing countries risked damaging the Doha Round world trade negotiations if they were to file new dispute cases aimed at forcing the US to dismantle its farm subsidy programs'.[41] This chapter suggests that WTO dispute settlement proceedings should

---

[40] Josling and Tangermann, *supra* n. 26, at 225.
[41] US Trade Representative R. Zoellick, commenting on the preliminary WTO Panel finding that US subsidies for cotton growers violate WTO rules, quoted in *Financial Times* 29 April 2004 at 3: 'If other countries decide to stand back and litigate their way, as opposed to negotiate, I think it's going to be a very complicated and non-productive result for everybody.'

not be viewed as inconsistent with WTO negotiations: 'litigating (where the facts warrant, of course) and negotiating are *complementary* means of motivating the reduction of particular trade-distorting subsidies, whereas failing to demonstrate a clear willingness to invoke dispute settlement may actually be the best way to keep the negotiations stalled. . . . initiating a case does not necessarily mean pursuing it all the way through to judgment; merely waving around a ready-to-file complaint, or holding consultations under the DSU, may be sufficient to concentrate the minds of potential defenders.'[42] Many trade negotiators commented on the WTO cotton ruling by saying that it 'could have a significant impact on continuing multilateral agriculture negotiations by increasing pressure on the U.S. and other developed countries to ensure that negotiations move forward in order to avoid a host of new legal challenges from developing countries.'[43] The special provisions on liberalization of trade barriers and trade distortions for cotton in the WTO Decision of 1 August 2004 confirm this view. Lack of progress in WTO negotiations could trigger additional WTO dispute settlement proceedings challenging the legality of existing subsidy programmes.

The expiry of the peace clause has rendered EC and US agricultural subsidies more vulnerable to legal challenges (e.g. under Articles 5 and 6 of the Subsidy Agreement).[44] The WTO dispute settlement findings on EC sugar and US cotton subsidies confirm the enhanced 'bargaining power of non-subsidizing countries, which may demand "payment" in the form of further subsidy reduction commitments and a shift toward tariffs-and-decoupled-payments systems in exchange for extending the peace clause. Ultimately, expiry of the peace clause will do what it was intended to do: light a fire under negotiations on trade-distorting agricultural subsidies.'[45] The US Cotton Panel finding that several US support measures for cotton are not covered by the peace clause and violate WTO rules, further suggests that—following the GATT Panel finding in the 1958 French Wheat Flour case that French subsidies on the export of wheat flour had resulted in 'more than an equitable share' of world export trade in violation of GATT Article XVI:3[46]—WTO Panels are

---

[42] J. R. Magnus, 'The Evils of a Long Peace: Legal Consequences of WTO 'Peace Clause' Expiry and Practical Issues for New Litigation over Farm Subsidies', paper presented at Washington, DC, 4 December 2003 at 3.

[43] Cf. 'Cotton Decision Could Increase Pressure to Reach Framework Deal' in *Inside US Trade* 30 April 2004.

[44] Cf. e.g. R. H. Steinberg and T. E. Josling, 'When the Peace Ends: The Vulnerability of EC and US Agricultural Subsidies to WTO Legal Challenge' in *Journal of International Economic Law* (2003) 369–417.   [45] *Ibid.* at 372.

[46] *BISD* 7S/46 at 50–51. In several subsequent GATT dispute settlement proceedings relating to GATT Art. XVI:3, the Panels concluded that the complainant had not been able to prove the causal relationship between agricultural subsidies and displacement of sales of non-subsidized, competing products.

capable of applying the often vaguely drafted WTO subsidy disciplines if the complainants can demonstrate trade-distorting effects.[47]

VI. SECOND CONCLUSION: THE 'WTO TRICYCLE' NEEDS TO BE TRANSFORMED INTO A FOUR-WHEEL VEHICLE SO AS TO IMPROVE THE QUALITY AND CULTURE OF WTO BARGAINING

Conflicts of interests are inevitable facts of life, as much in international trade relations as elsewhere. Just as individual rationality and justice require 'examining', 'reviewing', and impartially 'judging' contested facts, contrary arguments, and self-imposed disciplines in one's own mind, so the normality of trade conflicts justifies the large number of WTO provisions on dispute prevention (e.g. by negotiations, rule-making, and rule-application) and dispute settlement through recourse to domestic courts (cf. Article X:3 GATT) or to the compulsory WTO/DSU jurisdiction for intergovernmental consultations, good offices, mediation, conciliation, panel, appellate or arbitration procedures. Frequent recourse to these WTO dispute settlement proceedings is a sign of well-functioning legal and judicial systems, rather than of socially harmful conflicts. Most WTO disputes can be seen positively as serving legitimate functions for the (quasi-)judicial clarification and protection of agreed rights and obligations, without detriment to the different functions of legislatures (e.g. rule-making by WTO Members) and executives (e.g. rule-application by trade bureaucracies).

Dialectic 'checks and balances' among the legislative, executive and (quasi-)judicial branches of the WTO are likely to improve the quality of arguments, negotiations and agreements among the 148 WTO Members. For example, when in the Canada—Dairy dispute the Appellate Body reversed the finding of an Article 21.5 report relating to the interpretation of the WTO export subsidy disciplines, the extensive discussion in the WTO's Dispute Settlement Body (DSB) on the relative merits of the Appellate Body and Panel interpretations led to severe criticism by WTO Members that the Appellate Body had developed a new definition of 'payment' (based on the cost of production of individual farmers) which:

- had no basis in the treaty texts;
- had never been discussed before;

---

[47] On the interpretative problems of applying cumulatively the subsidy disciplines in the WTO Agreements on Agriculture and on Subsidies, see e.g. D. Chambovey, 'How the Expiry of the Peace Clause (Article 13 of the WTO Agreement on Agriculture) Might Alter Disciplines on Agricultural Subsidies in the WTO Framework' in *Journal of World Trade* (2002) 305–352.

- offered a 'particularly unworkable standard';
- 'should be of concern to other Members from a systemic standpoint'.[48]

As the Appellate Body's Article 21.5 report had not applied the new legal findings to the complex factual situation, the complainants requested a second Article 21.5 Panel report whose findings were again appealed. The second Article 21.5 Appellate Body report was, once more, criticized in the DSB because—in the view of some WTO Members—the new 'cross-subsidization standard' clearly 'went beyond the ordinary meaning of the words in the Agreement on Agriculture' and 'had found its way into another WTO dispute',[49] namely the WTO Panel proceeding over *EC—Export Subsidies on Sugar*.[50] The examples illustrate that WTO dispute settlement proceedings, apart from their judicial function for the settlement of disputes through legally binding rulings, do not curtail the right of WTO Members to criticize judicial interpretations and negotiate agreements on more precise and more coherent rules.

This chapter has shown that bi-level trade negotiations in GATT and the WTO over the reciprocal liberalization of domestic and foreign trade barriers, and also over general rule-making, have become increasingly influenced by (quasi-)judicial GATT and WTO dispute settlement findings. The transformation of the old 'GATT 1947 bicycle' into a 'WTO tricycle'—driven forward by intergovernmental negotiations, ever more comprehensive WTO jurisprudence, and domestic implementing measures—has resulted in imbalances between the protracted slowness of consensus-based rule-making processes, on the one side, and the dynamically progressing (quasi-)judicial clarification of the contested meaning of WTO rules, on the other. WTO Members clearly prefer resorting to WTO dispute settlement proceedings rather than to WTO rule-making by majority decisions: given the lack of democratic governance in many WTO Members, the redistributive effects of many WTO decisions, and the fact that only 30 WTO Members account for about 90 per cent of world trade, WTO majority decisions could lack legitimacy and unduly limit policy autonomy and democratic governance at the national level. The prevailing mantra of a 'member-driven WTO' needs to be replaced by adding a

---

[48] Cf. the discussion in the DSB meeting of 18 December 2001 on the *Canada—Dairy* dispute reported in WT/DSB/M/116 at 7–13.   [49] Cf. WT/DSB/M/141 at 2–6.

[50] The three complainants (Australia, Brazil, and Thailand) claimed, *inter alia*, that the EC is cross-subsidizing sugar exports by the high price guarantees for internally sold sugar. EU trade diplomats were quoted in the press as saying that 'a panel finding in favor of this claim would have huge implications for major subsidizers and exporters such as the EU and the United States . . . since many commodities—such as sugar, cotton, and dairy—are sold on global markets below the cost of production' (*WTO Reporter* 5 April 2004 at 2).

fourth wheel to the WTO tricycle, i.e. empowering the WTO Director-General to defend more effectively the general interests of WTO Members in a consumer-driven, mutually beneficial, and socially just world trading system. Just as European integration processes tend to be driven by independent Commission proposals protecting the 'Community interest' and by more flexible 'enhanced cooperation' among 'coalitions of the willing', so could WTO negotiations and rule-making processes benefit from empowering the WTO Director-General to initiate 'public interest proposals' and from increased recourse to 'plurilateral agreements' among interested WTO Members inside the WTO, rather than to the ever increasing number of free trade agreements outside the WTO.

The numerous producer-biases of GATT and WTO rules (e.g. on anti-dumping measures) confirm that national trade politicians have proven to be highly ineffective guardians of general consumer welfare. The more than US$270 billion of financial support for farmers in rich countries in 2003, amounting to 32 per cent of their gross receipts,[51] could certainly be used in more efficient, less trade-distorting, and more equitable ways. Also national parliaments in European and many other WTO member countries have shown little interest in effectively controlling rule-making in the WTO; the 1994 Uruguay Round Agreements, for instance, were ratified by most national parliaments after only a few hours of parliamentary debates, sometimes even without a complete translation of the more than 500 pages of treaty texts into the official national language (e.g. in the German Parliament).[52] Empowering the WTO Director-General to initiate *collective interest proposals* could promote 'principled bargaining'[53] in the WTO and be crucial for overcoming *collective action problems*. The modern literature on deliberative politics demonstrates that the quality and output of political discourse and of positional bargaining can be improved—especially in 'two-level' negotiations (as in the WTO) where the intergovernmental bargaining requires consensus and its ratification in domestic parliaments requires democratic legitimacy and majority voting—by institutional rules that promote a 'spirit of accommodation' and 'principled negotiations' which attach more importance to better arguments (in terms of the common good) than to bargaining power

---

[51] See the 2004 OECD report on agricultural policies in OECD countries, summarized in *Financial Times* 11 June 2004 at 6.

[52] Cf. the comparative studies in J. Jackson and A. Sykes (eds), *Implementing the Uruguay Round Agreements* (1997).

[53] On the advantages of 'principled' over 'positional bargaining' see R. Fisher and W. Ury, *Getting to Yes: Negotiating Agreement without Giving In* (2nd edn 1991) ch. 1. In the WTO Preamble, WTO Members express their determination 'to preserve the basic principles . . . underlying this multilateral trading system'.

(in terms of threats of punishment and promises of reward).[54] Additional powers of the WTO Director-General to influence WTO bargaining by independent public interest proposals could also help to improve the public image and democratic legitimacy of WTO negotiations by forcing WTO diplomats to pursue not only narrow national self-interests and group interests, but also to justify their national and individual preferences against alternative proposals focusing on *collective interests* and better arguments.

[54] Cf. J. Steiner *et al.* (eds), *Deliberative Politics in Action* (2004).

PART IV

THE DOHA ROUND NEGOTIATIONS ON SERVICES TRADE

7

Developing Country Proposals for the Liberalization of Movements of Natural Service Suppliers

L. ALAN WINTERS[1]

This chapter is about the developing countries' proposals in the General Agreement on Trade in Services (GATS) negotiations on the liberalization of the movement of natural persons to provide services—Mode 4. Trade negotiations in the Doha Round are as mercantilist as ever, and so typically 'proposals for liberalization' are proposals that other countries should liberalize their imports while the proposing country does next to nothing. As well as being bad economics this also makes it difficult to sort out from initial public positions exactly what the parties want, or even expect, to emerge, i.e. what is actually and realistically proposed and what is just rhetoric. At this early stage in the process of the Doha Round (early in terms of substance if not of calendar time), I have not been able to solve this riddle, so I have set myself a slightly more modest objective.

This chapter considers the offers that have been made on Mode 4 by developing countries during the round to date—in part to try to gauge the seriousness of their intent on Mode 4—and also the generalized demands that they have made of developed countries. (I have no access to their specific negotiating requests and therefore cannot comment on these.) I observe, as predicted above, that there is a huge difference in the level of ambition of the two parts of the putative equation. Then, having very briefly noted the extreme caution of developed country offers, and concluded that we are not going to see much progress on Mode 4 during this round, I ask why this is. While the pressures for

[1] I am grateful to, but do not implicate, Sumanta Chaudhuri, Bernard Hoekman, and Aaditya Mattoo for comments and to Audrey Kitson-Walters for logistical help. The findings, interpretations, and conclusions expressed in this chapter are entirely those of the author and do not necessarily reflect the views of the Board of Executive Directors of the World Bank or the governments they represent.

temporary mobility seem likely to grow as developed countries try to balance their ageing populations with their distaste for permanent migration (at least in Europe), neither side of the developed–developing country debate on Mode 4 seems to expect, or perhaps even wish, much from the process this time around.[2] Hence as well as considering the usual frictions to trade liberalization—entrenched interests, etc.—I also ask whether the GATS is delivering what we need.

There is a lot to discuss about the economics of the temporary movement of natural persons, but I have done that elsewhere.[3] Thus, this chapter is more about the negotiations and their architecture than economics *per se*.

I. DEVELOPING COUNTRY OFFERS

Table 7.1 lists the developing countries that have made offers on services by April 2004. These cover all four modes but we consider only their Mode 4 components here. They are also, of course, preliminary in the sense that serious negotiation of their content (as opposed to their form) has yet to start. Of the 28, three of these offers are published on the WTO website and a few others are available via national sites or unofficially. Hence a full and formal analysis of the complete set is not feasible at this stage. On the other hand, private conversations with participants suggest to me a good deal of commonality across offers and that the general tendencies I identify below are not seriously misleading.

Table 7.2 reports the horizontal commitments in the three schedules that are given on the WTO website. They are fairly typical of the others that I have seen although I am told that yet others (e.g. India's) are more ambitious. The text reported is extracted and occasionally paraphrased from the initial offers deposited by these countries in 2003. Hence while the information is authentic, the wording is not always that of the official document.

---

[2] One interesting reflection due to Aaditya Mattoo is that the relative importance of cultural and displacement fears may influence host countries' preferences between temporary and permanent migration. In Europe, intense cultural xenophobia coupled with relatively benign policies for displaced workers favour temporary mobility. In the US, on the other hand, with a historical disposition towards migration and a relatively harsh labour market, politics favour permanent immigrants who can be unionized and incorporated into 'the system' to potential 'hit-and-run' competition from temporary migrants.

[3] E.g. L. A. Winters, 'The Economic Implications of Liberalising Mode 4 Trade' in A. Mattoo and A. Carzaniga (eds) *Moving People to Deliver Services* (2003) 59–92; L. A. Winters, T. L. Walmsley, Z. K. Wang, and R. Grynberg, *Liberalizing Labour Mobility under the GATS*, Economic Paper No. 53, Commonwealth Secretariat (2003); L. A. Winters, T. L. Walmsley, Z. K. Wang, and R. Grynberg, 'Negotiating the Temporary Movement of Natural Persons: An Agenda for the Development Round', 26(8) *World Economy* (2003) 1137–1162.

TABLE 7.1. Developing and transition country services offers up to April 2004

Argentina	Mexico
Bahrain	Panama
Bolivia	Paraguay
Bulgaria	Peru
Chile	Poland
China	St Christopher and Nevis
Colombia	Singapore
Costa Rica	Slovak Republic
Czech Republic	Slovenia
Fiji	Sri Lanka
Guatemala	Suriname
India	Thailand
Macao, China	Turkey
Mauritius	Uruguay

The horizontal schedules are not uniform, but they share a number of themes. All three countries provide market access concessions on senior and skilled intra-corporate transferees and on business sellers (although the terminologies vary). In all cases only 'key' workers are permitted under the intra-corporate rubric and business sellers are precluded from selling directly to the public. Among the differences, the conditions applied to mobile workers differ, with varying periods of stay and of qualification for intra-corporate status. Chile appears to apply a sort of economic needs test to intra-corporate specialists, and she certainly restricts foreign workers to a defined share (15 per cent) of the workforce.

Developing country schedules overall share most of these features. Most of the countries that have made offers are said to be conceding intra-corporate transfers and business sellers and in Latin America maximum shares of the workforce or the wage bill are enforced locally and will be scheduled under the GATS. No developing countries are known to have made horizontal offers on lower-skilled professionals or workers (as they wish industrial countries to do) and very few have done so on independent professionals; several impose specific or vague (implicit) economic needs tests. Overall, so far as I can ascertain, developing countries continue to be actually or potentially quite restrictive on the movement of natural persons in general; they have made concessions in the key areas of interest to developed countries, which are also in their own interests in terms of improving service provision in their own economies.

Table 7.3 summarizes the initial sectoral offers from Turkey and Slovenia: Chile has made none, although she promises to strive to

TABLE 7.2. Horizontal commitments: Turkey, Slovenia, Chile

Turkey[a]

Market access

Unbound except for the entry and temporary stay of natural persons in the following categories:

(A) Administrative and technical personnel of established foreign service providers. Work permits and residence permits are valid up to two years, and subject to renewal. This includes: managers–executives, specialists, and service sellers.

(B) Service sellers. It is not necessary to obtain work permits and residence permits for service sellers who stay in Turkey for not more than 30 days, for the purpose of participating in business meetings, business contracts including negotiations for the sale of services, entry into contract to sell services and visits of business establishments, or other similar activities. Service sellers may not sell services directly to the general public.

National treatment

The professional services which are assigned only to Turkish citizens by the specific laws cannot be rendered by foreigners either as service providers or as the personnel of service providers. On the other hand foreign citizens with Turkish origin may work in professions which are assigned only to Turkish citizens with the permission obtained from the Ministry of Interior. Those professions which are assigned only to Turkish citizens are given below:

(1) Doctors, (2) Pharmacists, (3) Nurses, (4) Veterinarians, (5) Responsible directors of the factories producing medicine, (6) Guides, (7) Responsible directors of private hospitals, (8) Responsible directors of travel agencies, (9) Directors of newspaper, (10) Dentists, (11) Notaries, (12) Those personnel working in Free Trade Zones other than managers and qualified personnel, (13) Those personnel undertaking coastal commerce and related activities, (14) Opticians, (15) Doctors, pharmacists, and veterinarians dealing with laboratory services, (16) Lawyers who practice in Turkish Courts, (17) Accountants and Certified Public Accountants.

Slovenia

Market access

Unbound, except for measures concerning the entry into and temporary stay, without requiring compliance with an economic need test[b], of a natural person which falls in one of the following categories:

Business visitors

A natural person, who stays in the Republic of Slovenia without acquiring remuneration from or within the Republic of Slovenia and without engaging in making direct sales to the general public or supplying services, for the purpose of participating in business meetings, business contacts, including those to prepare the establishment of commercial presence in the Republic of Slovenia. The duration of temporary stay is limited with a 90-day visa.

Intra-Corporate Transferee[c]

Natural persons of another Member who have been employed by juridical persons of another Member for a period of not less than three years immediately preceding the entry or have been partners in it (other than majority shareholders):

(a) Natural persons occupying a senior position.
(b) Natural persons working who possess special knowledge and uncommon qualifications essential to the establishment's service, research equipment, techniques or management.

The duration of temporary stay for 'intra-corporate transferees' is limited with a residence permit, which may be granted for up to one year with extensions.

National treatment

Unbound except for measures concerning the categories of natural persons referred to in the Market Access Column. To the extent that any subsidy is made available to natural persons, their availability may be limited to nationals of the Republic of Slovenia.

Chile

Market access

Unbound, except for transfers of senior and specialized natural persons within a foreign enterprise established in Chile, who have been in the employ of the organization for a period of at least two years immediately preceding the date of their application for admission. Foreign natural persons may not make up more than 15 per cent of the total staff employed in Chile. For all legal purposes, senior and specialized personnel must establish domicile or residence in Chile. Senior personnel are executives and specialists with indispensable skills.

Specialists must have skills not available in Chile.

Service providers are admitted into Chile temporarily for a period of two years which can be extended for a further two years. Personnel admitted under these conditions will be subject to the labour and social security legislation in force.

National treatment

Unbound, except for the categories of natural persons listed under market access.

[a] Turkish legislation related to taxation, prudential and professional competency requirements, immigration policies has not been listed separately in this schedule.
[b] All other requirements of laws and regulations regarding entry, stay, work and social security measures shall continue to apply, including regulations concerning period of stay, minimum wages as well as collective wage agreements.
[c] An 'intra-corporate transferee' is defined as a natural person working within a juridical person, other than a non-profit making organization, established in the territory of a WTO Member, and being temporarily transferred in the context of the provision of a service through commercial presence in the territory of the Republic of Slovenia; the juridical persons concerned must have their principal place of business in the territory of a WTO Member and the transfer must be to an establishment of that juridical person, effectively providing like services in the territory of the Republic of Slovenia.

TABLE 7.3. Sectoral commitments: Turkey, Slovakia

Sector	Market access
Turkey	
Primary, secondary and other educational services	Foreign teachers and experts may work in pre-primary, primary, and secondary educational institutions and in non-formal educational institutions (i.e. in language teaching and vocational training centres) after obtaining permission from the Ministry of Education.
Insurance	Engaging of natural persons in a brokerage business or establishment of an insurance and reinsurance broker company or opening of a branch of a foreign insurance and reinsurance broker company in Turkey is subject to prior permission and obtaining an operation licence from Undersecretariat of Treasury. Such a firm must be founded in the form of a joint-stock or a limited liability company, and must possess the required minimum paid-in capital.
Services auxiliary to insurance	Foreign commercial presence or presence of foreign natural persons regarding services auxiliary to insurance is permitted only for consultancy and risk management. Natural person insurance and reinsurance brokers have to reside in Turkey and they must have at least five years experience as brokers in their countries of origin. Unbound except administrative and technical personnel. Foreign natural person insurance and reinsurance brokers must have at least five years experience as a broker abroad.
Collective investment management	The majority of the members of the board of directors of an investment corporation must have Turkish nationality.
Hotel and restaurants	After receiving the permission of the Ministry of Interior based on the affirmative opinion of the Ministry of Culture and Tourism, hotels and restaurants with the tourism encouragement certificate may employ foreign personnel. But the amount of foreign personnel employed in an enterprise should not exceed 10 per cent of the total personnel. This amount could be increased up to 20 per cent by the decision of the related Ministry.
Passenger and freight transportation	Captain and crew of Turkish flag vessels should be Turkish residents.

Slovenia

Accounting, auditing and Bookkeeping services[a]	Unbound except as indicated in Part I and subject to limitations on natural persons employed by juridical persons only.
Services auxiliary to insurance	Unbound except as indicated in Part I and for actuarial and risk assessment for which residence is required in addition to a qualifying examination, membership in the Actuarial Association of the Republic of Slovenia and proficiency in the Slovene language.
Travel agencies and tour operators	Unbound except as indicated in Part I and that a licence of the Slovenian Chamber of Commerce is required (for consumer protection purposes).
Other:	Registration is required (for consumer protection and safety purposes).
Mountain guides services	Unbound, except as indicated in Part I and training, one year of apprenticeship and examination are required for acquiring mountain guide qualifications. Registration in the Register of active mountain guides is required.[b]

[a] According to Slovene law, auditing services are a matter of firms, not natural persons.
[b] Mountain guides from abroad are temporarily allowed to guide groups from their country being subject to membership of the IFMGA and registration in the national register of active mountain guides is required.

improve her offer, while simultaneously reminding her partners that she has requests as well. The sectoral offers are interesting in detail but given their paucity, the horizontal section of the schedule is the key indicator of progress. Although it is not entirely clear, the way to read the schedules appears to be to take the more restrictive of the horizontal or the sectoral schedules, unless the latter explicitly liberalizes or over-rules the former. Specifically, 'none' in the horizontal section—where 'none' is the official term for no restrictions—means 'none except the conditions set out in the horizontal section'.[4] Sectors are exempt from the horizontal restrictions only if the exemption is explicitly noted. This rarely happens, and indeed most sectoral entries add further restrictions, often recording 'unbound', which means that even the restricted hori-zontal concessions do not apply to that sector, or 'unbound except as indicated in the horizontal section', which means that the horizontal concessions are the only ones that apply. Table 7.3 records text only where it differs from 'unbound', 'none', or the ubiquitous 'unbound except as in the horizontal schedule'.

In Turkey education has a potentially more liberal regime than other service sectors, although the basis for licensing teachers is not spelt out. Insurance, on the other hand, has a more restrictive regime with licensing, residence, experience, and capital restrictions even for key personnel. Hotels and restaurants have quantitative limits on foreign employment as does shipping (with a 0 per cent quota for foreigners!). Slovenia also further restricts the insurance sector, as well as the accountancy profes-sions and travel agencies. In a piece of local liberalism it permits, how-ever, foreign apprentice mountain guides. This presumably reflects the fact that tour companies have greater political clout than do local young seasonal workers and the need for foreign language skills for an international service.

Most of the remaining schedules are, I believe, not greatly different in flavour from these two. They have very few sectoral commitments and those that are recorded tend to further restrict financial services but liberalize teachers and the hotel trade. Less frequent, but still detectable, are constraints on legal workers, more favourable provisions for foreign doctors, a liberal regime for artists and at least one other country relax-ing restrictions for tour guides.

In economic and negotiating terms these offers are fine so far as they go although, as has been noted many times elsewhere, it is difficult to know from the schedules alone exactly how far that is. (One needs country-specific detail and implementation information for that.) Moreover, they are, of course, minimal not actual levels of market

---

[4] WTO, *Guidelines for Scheduling*, L/S/92.

access. However, they do not indicate an enthusiasm for foreign workers at any level of skill and they certainly make it difficult for local firms in developing countries to recruit specialists and leaders abroad. If they were keen to see progress on less-skilled workers, developing countries could usefully have established a precedent by scheduling some themselves. If they have excesses of such workers, as one would expect, presumably the inflow would be modest. Where local conditions mean that flows may be larger (e.g. South Africa), developing countries' reticence presumably reflects the same nervousness that developed countries feel about disruption to labour markets and social stresses. By failing to confront it they hardly increase their chances of getting their partners to do so. Overall, these schedules suggest that liberalizing flows of less-skilled workers is not just a North–South issue.

II. DEVELOPING COUNTRY ASPIRATIONS

Several developing countries have made statements about Mode 4 in general. These naturally say rather little explicitly about what they would offer and they are not the specific requests that will ultimately drive the negotiation process. Rather, they are broad statements of objectives and motivations for negotiating in the area. Two among these are notable: an early one from India and a later paper by 14 countries.

The most comprehensive developing country proposal on Mode 4 is from India which is closely related to the one by Chanda who provided the analysis.[5] The proposal provides not only concrete suggestions for areas of further liberalization in Mode 4, but also detailed administrative procedures relating to Mode 4 visas and work permits and the recognition of qualifications. It is motivated by the view that there is a huge imbalance between current commitments on Mode 3, commercial presence, and those on Mode 4, natural persons.

The communication first points out that existing Mode 4 commitments are largely linked to commercial presence which is of very limited use to developing countries which are interested primarily in the movement of independent professionals and other persons. It argues for adding another category 'individual professionals' to the existing categories, in line with India's perceived comparative advantage in the competitive end of the professional market where the competition from large transnational suppliers is least. Relatedly, it calls for further expansion in the scope of occupational categories to include middle and lower-level

---

[5] R. Chanda, 'Movement of Natural Persons and the GATS' 24(5) *World Economy* (2001) 631–654.

professionals in the existing coverage of 'other persons' and 'specialists'. This is of interest to many developing countries, who see their comparative advantage lying, if anywhere in skills, in the lower levels. It does not, however, do much for the many relatively small and very poor WTO members which are short of skills and abundant in unskilled labour and hence face potential brain-drain problems. These countries really need to press for low-skilled access, but so far have remained silent.

In support of their objective of extending coverage, the Indians call for uniform definitions of these broader service personnel categories, and propose using the International Labour Organization's (ILO) International Standard Classification of Occupations for the WTO services Sectoral Classification. This is potentially important because specially negotiated classifications can be manipulated to provide tailor-made protection for the sectors in developed countries most at risk from foreign competition, i.e. for sectors where developing countries are most competitive.

India identifies the need for clarity in the definition of and multilateral disciplines on the application of Economic Needs Tests. It calls for the establishment of Multilateral Norms to reduce the scope of discriminatory practices in the use of Economic Needs Tests, for fewer occupational categories to be made subject to such tests and for consensus to be achieved on what such categories should be. On the recognition of qualifications—a major barrier to temporary mobility—India proposes the establishment of multilateral norms to facilitate the recognition of academic qualifications, as well as the recognition of work-related qualifications. The Indians also propose exempting temporary workers from social security contributions.

Perhaps most significantly and innovatively, India makes concrete proposals to separate temporary service providers under the GATS from permanent labour flows, so that normal immigration procedures do not hinder the commitments made on temporary mobility. She proposes introducing a special GATS visa for Mode 4 temporaries outside the normal immigration procedures, with the following features:

- strict time-frames for granting the visa (two to four weeks maximum);
- flexibility for visas on shorter notice for select categories of service providers;
- transparent and streamlined application processes;
- mechanisms to find out the status of applications, causes of rejection, and requirements to be fulfilled;
- easier renewal and transfer procedures;
- GATS visas for select companies for use by its employees deputed abroad temporarily;

- adequate in-built safeguard mechanisms to prevent temporary service providers entering the permanent labour market.

Other developing country submissions—e.g. by Colombia, Pakistan, and Brazil—echo many of the points in the Indian paper—e.g. on economic needs tests and qualifications. The Brazilians also urge the negotiation of a framework before specific issues are tackled. This approach seems very likely to founder at the first stage, which may not be wholly unintentional.

Two and a half years after the Indian submission, a joint statement by 14 developing countries—Argentina, Bolivia, Chile, The People's Republic of China, Colombia, Dominican Republic, Egypt, Guatemala, India, Mexico, Pakistan, Peru, Philippines, and Thailand—made an eloquent and coherent plea for more progress on Mode 4 in many of the same directions as India.[6] It is not an offer, *per se*, because even where it makes commitments, it is non-binding on the authors, but nonetheless it identifies clearly the problems that developing countries face in this area. It argues that Mode 4 is the principal way in which developing countries might expect to reap market access benefits in services and cites indicative evidence on the large magnitude of the gains for both developed and developing countries.[7] It comments, as we do above, that offers to date are modest and barely advance beyond existing schedules. In particular most are horizontal, with no specific sectoral 'flesh' to hang on the horizontal 'bones', and most pertain to service providers associated with commercial presence (intra-corporate transferees) or the highly skilled.

The proponents suggest a special session of the Council for Trade in Services to consider several issues, including:

- the adoption of a classification of service providers separating intra-corporate transferees, business visitors, contractual service providers, and independent service providers;
- serious work to develop sectoral commitments to complement horizontal commitments, and, expressed very mildly, to extend the concessions to lower-skilled workers;
- to separate temporary from permanent movement, and specifically to establish a GATS visa, or equivalent;
- to codify or abolish economic needs tests;
- to improve the recognition of qualifications and to ensure that additional testing satisfies a necessity test, i.e. is necessary on objective grounds to test or instil necessary skills to operate in the host markets;
- to devise a model schedule for Mode 4.

---

[6] TN/S/W/14.   [7] Winters, *supra* n. 3.

In addition to the major papers, I note in passing some recent advances. Colombia has tabled a proposal on Administrative Procedures relating to visas. India has tabled informal proposals relating to implementation of Article VII of GATS (recognition agreements) and on the recognition of qualifications. And the group of developing countries who had sponsored TN/S/W/14 have co-sponsored an informal proposal on Transparency in Mode 4.

III. DEVELOPED COUNTRY RESPONSES

It is early days yet, but one cannot help observing that the developing countries' requests have not been handsomely treated. It is true that the European Union (EU) has made some concessions in its initial offer. In the latter, service companies with graduate training programmes will be able to transfer their 'managers of the future' for up to one year training with an affiliated company in the EU. Other intra-corporate transfers are possible for managers and specialists for a maximum of three years without an economic needs test. Companies in specified sectors which have contracts to provide services with a client in the EU will be able to send *highly skilled* personnel to the EU to provide these services for up to six months at a time.[8] Finally, self-employed skilled professionals, again only in certain sectors (for example computer services, engineers) and who are based overseas will be able to enter the EU for up to six months to provide services to EU clients. Under the EC offer, member states will continue to be able to refuse entry to persons that pose a security threat or that are considered to be at risk of abusing the terms of their entry. This is not a handsome offer, despite the EU's evident pride in its boldness, and there is even some debate as to whether it lies within the competence of the EU to offer even such modest concessions on behalf of its members.

Other developed countries have done no better, at least formally through the GATS, although via unilateral actions we have seen a bit more progress. The UK has liberalized its regime somewhat with GATS visas in certain sectors, increased quotas in others and a general loosening of implementation barriers (and an associated liberalization in official rhetoric). Similarly the US has proposed ways of regularizing illegal workers and increasing their flow. Overall, however, we are little nearer

---

[8] The person must possess (i) a university degree or equivalent technical qualification, (ii) professional qualifications where this is required to exercise an activity in the sector concerned according to EC law or the law of the Member State where the service is provided, and (iii) at least three years of professional experience in the sector.

to liberalizing lower-skilled mobility nor to addressing issues such as economic needs tests, qualifications, or social security.

IV. WHY SO MODEST?

The aggregate gains from increased labour mobility are potentially huge. One does not have to take the various estimates literally to see that the possibilities far outweigh those of further liberalizing goods trade.[9] This section explores why we are seeing such slow progress.

One argument is that I may have the wrong measure: negotiations have not become serious yet and so one can read little into the initial offers. Clearly there is some truth to this, but in goods we do observe initial offers being used both as challenges to partners to make concessions in specific areas and as ways of signalling intent to press for far-reaching deals. I do not detect these forces in the services schedules, although I do expect offers to become a little more daring over time.

Relatedly, the explicit trade-off in the Uruguay Round, and the expected one in this Round, was Mode 3 concessions by developing countries in return for Mode 4 concessions by developed countries. Since developing countries are making fewer offers in Mode 3, perhaps they feel no need to make them in Mode 4. Again, there is truth in this, but the trade-off did not work very well before and so the bargain is very likely to become 'within Mode 4' this time as well. Hence, making offers in Mode 4 would be likely to facilitate receiving them.

It is also argued that until the developed countries show a willingness to engage in Mode 4, it is unreasonable to ask the developing countries who, outside intra-corporate transferees, are the *demandeurs* to make extensive offers. This is the stalemate that I hope will be broken and the fact that it has not been so far bodes ill for the future and leads me to believe that developing countries are substantively nervous about this area.

This nervousness partly reflects the fact that migration and temporary mobility are more threatening than ordinary trade liberalization because they raise the spectre of cultural and social strife. A well-run temporary mobility scheme (which ensures, by and large, temporariness) should circumvent long-run fears of this kind because it shows the local population

---

[9] E.g. L. A. Winters, 'Assessing the Efficiency Gain from Further Liberalization: A Comment' in P. Sauve and A. Subramanian (eds) *Efficiency, Equity and Legitimacy: The Multilateral Trading System and the Millennium* (2001) 106–113; Winters, Walmsley, Wang, and Grynberg, *supra* n. 3; D. Rodrik, *How to Make the Trade System Work for Development* (2004) mimeo, online at http://ksghome.harvard.edu/~.drodrik. academic.ksg/How%20to%20Make%20Trade%20Work.pdf.

that integration is not intended. On the other hand, by leaving the temporary migrants out of the mainstream one makes them more isolated and more visible, which could exacerbate short-run frictions. My own belief is that the former effect should dominate (especially if the rhetoric shifts from 'sponging aliens' to 'essential service providers'). However, I note that the eminent Copenhagen Consensus[10] castigated guest worker schemes on the grounds that they prevented the integration of the migrants into local society.[11] The issue remains open.

A further related worry is that temporary mobility is seen as the first step towards permanent or very long-lived migration—as, for example, Germany's *Gastarbeiter* system turned out and the US's H1–B visa scheme is basically intended to be. Thus issues of migration and labour market policies become involved very directly and these typically lie with ministries that are not instinctively outward-looking. Moreover, temporary schemes are complex to legislate and administer, so these ministries have concrete objections as well. Immigration officials dislike sector-specific visa regulations—as GATS calls for—because they increase the administrative burden.[12] These latter issues apply to genuinely temporary as well as pseudo-permanent mobility.

The labour market effects of the temporary mobility of the lower-skilled fall heavily on local less-skilled workers. In high- and middle-income countries these have long been a favoured group in trade-policy terms, ostensibly being the main beneficiaries of protection—e.g. in agriculture, clothing, and footwear. Moreover, in arguing for the liberalization of imports of unskilled labour-intensive goods, protagonists have often implicitly fallen back on the existence of less-skilled jobs in the non-traded sector ('a nation of hamburger-flippers'). Mobility threatens these jobs (or the wages in them) too, and so encounters even more strongly the traditional biases and concerns. Moreover, although I have argued previously that the educated and ageing rich countries are going to run out of unskilled labour soon, the higher levels of unemployment among the less-skilled in those countries suggest that we haven't got there yet.

It is worth reiterating that the resistance of unskilled workers to immigration is not restricted to richer countries. Even in poor developing countries such fears are heard. This—along with social/racial concerns—could well explain why developing countries have not been bolder in their schedules.[13]

[10] *The Economist* 11 June 2004.

[11] Has anyone else noted the irony of a group of temporary workers—the Consensus Panel travelled to Denmark and worked there—castigating temporary mobility?

[12] S. Chaudhuri, A. Mattoo, and R. Self, *Moving People to Deliver Services: How Can the WTO Help?* Policy Research Working Paper No. 3238, The World Bank (2004).

[13] It is possible that the Indian proposals on contractual service providers could extend to less-skilled workers, but it does not seem very likely.

Competition from abroad is now visiting itself upon more-skilled, middle-class, jobs as well as the unskilled. The outsourcing debate partly reflects this phenomenon, but so too do the debates over the regulation and qualifications of foreign workers. The traditionally self-regulating professions have long sought to control competition by managing trainee numbers, and are now active in trying to preclude foreign competition via qualification restrictions; for example, the US State Bar Associations significantly restrict inter-state commerce in lawyers. Thus, interest groups throughout the economy are resistant to admitting competing labour. Moreover, middle classes are much more articulate, networked, and influential than less-skilled workers, so we must expect the opposition to be fierce, especially in developing countries where the relatively smaller middle class reaps all the adverse consequences of competition but only a share of the consumer gains from lower prices and more choice.

As always, export interests are less well organized and motivated than import-competing ones: the identities of the gainers are less clear and the gains may be eroded by future entry anyway. In Mode 4 the Indians have led on independent professionals, however. Several possible rationales exist: to try to cement down the willingness of the EU to grant concessions in this area, because India's strong endowment of such workers makes this a national interest and because Indian decision-makers have children entering the professions whose levels of education are sufficient to practice in the US or Europe and whose incomes would be greatly enhanced by doing so. Thus pushing on 'independent professions' marries public and private policy. Such pushing, however, may not be to the advantage of smaller, poorer developing countries with scarce professional skills. They may suffer more seriously from a 'brain drain'.[14] This possible division of interests in the developing world could also help to explain why we have not seen strong coalitions growing up. The traditional 'foot-soldiers' of the developing country caucus may recognize that they have different interests from the traditional 'captains'.

An important counteracting force—as in intermediate goods trade—is firms that wish to use foreign labour; these are likely to push for increased mobility. Examples include the IT sectors in the US, UK, and Germany in the early 2000s, the medical profession seeking nurses and doctors, and agriculture seeking pickers and packers. These groups are certainly behind the expansion of mobility schemes but, naturally, mainly for their own specific requirements rather than for labour in

---

[14] The brain drain is less of an issue with temporary than with permanent mobility, but problems cannot be ruled out.

general. In goods trade, users lobby for free trade in their inputs and also quite often for liberalization elsewhere in their economies so that, via reciprocity, other countries will relax restrictions on the users' exports. In labour mobility, the pressure for general liberalization is lost because, with one exception, none of the users exports labour. The exception, of course, is multinational companies whose desire to both 'export' and 'import' their own employees lies behind the progress on intra-corporate transferees.

Finally, having spent much of the last few years exploring issues of migration—permanent and temporary—I can assert that they are very complicated. Even qualitative results are hard to establish unambiguously and quantitative ones are rarely credible. In the absence of a well-defined calculus of net benefits, policy-makers will tend to be cautious—exactly as they were over agriculture until the Organisation for Economic Co-operation and Development (OECD) provided some clear numbers in the mid-1980s.

To ask why there is so little movement on the GATS is not to imply that there is no movement on temporary labour mobility, however. In fact there is, but not via the GATS. Temporary labour schemes currently exist, and, as I noted above, are being extended and improved. But not multilaterally. This may indicate either that there is no demand for a multilateral input on labour mobility or that there is demand but the GATS cannot satisfy it.

One possibility is that the constituencies that would naturally lobby for agreements on Mode 4 can be satisfied without it. On the unskilled labour front the safety valve for the agriculture, hotels and tourism, and clothing sectors may well be illegal migration. If, despite the hostile rhetoric towards foreign workers, these sectors get the labour they want, why bring things out into the open? On more skilled labour the situation is probably that direct targeting of specific sources of labour is cheaper and more reliable (because there are fewer qualifications and education systems to understand) than global search, so that that is what users lobby for.

Breining, Chadha, and Winters consider this question in a study of temporary mobility in the health sector, specifically, the flow of doctors from India to the UK.[15] They observe that medical mobility already satisfies many of the conditions that informed scholars of Mode 4 such as Mattoo urge on negotiators.[16] For example, to qualify to practice in

[15] C. Breining, R. Chadha, and L. A. Winters, 'The Temporary Movement of Workers: GATS Mode 4' in L. Alan Winters and Pradeep S. Mehta (eds) *Bridging the Differences: Analyses of Five Issues of the WTO Agenda, Consumer Unity Trust Society* (2003) 111–146, Cuts, Jaipur.

[16] A. Mattoo, 'Developing Countries in the New Round of GATS: Towards a Pro-Active Role' 23 *World Economy* (2000), 471–490.

the UK doctors need to prove their suitability via a test of competence and language (the PLAB); they do not need to undergo duplicative training or meet extensive residence requirements such as are found with some other professions. That is, the qualifications test focuses on necessary fiduciary issues rather than irrelevant formalities. Moreover, the World Health Organization (WHO) accreditation of medical training facilities goes a long way towards achieving mutual recognition of primary medical qualifications, for the UK recognizes preliminary medical training given in any WHO accredited institution. Moreover, India and the UK are almost as good a pair of negotiating partners as one is likely to find.[17] India is the UK's principal supplier of non-EEA doctors and the UK one of India's principal markets.[18] This maximizes the internalization of the negotiation, and in so doing will encourage agreement.[19]

Despite these apparent advantages, doctors never figure explicitly in GATS Mode 4 commitments and medicine is not included in the sectors for which the UK will now issue 'GATS visas' or in the favoured sectors in the EU's GATS offer. Partly this may just be because the mobility of health workers is well established and is seen by government as part of the health and employment portfolios rather than the trade nexus—i.e. no one thought of using the GATS in this context. It might also be because the current balance between supply and demand means that there is not much value-added to the GATS. Indeed, the GATS could increase the bureaucratic cost of medical mobility, since the UK's current 'permit-free' schemes for doctors are light-handed relative to other international mobility.[20]

A more likely candidate, however, is concern about the inflexibility of the GATS. In the absence of a safeguards clause it would be arduous to reduce inward mobility below bound levels if circumstances changed. And given the very long gestation period for doctors, the authorities will wish almost all short- to medium-term demand fluctuation to be accommodated by 'imports'. A cohort of unemployed domestic doctors would

[17] Even though health and education are national competences in the EU, the formal negotiation would be between the EU and India, because the Commission has responsibility for all negotiations in the WTO, even where, as here, the issues at stake are national competences.

[18] The UK is obliged to recognize qualifications from the European Economic Area (EEA) and to impose no restrictions on the employment of EEA nationals.

[19] See on internalization in GATT negotiations: J. M. Finger, 'Trade Liberalization: A Public Choice Perspective' in R. C. Amarcher, G. Haberler, and T. D. Willet (eds), *Challenges to a Liberal Economic Order* (1979) 421–461; L. A. Winters, 'Reciprocity' in J. M. Finger and A. Olechowski (eds), *A Handbook on the Multilateral Trade Negotiations*, (1987) 45–51.

[20] Once an overseas doctor has a training job in a UK hospital he/she has no need to apply for a work permit. By 'training jobs' I mean jobs for junior doctors who undertake a great deal of clinical work, but who also receive advanced training in their specialties. These jobs are typically time-limited and expire when training is completed.

be a very awkward political constituency. Also both sides wish to avoid the most-favoured-nation (MFN) clause. European countries appear to want to be able to target specific countries for specific services. This is especially true where language, culture, or qualifications are concerned—for example Commonwealth citizens receive favourable treatment in several UK temporary immigration schemes—or where they offer training, in which case 'aid-like' considerations occur. On the Indian side, applying the MFN clause would increase competition in the UK for migrant doctors' places, almost certainly reducing the numbers of Indians or their rewards. That is, binding in the GATS would reduce internalization. These arguments, of course, also apply to preferential trade in goods, and, at least for around 40 years, we largely overcame them in the GATT. However, given that integrating people is more demanding than accepting foreign goods, they are possibly stronger for Mode 4.

The MFN obligation in the GATS applies to all services trade whether scheduled or not (unless a measure has been explicitly excepted from MFN, and even that is time-limited). Thus there is some chance that all bilateral labour mobility arrangements, except those forming part of a full-blown preferential arrangement, could be challenged and possibly ruled WTO-inconsistent. That would not be helpful. Some commentators are starting to say that since the issues are so sensitive and so case-specific that progress will be possible only bilaterally, we should bow to the inevitable and let the GATS recognize bilateral deals. I agree that for many years most temporary mobility deals will be bilateral, but I would rather leave them out of the GATS than dilute the fundamental non-discrimination principle of the GATS and the WTO. Thus while there is clearly a case for ensuring that bilateral deals on Mode 4 cannot be taken to the dispute settlement procedure, I would not recognize them formally under the GATS and would certainly not allow them to be scheduled or enforced via its procedures. Bilateralism is likely to create friction in temporary mobility and there is a case for keeping that friction out of the WTO. Moreover, bilateralism in goods is economically and politically destructive and will become (even) harder to resist if we concede on Mode 4.

V. CONCLUSIONS

Developing country offers in Mode 4 are unambitious; their general demands are reasonable, but these are not supported by their offers or negotiating tactics, partly because interests differ across developing countries. The developed countries, on the other hand, have breathed a sigh of relief and offered almost nothing under Mode 4, despite stealthily liberalizing labour mobility via other mechanisms. The forces ranged against Mode 4 are formidable, so it will be a long and uphill struggle to establish it, not least because bilateralism looks more feasible in most cases. Nonetheless, I would oppose dropping demands for the liberalization of lower-skilled labour mobility under the GATS, and I would have the GATS ignore rather than condone bilateral arrangements. By seeking to keep unskilled labour in and bilateral deals out, I would clearly be reducing the amount of liberalization that could be attributed to the GATS, but at least, I would be upholding the fundamental principles of equity and non-discrimination.

8

Navigating between the Poles: Unpacking the Debate on the Implications for Development of GATS Obligations relating to Health and Education Services

J. ANTHONY VANDUZER

I. INTRODUCTION

Differences of opinion are stark regarding the implications of the General Agreement on Trade in Services (GATS) for public services like health and education in developing countries. Some believe that GATS poses no threat at all to these essential services and, in some circumstances, may contribute to their more effective delivery and regulation. Others are vehemently opposed to trade liberalization commitments of any kind in these areas and view GATS as a significant threat to the effectiveness and even the viability of national health and education systems.

GATS proponents emphasize that GATS allows countries to tailor their commitments to calibrate the level of obligation in ways consistent with national policy objectives. They point out that there is no obligation on any World Trade Organization (WTO) Member to accept the higher tier of GATS obligations, including national treatment and market access, for any particular service and the basic obligations applicable to all services, like most-favoured-nation (MFN) treatment, do not represent any meaningful limitation on regulatory flexibility. In any case, GATS does not apply to most publicly delivered health and education services. These are completely excluded from the scope of all GATS obligations. Most GATS proponents readily admit the fundamental importance of equitable access and other non-commercial goals that inform national policies in health and education. They assert, however, that GATS commitments to liberalize trade not only can be compatible with such goals but can make their achievement more likely.[1]

Many GATS critics start from a philosophical objection to a trade regime in which health and education services are treated like commodities. Trade liberalization commitments are viewed as serious constraints on the ability of developing country governments to achieve equitable access to basic health and education services and other objectives sought to be fulfilled by government schemes for the regulation and delivery of these services. In particular, liberalization commitments are seen as contributing to the development of two-tier markets in health and education under which public services will be undermined and developing country citizens who are the poorest or in rural areas will see a diminution of badly needed health and education services so that already better off and better served urban segments of the population will benefit.[2]

GATS critics assert that GATS' vaunted flexibility is constrained in practice for developing countries by the power dynamics of trade negotiations and capacity limitations that systematically disfavour developing countries. GATS obligation to engage in successive rounds of negotiations with a view to progressively liberalizing trade in services ensures that there is ongoing pressure to improve liberalization commitments. The critics argue that any flexibility that may be accorded in the architecture of the agreement is lost when commitments are undertaken. In their view, GATS commitments lock in liberalization programmes such that subsequent policy reform to return to local private or public delivery is precluded. The dynamic nature of regulation and services delivery in health and education combined with the uncertain scope of GATS obligations make locking in a specific approach to regulation and delivery inappropriate and undesirable.

The reality for developing countries, of course, is much more complex than either of these polar positions suggests. Before deciding on what GATS commitments to undertake in health and education, developing countries must make prior policy choices regarding how

---

[1] Examples of commentators who, in general, argue in favour of this view include R. Adlung, 'The GATS Negotiations: Implications for Health and Social Services' (2003) 38 *Intereconomics* 147; and P. Sauvé, *Trade, Education and The GATS: What's In, What's Out, What's All The Fuss About?* (2002).

[2] E.g. South Africa's Minister of Education, Kamal Asmal, once warned the South African parliament that 'We must avoid at all costs a GATS in education,' quoted in L. Mabuza, 'Who's In and Who's Out? Country Responses to Education and GATS' in *Report of the 15th CCEM Preliminary Meeting on Education and the General Agreement on Trade in Services: What Does the Future Hold?* (May 2003). A similar view was expressed in the 'Porto Alegre Declaration' by a conference of Latin American and Iberian universities in Porto Alegre, Brazil on 27 April 2002.

much private-sector participation to permit in the delivery of these services. Both health and education are basic government responsibilities and states are extensively involved in regulating, funding, and delivering services in these areas. But governments everywhere are considering, or are actually engaged in, reforms to privatize public services or commercialize services delivery in an effort to improve accessibility and control costs. Whether and how to move forward with such reforms are fundamental and often hotly debated domestic issues. Developing country governments must assess the costs and benefits of privatization and commercialization in health and education services measured against the achievement of their development objectives. The desirability and impact of privatization and commercialization on development in each country will depend very much on local conditions including the state's capacity for effective domestic regulation of private-sector suppliers.

One question for developing countries in this regard is whether there would be benefits resulting from permitting foreign firms to provide privatized or commercialized services. For example, countries must determine the extent to which opening health and education sectors to foreign investors would lead to more money flowing to improving health and education facilities and better access to desperately needed health and education services than if investment were limited to domestic sources.

A secondary question for developing countries that have decided to liberalize their markets for health and education services is to determine the prospective contribution of GATS commitments in health and education services to obtaining the net benefits of trade liberalization. Many states are successfully liberalizing their regimes relating to health and education services without making GATS commitments to do so. In the current round of GATS negotiations there is little pressure on developing countries to adopt stronger commitments in these areas from WTO Members. At the same time, there is some uncertainty regarding both the scope and nature of GATS obligations and the trade benefits associated with making specific GATS commitments in these sectors. In this context, many developing countries are understandably reluctant to undertake commitments that would limit their future policy options.

This chapter sketches the by now familiar outlines of the debate on the liberalization of public services in developing countries focusing on health and education. It then provides a brief overview of the relatively limited existing GATS commitments in these sectors and the low priority attached to improving commitments in the current negotiations. The final sections of the chapter look at why there is so little interest in GATS commitments among WTO Members and suggest some possible strategies for making the GATS more relevant to improving the regulation and delivery of health and education services in developing countries.

II. AN UNSCANDALIZED DISCUSSION OF TRADE LIBERALIZATION IN HEALTH AND EDUCATION

A. Introduction: health and education services under the GATS

GATS applies to all measures affecting trade in health and education services. The only true exclusion from the application of the agreement is for services 'supplied in the exercise of governmental authority' which would include, at least, health and education services provided exclusively by the state without charge to its citizens. In terms of obligations, GATS creates both a general framework that applies to all services subject to the agreement and a set of additional obligations for each WTO Member that apply to the treatment of particular services activities that the Member has agreed to list in a national schedule of commitments.

The most important general rule is the obligation to grant MFN treatment to foreign services and service suppliers of other Members. This means that Members must treat services and service suppliers from other Member states no less favourably than those from any other country. For this obligation to apply, services or the service suppliers must be in similar categories. In the language of the WTO agreements, they must be 'like'.

For every services activity that is listed in its national schedule, a Member commits to a higher level of obligation. A Member must grant foreign services and service suppliers national treatment (meaning treatment no less favourable than the treatment of like domestic businesses) and cannot impose certain restrictions on market access. The national treatment and market access obligations for listed sectors may be circumscribed by express limitations inscribed by each Member in its schedule.

As well, for listed sectors, each Member must ensure that all measures of general application are administered in a reasonable, objective, and impartial manner. Measures relating to qualification requirements and procedures, technical standards, and licensing requirements in these sectors cannot nullify or impair the Member's specific commitments in listed sectors by imposing requirements or standards not based on objective and transparent criteria, such as competence and ability to provide the service, or that are more burdensome than necessary to ensure the quality of the service. In the case of licensing procedures, the procedures themselves must not be a restriction on the supply of a service.

GATS contains no definition of health or education services. Most WTO Members scheduled their specific commitments for particular services with reference to the Services Sectoral Classification List developed during the Uruguay Round of negotiations which is based on and refers to the categories in the United Nations Provisional Central Product Classification.[3] In the Classification List, 'Health related and social services' is a distinct category of activity including hospital services and an undefined array of 'other human health services not elsewhere classified' that includes the services of long-term residential health-care facilities and ambulance services and likely extends to public health and health promotion, laboratory services, and diagnostic services. The services of health professionals, including physicians, dentists, nurses, and others, are listed under 'Business services'. Health insurance is categorized as a financial service. Education services referred to in the Classification List include not only primary and secondary education and higher education at colleges and universities, but also adult education and 'other education'. This last category likely encompasses a wide variety of commercial training programmes and in-house training by businesses. The Classification List provides little guidance on how to define education services beyond these basic categories.[4]

B. The national policy context for trade in health and education

One of the distinctive features of national regimes governing health and education services, as compared to most other services, is that they must be responsive to a complex matrix of important policy objectives and involve a high level of state engagement as a funder, regulator, and service provider.[5] These characteristics make health and education services particularly challenging to address in a trade agreement, like

[3] GATT, *Services Sectoral Classification List*, Note by the Secretariat (10 July 1991), GATT Doc. MTN.GNS/W/120. This classification is based on the United Nations, *Provisional Central Product Classification*, Statistical Paper Series M No. 77 (1991). Most Members identified the services activities with respect to which they were assuming obligations by reference to the Secretariat's classification and the corresponding categories in the Provisional CPC Classification, though, as noted below, many customized their commitments in health and education by adopting additional distinctions.

[4] The Provisional CPC (*supra* n. 3) adds little in the way of elaboration. See Provisional CPC code 92.

[5] The WTO Secretariat describes health as operating at the 'borderline between public and private spheres': WTO, Council on Trade in Services, Health and Social Services: Background Note by the Secretariat (1998) S/C/W/50 at 8.

GATS, that creates disciplines applicable across a broad range of services activities.[6]

Equitable access to a basic level of health and education is widely considered to be a human right and a fundamental responsibility of the state. Public policy in health and education is related not just to quality, the central preoccupation of policy-making in most other services areas, but also to a variety of other objectives including equitable access to services and consumer protection as well as the efficient allocation of resources.[7] In health, the greatest challenge for government policy-makers in all countries continues to be how to manage escalating expenses resulting from increased costs of treatment and demographic shifts while ensuring the quality and accessibility of treatment. Education policy must deal with cost pressures, consumer protection, and access concerns as well but must also safeguard the role of education as the primary mechanism for the transmission of national values and culture and in preparing a nation's people for citizenship.

For developing countries especially, improvements in health and education are closely linked to economic development. With respect to health, the recent report of the World Health Organization (WHO) Commission on Macroeconomics and Health has demonstrated the relationship between health and poverty reduction. The Commission found that better health contributes to:

- higher rates of labour productivity;
- higher rates of domestic and foreign investment;
- improved human capital;
- higher rates of national savings.[8]

The contribution of education to development is also well established.[9] Indeed improvements in health and education outcomes are related. For example, education is one of the most effective means of

---

[6] That is not to say that other services do not operate in an environment defined by important non-commercial policy considerations and complicated regulatory structures. Financial services and telecommunications are examples. The direct human impact and level of public-sector engagement in regulation and direct delivery in every country, however, make education and health distinctive.

[7] D. Lipson, Comments, *OECD–WB Services Experts Meeting*, 4–5 March 2002.

[8] World Health Organization, Commission on Macroeconomics and Health, *Investing in Health for Economic Development*, online at http://www.cid.harvard.edu/cidcmh/CMHReport.pdf; see also World Bank, *Development Report for 2004: Making Services Work for Poor People* ch. 8, online at http://econ.worldbank.org/wdr/wdr2004/text-30023/.

[9] UNESCO/OECD, *Financing Education—Investments and Returns, Analysis of the World Education Indicators 2002 Edition* (2003); World Bank, *supra* n. 8 ch. 7.

combating the transfer of HIV/AIDS.[10] In recognition of the key role of health and education in development, improvements in both areas are implicated in the first six of the eight millennium development goals set by the United Nations (UN).

Another distinctive attribute of the health and education sectors is that both are characterized by market failures. Simply stated, this means that because of a lack of consumer resources, information asymmetries between consumers and providers of health and education services and other market distortions, private-sector suppliers on their own would not supply health or education services at minimally necessary levels of quantity and quality.[11]

The combination of these factors has meant that a very large segment of both health and education services are delivered or funded, in whole or in part, by the state in all countries. Approximately 50 per cent of health services in developing countries are publicly funded.[12] Public spending on education varies substantially from one country to the next but represents more than one-half of total education expenditure in every country.[13]

In almost all developing countries, the extensive presence of the state is complemented by some level of private funding and delivery of health and education services. In part, this is because of the inability of developing country governments to provide fully adequate services in these areas. Private and public systems may operate in parallel but in most developing countries are closely intertwined. Typically some form of public funding is provided to support the private delivery of basic health and education services. The role of the private sector is expanding in many jurisdictions as governments seek new ways to enhance service delivery and manage escalating costs, such as by privatizing state-run services or introducing competition or other commercial considerations into services delivery. Because of the compelling and varied policy objectives associated with health and education and the state's role as a major funder, private services in these areas are closely regulated.

---

[10] OECD, 'Poverty and Health in Developing Countries: Key Actions' in *OECD Observer* (November 2003).

[11] C. Blouin, 'Economic Dimensions and Impact Assessment of GATS to Promote and Protect Health' in C. Blouin, N. Drager, and R. Smith (eds), *Trade in Health Services, Developing Countries and the General Agreement on Trade in Services (GATS): A Handbook* (2004).

[12] WTO Secretariat Note on Health and Social Services, *supra* n. 5.

[13] UNESCO, *Global Education Digest 2004: Comparing Education Statistics Across the World* (2004). Within OECD countries as much as 98 per cent of education spending is public, though the average is around 88 per cent. Percentages in developing countries are typically lower, but remain substantial.

C. Growth in health and education services trade

Despite the extensive role of the state, both health and education services are increasingly traded. Trade in services means services delivered in any of the four modes of supply contemplated in GATS:

- Mode 1—cross-border supply: a service is supplied from the territory of one WTO Member into the territory of any other Member such as over the telephone;
- Mode 2—consumption abroad: a service is supplied in the territory of one Member to a service consumer of any other Member where the service consumer travels to the supplier's country to consume the service;
- Mode 3—commercial presence: a service is supplied by a service supplier of one Member through a commercial presence in the territory of any other Member;
- Mode 4—presence of natural persons: a service is supplied by a service supplier of one Member through the presence of natural persons of that Member in the territory of any other Member.

Health-care and education services may be traded in all four of these modes of supply. Though reliable global data on the magnitude of such trade is not available, existing evidence suggests that it is modest but growing strongly. In part, this has been driven by experiments in many countries with increased private-sector delivery, including delivery by foreign suppliers. While most exporters are developed countries, a growing number of developing countries, including Cuba, India, Jordan, and Thailand, are engaged in exports of health and education services.

The most important mode for international trade in both health and education services is consumption abroad (GATS Mode 2). Large numbers of students attend foreign education programmes, especially those offered by universities and other higher education institutions. China is the source of the largest number of students studying abroad. Many students from other developing countries, including India, Indonesia, Malaysia, Mexico, Pakistan, and Thailand, also study outside their countries of origin.[14] As well, every year more and more patients are visiting other countries to consume health services. An increase in the number and mobility of affluent consumers in developing countries and their rising expectations regarding service quality is driving growth in Mode 2 imports into developing countries as these consumers travel abroad for health and education.

---

[14] In 2002, there were 2.3 million foreign students studying at higher education institutions in the OECD countries, compared to 1.47 million in 1999.

In the area of health services, exports from developing countries through GATS Mode 2 are becoming increasingly significant. Interest in non-traditional medicine and competitive pricing of high-quality services in some developing countries has encouraged developed country consumers to travel to developing countries for health care. The price of a liver transplant in India, for example, is one-tenth the price of the same procedure in the United States (US).[15] India also attracts such 'health tourism' from neighbouring developing countries like Bangladesh.

Though statistics on cross-border supply (GATS Mode 1) are notoriously difficult to come by, there is no doubt that enhancements in technology are permitting increasing numbers of patients to consume cross-border health services from foreign professionals around the globe through various 'telehealth' applications, such as the remote diagnosis of a patient's condition by a physician outside the country evaluating X-rays and other information provided electronically.[16] As well, information technology is facilitating an explosion in the remote delivery of education and training across national borders.[17]

Also increasing in importance is the delivery of services through a commercial presence (GATS Mode 3). Foreign hospitals, clinics, and other treatment and long-term care facilities are permitted to enter markets in many developing countries like India, Indonesia, Nepal, Sri Lanka, and Thailand. Some education institutions have set up a commercial presence abroad to offer programmes either in the form of green-field investments or in partnership with local institutions in developing countries. The Massachusetts Institute of Technology for example has established a partnership with some Malaysian institutions to offer programmes in Malaysia. Such partnerships with prestigious foreign institutions are growing and their services may replace, to some extent, services consumed abroad.[18]

Finally, more and more individual health and education professionals from developing countries provide their services abroad each year (GATS Mode 4). This has been modestly facilitated in health services

---

[15] R. Chanda, 'Trade in Health Services' in 80 *Bulletin of the World Health Organization* (2002) 158.

[16] G. Wolvaardt, 'Opportunities and Challenges for Developing Countries in the Health Sector' in S. Zarrilli and C. Kinnon (eds), *International Trade in Health Services: A Development Perspective* (1998) at 63.

[17] Distance education represents 6 per cent of international student enrolment and has been growing steadily since 1996: K. Larsen and S. Vincent-Lancrin, 'International Trade in Education Services: Good or Bad?' in 14 *Higher Education and Management Policy* (2002) 9.

[18] By 1996, 140,000 students were enrolled in foreign subsidiaries of British institutions of higher education outside the UK compared to 200,000 foreign students studying in the UK: Larsen and Vincent-Lancrin, *supra* n. 17.

by a trend toward globalization of medical education and information, standards, and practice.[19] For both health and education the non-recognition in developed countries of domestic qualifications and experience acquired in developing countries as well as visa and immigration constraints continue to represent a significant impediment to the movement of developing country professionals abroad.

D. A taxonomy of possible effects of trade liberalization in health and education[20]

In this section, the costs and benefits of service trade liberalization are set out for each of the four modes of supply contemplated in GATS. This taxonomy suggests the nature and direction of trade effects but not their relative magnitude or the corresponding policy implications which are likely to be different for each developing country, depending on local conditions.

1. Mode 1: Cross-border supply

Cross-border supply typically involves the delivery of a service from a foreign location via the internet or some other kind of communications technology. From the perspective of a developing country considering the import of health and education services through this mode, a wide range of possible benefits, both economic and non-economic, may be identified. With respect to health, technologically mediated supply could mean better access to a wider range of services and treatments and better disease monitoring, especially in remote areas. Similarly in education, all manner of educational programmes could become accessible in this way enhancing student choices for developing country consumers. In areas in which conventional face-to-face education is limited or non-existent the potential gains in access may be enormous. Enhanced availability of education and health services and access to expertise in these areas especially in remote regions may also contribute to higher rates of local staff retention as well as reduced internal and foreign migration. Both would have a positive impact on the delivery of local services.

The main barrier to the delivery of services through this mode is the absence of the necessary telecommunications infrastructure and technology in many developing countries. Given the magnitude of the need for improved access to health and education services in developing

---

[19] D. Warner, 'The Globalization of Medical Care' in S. Zarrilli and C. Kinnon (eds), *International Trade in Health Services: A Development Perspective* (1998) at 71.

[20] See Chanda, *supra* n. 15, and Blouin, *supra* n. 11, for further discussion of the possible effects of trade liberalization in health services. Regarding education services see Larsen and Vincent-Lancrin, *supra* n. 17.

countries, the scarce state resources necessary to put such infrastructure and technology in place may be better spent on the direct provision of basic health and education services. Nevertheless, in terms of cost-effectiveness, it is possible that the use of technology may offer certain efficiencies. Technology may increase the productivity of health and education workers, for example. As well, the same technology may be used to support both education and health services delivery.

Apart from the cost of enabling technology, the main concern for governments associated with cross-border supply from abroad is how to ensure that foreign suppliers meet domestic quality standards.[21] Recognition of foreign qualifications in the areas of education and especially health remains limited. Imposing quality standards on health and education services suppliers who never physically enter the country poses additional challenges.

Export opportunities through the cross-border supply of health and education services may be non-existent or limited for many developing countries. Nevertheless, there may be areas in which opportunities exist. It may be cost-effective to locate back-office functions related to health and education services, like health insurance claims processing and medical record-keeping and transcription, in developing countries that offer lower labour costs and the availability of well-trained workers with appropriate linguistic and technological skills, such as India and the Philippines.[22] Where concerns of importing states regarding the qualifications of health and education professionals can be overcome, there may be some prospect for the cross-border export of services, particularly to other developing countries. In order to be able to take advantage of any such prospects, public investment in telecommunications infrastructure may be required. Again, the opportunity costs of such an investment, taking into account any offsetting efficiencies and other gains from trade, would have to be considered.

2. Mode 2: Consumption abroad

The import of health and education services through Mode 2 involves the citizens of a country going abroad for medical treatment or to

---

[21] For further discussion of the costs and benefits of 'telehealth', see S. Mandill, 'Telehealth: What is it? Will it Propel Cross-Border Trade in Health Services?' in S. Zarrilli and C. Kinnon (eds), *International Trade in Health Services: A Development Perspective* (1998) at 79. Regarding cross-border trade in education see S. Bjarnason, 'Debate on Education and GATS: Where Do We Stand?' in *Report of the 15th CCEM Preliminary Meeting on Education and the General Agreement on Trade in Services: What Does the Future Hold?* (May 2003).

[22] D. Lipson, 'GATS and Trade in Health Insurance Services: Background Note for the WHO Commission on Macroeconomics and Health' in *Working Paper for Commission on Macroeconomics and Health* (2001).

participate in education programmes. For a developing country, imports through Mode 2 may be a substitute for foreign services provided to the same domestic population though services suppliers who enter the local market through a commercial presence (Mode 3) or individually (Mode 4). Mode 2 imports involve certain costs. Most directly, domestic resources will be spent abroad. In education services, any negative effects will be offset to some extent if citizens who complete education abroad return to enhance the human capital of their home country. When high-achieving local students go abroad to study but never return, Mode 2 imports risk contributing to a loss of human capital or 'brain drain' from developing countries.

Since, inevitably, it will be the more affluent among a country's population who will be aware of and able to engage in consumption abroad, a less direct problem may be the development of a two-tier market, where the rich travel abroad for education and medical treatment while the poor must rely on inferior services available at home. Such a two-tier market may have some offsetting benefits to the extent that consumption abroad relieves pressures on the limited resources of domestic public health and education systems. At the same time, however, a two-tier market may weaken political support for public systems. If an influential segment of the population does not see its direct interests being served by public health and education services, its support for such services may erode.

The export of health and education services by a developing country through Mode 2 consists of foreign individuals coming to the country to consume these services. Particularly in health care this form of consumption abroad may be attractive to citizens in developed countries. The burgeoning numbers of retirees in developed countries with increasing health-care needs may lead to increased interest in cheaper care in developing countries, especially among those who have ethnic, cultural, or other ties. The comparatively low cost of high-quality services and access to alternative treatments may draw developed country consumers to developing country services. For a developing country, such 'health tourism' would be a source of foreign exchange and domestic employment. The prospect of serving a richer foreign clientele may encourage local investment and foreign investment (trade in services through Mode 3) in new health and education facilities and the provision of a wider range of higher-quality services. In education, there may be cultural benefits in having foreign students studying domestically. In developing country markets that are geographically close to major developed countries, like Mexico and Morocco, the potential for gains from Mode 2 exports would likely be greatest. At the same time, improved local services will tend to discourage locals from engaging in consumption abroad (Mode 2 imports), mitigating the costs associated with Mode 2 imports described above. Improved opportunities for local health and education professionals may reduce incentives for them to emigrate.

Exporting health and education services through Mode 2 would have little impact on improved provision to the poor, unless some of the returns to local suppliers could be recovered by the state through taxes, and government receipts were used to fund services to poorer segments of the population. This is because investment in health and education facilities to provide services to foreign clients will be most attractive in the most lucrative services. Such 'cream-skimming' leaves the expensive remainder of services to be supplied by the state.[23] There may be other disadvantages associated with local investment in private health and education services catering to affluent foreign consumers, such as contributing to the development of a two-tier local market for these services. Well-off local consumers may abandon public services in favour of new private services. While this may relieve pressure on public services, in such a two-tier market there may be an internal brain drain as local health and education professionals migrate from public-sector to private-sector suppliers. Finally, to the extent that the two-tier market becomes entrenched, political support for public services may be undermined.

These possible threats to equity and access must be viewed in the appropriate context. Existing public systems of health and education services in developing countries are far from perfect. Some existing public systems already serve the rich disproportionately or, as a result of corruption and inefficiency, are substantially impaired in terms of achieving their social and development objectives.

Also, as discussed in more detail in the following sections, some negative side-effects may be managed if not eliminated by appropriate domestic regulation. GATS does not preclude governments from adopting measures to address internal brain drain by discouraging the movement of health and education professionals from the public to the private sector. Equally no provision in GATS restricts measures by governments relating to foreign patients. Even if full commitments were undertaken in hospital services, for example, GATS would permit a Member to tax the fees paid by foreign patients.[24] The feasibility of

[23] In health, for example, private investors may only be interested in providing a limited range of services at high prices to wealthy patients, leaving the state to deliver complex and expensive treatments to indigent patients.

[24] R. Adlung and A. Carzaniga, 'Trade in Health Services Under GATS' in 79 *Bulletin of the World Health Organization* (2001) 352. The authors have produced an updated version of their paper dated June 2003.

imposing regulatory solutions such as these in a particular state will depend on an appreciation by the government of the potential problems and the presence of the political will to address them, as well as on the state's regulatory capacity to implement these kinds of measures to complement its liberalization initiatives. In many developing countries, a chronic lack of capacity to regulate private suppliers may impair the prospects for effectively ensuring that the public interest is served and progress toward development objectives is achieved where private supply is permitted.

3. *Mode 3: Commercial presence*

As noted above, foreign investment in health and education services would result in the inflow of capital, expansion of employment, and, possibly, the provision of new and improved services. The efficiency and quality of services may be enhanced through the introduction by foreign investors of new technologies in developing countries. Local expertise may be enhanced through opportunities to work with these technologies at facilities established or expanded through foreign investment. In the area of health, at least, the available empirical evidence does not consistently show improvements in cost-effectiveness and service quality associated with the supply of health services by private suppliers, domestic or foreign.[25] Perhaps a more certain benefit from the augmentation of local services through foreign direct investment is that resources for the public-sector would be freed up as a result of reduced demand for public-sector services.

The development of high-quality private facilities through foreign direct investment may have an effect on trade in other modes. Improved local services through foreign investment may reduce reliance on consumption abroad (reducing Mode 2 imports) for the segment of the population for whom that is an alternative and stem the associated loss of foreign exchange. At the same time, such services may enhance opportunities to attract foreign consumers, contributing to Mode 2 exports. Opportunities to work in foreign-owned facilities may reduce the pressure for professionals to emigrate, curtailing trade through the presence of natural persons abroad, reducing exports in Mode 4.

Possible negative effects may also be identified. Most obviously, foreign investment would lead to an outflow of profits to foreign owners. As well, there may be a significant opportunity cost associated with the public investment that may be required in order to attract private investment in developing countries. Foreign investors may crowd out local suppliers. Given the serious and chronic shortages in

---

[25] Blouin, *supra* n. 11.

health care and many education services in most developing countries, however, crowding may not be a serious problem in many cases. The presence of foreign private services suppliers may also contribute to the development of two-tier markets for health and education services. Investment may not flow to where it is most needed from a health and education policy point of view. As noted above, foreign investors are likely to try to cream-skim the most lucrative services leaving the remainder of services to the state and local firms. To the extent that new private firms siphon off workers from public sector and local private sector suppliers foreign investment could contribute to an internal brain drain.[26] Finally, if a two-tier market becomes entrenched, there may be a political cost to the extent that some local consumers no longer see their interests as being served by publicly funded services.

Again, the significance of these possible negative effects will depend on the domestic context. For example, the cost of any public investment necessary to attract foreign direct investment will depend on the degree to which factors encouraging such investment are already present, including local market size. As well, one must ask how the results of a liberalized system would compare with the existing public systems of health and education. It may be possible to address some of the negative effects by GATS consistent domestic policies. The development of cream-skimming and a two-tier market, for example, could be avoided by the imposition of requirements for foreign services suppliers to locate in underserved areas combined with obligations to provide an identified range of services to all citizens at government specified rates. In health care, less intrusive regulation could require a specific number of hospital beds to be set aside for low-income patients at prescribed rates. Similarly, places in schools set up with the assistance of foreign investors could be reserved for disadvantaged segments of the population. The internal brain-drain problem could be mitigated if requirements to train local staff were imposed on foreign investors or measures were adopted to make moving to the private sector unattractive.

The GATS preamble contains a general recognition of the right of WTO Members to regulate and no provision in GATS precludes these kinds of measures. Where a Member has listed a health or education service in its national schedule of commitments, however, the Member's freedom to impose some of these kinds of policies would require that they be covered by a limitation on the Member's obligations. In order to preserve the Member's freedom to limit the number of suppliers in

---

[26] Apparently this occurred in connection with reforms to permit foreign investment in hospitals in Thailand: Chanda, *supra* n. 15.

a particular area, for example, a limitation on the Member's market-access obligation to this effect would be required.

While foreign direct investment originating in developing countries may not be substantial, it does occur in the health and education sectors. For example, one Indian hospital group is seeking to build hospitals in Malaysia, Nepal, and Sri Lanka.[27] The main benefit of these kinds of investments is that they may generate financial benefits in terms of profits repatriated.

4. Mode 4: Presence of natural persons

The movement of health and education professionals from developing countries to provide services abroad has a variety of both costs and benefits. Significantly, developing country professionals working abroad generate remittances to their country of origin. Working in another country may allow professionals to acquire new knowledge and skills which may be employed usefully on their return home.

As against these benefits there are also costs. Providing services abroad results in a reduction in the human resources available for delivery of health and education services in developing countries. The significance of this effect will be highly variable. For some professions in some countries movement abroad will cause or exacerbate local shortages, sometimes severely. In other cases, local surpluses may exist. As well, it may be feasible and cost-effective for some countries to import professionals to replace locally trained professionals who move abroad. Jamaican nurses, for example, commonly move abroad to provide services in the US and Canada and are replaced, to some extent, in Jamaica by nurses from Nigeria, Ghana, and Myanmar.[28] The net effect, however, has been serious shortage of nurses in Jamaica.

Where stays abroad become permanent the movement of health and education professionals becomes a brain drain with the attendant loss of public investment in the education of departed professionals. There is also the question of the distributive impact of remittances which are received by private rather than public hands. While there will be dispersed economic benefits to the use of remitted funds in the local economy, remittances are not directly available to the state to be applied to ensure the achievement of public policy goals.

Again, there are a variety of GATS consistent regulatory measures that may be adopted to counteract possible negative effects associated with increased export trade in Mode 4. Public investment in education

---

[27] Chanda, *supra* n. 15.
[28] WTO Secretariat Note on Health and Social Services, *supra* n. 5.

and training can be safeguarded by requirements to work locally for a period of time upon completion of education and training programmes. India and South Africa impose such requirements. Alternatively, departing professionals could be required to post a bond recoverable upon their return.

The likely effect of migration of health and education professionals to developing countries has been and will continue to be less significant than migration in the other direction. Nevertheless, to the extent that foreign health and education professionals from developed countries may work in developing countries local shortages in particular areas may be overcome. Migration from one developing country to another to address local shortages may be a more common occurrence, as illustrated by the Jamaican nursing example cited above.

III. A PROFILE OF CURRENT GATS OBLIGATIONS: LOW LEVELS OF SPECIFIC COMMITMENTS[29]

A. Introduction

In this section the specific commitments undertaken by WTO Members in health and education services under GATS are discussed. By specifically listing a services sector in its national schedule of commitments, each WTO Member commits to complying with a higher level of obligation under GATS including providing national treatment and not imposing certain restrictions on market access. The level of obligation may be reduced by limitations inscribed by the Member in its national schedule. Even in the absence of specific commitments, health and education services are subject to the limited general disciplines of the GATS, including transparency and the MFN obligation, unless they are excluded as services supplied 'in the exercise of governmental authority'.

B. Health

Along with education, health services are among the least committed services sectors. Only 42 per cent of Members have undertaken

---

[29] The commitments of WTO Members in health and related services are described in more detail in Adlung and Carzaniga, *supra* n. 24. The commitments of countries in education services are summarized in OECD, *CERI Background Document: Current Commitments under the GATS in Education Services* (2002) prepared for the OECD/US Forum on Trade in Education, held in Washington, DC in June 2002.

any specific commitment in relation to a health service.[30] Overall, commitments tend to be positively related to the level of development— only about one-third of the 100 developing and least developed country Members[31] have made commitments in health—though there are some significant exceptions. Botswana, Burundi, the Gambia, Lesotho, Malawi, Sierra Leone, and Zambia, all least-developed countries, undertook commitments in at least one health sector. All but one[32] of the developing countries that have joined the WTO since 1995 have accepted some commitments in health services reflecting the greater negotiating pressure to make commitments experienced by such countries in relation to all services sectors. As well, some developed countries, like Canada, have accepted no obligations in health services. Commitments by the US and Japan are limited to hospital services.

For WTO Members that have made commitments, most have been in medical and dental services (50 of 146 or 34 per cent of all Members) followed by hospital services (41 of 146 or 28 per cent of all Members), 'other health services' (23 of 146 or 16 per cent of all Members), and the services of nurses and other health professionals (21 of 146 or 14 per cent of all Members). Commitments by developing countries follow this same pattern, though the percentage of developing countries making commitments was lower in each category of health services (25 per cent for medical and dental services, 23 per cent for hospital services, 10 per cent for other health services, and 7 per cent for the services of nurses and other health professionals). This pattern suggests that more WTO Members were willing to make commitments in capital-intensive services like hospitals and highly specialized services like those of physicians and dentists as compared to more labour-intensive services, like nursing.[33]

The precise content of Members' commitments varies to some extent based on the express wording of the commitment. Typically, the open-ended category of 'other health services' was left undefined, but a few countries provided their own definitions for the purposes of their commitments. Australia listed only chiropody and podiatry in this category and Belize accepted commitments for epidemiological

---

[30] All statistics in this section were calculated as of 1 January 2004 and so do not include the commitments of Nepal which became a WTO Member in April 2004. Also the statistics are based on the 12 countries that were members of the European Community prior to 1995 constituting one Member. Health insurance is not discussed, though the availability of private health insurance will have implications for access to health services. See Lipson, *supra* n. 22.

[31] For the purposes of this paper, statistics referring to developing countries include least-developed countries. All transition economies have been removed from the category of developing countries except China and Mongolia.

[32] The sole exception is Mongolia.   [33] Adlung, *supra* n. 1.

services and some diagnostic services. Some Members restricted their commitments to granting market access for private hospitals.

In terms of modes of supply, WTO Members making commitments in health services imposed the fewest limitations on their obligations in Mode 2, probably reflecting the view that restrictions on this mode of supply would not be effective, even if they were desirable for some reason. A higher percentage of developing countries made full commitments for Mode 2 trade in health services (except for other health services) compared to the percentage of all WTO Members. A full commitment means that a Member imposed no limit on either the national treatment or market access obligation. Of those Members listing limitations on their obligations in Mode 2 most related to restrictions on the portability of health insurance or horizontal limitations relating to subsidies. These limitations preserve Members' flexibility to refuse to subsidize or reimburse patients for payments made for foreign medical services consumed outside the country.

The relative openness of large developed and developing country markets in Mode 2, including the European Communities for all health services, China for medical and dental services, and the US and Japan for hospital services, suggests a market opportunity for services suppliers from developing countries providing cost-effective or unique health services to attract foreign consumers from those states. Limitations on the availability of public funding to patients who travel abroad would curtail this opportunity somewhat.

Roughly half the WTO Members accepting commitments in health services sectors made full commitments in Mode 1. For all health services, a higher percentage of the developing country Members accepting commitments undertook full commitments. Most Members that did not accept full commitments to provide national treatment and market access for Mode 1 simply recorded their commitments as 'unbound', meaning that no commitment at all was accepted by the Member for that mode. Some of the unbound listings were due to the belief that the delivery of these services was technically unfeasible. Others may reflect uncertainty regarding the scope of the commitment given the fast-evolving nature of electronic delivery of services or concerns about how to regulate service quality. In one of the few specific limitations that cut back Member's obligations in Mode 1, Poland's schedule provides that public insurance need not cover medical care supplied through Mode 1.

Aside from the category of other health services, less than half of WTO Members making commitments in health services gave a full commitment for supply of health services through a commercial presence (Mode 3), though again the percentage of developing countries giving full commitments was higher, especially in relation to the services of nurses and other health professionals. Few Members, however, recorded their Mode 3 commitments as unbound. Many limitations imposed by Members on their obligations in Mode 3 consist of horizontal limitations relating to all services sectors that allow Members to restrict the percentage of permissible foreign ownership or the type of legal form that foreign services suppliers may employ for the purposes of their commercial presence or to require approval of foreign investments. In some cases, countries preserved their ability to impose a requirement for the satisfaction of an economic-needs test before the establishment of a commercial presence would be permitted. Often no specific criteria for the application of the test were set out, contrary to the WTO's scheduling guidelines, leaving a wide discretion to governments regarding its application. Such discretion would permit a Member to impose limits on the number of operations in specific locations and other limitations which are measures that could be used to address some of the possible negative effects of liberalization noted in the taxonomy of possible trade effects but which would otherwise be contrary to the market access obligation. In some cases, requirements for economic-needs tests were included in sector specific commitments for medical, dental, and hospital services. Of developing countries, only Malaysia included such a limitation and only in relation to its commitments for hospital services.

Almost all Members accepting commitments in health services, including most developing country Members, imposed significant limitations on their obligations to permit the presence of natural persons supplying health services (Mode 4). Some Members set out specific limitations on their obligations, but more than 75 per cent described their obligations as 'unbound' for all health services sectors. Limitations specifically applicable to Mode 4 obligations found in Member's schedules consist of quotas and specific training and language requirements. In many cases, Members who listed their obligations as unbound indicated that their obligations were nevertheless subject to their horizontal commitments. Many of these countries undertook to grant Mode 4 access to certain intra-corporate transferees. Typically these commitments relate to certain kinds of persons who work for a foreign business that has operations in a Member's country and who are permitted to enter the country on a temporary basis to work at the business's local operations. Such a commitment in Mode 4 means that access for individuals is conditional on the establishment of a commercial presence. This kind of access is likely to be of marginal value to developing countries who are not engaged in significant outward foreign direct investment, though as noted above, there are some exceptions in this regard. In some cases, Members listed horizontal obligations to provide access that are restricted to a small range of specialists, though often only if labour-market tests are satisfied. The magnitude of restrictions on Mode 4 reflect the political sensitivity of access to the local labour market.

C. Education

Approximately 30 per cent of Members have undertaken a specific commitment in some education sector (44 of 146 Members). Twenty-five out of 30 OECD countries have made a commitment in at least one education sub-sector.[34] For the 100 developing country Members, the percentage taking on commitments was only 17 per cent. As with health services, developing countries that became WTO Members after the Uruguay Round have committed to a higher level of obligation in a wider range of education sectors than the countries that made commitments at the conclusion of the Uruguay Round.

For Members making commitments, all education sectors were the subject of a similar number of commitments: 30 for primary education, 34 for secondary education, 33 for higher education, and 32 for adult education. Only 20 Members made commitments for other education, most leaving this category undefined. In general, WTO Members have put more limitations on their obligations relating to trade in primary and secondary education than on those relating to higher and adult education. Adult education is the sector in which countries have made most full commitments in Modes 1 to 3.

In defining the scope of their commitments in education many Members deviated from the WTO's Classification List and the more detailed Provisional CPC. In primary education, 12 of 30 Members restricted their commitments to a distinctive category of services. Eight of these Members limited their commitments to private education. In secondary education, 16 of 33 Members adopted distinctions not present in the Classification List or the Provisional CPC. Again, most of these restricted commitments to private education. In higher education, 15 of 33 countries adopted their own categories, 10 limiting their commitments to private education. The only developing country to limit its commitments to privately funded education was Mexico. China, however, may have achieved a similar result by excluding national compulsory education from its commitments in primary and secondary education.

---

[34] The five OECD countries that have not made commitments in education services are Canada, Finland, Iceland, Korea, and Sweden.

In terms of modes of supply, all WTO Members accepting commitments in an education sector committed to a high degree of freedom with respect to the consumption by their citizens of education services abroad (Mode 2). Over 85 per cent of Members accepting a commitment in an education services sector gave a full commitment for trade in services in this mode. Few countries either listed their commitments as unbound or inscribed some specific limitation on their obligations. Specific limitations in some countries' schedules relating to Mode 2 allow them to restrict the availability of scholarships for education services provided abroad or to non-nationals. The pattern of commitments for developing country Members is essentially the same as for all Members making commitments.

A high percentage of WTO Members that accepted commitments in education sectors gave full commitments for Mode 1, though the percentages were lower for primary and secondary education than for other education sectors. The pattern of commitments for developing countries who accepted commitments in Mode 1 was the same as for other countries, though a higher percentage recorded their commitments as 'unbound', perhaps reflecting the relatively greater challenge of drafting satisfactory limitations for developing countries. A few Members' schedules allow them to restrict the availability of scholarships for education services provided abroad or to non-nationals.

As with health services, less than one-half of countries accepting commitments in most sectors of education services gave full commitments with respect to Mode 3, commercial presence. The only exception in this regard was adult education which attracted a full commitment from just less than 60 per cent of countries accepting commitments. On the other hand, fewer than 10 per cent of countries accepted no commitments at all in the education sectors listed in their national schedules for Mode 3. All countries recording their commitments as 'unbound' are developing countries.

National schedules thus demonstrate a relatively low commitment to giving full market access and national treatment for education services suppliers operating through a commercial presence, even for those WTO Members undertaking commitments, but a willingness to accept commercial presence with specific or horizontal limitations. The horizontal limitations referred to in relation to health services delivered in Mode 3 and discussed above apply as well to education services supplied in this mode. Few of these limitations appear to be targeted directly at the kinds of measures suggested in the taxonomy of possible effects of trade liberalization as being useful to counteract the negative effects of foreign investment in education services, such as limiting the number of suppliers permitted to serve a particular area, though some broad horizontal limitations may preserve this flexibility. There is little difference in this regard between the commitments of developing countries and other WTO Members.

As with health services, Mode 4 received the lowest level of commitments in education services. Only one country gave a full commitment in any education sector for this mode. Most of the countries that recorded their obligations as 'unbound' referred to their horizontal commitments. In many of these horizontal commitments, Members have provided a limited undertaking to provide market access for some intra-corporate transferees and some specialist professionals that, as indicated previously, will be of limited value to most developing countries. The pattern of commitments for developing country Members is essentially the same as for all Members.

IV. GATS NEGOTIATIONS TO DATE: HEALTH AND EDUCATION ON THE BACK BURNER

There is no sector, including health and education, that is *a priori* excluded from the current round of negotiations. As well, strong export interests exist in some countries in these services. With respect to education, Australia, Canada, New Zealand, the UK and the US are all significant exporters.[35] In health services, the US and many other developed countries as well as a few developing countries have export interests.

Despite these interests, health and education have not been significant subjects of discussion in the current round of negotiations. Health was not the subject of any specific negotiating proposal. Four countries, Australia,[36] Japan,[37] New Zealand,[38] and the US[39] have filed negotiating proposals related to education but none could be characterized as suggesting an aggressive approach to liberalizing trade in education

---

[35] Larsen and Vincent-Lancrin, *supra* n. 17. For example, in 2000, education exports represented 11.8 per cent of Australia's total services exports and ranked as the third largest category of services exports and the 14th largest category of all exports.

[36] *Communication from Australia: Negotiating Proposal for Education Services*, 2001 (S/CSS/W/110).

[37] *Communication from Japan: Negotiating Proposal on Education Services*, 2002 (S/CSS/W/137).

[38] *Communication from New Zealand: Negotiating Proposal for Education Services*, 2001 (S/CSS/W/93).

[39] *Communication from the United States: Higher (Tertiary) Education, Adult Education, and Training*, 2000 (S/CSS/W/23).

services. Each expressly recognizes the important role played by the state in funding, delivering, and regulating education as well as the important link between education and social and economic development. As well, each is limited in its scope. The US proposal only relates to higher and adult education and training by private operators. New Zealand's is largely restricted to some suggestions for clarifications regarding the categories of education services used to schedule specific commitments. The main emphasis in Japan's proposal is the need to maintain quality in education, especially education services supplied cross-border. Australia's communication identifies possible benefits associated with more liberal trade in education services as well as some of the barriers currently impeding trade but the proposal itself is restricted to five principles that are relevant to liberalization initiatives, most of which focus on the maintenance of state sovereignty in this area.

The requests and offers of WTO Members that have been filed with the WTO are confidential. A review of those requests and offers that have been made public to date, however, reveals few that deal with health or education services. With a couple of modest exceptions, the market-access offers that have been made public do not contain improved commitments specifically relating to health or education.[40] Similarly, while the fragmentary nature of the available public information precludes anything like a complete picture, it also appears that few requests have been made for improved market access in health and education services.

All of the EU's requests are publicly available and only two relate to health or education. The EU has asked the US for improved access for private suppliers in the higher education sector and asked the Dominican Republic to drop its MFN exemption for medical, dental, and nursing services.[41]

India has provided comprehensive information on the requests that it has made and received though has not identified the recipient of its requests or the countries from which requests have been

[40] Offers from the following have been made public and can be found on the WTO website in the TN/S/O document series: Australia, Canada, Chile, EU, Iceland, Japan, Liechtenstein, New Zealand, Norway, Slovenia, Turkey, and the US, online at http://www.wto.org/english/tratop_e/serv_e/s_negs_e.htm. Japan has offered some improvements in its commitments regarding Mode 2 trade in higher education services and the US and the EU have offered slight improvements in their commitments in higher education services.

[41] The complete text of the EU's requests has been posted on the internet by the non-governmental organization GATSwatch, online at http://www.gatswatch.org/requests-offers.html. The EU itself has provided a summary of its requests (Summary of the EC's Initial Requests to Third Countries in the GATS Negotiations (1 July 2002), online at http://europa.eu.int/comm/trade/services/gats_sum.htm.

received.[42] In relation to health services, India currently has a commitment only in hospital services. It has received requests for full market access for medical and dental services, and the services of nurses and other health professionals in Modes 1, 2, and 3 as well as some commitments to permit foreign health professionals to operate in India through Mode 4. With respect to hospital services, India has received requests for full commitments in Modes 2 and 4, as well as the removal of its 51 per cent equity limit on foreign investment in hospitals. For its part, India has made requests for full commitments in health professionals in Modes 2 and 4, including the removal of residency and nationality commitments and, with respect to Mode 4, commitments to permit access for health professionals unrelated to businesses operating in Mode 3. As additional commitments, India has requested recognition for the qualifications of Indian medical and dental professionals and nurses.

In education services, India currently has no commitments and has been asked to provide full commitments for higher education, adult education, and other education, including educational testing, community education, and education agency services in Modes 1, 2, and 3. India has requested as additional commitments more transparent mechanisms for the accreditation of courses and programmes provided by education service suppliers, including an appeal process with respect to accreditation decisions.

Australia has made public its request for improved market access for private hospital and private care for the aged services. Australia has not identified the recipient(s) of its request.[43] Other publicly available information disclosed no other requests relating to health or education.

In summary, while both health and education have been the subject of some requests, there is little to indicate that these services have been accorded a high priority in the negotiations by WTO Members.[44] One possible exception is Australia which has described its interest in improved market access for its suppliers of private hospital and care for the aged services as a negotiating priority. Also, India has expressed

---

[42] Government of India, Ministry of Commerce and Industry, Department of Commerce, Trade Policy Division, *Consultation Document on the WTO Negotiations Under the General Agreement on Trade in Services (GATS)*, online at http://commerce.nic.in/wto_counsel_paper.htm.

[43] 'Australia Pushes Export Opportunities for Tourism, Healthcare Businesses', *Media Release* (29 October 2002), online at http://www.trademinister.gov.au/releases/2002/mvt139_02.html.

[44] 'Director-General of WTO and Chairman of WTO Services Negotiations Reject Misguided Claims that Public Services Are under Threat' *WTO Press Release/299* (28 June 2002).

a significant interest in greater mobility for its medical and other health professionals.

V. WHY SO LITTLE INTEREST IN GATS COMMITMENTS IN HEALTH AND EDUCATION?

A. Introduction

The taxonomy of possible effects of trade liberalization set out above shows that there may be benefits arising from liberalization of trade in health and education services. There are likely to be costs as well, though appropriate policies complementing liberalization initiatives can address at least some of the possible negative consequences in a manner consistent with GATS. Nevertheless, so far relatively few countries have made specific commitments in these services and publicly available evidence does not show a strong interest in additional commitments in the current round of negotiations. Why is this?

A variety of possible explanations may be suggested. The most straightforward reason for the low level of existing commitments may be simply that, in some cases at least, no one asked developing country Members for commitments in these sectors during the Uruguay Round. These sectors were not high on negotiators' lists of priorities. As well, in countries in which health and education services are largely supplied through government monopolies, it might have been thought that there was no point in undertaking commitments. It has also been suggested that the commitments in health and education were impeded by a low level of familiarity with GATS among health and education officials and inadequate dialogue between them and trade officials.[45]

The reason most frequently cited for avoiding commitments in health and education services in the current negotiations, however, is uncertainty regarding the nature and effect of GATS commitments. The three main categories of uncertainty may be identified as uncertainty regarding:

- the scope and nature of GATS obligations;
- the trade impact of GATS commitments;
- the likelihood that governments may need or want to adopt future policies in health and education that may be inconsistent with specific commitments in GATS.

[45] OECD Observer, *supra* n. 10.

B. The three uncertainties of GATS

1. *Uncertainty regarding the scope and nature of GATS obligations*

When GATS came into force on 1 January 1995, it was the first set of comprehensive multilateral rules dealing with trade in services. Many provisions in the agreement are novel, including the application to services of concepts like MFN and national treatment that are well known in trade agreements relating to goods but new in the area of services. The scope and nature of GATS is only beginning to be fleshed out in WTO dispute settlement proceedings.

Many commentators and even the WTO Secretariat have expressed some concerns regarding the precise scope of the services agreement because of uncertainty regarding the carve-out for 'services supplied in the exercise of governmental authority'.[46] This expression is defined to mean 'any service that is supplied neither on a commercial basis nor in competition with one or more service suppliers'. The application of the criteria in this definition to health and education services is not straightforward because in many countries private and public providers of health and education coexist and public provision may be implemented through private-sector suppliers. As a result, some aspects of national public health and education systems may be subject to the agreement. For example, if universally available publicly funded health services provided free to consumers were supplied by hospitals or physicians that are organized on a for-profit basis, it could be that such services are provided on a commercial basis and are thus outside the exclusion and subject to the GATS. Some have worried that even if services are delivered directly by the state, such as public schools, the mere existence of private schools seeking to serve the same students means that the exclusion has no application because the public and private schools will be found to be in competition and the services of public schools would then be subject to the agreement.[47]

In response, it must be said that some level of uncertainty is the inevitable consequence of applying a short, broadly worded treaty provision, like the exclusion for services supplied in the exercise of governmental authority, to services that are the subject of a range of complex regulations and methods of delivery like health and education.

---

[46] E.g. M. Krajewski, 'Public Services and Trade Liberalization: Mapping the Legal Framework' in *Journal of International Economic Law* (2003) 341; WTO, Council for Trade in Services, Environmental Services: Background Note by the Secretariat (1998) (S/C/W/46) at 14, 15; WTO, Council for Trade in Services, Education Services: Background Note by the Secretariat (1998) (S/C/W/49) at 4–6.

[47] Among the most prominent critical analyses are S. Sinclair, *GATS: How the World Trade Organization's New 'Services' Negotiations Threaten Democracy* (2000); and J. Grieshaber-Otto and S. Sinclair, *Facing the Facts: A Guide to the GATS Debate* (2002).

As well, the exclusion is likely to be interpreted more generously than the critics fear. The simple coexistence of public and private services should not lead to the conclusion that public services are in competition.[48] Nevertheless, the inability of governments in WTO Member states to define precisely which aspects of national health and education systems are subject to the agreement and which are not has made it difficult to reassure domestic interests that public services are not threatened in any way by GATS and has impeded the progress of domestic discussions regarding how GATS obligations could be helpful in promoting better outcomes in health and education.

This is unfortunate because the application of this exclusion should not be the key concern of policy-makers or those with a stake in health and education. So long as a government has not taken the additional step of accepting specific commitments for health or education services, the remaining GATS obligations that do apply are unlikely to impose meaningful constraints on governments.[49] The main substantive obligation is MFN treatment which does not require providing any degree of access for foreigners to domestic markets.

Uncertainty regarding the scope of the substantive obligations in the GATS that become applicable when specific commitments are undertaken has also been raised as a concern. The national treatment obligation only requires that foreign service suppliers and services be treated no less favourably than like domestic service suppliers and services. Because it is necessary to make an assessment of the likeness of service suppliers or services, the precise impact of this obligation will depend on the facts of each case. In determining the likeness of goods, WTO panels have focused on the attributes of the products and whether they are competitive substitutes in the market. It remains to be seen whether services that are substitutes in this sense may nevertheless be found not to be like for the purposes of the national treatment obligation on other grounds. It is not clear, for example, whether foreign services that are treated differently from domestic services in order to achieve legitimate regulatory objectives, such as consumer protection, should not be considered like services and therefore not protected from such discrimination by the national treatment obligation.[50] Where the national treatment obligation applies, it is

---

[48] J. A. VanDuzer, 'Health, Education and Social Services in Canada: The Impact of the GATS' in *Trade Policy Research* (2004) 303.

[49] D. Luff, 'Regulation of Health Services and International Trade Law' in A. Matoo and P. Sauvé (eds), *Domestic Regulation and Services Trade Liberalization* (2003) 191.

[50] As an example of the kind of uncertainty that could arise in the services context, imagine an Indian medical laboratory that does diagnostic work for patients in India and a British laboratory that performs the same diagnostic work for the same Indian patients over the internet from its location in the UK. Because of its remote location, it may be

not yet clear what differences in treatment will result in less favourable treatment contrary to the obligation.[51] In the few cases dealing with the GATS to date, WTO panels have provided little guidance on these issues. As a result, the effective scope of the national treatment obligation under the GATS is much less certain than the analogous obligation for goods under the GATT, discouraging the making of commitments.[52]

Perhaps the most important area of concern regarding the scope of the substantive obligations in GATS is the application of GATS disciplines on domestic regulation. The preamble of the GATS expressly acknowledges the 'right of Members to regulate' as well as the need to give 'respect to national policy objectives' and the 'particular need for developing countries to exercise this right'. These preambular statements provide an important part of the interpretive context for understanding the substantive standards of the agreement, but are not substantive rules in themselves. With respect to the substantive rules on domestic regulation, the GATS requires that measures relating to qualification requirements and procedures, technical standards, and licensing requirements not nullify or impair a Member's specific commitments in listed sectors by imposing requirements or standards not based on objective and transparent criteria, such as competence

harder for Indian regulators to detect and impose sanctions for non-compliance with quality standards on the British laboratory. The Indian government may want to impose additional regulatory requirements on a foreign-based laboratory to ensure the protection of Indian consumers and the achievement of other regulatory objectives. These might include more onerous reporting requirements or requiring a cash deposit to ensure that any fine imposed to sanction non-compliance would be paid. Consistent with the national treatment obligation, what scope is there to impose these kinds of different regulatory requirements on the British laboratory? For there to be a breach of national treatment, these two service suppliers (or their services) must be found to be like and any difference in treatment must be such as to impair the competitive opportunities in the Indian market for the British laboratory as compared to the Indian laboratory. The scope of the national treatment obligation and the corresponding freedom to treat foreign suppliers differently in these sorts of situations is not clear.

[51] G. Verhoosel, *National Treatment and WTO Dispute Settlement: Adjudicating the Boundaries of Regulatory Autonomy* (2002) at 14–18. These same issues arise with respect to MFN. Abu-Akeel concludes that these issues in the MFN context are difficult and not capable of being resolved by WTO dispute settlement panels. He argues that the Council on Trade in Services should issue guidelines to address these issues: A. K. Abu-Akeel, 'The MFN as it applies to Service Trade: New Problems for an Old Concept' in 33 *Journal of World Trade* (1999) 103, at 115. Matoo suggests that the MFN obligation should only be breached when differences in treatment cannot be justified as necessary to achieve a legitimate non-discriminatory policy objective: A. Matoo, 'MFN and GATS' in T. Cottier and P. Mavroidis (eds), *Regulatory Barriers and the Principle of Non-Discrimination in World Trade Law* (2000) at 77–79.

[52] Some of the difficulties associated with interpreting the national treatment obligation are discussed in J. Trachtman, 'Negotiations on Domestic Regulation and Trade in Services: (GATS Article VI): A Legal Analysis of Selected Issues' in this volume.

and ability to provide the service, or that are more burdensome than necessary to ensure the quality of the service. These vague requirements are hard to apply in the context of health and education services where a variety of goals other than quality of the service, narrowly conceived, are fundamental determinants of public policy. It is not clear to what extent a measure related to, for example, imposing a new universal service obligation as a condition of being permitted to offer hospital services would be considered to relate to the quality of the service. If the measure was found to relate to quality, one may still wonder whether a new universal service obligation would be considered no more burdensome than necessary to ensure the quality of the service.[53] Alternative ways of ensuring the availability of hospital services to the population, such as through the use of some form of incentive, are certainly conceivable. Perhaps one could make arguments regarding the consistency of new universal service obligations and other measures common in the health and education sectors with the domestic regulation requirements. Nevertheless, uncertainty regarding the application of these requirements will discourage listing health and education services and becoming subject to GATS domestic regulation obligations as a result.[54]

Members' decisions regarding what to commit under the GATS have been made more difficult by the unrefined and imprecise categories of education and health services in the WTO's Sectoral Services Classification List and the corresponding divisions under the UN Provisional Central Product Classification. The distinctive architecture of GATS requires each Member to define the category of services activity in which it is willing to accept commitments. In both health and especially education, the Classification List and the Provisional CPC have proven to be inadequate models for countries seeking to make commitments. This is amply demonstrated by the fact that almost half of Members making commitments in education have used different categories of their own invention in their schedules and by the concerns and suggestions regarding education services classifications from two of the countries who have thought most about commitments in education—the US and New Zealand—both of whom focused on classification problems in their proposals for negotiations on education services. The content of 'other education services' in particular requires some further specification. In health as well, concerns have been expressed by WTO Members about the adequacy of the categories for

---

[53] This example is taken from Luff, *supra* n. 49 at 204–206.

[54] A much more comprehensive analysis of the challenges associated with interpreting the domestic regulation obligations is provided in Trachtman, *supra* n. 52.

scheduling services.[55] A simple issue, but one which arises under virtually every national health system, is whether services performed by physicians in a hospital, like most surgery, are hospital services or medical services.[56] While nothing prevents a Member from attempting to resolve these uncertainties by adopting its own classification system and nomenclature, the development and adoption of a single more specific and refined classification system would facilitate scheduling of commitments in a consistent manner and contribute to a common understanding among WTO Members regarding the nature of obligations undertaken.

2. Uncertainty regarding the trade impact of GATS commitments

GATS proponents advocate commitments in health and education that guarantee improved market access for foreign suppliers on the basis that such commitments will promote trade and investment leading to efficiency gains, increased consumer choice, reduced prices, innovation, and technology transfer. The taxonomy of possible effects of trade liberalization set out above describes the process by which such beneficial effects may occur. By creating binding commitments, GATS imposes disciplines on domestic policy-makers who may be tempted to retreat from liberalization to engage in renewed protectionism as well as contributing to the transparency and predictability of domestic regulatory regimes. This is true even if GATS specific commitments simply confirm the status quo, as is the case in many national schedules. The enhanced predictability of a domestic regime bound by GATS commitments should encourage foreign businesses to participate in the market, especially through foreign direct investment.

But it is not clear how much of an effect GATS actually has in terms of increasing trade and investment, much less on the broader development outcomes critical to shaping health and education policy. To date, there is no empirical evidence demonstrating strong linkages between GATS commitments and increased trade or investment.[57]

This does not necessarily mean that GATS has not had any effect or that it could not have effects in the future. Nevertheless, in the areas of health and education, its impact will be restricted by the

---

[55] *Communication from the United States, Health and Social Services*, S/C/W/56 (1998).

[56] Luff, *supra* n. 49 at 198.

[57] WHO and WTO, *WTO Agreements and Public Health: A Joint Study by the WHO and WTO Secretariats* (2002) at 117–118.

existence of significant impediments to trade that operate largely outside existing GATS disciplines. The following are some examples:

- lack of recognition of foreign credentials impeding the movement of professionals abroad and discouraging students from obtaining foreign credentials;
- lack of quality-assurance standards and procedures for assessment which discourage countries from permitting foreign suppliers to deliver services in all modes;
- restrictions on the physical and electronic transmission of educational materials;
- difficulties in obtaining authorization to enter and leave the country for individual services suppliers—including managers, computer specialists, academics and health professionals;
- rules regarding the employment of academics.[58]

The lack of strong evidence of benefits associated with GATS commitments combined with the fact that many barriers to trade in health and education services cannot be readily addressed through existing GATS disciplines discourages countries from negotiating GATS commitments.

3. *Uncertainty regarding the extent to which specific commitments in GATS may preclude future changes in health and education policies*

One of the particular concerns expressed regarding accepting commitments in health and education is that once a state takes this step, its flexibility subsequently to shift direction is lost. Potentially, this could be an important consideration for governments because experiments with market-opening reforms, at least in health care, have often been followed by subsequent rounds of reforms to correct for problems arising with initial reforms.[59] Critics of the GATS worry that if a country decided to commit to national treatment and market access for foreign hospitals operating through a commercial presence, for example, it would be precluded from deciding subsequently to return to a regime requiring the delivery of hospital services through domestic suppliers or under which the state provides the services.

---

[58] These are some of the barriers to trade in education noted in United States: Proposal on Higher (Tertiary) Education, Adult Education, and Training, *supra* n. 39, and Australia: Negotiating Proposal for Education Services, *supra* n. 36. Adlung describes some of these barriers to trade in health services in Adlung, *supra* n. 1.

[59] Epps and Flood discuss experience with several specific types of market reforms in health care which involve increased foreign private participation and the frequent need for a second round of reforms: T. Epps and C. Flood, 'Have We Traded Away the Opportunity for Innovative Health Care Reform? The Implications of the NAFTA for Medicare' in 47 *McGill Law Journal* (2002) 747.

One short answer to this concern is that GATS does not prohibit such a policy change. The agreement expressly contemplates that a Member may withdraw trade concessions made in its national schedule in relation to any service sector at any time on three months' notice to the WTO Council on Trade in Services. Where another WTO Member feels the withdrawal may affect the benefits it receives under the agreement, it may request that the withdrawing Member enter into negotiations with a view to agreeing on a compensating adjustment typically in the form of other trade concessions. Compensatory adjustments must be extended to all WTO Members on an MFN basis. In the event of failed compensation negotiations, the affected Member country may seek arbitration. Where arbitration has been requested, the withdrawing Member cannot make the modification until it has given trade compensation in accordance with the arbitration award. If the withdrawing Member does not do so, any Member who participated in the arbitration may withdraw substantially equivalent concessions in retaliation. If arbitration is not requested by another Member, the withdrawing Member is free to implement the proposed change to its schedule of commitments.

A state could avoid the risk of such a compensation claim by expressly recording any flexibility it foresees as possibly important in the future in the form of an express limitation on its obligations in its national schedule at the time it undertakes specific commitments for health and education.[60] Taking advantage of this feature of GATS, however, requires a very high level of understanding of the demographic, economic, and technological trends affecting such services, which few developing country governments may possess. The challenge of inscribing appropriate limitations may be exacerbated by a lack of engagement by health and education ministries in the trade policy development process. To the extent that scheduling limitations is not a straightforward strategy to safeguard policy flexibility that is thought to be required, countries may choose not to list health and education sectors in their schedules, notwithstanding their right subsequently to withdraw their commitments.

C. Summary

The result of these three uncertainties of GATS is that even where developing countries are willing to liberalize trade in health and education services, the case for expressing such willingness in the form

---

[60] The possible application of the general exceptions in GATS Art. XIV would also have to be considered.

of GATS commitments may not be convincing. Many developing countries may see GATS commitments, including commitments simply to maintain the status quo, as having few certain benefits while imposing constraints, the precise scope of which is hard to predict. While the architecture of the agreement permits Members to preserve their policy flexibility by inscribing limitations on their obligations in their national schedules, doing so imposes a burden that developing countries may be unwilling to bear. In light of the risks to the achievement of the important social policy objectives of domestic health and education systems that are associated with trade liberalization, developing countries may be reluctant to make commitments that may restrict their policy options in any way.

VI. CONCLUSIONS: TOWARD A GATS THAT IS MORE RELEVANT TO HEALTH AND EDUCATION

GATS is not inherently unfriendly to the regulation and delivery of health and education services in ways that achieve development objectives in developing countries. Trade liberalization in health and education services secured under GATS commitments can have some real benefits and many of the negative effects can be addressed through GATS-consistent regulation. GATS does permit Members to decide whether to accept commitments in any area and, if they do, to tailor them in ways consistent with their national policies. It is not surprising, then, that a number of developing and least-developed countries have chosen to make commitments in both areas. Still, most developing countries have not undertaken commitments. Among the main impediments to a GATS that operates more effectively as an instrument to facilitate trade in health and education services consistent with development objectives are the three uncertainties described in the preceding section.

The first step to addressing this problem is to improve understanding of the operation of GATS especially among the health and education communities in developing countries. Efforts by the WTO, the OECD, and others to date have proved insufficient to dispel the misinformation regarding issues like the impact of the agreement on public services that has played such a significant role in the debate over GATS and its effects on health and education. More work is needed to give practical operational content to GATS obligations in order to assist developing country policy-makers to appreciate the impact and the limits of GATS obligations. While this could be undertaken by international organizations and development agencies, some of this work is already being done by developed country governments, such as Canada's, for their internal purposes and could be made available to developing countries.

In terms of other definite steps that may be taken to address the uncertainties of GATS, one option would be to develop reference papers for health and education as was done in the telecommunications sector. The telecommunications reference paper addressed a range of sector-specific issues. It provided some basic, commonly accepted definitions and clarified and established the modalities for the application of key obligations in terms specific to the telecommunications sector. Ultimately, the reference paper was incorporated by reference in the national schedules of many Members. The same approach could be used in relation to health and education services. Developing a common template for specific commitments would economize on scarce negotiating resources in developing countries. As well, in the telecommunications negotiations, the reference paper provided reassurance to domestic regulators regarding the scope and impact of GATS obligations by acknowledging the importance of relevant policy goals in the telecommunication sector, including the right of Members to impose universal service obligations.[61] Given the highly charged negative response to the application of GATS in the areas of health and education, there is widespread suspicion regarding GATS. The adoption of instruments specifically tailored to the exigencies of health and education would help to reassure key national stakeholders. Such confidence building will be an essential condition to the development of Members' interest in GATS commitments.

It is not clear that it is possible to address the uncertainties regarding the application of GATS domestic regulation rules through a reference paper. As a part of the specific commitments of those individual WTO Members that incorporate it in their schedules, a reference paper could only express limitations relating to the Member's market access and national treatment obligations or additional commitments. Nothing in a national schedule can affect the domestic regulations obligations. It would be more appropriate to address the uncertainty related to current domestic regulation rules in the context of the negotiations on these rules. Sector-specific disciplines, like those adopted for accounting services, could be developed to define what kinds of measures relate to the quality of health and education services and how to apply the rule that qualification requirements and procedures, technical standards, and licensing requirements cannot nullify or impair the Member's

---

[61] Luff, *supra* n. 49, and Adlung, *supra* n. 1. Lipson has suggested going much farther to adopt some form of special and differential treatment for developing countries (Lipson, *supra* n. 22).

specific commitments in listed sectors by imposing requirements or standards that are more burdensome than necessary to ensure the quality of the service. To date, such sector-specific work in health and education has not been on the agenda of the Working Party on Domestic Regulation.

Alternatively, separate international instruments dealing with these issues could be negotiated in other multilateral fora, such as the UN Educational, Scientific and Cultural Organization (UNESCO) or the WHO. GATS Article VI.5(b) expressly requires that in determining whether a Member is in conformity with its obligations related to domestic regulation, 'account shall be taken of international standards of relevant international organizations applied by that Member'. In this way, the development of international standards to which a Member subscribed would assist in defining the scope of the Member's obligation.

As well, the development and adoption of a more specific and refined classification system for health and education services would facilitate more consistent scheduling of commitments and contribute to a common understanding among the Members of the WTO regarding the nature of obligations undertaken. Again, especially for developing countries, collective efforts to resolve existing uncertainty are more likely to encourage commitments than leaving it up to individual members to establish their own categories. At the same time, clarity and predictability of GATS obligations would be enhanced by more uniform categories of commitments. This work might be undertaken by the Committee on Specific Commitments, but, so far, has not been. Classification issues could also be addressed in a reference paper.

Support for individual developing countries would also help them to make more effective use of specific GATS commitments in health and education. A significant challenge for many developing countries is the absence of adequate capacity to assess the costs and benefits of GATS commitments in health and education and to conceive and implement an appropriate regulatory regime capable of ensuring that the benefits of trade liberalization are attained in a manner consistent with the achievement of the range of objectives informing government policy related to these areas. At the country level, international development agencies may support local assessment of the costs and benefits of liberalization initiatives, including identifying areas of export potential, such as traditional medicines, and the feasibility of complementary measures in the context of local regulatory capacity and other local conditions. In a recently completed pilot project, the International Trade Centre carried out assessments of trade liberalization with ten developing countries. While this work focused on business-to-business services rather than business-to-consumer services like health and education, it is an example of the kind of support that could be provided.

Whatever improvements are made relating to GATS, inevitably, the agreement will serve only as a complement to other liberalization initiatives. The role of GATS is necessarily limited because many of the impediments to increased trade in health and education lie outside the disciplines of the agreement. International development agencies and international organizations will play a number of key roles in addressing these barriers. Continued research on the effects of liberalization in health and education services not only on trade and investment, but also on accessibility, internal and international migration of health and education professionals, and the scope for domestic policy measures to complement and manage the effects of liberalization by organizations like the WHO, UNESCO, the OECD, the World Bank, and others will be essential.[62] One of the largest impediments to trade in health and education will continue to be the absence of recognition of foreign credentials and experience of health and education professionals. Quality-assurance and accreditation standards are still largely national. UNESCO has played a useful role in coordinating the development of international standards agreements in education.[63] The WHO has developed accreditation guidelines for hospitals and medical laboratories that can be applied by national agencies. These kinds of efforts facilitate international trade in health and education and help to provide a basis for regulating the globalized aspects of these activities so as to ensure that consumer protection and other domestic policy priorities are promoted. International development agencies may also play a role in facilitating adoption of technology forming the backbone of electronic supply of health and education services. This mode of supply promises significant benefits in terms of increasing access while involving few negative effects for developing countries.

All these efforts and others outside the scope of GATS are likely to have a more substantial impact on trade in health and education services than commitments under the GATS. Nevertheless, GATS has the potential to play an important complementary role. Taking the steps identified above could assist in the realization of this potential. Whether

---

[62] Chanda, *supra* n. 15.

[63] See e.g. *Convention on the Recognition of Qualifications Concerning Higher Education in the European Region*, co-sponsored by the Council of Europe and UNESCO, which was concluded in April 1997 to facilitate international exchanges of students and scholars by establishing standards for the international evaluation of secondary and post-secondary credentials. Signatories include the EU, many Eastern European countries, Australia, Israel, the US, and Canada. Appendix II to WTO Secretariat Note on Education Services, *supra* n. 46, lists other recognition instruments.

WTO Members are willing to take these or other steps to facilitate GATS commitments in health and education, however, is not obvious. To date, health and education have not received significant attention from WTO Members. No doubt, this is because the commercial opportunities in these sectors pale in comparison to those in other areas. As well, there is a fierce debate in many countries regarding the virtues of private commercial participation in health care and education. This has created a difficult domestic political environment in many countries that may discourage them from attaching priority to improving health and education disciplines in the WTO. Nevertheless, widespread concerns about the impact of the GATS on health and education have been the source of impassioned critiques of the agreement that have seriously tainted the public view of GATS. The public rehabilitation of the agreement in addition to the economic benefits that may flow from GATS-secured liberalization in health and education argue in favour of greater attention to the application of GATS to health and education services.

9

Negotiations on Domestic Regulation and Trade in Services (GATS Article VI): A Legal Analysis of Selected Current Issues

JOEL P. TRACHTMAN

I. INTRODUCTION

Services negotiations will be an important component of the Doha Development Round. One critical potential limit on liberalization of trade in services is domestic regulation that is intended to achieve purposes other than protection from competition. Here, developing countries, like other countries, have two goals. They wish to open up foreign markets, but they wish to retain as much domestic policy flexibility as possible.

Regulatory criteria have already served as barriers to developing country provision of services in developed countries.[1] And, in general, developed countries maintain more extensive regulation of services than developing countries. So, developing countries may be served by further disciplines on domestic regulation. On the other hand, developing countries require flexibility to maintain, and to extend, their prudential regulation. As economies develop, the need for additional regulation may arise. Therefore, it is important for developing countries to retain flexibility to apply regulation suited to their developmental goals and stage of development.

There are many ways to negotiate disciplines on domestic regulation.

- First, horizontal disciplines may be applied. These horizontal disciplines are generally rather broad in structure, including rules of non-discrimination, proportionality tests, least trade restrictive alternative tests, requirements for compliance with international

---

[1] E.g. *Final Report of the Panel in the Matter of Cross-Border Trucking Services*, NAFTA Arbitral Panel, Secretariat File No. USA-MEX-98-2008-01 (6 February 2001), online at http://www.ustr.gov/enforcement/trucking.pdf; *United States—Measures Affecting the Offshore Supply of Gambling and Betting Services*, WT/DS285/4.

standards, and requirements for recognition of foreign regulation. These types of horizontal disciplines generally leave some room for interpretation through dispute settlement. Under the General Agreement on Trade in Services (GATS) as originally agreed, only the most-favoured-nation (MFN) and national treatment non-discrimination rules applied directly, and the national treatment obligation only applied to the extent that the sector was included in the Member state's schedule and only to the extent that the Member state did not qualify its adherence to the national treatment requirement. We discuss below the weakness of original GATS proportionality tests.

- Second, these same types of disciplines may be applied instead on a sectoral basis. This is the main project of the Article VI:4 Work Programme with respect to requirements beyond national treatment and MFN.
- Third, and less explicitly, particular regulatory barriers may be requested specifically to be reduced or otherwise ameliorated. So, instead of relying on the interpretation and application of a general requirement, a Member state may specifically request reduction of a particular barrier. This type of approach has the advantage of specificity: Member states know what they must give up in terms of their regulatory structure and can make a specific and considered decision to do so or not. Article XVIII of GATS specifically provides for additional types of commitments. However, this approach does not appear to be in common usage.

It may be difficult for developing countries to argue for asymmetric obligations in this area, i.e. greater disciplines on developed countries than on developing countries. Equal general obligations should be evaluated before acceptance to determine their impact on existing and potential developing country regulation. The general disciplines that exist today are somewhat asymmetric in the wrong direction: they seem to discipline new regulation more strongly than existing regulation, and so may be expected to have a greater restrictive effect on developing countries.

While this asymmetry should be revised, developing countries should not broadly reject the possibility of greater disciplines on domestic regulation, especially if GATS commitments may begin otherwise to address service areas of interest to developing countries. For example, immigration controls should be understood as largely motivated by protectionism, and should be understood as a barrier to trade in services. Whether immigration controls are understood as pure protectionism, like a quota on goods, or as a kind of regulatory protectionism, with a valid collateral purpose, they are intensely relevant to negotiations on trade in services.

II. STATE OF PLAY

This section is intended to describe the current GATS treatment of domestic regulation. While our main concern is Article VI, it is important to examine first the existing disciplines on domestic regulation under the national treatment obligation of GATS. This examination will allow us to evaluate the extent of existing discipline on domestic regulation. Furthermore, there seems to be some level of agreement among negotiators that disciplines under Article VI:4 should not overlap those under Articles XVI (market access) and XVII (national treatment).[2]

A. National treatment under Article XVII

Article XVII:1 of GATS provides that:

In the sectors inscribed in its schedule, and subject to any conditions and qualifications set out therein, each Member shall accord to services and service suppliers of any other Member, in respect of all measures affecting the supply of services, treatment no less favourable than that it accords to its own like services and service suppliers.

Thus, national treatment under GATS is not universal, but is subject to the positive listing of the relevant service sector in the relevant state's schedule.[3] In addition, it is subject within each listed sector to the negative listing of any exception to the national treatment obligation in that schedule. Deciding that national treatment should not be a general principle as in the General Agreement on Tariffs and Trade (GATT), but a concession to be bargained over is one of the distinctive features of the GATS. The core of a non-discrimination obligation such as national treatment is the comparison between the favoured good, service, or service supplier and the disfavoured one. Article XVII sets up the comparison as being one between 'like' services or service suppliers, referring on its face to the 'like products' concept articulated pursuant to Article III of GATT.

---

[2] In November 2005, an Appellate Body report with respect to *US—Measures Affecting the Cross-border Supply of Gambling and Betting Services* was delivered, just as this volume went to press. In a case of first instance, the Appellate Body misinterpreted the scope of the prohibition of the market access requirements of the GATS, breaching the divide between Article VI:4 and Article XVI. Article XVI prohibits limitations on the number of service suppliers, or the total value of service transactions, in the form of numerical quotas. The Appellate Body found that a qualitative regulatory ban on electronic gambling, which naturally includes electronic gambling supplied from abroad, is covered by this prohibition of numerical quotas. While it is true that ban can be assimilated to 'zero quotas' as a matter of theory, the Appellate Body failed to attend to the purpose of the ban in this case.

[3] See A. Mattoo, 'National Treatment in the GATS: Corner-Stone or Pandora's Box?' in *Journal of World Trade* (1997) at 107.

What makes two services 'like'? For example, is the underwriting of a bond issue 'like' a bank lending transaction? If so, why are different reserve requirements and capital requirements applicable? Does it matter for regulatory purposes that one transaction is effected by a bank that accepts insured deposits? Similarly, is internet telephony 'like' standard telephone service? More fundamentally, is it permissible to make distinctions between services on the basis of the identity and structure of the service supplier as well as the way the service appears to the consumer? While it would be plausible to attempt to apply the *Border Tax Adjustments* factors to services, it is not clear that these parameters of likeness make sense even in GATT. And of course, the word 'like' has meant different things in different contexts, even within GATT.

The majority of the Appellate Body in *EC—Asbestos* found that 'likeness' under Article III:4 is, 'fundamentally, a determination about the nature and extent of a competitive relationship between and among products'.[4] To perform such an assessment the Appellate Body recalled that the four classic, and basic, criteria, derived from the *Border Tax Adjustment* report[5]—(i) the physical properties of the products in question, (ii) their end uses, (iii) consumer tastes and habits vis-à-vis those products, and (iv) tariff classification[6]—are to be used as tools in the determination of this competitive relationship between products. These criteria do not exhaust inquiry.[7] This approach is intended to approximate the competitive relationship between the relevant goods—it is not as accurate or refined as simply testing cross-elasticity of demand. But the more important point is that this test is relatively ignorant of factors that motivate regulation. The economic theory of regulation suggests that regulation is necessary precisely where consumers cannot adequately distinguish relevant goods—where they are in close competitive relation. Thus, a competitive relationship test for likeness will often result in a finding that goods that differ by the parameter addressed by regulation are indeed like, and should be treated the same.

Under pre-World Trade Organization (WTO) GATT Article III jurisprudence, regulation of production processes has been considered not 'subject to' Article III, and is therefore an illegal quantitative restriction under Article XI, unless an exception applies under Article XX. The product/process distinction serves as a kind of territorially based allocation of jurisdiction, in which the product, which travels to the importing state, is permitted to be regulated by the importing state. On the other hand, the production process, which is assumed to take place in the

---

[4] Appellate Body Report, *EC—Asbestos*, WT/DS135/AB/R at para. 99. Note the different opinion with regard to the very specific aspects mentioned in para. 154.
[5] Working Party Report, *Border Tax Adjustments*, adopted 2 December 1970, *BISD* 18S/97.   [6] *Ibid.*
[7] *EC–Asbestos*, *supra* n. 4 at para. 101.

exporting state, is not 'subject to' Article III, and therefore unprotected from the strict scrutiny of Article XI (and regulation by the host state is only permitted if justified under Article XX).

The situation is quite different in GATS, where regulation of service providers is expressly validated, and subjected to the national treatment criterion.[8] Because of the fact that in many services, the service provider—person or firm—may itself be a part of the continuing nature of the service, a different arrangement seems appropriate. That is, it seems less obvious (if it is at all obvious in the goods sector) that the service importing state should not have equal rights to regulate the service provider itself, even though on the territory of the home country. In other words, the process by which a service is 'produced' (a loan issued, a professional trained) may determine the actual characteristics of the ultimate service 'product' (the loan, the advice, the treatment). This would validate traditional institutional regulation of most types of financial institutions, as well as regulation of the structure of law firms or other types of service providers.

Furthermore, we must distinguish between the two main vehicles for trade in services: cross-border provision (including consumption abroad) and commercial presence. In cases of commercial presence, the foreign service provider would, at least to some extent, be present in the territory of the service 'importing' state, and thus would be more naturally subject to the full territorial jurisdiction of that state. The need for commercial presence indeed reflects the fact that a service is often 'produced' and 'consumed' simultaneously and in the same place. We have a much less 'natural'—and more difficult—problem of allocation of regulatory jurisdiction in connection with cross-border provision of services, whereby production and consumption need not happen in the same place. However, as seems to be recognized in Article XVII, the 'importing' state should not, *prima facie*, be prevented from regulating the service provider in these cases.

Interestingly, the structure of Article XVII seems, on its face, to indicate that a national service regulation imposed on a foreign service provider must meet two tests: it must provide (i) treatment no less favourable than that accorded domestic like services, and (ii) treatment no less favourable than that accorded domestic like-service providers. Therefore, even if the service providers are not 'like', and there is thus no possible basis for finding illegal discrimination between them, it is still possible that the services they provide may be 'like', giving rise to a claim of violation of the requirement of national treatment. This might on its face seem an absurd result, and might invalidate, for example, a regulation that requires a bank to maintain reserves different from those

---

[8] Mattoo, *supra* n. 3.

maintained by an insurance company prior to making a loan, as while the service providers might not be 'like', the services are.

Thus, a better reading would read the two requirements above in the disjunctive, i.e. to separate the evaluation of treatment of services from the evaluation of treatment of service providers.[9] It would simply evaluate regulation of services, as services, by determining whether the regulation treats 'like' services alike, full stop. If this were the case, regulation of service providers would be evaluated to determine only whether like service providers, as service providers, are treated alike. Using this interpretation, there would be no violation of national treatment if like services were treated differently where the reason for the difference in treatment is the regulation of the service provider, as service provider. This is likely to be the interpretation that a WTO panel or the Appellate Body would apply.

In effect, such an approach would replicate a kind of product/process distinction as a service/service provider distinction. But by contrast to the case of products, host state regulation of the 'process' or the service provider—often geographically located in the host state—would be validated (subject only to a strict national treatment constraint). Regulations regulating the service, as such, would only be evaluated to determine whether like services are treated alike, while regulations regulating the service provider, as such, would only be evaluated to determine whether like service providers are treated alike. The WTO Dispute Settlement Body would be required to distinguish between regulation of services and regulation of service providers. In addition, the analogy to products might be taken one step further, suggesting stronger constraints on host state regulation of the service provider than on the service.

Thus far, GATT–WTO dispute resolution has been unable to provide a predictable, consistent approach to determining when products are 'like'. We cannot expect GATS dispute resolution to do better. Thus, for example, we might ask whether two accountants, each with advanced university degrees from universities in different states, are 'like service providers'. Are two banks, each from different states where they are required to establish different levels of reserves, 'like service providers'? Similarly, are the loans provided by these two banks 'like services'? Under GATT jurisprudence, these questions cannot be answered predictably, or in the abstract, but must be determined on a case-by-case basis. While this jurisprudence results in a degree of unpredictability, the Appellate Body has now addressed several cases, providing experience in how these multiple factors are likely to be viewed and applied. The question

---

[9] But see Panel Report, *EC—Bananas*, WT/DS27/R/USA para. 7.322 (considering that 'like' service suppliers are producers of 'like' services).

for us is whether this situation of case-by-case analysis by the dispute settlement mechanism is superior to a more discrete, *ex ante*, specification that could be provided by treaty-making or other quasi-legislative processes?

Once services or service providers are determined to be 'like', it is necessary to determine that the measure imposes 'less favourable treatment' on the foreign service or service provider, compared to the domestic ones. In its *EC—Asbestos* decision, the Appellate Body emphasized that this is a distinct analysis, and that not every national measure that treats foreign goods differently from domestic goods would result in *less favourable treatment*.

To summarize, the national treatment obligation is theoretically capable of being used to scrutinize and find illegal domestic regulation that (i) treats like products differently, and (ii) less favourably. These terms are difficult to define, and are in flux, but where there is a compelling sense of protectionism, as opposed to good faith regulatory differentiation, panels and the Appellate Body are likely to find a violation.

B. Article VI

Article VI (domestic regulation) spells out general obligations for service sectors that have been included by contracting parties in their national schedules, except for measures that are covered by reservations in these schedules under Article XVII (national treatment) and XVI (market access).

In vague terms, Article VI:1 provides that domestic regulations, applied in a sector that a Member has agreed to include under specific liberalization commitments, must be administered in a 'reasonable, objective, and impartial manner'. It is possible that this requirement—especially its reasonableness prong—may be employed and developed in WTO dispute settlement to impose substantive obligations of proportionality in connection with domestic regulation. Interestingly, and provocatively, the relevant portions of the dictionary definition of 'reasonable' include 'in accordance with reason; not irrational or absurd', 'proportionate', and 'within the limits of reason; not greatly less or more than might be thought likely or appropriate'.[10] The limitation of this discipline to the 'manner of administration' may be important, although it will be difficult to separate the manner of administration from the substance of rules.

Article VI also includes procedural guidelines requiring that decisions in cases where the supply of a service requires authorization in the host country must be issued 'within a reasonable period of time', and that

---

[10] *The New Shorter Oxford English Dictionary* (1993).

signatories establish tribunals and procedures to process potential complaints by foreign service suppliers.

Article VI:4 of GATS calls on the Council for Trade in Services (CTS) to develop any necessary disciplines to ensure that measures relating to qualification requirements and procedures, technical standards, and licensing requirements do not constitute unnecessary barriers to trade in services. We will discuss the Article VI:4 Work Programme and its fruits below.

Prior to the agreement and entry into force of more specific rules under Article VI:4, disciplines on national measures are available under Article VI:5 in sectors in which the importing Member has undertaken specific commitments. In order for these disciplines to apply, two sets of criteria must be satisfied:

(1) The licensing or qualification requirements or technical standards must nullify or impair specific commitments in a manner that could not reasonably have been expected at the time the specific commitments were made;
(2) the measure must be (a) not based on objective and transparent criteria, or (b) more burdensome than necessary to ensure the quality of the service, or (c) in the case of licensing procedures, in itself a restriction on the supply of the service.

We examine these two criteria in turn.

1. Nullification or impairment

Nullification or impairment (N/I) has served as a central feature in GATT and WTO dispute resolution. Under Article XXIII of GATT, redress pursuant to the dispute resolution system of GATT is only available in the event of N/I. Where a provision of WTO law is violated, nullification or impairment is presumed. On the other hand, it is possible, although infrequent, for N/I to serve as the basis for a successful complaint in the absence of an actual violation of GATT: so-called non-violation nullification or impairment. Article VI:5 of GATS incorporates this concept of non-violation nullification or impairment.

In the leading non-violation nullification or impairment case, *Film*,[11] the Panel reviewed in detail the basis for certain United States (US) expectations, in order to decide whether the US had 'legitimate expectations' of benefits after successive tariff negotiation rounds. As the complaining party, the US was allocated the burden of proof as to its

---

[11] Panel Report, *Japan—Measures affecting Consumer Photographic Film and Paper*, WT/DS44/R (98-088VI), adopted by Dispute Settlement Body 22 April 1998.

legitimate expectations. In order for the US to meet this burden, it was required to show that the Japanese measures at issue were not reasonably anticipated at the time the concessions were granted. Where the measure at issue was adopted after the relevant tariff concession, the Panel established a presumption, rebuttable by Japan, that the US could not have reasonably anticipated the measure.

The import of this approach in the services context is clear. The complaining party must show that the measures attacked were not reasonably anticipated. Thus, long-standing regulatory practices or circumstances are protected. This provides a certain advantage to developed countries, as compared to developing countries that may be establishing new regulatory regimes. Furthermore, this understanding means that the domestic circumstances as they are form a background for all concessions; as a matter of negotiation strategy, members of GATS must recognize this and bear the burden of negotiating an end to existing measures that reduce the benefits for which they negotiate. It is also clear, as described in more detail below, that Article VI:5 will not impose substantial discipline on existing domestic regulation, placing a greater burden on Article VI:4 as a source of discipline.

It is worthwhile to compare this structure with that applicable to goods under the GATT and under the two WTO agreements applicable to regulatory standards: the Agreement on Technical Barriers to Trade (TBT) and the Agreement on the Application of Sanitary and Phytosanitary Standards (SPS). Neither GATT nor these agreements include the N/I requirement in the prohibition itself. Therefore, in connection with trade in goods, determination of a violation of a provision of a covered agreement results in *prima facie* N/I under Article 3:8 of the Dispute Settlement Understanding (DSU), placing the burden of rebutting the existence of N/I on the respondent. In the context of Article VI:5 of GATS, without N/I, there is no violation. Without a violation, there is no *prima facie* N/I. Consequently, it will be for the complaining party to show nullification or impairment. This will make it more difficult for national services regulation to be addressed under Article VI:5.

We may speculate as to why GATS relies on the N/I concept so heavily in this context. N/I is an extremely vague standard, but one which by itself has been difficult to meet. Thus, in the absence of an ability to negotiate more specific disciplines on national regulation, N/I provides a modicum of more general discipline. It might be viewed as a 'least common denominator', insofar as the parties could agree not to nullify or impair concessions earnestly made, but could not agree on more pervasive, blanket restrictions on their national regulatory sovereignty. Thus, Article VI:5 is first and foremost merely a standstill obligation.

2. *The necessity test*

Under this additional component of the GATS Article VI:5 test, we focus on the requirement (incorporated from Article VI:4(b)) that the national measure not be more burdensome than necessary to ensure the quality of the service. Even if it is possible to show that a national measure nullifies or impairs service commitments, a complainant would still be required to show that the national measure does not comply with the criteria listed in Article VI:4, the most likely of which is the necessity test examined here.

Until the *EC—Asbestos* and *Korea—Various Measures on Beef* decisions of the Appellate Body, 'necessity' was generally interpreted as requiring the domestic regulation to be the least trade restrictive method of achieving the desired goal. In *Korea—Various Measures on Beef*, the Appellate Body interpreted the necessity test of Article XX(d) to imply a requirement for balancing among at least three variables:

> In sum, determination of whether a measure, which is not 'indispensable', may nevertheless be 'necessary' within the contemplation of Article XX(d), involves in every case a process of weighing and balancing a series of factors which prominently include the contribution made by the compliance measure to the enforcement of the law or regulation at issue, the importance of the common interests or values protected by that law or regulation, and the accompanying impact of the law or regulation on imports or exports.[12]

In the context of Article VI:4(b), the reference is to measures 'not more burdensome than necessary to ensure the quality of the service'. The last clause could be very interventionist. It could restrict not just the means to attain a given regulatory goal but even the types of regulatory goals that might be achieved, as when the regulatory goal is not to maintain the quality of the service but to avoid some other externalization or regulatory harm by the service provider. For example, if a bank is required to maintain a particular reserve in relation to a loan, is that necessary to ensure the quality of the service? Many types of service regulation might be subject to similar, inappropriate, attack. This provision should be revised.

Furthermore, in a placement comparable to the inclusion of the N/I criterion in the substantive prohibition, here the necessity criterion is included as a parameter of the substantive prohibition, in addition to being included in the exceptional provisions of Article XIV(c). Therefore, in order to make out a violation of Article VI:5 under this clause, the national measure will be required to be shown to be unnecessary in the sense described above. Then, in order for the respondent to claim an

---

[12] Appellate Body Report, *Korea—Various Measures on Beef*, WT/DS161/AB/R and WT/DS169/AB/R at para. 164.

exception under XIV(c), it will be required to show that it is necessary in the broader sense defined there. One interesting question involves the burden of proof. Under the products jurisprudence of the Appellate Body, it appears that the complainant will be required to show the lack of necessity under Article VI:5, while the responding state would ordinarily be required to prove the affirmative defence of necessity under Article XIV(c). This is at least an odd legal circumstance, where each side is allocated the burden of proof on the same issue at different phases. The complaining state, say for example the European Community (EC) in an attack on US separation of commercial from investment banking, would be required to show that the US regulatory approach is 'unnecessary' under Article VI:5, while the US would be required to demonstrate its necessity under Article XIV(c).

In 1998, the CTS adopted the *Disciplines on Domestic Regulation in the Accountancy Sector* (the 'Accountancy Disciplines'),[13] developed by the GATS Working Party on Professional Services (now the Working Party on Domestic Regulation). These disciplines apply to all Member states that have made specific commitments in accountancy (positive list) but do not apply to national measures listed as exceptions under Articles XVI and XVII (negative list). They generally articulate further and tighten the principle of necessity: that measures should be the least trade-restrictive method to effect a legitimate objective. In fact, these provisions replicate requirements that have been imposed in the EC pursuant to the European Court of Justice's (ECJ) single market jurisprudence. They also replicate the approach of the EC's General System Directives on professions, codifying principles of proportionality, or necessity. They have the following features relevant to this paper:

- Necessity: Member states are required to ensure that measures relating to licensing requirements and procedures, technical standards, and qualification requirements and procedures are not prepared, adopted or applied with a view to, or with the effect of creating unnecessary barriers to trade in accountancy services. Such measures may not be more trade restrictive than necessary to fulfil a legitimate objective, including protection of consumers, the quality of the service, professional competence, and the integrity of the profession. As will be clear from the discussion above, this necessity requirement is substantially stronger than that contained in Article VI:5 of GATS.

---

[13] WTO, *Disciplines on Domestic Regulation in the Accountancy Sector*, S/L/64 (17 December 1998) (reprinted in *WTO Focus* (December 1998) 10–11). There is an interesting issue, beyond the scope of this paper, regarding the legal status of this type of WTO 'secondary legislation', both within the WTO and in Member states.

- Qualification requirements: Member states must take account of qualifications acquired in the territory of another Member state, on the basis of equivalency of education, experience, and/or examination requirements. Examinations or other qualification requirements must be limited to subjects relevant to the activities for which authorization is sought.
- Technical standards: technical standards must be prepared, adopted, and applied only to fulfil legitimate objectives. In determining conformity, Member states must take account of internationally recognized standards (of international organizations) applied by that member.

It is worth noting that the EC has stated that the following should be considered in defining necessity under Article VI:4: 'A measure that is not the least trade restrictive to trade will not be considered more burdensome/ more trade restrictive than necessary so long as it is not disproportionate to the objective stated and pursued.'[14] This is substantially more lenient in respect of domestic regulation than the definition of 'necessity' developed in GATT–WTO jurisprudence. Furthermore, it is not clear precisely what 'disproportionate' means in this context. Proportionality *stricto sensu* inquires whether the means are 'proportionate' to the ends: whether the costs are excessive in relation to the benefits.[15] It might be viewed as cost–benefit analysis with a margin of appreciation, as it does not require that the costs be less than the benefits. At the same time that it prefers proportionality and necessity to a least trade-restrictive alternative test, the EC seems to suggest that 'the validity, or rationale, of the policy objective[s] must not be assessed'.[16]

C. Recognition and necessity

Necessity has a complex relationship with recognition. That is, a necessity test, interpreted as a requirement that the national measure be the least trade-restrictive alternative reasonably available to address the regulatory concern, can either be an absolute requirement or a relative requirement. Thus, a less restrictive option might make sense irrespective of the home regime or conversely might only be justified in reference to the home country regulatory regime, as a *complementary* measure. Judgments based on the former assessment reflect a high degree of judicial activism and are unlikely to be found legitimate.

[14] WTO, *Communication from the European Communities and Their Member States: Domestic Regulation: Necessity and Transparency*, S/WPDR/W/14 (1 May 2001) para. 22. Note that the Appellate Body may be understood to have adopted a similar position in *EC—Asbestos* and *Korea—Beef*.

[15] N. Emiliou, *The Principle of Proportionality in European Law: A Comparative Study* (1996) at 6.   [16] WTO, *supra* n. 14, para. 17.

In the latter case, where the home country regulatory regime satisfies the host country concerns, necessity may require recognition. This would be an extreme interpretation of necessity as least trade-restrictive alternative analysis, stating in effect that *no* regulatory intervention on the part of the importing country is necessary at all. The least restrictive alternative is to do nothing. We have seen this in the ECJ's jurisprudence, and there are also treaty provisions reflecting this concept in Article 4 of the SPS Agreement and Article 2.9 of the TBT Agreement. Under this interpretation, recognition may be mandated by *judicial fiat*.

Note that Article VII of GATS and paragraph 3 of the Annex on Financial Services, in contrast, do not require recognition, but merely authorize it. Although a strong GATS standard of necessity might eventually lead to such judicially required recognition, this is unlikely to be the case under current treaty language for reasons we will come to in the last section. But the necessity test might nevertheless mandate partial recognition of some regulations and not others, whereby partial recognition becomes the operational consequence of the principle of proportionality. It is important to note that the Accountancy Standards require recognition of professional qualifications in accountancy.

As noted above, the Accountancy Disciplines include a greatly enhanced necessity test, applicable within that sector.

D. International standards

GATS, like GATT, does not specifically require the use of international standards, and provides weaker incentives for the use of international standards than the SPS Agreement or the TBT Agreement. As noted above, Article VI:5(b) requires that account be taken of compliance with international standards where a Member state's compliance with Article VI:5(a) is being evaluated. This is a nod toward a safe harbour for states that comply with international standards, although it should provide only very modest incentive effects, because of the weakness of Article VI:5(a). It does not provide a presumption of compliance, as do Article 2.5 of the TBT Agreement and Article 3.2 of the SPS Agreement.

The Accountancy Disciplines require that Member states take account of internationally recognized standards of international organizations in determining conformity with technical standards.[17] This is a different and additional requirement. Under Article VI:5(b), compliance with international standards is taken into account in determining the compliance of a Member's regulation with WTO law.[18] Under the Accountancy

---

[17] WTO, *supra* n. 13, para. 26.
[18] Article VI(5)(b) refers to standards 'of relevant international organizations', which are defined as 'international bodies whose membership is open to the relevant bodies of

Disciplines, a Member state must take compliance with international standards into account in determining the acceptability of foreign service providers. This is a gentle shove toward recognition based on essential harmonization.

III. ADDITIONAL ISSUES

A. The Article VI:4 Work Programme

The Article VI:4 Work Programme was intended to deal over time with certain regulatory barriers to trade in services, through decisions made by the CTS under its authority. The WTO Secretariat, with the assistance of Member states, has prepared a list of examples of measures to be addressed by disciplines under GATS Article VI:4.[19] These examples included, *inter alia*, residency requirements, failure to recognize foreign qualifications, and national standards that diverge from international standards. By focusing on examples of regulatory barriers that service suppliers actually face, it is possible to target additional disciplines more precisely. Developing countries should participate actively in this process in order to focus attention on the barriers that their service providers face.

B. Sectoral versus horizontal treatment

So far, the Article VI:4 Work Programme has operated sectorally, and only in the single sector of accountancy. However, it may be that other professional service sectors, and even other service sectors, may be amenable to similar types of disciplines. Thus, it would be possible to evaluate application of similar necessity, equivalence, and other disciplines on a horizontal basis.

The proposed draft annex on domestic regulation prepared by Japan suggests adoption of the core disciplines contained in the Accountancy Disciplines, with some modifications, on a horizontal basis.[20] This would retain the possibility for separate, additional, or alternative disciplines on a sectoral basis.

at least all Members of the WTO'. This definition might exclude, for example, the Basle Committee.

[19] Informal Note by the Secretariat, Working Party on Domestic Regulation, *Examples of Measures to be Addressed by Disciplines under GATS Article VI:4*, JOB(01)/62 (10 May 2001) (latest version is JOB(02)/20/Rev.5, dated 29 April 2003). See also Note by the Secretariat, Council for Trade in Services, *Article VI:4 of the GATS: Disciplines on Domestic Regulation Applicable to All Services*, S/C/W/96 (1 March 1999).

[20] *Communication from Japan, Draft Annex on Domestic Regulation*, JOB(03)/45/Rev.1, revised 2 May 2003.

C. Relationship to immigration and Mode 4 interests of developing countries

Immigration and Mode 4 interests of developing countries have received much attention in the Doha Round. These issues should be addressed directly, with specific commitments regarding the relationship between immigration rules and market access. Immigration might be understood as a 'border measure' not unlike a tariff or a quota, while domestic regulation is an 'internal measure'. While this distinction should not be accorded great substantive impact, it may be useful to consider the approach to immigration and Mode 4 commitments as part of general liberalization, while domestic regulation issues are treated separately.

D. Dependence of domestic regulation disciplines on commitments

Existing disciplines in Article VI:1 and VI:5 are dependent on whether the Member state in question has undertaken specific commitments in the relevant sector. This is not the procedure followed in the TBT and SPS Agreements, but may seem more relevant in the field of services.

E. Mutual recognition and economic integration

Under GATS Article VII, Member states that develop mutual recognition arrangements are required to 'afford adequate opportunity for other interested Members to negotiate their accession to such an agreement or arrangement or to negotiate comparable ones with it'. GATS Article V permits economic integration arrangements. The relationship between these two provisions, and the circumstances under which developing countries will be permitted to participate in recognition arrangements among developed countries, is an emerging issue. Under the WTO Appellate Body's jurisprudence, it is at least arguable that recognition arrangements within regional integration arrangements are not protected by Article V, and would be required to comply with Article VII.

F. Prudential carve-out and regulation of regulatory goals

At some point, it will be worthwhile to reconsider the utility of the prudential carve-out in financial services, and to consider whether any discipline on the determination of regulatory goals is required in services more generally. Such a discipline could parallel disciplines in the TBT and SPS Agreements. At the extreme, services regulation might be required to have a prudential or other independent public policy basis, paralleling the requirement of a 'scientific basis' contained in the SPS Agreement.

PART V

LESS-DEVELOPED WTO MEMBERS IN THE DOHA ROUND NEGOTIATIONS

10

Operationalizing the Concept of Policy Space in the WTO: Beyond Special and Differential Treatment[1]

BERNARD HOEKMAN

I. INTRODUCTION

There are large differences between World Trade Organization (WTO) Members in terms of resource capacity constraints and national trade policy and investment priorities. These affect the ability and willingness to incur the costs associated with implementation of new rules, as well as the net benefits of doing so. The 'adjustment burden' of new rules mostly will fall on developing countries, as such rules will reflect the status quo in industrialized countries. This chapter discusses options that have been proposed to address country differences and increase the 'development relevance' of the WTO. These include shifting back to a club approach, more explicit special and differential treatment provisions in specific WTO agreements, and a concerted effort to establish a mechanism in the WTO where development concerns can be considered. A case is made for the latter—involving a serious effort to increase the transparency of applied policies, including assessments of their effectiveness and the magnitude of any negative spillovers imposed on other developing countries.

[1] Presented at the 3rd Annual Conference on *Preparing the Doha Development Round—WTO Negotiators Meet the Academics*, European University Institute, 2–3 July 2004. I am grateful to my discussant, Eduardo Varela, as well as Chad Bown, Stuart Harbinson, Faizel Ismail, Mathias Meyer, Dominique Njinkeu, Sheila Page, Eduardo Pérez-Motta, Susan Prowse, David Shark, Thierry Verdier, and Alan Winters for helpful comments, suggestions and discussions. The views expressed are personal and should not be attributed to the World Bank.

II. BEYOND SPECIAL AND DIFFERENTIAL TREATMENT

A major constraint impeding progress in the Doha Round is how to deal with demands by many developing country WTO Members for strengthened and more effective special and differential treatment (SDT). Traditionally, developing countries have sought 'differential and more favorable treatment' in the General Agreement on Tariffs and Trade (GATT)/WTO with a view to increasing the development relevance of the trading system.[2] Formally, SDT was made an element of the trading system in 1979 through the so-called 'Enabling Clause' (Differential and More Favourable Treatment, Reciprocity and Fuller Participation of Developing Countries). This calls for preferential market access for developing countries, limits reciprocity in negotiating rounds to levels 'consistent with development needs', and provides developing countries with greater freedom to use trade policies than would otherwise be permitted by GATT rules.

The premise behind SDT is couched in the belief that trade liberalization under most-favoured-nation (MFN) auspices does not necessarily help achieve growth and development insofar as industries in developing countries need to be protected from foreign competition for a period of time. This infant industry (import substitution) rationale is reflected in greater flexibility and 'policy space' for developing country trade policies, as well as the call for preferential access to rich country markets. However, SDT goes beyond market access and limited reciprocity—it also spans the cost of implementation of agreements and the approach towards the possible negotiation of disciplines on new issues (e.g. investment and competition policy).

The Doha Ministerial Declaration reaffirmed the importance of SDT by stating that 'provisions for special and differential treatment are an integral part of the WTO agreements'. It called for a review of WTO SDT provisions with the objective of 'strengthening them and making them more precise, effective and operational'.[3] The Declaration also states that 'modalities for further commitments, including provisions for special and differential treatment, be established no later than 31 March 2003'.[4]

Efforts to come to agreement on SDT during 2002–03 were not successful, reflecting deep divisions between WTO members on the appropriate scope and design of SDT. In part this reflects wide differences

---

[2] R. Hudec, *Developing Countries in the GATT Legal System* (1987); J. M. Finger, 'Development Economics and the GATT' in J. De Melo and A. Sapir (eds), *Trade Theory and Economic Reform* (1991).
[3] Doha Ministerial Declaration, WT/MIN(01)/DEC/W/1 of 14 November 2001, para. 44.   [4] *Ibid.* para. 14.

between WTO members in terms of resource capacity constraints and national policy and investment priorities, with consequent differences in the ability (willingness) to incur the costs associated with implementation of new rules, as well as differences in the net benefits of doing so. Implementation costs associated with new agreements will fall disproportionately on developing economies, as the associated disciplines often will reflect the prevailing practice in industrialized countries. Longer transition periods—the approach used in the Uruguay Round—is now recognized as an inadequate response, as these are arbitrary and are not accompanied by or based on an objective assessment of whether (and when) implementation of a specific set of (proposed) rules will be beneficial to a country. If the Doha Development Agenda is to live up to its name, the fact that country priorities and capacities differ enormously will need to be addressed. There are two basic options: shift back to a club approach, or pursue universal membership agreements that are accompanied with more effective development provisions.

While most of the Singapore issues have now been taken off the multilateral negotiating table, it seems clear that many members will continue to seek to expand the scope of the WTO (if only because this is also being pursued through regional agreements). One approach to moving forward on new areas that could address the problem of differences in priorities and capacities across the WTO membership is to expand the number of plurilateral agreements in the WTO. This would allow WTO members to decide whether to sign on to new disciplines on a voluntary basis, while allowing all countries to be involved in the negotiating process. Another option is to develop a set of general rules that in principle apply to all members but to adopt specific development provisions that apply to (subsets of) developing countries. Yet another is to seek to adopt a new 'development framework' in the WTO to determine the reach of disciplines.

Many of the provisions of the WTO make good sense from an economic development perspective. However, some agreements may not pass a cost–benefit analysis test. Insufficient attention is generally paid to issues related to the costs of (and preconditions for) implementation of resource-intensive agreements. These considerations suggest that an approach that allows for greater flexibility while at the same time maintaining—indeed, preferably, increasing—the accountability of governments for performance could provide the basis for a more effective approach to address development concerns and objectives in the WTO.

III. THE 'OLD APPROACH'

The traditional approach to SDT comprises trade preferences through the Generalized System of Preferences (GSP), limited reciprocity in trade negotiations, and temporary exemptions from certain rules, conditional on level of development (albeit undefined).

A. Non-reciprocal trade preferences

Non-reciprocal trade preferences have been a major feature of North–South trade relations for decades. Recent years have witnessed the deepening of trade preferences for least-developed countries (LDCs) and sub-Saharan Africa.[5] While these schemes can have a positive effect on the exports of beneficiary countries, much depends on their supply-side capacity—often very limited; the share of any associated rents that accrue to exporters—often much less than 100 per cent; and the impact of ancillary documentary requirements imposed by preference-granting countries, such as rules of origin, which have been shown to be a major impediment, especially for key sectors such as clothing, leading to low utilization rates. Research suggests that most countries have not benefited much from preferential trade programmes given uncertainty/costs created by 'political conditionality', product exclusions, and rules of origin.[6] The importance of liberal rules of origin has been demonstrated in the context of the African Growth and Opportunity Act, where (temporary) relaxation of triple transformation or yarn-forward rules underpinned an export boom in countries such as Lesotho.[7]

Preferences are discriminatory in nature—they not only imply but depend for any effects on not giving such access to others. In practice, there is a hierarchy of preferences, with the most preferred countries generally being members of reciprocal free trade agreements, followed by LDCs (which often enjoy free access to major markets), and other developing countries (which generally get GSP preferences). From a poverty reduction point of view a case can be made that preferences should focus on the poor, wherever they are geographically located, and not on a limited set of countries. In absolute terms, most poor people live in countries that are not LDCs—especially the large countries of East and South Asia. Moreover, efforts to maintain (or deepen) prefer-ence margins on a selective basis have the potential (indirect) downside of reducing pressure on high-income countries to reform their most

---

[5] Two examples of these are the EU Everything But Arms Initiative and the US African Growth and Opportunity Act.

[6] E.g. P. Brenton, 'Integrating the LDCs into the World Trading System: The Current Impact of EU Preferences under Everything But Arms' in 37(3) *Journal of World Trade* (2003) 623–646; World Bank, *Global Economic Prospects and the Developed Countries: Making Trade Work for the Poor* (2002).

[7] A. Mattoo, D. Roy, and A. Subramanian, *The Africa Growth and Opportunity Act and its Rules of Origin: Generosity Undermined?*, Policy Research Working Paper No. 2908, World Bank (2002).

trade-distorting policies—farm policies, tariff peaks, etc.—on an MFN basis, which is critical for these 'less preferred' countries. Finally, preferences are a costly way to transfer resources—it has been estimated that US$1 worth of additional income created by preference programmes may cost US$5.[8]

Giving priority to MFN liberalization of trade in goods and services in which developing countries have an export interest is superior in global welfare terms to piecemeal preferences.[9] The recent trend has been towards a mix of MFN liberalization (through tariff reductions, the phase-out of the Multi-Fibre Arrangement (MFA) as of 1 January 2005) and deepening of reciprocal preferential trade agreements (FTAs). The implication of both developments is that those non-reciprocal preferences with value to recipients are increasingly being eroded, independent of what may happen in the Doha Round. These trends, and the presumption that an MFN-based approach to liberalization is first-best for the world as a whole, suggest that efforts are needed to assist countries deal with the negative impacts of any erosion, as well as more generally to meet adjustment costs and enhance supply capacity. A credible commitment to replace trade preferences with more efficient instruments of assistance should be an important part of any new approach towards development and the WTO.

B. Market access, core disciplines, and reciprocity

Government interventions are justified where there are market distortions and to achieve social (equity) objectives. In the case of market failures, policy interventions should directly target the source of the failure. Trade policy will rarely do so. Even if trade policies are used, there is a clear efficiency ranking of trade policy instruments, with quotas and quota-like instruments being particularly costly. WTO rules that impose disciplines on the use of such instruments will benefit consumers and enhance welfare in developing countries. Similarly, there are benefits to binding tariffs—not least of which is that this is negotiating coin in trade rounds—and abiding by WTO rules and criteria for taking actions against imports that are deemed to injure a domestic industry.

There is a huge literature on these issues.[10] The main conclusion suggested by both theory and practice is that a good case can be made

---

[8] World Bank, *supra* n. 6.

[9] B. Hoekman, C. Michalopoulos, and L. A. Winters, 'Special and Differential Treatment in the WTO After Cancún' in 27(4) *World Economy* (2003) 481–506.

[10] See M. Noland and H. Pack, *Industrial Policy in an Era of Globalization: Lessons from Asia* (2003) for a review of the East Asian experience and the relevant literature; more generally, on the economics of the WTO, N. McCulloch, L. A. Winters, and X. Cirera, *Trade Liberalization and Poverty: A Handbook* (2001).

that the core trade policy rules of the WTO make good sense for all countries, developed and developing. Core rules arguably span MFN, the ban on quantitative restrictions, committing to ceiling bindings for tariffs, and engaging in the process of reciprocal trade liberalization.[11] Currently, these core principles do not apply equally to all members, due to SDT provisions and the Enabling Clause (which calls for reciprocity in negotiating rounds by developing countries to be limited to what is 'consistent with development needs').

Reciprocity is the engine of the WTO, the means through which to obtain concessions from trading partners. More important, it is also in a country's own interest insofar as what is being conceded is a 'bad', i.e. a policy that does not increase welfare. In practice, much of the benefit from trade policy reforms is generated by a country's own actions. Overuse of the 'non-reciprocity' clause has, in the past, excluded developing countries from the major source of gains from trade liberalization— namely the reform of their *own* policies. Non-reciprocity is also a reason why tariff peaks today are largely on goods produced in developing countries. While there is certainly a need for differentiation between developing countries in determining the extent of reciprocity in market access—some countries rely substantially on tariffs for revenue, and countries with high tariffs will need to reduce them gradually to manage adjustment costs—the WTO can, has, and is providing mechanisms through which market access liberalization can be tailored to reflect the interests of individual (groups) of countries. Not employing the 'technology' offered by the WTO—i.e. a commitment mechanism for credible, gradual market access reforms—reduces the value of membership.[12]

C. Regulatory and 'resource-intensive' disciplines

Increasingly, the focus of high-income WTO members has turned to international cooperation on 'behind the border' regulatory policies. Often these may entail pecuniary spillovers on other members, but this is not necessarily the case. In part the expansion of the agenda is driven by a need to mobilize (political) support for reducing the trade-distorting effects of policies in areas such as agriculture. The Uruguay Round was premised on such a grand bargain, with developing countries accepting new disciplines in a variety of areas (trade-related aspects of intellectual

---

[11] Hoekman, Michalopoulos, and Winters, *supra* n. 9.

[12] The foregoing is not to deny that weak institutional capacity, market imperfections, and lack of financial resources may require that developing countries pursue second best trade policies. However, existing WTO provisions—allowing tariff bindings above applied rates, safeguards, waivers, and renegotiation of concessions—arguably provide ample scope for countries to do so.

property rights (TRIPS), services) in return for the elimination of the MFA, outlawing of voluntary export restraints (VERs) and inclusion of agriculture into the WTO. The regulatory standards that are written into the WTO generally start from the status quo prevailing in Organization for Economic Co-operation and Development (OECD) countries, so that the lion's share of associated implementation costs tends to fall on developing countries. In recognition of the differential capacity of developing countries to incur the implementation costs associated with the new disciplines, SDT was provided in the form of longer transitional periods and offers of technical assistance from rich countries. By the end of the 1990s many countries had come to the view that the WTO was unbalanced, reflected *inter alia* in numerous implementation-related issues and concerns.[13] The net returns to implementation were perceived to be low, i.e. there was a lack of 'ownership' of agreements by domestic constituencies.[14]

If the Uruguay Round demonstrates that uniform transition periods are inadequate for agreements that require investments of scarce human and financial resources as well as institutional development and strengthening, the experience pre- and post-Seattle that culminated in the 2003 Cancún WTO Ministerial Conference illustrated that seeking to expand the negotiating set by adding 'behind the border' issues can be counterproductive. The strategy of adding investment, competition law, and procurement to the agenda proved divisive, with many poor countries in particular concerned that multilateral rules might not be in their interest and would do little to promote progress on key market access issues such as agriculture. Post-Cancún, an increasing number of calls could be heard on the part of *demandeurs* for new disciplines to consider shifting from a universal membership approach for new disciplines to a 'code' or club approach with voluntary membership as a way of avoiding the need to define SDT and allow movement on new areas. Many others argued instead that both the Uruguay Round itself and the ambitious proposals to expand the WTO's ambit further had clearly been misconceived and called for a return to 'basics'—a market-access agenda.

Trade-related technical assistance is an important part of the SDT agenda. A major problem with provisions in the WTO offering help to countries is that there were no mechanisms to link these to the actual provision of development assistance. Much has been done post-Seattle

[13] J. M. Finger and P. Schuler, 'Implementation of Uruguay Round Commitments: The Development Challenge' in 23 *World Economy* (2000) 511–526.
[14] One consequence has been that the relevant committees in the WTO—e.g. on customs valuation and technical barriers/SPS—became focal points for discussions on implementation and technical assistance. I argue below that the activities of such committees in considering capacity constraints could be the basis for a more general approach to address differences in circumstances across countries.

to integrate such assistance more fully into the activities of the WTO. A major example is the Integrated Framework for LDCs; more generally, there is a greater awareness of the need to incorporate trade into national processes through which policy reform and investment priorities are determined.[15] However, as discussed below, much more can and should be done to enhance the 'coherence' of trade and development policies and to assist poor developing countries make use of market access opportunities.

IV. OPTIONS FOR A NEW FRAMEWORK

The traditional approach to SDT sketched out above has not been effective. The predominant view among analysts and practitioners is that many if not most SDT provisions are either exhortatory or unlikely to be beneficial.[16] A solution will require actions (and concessions) by both rich and developing countries. One way forward is to distinguish between the market access and rule-making dimensions of the WTO. The approach could involve three basic elements:

- Acceptance by developing countries to commit to the core disciplines of the WTO on market access, including undertaking liberalization commitments, albeit differentiated across countries.
- Adoption of a cooperative, 'enabling' approach for the use of a to-be-determined (negotiated) set of WTO rules. This would span resource-intensive agreements requiring investments and complementary reforms, as well as disciplines where governments believe (continued) use of policies that are subject to WTO rules are warranted for development purposes. The approach would involve commitments by developing countries to identify clearly the underlying objectives that motivate the continued use of such policies, and accepting multilateral scrutiny to determine the impact of these policies. It would act as a 'circuit-breaker' in cases where otherwise dispute settlement procedures may have been launched, but would not remove issues from the reach of the Dispute Settlement Understanding (DSU)—if actions by one member are considered by another member to impose serious negative spillovers, recourse to the DSU would remain possible.

[15] S. Prowse, 'The Role of International and National Agencies in Trade-Related Capacity Building' in 25(9) *World Economy* (2002) 1235–1261.
[16] See Hoekman, Michalopoulos, and Winters, *supra* n. 9; M. Hart, and B. Dymond, 'Special and Differential Treatment and the Doha "Development" Round' in 37(2) *Journal of World Trade* (2003) 395–415; M. Pangestu, 'Special and Differential Treatment in the Millennium: Special for Whom and How Different?' in 23(9) *World Economy* (2000), 1285–1302; J. Whalley, 'Special and Differential Treatment in the Millennium Round' in 22(8) *World Economy* (1999) 1065–1093.

- Credible commitments by high-income countries to assist countries/ groups to benefit from trade opportunities, by removing policies that negatively affect developing countries, adoption of internal mechanisms to enhance the coherence of domestic policies, and the use of aid resource transfers to poor countries to assist in meeting adjustment costs from reforms.

A. A (very) short review of recent proposals on SDT

Several options have been proposed in the literature for a new approach to SDT:

- Acceptance of the principle of 'policy space'—implying flexibility for all developing countries as currently (self-)defined in the WTO whether to implement a specific set of (new) rules, as long as this does not impose significant negative (pecuniary) spillovers.[17]
- A country-specific approach that would make implementation of new rules a function of national priorities. WTO disciplines implying significant resources would be implemented only when this conforms with or supports the attainment of national development strategies. A process of multilateral monitoring and surveillance, with input by international development agencies, would be established to ensure that decisions are subject to scrutiny and debate.[18]
- An agreement-specific approach involving the *ex ante* setting of specific criteria on an agreement-by-agreement basis to determine whether countries could opt out of the application of negotiated disciplines for a limited time period. Criteria could include indicators of administrative capacity, country size and level of development, and implementation could be made conditional upon adequate financial and technical assistance being offered.[19]
- A simple rule-of-thumb approach that would allow opt-outs for resource-intensive agreements for all countries satisfying broad threshold criteria such as minimum level of per capita income, institutional capacity, or economic scale.[20] The presumption here is that this would

[17] As in practice small countries are likely not to be confronted with the DSU, in effect this would to some extent formalize the prevailing status quo. See C. Stevens, *The Future of SDT for Developing Countries in the WTO*, Working Paper No. 163, Institute for Development Studies, Sussex (2002).   [18] See Prowse, *supra* n. 15.

[19] Z. K. Wang and L. A. Winters, *Putting 'Humpty' Together Again: Including Developing Countries in a Consensus for the WTO*, CEPR Policy Paper No. 4 (2000); A. Keck and P. Low, *Special and Differential Treatment in the WTO: Why, When and How?* (2003) mimeo.

[20] See Hoekman, Michalopoulos, and Winters, *supra* n. 9. Some WTO disciplines may not be appropriate for very small countries if the institutions that are required are unduly costly— that is, countries may lack the scale needed for benefits to exceed implementation costs.

allow the bulk of identified difficulties to be tackled at little or no negotiating cost. The criteria would apply to *all* new resource-intensive agreements. Invocation of an opt-out would be voluntary. As countries come to surpass thresholds over time, disciplines automatically would become applicable.

A common element of all these proposals is that use is made of economic criteria to determine the applicability of (resource-intensive) rules.[21] This is controversial, as it implies differentiation among countries, something that is rejected by many developing country representatives in the WTO. Currently, whether SDT is invoked is left to individual Members (i.e. whether or not to self-declare as a developing country) and there is a mix of unilateral action and bargaining by developed country Members whether to accept this and provide SDT.

Country classification inevitably creates tensions among governments as to which countries would be counted in and which out. A major advantage of simple criteria is that it is 'clean'—there is no need for additional negotiation. The disadvantage is that criteria are inherently arbitrary, and of course this is not a route that has proven successful to date. The alternative is a case-by-case approach to determining the criteria that define the reach of rules. What constitutes 'resource-intensive', for example, and the extent to which specific agreements will give rise to implementation costs are questions that are country-specific. Past experience illustrates that agreeing on a rule- or agreement-specific set of criteria is feasible—witness the Subsidies Agreement per capita income threshold for the use of export subsidies or the net food importers group in the Agreement on Agriculture. The downside is that poor countries will be confronted with inevitable negotiation costs and the need to allocate scarce human resources to issues that may not be priorities.[22] Neither type of approach does much to engage governments and stakeholders, or to help them identify better policies or areas where complementary actions/investments are needed. Instead, the focus is purely 'legalistic': SDT is needed as a mechanism to prevent countries from undertaking investments or implementing rules they do not wish to and to avoid being confronted by the threat of retaliation for non-compliance.

B. Towards a more cooperative approach?

A basic issue that underlies the calls for strengthening of SDT by developing countries is a perception that many WTO rules are not beneficial.

---

[21] This is also the case in the first option, as implicitly this approach introduces a size criterion.

[22] L. A. Winters, 'Doha and the World Poverty Targets', paper presented at the *14th Annual World Bank Conference on Development Economics*, Washington, DC (2002).

One can also point to the disparity between the current binding enforcement regime—which does not permit blocking dispute settlement and delegates ultimate enforcement decisions to a very small number of people (panelists and Appellate Body members)—and the fact that most of the current disciplines were negotiated in an institutional framework where there was no such binding enforcement.[23] One way forward is to renegotiate the rules. Another, complementary approach is to focus on the enforcement side of the picture, and make recourse to the DSU conditional on a 'development test' for some issues. Various options could be considered to implement this, including the creation of a formal 'circuit-breaker' mechanism that would make recourse to panels under the DSU conditional on a prior process of consultation mediated by an independent body that focuses not solely on legal issues but on the likely net benefits of (non-)implementation and the magnitude of any negative spillovers associated with the use of policies that are subject to WTO disciplines.

A precondition for ownership of international agreements is that governments and stakeholders perceive the rules to benefit the economy overall. A more economically based discussion of instances where countries are not in conformity with WTO rules could help enhance such ownership. That is, rather than invoke the (immediate) threat of a panel, a more cooperative approach could be envisaged that is geared towards assisting countries attain their objectives in an efficient manner as opposed to one that is aimed solely at safeguarding or attaining market access or minimizing negative terms of trade externalities. An important corollary of such an approach would be greater accountability of governments for performance and outcomes—a determination of whether the policies that are used are effective.

Such an empowerment or enabling mechanism implies a shift at the margin towards a so-called 'soft law' approach.[24] Soft law involves establishment of a framework for international cooperation focusing on the provision of information and learning through regular interactions of relevant policy-makers and constituents (stakeholders), peer review, and (multilateral) monitoring of the impacts of policies and their effectiveness in attaining stated objectives. From an economic development perspective, depending on the issue, a soft law approach towards identifying 'good practices' may make good sense, as often these will differ across countries. There is an emerging literature that argues in favour of a 'learning' approach to international cooperation in complex

---

[23] I owe this point to Claus-Dieter Ehlermann.
[24] To some extent, this can be seen as building on the consultations part of the DSU, with the difference that the focus goes beyond compliance narrowly defined.

regulation-intensive domestic policy domains.[25] One premise that underlies arguments for soft law (be it implicit or explicit) is that the mechanism of reciprocity may be inappropriate to define common rules for 'behind the border' regulatory policies. The specific content of regulation should reflect national (or local) circumstances. Thus, what may be most appropriate from an economic welfare (development) perspective is to create a framework for assisting governments to identify good policies, not a system that aims at harmonization enforced by binding dispute settlement.[26] This could also allow a more considered and flexible approach towards determining at what level cooperation on new issues should occur—bilateral, regional, or multilateral.

C. Pros, cons, and open questions

Some of the advantages of a 'softer' approach have already been noted. A major advantage is that it could allow the WTO to avoid the vexed problem of agreeing on country classification and dealing with the issue of 'graduation'—matters that have proven to be hugely controversial, although in practice one can observe acceptance of greater differentiation in specific WTO discussions.[27] As there is currently no legal basis in the WTO for greater differentiation across developing countries, and insofar as a necessary element for any solution on SDT is that there is no a priori exclusion of any country (still an open issue, of course), a soft law option could help WTO Members advance on the 'development dimension'. The approach implies that the WTO would take development considerations more seriously—and this is after all a premise of the Doha Development Agenda. A mechanism that involves the need to explicitly assess the impact of trade policies on specified development objectives could also help raise the profile of trade issues in national capitals, a potentially significant benefit given the difficulty the national trade community often has in ensuring trade issues and problems are considered in domestic priority setting processes.

[25] E.g. K. Abbott and D. Snidal, 'Hard and Soft Law in International Governance' in 53(3) *International Organization* (2000) 421–456; A. Chayes and A. Handler Chayes, *The New Sovereignty: Compliance with International Regulatory Agreements* (1995); G. Helleiner, *Markets, Politics, and Globalization: Can the Global Economy be Civilized?*, 10th Prebisch Lecture, UNCTAD (2002); J. M. Finger, *The Doha Agenda and Development: A View From the Uruguay Round* (2002); C. Sabel and S. Reddy, *Learning to Learn: Undoing the Gordian Knot of Development Today* (2002), online at http://www.sopde.org/discussion.htm.

[26] This is clear-cut if there are no pecuniary spillovers.

[27] This is most prominent in Doha discussions on market access negotiating modalities on agriculture and non-agricultural market access (NAMA). The TRIPS/public health decision also differentiates between developing countries, as does the WTO subsidies agreement.

Related to this, another potential benefit is that it would provide a context to identify more efficient instruments that might be supported by the donor community to achieve specific objectives. For example, basic economics suggests that subsidies are more efficient instruments to address market failures than trade policies. If binding budget constraints in a developing country precludes the use of subsidy instruments, these may be overcome through development assistance. This also has the advantage of introducing a credible exit mechanism, a key condition to prevent capture and control rent seeking. The process can help reveal where such interventions can make trade policies redundant, in the process also enhancing policy coherence. Finally, and perhaps most important, an enabling-cum-peer review process can increase the accountability of governments by creating incentives—the need—to reveal (identify) true differences across countries (and true preferences of governments).

Among the concerns (cons) that are likely to arise regarding a move towards soft law are free riding and the possible negative spillovers created by the use of a policy that is otherwise subject to WTO rules if developing country status—and thus access to the mechanism—continues to be defined by self-declaration; the reduction in certainty associated with conditional enforcement or non-enforcement of rules for developing countries; a hollowing-out of the principle of a rules-based trading system; the likely difficulty of obtaining agreement on what set of rules the mechanism should apply to (i.e. what are the core rules that should apply to all WTO Members unconditionally and be subject to the DSU?); the transaction (and possible negotiation) costs that will be associated with the operation of the mechanism; and, more generally, the desirability of using the WTO as a forum for development-oriented policy dialogue on trade-related issues.

These are all valid concerns. Insofar as the policy (policies) in question impose negative pecuniary spillovers on other countries, one option would be to allow affected countries to document the magnitude of such spillovers, and agree that the soft law option is conditional on there not being significant spillovers—otherwise recourse could be made to renegotiation or the DSU. Spillovers could also be considered as part of the functioning of the relevant WTO monitoring mechanism, and perhaps factored into recommendations for the use of less trade-distorting policies (e.g. aid). In many cases, the developing economies concerned will be too small to impose substantial harm on large trading partners, although the impact of their policies on other small developing countries may be significant—one reason why recourse to the DSU should remain possible.

Arguments concerning the need for (benefits of) legal certainty and the importance of safeguarding the integrity of the rules-based trading system, while relevant in principle, do not have much force as long as it is clear what the rules of the game are. The process of determining the impact and effectiveness of a particular policy should in itself enhance both transparency and accountability of governments; indeed, the associated monitoring of the incidence (impact) of policies provides scope for those that pay for the use of inefficient policy instruments to press for policy changes. If the mechanism leads to replacement of inefficient trade instruments for less distorting subsidy type intervention—e.g. financed by aid—spillover effects will also be attenuated.

Perhaps the major potential downsides concern the possible hollowing-out of the reach of the DSU and the transactions costs associated with the process. The latter is very much a cost–benefit issue, i.e. will the benefits outweigh the costs? This cannot be determined *ex ante*, but clearly thought must be given to the potential for redundancy as the type of policy dialogue and review that is proposed is also undertaken to some extent by institutions such as the World Bank, the International Monetary Fund (IMF), and European Commission (in the context of accession negotiation, Association Agreements and assistance programmes). However, this also suggests there is potential for synergies. The Integrated Framework diagnostic process already brings together six agencies to identify technical assistance needs; a focal point in the WTO that focuses on the development impacts of trade-related policies of a country, as well as the effects of partner country policies, could help improve overall policy coherence. That said, it must be recognized that the suggested approach will impose a burden on already very scarce administrative and human resources in low-income countries. There is a strong counter-argument that it would be preferable to maintain the status quo and let development organizations take the lead on such policy dialogue.[28]

What about concerns pertaining to a hollowing-out of the DSU? Here again clarity regarding the conditions (limits) on the proposed soft law approach will be important. As mentioned, from an economic perspective a (temporary) 'circuit-breaker' that involves constraining access to panels (the Dispute Settlement Body (DSB)) is likely to generate downsides for developing countries primarily insofar as actions of one developing country impinge negatively on another developing country. The small size of most developing countries in world trade suggest that negative spillovers imposed on OECD members will be small. This suggests countries should have the opportunity to raise spillover objections in the context of the operation of the proposed WTO 'monitoring' or consultative body and that this should factor into the recommendations that

[28] Finger, *supra* n. 25.

are made. One could also envisage developing countries that perceive that a policy imposes a significant negative externality would continue to have the opportunity to invoke the DSU, whereas this would not be available to high-income countries.

D. Plurilateral agreements as an alternative?

Another option that can be used to reflect differences across countries in priorities and capacity is to adopt a dynamic variable geometry approach that would break issues and agreements into parts.[29] This might involve only some minimum disciplines applying to a set of countries, and stronger or additional rules applying to others. Over time, countries could elect on a voluntary basis to shift category and take on more disciplines.[30] In this approach, presumably either countries would recognize the value of the disciplines and have established the preconditions for benefiting from their implementation, or they could be induced to take on additional disciplines in the context of a quid pro quo elsewhere.[31] The most straightforward approach in pursuing such a variable geometry approach is to expand the use of plurilateral agreements.

WTO Article X:9 states: 'The Ministerial Conference, upon the request of the Members parties to a trade agreement, may decide exclusively by consensus to add that agreement to Annex 4.' Annex 4 lists so-called Plurilateral Trade Agreements that have been accepted by the membership.[32] WTO Article II:3 specifies that the agreements and associated legal instruments included in Annex 4 are part of the WTO Agreement 'for those Members that have accepted them, and are binding on those Members. The Plurilateral Trade Agreements do not create either obligations or rights for Members that have not accepted them.' Thus, (i) the creation and addition of new plurilateral agreements under Annex 4 requires consensus; and (ii) signatories are not required to apply them on an MFN basis.

Plurilateral agreements are close in effect to those SDT options that allow for countries to opt out from specific agreements. A key difference, however, is that in the case of a plurilateral, there is no presumption that eventually a country will join and thus be subject to the rules—this

---

[29] This terminology is due to Eduardo Perez-Motta.

[30] Alternatively, they could be required to do so if specific criteria or indicators have been met—although that raises the issue of country classification.

[31] Yet another approach that could address this issue in the case of new rules/agreements is to limit membership of (binding) agreements to the minimum set of countries that internalizes most of the spillovers—as was done with the Information Technology Agreement (ITA).

[32] Currently there are only two plurilateral agreements: the Agreement on Government Procurement and the Agreement on Civil Aircraft.

would be the case if the rules in principle apply to all. Plurilaterals used to be more prevalent under the pre-WTO GATT regime reflecting the difficulty of amending the GATT. In the Kennedy and Tokyo Rounds, for example, a number of agreements were negotiated that bound only signatories. Most of these agreements did not attract many developing country contracting parties. During the Uruguay Round, virtually all of the GATT codes of conduct were transformed into multilateral agreements that are binding on all WTO members.

Useful criteria in assessing the upsides and downsides of a plurilateral approach are (i) whether it permits all countries to engage in the negotiation of a proposed rule even if they may not apply it immediately, if at all; (ii) whether they are able to engage in a fully informed way, i.e. are able to determine the 'return' to applying a proposed rule (this requires taking into account direct administrative costs and the size of net economic impact of implementation); (iii) if agreements are implemented on an MFN basis; and (iv) whether and how the DSU would apply.[33]

Although a plurilateral approach to determining the country coverage of new disciplines would ensure that developing countries that do not want to apply new rules could opt out, there are nonetheless a number of downsides to the pursuit of this option. First, the approach would move the WTO towards a two-track regime. Many developing countries have argued that this is contrary to the basic character of the WTO and conflicts with the consensus-based approach that has historically been the norm.[34] A major advantage of continued efforts to agree to multilateral disciplines that apply in principle to all members—even if SDT implies that some will not implement for some time—is that all countries have a say in whether an issue belongs in the WTO.

Second, plurilateral agreements would define the rules of the game in a specific area. Even if countries opt out, over time there would undoubtedly be pressure for non-members to sign on.[35] Moreover, the rules are likely

---

[33] R. Lawrence, *Rule-Making Amidst Growing Diversity: A 'Club of Clubs' Approach to WTO Reform and New Issue Selection* (2004) mimeo, provides a set of criteria for plurilateral agreements to be consistent with the objectives of the WTO. Suggested requirements are that all members be able to participate in the negotiations, membership is voluntary, and cross-retaliation be prohibited—i.e. enforcement threats would be limited to withdrawal of the commitments made within the subject area covered by an agreement.

[34] *Singapore Issues: The Way Forward*, Joint Communication from Bangladesh (on behalf of the LDC Group), Botswana, China, Cuba, Egypt, India, Indonesia, Kenya, Malaysia, Nigeria, Philippines, Tanzania, Uganda, Venezuela, Zambia, and Zimbabwe, WTO document WT/GC/W/522 (12 December 2003).

[35] This has been emphasized by the non-governmental organization (NGO) community as a major downside of plurilateral agreements in the WTO. See e.g. D. Green and C. Melamed, *Four Arguments against a Plurilateral Investment Agreement in the WTO*, Paper on behalf of Cafod, Christian Aid, Oxfam, Action Aid, and World Development Movement (2003).

to reflect the interests and current practices of high-income countries, in part because of negotiating capacity constraints, and in part because of the expectation that many developing countries will not sign a specific agreement. This makes it less likely that the agreement will address issues that are of primary concern to low-income economies. Experience illustrates that it is very difficult to amend (renegotiate) disciplines, so that a plurilateral approach may well become analogous to the *Acquis Communautaire* for prospective members of the EU—i.e. non-negotiable.

E. Beyond access and rules: trade capacity and trade-related assistance

The discussion so far has centred mostly on the 'policy space' dimensions of the SDT debate. Also important is what rich countries could do proactively to assist developing countries. A major constraint limiting export growth in many small and low-income countries is a lack of supply capacity and a high-cost business environment. Firms in these countries may also find it difficult to deal with regulatory requirements such as health and safety standards that apply in export markets. In the literature a useful distinction between market access (trade policy) and market entry has been developed. The latter pertains to the ability of firms to make effective use of (benefit from) market access opportunities. A frequent example of such a 'barrier to entry' is health and safety standards, which may be excessively strict and weigh disproportionately heavily on low-income country producers. Within these countries trade facilitation and trade-related transactions costs—including the costs and quality of services inputs—are important determinants of competitiveness.

Development assistance can play an important role in helping to build the institutional and trade capacity needed to benefit from increased trade and better access to markets. This assistance must go beyond the implementation of trade agreement rules narrowly defined and focus on supply capacity more broadly, as well as addressing adjustment costs associated with reforms. While priorities will differ, in many cases assistance will be needed to address trade-related policy and public investment priorities, to help adapt to a reduction in trade preferences following further non-discriminatory trade liberalization, or to assist in dealing with the potential detrimental effects of a significant increase in world food prices should these materialize. The development community made commitments to this effect at the International Conference on Financing for Development in Monterrey in March 2002—what is needed is a clear articulation of trade-related requests by developing countries, complemented by action on the part of high-income countries to allocate funding to address the priority areas for finance and technical assistance.[36]

One option to be considered in connection with this is to establish a multilateral facility that would temporarily expand the financial envelope available to support the adjustment process that is associated with trade reforms. Mobilizing such funding should be feasible as the aggregate (global) gains from trade are much greater than the aggregate losses associated with restructuring. The problem is that in practice the compensation (transfers) that is called for often does not occur domestically, and barely occurs at all internationally, as reflected in low official development assistance (ODA) levels—in the US$55 billion range—relative to the estimates of the net income gains associated with past multilateral rounds (in the US$200–500 billion range), the magnitude of total support to farmers in OECD countries (currently some US$350 billion), or the potential gains from further global liberalization (upwards of US$500 billion, especially if services trade is included).[37]

There are various ways in which such redistribution could be realized. The most direct way would be through a small consumption tax on goods and services whose prices will be falling as a result of the implementation of negotiated multilateral liberalization commitments. Administrative convenience and collection cost considerations may make a small uniform levy on imports whose tariffs are being cut more feasible. To give a sense of the orders of magnitude involved, a 0.25 per cent levy on imports of OECD countries would be equivalent to over US$12 billion (total OECD imports are some US$5 trillion). However, as much of trade into OECD countries is duty-free, and it is not desirable to reimpose duties on such trade, any such levy should be restricted to currently dutiable imports where tariffs are subject to reduction commitments. An option to consider here would be to negotiate commitments that all or a certain share of currently collected revenue would be made available to low-income countries.[38] As tariffs are gradually lowered— as is the case in WTO agreements—the total revenue available would automatically decline over time, which is appropriate given that the motivation is to facilitate adjustment. Indeed, it is important that there

---

[36] In order to maximize financing for trade-related assistance *and* to ensure that assistance in this area addresses priority areas for intervention, the trade-related technical assistance and capacity-building agenda must be embedded in a country's national development plan or strategy. In the case of low-income countries the primary example of such an instrument is the Poverty Reduction Strategy Paper (PRSP)—implying that governments and stakeholders must take action to embed trade in PRSPs in those instances where trade is seen as a priority.

[37] See K. Anderson, 'Subsidies and Trade Barriers', paper prepared for the *Copenhagen Consensus Project*, World Bank (2004) mimeo, for a review of the estimates found in the literature.

[38] What follows draws on discussions and joint work in progress with Alan Winters.

be general acceptance that any such levy not be an additional tax, but is explicitly based on the recognition that any process of multilateral liberalization will create losers as well as winners. Despite the well-known case for and potential feasibility of compensating losers, in practice this often does not occur. A small reduction in the price gains/benefits that will accrue to consumers as a result of liberalization is one practical means of redistributing some of the gains from trade reform to those who gain less or may lose.[39]

V. CONCLUDING REMARKS

The traditional approach to SDT in the GATT–WTO has not been a success in promoting development. Indeed, it is fundamentally flawed. It has helped create incentives for developing countries not to engage in the WTO process, resulting in the highest trade barriers—in both the North and the South—being on goods in which developing countries have a comparative advantage. Trade preferences have proven to be a double-edged sword, offering only limited benefits and substantial downsides.[40] Further, the traditional approach has not helped the WTO move forward in the arena of rule-making by not taking differences in country circumstances and priorities seriously. In short, SDT has not focused on helping to put in place policies that will promote development. Hence the need for SDT to be recast if the WTO is to become more effective in helping poor countries use trade for development.

There is a basic choice to be made between the pursuit of universal rules that in principle apply to all members, and that will by necessity require SDT-type provisions to account for country differences, and a move to a two- or multi-track trading system based on a plurilateral approach (and regional trade agreements) without SDT. The latter appears to be an attractive way of allowing a subset of the membership to move forward in the absence of consensus. However, many developing countries are on record in the WTO as opposing moves towards

---

[39] This funding mechanism could also help to address the preference erosion problem that will emerge for those countries that rely heavily for export revenues on preferences. Research suggests the number of such countries is small, but that some countries may confront a substantial adjustment burden, ranging up to 5 per cent of current exports, or higher. For further discussion see K. Alexandraki and H. P. Lankes, *Estimating the Impact of Preference Erosion on Middle-Income Countries*, IMF Working Paper (2004); S. Page and P. Kleen, *Special and Differential Treatment of Developing Countries in the World Trade Organization*, Report for the Ministry of Foreign Affairs, Sweden (2004); C. Stevens and J. Kennan, *The Utilization of EU Preferences to the ACP*, presented at the *Seminar on Tariff Preferences and their Utilization*, WTO, Geneva, 31 March 2004.

[40] See B. Hoekman and C. Ozden, *Trade Preferences and Differential Treatment of Developing Countries: A Selective Survey* (2004), mimeo, for a review of the literature.

greater use of such agreements, primarily on the basis of resistance to the creation of a multi-tier trading system[41]. Such an approach also does little to help promote development. A recast framework that aims to take development concerns seriously could do much to make plurilateral agreements redundant by both facilitating new rule-making *and* improving the substance of disciplines from a development perspective. Key elements of a possible new approach could include:

- acceptance of the core rules by all WTO Members: MFN, the ban on quotas, and binding of maximum tariffs, as well as engagement in the market access dimension of WTO negotiating rounds;
- greater reliance on explicit cost–benefit analysis to identify net implementation benefits for countries and the magnitude of negative (pecuniary) spillovers created by development-motivated policies on other countries;
- movement towards the adoption of mechanisms that strengthen the consultative and 'pre-Panel' dimensions of WTO dispute settlement by mandating a focus not just on the legality of a policy instrument but consideration of the rationale and impact of policies used by developing countries that may be inconsistent with WTO disciplines, with the aim of assisting governments to attain their objectives in an efficient way;
- a credible commitment to strengthen global funding mechanisms to provide the resources to address adjustment costs, including those resulting from an erosion of trade preferences, and enhancing supply capacity, in recognition of the need to transfer some of the gains from trade from winners to losers.

Clearly this type of approach will be significantly more resource-intensive than a simple set of rules of thumb that allow countries to opt out from certain WTO agreements. The latter has a number of important advantages, including simplicity and minimal transactions (negotiating) costs.[42] However, it is vigorously resisted by many developing countries, and, as discussed, does not do much to actively assist countries in the development process. A shift away from opt-outs and arbitrary transition periods towards the creation of a process that involves policy dialogue and accountability on all sides could do much to enhance the development relevance of the WTO, while at the same time reducing the perceived downside risk of undertaking new commitments for developing countries.

A fundamental question that must be answered if members are to move down this track is whether the WTO should be the focal point

---

[41] See WTO document WT/GC/W/522, *supra* n. 34.
[42] See Hoekman, Michalopoulos, and Winters, *supra* n. 9.

for this type of international cooperation on trade-related policies. Compelling arguments have been made in the literature that the WTO should not become embroiled in development issues.[43] Many will agree that the WTO is not a development organization and should not become one—this is certainly my view as well.[44] Many of the questions that will come up in discussions will revolve around prioritization, sequencing, complementary reforms, and investment needs/decisions. Development banks and similar institutions have the mandate, mechanisms, and capacity to engage in such policy dialogue with governments. Will the benefits of engaging in such discussions in the WTO outweigh the costs? The potential for a positive return are certainly there, but much will also depend on how the mechanism is implemented, who is involved, how it relates to the activities of development institutions— who clearly will have to play a role in any policy dialogue that occurs in a WTO setting, etc. It is important to keep in mind that the focus of discussions in the WTO would be limited to policies that are covered by the institution—i.e. the review and dialogue process would have predefined boundaries. Moreover, while the suggested approach may seem a rather far-reaching change in the *modus operandi* of the WTO, there are already numerous mechanisms in the WTO that can be—and at times are—used to engage in policy discussions. These include the committees that oversee the operation of specific agreements and the Trade Policy Review Mechanism. One committee that explicitly includes a multilateral process of assessment of the prevailing economic situation in countries as a justification for the use of trade restrictions is the Balance of Payments Committee—which operates with inputs from the IMF on the balance-of-payments situation in a Member that invokes the relevant GATT articles as cover for trade barriers. In practice deliberations have mostly been 'cooperative', with only very few cases of recourse being made to the DSU.[45]

The foregoing has just sketched the outlines of a possible way forward. Much work will be required to map out how the suggested mechanisms might work. Issues to be determined include what agreements/rules the new development framework would apply to—what are 'core' disciplines in addition to market access commitments that should apply to all Members on an unconditional basis? What national and international entities would participate/have standing in the proposed multilateral monitoring process? To what extent could/should this be linked to the Trade Policy Review Mechanism? Under what conditions would countries

---

[43] E.g. Finger, *supra* n. 25.

[44] B. Hoekman, 'Strengthening the Global Trade Architecture for Development: The Post-Doha Agenda' in 1(1) *World Trade Review* (2002) 23–45.

[45] Prowse, *supra* n. 15.

be able to initiate panel proceedings under the DSU? How might a (global) trade adjustment facility be financed? What mechanisms would be used to allocate the revenue generated? Clearly there are many open questions. What matters most at this point is that a decision in principle be taken to consider a new approach to recognizing the huge disparities in capacity and priorities across the WTO membership. The options include simple country-based criteria; greater reliance on plurilateral agreements; and/or a shift to a case-by-case approach that relates multilateral disciplines to national circumstances and is accompanied by explicit and credible mechanisms through which to transfer additional financial resources to low-income countries—'aid for trade'. The latter will be the most challenging to operationalize, but offers the greatest potential to promote development and increase policy coherence.

11

Can WTO Technical Assistance and Capacity-Building Serve Developing Countries?

GREGORY SHAFFER[1]

> Should capacity-building aim to widen the scope of actual economic policy choices for developing countries? Or should it be limited to helping them cope with the burden of commitments they have taken on—sometimes lightly, it has turned out—for the benefit of their more developed partners?[2]

Technical assistance and capacity-building are large and complex issues. A sprawling literature has developed about them since World War II, picking up in the 1960s, and passing through various paradigm shifts through today. These issues, however, are rather new to the World Trade Organization (WTO). They gained particular salience following the expiration of the transition periods for developing country implementation of obligations under the 1995 Uruguay Round agreements and the launch of the Doha negotiating round in November 2001. As the transition periods elapsed, many developing countries balked at implementing WTO requirements on account of the costs of doing so and the perception that they had not benefited from market access as promised. They received intellectual support from a number of international economists

[1] I give my sincere and warm thanks to the 26 individuals whom I interviewed for purposes of this project and who took time out of their demanding schedules to meet with me, and, in some cases, to read earlier versions of this chapter. These hard-working and committed individuals respectively work for the WTO, international development agencies, member delegations to the WTO, and development-oriented NGOs. I also wish to thank Peng Zhao for his research assistance. All errors of course remain my own.

[2] H.-B. Solignac Lecomte, 'Capacity-Building and Technical Assistance for Developing Countries after Doha' in *Bridges (ICTSD)* (January 2002) 3. Solignac Lecomte is an official at the OECD writing in his own capacity.

and development specialists. As Michael Finger and Philip Schuler of the World Bank wrote:

Our analysis indicates that WTO regulations reflect little awareness of development problems and little appreciation of the capacities of the least developed countries to carry out the functions that [sanitary and phytosanitary standards], customs valuation, intellectual property, etc. regulations address. For most of the developing and transition economies—some 100 countries—money spent to implement the WTO rules in these areas would be money unproductively invested.[3]

Leading trade economists noted that the Agreement on Trade-Related Aspects of Intellectual Property Rights (TRIPS Agreement) 'is almost certain to redistribute welfare away from developing countries' to the developed world.[4] In these circumstances, WTO 'capacity-building' programmes, if they are simply designed to assist developing countries in the implementation of WTO contractual obligations, could actually work against developing country interests. On the other hand, as one Secretariat official noted to the author, 'if WTO capacity building restricts itself to explaining the existing obligations to developing country officials, it is already preparing them to take a critical view of these obligations'.

When developing countries agreed to enter into new trade negotiations at Doha, they obtained a commitment that the round, dubbed the 'Doha Development Round', would address issues important to their development, and that they would receive capacity-building assistance to facilitate their participation in the negotiations and the eventual integration of their economies into the international trading system. The Doha Ministerial Declaration dedicated more text to capacity building than to any other issue, including four paragraphs on technical assistance, one paragraph on trade and technology transfer, two paragraphs on least-developed

---

[3] J. M. Finger and P. Schuler, 'Implementation of Uruguay Round Commitments: The Development Challenge' in 23 *World Economy* (2000) 511. See also J. M. Finger, 'Implementing the Uruguay Round Agreements: Problems for Developing Countries' in 24 *World Economy* (2001) 1097. Finger was Lead Economist and former Chief of the World Bank's Trade Research division. Schuler is a senior economist in the World Bank.

[4] The quotation is from A. Deardorff, 'Should Patent Protection Be Extended to All Developing Countries?' in 13 *World Economy* (1990) 497, 507. See also C. Fink and K. E. Maskus (eds), *Intellectual Property and Development: Lessons from Recent Economic Research* (2004); K. Maskus, *Intellectual Property Rights in the Global Economy* (2000); K. Maskus, 'Intellectual Property Issues for the New Round' in J. Scott (ed.), *The WTO after Seattle* (2000) at 142 (noting an estimate of 'static risk transfers . . . of some \$5.8 billion per year' to the US, and 'a net outward transfer of around \$1.2 billion per year' for Brazil); C. Correa, *Intellectual Property Rights, the WTO and Developing Countries: The TRIPS Agreement and Policy Options* (2000) at 35 (citing World Bank and IMF studies on detrimental impacts of TRIPS on developing countries); F. M. Abbott, 'The WTO TRIPS Agreement and Global Economic Development' in F. Abbott and D. Gerber (eds), *Public Policy and Global Technological Integration* (1997).

countries, and other references sprinkled throughout the document.[5] The *2003 World Trade Report* declared, 'The Doha Declaration marked a new departure in the GATT–WTO approach to technical assistance and capacity-building.'[6] One member of the Secretariat characterized the WTO's capacity-building programme as a 'sea change' for the organization, one that 'we [at the WTO] are still digesting'.[7]

Whether these capacity-building commitments are tailored toward contractual negotiations that will serve developing country interests, however, remains under challenge, as noted below. Many of the promises for technical assistance were in exchange for developing country agreement to negotiate over the four 'Singapore issues' advanced by the European Union ('EU'), concerning trade and investment, competition policy, government procurement, and trade facilitation.[8] Indeed, when WTO Director-General Mike Moore cautioned that the provision of technical assistance and capacity-building was a 'condition of further progress on the development dimension', he was referring expressly to the Singapore issues.[9] Now that developing countries have refused to negotiate over three of these issues—trade and investment, competition policy, and government procurement—one wonders whether donor funding of developing country trade-related capacity-building requests will be cut back, even though it has not been so far.

A central conundrum for effective WTO technical assistance lies in how the Secretariat views its capacity-building role in relation to its

---

[5] Paras. 38–41 of the Doha Ministerial Declaration address overall technical assistance and capacity-building. Para. 38 explicitly calls for the Secretariat 'to support domestic efforts for mainstreaming trade into national plans for economic development and strategies for poverty reduction'. Para. 39 calls for coordination between the relevant international agencies, bilateral donors, and beneficiaries so as to rationalize the Integrated Framework and JITAP programmes (see below). Para. 40 calls for a plan to ensure long-term funding for WTO technical assistance, which eventually led to the establishment of the Doha Development Agenda Global Trust Fund in December 2001. Paras. 42–43 focus on assistance to least-developed countries, and paras. 2, 20–21, 23–24, 26, 27, and 33 respectively address assistance in respect of trade and investment, trade and competition policy, transparency in government procurement, trade facilitation, and trade and environment. Specific technical assistance provisions were also contained in paras. 2.2, 3.5, 3.6, 5.1, 5.4, and 14 of the Decision on implementation-related issues and concerns. See WT/MIN (01)/W/17.

[6] See WTO, *World Trade Report 2003* at xix. The *Report* also highlighted 'that technology transfer had never been included explicitly on the GATT–WTO agenda before', but now was part of the work programme: *ibid.* at 164. GATT refers to the General Agreement on Tariffs and Trade.   [7] Interview, 23 June 2004, Geneva.

[8] At the WTO Ministerial Meeting in Singapore in 1997, WTO Members agreed to establish working groups to examine these four issues and their potential integration into the WTO system.

[9] See 'Report to the Council by the Director-General' in *WTO News* (13 February 2002) at para. 6, online at http://www.wto.org/english/news_e/news2002_e.htm. See also the remarks of Director-General Mike Moore concerning the 'conditionality' of technical assistance and capacity-building, *WTO Press Release 279* 11 March 2002.

conventional sense of its 'mandate'. WTO Members and the WTO Secretariat often refer to the WTO as a 'contract organization'. By contract organization, they refer to a 'Member-driven' institution that facilitates the negotiation of trade agreements (the 'contracts'), helps oversee implementation of the resulting contractual commitments, and, where requested, issues judicial decisions over these commitments. WTO Secretariat officials thus view their role as one of servicing negotiations (occurring in various negotiating groups), servicing Member oversight of obligations (through various 'committees and councils'), and assisting with dispute resolution (before the dispute settlement panels and the Appellate Body). Capacity-building, however, is a quite different endeavour.

One's view of WTO substantive rules will shape one's appreciation of WTO capacity-building projects. Should WTO rules be viewed as contingent in time, and subject to debate and modification in relation to changing development challenges, as in domestic political and contractual contexts? Or should they be viewed as fundamental, 'constitutional', 'rule of law'-type commitments that domestic administrations must internalize? As Finger, Schuler, and others point out, many WTO rules represent political choices reflective of contractual bargaining rather than constitutive rules for a global 'constitutional' order. Yet unlike in domestic political and contractual settings, WTO rules are much more difficult to modify over time. WTO Secretariat officials therefore face a dilemma. If they travel to developing countries simply to promote existing WTO rules, they elide the political and development choices implicated by the rules. They cut off what could be valuable discussion, in meetings with those most up-to-date about WTO developments, as to how developing countries can shape the rules though implementation and renegotiation in order to advance trade-related development objectives. If the Secretariat views WTO rules as fundamental commitments, then WTO technical assistance will tend to operate as a form of 'soft' power to shape understandings of WTO obligations and thereby alleviate the need for 'harder' enforcement measures through formal WTO dispute settlement. If, on the other hand, the Secretariat provides a forum for raising awareness about the current rules and different positions regarding them, then it can help developing country officials critically engage with the rules in light of their perceptions of their national interests.

WTO Secretariat officials stress that the WTO is not a development agency mandated to provide development consulting or to finance the provision of roads, port facilities, sanitary testing equipment, information technology, and other trade infrastructure needs. These development tasks lie within the competence of other international organizations, such as the World Bank and the United Nations Development Programme (UNDP). However, now that the WTO has received significant funding for trade-related capacity-building, the WTO Secretariat also receives requests for programmatic funding from developing country members.[10] As a result, there is again tension between the Secretariat's internal understanding of its 'mandate' and the call for enhanced WTO trade-related 'capacity-building' initiatives. All the WTO Secretariat can do in these situations is to refer the matter to relevant development agencies in a more coordinated manner.

This chapter is in four parts. Section I sets forth the competing (and sometimes conflicting) rationales for WTO trade-related capacity-building and technical assistance efforts. These competing rationales have led to contention over how the funding is used. Section II addresses the political and operational constraints on the Secretariat's implementation of a meaningful WTO capacity-building programme. Section III provides historical background to, and a summary of, the WTO's technical assistance and capacity-building initiatives and some of the criticisms that they have generated. Section IV concludes by suggesting how developing countries, donors, and the WTO Secretariat could build from current initiatives, while noting the challenges posed.

As any empirically grounded work, this one is bound to reflect a subjective element as to where it casts its lens, as to what it emphasizes and does not. Its aim, however, is to provide a critical, but ultimately constructive, assessment of WTO capacity-building initiatives, highlighting responses to WTO technical assistance programmes so that these programmes can be made more effective over time.

I. COMPETING RATIONALES FOR TRADE-RELATED CAPACITY-BUILDING AND TECHNICAL ASSISTANCE

At first glance, enhancing trade-related capacity in poor countries seems uncontroversial. All developing countries suffer from capacity constraints that impede their ability to promote their interests through the WTO. The least-developed members are in the most strained situation. A number of WTO members do not have a single representative in Geneva to even consider choosing among over 70 different WTO councils, committees, working parties, and other groupings, involving over 2,800 meetings each year.[11] Because of capacity constraints, developing

---

[10] Interviews with Secretariat officials, June 2004, Geneva.

[11] See G. Sampson, *Trade, Environment and the WTO: The Post-Seattle Agenda* (2000) at 24. As Sampson, the former Director of the WTO's Trade and Environment Division notes, the Egyptian delegation to the WTO has estimated that there were 2,847 meetings in the WTO in 1997, or an average of 10 meetings per working day (citing

countries are less able to advance their interests in WTO negotiations, before WTO committees, and in dispute settlement. Not surprisingly, they face considerable trade barriers for the product markets of greatest importance to their economies, which developed countries label as 'sensitive'. A 2001 World Bank report maintained, 'The prevailing pattern of protection in the world today is biased against the poor in that barriers are highest on goods produced by poor people—agriculture and unskilled labor-intensive manufacturers and services.'[12] Similarly, many developing countries are less able to shape their internal implementation of WTO rules in a manner that protects their interests.

In practice, however, capacity-building programmes can be controversial. Who defines the purpose of technical assistance and capacity-building, and who oversees how funding is used, can shape programmes toward different ends. Technical assistance programmes can be relatively donor-driven to serve donor-defined interests, or they can be relatively demand-driven to serve interests defined within the recipient countries. Constituency interests in developing countries can differ, fragmenting, and spurring conflict over, capacity-building projects. Donors can work through allies in developing country bureaucracies to act as brokers to serve both personal and donor interests. What looks like a 'demand-driven' request can actually be donor-driven. In the words of Thandika Mkandawire, director of the UN Research Institute for Social Development, developing country 'nationals' may simply serve to champion 'externally driven policy agendas', so that the resulting 'dialogue' between donor and recipient can take on 'the character of the conversation between a ventriloquist and a puppet'.[13] As one African representative to the WTO contends, 'The problem [with the WTO Secretariat's

---

Communication from Egypt, *High Level Symposium on Trade and Development*, WTO 17 March 1997 mimeo); *ibid.* at 30. In consequence, many countries' representatives simply do not attend or keep up with developments in most WTO committees. Developing countries may lack the capacity to attend meetings in Geneva scheduled for their express benefit. As reported by a WTO official interviewed by Braithwaite and Drahos, 'We set up a Subcommittee with a Chair and a Secretary who turned up for the first meeting on trade needs of LDCs [least-developed countries]. No LDCs came. No developed countries came. No one came. Not one country showed up. If it had been telecoms, the chamber would have been packed [with special interests and states pushed by telecom interests].' J. Braithwaite and P. Drahos, *Global Business Regulation* (2000) at 196. As of November 1999, 28 WTO Members did not even maintain permanent offices in Geneva because of a lack of resources. See 'WTO Organizes Geneva Week for Non-Resident Delegations' in 43 *WTO Focus* (1999) 16.

[12] See World Bank, *Global Economic Prospects and the Developing Countries: Making Trade Work for the World's Poor* (2001). See also B. Hoekman, 'Strengthening the Global Trade Architecture for Development' in 1(1) *World Trade Review* (2002) 1, 29.

[13] T. Mkandawire, 'Incentives, Governance and Capacity Development in Africa' in S. Fukuda-Parr, C. Lopes, and K. Malik (eds), *Capacity for Development: New Solutions to Old Problems*, (2002) 147, 155.

capacity-building programme] is that it is ideological. They come to tell us what to think, what our positions should be.'[14] As he states, WTO technical assistance is often about 'the use of ideas to transform developing country negotiating positions'.[15] Even if donor-driven technical assistance does not directly conflict with a developing country's interests, in a world of limited resources, technical assistance in one area can divert human and material resources from others that may be of greater priority.

There are at least four competing rationales for WTO trade-related technical assistance efforts:

(1) To facilitate trade liberalization.
(2) To support specific trade-related aspects of a country's development strategy.
(3) To assist with the costs of the implementation of WTO agreements.
(4) To enhance the capacity of developing countries to participate in the shaping of international trade rules, their interpretation and understanding, and their monitoring and enforcement.

These four rationales can overlap and conflict. Trade is widely recognized as important for development, especially for countries with small internal markets. Because of their small markets, these countries do not benefit from specialization, economies of scale, and competition. There is considerable evidence that a larger market, made possible through trade, facilitates specialization so that productivity improves and costs decrease.[16] The import substitution model for development is now widely viewed as unsuccessful. In contrast, the great development stories since World War II were those from East Asia that benefited from competitive export sectors.[17] Developing countries can benefit, in particular, from opening their markets to each other's products, as some Asian countries now demonstrate.[18]

Development, however, is a much broader objective than trade liberalization. From a development perspective, trade is a tool. As the Organization for Economic Co-operation and Development (OECD) technical assistance guidelines state, 'Trade and trade liberalisation are not ends in themselves . . . [although] they can enhance a country's access to a wider range of goods, services, technologies and knowledge.'[19]

---

[14] Interview July 2004.   [15] *Ibid.*   [16] WTO, *supra* n. 6 at 85.

[17] Growth rates in East Asia were on average 5.5 per cent per year from 1965 to 1990, implying a doubling of national income every 13 years. See S. Radelet and J. Sachs, 'The East Asian Financial Crisis: Diagnosis, Remedies and Prospects' in *Brookings Papers on Economic Activity* (1998).   [18] WTO, *supra* n. 6.

[19] Organization for Economic Cooperation and Development (OECD), *The DAC Guidelines: Strengthening Trade Capacity for Development* (2001) at 17, online at

Development analysts may agree on the importance of trade, but they also disagree over the scope and timing of internal trade liberalization.[20] Some high-growth Asian countries were more free-trade oriented, such as Hong Kong and Singapore, while others were more mercantilist, such as Japan, Korea, China, and Chinese Taipei. While all of these WTO members have moved toward freer trade, the rapid jump in their development was not because of uniformly liberal trade policies.

The East Asian countries' experience demonstrates the importance of internal trade-related capacity both in government and in the private sector. Exports may have been central to the growth models of East Asian countries, but so was a strong state having a competent bureaucracy and a private sector subject to internal competition.[21] These countries understood the importance of investing in education and skills development, and of transferring skills through the private sector, so that they had broader-based internal capacity to absorb and deploy technical assistance.[22] Although all development contexts differ, countries can learn from each other's successes and failures. In a globalizing world, they can 'scan globally, reinvent locally'.[23] The East Asian experience

http://www.oecd.org/dac/trade. The guidelines call for collaboration 'in formulating and implementing a trade development strategy that is embedded in a broader national development strategy'. See also United Nations Conference on Trade and Development (UNCTAD), *The Least Developed Countries Report 2004: Linking International Trade with Poverty Reduction* (2004).

[20] Cf. D. Dollar and A. Kray, *Growth is Good for the Poor*, Policy Department Working Paper No. 2587, World Bank (2001); T.N. Srinivasan and J. Bhagwati, *Outward Orientation: Are the Revisionists Right?*, Center Discussion Paper No. 806, Yale University (1999); D. Rodrik, *The Global Governance of Trade as if Development Really Mattered*, online at http://www.cid.harvard.edu/cidtrade/issues/developmentpapers; D. Rodrik, 'Development Strategies for the 21st century' in *Annual World Bank Conference on Development Economics 2000* (2001) 85–101; A. Winters, *Trade Liberalization and Poverty: The Empirical Evidence* (2002) at 64, online at http://www.sussex.ac.uk/Units/economics/dp/Wintersetal88.pdf (concluding 'The evidence surveyed in this paper demonstrates that there can be no simple generalisable conclusion about the relationship between trade liberalisation and poverty'); and Oxfam, *Rigged Rules and Double Standards: Make Trade Fair* (2002).

[21] See e.g. R. Wade, *Governing the Market: Economic Theory and the Role of Government in East Asian Industrialization* (1990); M. Woo-Cumings (ed.), *The Developmental State* (1999). Interestingly, a study by Schiavo-Campo has 'measured the share of the number of civil servants for 100 people', and found that 'the average ratio for sub-Saharan Africa (1.5) is less than that of Asia (2.6) or of Latin America (3.0)', although 'Mauritius and Botswana—the best-performing countries in terms of growth, and with bureaucracies touted as efficient—have more than three times the African average: 5.5 and 5.8 respectively: Mkandawire, *supra* n. 13 at 151.

[22] Korea, for example, has a large programme for promoting technological development in the private sector. See S. Lall, 'Social Capital and Industrial Transformation' in S. Fukuda-Parr, C. Lopes, and K. Malik (eds), *Capacity for Development: New Solutions to Old Problems* (2002) 101, 114 at 115.

[23] S. Fukuda-Parr, C. Lopes, and K. Malik, 'Institutional Innovations for Capacity Building' in S. Fukuda-Parr, C. Lopes, and K. Malik (eds), *Capacity for*

suggests that technical assistance will be of less value without a competent state bureaucracy, engaged private sector, and civil society with a developing skill base to absorb it. That being said, there is little that the WTO can do in this respect except improve the way in which it coordinates with other development institutions, as noted below.

Technical assistance for the implementation of WTO obligations is a conceptually different goal than those of trade liberalization and development promotion. No longer is the WTO and General Agreement on Tariffs and Trade (GATT) system just about trade liberalization, if it ever was. The WTO's mandate has expanded to include intellectual property and other regulatory issues. Implementing obligations under these new agreements entails significant costs, distracting resource-strapped developing country officials from other priorities. If trade-related capacity-building programmes are simply created to help developing countries implement their WTO obligations, these programmes will serve more limited (and possibly donor-driven) goals.[24]

Finally, the primary aim of a WTO capacity-building programme can be to empower developing countries to better define their trade objectives, to integrate these objectives in development plans, and to advance them in international trade negotiations, monitoring, and enforcement, as well as in the shaping and sequencing of internal regulatory policies. These aims could be advanced through close coordination with other development institutions. As Henri Bernard Solignac Lecomte of the OECD writes, 'There can only be one ultimate objective: to empower developing countries in the multilateral trade system, and help their products to penetrate OECD and other world markets.'[25] Although this latter empowerment objective may overlap with the others, it is much broader, adopting more of a process-based approach. Its aim is to enhance developing countries' capacity to define their own objectives

Development: New Solutions to Old Problems (2002) 1, 18. See also C. Sable and S. Reddy, *Learning to Learn: Undoing the Gordian Knot of Development Today*, mimeo, online at http://www.sopde.org/discussion.htm; P. Evans, 'Transferable Lessons? Re-Examining the Institutional Prerequisites of East Asian Economic Policies' in Y. Akyuz (ed.), *East Asian Development: New Perspectives* (1999); and Lall, *supra* n. 22 (noting that there is a debate as to whether 'social capital' is inherent in the Confucian ethic in Asian culture, or grew through their development strategies).

[24] Implementation of WTO obligations is a complex issue. Countries need to analyse the trade-offs in choices over how they implement WTO requirements in order to facilitate their development strategies. See e.g. C. Correa, *Intellectual Property Rights, the WTO and Developing Countries: The TRIPS Agreement and Policy Options* (2000); J. H. Reichman, *Managing the Challenge of a Globalized Intellectual Property Regime*, draft for the 2nd Bellagio meeting on *Intellectual Property and Development* (2003) (on file).

[25] H. B. Solignac Lecomte, *Building Capacity to Trade: A Road Map for Development Partners: Insights from Africa and the Caribbean*, Overseas Development Institute Paper (July 2001) (on file) at 7.

and policies, as opposed to enhance 'ownership' of substantive policies that others may have defined for them.

II. POLITICAL AND OPERATIONAL CHALLENGES TO IMPLEMENTING A WTO CAPACITY-BUILDING PROGRAMME

WTO technical assistance and capacity-building programmes face at least four major interrelated challenges. They are: (i) the difficulty of ensuring that WTO technical assistance is coherently integrated into larger development strategies, and consists of more than a fragmented hotchpotch of 'one-off' events; (ii) the incentives of donors to frame capacity-building projects to advance donor constituency interests; (iii) the risk of dependency, which can undermine local capacity, unless technical assistance is absorbed institutionally; and (iv) the threat of discontinuation of significant WTO and other trade-related technical assistance after the completion (or termination) of the Doha Round, so that trade-related capacity-building does not remain a significant WTO function.

A. The challenge of coherence with broader development strategies

Technical assistance projects can appear to be random and uncoordinated. Because donors like to take 'credit' for assistance projects, they prefer not to provide substantial funding through an international organization or a common fund.[26] As Susan Prowse of the United Kingdom's (UK) Department for International Development writes, different agencies thus often support 'a vertical multiplicity of trade-related assistance initiatives with little to no horizontal coordination'.[27] The resulting challenge is to ensure greater coherence of trade-related technical assistance programmes in relation to a recipient's overall development strategy.

The WTO has struggled with its attempts to provide a coherent capacity-building programme. As the former Director of the Trade and Development Division, Chiedhu Osakwe, stated, 'we have to realize that we have a monumental problem with coordination . . . There are coordination challenges at every level, there are coordination challenges within the Secretariat, . . . among the beneficiary countries, . . . and amongst the donors. Frequently we are in the middle of friendly fire

---

[26] Interview with a developed country representative to the WTO, June 2004.

[27] S. Prowse, 'The Role of International and National Agencies in Trade-Related Capacity Building' in 25 *World Economy* (2002) 1197 at 1239 (citing OECD, *Building Trade Policy Capacity in Developing Countries and Transition: A Practical Guide to Planning Technical Cooperation Programmes* (2001)).

with regard to the same Missions and their capitals.'[28] The WTO's Technical Cooperation Audit Report for 2002 found:

The activities of the TA Plan in 2002 were not planned, designed or implemented as part of a systematically and coherently developed multi-year technical cooperation project or programme for a technical sector, a country or a region or sub-region. The plan lives and dies from one year to the next. Therefore, the cumulative benefits of the current TAs for the beneficiaries are more the result of coincidence than systematically thought out efforts.[29]

Most activities were of short duration and involved the 'dissemination of information . . . rather than real skill development and capacity-building'.[30] Early WTO technical assistance reports merely described activities in such terms as: 'present detailed information', 'inform the government', or 'explain the structure of GATS'.[31] The WTO's 2003 technical assistance plan admitted 'coordination challenges remain acute . . . at the national level, amongst agencies, and amongst bilateral donors'. The report found too many 'ad hoc demands and fitful Secretariat responses'.[32] The Secretariat nonetheless maintains that, having learned from these experiences, it has built a more effective plan for 2004 and the future, involving a more coherent set of products, each with a clear capacity-building objective.

Conceptualizing capacity-building goals is much easier than implementing them. Part of the conundrum is that a country needs capacity to coordinate, rationalize, and absorb the technical assistance provided. As development analyst Devendra Panday writes, 'integrating and transforming [donor assistance] into a coherent national strategy and then implementing the strategy is a very difficult proposition for a poor country whose coordinating capacity is swamped from all directions'.[33] Thus, some countries have told the Secretariat that 'they need technical assistance to identify their domestic technical assistance needs'.[34] They also need resources just to manage the assistance provided. They admit that 'seminars and workshops . . . will be of little value as we are finding out, . . . if the objective is to develop capacity in the broad sense'.[35]

---

[28] Report to the Secretariat, *High Level Briefing/Meeting on Technical Cooperation and Capacity Building for Capital-Based Senior Officials*, WT/COMTD/43 (20 September 2002) at 10.

[29] See Note by the Secretariat, *Technical Cooperation Audit Report for 2002*, WT/COMTD/W/111 (28 March 2003) at 5.   [30] *Ibid.* at 5.

[31] 'Only six per cent of the back-to-office reports' included reference to 'pre-set indicators' of capacity objectives. WTO Secretariat, *supra* n. 29 at 8.

[32] See Note by the Secretariat, *Coordinated WTO Secretariat Annual Technical Assistance Plan 2003*, WT/COMTD/W/104 (3 October 2002) at 8.

[33] See D. R. Panday, 'Technical Cooperation and Institutional Capacity Building for Development: Back to the Basics' in S. Fukuda-Parr, C. Lopes, and K. Malik (eds), *Capacity for Development: New Solutions to Old Problems* (2002) 61, 79.

[34] WTO Secretariat, *supra* n. 32 at 8.   [35] WTO Secretariat, *supra* n. 28 at 21.

Yet *ad hoc* demands are much easier to formulate, especially when a country lacks internal capacity.

Implementing a trade-related technical assistance strategy, moreover, must respond to the dynamic of WTO negotiations and dispute settlement.[36] The WTO Director-General has consistently emphasized 'the urgency underpinning the on-going Doha trade negotiations and work programme . . . Time frames and deadlines need to be adhered to.'[37] Developing countries must also respond to regional and bilateral trade negotiations. They thus need 'flexibility' in the formulation of technical assistance requests in order for them to participate effectively in multiple, complex negotiations.[38] They do not wish to finalize technical assistance requests six months or a year in advance when the dynamics of negotiations and disputes can raise new needs. This understandable desire for 'flexibility' can conflict with the aim of integrating WTO technical assistance into long-term strategies unless the requests fit into a coherent umbrella framework.

B. The political context

A major challenge for the creation of a meaningful WTO capacity-building programme is that development objectives can conflict with the interests of powerful constituents within donor countries. Government officials in every country respond to their constituents, whether they be protectionist or export-oriented. Not surprisingly, donors respond to the demands of constituents that wish to impede access to 'sensitive sectors' and to press for immediate implementation of intellectual property and other requirements, regardless of another country's development priorities. Donors may 'tie' aid to profit national companies and consultants.[39] Technical assistance is not necessarily 'free'.

---

[36] WTO Secretariat, *supra* n. 28 at 24. The representative of Chile remarked: 'it is very difficult to anticipate what specific needs a developing country will have next year, because we don't know exactly what it is that is going to be required, and the challenges that will have to be faced in the course of the negotiations'. *Ibid.* at 25. The negotiating dynamic reflects the 'bicycle theory' of trade policy which claims that, 'unless there is forward movement, the bicycle will fall over'. See J. H. Jackson, *The World Trade Organization: Constitution and Jurisprudence* (1998) at 24.

[37] See *Report on the Mainstreaming Seminar II*, 31 October–1 November 2002, WT/IFSC/2, at 17.

[38] For example, Colombia asked for technical cooperation for home officials to be conducted back-to-back with meetings of negotiating groups. See WTO Secretariat, *supra* n. 28 at 30. Similarly, Kenya spoke of the need to 'focus on upgrading technical skills and capacity . . . to negotiate on various subjects under discussion in the WTO': *ibid.* at 10. Mauritania expressed a similar need. See *Note on the Meeting of 27 and 28 November 2003*, WT/COMTD/M/47 (14 January 2004) at 12.

[39] See, for example, efforts within the OECD to eliminate 'tied aid,' where development assistance is subject to conditions, such as a requirement that the recipient use companies

One may thus question whether developing countries are 'beneficiaries' of some WTO 'technical assistance' initiatives. For most development analysts, implementation of intellectual property protection, especially in the manner desired by some richer countries, is not a priority for the poor.[40] Yet the first organization with which the WTO signed a 'Cooperation Agreement' for the provision of technical assistance was the World Intellectual Property Organization (WIPO).[41] In July 1998, the WTO and WIPO announced a new joint initiative 'to help developing countries which are members of the WTO meet the 1 January 2000 deadline—less than a year and a half away—for conforming with the [TRIPS Agreement]'.[42] Similarly, other early WTO capacity-building plans consistently referred to 'technical missions . . . aimed at helping individual countries to adapt their existing legislation and regulations to the WTO Agreements in areas such as customs valuation, trade remedies and TRIPS, and transposition of tariff schedules'.[43] A special initiative for African countries likewise proclaimed that it was 'assisting beneficiary countries implement their obligations under the WTO'.[44] In the build-up to the Cancún Ministerial Meeting in 2003, 'of the 1048 TA/CB priorities communicated by Members to the WTO Secretariat, the largest number were to be 'Singapore issues' (investment, competition policy, transparency in government procurement, and trade facilitation)', which were the primary demands of the EU.[45] Of course, one may validly counter that without such technical assistance, developing countries would have been less effective in engaging with the Singapore issues, and many developing countries did not oppose their inclusion.

---

from the granting state. See *Report on Export Credits in the OECD* (2002), online at http://www.oecd.org/publications&documents/guidelines/2002.htm.

[40] See Finger and Schuler, *supra* n. 4. (Estimating that the implementation of the TRIPS, Customs Valuation, and SPS Agreements would cost developing countries around US$150 million dollars, which equals a year's development budget for most LDCs); and the sources cited in *supra* n. 4.

[41] See Note by the Secretariat, *A New Strategy for WTO Technical Cooperation: Technical Cooperation for Capacity Building, Growth and Integration*, WT/COMTD/W/90 (21 September 2001) at 3 (referring to the 1995 document).

[42] See *WTO Press Release 108* 21 July 1998.

[43] E.g. Note by the Secretariat, *Report on Technical Assistance 2000*, WT/COMTD/W/83, (2 May 2001) at 31. The report maintained, for example, that a 'systematic' purpose in the 'cooperation' was to assist developing countries with their notification obligations. In the words of the WTO report, 'In order to raise Members' awareness of their notification obligations, the Secretariat almost systematically includes a module on notification requirements in national as well as in regional seminars'. *Ibid.* at 13. Interestingly, Santa Lucia (a non-resident member of the WTO) expressed the need for flexibility to respond to developing country needs, but the example that it cited was its need 'to do notifications' to the subsidies committee concerning 'subsidy programs'. See WTO Secretariat, *supra* n. 28 at 29.   [44] *Ibid.* at 20 (referring to the JITAP; see below).

[45] 'Technical Assistance and Capacity-building', *ICTSD Doha Round Briefing Series* (February 2003) at 3.

The point remains, however, that the primary demander of the incorporation of these negotiating issues was the EU. When it appeared that implementation issues were being given less attention in the 2004 capacity-building plan, the EU complained that 'no TA was foreseen for the actual implementation and application of existing WTO Agreements'.[46] Even if one takes a favourable view of WTO-promoted regulatory change, in a world of limited resources, there are opportunity costs when development assistance is provided in one area—say for intellectual property protection—and not in another.[47]

Developing countries often view the WTO Secretariat's provision of technical assistance with circumspection because the Secretariat could be advancing the interests of those who oversee the WTO budget—the major donors.[48] An official at an international development agency complains that WTO Secretariat members, when they travel to a developing country to provide technical assistance, 'do not engage in exchange with stakeholders where it is an open question as to whether a WTO rule is good or bad for development, and what are the implementation options and their tradeoffs for a country'.[49] He maintains that WTO Secretariat officials are discouraged from offering counsel as to how a WTO obligation could be interpreted by a country to facilitate a development objective. In at least one case, a WTO Secretariat official complained that officials from other development agencies that might be critical of a WTO rule are 'not being helpful for the WTO agenda'.[50] As one representative from Africa remarked, 'you have to be wary of them [members of the WTO Secretariat],' and 'need to fight constantly' for your interests to be respected.[51] Developing country experiences of course will vary as a function of the country, the country official, and the Secretariat member providing the assistance. Developing countries generally appear to be grateful for the assistance that they receive. The point remains that capacity-building is likely to be more effective if the Secretariat member conducts the mission not to 'promote' a rule, but rather to clarify it and engage about it in an open-ended manner.

In the 2004 capacity-building plan, the Secretariat spoke of the need for Secretariat 'management of the demand' for technical assistance because of the Secretariat's limited resources and the potentially unlimited

---

[46] See *Note on the Meeting of 16 and 23 October 2003*, WT/COMTED/M/46 at 15.

[47] Unlike for the US and Europe, implementation of WTO obligations often requires developing countries to create entirely new regulatory institutions and regimes.

[48] See e.g. Braithwaite and Drahos, *supra* n. 11 at 196 (maintaining that the WTO's upper management faces an incentive structure 'which is symbiotically linked to the power of the US and EC'). [49] Discussion, June 2004.

[50] *Ibid.* [51] Discussion, June 2004.

requests.[52] The EU supported the idea that 'the WTO Secretariat assumes a more proactive and strategic role in assisting those members that have difficulties in identifying their technical assistance needs'.[53] Although there is a strong rationale for bureaucratic coordination to ensure greater coherence, many developing countries distrust Secretariat discretion. They demand that the Secretariat serve their requests in a 'transparent' manner. India, for example, stressed that technical assist-ance must remain 'demand-driven rather than having any aspects that might suggest a prescriptive approach from the part of the Secretariat'.[54] Morocco expressed concern that the Secretariat's approach for 2004 will give the Secretariat too much 'discretionary power'.[55] Costa Rica likewise supported the need to 'provide more flexibility to individual members in deciding national activities'.[56] So did Kenya.[57] At the follow-ing meeting of the Committee on Trade and Development, Mauritania expressed similar views on behalf of the Africa Group, a perspective that Thailand, Colombia, and Morocco also supported.[58]

C. The need to avoid dependency

For most development specialists, the measurement of a development project's success lies not in the quantity of assistance, but in the extent to which the project empowers a country to devise and implement effective strategies on its own over time. As David Ellerman writes, the 'fun-damental conundrum' will remain the paradox of 'supplying help to self-help'.[59] The OECD guidelines similarly speak of the need for approaches that 'strengthen the ability of partner countries to continue helping themselves after the donors have left'.[60] The challenge is to avoid what Ellerman dubs 'Say's Law of Development Aid—the supply of aid seems to create and perpetuate the demand for it.'[61] The temptation to become dependent on aid is high. Developing countries strapped for funds may conform to donor demands simply to get the funds. 'In 1989,

---

[52] See WTO secretariat, *supra* n. 28 at 7. The Secretariat notes the need 'to move away from demand-driven TA' to one in which Members set priorities for managed TA: *ibid.* at 11.
[53] *Ibid.* at 22.   [54] See WTO, *supra* n. 46 at 18.   [55] *Ibid.* at 12.
[56] *Ibid.* at 23.   [57] *Ibid.* at 26.
[58] See *Note on the Meeting of 27 and 28 November 2003*, WT/COMTD/M/47 at 12.
[59] D. Ellerman, 'Autonomy-Respecting Assistance: Towards New Strategies for Capacity-Building and Development Assistance' in S. Fukuda-Parr, C. Lopes, and K. Malik (eds), *Capacity for Development: New Solutions to Old Problems*, (2002) at 43.
[60] OECD, *The DAC Guidelines: Strengthening Trade Capacity for Development*, (2001), online at http://www.oecd.org/dac/trade at 17.
[61] Ellerman, *supra* n. 59 at 50. See also P. Morgan, 'Technical Assistance: Correcting the Precedents' in *Development Policy Journal* (December 2002) 1, 5 ('TA in many instances led to the erosion of ownership, commitment and independent action of national actors. Put in place to help generate independence, TA led in too many cases to a sense of dependence').

for example, for the countries of sub-Saharan Africa, excluding Nigeria, technical cooperation was equivalent to 14 per cent of government revenues. For ten countries, it was equivalent to at least 30 per cent.'[62] Not surprisingly, beneficiaries of a current WTO assistance programme for Africa do not wish to 'graduate' from it, although they may have to do so if the programme is to be extended to other African countries. When developing countries become dependent on external funding, whether for WTO matters or otherwise, technical assistance programmes can actually undermine the development of local capacity. WTO resources are probably too limited and missions too sporadic to create such dependency, at least in the short term. Yet the conundrum of 'supplying help to self-help' to countries that lack underlying capacity remains.

D. The challenge of ensuring sustainability in light of short-term negotiating goals

Donors wish to see pay-offs from the funds that they provide. If trade-related technical assistance does not generate desirable results, then it may be discontinued. Donor governments have thus demanded improvements in the evaluation and reporting of how WTO capacity-building efforts work.[63] The WTO Secretariat now organizes meetings about every six weeks between it, donors, and beneficiaries regarding the use of WTO capacity-building products.[64]

The problem, however, arises in the definition of success and its timeline. Is success to be measured by whether the Doha Round is concluded? Is it to be measured by whether the Doha Round leads to market access in sectors desired by developing countries? Or are capacity-building programmes now institutionalized within the WTO so that their objectives are longer-term? Certainly the Doha Round will not in itself resolve developing countries' trade-related capacity needs.

There exists some pressure to link WTO capacity-building initiatives to the conclusion of the Doha negotiating round. The technical assistance now provided was granted 'explicitly and implicitly' in response to developing countries' agreement to launch the round, which included the Singapore issues.[65] When three of the Singapore issues dropped out of the negotiations in July 2004, the future of donor funding was put in question. As the EU representative warned following the Cancún Ministerial Meeting when developing countries rebelled against inclusion of these issues in the work programme: 'The Cancún outcome required

[62] Fukuda-Parr, Lopes, and Mahik, *supra* n. 23 at 12.
[63] See *Meeting of 22 May and 12 June 2003*, WT/COMTD/M/45 at 14 (US remarks).
[64] Interview with Secretariat member, 23 June 2004.
[65] Interview with a developed country representative to the WTO, June 2004, Geneva.

a re-assessment of TA [technical assistance] priorities . . . Members needed to reconsider the scope of future TA since it was not clear what the scope of the DDA would be in the future.'[66] Canada suggested that the Secretariat reduce trade-related technical assistance over time, and become coordinator, rather than a deliverer, of such assistance.[67]

Developing countries, in contrast, generally insist that 'technical cooperation and capacity-building should be considered as a fundamental aspect of the activities of the WTO'.[68] Some Secretariat observers maintain that it may be politically difficult for donors to significantly curtail technical assistance now that it has been institutionalized within the WTO. At a high-level WTO meeting, a US representative agreed that capacity-building should be 'an enduring component of the work of the WTO'.[69] Nonetheless, donors' perceptions of WTO capacity-building projects' effectiveness in achieving the programme's goals, however those goals might be defined, will shape future funding decisions.

III. HISTORICAL OVERVIEW: THE WTO'S CAPACITY-BUILDING PROGRAMMES IN CONTEXT

Countries have obtained technical expertise from foreign experts throughout history in furtherance of development goals, but technical assistance efforts have become more central aspects of policy since World War II. As Peter Morgan remarks, 'the approach to TA that began in the late 1940s departed radically from much of what had gone before . . . TA became, for the first time, an issue of public policy . . . TA was now to be managed as a public sector activity . . . [as] part of projects and programmes for which staff in new international development organizations were accountable.'[70] In the first decades following World War II, 'thousands of experts and consultants fanned around the world, taking up residence in ministries and project offices, partly to supervise aid projects, but also to plant the skills and expertise . . . The underlying assumption was that developing countries lacked important skills and abilities—and that outsiders could fill these gaps with quick injections of know-how.'[71] The term 'technical assistance' referred to skill transfers to foster modernization.

---

[66] WT/COMTD/M/46 at 14 (the DDA refers to the Doha Development Agenda).

[67] See WTO Secretariat, *supra* n. 28 at 22.

[68] *Ibid.* at 30 (remarks of Colombian official in reference to para. 38 of the Doha Declaration). Confirmed in numerous interviews in Geneva, June 2004.

[69] WTO Secretariat, *supra* n. 28 at 26.

[70] P. Morgan, 'Technical Assistance: Correcting the Precedents' in *Development Policy Journal* (December 2002) at 1–2.

[71] Fukuda-Parr, Lopes, and Malik, *supra* n. 23 at 2.

After a couple of decades, development analysts switched their focus to that of 'technical cooperation' to emphasize that development programmes should work through a collaborative process. This term was later complemented by that of 'capacity-building' to highlight the importance of local 'ownership' and 'absorption' of technical assistance to bolster recipients' ability to pursue their development goals.[72] The OECD's development guidelines, for example, now call for 'local ownership and participation in all trade-related development cooperation activities'.[73] The lack of local ownership in previous development assistance efforts is shown by the fact that of 113 public expenditure review exercises completed up to 1993, 'only three included local members on the review team, not one in Africa where most were done and where the ownership problem was most acute'.[74] Capacity-building efforts have also shifted toward the development of broader-based 'social capital', defined as 'the norms and networks facilitating collective action for mutual benefit'.[75] Initiatives that focus on the development of social capital target private and civil groups, as well as public officials.

The provision of technical assistance and capacity-building has changed over time within the GATT and WTO, although the type of assistance that the WTO secretariat can deliver remains limited by the Secretariat's human resources and its perception of its mandate.[76] Although Secretariat officials refer to a 'Member-driven' mandate, some Members play more predominant roles than others. Donor governments play a central role on the WTO's budget committee, which is a primary means through which they oversee and constrain what the Secretariat does.

Until the creation of the WTO, GATT technical assistance largely took the form of 'trade policy courses' taught in Geneva. The Secretariat organized around 77 of these courses during the GATT's 47-year history.[77] As WTO membership grew, and as WTO rules proliferated and their

---

[72] See e.g. Organization for Economic Co-operation and Development/Development Assistance Committee (OECD/DAC), *Principles of New Orientations in Technical Cooperation* (1991); E. Berg and the United Nations Development Programme, *Rethinking Technical Cooperation: Reforms for Capacity-Building in Africa* (1993).

[73] OECD, *supra* n. 19.

[74] See E. Berg, 'Why Aren't Aid Organizations Better Learners?' in J. Carlsson and L. Wohlgemuth (eds), *Learning in Development Co-operation* (2000) at 25.

[75] See S. Woolcock, 'The Place of Social Capital in Understanding Social and Economic Outcomes' in 2(1) *Canadian Journal of Policy Research* (2000) 11; Lall, *supra* n. 22. See also the work of F. Fukuyama, *Trust: The Social Virtues and the Creation of Prosperity* (1995); R. Putnam, 'The Prosperous Community: Social Capital and Public Life', 4 *The American Prospect* (1993) 13.

[76] The total size of the WTO Secretariat remains under 600 persons, over 200 of which are translators or providers of secretarial and cataloguing services. Compare these figures to that of a World Bank staff of around 9,300 and of an IMF staff of around 2,700.

[77] See 'Second WTO Trade Policy Course opens in Geneva' in *WTO Press Release*, 28 August 1995.

scope expanded, more developing countries complained about the demands of WTO developments. The WTO launched a fund for technical assistance for least-developed countries in September 1995.[78] In 1996, the WTO published guidelines for WTO Technical Cooperation 'to improve knowledge of multilateral trade rules', and 'to assist in the implementation of commitments and full use of its provisions.' The first 'modes of delivery' were, once again, 'training courses' and the 'development of information and training material', complemented by 'specialized technical seminars'.[79]

At the Singapore Ministerial Meeting of December 1996, the WTO announced a broader Integrated Framework for Trade-Related Technical Assistance to Least-Developed Countries. The Integrated Framework, coordinated out of the WTO, brings together six international agencies (United Nations Conference on Trade and Development (UNCTAD), International Trade Center (ITC), United Nations Development Programme (UNDP), WTO, the International Monetary Fund (IMF), and the World Bank) to collaborate with bilateral donors to ensure greater coherence in the provision of trade-related technical assistance in least-developed countries.[80] The WTO, UNCTAD, and ITC concurrently launched a Joint Integrated Technical Assistance Programme to selected Least Developed and other African countries (JITAP).[81] The WTO's portion of JITAP's work has

---

[78] 'Norway provides $2.5 Million to Launch a WTO Fund for Least-Developed Countries' in *WTO Press Release*, 29 September 1995.

[79] See *Guidelines for WTO Technical Cooperation*, Committee on Trade and Development, WT/COMTD/8 at 1. (16 October 1996).

[80] The Integrated Framework has taken a 'process'-oriented approach of awareness-building combined with diagnosis of trade-related challenges, with the aim of integrating trade strategies in national development plans. As part of a revised IMF/World Bank strategy, between 1999 and 2001, around 50 countries prepared 'Poverty Reduction Strategy Papers' (PRSPs) in which they define priorities. However, trade initially did not figure prominently in most PRSPs. See discussion in K. Malik and S. Wagle, 'Civic Engagement and Development: Introducing the Issues' in S. Fukuda-Parr, C. Lopes, and K. Malik (eds), *Capacity for Development: New Solutions to Old Problems* (2002) 85, 96. According to Prowse, one of the objectives of the Integrated Framework was that trade-related capacity-building be granted greater attention 'in relation to other development assistance needs': Prowse, *supra* n. 27 at 1242. See also Terms of reference for Integrated Framework pilot programme, WT/LDC/SWG/IF/13. In most developing countries, trade ministries play an extremely weak role compared to finance and other ministries: interviews with members of WTO, UNCTAD, and ITC Secretariats, June 2004, Geneva. These interviewees also noted the problem of rapid turnover in the trade bureaucracies in developing countries, and, in particular, in the least developed countries. The Integrated Framework was endorsed at a WTO high-level meeting on 27 October 1997. See 'Inter-Agency Trade Assistance Programme Launched for Least-Developed Countries', *WTO Press Release* 83, 30 October 1997. The Integrated Framework received US$19 million in pledges through 2003, of which around US$10 million was disbursed through 2003. The International Trade Centre (ITC) is a joint venture of the WTO and UNCTAD.

[81] The JITAP is a 'results-oriented' programme involving specific activities and products. JITAP was first announced at UNCTAD IX in Midran, South Africa in 1996. By September 2003, the JITAP had received US$12.6 million in its Common Trust Fund, of

focused on strengthening WTO 'reference centres' located in these countries, which include computer terminals and internet access, and on providing updates to officials on WTO developments.

Analysts criticized the early WTO technical assistance programmes, including the Integrated Framework and JITAP efforts.[82] Overall funding was limited. The WTO Secretariat was unschooled in the provision of technical assistance, which lay outside its traditional competence. Requests for assistance largely came from Geneva-based representatives so that capacity-building efforts were not well coordinated with national capitals, with a resulting lack of local ownership. Although there were some successes,[83] the system allegedly operated in a 'rigid' manner, with requests for assistance required to be fixed at least six months prior to the start of the annual plan's implementation.[84] Many of the activities were considered to be 'one-off' events that would have little sustainable impact, so that there was an overall focus on quantity rather than quality.[85] A representative of one development organization characterized WTO technical assistance as 'a joke'.[86]

With the launch of the Doha Round in 2001 and the creation of the Doha Development Agenda Global Trust Fund, trade-related technical assistance and capacity-building programmes increased. Members pledged over 21.5 million Swiss francs (about US\$15.7 million) in 2002.[87] In 2003,

which US\$11 million had been pledged by donors. In JITAP, UNCTAD's work focuses on providing support for the beneficiaries' development of trade policies through 'inter-institutional committees'. The ITC focuses on trade capacity issues that are more commercially oriented. Interview, WTO Secretariat member, 23 June 2004, Geneva, and with ITC officials, 28 June 2004.

[82] See generally M. Kostecki, *Technical Assistance Services in Trade-Policy: A Contribution to the Discussion on Capacity-Building in the WTO*, ICTSD Resource Paper No. 2 (November 2001); S. Prowse, *The Role of International and National Agencies in Trade-related Capacity-Building*, online at http://www.unido.org/file-storage/download/?file_id=12962; B. Larson, 'Meaningful Technical Assistance in the WTO' in 6 *Wisconsin Law Review* (2003) 1164, 1194–1195.

[83] The JITAP received a positive evaluation in 2002 (document on file with author). The JITAP helped establish WTO 'resource centres' in its beneficiary countries, a programme that was then expanded to cover developing country members generally. JITAP also allegedly facilitated the coordination of trade policy within beneficiaries through 'inter-institutional committees'. Interview with a member of the WTO Secretariat, 23 June 2004, Geneva.

[84] Interview with member of the WTO Secretariat, 23 June 2004, Geneva.

[85] WTO Secretariat, *supra* n. 29 at 11. To give an example, the WTO's 2000 report on technical assistance largely consisted of *ad hoc* examples broken down by WTO agreement, mode of delivery, numbers of activities, and percentage of geographical distribution.

[86] Discussion, July 2004.

[87] 'Technical Assistance and Capacity-Building', *ICTSD Doha Round Briefing Series* (February 2003). Governments pledged 30 million Swiss francs to the Doha Development Agenda Global Trust Fund at a pledging conference held on 11 March 2002 at the WTO: *WTO Press Release* 279, 11 March 2002. As Larson notes, the trust fund 'grew to three times the size of [the Integrated Framework's funding] overnight': Larson, *supra* n. 82 at 1195. The 2004 technical assistance plan was estimated to cost around 36.2 million Swiss francs, with around 30 million Swiss francs coming from WTO sources. About 6

funds for WTO capacity-building projects from the annual budget and the new trust fund slightly exceeded 30 million Swiss Francs. The same amount was also budgeted for 2004.[88] These figures do not include overhead costs, including the salaries of around 38 officials in the WTO Institute for Training and Technical Cooperation, 19 'L' officials hired on fixed-term contracts to provide assistance, and other 'operational staff' asked to help.[89] Moreover, these funds complement the considerably greater amounts of trade-related capacity building that donors provide directly or through other international organizations.[90]

Problems with WTO technical assistance efforts spurred the WTO to announce a 'new strategy' in 2001 whose stated aims were to make technical assistance more demand-driven, to create financial stability through the Doha trust fund, and to enhance the capability of the WTO Secretariat to deliver products within its mandate in a manner that was both coherent and flexible to meet developing country needs.[91] The WTO's 'new strategy' nonetheless initially continued to focus on the more limited objectives of trade liberalization and rule implementation. The opening paragraph of the new strategy stated: 'The core mandate of the WTO is trade liberalization . . . WTO technical assistance . . . provides enabling assistance for Members to undertake trade liberalization . . . [The role of the Secretariat is] to assist them in understanding WTO rules and disciplines.'[92]

WTO trade-related capacity-building plans were, however, modified and became somewhat more sophisticated over time. The plans have taken account of audits of the previous year's activities. An audit of the Technical Assistance Plan for 2003, for example, criticized the plan's implementation for a lack of coherence, maintaining that the Secretariat was largely servicing *ad hoc* requests.[93] In response, the Secretariat

---

million Swiss francs was to come out of the WTO's general budget and about 24 million out of the Doha Development Agenda Global Trust Fund.

[88] WTO members contributed 24.6 million Swiss francs to the Doha Trust Fund in 2003, of which only 14.4 million Swiss francs was expended. See *WTO 2004 World Trade Report* at 131.

[89] Interview with WTO Secretariat official, 22 June 2004, Geneva.

[90] The second joint WTO/OECD report on trade-related technical assistance and capacity-building of 2003 divided trade-related capacity-building programmes into three categories which had generated the following amounts of funding: (i) trade policy and regulations, US$719 million; (ii) trade/business development, US$1.4 billion; and (iii) infrastructure, US$8.1 billion. The total of these three items constituted about 4.8 per cent of total aid, more than went to basic education or basic health: *2nd Joint WTO/OECD Report on Trade-Related Technical Assistance and Capacity-building (TRTA/CB)* (2003), online at http://www.oecd.org/dataoecd/27/4/11422694.htm.

[91] WTO Secretariat, *supra* n. 41. Note, however, that the 1996 guidelines for WTO Technical Cooperation also proclaimed that they should 'be demand-driven'. See WT/COMTD/8 at 1.   [92] WTO Secretariat, *supra* n. 41 at 1.

[93] The 2003 Technical Assistance Plan focused on the need to build capacity to understand the rules and implement WTO agreements, on the one hand, and to develop

prepared a plan for 2004 that was to be more 'quality-oriented, aiming at building long-term—i.e. sustainable, human and institutional capacity,' setting forth clearer 'objectives' for each type of capacity-building 'product'.[94] The 2004 Plan set forth a long list of 'products' that included Geneva-based, region-based, nation-based, and distance-learning activities, as follows:

- Four three-month trade policy courses at the WTO in Geneva, two in English, and one each in French and Spanish, for which participants first undergo a selection process.

- Four three-month regional trade policy courses: in Nairobi, Kenya for Anglophone Africa; in Rabat, Morocco for Francophone Africa; in Hong Kong for Asia/Pacific members; and at the University of West Indies, Jamaica for the Caribbean. The Secretariat hopes to hold regional courses in other regions in the future for 'Arab and Middle East Countries, Latin America, Central and Eastern Europe, Central Asia and the Caucasus'.[95] Through these regional courses, the Secretariat hopes to build regional institutional partnerships and academic networks.

- Two- to- five-day regional seminars on specific WTO issues, from agriculture to textiles, dispute settlement to the TRIPS Agreement. These seminars, which aim to provide 'more advanced levels of training' that may build on previous programmes, are to be conducted in partnership with other international and regional agencies.

- Shorter Doha Development Agenda courses for senior government officials that focus on the state and process of the Doha negotiations, which are 'held in each region'.

- National seminars which are provided flexibly in response to developing country requests, with up to two seminars allocated for each developing country, and three for least-developed countries (in addition to the assistance that the latter may receive under the JITAP and Integrated Framework programmes).

- Five specialized courses held in Geneva on dispute settlement and trade negotiation theory and practice.

- Two introductory courses in Geneva for least-developed countries.

negotiating capacity, on the other, although it called for 'capacity-building based on Members' explicitly determined priorities'. See Note by the Secretariat, *Coordinated WTO Secretariat Annual Technical Assistance Plan 2003*, WT/COMTD/W/104/Rev.2 (22 November 2002) para. 15.

[94] WTO, *Technical Assistance and Training Plan 2004*, WT/COMTD/W/119/Rev.3 (18 February 2004). The 2004 Plan aimed 'to enhance institutional and human capacity in beneficiary countries and to address trade policy issues and concerns, "mainstreaming" trade into national development and poverty reduction policies and facilitating a fuller participation of beneficiaries in the Multilateral Trading System and effective participation in the negotiations'. *Ibid.* at 1.   [95] WTO, *supra* n. 93 at 7.

- Other Geneva-based support, including an induction day for new diplomats, two 'Geneva weeks' for those WTO members without permanent representation in Geneva, video conferencing, advisory assistance on dispute settlement issues, and *ad hoc* assistance.
- Distance learning courses through computer-based training modules, interactive guides, and on-line fora.[96]
- Establishment and upgrading of 'WTO Reference Centres', of which around 130 operated in 90 countries as of June 2004.[97] For poorer countries, the WTO has provided information technology equipment and helped with internet access outside of the local power grid. (One of the aims is to facilitate trainees' ability to maintain contact with members of the WTO secretariat and with each other).
- WTO internship and trainee programmes to build hands-on practical learning.
- Through collaboration with the OECD, creation of a database of trade-related technical assistance activities to facilitate greater coordination.[98]

According to the Secretariat, beneficiaries and donors have supported the way that the 2004 Plan has operated.[99] The Secretariat hopes that courses held in developing countries, in particular, can foster the creation of 'academic networks with institutions of higher learning' in developing countries.[100] Over time, the Secretariat would like the regional partners to assume 'a growing share of the responsibility of the courses', with the Secretariat overseeing quality control.[101] The Secretariat also plans to begin a PhD mentor programme in Geneva, where PhD candidates from developing countries can have space in the WTO library and be assigned a mentor from within the Secretariat.[102]

The Integrated Framework and JITAP programmes were revamped in 2003 and 2004 in order to better 'aim at mainstreaming trade within national development strategies by promoting trade policies supportive of the poverty reduction objectives of those countries'.[103] The JITAP programme was expanded in 2003 to include 16 countries, and its modules

---

[96] The first WTO eTraining programme was scheduled for 21 June to 30 July 2004. See 'First WTO eTraining Course for Government Officials' in *WTO News* (14 May 2004), online at http://www.wto.org/news/news2004.htm.

[97] Email from a member of the WTO Secretariat, June 2004.

[98] See Doha Development Agenda Trade-Related Technical Assistance and Capacity-Building Database, online at http:/tcbdb.wto.org.

[99] Interview with Secretariat official, 22 June 2004, Geneva.

[100] One of the plan's objectives is to 'enhance the capacity of [local] academic institutions to backstop policy-making': WTO, *supra* n. 94 at 6. See also WTO *supra* n. 46 (remarks of Secretariat). Confirmed in interviews with Secretariat members, 22 June 2004, Geneva.   [101] See WTO, *supra* n. 94.

[102] See WTO, *supra* n. 46 at 29.

[103] The quote is from Integrated Framework Steering Committee, *Financial Report on the Integrated Framework Trust Fund*, WT/IFSC/W/7/Add.1 (1 May 2002).

were reduced to five core programmes, from 15. The Integrated
Framework's coverage was expanded from three to 14 countries in 2003,
and to 32 by October 2004.[104] The Integrated Framework opened a second
'window' to include 'bridging' funding of up to US$1 million per country
for priority needs, in addition to diagnostic studies (its 'first window').[105]

Sceptics outside of the WTO nonetheless question whether WTO trade-
related capacity-building will be reoriented in practice. They suspect that
WTO capacity-building programmes will continue to focus on Powerpoint
presentations of 'rules' and on developing countries' implementation
obligations because of a restrictive 'interpretation' of the WTO's rule-
orientated mandate which is pressed by donor countries monitoring the
WTO's budget.[106] As one developing country representative remarked,
'the donors were careful that the Doha trust fund went into the WTO
where they could control it, and not into another organization'.[107] As he
concluded:

the delivery modes [of the Secretariat's new plan] may be better, but the orientation is likely to be the same. Ultimately, the donors will control how the
money is used. For example, when technical assistance is provided on WTO
agricultural issues, the US Department of Agriculture will send an expert who
will tell you what your position should be in the Doha round agricultural negotiations. They and the WTO guys go to countries to tell them what to do, not
how to analyze and review options and their implications. WTO capacity building and technical assistance are important, but we need to fight all the time over
how they are applied.[108]

---

[104] Email from WTO Secretariat member, 12 October 2004. One interviewee in the
WTO Secretariat characterized this as a 'mini-crisis of success' for the Integrated
Framework Interview, June 2004, Geneva.

[105] The 'first window' consisted of diagnostic studies prepared on a pilot basis for three
least-developed countries (LDCs). It was then extended to 14 LDCs in 2003. See WTO,
supra n. 94 at 21. Confirmed in interview with WTO Secretariat member, 22 June 2004,
Geneva. Following the diagnostic studies, Integrated Framework beneficiaries were to
obtain funding from donor organizations, but it allegedly turned out that there was little
follow-up. A World Bank official blamed the donors for not coming through with funding. Discussion, July 2004. A donor representative, in contrast, blamed the World Bank
for, among other matters, hiring consultants from Washington to prepare 'huge fat' diagnostic studies instead of using the Bank's local people. Discussion with a donor representative, July 2004. Because it has taken so long to move beyond the diagnostic and pilot
stages, some development analysts have labelled the Integrated Framework 'if and when'.
Interview with an official at a development organization, 29 June 2004, Geneva.

[106] Many developing countries would like to have the WTO mandate explicitly
include 'development' issues, but developed countries prefer to keep it narrow, focusing
on the 'rules' of a 'contract' organization. Interviews with officials in other Geneva-based
international organizations and developing country non-governmental organizations,
June 2004, Geneva (noting who is 'interpreting' and 'defining' the 'mandate'). One interviewee from another international organization characterized changes in the WTO
regarding development issues as ones of 'rhetoric', since the WTO will remain a 'rule-
based system', 29 June 2004, Geneva.   [107] Discussion, July 2004.
[108] *Ibid.*

IV. CONCLUSION: SOME POTENTIAL ADAPTATIONS WITHIN DEVELOPING COUNTRIES, THE WTO, AND DONORS

The role of capacity-building programmes should be to empower developing countries to take advantage of trade-related opportunities, whether through shaping WTO law and tariff concessions to facilitate development goals, through deploying WTO rights in dispute settlement, through implementing WTO law more effectively, or otherwise. It is, of course, always easier to examine challenges and failures than to implement strategies to capitalize on new opportunities. This concluding section aims to highlight positive developments in WTO capacity-building efforts and some potential adaptations to be considered.

First, we should recognize that donors came through with a significantly greater amount of funding for trade-related technical assistance and that the WTO Secretariat improved in delivering its part. The Secretariat now provides a broader spectrum of products that include regional courses hosted by local universities, specialized regional courses, workshops on negotiation techniques,[109] partnerships with academic and other institutions, and WTO reference centres set up around the world. The provision of this assistance has been somewhat more demand-driven, resulting in a better understanding of WTO rules and negotiating dynamics among a broader network of developing country government officials. WTO observers note that developing countries have been much more engaged in the Doha Round of trade negotiations than they were in the past, indicating much greater 'ownership' of the technical assistance provided.[110] Such engagement could, however, result from assistance from organizations and networks that are independent of the WTO, rather than through the WTO itself.

How can developing countries, donors, and the WTO Secretariat build on past developments? First, developing countries need to increase their institutional coordination at multiple levels in a broader-based manner to include government departments, the private sector, and civil

---

[109] The WTO held its first course on 'Negotiating Trade Agreements: From Theory to Practice' on 2–13 December 2002, and its second on 16–27 June 2003.

[110] As Faizel Ismail, the head of the South African delegation to the WTO, said following the Cancún meeting, 'The only silver lining to the disappointment felt by G20 members at the abrupt end of the WTO Cancún Ministerial Conference was that developing country negotiators had come of age. They had galvanized a formidable group of developing countries and skillfully built a common negotiation position that provided a sound platform to continue negotiations for a fair and freer global market for developing countries' agricultural products'. F. Ismail, 'Agricultural Trade Liberalization and the Poor: A Development Perspective on Cancún' in *Bridges* (January 2004) at 4.

society representatives.[111] Technical assistance and capacity-building endeavours will be most sustainable if they permeate broadly throughout institutions and societies. Donor capture is less likely if a broad array of stakeholders is included. The WTO's 2002 audit, however, showed that the 'representation of other economic sectors remains insignificant [with representatives being limited to officials from certain ministries], . . . despite general recognition that the involvement of the private sector and civil society representatives is desirable'.[112] If the focus of technical assistance were to remain on individual capacity instead of larger societal and institutional capacity, then the WTO could simply be training individuals whose objectives and career paths are unpredictable.[113] Trade-related capacity-building will be more effective if it also responds, directly or indirectly, to local constituent demands, including those of the private sector, academics, and other civil groups, as part of a bottom–up process.

If developing countries are to shape the international trading system to facilitate their economic development and if they are to take advantage of WTO rules, they will need to work with the private sector to enhance the resources at their disposal. They will also need strong civil society networks to provide government representatives with greater negotiating leverage. The US and Europe have learned how to harness private resources—informational and material—to advance their agendas.[114] Developing countries will need to develop strategies of their own that involve broader-based constituencies. To give a few examples, civil society organizations have been instrumental in reframing debates over the TRIPS Agreement and agricultural subsidies, and Brazil's private sector has helped finance WTO legal challenges against US cotton and EU sugar subsidies.

There are some signs that WTO capacity-building efforts are becoming broader-based. The Secretariat's 2004 Plan explores ways to increase the absorptive capacity of technical assistance projects through coordination with broader networks of actors. Developing country representatives have welcomed the Secretariat's initiative to work with

---

[111] The OECD guidelines refer to 'effective mechanisms for consultation among three key sets of stakeholders: government, the enterprise sector, and civil society': *supra* n. 19.

[112] See WTO Secretariat, *supra* n. 29 at 4.

[113] Some WTO trainees will leave government service or be assigned to agencies that do not work on trade matters. One interviewee noted that the trade policy course was extremely valuable for him and others, but that some students appeared to treat the course as an opportunity for 'tourism'. Interview with developing country representative, 30 June 2004, Geneva. Similarly, a WTO official questioned the extent to which some beneficiaries are 'serious' about capacity-building in light of the minimal efforts of some students in the courses. Interview, 23 June 2004, Geneva.

[114] G. Shaffer, *Defending Interests: Public-Private Partnerships in WTO Litigation* (2003).

developing country academic institutions and think-tanks, to provide WTO internships, and to organize a programme for their doctoral students to use the WTO library. Developing country hosts of WTO regional courses, in particular, hope that the courses stimulate greater awareness of WTO trade issues in government ministries and universities, as well as in the general public as a result of media coverage.[115] Nonetheless, some developing country representatives have been reticent about civil society and parliamentarian-oriented capacity-building projects, at least where the funding comes out of the WTO's technical assistance budget. India and Egypt have stated, for example, that they do not view 'outreach programmes for parliaments and civil society as TA activities but rather as national activities'.[116] Thailand agreed.[117]

Developing countries could also benefit from mechanisms to network and pool their resources at the regional and international levels. Most developing countries are small. These countries will never have the capacity to follow and advance their interests effectively in the WTO system by acting alone. Just as European countries, they could benefit from networking and pooling resources through regional and other institutions. The WTO's 'regional' technical assistance programmes could, at least in theory, facilitate this coordination. Although strategies for pooling resources have their limits, they need to be compared with the alternative of each developing country working on its own, in which case the trading powers can more easily play developing countries off against each other.[118]

As for the WTO Secretariat, although the WTO may be a Member-driven organization, it is not entirely so. Secretariat members are able to exercise authority in numerous contexts, including in the provision of technical assistance. Some of the Secretariat's assistance raises fewer tensions than others. For example, capacity-building programmes regarding

---

[115] Interview with a representative from an African country.

[116] See WTO, *supra* n. 46 at 22. Curiously, Pakistan's representative supported the inclusion of outreach programmes for parliamentarians and civil society. *Ibid.* at 23. So did the representative from Venezuela. See WTO, *supra* n. 58 at 20.   [117] *Ibid.* at 18.

[118] See e.g. P. Drahos, 'When the Weak Bargain with the Strong: Negotiations in the World Trade Organization' in 8 *International Negotiation* (2003) 79–109; G. Shaffer, *How to Make the WTO Dispute Settlement System Work for Developing Countries: Some Proactive Developing Country Strategies*, ICTSD Monograph, Geneva (March 2003) 1–65, online at http://www.ictsd.org/pubs/ictsd_series/resource_papers/DSU_2003.pdf. The proliferation of bilateral trade negotiations and agreements, and the manner of implementation of the general system of preferences, often divide developing countries, making it more difficult for them to coordinate across issues in a sustained manner. See G. Shaffer and Y. Apea, 'Putting the GSP Case in Context: Who Decides the Conditions for Trade Preferences?' in T. Cottier and J. Pauwelyn (eds), *Trade and Human Rights* (2005). Developing countries nonetheless would have to monitor and develop trust that the Secretariats of regional associations and the lead representatives in regional networks work effectively on their behalf.

trade negotiating practices and the use of the WTO's dispute settlement system address how developing countries can better defend and advance their objectives. Technical assistance for implementation, in contrast, can represent a form of 'soft' persuasion by the Secretariat of what developing countries must do in respect of other Members' demands. To put this in context, were Secretariat representatives to travel to Washington DC or to European capitals to tell administrative officials (in a potentially doctrinaire manner) what WTO rules require them to do and why these rules are 'good' for their countries, sparks could fly. If the WTO Secretariat believes that it lacks the independence to engage with developing country representatives and stakeholders in an open way about whether WTO rules serve varying development contexts and about how WTO disciplines might be flexibly interpreted to promote development objectives, then developing countries should be wary. In such a case, developing countries should be sure that representatives from development agencies and other consultants who have greater independence are included in relevant WTO trade-related 'capacity-building' projects.

Although the WTO's organizational culture is not that of a development institution, Members could further integrate certain development orientations. The Trade Policy Review Mechanism could be given a greater development orientation when applied to developing countries.[119] If trade strategies are to be integrated into development plans, as called for by the Integrated Framework, the JITAP, and the WTO's technical assistance programmes, then it makes sense to adapt the Trade Policy Review Mechanism accordingly. Trade Policy Review Mechanism implementation reviews could examine the ways in which a developing country has mainstreamed trade policy as part of a development strategy. Implementation of WTO requirements could be viewed through the lens of sequencing based on development thresholds. This adaptation could be applied on a trial basis with least-developed and other low-income countries. As Prowse points out, a development approach is not alien to GATT–WTO traditions that include such issues as infant industry promotion and balance-of-payment concerns.[120]

Similarly, as the scope of WTO rules continues to expand, a single set of disciplines becomes less appropriate for all WTO members. One can, and should, distinguish between core GATT rules of non-discrimination,

---

[119] See also OECD, *supra* n. 19 at 9 (suggesting that the TPRM be used 'to raise awareness of constraints to trade and investment in developing countries' so as 'to ensure coherence between trade policies and regulatory regimes on the one hand, and overall development goals on the other').

[120] See Prowse, *supra* n. 27 at 1242 (referring to GATT Arts. XVIII:B and XII).

which apply to all members, and other substantive rules.[121] Article XXXVI of Part IV of GATT 1994 expressly provides that 'developed countries do not expect reciprocity for commitments made to them in trade negotiations [from] . . . less-developed contracting parties'. It further specifies that 'the less-developed countries should not be expected, in the course of trade negotiations, to make contributions which are inconsistent with their individual development, financial and trade needs, taking into consideration past trade developments'. In practice, however, developing countries often have only received longer transition periods to implement WTO obligations, periods that by now have largely elapsed. There is a role for greater differentiation of Members based on less-developed countries' capacities and levels of development. That variation can be implemented through conditioning implementation on defined development thresholds and through enhanced Special and Differential Treatment (SDT) provisions.[122]

Institutionalizing a capacity-building component in the WTO could play a transformative role for the Secretariat itself. Such institutionalization could induce the Secretariat to become more conscious of the development context of trade. Just as the Secretariat admirably has been self-critical regarding its past provision of technical assistance, so it could be self-critical in its understanding of the role of trade in development. It could view trade rules not as ends in themselves, but rather as tools that can be applied to different development contexts. The WTO could, in particular, open permanent WTO regional offices where WTO staff can become more attuned to region- and country-specific needs.[123]

As regards donors, they will continue to be under pressure from domestic constituents to shape technical assistance to advance those constituents' interests. Constituents that lose from reduced donor government subsidies or increased access to donor markets will oppose technical assistance provided to developing countries that facilitates these objectives. Capacity-building initiatives, however, are more likely to be effective if donors view them as longer-term foundational issues to enhance developing country trading options in the global economy, and not as shorter-term concessions as part of a trade negotiation package. Initiatives will also be more effective if donors coordinate among, and do not compete between, each other. Donors will need to support these programmes before their own publics in this light.

---

[121] See B. Hoekman, 'Operationalizing the Concept of Policy Space in the WTO: Beyond Special and Differential Treatment of Developing Countries' in this volume.

[122] The national treatment obligations under the General Agreement on Trade in Services (GATS), for example, only apply to sectors listed in a country's GATS schedule.

[123] This idea was considered in *Technical Cooperation Audit Report for 2002, supra* n. 29 at 11.

The unstable security situation that the world now confronts offers opportunities and sets constraints for trade-related development strategies. On the one hand, the threat of terrorism can impede and disrupt trade, which could particularly harm countries with small internal markets. On the other hand, global concern with terrorism could focus developed countries' attention toward the development of stable developing states that can serve as critical allies. In this regard, there are analogies between the current situation and the past, in which East Asian countries benefited from the US desire for strong and economically successful allies during the Cold War. Developed and developing countries' security interests are both ultimately linked with global development. As one high-level member of the WTO Secretariat quipped, 'the Doha round was a gift of Osama bin Ladin'.[124] Similarly, the 2002 US *National Security Strategy* states, 'A world where some live in comfort and plenty, while half of the human race lives on less than $2 a day, is neither just nor stable. Including all of the world's poor in an expanding circle of development and opportunity is a moral imperative and one of the top priorities of U.S. international policy.'[125] The test of such a 'security policy' will be in the doing. WTO capacity-building programmes could play a small, but beneficial, part.

---

[124] Interview, June 2002, Geneva.

[125] The policy is set force in a document entitled *The National Security Strategy of the United States* (17 September 2002), online at http://www.whitehouse.gov/nsc/nss.pdf. The strategy is best known for its justification of the need for pre-emptive strikes, so that its development dimension is often overlooked.

PART VI

ARE WTO RULES PROTECTING CONSUMER WELFARE?

12

Come Together? Producer Welfare, Consumer Welfare, and WTO Rules

PETROS C. MAVROIDIS[1]

I. SOME BRIEF INTRODUCTORY REMARKS

World Trade Organization (WTO) rules concerned with trade liberalization (that is the General Agreement on Tariffs and Trade (GATT), the General Agreement on Trade in Services (GATS), and their Annexes) are based on the premise that trade liberalization has overall positive welfare implications for the liberalizing state. This much is commonplace in economics.

Trade liberalization in the WTO is a matter of degree and a subject of multilateral negotiations. It is not the case that WTO Members have unilaterally adopted equally open trade policies. What is horizontally (i.e. for all WTO Members) true is that their trade openness must, *in principle*, be non-discriminatory. What exactly non-discriminatory access amounts to is very much a matter of discussion.[2]

Non-discrimination, however, does not prejudge the quality of regulatory intervention. That is, a WTO Member might be adopting a series of inefficient policies that will not sufficiently take account of consumer welfare but, to the extent that it applies to them in a non-discriminatory manner will not be running the risk of seeing its choices successfully challenged before WTO adjudicating bodies. This is the direct outcome of the fact that both the GATT and the GATS are largely negative integration-type contracts where policies affecting trade are defined

[1] As always, I am indebted for never ending discussions on the issue and very helpful comments on a previous draft to Henrik Horn. I would further like to thank Panagiotis Delimatsis, Patrick Messerlin, Tim Groser, and Sebastian Herreros as well as participants at the EUI conference (27–28 June 2003) for many helpful comments.
[2] See, for example, the analysis of positive case law on this issue in H. Henrik and P. C. Mavroidis, 'Still Hazy after All These Years: The Interpretation of National Treatment in the GATT/WTO Case-Law on Tax Discrimination' in 15 *European Journal of International Law* (2004) 39–69.

unilaterally and their international spillovers have to simply obey the non-discrimination principle.[3]

The WTO contract contains safeguards:[4] the GATT knows of four contingent protection instruments (anti-dumping, subsidies, safeguards, balance of payments) alongside the GATT waiver (which could be used in this way). The GATS, on the other hand, contains no formal safeguards (although it was agreed that a Working Party discuss this issue), but is, in Hoekman's expression, full of in-built safeguards anyway.[5]

GATT contingent protection instruments allow for WTO Members the possibility to increase their multilaterally negotiated and agreed protection (either by raising their import duties or by restricting the volume of imports, or even through a combination of both options) whenever an event occurs that justifies recourse to such instruments: dumping might lead to anti-dumping duties, increased imports to safeguards, etc. Recourse to contingent protection instruments is WTO-consistent when the event at hand is causing injury to the domestic producer and irrespective of beneficial spillovers that the event at hand (say dumping) might have on consumer welfare.

The overall picture however that emerges could be described as follows:

- the GATT and the GATS share as their intellectual foundation the economic theory that trade liberalization has overall positive welfare implications for those opting for free trade;
- both the GATT and the GATS are essentially negative integration-type contracts. Hence, once the permissible level of protection has been negotiated, the quality of regulatory intervention affecting trade is not put into question by the relevant WTO rules if adherence to the non-discrimination principle is guaranteed (section II);
- the GATT allows its Members to increase their protection through use of the so-called contingent protection instruments. Recourse to such instruments is justified when, as a result of an exogenous action, the domestic industry has suffered injury. These instruments reflect an injury to competitors standard only (section III).[6]

In a nutshell the thesis of this chapter is that the WTO contract, in its *static* expression, only tangentially requests from WTO Members to

---

[3] True, some obligations move beyond a pure negative integration-type approach. With the exception of TRIPS, however, most such obligations are of procedural as opposed to substantive nature.   [4] I use the term in its generic sense here.

[5] See B. M. Hoekman, and P. C. Mavroidis, 'Dumping, Antidumping and Antitrust' in 30 *Journal of World Trade* (1996) 27–42.

[6] In this chapter, when discussing contingent protection instruments, I will refrain from discussing the balance of payments provisions in the GATT contract (Art. XII and Art. XVIII). These Articles know of very limited use nowadays and anyway espouse the injury to competitors standard. I will also not discuss TRIPs either. TRIPs might indirectly facilitate trade liberalization (and even this is debatable).

account for consumer welfare alongside producer welfare.[7] The history of trade negotiations[8] and the economic analysis of the function of interest groups[9] provide ample evidence that this is the case. The WTO contract in its *dynamic* expression looks, in principle, a more promising avenue when it comes to taking into account consumer welfare: duties are being continuously reduced as a result of negotiating rounds and contingent protection instruments are more and more put into question. The institutional implication has so far been an undeniable 'tightening of the screws' in this respect.

II. NON-DISCRIMINATION

A. The arduous task of defining non-discrimination

The non-discrimination principle in the WTO legal order has two legs: the most-favoured-nation (MFN)[10] leg and the national treatment (NT) leg. The latter comes into play when the ticket to entry into a particular market has been paid.[11] WTO rules make it clear that non-discrimination covers both trade (border) policies as well as all domestic policies affecting trade with the notable exceptions of subsidies and government procurement. This is definitely true for GATT. As far as GATS is concerned, the MFN leg is a general obligation (that is, it binds WTO Members irrespective of their specific commitments) and exceptions to it are legal and political (GATS Article II).[12] The NT provision in GATS does not come into play absent specific commitments.

1. First observation: the non-discrimination principle in GATS is a watered-down version of its GATT equivalent

GATT case law has made it clear that for a violation of non-discrimination to occur, there is no need of trade effects.[13] In its classic

---

[7] By this, I do not mean that binding concessions do not act beneficially on consumer welfare. Of course they do, since the counterfactual (volatility of customs protection) could prove disastrous in this respect. All I mean is that the WTO law does not prejudge the level of consolidation.

[8] See K. Bagwell and R. W. Staiger, *The Economics of the World Trading System* (2002) 43ff.

[9] See the relevant chapters in G. M. Grossman and E. Helpman, *Interest Groups and Trade Policy* (2002).

[10] Whatever MFN means nowadays where more than 160 preferential schemes have been notified to the WTO.

[11] Even when the ticket to entry bears no cost to exporters (no customs duties).

[12] Much of the analysis here borrows from H. Henrik and P. C. Mavroidis, 'Legal and Economic Aspects of the Most-Favoured Nation Clause' in 17 *European Journal of Political Economy* (2001) 233–279.

[13] If there was any doubt to this effect, the WTO *Bananas* jurisprudence made it clear that the interpretation of the substantive content of the non-discrimination obligation in the GATT is relevant for GATS purposes as well.

Superfund expression, a GATT panel stated that GATT Article III is about competitive opportunities and protects legitimate expectations that post-payment of the ticket to entry into a particular market, domestic laws will adopt an origin-neutral attitude vis-à-vis all products circulating in the market. This approach is valid for customs duties (GATT Article II) and quantitative restrictions (GATT Article XI) as well. We should note however, that the GATT Article XI obligation is not subjected to a non-discrimination test, as things stand right now.

2. Second observation: the non-discrimination principle is about competitive opportunities and must be respected irrespective of the trade effects its violation might incur

In its *Bananas* jurisprudence, the panel and the Appellate Body dealt, *inter alia*, with a clause in the European Community (EC) schedule of concessions whereby some WTO Members were treated better than others. The Appellate Body confirmed the Panel's interpretation that concessions have to be granted in a non-discriminatory manner.

3. Third observation: WTO Members know ex ante (i.e. before negotiations start) that their eventual concessions will be applied in a non-discriminatory manner, hence, there is no way around the non-discrimination principle during the negotiations

So much is clear.[14] But of course, so much is not enough. All observations mentioned above have to do with the function of the non-discrimination principle. None of them deals with its precise scope. For this latter exercise, we need to delve into concepts such as 'so as to afford protection' and 'like products'.

And this is where our troubles begin. Let us kick off our discussion with one (to my mind, correct) observation by the Appellate Body: the term 'like products' cannot have the same meaning throughout the GATT, not even throughout one GATT Article. Horn and Mavroidis[15] describe in the following terms their understanding of the status quo of

---

[14] I am tempted to add for the sake of completeness, the WTO case law on *Korea—Beef*. There the AB interpreted the NT obligation in as yet novel manner: in its view, a change in the domestic regulation of Korea which results in a *reformatio in pejus* (worsening of competitive conditions) for imports is Art. III-inconsistent and that independently of whether such a *reformatio in pejus* results for domestic products as well. The reason why I decided to relegate this observation to a footnote has to do with my belief that on this occasion the AB mixed two distinct legal concepts, that of violation and that of non-violation, and my wish that because of this legal error this reasoning will not be repeated in future case law.

[15] Horn and Mavroidis, *supra* n. 2 at 51f.

the understanding by the Appellate Body of the terms appearing in GATT Article III.2:

(1) The legal test for demonstrating conformity (or lack of it) of a domestic taxation scheme with Article III.2 is also clear: when it comes to Article III.2, first sentence, the satisfaction of the likeness and taxation in excess-criteria *ipso facto* amounts to a violation of Article III.1 (two-prong test). Even a minute difference in taxes can satisfy the 'in excess' criterion. When it comes to Article III.2, second sentence, the complainant must show, beyond a DCS relationship between two products and a tax differential, that the latter operates SATAP (three-prong test).[16] In this case, sometimes a more than *de minimis* tax differential will suffice to satisfy the SATAP criterion, and sometimes recourse will be made to other factors indicating the protective application of the measure at hand. The Appellate Body has provided an indicative list of such factors but has yet to explain which cases fall under the first and which under the second category.

(2) Article III.2 covers cases of both *de jure* and *de facto* discrimination.

(3) The Appellate Body has also made it clear that intent is immaterial when interpreting Article III: in its view, Article III addresses protective application of any given domestic legislation without addressing its underlying intent.

(4) We further know that in order to establish whether two products are DCS, WTO adjudicating bodies must look at factors like cross-price elasticity, elasticity of substitution, end uses, consumers' tastes and habits, and the products' properties and nature. The Appellate Body has not clarified the weight to be given to each of the mentioned elements, but it stated that cross-price elasticity is not the decisive criterion. The list of relevant criteria is not exhaustive; WTO adjudicating bodies might add other (as yet unidentified) factors to the list. The term 'direct' in DCS refers to the degree of proximity between two products. The Appellate Body, however, does not specify what level of proximity is required for two products to be DCS. Thus, two products can be competitive but not directly competitive—i.e. they may not share a satisfactory degree of proximity. Potential competition is relevant to establish DCS relationship especially in cases of 'latent demand'. Evidence from other markets concerning the DCS relationship between two products is welcome at least in cases where a potentially DCS product

---

[16] DCS refers to 'directly competitive or substitutable' in the sense of the interpretative note to GATT Art. III. SATAP refers to 'so as to avoid protection' in the sense of Art. III.1 of GATT.

has not made its way in a particular market as a result of a regulatory intervention. The Appellate Body again does not offer any precise criteria as to the appropriateness of comparability between two markets. Since like products constitute a subset of DCS products, and since tariff classification may be relevant to establish likeness, it is also relevant to establish DCS.

(5) To establish likeness, a complainant needs to show, besides what is needed to establish DCS relationship, additional factors that might argue in favour of likeness. The only such factor mentioned in case law so far is tariff classification. However, the description in tariff classification must be quite comprehensive. General categories such as those often encountered in schedules of concessions of some developing countries will not be taken into account. Generally speaking, there is tendency in case law to construe like products in a narrow manner, in the mind of adjudicating bodies.

(6) We are also clear as to the relationship between like and DCS products: all like products are, by definition, DCS products. Hence, the complainant who succeeds in showing that two products are like has, by definition, also shown that the two products are DCS.

(7) Finally, an observation which does not stem directly from what has been discussed so far. It is by now settled case law that a WTO Member whose practices are found to be in violation of Article III can still justify these through recourse to Article XX. Violation of Article III does not *ipso facto* amount to violation of the GATT. Article XX can 'heal' the violation of Article III and intent is relevant in the context of Article XX. In other words, what the AB has done in the tax discrimination cases that it has treated so far is to provide a 'dividing line' between Article III and Article XX: the applicability of Article III is determined in the marketplace, whereas an evaluation under Article XX may involve other considerations (the Japan Panel report reflects similar thoughts, which were not overturned by the Appellate Body).

The inescapable conclusion is that we simply do not know what is the precise methodology for defining likeness in GATT law. Beyond the sometimes confusing Appellate Body case law (likeness is not a matter of effects and not a matter of intent either), lies one important observation that to some extent justifies the back and forth in the Appellate Body case law: in the words of Horn and Mavroidis there is an inherent indeterminacy when it comes to defining the non-protectionist counterfactual.[17] Absent this definition (which is legally crucial, since the institutional promise of WTO Members as expressed in Article III.1 is to avoid

---

[17] *Supra*, n. 15 at 57f.

protectionist domestic legislation), it is impossible to distinguish wheat from chaff.

The situation is probably more complex when it comes to discussing likeness in the context of Article III.4 post-*Asbestos*. There, the Appellate Body seems to suggest that some product characteristics must be presumed to affect consumers' choices without however, evidence *in casu* of consumers' reactions to such characteristics. The test for likeness thus is nominally still the marketplace but, for all practical purposes, it has been removed from the market.

I think it is not an exaggeration to state that we still lack a methodology that will help us define likeness with a satisfactory amount of foresight in future cases. Hence, what exactly non-discrimination means depends, in the Appellate Body's words, 'on the tuning of the accordion'. We know who will do it, we do not know how.[18]

At the end of the day, recourse to GATT Article XX might give us a better idea as to the presence or absence of a protectionist motive (see *infra*, under section II.B).

The situation is even more problematic when it comes to defining 'likeness' under GATT Article I (MFN). Davey and Pauwelyn offer an exhaustive analysis of the concept as interpreted in GATT–WTO case law.[19] What stems from their analysis is that so far, WTO adjudicating bodies did not have 'hot potatoes' in their hands.

Article 3.3 of the Harmonized System (HS) Convention reads:

Nothing in this Article shall prevent a Contracting Party from establishing, in its Customs tariff or statistical nomenclature, subdivisions classifying goods beyond the level of the Harmonized System, provided that any such subdivision is added and coded at a level beyond that of the six-digit numerical code set out in the Annex to this Convention.

Take the following example now. In the Doha Round, the United States (US) insert at the eight-digit level the following two classifications:

- footballs produced with fair-labour standards   0%
- footballs produced with unfair-labour standards   30%

---

[18] In his wonderful collection of articles, Posner (R. Posner, *Overcoming Law* (1995)) states that at the end of the day we will need a judge (probably borrowing from Avinash Dixit's affirmation that 'all feasible contracts are incomplete' and adding his thought that judges are there to complete them). I can side with this approach. My comments here should be understood as a plea for methodology and not as a negation of the role of the judge.

[19] W. J. Davey and J. Pauwelyn, 'MFN Unconditionality: A Legal Analysis of the Concept in View of its Evolution in the GATT/WTO Jurisprudence with Particular Reference to the Issue of "Like Product," ' in T. Cottier and P. C. Mavroidis (eds), *Regulatory Barriers and the Principle of Non-Discrimination in World Trade Law* (2000) 1–50.

Is such a classification inconsistent with Article II? It should be remembered that in *Bananas*, the Appellate Body outlawed origin-based distinctions. This is not the case here. Does the prior case law help us in any way to pronounce in an unambiguous manner that such a classification is GATT-inconsistent or GATT-consistent? The short answer is no. Such a question has not been put to the test.

My conclusion stemming from the preceding analysis is that so far we probably know what non-discrimination aims to achieve but we are still in the dark as to the precise ambit of what has been time and again described as the 'cornerstone' of the GATT edifice.

B. The new-generation agreements

The situation is marginally better with respect to the new-generation agreements, Technical Barriers to Trade (TBT) and Sanitary and Phytosanitary Standards (SPS). There, for a violation to be the case, a WTO panel needs to regard not only the non-discrimination principle but also the necessity principle and, as far as SPS is concerned, the requirement that regulatory interventions must be based on scientific principles.[20]

One way to describe our discussion under II.A could be the following: the judge will be called to discuss non-discrimination in an, for all practical purposes, asymmetry of information context: he/she will be called to establish whether a regulatory intervention is GATT-consistent months, years later after such an intervention took place and probably without the benefit of all the preparatory work leading to the intervention at hand.

Take the classic GATT Articles III–XX analysis as summarized under II.A: intent is relevant when moving to GATT Article XX and there, on occasions, the judge can benefit from proxies that help establish the authenticity of the intervention; this is the role, for example, of the 'necessity' principle. The rationale for the principle is that, although social choices are unaffected by a negative integration-type contract (like the GATT), when expressing such choices (preferences), the regulating state should choose the least onerous to international trade means. Implicitly, whenever the necessity principle is followed, we can deduce that the intervening state was authentic about the ends its intervention purportedly serves, since the side-effects of the intervention have been minimized.

Necessity serves thus as proxy to deduce intent.

---

[20] Provided, of course, that recourse to the precautionary principle has not taken place.

The new-generation agreements incorporate necessity in the original test for consistency of a regulatory intervention.[21] Consequently, in case the necessity requirement is respected, we have a better idea as to presence or absence of protectionist intent in a TBT/SPS case than we do in the context of an Article III case.

The SPS beyond necessity also requests that SPS-covered interventions are, in principle, based on scientific evidence. It will be quite hard in practice to come up with examples where an SPS measure respects the necessity principle, is based on scientific evidence, and still could have been motivated by protectionist intent. This 'double check' arms pronouncements by WTO adjudicating bodies of WTO-consistency for such measures with a considerable amount of certainty.

It is reasonable hence to conclude that, because of the proxies inserted in the new-generation WTO Agreements, we have a better idea as to the protectionist character of measures.

C. Non-discrimination and consumer welfare

However, even the new-generation agreements stop short of going beyond non-discrimination. Let me explain this sentence, because at first glance, it might seem as contradictory to what I have described above.

The thesis I want to defend here is that proxies such as necessity, or scientific evidence, help us better delineate the non-discrimination principle by reference to protectionist policies. The latter could be loosely defined as policies the prime objective of which is to subsidize (through regulatory means) the income of the domestic producer.[22]

A measure necessary to achieve an objective by definition imposes the least amount of hardship on imports. Hence, even if it does *de facto* burden imports it does not do so in a disproportionate manner. By the same token, a measure based on a scientific basis (provided that we can move to a better definition of 'science' than that offered in the AB *Hormones* jurisprudence) has an acceptable rationale for its existence beyond simply subsidizing domestic interest groups.

Is this enough? No, clearly not. Hopefully future research will help us add to the present list of proxies. Be it as it may though, these concepts give us some ammunition to move away from the thesis that a measure was enacted with protectionism in mind.

---

[21] In practice, this is not a mundane observation: there are many reported cases where, for one reason or another, recourse to GATT Art. XX did not take place (see, for example the recent *Korea—Beef* and *Chile—Taxes on Alcoholic Beverages* cases).

[22] I still believe that as exposed in Horn and Mavroidis, *supra* n. 2, this is not a very satisfactory proposition. I use it *faute de mieux*.

However, having said that, we should keep in mind that under either the old or the new-generation agreements, it is the means chosen to reveal a preference and not the ends (the preference itself) that can be put into question by the WTO judge.

This means that a WTO Member can be as inefficient as it wishes, as pro-domestic producer as it finds it warranted and still see its regulatory interventions immunized by WTO adjudicating bodies, provided that it respects the non-discrimination obligation. Some telling examples can serve as an illustration: a 1,000 per cent sales tax applied to domestic and foreign cars alike does not violate GATT Article III;[23] a banning of all advertisement could hardly be found to be inconsistent with GATT Article III.4.[24]

On the other hand, the negotiation of concessions, that is the degree of openness of an economy, is not a matter of concern for WTO law: it is purely a matter of concern of national governments. The WTO law will apply independently of the degree of openness of a national economy.

My conclusion is that non-discriminatory market access of goods (and services) as interpreted so far by WTO adjudicating bodies has very little to do with consumer welfare concerns. This conclusion is the natural outcome of the predominant (i.e. with the exception of Trade-Related Aspects of Intellectual Property Rights (TRIPs)) legal nature of the WTO contract: negative integration entails, among other things, that consumer preferences might or might not be taken into account in the formulation of trade policy. At any rate, their inclusion is done for reasons exogenous to the WTO contract.

III. CONTINGENT PROTECTION INSTRUMENTS

A. Hard law for producer welfare: injury to competitors

Turning now to contingent protection instruments, one observation seems warranted before we move to a discussion of the injury standard. As Messerlin's comprehensive study shows, the trade impact of such

---

[23] It could form the subject-matter of a non-violation complaint, provided, however, that a number of conditions are met. See, on this issue, K. Bagwell, P. C. Mavroidis, and R. W. Staiger, 'It's a Question of Market Access' in 96 *American Journal of International Law* (2002) 56–76.

[24] As the Advocate-General of the European Court of Justice acknowledged in *Leclerc—Siplec*, in a country where investment is not liberalized, such measures might have a discriminatory impact on foreign goods. Such case law seems hardly reconcilable with WTO law. At any rate it is consumer welfare that will be affected by such measures since consumers will not be in a position to acquire information about other products.

measures, at least for some WTO players, is quite significant (in terms not only of increased protection but also of frequency of invocation of the instrument).[25] A statement to the effect that the aggregate rate of duties for *x* products is less than 5 per cent nowadays is meaningless. The careful analyst will try to reflect whatever other duties are legally added to the MFN rate in order to provide the actual picture of trade liberalization. Adding to the duties has an *a priori* detrimental welfare implication for consumers. As we will see *infra*, the rationale for this implication is subsidization of the income of the domestic producer.

Turning now to the legal requirements for a lawful imposition of an anti-dumping or countervailing (CVD) duty or a safeguard:

All three agreements request that in the presence of (i) dumping (subsidy/increased imports) which (ii) cause (iii) injury to the domestic industry producing the like product, a WTO Member can lawfully increase its protection. It goes without saying that increasing the protection *ipso facto* means that consumer welfare will be negatively influenced. That much is clear. However, as we know from antitrust analysis, sometimes measures against low prices are justified in economic theory (predation). The rationale for outlawing such policies is the injury to competition standard (the fear that subsequently, because of high barriers to entry, the now cheap-selling entity will be in a position to recoup its investment).

The injury in all three contingent protection instruments is the drastically different injury to competitors-standard. Article 3.4 of the Antidumping Agreement (AD), Articles 5 and 15 of the Subsidies Agreement (SCM), and Article 4 of the Safeguards Agreement (SG) all share one common feature: action is lawful when the producer welfare has been (or threatens to be) negatively affected as a result of cheap prices, subsidies to foreign producers, or increased imports.

Consumer welfare considerations are institutionally absent in the provisions of the aforesaid Agreements.

The natural conclusion is that lawful increased protection beyond the MFN rate is legal under WTO law when the producer welfare is affected. When it comes hence to contingent protection instruments, the WTO rules do not stand on the fence (as is the case with non-discrimination). They take an active pro-producer welfare stance.

B. Soft law for (against?) consumers interests

To complete the analysis, I should probably also refer to Articles 6.12 AD, 12.10 SCM, and 3.1 SG. These Articles request from WTO

---

[25] P. Messerlin, *Measuring the Cost of Protection in Europe* (2001) at 29f.

Members opportunities to other interested parties (including consumers' organizations) to provide their views during the proceedings. The strongest language is that of Article 3.1 SG but even that falls short of imposing on WTO Members the control of consumer welfare implications as a matter of WTO law when imposing safeguards.[26]

Some domestic statutes do provide for enhanced opportunities for consumers: the EC AD regulation requests that all AD duties imposed by the EC must be in the Community interest (which must, at least *a priori*, include consumer welfare). The empirical analysis by Hoekman and Mavroidis demonstrates that, even in the presence of a legal requirement to this effect, this has hardly been the case.[27]

The inescapable conclusion is that activation of all safeguards to the WTO contract (the three instruments described above) are contingent, as a matter of WTO law, exclusively upon producer welfare considerations only.

IV. CONCLUSIONS

In this chapter, I have offered a diagnosis which can be summarized as follows: the foundation of WTO rules (the non-discrimination principle) does not take a stance on the issue of whether producer or consumer interests or a balancing of both should guide trade liberalization. The safeguard clauses in the WTO Agreement are there to ensure that producers' interests are not negatively affected because of a threshold (which is endogenously defined in every society) of acceptable trade liberalization. Because of the importance of the latter, it is fair to conclude that the WTO rules in this respect are producer-oriented.

Negotiating positions are designed at home. The degree of trade liberalization for the EC is first discussed in Brussels and the national capitals, for India in Delhi, and so on and so forth. It is there where the game is played and not in Geneva. It is there where the change can happen.

European governments have not done a great job so far (because most likely as a continuous string of public-choice theorists have explained, they have no incentive to do so) in making the European *demos* (or *demoi*) aware of the intellectual merits of trade liberalization.

If at all, the WTO machinery can be used as the machinery to facilitate change of domestic policies ('use GATT as an excuse', as Hudec, in his inimitable way used to write). Not much can be achieved through

---

[26] A point that Aaditya Mattoo in his astute manner noticed first.
[27] *Supra* n. 5 at 31f.

dispute settlement activities. For a start, through adjudication one can only adjudicate what has been agreed at the table of negotiations (and this is precisely where change is needed). Moreover, adjudication suffers from its *ad hoc* character: outcomes have limited value for non-participants.

Hence, it is at the table of negotiations where things can change. In what has been described above, it is contingent protection instruments that bind everyone. This is where change should occur (for example, by introducing one safeguard mechanism only coupled with a public interest clause and thus, abolishing the existing mechanism of *de facto* overlapping safeguards). Such a change could result in tangible benefits for consumer welfare.

13

Non-Discrimination, Welfare Balances, and WTO Rules: An Historical Perspective

PATRICK A. MESSERLIN

Petros Mavroidis' 'twin' chapter provides a very clear and detailed analysis of the current tensions between non-discrimination, the (producer and consumer) welfare balances, and World Trade Organization (WTO) rules. This chapter tries to understand why such tensions are still there, unabated and even perhaps deeper and stronger than ever—after half a century of refined economic analysis and of its improved operationability (that is, its capacity to be put in terms and forms fit for decision-makers) and after half a century of a General Agreement on Tariffs and Trade (GATT) trade regime so successful that new domains (agriculture, services, etc.) are now covered by its successor, the WTO.

In order to understand the sources and the evolution of these tensions between WTO rules and economic analysis, this chapter adopts an historical approach which reveals the increasing understanding and operationability of the welfare economic analysis of trade policy on the one hand, and, on the other hand, the continued resistance of WTO rules to fully taking into account cost–benefit analysis based on welfare balances. Some lessons are then drawn—whether one could expect these tensions to decrease, and, if not, how to live with them.

The chapter gives to WTO rules the widest possible definition (it covers both the so-called 'static' and 'dynamic' aspects in the Mavroidis chapter). Such rules thus cover all the provisions dealing with goods and services since the Uruguay Round—GATT, General Agreement on Trade in Services (GATS), and their Codes or Agreements of Interpretation. They also cover all the decisions taken during the successive GATT and WTO Rounds, that is, decreases of tariff rates, reductions of non-tariff barriers, etc., and those taken under GATT provisions, such as anti-dumping, anti-subsidy, or safeguard measures.

I. THE SHAPING OF THE GATT (FROM THE LATE 1940s TO THE LATE 1950s)

When looking at a system which has been in an almost permanent process of reshuffling and extension, it is important not to create historical non-senses. The first thing to do when looking at the welfare balances in GATT 1947 is to carefully assess the state of welfare economic theory applied to trade policy (in what follows, trade policy is distinct from trade theory which examines the economic gains from freer trade) in the late 1940s, at the time of the signing of GATT.

A quick review of the few trade books prevalent in the 1950s and 1960s suggests that the notions of producer and consumer welfare in trade policy were generally dealt with quickly and not in a very operational way. If the key economic concepts were largely discovered by the late 1800s and formalized by the 1930s,[1] their operational form, that is, their capacity to answer questions raised by decision makers in a straight forward and computable manner, was non-existent. The ranking of the instruments of protection in terms of welfare impact was also quite embryonic. Hence, the capacity of the existing economic analysis to generate sound GATT–WTO rules was *de facto* very limited.

In fact, the focus on trade matters in the late 1940s and early 1950s (that is, during the years where GATT was created and took shape) was not on the welfare balances. For instance, Meade's highly influential textbook[2] devotes most of its chapter on 'taxes (i.e. tariffs) and sub-sidies' to their impact on the public budget. Most of its developments related to welfare balances as conceived today were largely limited to the mere evocation of changes in prices. That is not so surprising. The key elements of modern trade literature on producer and consumer welfare as we know them today have been mostly developed in papers written by Haberger, Johnson, Corden, and a handful of other authors during the late 1950s and early 1960s, before being cast in the form we are used to by authors writing in the late 1960s and early 1970s, such as Bhagwati, Kemp, or Srinivasan.

This brief review of economic thought on trade policy issues is not so astonishing after all. International trade started to boom only during the late 1950s and early 1960s, after several decades of severe decline and stagnation. The nitty-gritty details of trade policy were thus unlikely to trigger deep interests from the economic profession. More generally, one should not forget that markets were suspicious of many 'economists' of

---

[1] T. O. Yntema, *A Mathematical Reformulation of the General Theory of International Trade* (1932).

[2] J. E. Meade, *The Theory of International Economic Policy, Vol. II: Trade and Welfare* (1955).

this period—planning was then a much more fashionable approach among policy-makers and the economists close to them.

In this context, it is not difficult to understand that the GATT drafters paid little attention to producer and consumer welfare. They were mostly sensitive to the mess of the existing bilateral and discriminatory trade policies—a mess which begun to emerge as early as in the 1880s, with the first 'trade wars', for instance between France and Italy, and which led to the highly protectionist policies of the 1920s and 1930s. For the trade negotiators of the 1950s, the most desirable objective was to introduce some kind of systemic 'simplicity' in the spaghetti bowl inherited from the nineteenth century by generating a level playing-field between all foreign competitors—hence the focus on non-discrimination. As Tumlir[3] was the first to observe, the principle of non-discrimination was not strongly included in the complex web of trade agreements of the second half of the nineteenth century. It was sneaked in through indirect means, often politically quite awkward (such as the Treaty of Frankfurt which ended the 1870 Franco-Prussian war) and as a result, it left wide open the door to bilateral, fast-spreading, trade wars.

Nowadays, the non-discrimination principle tends to be taken for granted. It should be stressed that it defines the level of competition between foreign competitors by drawing the line between 'fake' liberalization (opening domestic markets to relatively inefficient foreign producers, as often discriminatory liberalization does) and 'effective' liberalization (opening domestic markets to the most efficient foreign producers, as does non-discriminatory liberalization). This division is important because fake liberalization can be a source of consumer welfare opportunity losses, in the form of transfers from domestic consumers to inefficient foreign producers.

It is important to note that the GATT text develops only one dimension of the non-discriminatory principle—the one referring to the source of imports for a given product (hereafter geographical non-discrimination). By allowing the possibility of different tariffs for different products, the GATT text ignores the other possible dimension of non-discrimination—between products. The only tariff structure which respects the two dimensions of non-discrimination is the so-called uniform tariff structure, be the tariff rate equal to zero (the free trade case) or to some positive number. The GATT regime had to wait until 1984 to witness the first clear example of the product dimension of non-discrimination, with the unilateral adoption by Chile of a uniform tariff schedule (at the very high rate of 35 per cent, reduced the year after to 20 per cent, and then followed by a series of mostly unilateral reductions, up to its current level of 6 per cent).

[3] J. Tumlir, *Economic Policy as a Constitutional Problem* (1984).

Geographical non-discrimination raises a question for the many existing bilateral trade agreements (contrary to the usual understanding, regional trade agreements are very rare). So far, many of these trade agreements have had little content, and they are disappearing slowly under the dust on the shelves of the Trade Ministries of the signatories. The question is whether the new generation of bilateral trade agreements will be as mildly bothering for geographical non-discrimination as the old ones. The world trade regime is in a better situation to cope with infringements to the non-discrimination principle in the realm of goods, simply because the most-favoured-nation (MFN) tariffs on goods are lower than those in the late 1940s, so that trade preferences and their potential costs are likely to be smaller.[4]

The above review of the economic literature on trade policy suggests that the GATT 1947 text could hardly give some room to the welfare balances, since its basic notions and concerns were too far away from the main trends of a still undeveloped economic literature on trade policy.

Finally, it remains to underline that the welfare balances are *de facto* present in the GATT machinery, if not in the GATT text. As is well known, rounds put in place trade negotiators who, because of the political situation in trade matters, behave essentially under the pressures of the domestic export lobbies which are convinced that access to foreign markets will provide them additional consumers, thanks to their comparative advantages over their foreign competitors. However, every time a trade negotiator speaks on behalf of its export lobbies, he/she is *ipso facto* advocating the interests of the foreign consumers (if the domestic exporting firms are correct when assessing their comparative advantages). In other words, each trade negotiator is improving the welfare of both domestic producers and foreign consumers (at a 'cost' for foreign producers and possibly for domestic consumers, if the price of the exported good increases in the exporting country, compared to the pre-liberalization price because of the additional foreign demand). This improvement is most likely to be maximum if the round covers the whole universe of goods and WTO members.

Much less often recognized is the sound approach of the GATT text in terms of the ranking of the instruments of protection to be used. GATT includes a classification of the instruments of protection which give countries a relatively clear view of what to do in trade in goods. Tariffs are preferred to other border barriers, such as quantitative restrictions, export taxes and subsidies, and tariff-rate quotas. Non-border instruments (production subsidies and consumption taxes) are seen as

---

[4] The same observation cannot be made for services where today's situation seems much closer to what existed in goods in the late 1940s. However, preferential agreements in services are still very limited in numbers, scope and depth.

preferable. This classification is broadly consistent with the welfare balances that trade policy analysis associates with these trade instruments.

The still missing economic analysis of trade instruments could not be the main motive behind these sound GATT rules. Two other reasons have worked in the same direction: tariffs provide public revenues, and quotas provide rents, which can be used by the beneficiaries for capturing the government's trade policy. The first of these two arguments (public finance) has probably been the dominant one.

In sum, the situation in the late 1940s and in the 1950s is quite ambiguous. On the one hand, sound competition came back through the non-discrimination principle—hence the unprecedented rapid growth of the Western economies supported and amplified by the series of GATT Rounds. On the other hand, the GATT–WTO rules show little knowledge about the emerging analysis of welfare balances—hence, leaving wide open a back door to protection as soon as liberalization may require severe adjustments.

II. THE GATT CODES (FROM THE EARLY 1960s TO THE LATE 1980s)

In what follows, the generic term of 'Codes' covers not only the texts which have been entitled as such (for instance, the Codes or Agreements of interpretation of the GATT Articles on Anti-dumping, Anti-subsidy, and Safeguard) but also those which have introduced the Special and Differential Treatment (SDT) in the GATT text itself during its first 20 years of existence (GATT Article XVIII and the whole of Part IV).

Have these Codes taken into consideration the trade policy theory, which has flourished during this period? At this time, the theory of trade policy has already 'solidified' most of its operational capacities by providing simple (partial equilibrium) computational methods allowing for the estimation of producer and consumer surpluses (including by beginning to gather estimates of the various elasticities necessary to make such computations), by ranking the various instruments of protection in terms of welfare balances, and by developing the analysis of the optimal instruments to be used in case of specific distortions in an economy—an analysis which strongly suggests that most distortions should be addressed by non-trade instruments.

The GATT Codes have not used this opportunity to take on board all these improvements. First, all the SDT-related texts fundamentally ignore consumer welfare and the fact that the net welfare gains from liberalization flow from a country's own liberalization—not from the liberalization of the country's trading partners. They tend to deny the freedom of choice to the domestic consumers of a country by expanding without limits the right of a government to make choices on the basis of undefined 'development needs', meaning *de facto* what is good for the domestic producers and possibly the government. This wide divergence between the SDT premises and economic analysis explains the subsequent failure of this SDT approach.[5]

Second, as is abundantly pointed out by Mavroidis, the Codes for contingent protection did not reduce the initial bias in favour of domestic producers. In fact, the more time was passing, the more these Codes have shifted away from economically sound concepts. They drifted away from safeguard (which at least recognizes that domestic producers may be eligible for some breathing space, i.e. allows only transitory re-protection) to anti-dumping. In the 1970s and 1980s, anti-dumping (and anti-subsidy) have shown a sharply decreasing interest for adopting cost–benefit analyses based on welfare balances, with an increasingly deeper neglect of economically sound definitions of their key legal notions (for instance, domestic industry, major proportion, like-product, injury, etc.). During the whole period, anti-dumping and anti-subsidy national regulations have also shown an equally sharp decrease of references to consumers' interests and to competition combined with an increasing capture of concepts, as best illustrated by the 'national interest' interpreted as an argument in favour of the survival of domestic producers (instead of its original intent of being the voice of the domestic consumers).

How to explain such an increasing gap between key economic concepts and trade policy? The first answer may be narrow, but it has some weight. During this period, few people involved in the day-to-day trade policy (GATT negotiators, decision-makers in the capital cities, etc.) were trained as economists. The same observation could be made for the staff of the GATT Secretariat and of other international institutions. Moreover, one could argue that, had all these actors been economists, the result might not have been so different because the consensus among economists on trade policy issues was still building up. For instance, Hollis Chenery, Chief Economist of the World Bank in the 1970s, stated that 'industrialization consists primarily in the substitution of domestic production of manufactured goods for imports'.[6]

In fact, there is only one clear indication of the nascent but limited influence of economic thinking during these 20–25 years. The use of the

---

[5] But one could think about an SDT approach more respectful of economic analysis because it is based on the product dimension of non-discrimination: P. A. Messerlin, *Rethinking Fair Trade: Making the Doha Development Round Work for the Poorest Developing Countries* (2003) mimeo.

[6] A. O. Krueger (ed.), *The WTO as an International Organization* (1998).

cost–benefit analysis of welfare balances made its first clear apparition in the GATT context with the so-called Leutwiller Report.[7] But this Report was largely shaped by the very specific experience of the Australian Tariff Commission (itself relying on specific circumstances concerning trade economists in this country.)[8]

The second answer to the increasing gap between GATT rules and the economic analysis is more profound—and also more debatable. It lies in the deep relations between economics and politics. Economic analysis insists on the fact that what counts for assessing trade policy decisions are the 'dead-weight triangles', that is, the net effect on the whole economy of a trade measure (be it of liberalization or of protection). Traditionally, the estimates of these dead-weight triangles are small, suggesting that liberalization policies improve national income by a small percentage. This 'smallness' has generated scepticism about the importance of the economic analysis for taking trade policy decisions.

There were two reactions to this situation. First was that the dead-weight triangles associated with other policies for increasing national income were also small (indeed often significantly smaller). Second, the traditional trade analysis relies on the assumption that transfers between producers, consumers, and the government should be treated as domestic transfers, hence not counted when estimating the welfare effects on the 'national' economy. This approach may have made sense in the 1960s, when it became the standard. But it tends to ignore many aspects, which have become increasingly important since the 1960s. For instance, the fact that not taking tariff revenues into account in the dead-weight triangles could be subjected to serious caveats. For instance, tariff revenues from low tariffs (again frequent in industrial countries nowadays) may be entirely spent by paying the customs officers needed for levying these tariffs. Another example is that it can be shown that a euro spent by the government has not necessarily the same 'value' as a euro spent by the consumers themselves. Hence, in the case of highly taxed countries (as industrial countries nowadays) it may be the case that its value is smaller (the government has 'too much' revenue, and wastes it compared to the potential use by the consumers). Looking at quota rents (instead of tariff revenues) and at producers' surplus, a portion of them could leave the country if their beneficiaries have close links with foreign traders or producers. In all these cases, the traditional approach of the economic analysis underestimates the costs of protection.

[7] GATT (Leutwiller Report), *Trade Policy and Prosperity* (1985).
[8] I. A. McDougall and R. H. Snape, *Studies in International Economics* (1970).

III. THE POST-URUGUAY ROUND PERIOD

The period from the late 1980s up to today has witnessed huge improvements in the operational capacity of economic analysis to estimate welfare changes triggered by trade measures for the various agents of the domestic economy. They have also seen notable improvements in the capacity of economic analysis to take into account certain aspects of imperfect competition in a theoretical and operational way. Moreover, this increasingly wide and operational economic analysis seems to have been accompanied by an increase of the economic skills of trade negotiators.[9]

However, once again, the WTO rules written down during these years do not reflect these substantive changes. In fact, the Uruguay Round may even show a worrisome evolution, compared to the previous ones. Whereas the successive GATT Rounds of the 1960s and 1970s have been able to deliver a healthy dose of competition through non-discriminatory liberalization, the Uruguay Round is characterized by modest results in this respect. Agriculture has been integrated in the legal framework, but it has not been liberalized. Progress has been limited in manufactures, if one excludes the scheduled (but still to come) dismantlement of Multi-Fibre Arrangement (MFA) quotas by industrial countries and the unilateral (autonomous) liberalization of a substantial number of developing countries. Increases in market access in services have been almost nil.

Turning to the Uruguay texts themselves, it is interesting to focus on the most stable innovation of the Uruguay Round—GATS. References in the GATS text to the welfare balances are not notably different to those in GATT. This observation is not so surprising to the extent that what characterized the initial (in the late 1980s) situation in services is, once again, a highly discriminatory trade regime more than the level of protection per se. Prior to the Uruguay Round (and leaving aside the European Community (EC)), all the agreements on trade in services were bilateral agreements (including those between a WTO member and a sub-federal entity of another WTO member, such as the agreement between Britain and Pennsylvania in insurance services). In some instances, they were even the ultimate expression of the highest and most systematic discrimination at the world level (such as the

---

[9] Based on anecdotal observations (it would be interesting to have some systematic evidence on this point), the share of negotiators and decision-makers on trade issues with a substantial economic training seems to have increased. However, this observation may not be correct at the level of dispute settlements. If many lawyers have economic skills, they do not necessarily use them, all the more because economists have a tendency to fight each other with such an energy that it makes for nervous or dubious lawyers.

Chicago Convention in air transport). In sum, the Uruguay Round negotiators in services faced the same situation of a highly discriminatory world as the founding fathers of GATT dealing with goods 50 years before.

However, there are two interesting differences between the GATS and GATT texts with respect to welfare balances. The first is to the advantage of GATS, as compared with GATT. GATS Article X text on the emergency safeguard measure (ESM) is an empty shell. It provides for a non-discriminatory ESM, but it has left for future discussion all the other possible provisions necessary for designing a fully-fledged ESM. Since 1995, WTO members have tried several times to define these appropriate provisions, without success so far. Industrial countries argue that such an ESM is not necessary, whereas a relatively large group of developing countries (mostly from those Asian and Latin American countries recently hit by financial crises) insist on such an ESM as necessary for facing the 'unforeseen developments' which could be caused by further liberalization in services.

The still empty shell of GATS Article X can be seen as a recognition that the welfare balances in safeguard matters were not achieved in a satisfactory manner in GATT. However, there is a competing, less optimistic, interpretation. There are a large number of provisions in the existing WTO commitments conditioning market access to 'economic-need tests', or to 'proofs of public convenience', etc. These tests or proofs (particularly numerous and obscure for provisions under Mode 4) constitute a severe threat to the effectiveness of the existing commitments, and they are far away from any consideration of the appropriate balances between the various welfare aspects. In many respects, they constitute *ex ante* safeguards defined on a sectoral and country basis. Moreover, their existence raises the possibility of a trade-off between them and the creation of a fully-fledged EMS.

The second key difference between GATS and GATT is to the detriment of GATS, compared with GATT. The GATS text defines liberalization by the elimination of quotas—be it on the number of service suppliers allowed, on the value or quantity of services supplied, on the number of foreign persons employed, on the participation of foreign capital, or on the legal entities (GATS Article XVI). But, it shows no effort to envisage and promote the use of taxes as alternative trade instruments in services, be they on imports (Mode 1), on entry, input, output or profit (Mode 3), or on labour entry (Mode 4). This renunciation of instruments facilitating a non-discriminatory approach in services represents a sharp difference from the GATT text. One could argue that such a non-discrimination may be difficult in services, but making progress in this direction would nevertheless provide benefits.

The absence of interest of GATS in price-based instruments and the pervasive use of quantitative restraints in trade in services is likely to make progressive liberalization difficult to achieve in services. The protectionist power of a quota may remain almost intact until some threshold (hard to know in the real world) is reached, but it may vanish rapidly beyond the threshold. The focus on quantitative restraints may also favour the creation of huge and unsustainable (in the long run) differences among the protection rates granted to different services, as best illustrated by Korea where short-term foreign borrowing (capital imports) was largely liberalized, while long-term borrowing was banned. Lastly, the absence of price-based instruments makes the introduction of acceptable safeguards more difficult (for instance, how is it possible to revoke granted licences without risking a collapse of the whole system?).

Why then so little progress to include welfare balances in WTO rules in services? There are several answers. First is that the Uruguay negotiators believed that services were 'different'. Indeed, they did so partly under the influence of many economists who have been unable to anticipate the consequence of technical progress on services, and its interactions with market liberalization (see, for instance, the huge literature of the late 1980s on the 'non-tradability' of services).

Second, trade negotiators have little or no knowledge of the potential comparative advantages of their countries in services (contrary to what they believe for goods.) Even if imprecise or inaccurate (estimates are often too conservative, and certain sectors will boom unexpectedly post-liberalization), such knowledge is seen as a necessary guide for negotiators during trade talks when the time comes to define which foreign markets should be opened, and in exchange, which domestic markets could be opened or kept closed). The years devoted to the Uruguay Round negotiations have provided clear examples of wrong expectations in this respect. For instance, it was often said that industrialized countries had comparative advantages in services because services were seen as intensive users of capital and skilled labour. Opinions have shifted rapidly and significantly on this matter, with emerging success stories, during the last decade, of developing countries in all kinds of services—from low-skilled (construction) to medium-skilled (maritime transport) to high-skilled services (from Indian software services to South African or Thai health services). By contrast, tourism (the service sector in which developing countries were the most confident of their comparative advantage, and the sector that makes up a large share of their total export revenues) has had surprisingly mixed success. Its reliance on key input services (airlines, travel agencies, etc.) based in the home countries of tourists (mostly industrialized countries) and on high-quality infrastructure services (from roads to security) in the destination countries (developing countries) makes tourism a sector where developing-country comparative advantages may indeed be very volatile. Such an unpredictable environment may have induced trade negotiators to loose faith in the usual analytical framework behind welfare balances.

Last but not least, services are more prone to differentiation than goods (the range of varieties for a broadly defined given service is likely to be much larger than the one for a given product). In such a context, welfare balances are more complex to examine because prices and quantities do not grasp the whole picture (there is a third component which influences each component of the welfare balances, that is, the number of available varieties of a given 'product'). Operational models fully capturing the expected welfare changes caused by a variable number of varieties are not yet available.

IV. CONCLUDING REMARKS

This brief overview of the GATT and trade policy evolutions leads to two questions. First, should one expect WTO rules to better take into account welfare balances in the future? The answer is 'yes' if the Doha Round and its successors do the basic job that any round is supposed to do—improving market access (but the Uruguay Round has shown that such a goal can be missed).

However, the answer is probably 'no' when the rest of the WTO rules are considered. Being based on a contract between sovereign states, it is hard to see how a well-defined procedure for assessing a policy and for judging its consequences (a cost–benefit analysis of the welfare balances) could be imposed on WTO members through the WTO framework. One could even argue that there should be no attempt to do so for two reasons (leaving aside all the legal and political difficulties). Were such a procedure to be imposed, it is likely that, even if sovereign states behave in good faith, they would put different weightings on the various components of the welfare balances. This situation may have already occurred in transatlantic competition cases, such as in the Boeing—MDD case.[10] Different weightings could lead to different outcomes in the various WTO members concerned, even if the analysis is based on the same initial welfare components and methodology. As a result, it is not even sure that the outcomes of such procedures would be very different from those prevailing in their absence.

---

[10] S. Evenett, A. Lehmann, and B. Steil (eds), *Antitrust Goes Global: What Future for Transatlantic Co-operation?* (2000).

The second reason is that WTO rules should not be seen as similar to laws voted by a parliament and enforced on citizens. WTO members define rules that they apply to themselves. This situation induces them to look for strong terms for their partners, but loose terms for them-selves, and it is hard to see how this game could end as long as the net gains or costs of WTO rules are not the same for every member. For instance, the fact that ten large economies (four developed and six developing) have initiated 90 per cent of the stock of anti-dumping cases, but are the targets of 30 per cent of this stock leaves little hope that the Uruguay Anti-dumping Agreement could be amended by the introduction of a cost–benefit analysis based on the 'national interest'.

In sum, it is hard to see the benefits of introducing a strong competi-tion culture *directly* in the WTO system (other than through improved market access). Indeed, it is easy to foresee the perverse effects of such a direct approach. As amply shown in the Mavroidis chapter, the subtle definitions on which an economically sound use of the welfare balances approach is based require an intimate conviction of their usefulness by users. Without such a conviction, welfare balances may be useless, even counter-productive. And if improving WTO texts are useful only for members already 'convinced' by the usefulness of the welfare balances, what is the value of such 'improvements'?

The second basic question is: what can then be done? There are two complementary options. First is to recognize that the fundamental layer for introducing the competition culture is every WTO Member, as indeed stressed by the Leutwiller Report 30 years ago. For instance, the fact that, within the last few months, the EC has excluded services of 'public interest' from both the full reach of domestic competition rules and the Doha negotiations is likely to be more than an unfortunate cor-relation.[11]

The second possible option is to recognize that, at the WTO level, the only available assets are market access and renegotiations. They should be used more intensively, hence the two following suggestions. First, when negotiating in a round on anti-dumping rules, small countries should make a coalition for increasing *de minimis* thresholds which are crude, but hard to manipulate, rules of thumb for assessing the real impact of their exports on the importing markets. Second, instead of refining endlessly the legal definitions of like-product, injury, etc., in anti-dumping procedures, it would be more efficient to draw the full con-sequences of the political necessity of certain trade actions. This approach would suggest favouring a progressive shift away from anti-dumping

---

[11] Despite the fact that some of them are already under worldwide competition, such as university education (with vast movements of students, and more modest movements of professors) or some health services (with notable movements of doctors and patients).

and anti-subsidy (dumping and subsidies becoming simply an excuse for triggering protection) and towards safeguard, to subject such safeguard measures to the WTO basic discipline of renegotiations—meaning that after x years of enforcing a safeguard, a country will abolish it, or, if it will decide to keep it, foreign countries will be entitled to compensations under the form of new liberalization from the country having imposed the safeguard.[12] Indeed, such rights could be automatically granted in cases where a safeguard is ruled as illegal in a dispute settlement case. This measure will allow management of the fact that unrestrained safeguards could be worse than antidumping actions (for instance, the EC steel safeguard alone is equivalent to more than 60 anti-dumping cases).

[12] P. A. Messerlin, 'Antidumping and Safeguards' in J. J. Schott (ed.), *The WTO after Seattle* (2000).

14

Is There a Need for Additional WTO Competition Rules Promoting Non-Discriminatory Competition Laws and Competition Institutions in WTO Members?

FRANÇOIS SOUTY

I. INTRODUCTION

When the World Trade Organization (WTO) Working Group to study the Interrelation between Trade and Competition Policy was constituted in 1997 pursuant to the Singapore Declaration, initial discussions were shaped by two reference studies that were stimulated by the 'globalization' in the early 1990s: the so-called Draft International Antitrust Code elaborated by a group of private scholars from the European Union (EU) and the United States (US)[1] and the Report of the so-called Van Miert Expert group established by the European Community (EC) then Commissioner in charge of Competition Policy Karel Van Miert.[2] The first study resulted in a detailed Code modelled after the experience of the most advanced economies, to be incorporated into WTO law and to be administered by an 'International Antitrust Authority' vested with,

---

[1] H. Hauser and E. U. Petersmann (eds), 'International Competition Rules in the GATT/WTO System' in *Swiss Review of International Economic Relations* (1994) 169–424 (see in particular pp. 310–325). A further edition of the Draft International Antitrust Code which was presented at the OECD Committee on Competition Law and Policy was published by W. Fikentscher and U. Immenga (eds), *Draft International Antitrust Code* (1995). See also E. U. Petersmann, *The Need for Integrating Trade and Competition Rules in the WTO World Trade and Legal System*, PSIO Occasional Papers, WTO Series No. 3 (1996) at 43.

[2] EC Commission, *Competition Policy in the New Trade Order: Strengthening International Cooperation and Rules* (1995).

inter alia, a 'right to ask for actions in individual antitrust cases or groups of cases to be initiated by a national antitrust authority' and:

[A] right to bring actions against national antitrust authorities in individual cases or groups of cases before national law courts, whenever a national antitrust authority refuses to take appropriate measures against individual restraints of competition (Article 19:2).

The second study drew on the experience gained by the EU Commission in its tackling of global anti-competitive behaviours in differentiated situations including international cartels (1989–91 wood pulp case), abuses of dominance on several major markets (1994 Microsoft), anti-competitive effects of vertical restraints (1994 Kodak–Fuji case), and global mega-mergers (1991 Aerospatiale–Alenia–De Havilland and 1995 Mc Donnell–Douglas cases). This study focused on 'competition problems that transcend national boundaries: international cartels, export cartels, restrictive practices in fields which are international by nature (such as air and sea transport)'. It identified problems arising chiefly on the part of American businesses but not exclusively (the 1991 prohibition of the Aerospatiale–Alenia merger case concerned French, Italian, and Canadian firms, and the 1994 Kodak–Fuji case also involved a Japanese firm) and focused on diverging views about enforcing competition laws on both sides of the Atlantic (e.g. the unilateral extraterritorial enforcement of US antitrust and trade laws vis-à-vis foreign anti-competitive practices leading to international conflicts of laws on jurisdictions, unilateral sanctions and counter-measures, and enforcement problems such as information-gathering abroad and foreign 'blocking statutes'). Even though the developing countries situation was touched by the second study, the developing countries were only considered as being subject to some types of anti-competitive practices (e.g. use of intellectual property rights for limiting domestic competition) and 'extraterritorial application of other countries' competition laws' (i.e. chiefly the laws of the US and of the EU).

However, it would be completely misleading, and unfair, to consider that global competition studies and multilateral projects emanated only from Europe. For instance, the American Bar Association international antitrust proposal was one of the first and most prominent of these studies a decade ago. As early as 1991, a Special Committee on International Antitrust, chaired by Professor Barry Hawk, of the Section of Antitrust Law of the American Bar Association issued a report in which it recommended that 'all countries should enter into an agreement to repeal their statutes granting immunity to export cartels at least to the extent that the statutes allow conduct in or into foreign markets that would be unlawful in their domestic markets'; that a mechanism should be developed to resolve international disputes regarding conduct by export cartels that is alleged to have effects solely in foreign markets'; and that:

[A]lternative methods of resolving international conflicts over the behaviour of export ventures include the formation of a multinational tribunal to make findings or to recommend resolutions to such disputes, or to establish a system of binding arbitration.[3]

Furthermore, Professor Scherer made the insightful proposal, similar to the Munich Group's recommendation, providing for a gradual, phased approach over approximately seven years to allow all signatory nations to comply with the full set of commitments. His book proposed to create an 'International Competition Policy Office' (ICPO) that would be situated 'within the ambit of the new World Trade Organization' and would 'have both investigative and (in a second stage) enforcement responsibilities'. This ICPO would at first be an information-gathering agency, thereby following the model of the US Federal Trade Commission that was initially proposed by President Woodrow Wilson.[4] This scheme would also follow the British model that was developed in the late 1940s and in the 1950s and which developed competition authorities essentially vested with registration powers in their initial stages of functioning.[5] Furthermore:

[O]ne year after a new international competition policy agreement has been ratified, all substantial single-nation export and import cartels and all cartels operating across national boundaries [should] be registered, and the mechanism of their operations [should] be documented, with the ICPO.[6]

Later, over a period of five to ten years, having gained in experience, the Scherer-proposed ICPO would become more like an action-taking body up to the point where:

[B]eginning seven years after its creation, the ICPO will receive complaints from the competition policy authorities of signatory nations concerning monopolistic practices that distort international trade but that are not expressly covered by the policies specified here. It will investigate those complaints and make recommendations for appropriate corrective action by the competition policy authorities of nations in which the alleged practices occur. If the ICPO finds that international trade has in fact been distorted and if the problem is not remedied through national action, individual nations will be authorized to take

---

[3] American Bar Association, Special Committee on International Antitrust, *Report* (1991) at 8–9.
[4] F. M. Scherer, *Competition Policies for an Integrated World Economy* (1994) at 92.
[5] F. Souty, *La Politique de la concurrence au Royaume-Uni* (1996) at 128.
[6] Scherer, *supra* n. 4 at 92.

appropriately graduated countermeasures against the nation(s) or industries in which the distorting practices occur.[7]

In this proposal by Scherer, the ICPO would also have had a major role with regard to mega-mergers that would have resulted in the concentration of 40 per cent or more of the world trade under the control of a single enterprise or group of jointly acting enterprises. In that case, suggested Scherer:

[I]f the ICPO [determined] that competition in international trade [would be] likely to be jeopardized by such mergers to the detriment of consumers, it [would] recommend corrective measures to signatory nations, which [would] use their national laws and policies to remedy the problem.[8]

Because of the high-level political involvement of EU Commissioners, it was no surprise that, at the Singapore WTO Ministerial Conference in 1996, Vice-President of the EU Commission (and former Commissioner in charge of Competition) Sir Leon Brittan strongly supported the creation of a working group at the WTO, with full backing of then Competition Commissioner Van Miert. The EC also suggested an examination in the WTO of the following:

• the relationship between objectives, principles, concepts, scope and instruments of trade and competition policy, and their relation to development and growth;
• analysis of existing instruments, standards, and activities regarding trade and competition, including experience with their application;
• the interaction between trade and competition policy, considering in particular: (1) the impact of anti-competitive practices of enterprises and associations on international trade; (2) the influence of state monopolies, exclusive rights, and regulatory policies on competition and international trade; (3) the relationship between trade-related aspects of intellectual property rights and competition policy; (4) the relationship between investment and competition policy; and (5) the impact of trade policy on competition.[9]

Debates at the WTO started to focus on issues that were chiefly related to developed countries that are already equipped with competition or antitrust institutions, as these concerns were reflected by legally non-binding multilateral guidelines. Over time, with progress made in symposia including civil society (notably non-governmental organizations (NGOs) such as consumers' organizations)[10] and all multilateral

[7] Scherer, *supra* n. 4 at 95.   [8] *Ibid.* at 94.
[9] See para. 20 of the WTO Singapore Ministerial Declaration adopted on 13 December 1996.
[10] Five symposia held in Geneva, 1997–2002, jointly organized by the Secretariats of the WTO, UNCTD, OECD, and the World Bank.

international organizations involved with competition policy activities (the Organisation for Economic Co-operation and Development (OECD), the United Nations Conference on Trade and Development (UNCTAD), the WTO, and the World Bank), discussions focused more and more on issues related to developing countries, especially so after the Doha Ministerial Conference in November 2001.

During the period 1997–2003, the WTO Working Group on Trade and Competition Policy (WGTCP) identified all existing WTO provisions regarding private anti-competitive practices. Few of these WTO provisions on competition had led to WTO disputes. The WGTCP identified that international hard-core cartels affected both developed and developing countries in the same way. The debates in preparation of the WTO conference at Cancún showed the need for competition rules in the WTO to cope with issues of substance (i.e. anti-competitive behaviours) and to make the world trading system more efficient.

II. EXISTING WTO PROVISIONS REGARDING PRIVATE ANTI-COMPETITIVE PRACTICES

This section briefly reviews the competition-related provisions in existing WTO Agreements, namely:

- GATS Article VIII: members are to ensure that state monopolies do not act in a manner inconsistent with their obligations/specific commitments;
- Trade-Related Aspects of Intellectual Property Rights (TRIPS) Articles 8 and 40: authority to take measures against abuses of intellectual property rights such as anti-competitive licensing practices;
- Basic telecom negotiations: reference paper on regulatory principles— commitments to adopt appropriate measures to prevent anti-competitive practices by major suppliers;
- Agreement on Safeguards Article 11.3: Members are not to encourage/ support the adoption of non-governmental measures equivalent to voluntary export restraints, orderly marketing arrangements or other governmental arrangements prohibited under Article 11;
- Government Procurement Agreement: raises the level of burden on Members to strengthen the openness, transparency, and predictability of procurement systems, thereby raising the risks of international collusion and cartellization: a recent and spectacular case has been made public by investigations conducted by the *Financial Times* which alleges that US energy groups AES and Enron colluded to rig the auction for the largest electric distribution company in Latin

America, thereby depriving the government of Brazil of several hundreds of US$ millions of benefits;[11]

- Consultation arrangements under GATT and GATS: recognition that business practices that restrict competition in international trade may hamper the expansion of world trade and economic development.

So far, few of these WTO provisions on competition have led to cases or enforcement within the WTO dispute settlement system. One reason for this may be the absence of any specific competition institution in the WTO which specializes in competition-related issues. Another major reason for this lack of enforcement is the dispersion of these provisions in several sets of documents which are not easily and frequently consulted by competition authorities in Member States nor by market operators (which remain unfamiliar with current WTO proceedings that only concern Member States of that organization and not corporations).

III. WGTCP DEBATES AND NEGATIVE CONSEQUENCES OF ANTI-COMPETITIVE PRACTICES FOR DEVELOPING ECONOMIES

The WGTCP has greatly contributed in identifying anti-competitive practices that affect trade. Two types of practices can be identified. First, practices that contribute to defeating trade liberalization, including import cartels, domestic abuses of a dominant position and monopolization, vertical restraints, and some international cartels. Second, practices that more directly deprive nations of the benefit of trade, such as export cartels, anti-competitive transnational mergers, and international cartels.

Contrary to frequently held misconceptions, transnational anti-competitive practices have important costs: they inflict serious harm on consumers (for instance in the graphite electrode case, the cartel members increased their prices by 60 per cent resulting in overcharging of nearly US$1 billion a year; in the lysine cartel, prices were doubled over several years).[12] As Anderson and Jenny put it:

[C]oncern over the impact of international cartels on trade and development receded somewhat in the 1970s and 1980s. However, in the 1990s evidence surfaced that they were far from being a problem only of the past and, indeed, that cartels were alive and flourishing in the 'globalizing' economic environment.

---

[11] D. Sevastopoulo, 'AES Colluded with Enron to Rig a Bid for Latin American Energy Group' in *Financial Times* 21 May 2003 at 1 and 20.

[12] F. Jenny, 'Competition Law and Policy: Global Governance Issues' in *Globalization and Its Discontent Colloquium*, New York University, 4 March 2003.

Investigations conducted by the US Department of Justice, the European Commission, the Canadian Competition Bureau and other jurisdictions revealed the existence of major cartels.[13]

In the particular case of cartels, they can be very stable over time: the average duration of cartels for which there is publicly available information is six to eight years but some cartels may last considerably longer (up to 40 years for the International Equipment cartel). And these cartels may affect a large and diversified number of industries (e.g. steel, plastic dinnerware, thermal fax paper, heavy electrical equipment, construction materials and cement, glass, graphite electrode, vitamins, lysine, citric acid, etc.)

Besides identification of the harmful effects of anti-competitive practices on economic development, the WGTCP work has also shown that relatively few developing countries have effective and operational competition institutions, due to a lack of human and financial resources, which means that they are unable to fight against these anti-competitive practices. Indeed one of the major requests of participants from developing countries attending the WGTCP sessions is focused on assistance for institutional capacity building, with the major problem created by scarcity of skilled human resources in some least developed countries (thereby inducing a high turnover of the skilled workforce within the civil service who tend to be drawn by better terms and conditions offered by private enterprises).

IV. INTERNATIONAL HARD-CORE CARTELS AFFECTING BOTH DEVELOPED AND DEVELOPING COUNTRIES

It was Professors Graham and Richardson who first identified the areas of anti-competitive practices where consensus was beginning to emerge because of existing worldwide convergence of enforcement and those areas where the economic analysis might lead to persisting disagreements.[14]

More recently, several studies sponsored by the World Bank, the OECD, and UNCTAD have started to evaluate the actual prejudice to economic development and to international trade. In particular, with respect to developing countries, experiences have shown that international anti-competitive practices are often aimed at preventing the

---

[13] R. Anderson and F. Jenny, *Competition Policy, Economic Development and the Multilateral Trading System* (2002).
[14] E. M. Graham and J. D. Richardson, *Global Competition Policy* (1997) at 591.

emergence of local industries in developing countries (i.e. use of dumping by manufacturers of heavy electrical equipment and in the steel industry). They are most harmful in countries which do not have strong antitrust laws, now mainly developing countries, and they hurt developing countries which are particularly dependent on imports for access to basic industrial products not produced locally or on exports (for their growth) and countries which have weak industrial structures. Some studies have shown the importance of cartels and the extent of the damage they have inflicted upon developing countries. For example, in 1997, developing countries imported US$81 billion of goods from industries which had been affected by price-fixing conspiracies during the 1990s. These imports represented 6.7 per cent of total imports and 1.2 per cent of the gross domestic product (GDP) of the developing countries.[15] To put this statistic into proper perspective, international aid for development is about US$50 billion per annum. Thus, at a minimum, the existence of anti-competitive international cartels implies transfers in the form of overcharge from developing countries to cartel members (often if not mostly firms from developed countries) which represent at least half of the value of the development aid given by governments of developed countries to developing countries.[16]

Lastly, a study from UNCTAD estimates the welfare impact of various hypothetical trade liberalization measures and states:

[A] world-wide reduction of 50% in all agriculture tariffs brings about an aggregate welfare gain of USD 21.5 billions. The largest absolute gains are captured by Japan, North America, the NICs, North Africa and the Middle East and Oceania. The estimates for the percentage gains for sub-Saharan Africa and Latin America are lower than in other studies conducted under similar assumptions. Since Africa and Latin America are among the major beneficiaries of preferential schemes, it seems likely that gains from liberalization for these countries in other studies could be overstated when full account is not taken of tariff preferences as has been done here.[17]

A further analysis using the UNCTAD figures shows that the net welfare benefit for developing countries from such an agreement would be equal to US$13.4 billion, out of the US$21.5 billion in total. This US$13.4 billion, which represents the theoretical gains to result from a drastic multilateral reduction in agricultural tariffs, is about half the minimum estimate of the direct benefit developing countries would

[15] S. Evenett, M. C. Levenstein, and V. Y. Suslow, 'International Cartel Enforcement: Lessons from the 1990s' in *World Economy* (2001). This was a background paper prepared for the World Bank's *World Development Report 2001*.

[16] Jenny, *supra* n. 12.

[17] UNCTAD, *Back to Basics: Market Access Issues in the Doha Agenda* (2003) ch. V, 'Estimated Gains from Multilateral Trade Liberalization'.

obtain if a multilateral agreement on competition enabled the elimination of international cartels and therefore the supra-competitive margin developing countries have to pay to cartel members when they import goods (US$20–25 billion according to World Bank sources).[18]

The definition of hard-core cartels may be an issue. So far, only the OECD has attempted to define hard-core cartels in a recommendation to fight these cartels.[19] Lastly, a study was prepared by the WTO Secretariat which attempts an inventory of the effects of 'private international cartels' on developing economies and stresses the harm done to these countries:

[A]lthough estimates vary the price increases caused by international cartels are of the order of 20–40 percent. The price increases generate sizeable overcharges, especially given the large amount of imports by developing economies of cartelized products.[20]

V. NEED FOR WTO COMPETITION RULES

Already by 2001 it had been proposed by the EU at the WTO that:

[T]he potential development benefits of a WTO competition agreement would be a combination of three factors: a) a framework of rules which supports domestic competition institutions, b) flexibility and progressivity in commitments, c) providing an effective response to developing countries co-operation needs, including capacity building.[21]

What are now the parameters of the discussion especially in view of the EU proposals?[22]

First, the discussion at the WTO is neither about creating a supranational antitrust agency, nor about the harmonization of national competition laws. There is agreement not to subject individual decisions of national competition authorities to the WTO Dispute Settlement Understanding, and there are no discussions in the WGTCP to change existing anti-dumping laws. Rather, the discussion focuses on how to address the issue of transnational cartels which defeat the purpose of trade liberalization and deprive trading nations of the benefits of trade

---

[18] Jenny, *supra* n. 12.

[19] OECD, *Recommendation of the Council concerning Effective Action against Hard Core Cartels* (1998).

[20] S. Evenett, *Study on Issues Relating to a Possible Multilateral Framework on Competition Policy* (2003) (WT/WGTCP/W/228), 92.

[21] EU and its Member States Submission, 26 July 2001.

[22] This section draws on a presentation made by F. Jenny at a WTO Post-Doha Regional Seminar at Nairobi in April 2003.

liberalization as mentioned above. At present, the EU proposals are suggesting that every country should be covered by a competition law regime, that all national or regional competition or antitrust laws would include a provision prohibiting hard-core cartels, and that each country would remain free to include other provisions (e.g. on vertical restraints, abuses of dominance, merger control, etc.). The national competition laws would have to meet the WTO standards of transparency, non-discrimination, and procedural fairness.[23] Furthermore a mechanism of consultation and voluntary cooperation on transnational hard-core cartels and a WTO Competition Committee would be established to monitor the agreement and facilitate cooperation between countries, for example through peer reviews.[24] Finally, technical assistance would be offered to countries that do not have extensive experience nor resources in competition enforcement.

These elements suggest further reflections after Cancún particularly on the following issues: a definition of hard-core cartels; the means for integrating or translating WTO core principles of non-discrimination, transparency, procedural fairness, and due process into national or regional competition and antitrust laws; the ban on hard-core cartels as so defined; international cooperation and special and differential treatment for less-developed countries; co-operation and consultation including peer reviews within the proposed Competition Committee; and the relationships to WTO dispute settlement procedures.

VI. CONCLUSION

The occurrence of such a significant number of global and regional private anti-competitive practices more than justifies competition rules in the WTO. However, the agenda in WTO discussions has so far narrowed to five areas, which can be summarized as follows:

(1) A commitment to the adoption of national competition law and policy rules by all Member States, or at least a commitment to respect some basic principles.
(2) A general ban on hard-core cartels (with an agreement among Member States on an explicit definition of them that could be acceptable both to developed and developing countries).
(3) The submission of competition law disciplines to WTO dispute settlement procedures.

---

[23] See EU and its Member States submission at WGTCP No. 1, May 2003.
[24] See EU and its Member States communication, No. 2, May 2003.

(4) The institution of a Competition Committee within the WTO to work on competition issues.

(5) The adoption of peer reviews.

Some major competition issues—such as merger control—may have to remain outside the terms of the debates at the WTO because they have been pre-empted by the International Competition Network established among more than 50 competition authorities outside the WTO in 2001.

VII. ADDENDUM

The Decision adopted by the WTO General Council on 1 August 2004 provides, however, that—among the four 'Singapore issues' (trade-related competition rules, investment rules, transparency in government procurement, trade facilitation)—only negotiations on trade facilitation will commence in 2004; negotiations on the other three issues, including trade-related competition rules, will not take place within the Doha Round.

15

Are the Competition Rules in the WTO Agreement on Trade-Related Aspects of Intellectual Property Rights Adequate?

FREDERICK M. ABBOTT

In connection with the run-up to the Cancún Ministerial Conference, the author was asked whether there are grounds for recommending amendment of the World Trade Organization (WTO) Agreement on Trade-Related Aspects of Intellectual Property Rights (TRIPS) rules addressing competition. The general conclusion of the study is that the TRIPS Agreement in its present form provides substantial discretion to WTO Members in the formulation and application of competition rules regulating intellectual property, and this arrangement serves the best interests of developed and developing countries. Potential amendments were considered across a matrix of interested country groups: North–North, North–South, South–North, and South–South. Although country groups with different interests might seek to modify TRIPS competition-related rules to their perceived advantage, there is little reason to believe that consensus would be reached on such changes. The study acknowledges that global welfare benefits might flow from a more highly integrated international competition regime with powers to investigate and enforce agreed upon rules. There is, however, little identifiable near-term impetus for building such a regime, whether at the WTO or elsewhere. Competition laws of certain developed countries expressly exempt conduct with wholly foreign effects from the application of rules regulating anti-competitive practices, including those concerning intellectual property. Such exemptions appear inconsistent with advocacy of liberal market principles, and they are damaging to developing country interests. As part of the Doha Development Round commitment to developing countries, a decision by developed countries to eliminate these exemptions would be constructive.

I. COMPETITION RULES IN THE TRIPS AGREEMENT

A. Brief historical background

Article 46 of the 1948 Havana Charter for the International Trade Organization (ITO) contained an undertaking by Members to prevent restraints on competition (and to cooperate with the Organization in preventing such restraints), and permitted a Member to bring a complaint to the Organization on the basis that another Member was failing to deal with a competition-related situation. Included within the specific kinds of practices which the Organization's dispute settlement procedure would have addressed was commercial conduct:

3(e) preventing by agreement the development or application of technology or invention whether patented or unpatented;
(f) extending the use of rights under patents, trade marks or copyrights granted by any Member to matters which, according to its laws and regulations, are not within the scope of such grants, or to products or conditions of production, use or sale which are likewise not the subjects of such grants.[1]

The ITO would have had the authority to 'request each Member concerned to take every possible remedial action, and . . . recommend to the Members concerned remedial measures to be carried out in accordance with their respective laws and procedures'.[2] The Organization would have prepared, distributed to Members, and made public a report on its decisions, and the remedial actions taken by Members.[3]

From the late 1960s through the early 1980s there was considerable attention to the relationship between intellectual property rights (IPRs), transfer of technology, and competition in the context of debate on a New International Economic Order. In 1980, the United Nations General Assembly adopted as a resolution 'The Set of Multilaterally Agreed Equitable Principles and Rules for the Control of Restrictive Business Practices', which includes rules relating to abusive practices in the field of IPRs.[4]

The negotiating history of the TRIPS Agreement reflects concerns expressed by developing countries with the potential market restricting/anti-competitive effects of IPRs.[5] Proposals to incorporate

---

[1] Havana Charter for an International Trade Organization, United States Conference on Trade and Employment, held at Havana, Cuba, 21 November 1947 to 24 March 1948, *Final Act and Related Documents* (March 1948) Ch. V, Restrictive Business Practices, Art. 46. See F. M. Abbott, 'Public Policy and Global Technological Integration: An Introduction' in F. M. Abbott and D. Gerber (eds), *Public Policy and Global Technological Integration* (1997) 3.   [2] Havana Charter, *supra* n. 1, Arts. 8 and 48(7).
[3] Ibid., Arts. 48(9) and (10).
[4] E.g. Section D4, reprinted in 19 *International Legal Materials* (1980) 813.
[5] E.g. Communication from India of 10 July 1989 MTN.GNG./NG11/W/37 sub. 2 and VI.

provisions addressing the potential anti-competitive effects of IPRs originated with the developing countries. For example, draft Article 43, para 2B (developing) of the Brussels Ministerial (December 1990) Text included more specific references to anti-competitive practices and remedies than were ultimately incorporated in Article 40.2, TRIPS Agreement.

Article 43
1. PARTIES agree that some licensing practices or conditions pertaining to intellectual property rights which restrain competition may have adverse effects on trade and may impede the transfer and dissemination of technology.
2B. PARTIES may specify in their national legislation licensing practices or conditions that may be deemed to constitute an abuse of intellectual property rights or to have an adverse effect on competition in the relevant market, and may adopt appropriate measures to prevent or control such practices and conditions, including non-voluntary licensing in accordance with the provisions of Article 34 and the annulment of the contract or of those clauses of the contract deemed contrary to the laws and regulations governing competition and/or transfer of technology. The following practices and conditions may be subject to such measures where they are deemed to be abusive or anti-competitive: (i) grant-back provisions; (ii) challenges to validity; (iii) exclusive dealing; (iv) restrictions on research; (v) restrictions on use of personnel; (vi) price fixing; (vii) restrictions on adaptations; (viii) exclusive sales or representation agreements; (ix) tying arrangements; (x) export restrictions; (xi) patent pooling or cross-licensing agreements and other arrangements; (xii) restrictions on publicity; (xiii) payments and other obligations after expiration of industrial property rights; (xiv) restrictions after expiration of an arrangement.[6]

The Brussels Ministerial Text of Article 8.2 differed from the final TRIPS Agreement text, using a 'do not derogate from the obligations' formula instead of the final 'consistent with the provisions of' formula as the control mechanism.[7]

---

[6] Draft Final Act Embodying the Results of the Uruguay Round of Multilateral Trade Negotiations, Trade-Related Aspects of Intellectual Property Rights, Including Trade in Counterfeit Goods, MTN.TNC/W/35/Rev. 1, 3 December 1990 ('Brussels Ministerial Text'). The TRIPS Negotiation Group Chairman noted in his comments: 'Further basic issues needing to be resolved are . . . the content of the provisions on the Control of Abusive or Anti-Competitive Practices in Contractual Licences (Section 8 of Part II).'

[7] The Brussels Ministerial Text (*supra* n. 6) provided:

Article 8: Principles
   2. Appropriate measures, provided that they do not derogate from the obligations arising under this Agreement, may be needed to prevent the abuse of intellectual property rights by right holders or the resort to practices which unreasonably restrain trade or adversely affect the international transfer of technology.

B. TRIPS provisions

There are three provisions of the TRIPS Agreement expressly addressing competition. The first, Article 8.2, acknowledges the right of Members to act against abuse of IPRs, provided such action is consistent with the provisions of the Agreement.

Article 8, Principles

2. Appropriate measures, provided that they are consistent with the provisions of this Agreement, may be needed to prevent the abuse of intellectual property rights by right holders or the resort to practices which unreasonably restrain trade or adversely affect the international transfer of technology.

The second, Article 40, is a more detailed provision that, by its title and terms, is addressed to anti-competitive licensing practices or conditions.

SECTION 8: CONTROL OF ANTI-COMPETITIVE PRACTICES IN CONTRACTUAL LICENCES

Article 40

1. Members agree that some licensing practices or conditions pertaining to intellectual property rights which restrain competition may have adverse effects on trade and may impede the transfer and dissemination of technology.
2. Nothing in this Agreement shall prevent Members from specifying in their legislation licensing practices or conditions that may in particular cases constitute an abuse of intellectual property rights having an adverse effect on competition in the relevant market. As provided above, a Member may adopt, consistently with the other provisions of this Agreement, appropriate measures to prevent or control such practices, which may include for example exclusive grantback conditions, conditions preventing challenges to validity and coercive package licensing, in the light of the relevant laws and regulations of that Member.[8]

---

[8] Article 40, TRIPS Agreement, continues:

3. Each Member shall enter, upon request, into consultations with any other Member which has cause to believe that an intellectual property right owner that is a national or domiciliary of the Member to which the request for consultations has been addressed is undertaking practices in violation of the requesting Member's laws and regulations on the subject matter of this Section, and which wishes to secure compliance with such legislation, without prejudice to any action under the law and to the full freedom of an ultimate decision of either Member. The Member addressed shall accord full and sympathetic consideration to, and shall afford adequate opportunity for, consultations with the requesting Member, and shall cooperate through supply of publicly available non-confidential information of relevance to the matter in question and of other information available to the Member, subject to domestic law and to the conclusion of mutually satisfactory agreements concerning the safeguarding of its confidentiality by the requesting Member.

4. A Member whose nationals or domiciliaries are subject to proceedings in another Member concerning alleged violation of that other Member's laws and regulations on the subject matter of this Section shall, upon request, be granted an opportunity for consultations by the other Member under the same conditions as those foreseen in paragraph 3.

Article 31(k), TRIPS Agreement, acknowledges that compulsory licensing is a remedy available to correct abuse of patents,[9] providing:

(k) Members are not obliged to apply the conditions set forth in subparagraphs (b) and (f) where such use is permitted to remedy a practice determined after judicial or administrative process to be anti-competitive. The need to correct anti-competitive practices may be taken into account in determining the amount of remuneration in such cases. Competent authorities shall have the authority to refuse termination of authorization if and when the conditions which led to such authorization are likely to recur;

Article 31(k) is the only part of the TRIPS compulsory licensing rules that incorporates a waiver of the condition that compulsory licenses must be issued 'predominantly' for the supply of the domestic market.[10]

At an indirect level, Article 6, TRIPS Agreement, as confirmed by the Doha Declaration on the TRIPS Agreement and Public Health, authorizes each WTO Member to adopt its own policies and rules on the subject of exhaustion of rights.

Article 6
Exhaustion
For the purposes of dispute settlement under this Agreement, subject to the provisions of Articles 3 and 4 nothing in this Agreement shall be used to address the issue of the exhaustion of intellectual property rights.

Doha Declaration
5(d) The effect of the provisions in the TRIPS Agreement that are relevant to the exhaustion of intellectual property rights is to leave each Member free to establish its own regime for such exhaustion without challenge, subject to the MFN and national treatment provisions of Articles 3 and 4.[11]

The exhaustion principle is fundamentally directed at maintaining competitive markets in trade.[12] The general recognition of flexibility in implementing methods in Article 1.1, TRIPS Agreement, will apply in the competition context.

---

[9] Article 31(l), TRIPS Agreement, addresses the problem of dependent patents whose exploitation might otherwise be blocked. This is also a competition-related provision.

[10] Of course, compulsory licensing is not the only remedy available for anti-competitive abuse of IPRs, which may include, *inter alia*, injunction and fines. This paper was presented prior to adoption on 30 August 2003 of the Decision on Implementation of Paragraph 6 of the Doha *Declaration on the TRIPS Agreement and Public Health*, which provides for a waiver of the Article 31(f) condition.

[11] WTO Ministerial Conference, Declaration on the Trips Agreement and Public Health, adopted 14 November 2001, 4th Session, Doha, WT/MIN(01)/DEC/2 (20 November 2001).

[12] E.g. F. M. Abbott, 'First Report (Final) to the Committee on International Trade Law of the International Law Association on the Subject of Parallel Importation' in 1 *Journal of International Economic Law* (1998) 607.

The first paragraph of the preamble to the agreement notes that IPRs should not themselves act to distort trade:

Desiring to reduce distortions and impediments to international trade, and taking into account the need to promote effective and adequate protection of intellectual property rights, and to ensure that measures and procedures to enforce intellectual property rights do not themselves become barriers to legitimate trade;

Part III, TRIPS Agreement, on enforcement of IPRs is of course generally applicable to enforcement in the competition context as well requiring, for example, due process of law.

C. Interpretation

The TRIPS Agreement provides WTO Members with substantial discretion in the development and application of competition law to arrangements and conduct in the field of IPRs. The text of Article 8.2 requires that competition measures be 'consistent' with the TRIPS Agreement, and this suggests that competition law should not be used as a disguised mechanism for undermining the basic rights accorded under it. Measures may be taken to prevent abuse of IPRs, or resort to practices that 'unreasonably' restrain trade or that 'adversely affect' the 'international transfer of technology'. The question whether a particular practice 'unreasonably' restrains trade involves a classical balancing test taking into account the effects of conduct on consumers or industrial policy interests, and has been applied with significantly different results not only in different legal systems, but in the same legal systems over time. From the standpoint of competition rules customarily applied to IPRs-related practices in developed and developing Members, it is doubtful that such application in good faith will be limited by the text of Article 8.2.

Article 40.2 expressly envisions that Members may 'specify' in their legislation licensing practices that 'may in particular cases constitute an abuse' of IPRs. This language encompasses the adoption of *per se* rules in respect to certain types of licensing practices, such as applied by the EC in its technology transfer regulation.[13] The 'in particular cases' language, which is acknowledged to represent less than ideal drafting, is intended to require that Members define such practices on the basis of their competitive merits, rather than in an overly abstract manner (and not to prevent the adoption of *per se* rules).[14]

---

[13] See discussion of EC technology transfer regulation, *supra*, nn. 19–24.
[14] See Part 3, Intellectual Property Rights and Competition, in *UNCTAD–ICTSD TRIPS Resource Book: An Authoritative and Practical Guide to the TRIPS Agreement*, (2003) . . . online at http://www.iprsonline.org.

While there might be ways to improve the drafting of Articles 8.2 or 40 so as to improve clarity, as a practical matter these provisions do not appear to substantially impinge upon Member discretion in the formulation and application of competition rules to IPRs, and it is doubtful that a new set of negotiations is needed to establish the presence of discretion from a legal standpoint. Moreover, the Doha Declaration on the TRIPS Agreement and Public Health, paragraph 5, has confirmed the flexibility inherent in parallel trade and compulsory licensing rules.

The TRIPS Agreement does not limit the remedial measures that may be imposed by competition authorities and courts. For example, it does not preclude the award of treble damages that may be imposed as a remedy in United States (US) antitrust proceedings. Remedies may include injunction, damages, fines, and, as noted above, compulsory licensing.[15]

The presence of discretion from a legal standpoint does not assure that developing Members will not come under pressure from developed Members should they choose to exercise it. Developed Members with some regularity assert political and economic pressure on developing Members not to act in ways permitted under WTO agreements.

It may not be the most productive use of this brief chapter and the attention of this distinguished readership to focus on narrow interpretive issues that are likely to influence Members only at the margins.[16] The real question and centrepiece for this discussion is: what would or might be gained from changing the present rules?

II. PROSPECTIVE NEW COMPETITION RULES FOR TRIPS

A. A trade and competition agreement

There is a general question whether a multilateral or plurilateral trade and competition agreement should be agreed upon at the WTO. While such evaluations are to a certain extent subjective, there appears to remain a fairly wide level of divergence regarding what Members think might or ought to be done regarding such an agreement. Developing Members are worried that national treatment rules will be used to force changes to national industrial policy, including preferences to small and medium enterprises. Members are unable to agree on what constitutes a 'hard-core cartel' (having moved from focusing on the 'hard export

---

[15] There are certain conditions placed on compulsory licensing as antitrust remedy, but the main effect is to allow reduction of remuneration based on the remedial nature of the license.

[16] A detailed analysis of the 'control' language of the competition provisions can be found at Part 3 of the *UNCTAD–ICTSD TRIPS Resource Book, supra,* n. 14.

cartel'), and whether such cartels could be justified in some circumstances based on economic efficiency. From the developed country side, there appears to be agreement that developing Members should adopt and implement competition laws (where they have not already done so), that measures should be transparent, and that national treatment rules should apply. While there seems to be agreement that restrictive business practices in the developed Members act to the detriment of developing Members, there is little in the way of explanation why those practices are presently tolerated in developed Members and why it should be necessary to adopt a multilateral agreement to address this problem. The antitrust laws of the US, for example, expressly exempt US-based anti-competitive conduct that affects only foreign markets, tolerating and encouraging the very conduct about which concern is expressed.[17]

However, the purpose of this chapter is not to consider the prospective contents, or advantages and disadvantages, of a multilateral agreement on trade and competition, but whether changes to the competition rules in the TRIPS Agreement are necessary or desirable.

B. The locus of change

A threshold question is whether any changes to TRIPS-related competition rules would be made in the text of the TRIPS Agreement, or would instead be embodied in a separate trade and competition agreement. There is nothing in the WTO agreements to preclude competition rules with effect on TRIPS being set out in a separate agreement and cross-referenced. As a practical matter, absent an express exclusion, it is inevitable that competition rules set out in a trade and competition agreement would affect TRIPS since IPRs regulation is traditionally

---

[17] The Sherman Act provides, for example:

15 USCS s. 6a (2003)

s. 6a. Conduct involving trade or commerce with foreign nations

This Act [15 USCS s. 1 et seq., commonly 'the Sherman Anti-Trust Act'] shall not apply to conduct involving trade or commerce (other than import trade or import commerce) with foreign nations unless—

(1) such conduct has a direct, substantial, and reasonably foreseeable effect—
(A) on trade or commerce which is not trade or commerce with foreign nations, or on import trade or import commerce with foreign nations; or
(B) on export trade or export commerce with foreign nations, of a person engaged in such trade or commerce in the United States; and
(2) such effect gives rise to a claim under the provisions of this Act [15 USCS s. 1 et seq.], other than this section.

If this Act [15 USCS s. 1 et seq.] applies to such conduct only because of the operation of paragraph (1)(B), then this Act [15 USCS s. 1 et seq.] shall apply to such conduct only for injury to export business in the United States.

within the general scope of competition law. For example, while the US Department of Justice and Federal Trade Commission have issued antitrust guidelines for the licensing of intellectual property,[18] these guidelines are based on interpretation of Sherman and Clayton Act rules and jurisprudence, and not on a body of rules specific to IPRs. Similarly, while the European Community (EC) has issued fairly extensive guidance on the licensing of technology, this guidance is framed as an application of Articles 81 and 82, EC Treaty, and not on a separate body of IPRs-specific competition law.[19]

Changes directly to TRIPS Agreement rules presuppose a reopening of the agreement, and whether that is desirable will depend on the perspective of the participating Members. Generally speaking, the imbalance of bargaining power at the WTO has made developing Members wary of reopening TRIPS. Reopening might be used by the US–EC–Japan–Swiss group to lobby for increased levels of protection, which are likely to further exacerbate the imbalanced static wealth transfer effects already in place.

At the WTO, parties bargain in their own interests, with Members typically representing their producers. For this reason, it is perhaps most useful to look first at prospective changes to TRIPS competition rules across a matrix of potential interests, with discussion of global public welfare effects reserved until later on.

C. North–North

As noted above, Articles 6, 8.2, and 40 of the TRIPS Agreement leave Members with substantial discretion as to whether and how to apply competition rules to IPRs-based restraints of trade and abuse of dominant position. The US and EC over time have taken substantially different views on appropriate industrial policy. It seems doubtful that competition authorities in either the US or EC would be anxious to formally harmonize or approximate rules in the IPRs field since this would involve a reduction of discretion. It is, in fact, difficult to see why, from

---

[18] US Department of Justice/Federal Trade Commission, *Antitrust Guidelines for the Licensing of Intellectual Property* (1995), online at http://www.usdoj.gov/atr/public/guidelines/ipguide.htm.

[19] 'Commission Regulation (EC) No 240/96 of 31 January 1996 on the application of Article 85(3) of the Treaty to Certain Categories of Technology Transfer Agreements' in *Official Journal* L 031, 9 February 1996 P. 0002–0013 (reference to unadjusted EC Treaty numbering) ('1996 Technology Transfer Regulation'). On 7 April 2004, the European Commission announced the adoption of a new block exemption on technology transfer agreements under Article 81(3) of the EC Treaty. Commission Regulation (EC) No 772/2004 of 27 April 2004 on the application of Article 81(3) of the Treaty to categories of technology transfer agreements, *Official Journal* L123, 27 April 2004, pp. 11–17 ('2004 Technology Transfer Regulation').

the perspective of the US or EC, approximation or harmonization—that is, 'freezing the industrial policy pendulum'—would be desirable.

In the 1960s and 1970s, US competition law authorities and courts were concerned that IPRs had a direct correlation with market power and potential abuse, and antitrust analysis began with a presumption that IPRs conferred market power. By the mid-1980s, and as reflected in the 1995 Licensing Guidelines, this perception shifted, and IPRs are presently treated as any other form of property (whether real, personal, or intangible), without the market power presumption. With few exceptions—price fixing, horizontal market segmentation, and output restraints (which also apply in goods markets)—technology acquisition and licensing agreements are evaluated under a rule of reason approach.[20] The rule of reason approach extends, for example, to exclusive grantback provisions. For the past two years the Federal Trade Commission has been studying the effects of IPRs on innovation markets in the US, with evident concern that overprotection of IPRs may present risks to future innovation. This may signal the beginning of a shift towards another view of IPRs and market power, though conclusions are not yet reached.

In April 2004 the EC revised its approach to the regulation of technology markets, enhancing flexibility and more closely approximating the US approach that de-emphasizes adverse presumptions toward licensing restrictions, up to certain levels of market power.[21] Prior to this revision, the EC took a substantially more direct approach to the regulation of technology markets.[22] Even under the new EC regime, certain important distinctions with respect to the US approach remain, such as the EC's continuing *per se* disapproval of exclusive grantbacks.[23] This represents yet again a swing in the pendulum of regulatory approach, this time on the European side.

With respect to licensing, both the US and EC use percentage of market formulas for establishing presumptions of market concentration in respect to technology and innovation.[24] The formulas are somewhat different, though this does not necessarily imply that competition authorities in the two Members would reach different results in a given case.

[20] The US Department of Justice/Federal Trade Commission Licensing Guidelines separately consider IPRs as they affect goods markets, technology markets, and innovation markets. The technology market refers to licensing and acquisition of existing technologies, while the innovation market essentially refers to the market in future R&D.

[21] See 2004 Technology Transfer Regulation, *supra* n. 19.

[22] These exempt from competition law scrutiny a range of licensing practices, impose certain *per se* prohibitions, and leave other areas for which parties must notify and effectively seek clearance from the Commission. See 1996 Technology Transfer Regulation, *supra*, n. 19, at e.g. Arts. 1–4.

[23] Art. 5(1), 2004 Technology Transfer Directive.

[24] *Ibid.*, e.g., Arts. 3, 7–8; US Department of Justice/Federal Trade Commission, *supra* n. 18 at e.g. section 4.3 (Antitrust 'safety zone').

The potential advantage of stronger North–North-oriented TRIPS and competition rules might be to force some industrialized countries to apply competition rules more vigorously (e.g. to redress the type of enforcement failures alleged in *Japan—Film and Photographic Paper*).[25] Yet even if more aggressive enforcement policies in some industrialized Members would be desirable, producer interests in the US and EC are unlikely to support the negotiation of strong enforcement obligations that may be used for the basis of investigations into their own activities.

In 1998, I commented on the prospects for a WTO trade and competition agreement in respect, *inter alia*, to the then-pending controversy between the US and EC involving the Boeing–McDonnell Douglas merger.[26] I asked, rhetorically, whether and what issue involved in that controversy would a WTO trade and competition agreement propose to 'cure'? I would ask today whether there is any defect in the TRIPS Agreement competition rules from a North–North perspective that we might propose to 'cure' in multilateral negotiations? From a pragmatic standpoint, it is difficult to see what that might be.[27]

D. North–South

Developed Members consistently evidence two principal objectives in WTO negotiations with developing Members. The first is to enhance their access to developing Member markets. The second is to prevent developing Members from exercising discretion in a way that would be considered unfavourable to the developed Members.

Although the practice appears presently out of favour,[28] some developing Members have sought to impose on the importation of goods or the undertaking of direct investment conditions requiring transfer of technology, typically in the form of patent and know-how licensing to a local enterprise.[29] This is not a restrictive licensing practice as such, nor does it involve use of IPRs for anti-competitive purposes. To the extent such practices are regarded as discriminatory, they are for the most part

[25] Report of the Panel, *Japan—Measures affecting Consumer Photographic Film and Paper*, WT/DS44/R, 31 March 1998.

[26] F. M. Abbott, 'The Prospects for World Competition Law: An American Perspective', address to the German-American Lawyers Association, Cologne, Germany, 9 November 1998 (unpublished, in author's files).

[27] This observation is made in light of the substantial ongoing cooperation between US and EC competition authorities under bilateral agreement.

[28] This is not based on an empirical study, but rather on the author's general perception that the volume of complaints about such practices has subsided.

[29] 'Civil offsets' or 'offsets' appear to remain a standard feature in military equipment procurement agreements but, as above, this is an impressionistic observation. Offsets in military procurement are by no means confined to developed–developing country arrangements, appearing to be a standard feature of developed–developed country procurement arrangements.

to be dealt with under the GATT.[30] Some of these conditions have been addressed in the Agreement on Government Procurement.[31] It is difficult to place this subject matter within the subject matter scope of the TRIPS Agreement.

From a market-access standpoint, developing Member enterprises do not seem likely for the near to medium term to be using IPRs licensing agreements—such as pooling arrangements or R&D joint ventures—as a means to restrict access of foreign goods or services to local markets. There would not appear to be a pressing need to develop additional rules to address potential future activities of this nature.

Government preferences in the grant of research funding might be considered an anti-competitive practice in the IPRs field. This is an issue that might be addressed by developing Members in relation to developed Members. It is doubtful there is significant concern in developed Members with respect to such grants in developing Members.

Developed Members might be concerned with potential 'overaggressive' pursuit of competition-based claims in the field of patents, and developed Members might seek to limit the potential exercise of discretion. So far, the principal limitation in the TRIPS Agreement is that competition measures be consistent with it. This is a 'soft' limitation. It would conceptually be possible for developed countries to seek negotiation of a list of prohibited or presumptively prohibited anti-competitive restraints that would act as the outer limit of discretion for competition authorities in developing Members. Such an exercise seems unlikely to succeed in light of the need to achieve consensus on a list of practices.

Developing Members might seek to impose conditions on technology licences in favour of local enterprise; for example, requirements that the licensee be trained in the use of the technology and be permitted to use it in competition with the licensor during or after the licence term. Although ongoing demands from developing Members for improved technology transfer might appear to favour such conditions, this does not mean that developed Members may not view TRIPS and competition negotiations as an opportunity to limit such practices. Again, however, there is little prospect for consensus agreement on such limitations.

To be clear, this report is not recommending that developed WTO Members pursue any of the foregoing negotiating objectives, but rather

---

[30] This set of issues is addressed in detail in F. M. Abbott, 'Reflection Paper on China in the World Trading System: Defining the Principles of Engagement' in F. M. Abbott (ed.), *China in the World Trading System, Vol. I* (1998) 13–18.

[31] These concerns have been raised, for example, in respect to purchases of civil aircraft, and were addressed at one stage under the Agreement on Trade in Civil Aircraft. *Ibid.*

is suggesting the types of outcomes that such Members might pursue in TRIPS and competition negotiations.

E. South–North

Developing countries presently have substantial discretion in the formulation and application of TRIPS and competition rules within their own territories. In many respects this may be the ideal position for them, and may argue against attempting to negotiate any new TRIPS and competition rules.

It is an important feature of US antitrust law that conduct which only affects external markets is not subject to scrutiny. In the general context of a multilateral competition agreement, it would be desirable from the standpoint of developing Members to obtain agreement that this sort of legislation is prohibited. That is, it is not permitted to discriminate against foreign markets in the application of competition rules. This general principle could well be transposed more specifically to the TRIPS and competition arena. That is, for example, licensing practices that are not tolerated in the home market will not be tolerated in a foreign market, and the enterprise subject of the complaint will face penalties in the home market for engaging in prohibited conduct overseas.[32]

As an illustration, the US Federal Trade Commission recently completed an in-depth study of so-called 'Orange Book' practices by certain pharmaceutical enterprises.[33] This study found that patents had been grossly abused at the Food and Drug Administration to prevent the entry of generic drugs onto the US market. A principal violator company has been the subject of consent injunction and has paid substantial fines.[34] The US market is subject to relative close monitoring by competition authorities and public interest groups. Yet potential competitive abuse of patents in foreign markets is not within the scope of US antitrust law (absent a direct and substantial impact on the US market, including on US exporters), and equivalent capacities for monitoring and enforcement would be the exception in developing Members. Thus, if US law prohibited equivalent anti-competitive acts

---

[32] This may raise difficult issues in the application of competition law. A *rule of reason* analysis will include such matters as a determination of the relevant market and the conditions of competition in that market. The fact that an analysis would be difficult does not mean it should be avoided. *Per se* rules might assist when applied to conduct abroad.

[33] US Federal Trade Commission, *Generic Drug Entry Prior to Patent Expiration: An FTC Study* (2002), online at http://www.ftc.gov/os/2002/07/genericdrugstudy.pdf.

[34] See *States and FTC Settle with Bristol-Myers Squibb in Buspar Monopolization Suit*, 28(2) Antitrust Multistate Review; p. 3, National Association of Attorneys General Antitrust Report (February 2003).

in foreign markets this might yield significant benefits to developing Members.[35]

On 14 June 2004, the US Supreme Court rendered a decision in *Hoffmann-La Roche v Empagran*,[36] in which it confirmed that:

The FTAIA seeks to make clear to American exporters (and to firms doing business abroad) that the Sherman Act does not prevent them from entering into business arrangements (say, joint selling arrangements), however anticompetitive, as long as those arrangements adversely affect only foreign markets.[37]

The Court held that a plaintiff injured solely by anti-competitive conduct outside the US could not sue a defendant within the US, even if that same defendant had caused independent anti-competitive harm in the US to another person. The Court's holding was grounded in 'comity' concerns; that foreign nations would be offended if the US acted to regulate conduct within their territories absent a direct effect on the US. Particular concern was expressed that foreign nations might take offence at the imposition of treble damages on their nationals as a remedy for Sherman Act violations. The Court acknowledged that comity considerations could be eveluted on a case-by-case basis, but said that this approach 'is too complex to prove workable'.

Comity concerns were expressed to the Court in amicus briefs from Canada, Germany, and Japan, and it may be that competition authorities in these countries are ready and willing to police the conduct of American companies within their territories. Friendly relations among nations might allow them to do that in the way they deem most appropriate. It is not so clear that giving a 'green light' to companies doing business in the US for engaging in conduct 'however anti-competitive' in developing countries serves the interests of those countries, or of the international community. Unlike in Canada, Japan, and Germany, competition authorities in many developing countries might find it diplomatically problematic to assess the conduct of and impose penalties on General Electric or Pfizer. Developing country governments might not be so sanguine about their capacity to prevent US-based export cartels from extracting anti-competitive rents from their economies. While the Supreme Court might have allowed a case-by-case balancing of comity considerations, it interpreted the will of the Congress to literally exempt the conduct of companies doing business in

---

[35] As of April 2004 there is a decision by the US Supreme Court pending regarding whether a plaintiff may bring suit in the US for antitrust injuries occurring in a foreign market if the predicate of a direct and substantial effect in the US market is satisfied, even if that predicate is not satisfied as to the particular plaintiff (*Hoffmann-La Roche v Empagran*, 124 S. Ct. 966, cert. granted).

[36] 124 S. Ct. 2359; 2004 US LEXIS 4174 (2004).

[37] *Ibid.* at *10–11 (preliminary pagination).

the US from 'bad behavior' solely engaged in abroad. This does not seem to send a promising message from the principal advocate of 'liberal trade' to the large majority of developing countries that do not have the resources needed to effectively police anti-competitive conduct within their borders.

Article 40.3 of the TRIPS Agreement provides for consultations and furnishing of non-confidential information, and for furnishing other information subject to the national law of the requested Member.[38] It is difficult to know the extent to which the national law of a Member will permit (or not) the mandatory furnishing of business information to the authorities (or private complainants) in another Member. Developing Members pursuing competition cases may have great difficulty obtaining critical information from private enterprises in developed Members, and a stronger form of cooperation agreement relating to such information might usefully be negotiated. However, it must be recognized that such information rules would run in both directions, and developing Members would also need to consider the extent to which they would be willing to furnish information in equivalent settings.[39]

The TRIPS Agreement contains a limited set of illustrative anti-competitive licensing practices: 'for example exclusive grantback conditions, conditions preventing challenges to validity and coercive package licensing' (Article 40.2). Because developing Members come under pressure from developed Members when they seek to act against the latter's perceived interests, there is an argument to be made for expanding the list of practices that may be considered anti-competitive. This could provide assurance to developing Members that actions taken against such conditions could not be successfully challenged before the Appellate Body. However, there are two arguments against pursuing expansion of the list. First, the negotiations might well result in reducing the flexibility presently enjoyed by developing Members. Second, if a developing Member is going to be threatened or intimidated by a developed Member for using flexibility existing in the TRIPS Agreement, adding text that is more supportive may not remedy the problem. The problem is rooted in an imbalance in political and economic power, not in the language of the TRIPS Agreement.

---

[38] '. . . The Member addressed shall accord full and sympathetic consideration to, and shall afford adequate opportunity for, consultations with the requesting Member, and shall cooperate through supply of publicly available non-confidential information of relevance to the matter in question and of other information available to the Member, subject to domestic law and to the conclusion of mutually satisfactory agreements concerning the safeguarding of its confidentiality by the requesting Member.' Article 40.3 TRIPS Agreement.

[39] An argument might be made in terms of special and differential treatment in the field of evidence sharing. An argument might be made that there is less capacity for local investigation in developing Members.

The US Patent Act establishes preferences that patents resulting from federally funded research be licensed to parties that will produce in the US.[40] This is arguably a legislative restriction on patent licensing that discriminates against foreign enterprises. A developing Member objective in TRIPS and competition negotiations might be to subject such licensing practices to further scrutiny.

Developing Members differ widely in their capacity to address competition issues. Some have relatively well developed legal and pro-secutorial infrastructure. In others, such infrastructure is very weak. Perhaps the most important aspect of any competition agreement at the WTO would be a hard commitment on financial contribution from the developed Members to training of competition law authorities and the furnishing of suitable investigatory facilities. Since the TRIPS Agreement has an essentially satisfactory set of competition rules at present, there is no need to change the TRIPS rules in order to establish training and infrastructure programmes. A critical aspect is to assure that training and infrastructure support be provided by persons whose interests are on the side of developing Members.

It is important to recall that some developing Members have in the past attempted to rebalance the international distribution of technolog-ical capacity through legislative means, in particular through rules governing technology licensing.[41] That experience should be studied carefully—in particular regarding the effects of a political/economic power imbalance on legislative solutions—as a prelude to considering additional rules in this area.

F. South–South

Might developing countries in the TRIPS and competition context bene-fit from additional rules in relations among themselves? Competitive markets restraints in the field of TRIPS might as readily affect developing Members as among themselves as they do in relations with developed Members, except that developing Members are at present largely importers of technology protected by IPRs.

The starting-point is existing discretion to develop and apply rules, and this may be the optimal situation.

---

[40] Section 204 of the US Patent Act, e.g., provides, *inter alia*:

no small business firm or non-profit organization which receives title to any subject invention [i.e. based on federally funded research] and no assignee of any such small business firm or non-profit organization shall grant to any person the exclusive right to use or sell any subject invention in the United States unless such person agrees that any products embodying the subject invention or produced through the use of the subject invention will be manufactured substantially in the United States.

[41] Recalling, in particular, Decisions 84 and 85 of the Andean Commission (1974).

Developing Members might gain from strengthened rules on furnishing of evidence, just as in South–North relations, bearing in mind again that this would be a two-way street.

Training of personnel and improvements in infrastructure may be just as useful in South–South relations as in South–North relations.

G. Global public welfare

It is reasonable to ask what might be the optimal TRIPS and competition result leaving aside the perspective of Member self-interest, and viewing the subject from the perspective of global public welfare. In this approach, TRIPS competition rules would seek to assure that producers did not obtain IPRs monopoly rents in excess of their economic contribution to social welfare, and WTO Members would cooperate in implementing this objective. Consumer protection and human rights interests (e.g. right to health) would play a role in implementation of competition rules at least equivalent to that of industrial policy interests. The grant and enforcement of patents in developed Members would not presuppose the grant and enforcement of patents in developing Members because of the different situations in the respective WTO Members. In developing Members, competition on the basis of marginal costs would be the objective in socially sensitive sectors of the economy.

Accomplishment of global public welfare maximizing objectives might require elaboration of a set of prohibited anti-competitive practices addressed to conduct occurring in any territory. Such a set of rules might take into account the differential capacities of enterprises based in countries at different levels of development. There might be created a multinational investigatory and enforcement body with power to compel production of evidence, to refer cases to a neutral tribunal, and to impose remedies.

Leaving aside concerns that might legitimately be raised regarding the implications of such multilateral rules and enforcement mechanisms from the standpoint of state sovereignty and individual rights, there is little reason to believe that the international community is prepared to embark on a law-making venture of such scope. In relation to the TRIPS Agreement and prospective changes to competition rules it is more practical to focus attention on whether incremental modifications are necessary or desirable.

III. CONCLUSION

The present situation under the TRIPS Agreement provides WTO Members with substantial discretion in the development and application of competition rules. A survey of potential interests from the perspective of differing circumstances does not suggest compelling grounds for change. However, as a 'down-payment' by developed Members in the Doha Development Agenda, they might agree to reform their competition laws such that exemptions are not provided for conduct undertaken abroad. If developed Members are serious about the pursuit of market liberalization, they should accept that it is entirely inconsistent with that objective to tolerate and encourage their enterprises to adopt restrictive business practices in foreign markets.

16

Investment and the Doha Development Agenda*

BIJIT BORA[1] AND EDWARD M. GRAHAM

I. INTRODUCTION

Although investment issues have been discussed and negotiated at the multilateral level for more than 50 years, they rose to prominence in the early 1980s with a limited mandated agenda on trade related investment measures during the Uruguay Round of negotiations. Progress on this limited mandate was slow. In contrast, the successful conclusion in 1994 of the North American Free Trade Agreement (NAFTA), which incorporated investment provisions and thus revitalized earlier ambitions to achieve a multilateral framework. Subsequently, the Organization for Economic Co-operation and Development (OECD) attempted to transform itself from a bureaucratic organization into a negotiating body with the objective of successfully concluding a Multilateral Agreement on Investment (MAI). As is well known, that effort failed in 1998.[2] At the multilateral level, the First Ministerial of the newly created World Trade Organization (WTO), held in 1996, initiated a Working Group on Trade and Investment.

Taken together these initiatives established the importance of foreign investment policy as an important component of the multilateral trading system. They also created new challenges for negotiators at the 4th WTO Ministerial with respect to how this policy might be incorporated into WTO rules. The Ministers responded by establishing a mandate in what now is known as the 'Doha Declaration' that, in effect, requires that key substantive decisions be made at the following (5th) Ministerial.

Most recent discussion on investment issues in the WTO in fact has been at the very generic stage such that even the most basic question is not fully settled as to whether a formal negotiation will take place.

---

* The main body of this article was completed prior to the Cancún WTO meeting of September, 2004. An epilogue updating the state of play since that meeting appears at the end of this article.

[1] The views in this paper are expressed in a personal capacity and should not in anyway be associated with the World Trade Organization or its Member states.

[2] A detailed account is provided in E. M. Graham, *Fighting the Wrong Enemy* (2000).

Indeed, if investment issues are not adopted as part of the negotiating agenda at the 5th WTO Ministerial to take place in September 2003 in Cancún, some WTO Members would take this as a victory. But, even if this were to happen, many investment policies that might have formed part of an overarching investment agreement will nonetheless be covered in a number of existing WTO agreements. Hence, the question that needs to be answered is, would additional investment rule-making as is proposed in the Doha mandate add new value beyond that which already exists? In particular, given the focus on economic development in poorer countries that is meant to be the focus of the new round, would a new agreement to create investment rules make a tangible and significant contribution to the development process, if such an agreement were eventually included in the WTO? Alternatively, could an equal contribution be achieved via the deepening of existing investment rules or negotiating new such rules within existing WTO agreements? The issue before WTO Members, therefore, is one of the extent to which investment issues in the WTO should be deepened and by what mode, as opposed to the binary question of whether or not the WTO will embark upon negotiation of an overarching investment agreement.

The approach taken in this chapter to responding to these questions is to review the current investment related provisions in the WTO in the next section. The third section examines the mandate for investment issues given by Ministers in Doha while the fourth section is a review of the state of play of the various components of the current mandate. Most of it supports the transition of developing country governments towards a more open and receptive policy framework for foreign direct investment (FDI). It emphasizes the assets possessed by multinational corporations and their ability to contribute to the economic growth and development of a host country.[3]

While the chapter is policy-oriented it is important to note the theoretical and empirical literature on the link between FDI and development. It highlights the fact that while there is very strong evidence supporting the case for investment liberalization there are also possible negative effects from opening up to FDI.[4] This is not surprising and in no way should be discounted. Any economic policy will have both positive welfare effects, which require associated adjustment. Some of the specifics of this literature is discussed in a previous paper by Bora and Graham[5] and will not be repeated in this chapter.

---

[3] These assets include additional capital, advanced technology, managerial expertise, and linkages to international markets.

[4] E.g. T. Moran, *Foreign Direct Investment and Development* (1998); UNCTAD, *World Investment Report 1999: FDI and the Challenge of Development* (1999).

[5] B. Bora and E. M. Graham, *Investment and the Doha Development Agenda*, Working Paper No. 30, Institute for International Economics (2003).

II. INVESTMENT-RELATED ISSUES BEARING ON EXISTING WTO AGREEMENTS[6]

As suggested earlier, critics of the investment agenda at the WTO tend to focus on the failure of the MAI, trying to use it as an example of why rule making on investment issues would not be in the best interests of countries, especially developing ones. However, this is to ignore the fact that many of the issues related to investment policy-making are already being covered within the multilateral rule making agenda.

One of the most contentious issues at stake, for example, is market access for foreign investors. This involves national and most favoured nation treatment for foreign investors, which were among the cornerstone principles of the MAI. The issue is taken up in some detail in the next section, since it is partly covered in two existing WTO agreements; the Agreement on Government Procurement (AGP) and the General Agreement on Trade in Services (GATS). The standard provided in these agreements, and indeed, other agreements such as Bilateral Investment Treaties and the NAFTA is national treatment for foreign investors. This means providing treatment to foreign investors which is no less favourable than that provided to domestic investors. A corresponding principle is the most-favoured-nation (MFN) principle, which prohibits discrimination between investors from different countries.

The AGP provides that there be no discrimination against foreign suppliers, and also no discrimination against locally established suppliers on the basis of their degree of foreign affiliation or ownership.[7] The GATS treats foreign investment in the service sector as a mode of supply.[8] This is done by defining the commercial presence of a foreign supply as:

[A]ny type of business or professional establishment, including through (i) the constitution, acquisition or maintenance of a juridical person or (ii) the creation or maintenance of a branch or a representative office, within the territory of a Member for the purpose of supplying a service.[9]

Another mode of supply is through the presence of 'natural persons'. Koulen argues that this is closely related to the commercial presence

---

[6] See for a more detailed discussion of the foreign investment related disciplines in the WTO; WTO, *Annual Report: Special Topic Foreign Direct Investment and Trade* (1996); M. Koulen, 'Foreign Investment in the WTO' in E. C. Nieuwenhuys and M. M. T. A. Brus (eds), *Multilateral Regulation of Investment* (2001) 181–203.

[7] The agreement also has a provision against the use of offsets, which for the most part is parallel to the issue of performance requirements.

[8] Investment aspects of GATS are dealt in some detail in P. Sauvé and C. Wilkie, 'Investment Liberalization in GATS' in P. Sauvé and R. M. Stern (eds), *GATS 2000: New Directions in Services Trade Liberalization* (2000).   [9] GATS Art. XXVIII (d).

mode since it includes the temporary entry of business visitors and intra-company transfers of managerial and other key personnel.[10]

One word of caution or clarification: while the GATS and the AGP have elements of market access for foreign investors, their architecture differs substantially from that proposed in the MAI or from Chapter 11 of NAFTA. One of the key differences, with respect to the GATS is that there is no general obligation. Members apply the standards of treatment through specific commitments. These commitments apply only to the listed sectors and the reservations and exceptions expressed by Members.

One final note with respect to market access is the role of the Agreement on Trade-Related Aspects of Intellectual Property Rights (TRIPS). While the agreement itself does not provide a standard of market access it does provide for a standard of intellectual property rights protection. One element of the determinants of FDI flows is the extent to which a firm specific asset can be protected from either expropriation or dissipation.[11] If intellectual property rights protection is of a sufficient standard it could induce FDI flows.

A second area where disciplines already exist is with respect to investment measures that can be linked to trade. In this respect there are measures which, on the one hand, condition the behaviour of affiliates of foreign enterprises, and on the other, used to attract foreign investment.

With respect to this second area, coverage is at least potentially already established in the Agreement on Subsidies and Countervailing Measures (ASCM) for industrial products, the Agreement on Agriculture for agricultural products, and the GATS for services. The establishment of the first of these agreements, which provides remedies to challenge the use of subsidies, was a major achievement of the Tokyo Round of Multilateral Trade negotiations; the agreement was further modified during the Uruguay Round. However, whether this Agreement and the two others fully cover investment incentives is not very clear. The main reason why is that these agreements explicitly cover trade in goods and services and not foreign investment. Therefore, if there is a link, it must be through the relationship between investments and trade in goods and services.

The ASCM in particular raises ambiguities. The ASCM is a very broad agreement and contains a number of specific steps that are used to determine whether or not a measure comes under its jurisdiction. For example, a three-part definition is used to determine whether the measure is indeed a subsidy; what must be established is that a clear

---

[10] Koulen, *supra* n. 6.

[11] K. Maskus, 'FDI and Intellectual Property' in B. Bora (ed.), *Foreign Direct Investment: Research Issues* (2002).

financial contribution has been provided by a government or public body within the territory of a Member that confers a benefit. A second condition is that the measure must then be specific to an enterprise, or group of enterprises.

Most measures that can be classified as investment incentives would indeed seem to fall within the jurisdiction of the ASCM on the basis of these criteria, or at least so with respect to industrial goods as covered by this Agreement. However, a number of additional factors must come into play before a subsidy is ruled as inconsistent with the ASCM and subject to discipline. To begin, it must be established whether the subsidy falls into a category of prohibited subsidies. This category includes specific trade-related subsidies, such as direct export subsidies and subsidies that are contingent on exporting. The burden of proof rests with the complaining party. If this is established, the complaining member must show that it has suffered adverse effects. This means that either its domestic industry producing like industrial goods has suffered injury from imports sourced from the country offering the incentive, serious prejudice arising from export displacement in either the market of the country offering the incentive or a third market. Finally, account must be taken of nullification and impairment of benefits from improved market access that is undercut by subsidization. Importantly, whether or not investment incentives can be shown to have these prejudicial effects has not been established in any case actually brought to the WTO where some sort of concrete precedent could be set.

The Agreement on Agriculture provides special provision for agricultural products. These provisions for the most part insulate subsidies to industries that produce agricultural products from the disciplines contained in the ASCM. However, after 1 January 2003 the ASCM agreement is meant to apply to subsidies for agricultural products.[12] But, again, no cases have come up whereby investment incentives to foreign investment in agriculture have been challenged under ASCM.

Therefore, for those types of measures that might be classified as investment incentives, the WTO Agreements provide potentially broad although as yet untested disciplines. The policy question is whether specific application of these agreements should be allowed to be determined by future dispute cases or, alternatively, should negotiations now be conducted so as to clarify how these agreements should be interpreted with respect to investment incentives?

As already noted, selective government intervention meant to affect performance of foreign investment is already partially covered under the Agreement on Trade-Related Investment Measures (TRIMS). Actually,

---

[12] Subject to the provisions of the agreement as set forth in Art. 21.

the fact that this text is considered to be a full-blown WTO Agreement is something of a mystery. This is because the TRIMS agreement at present does little more than clarify the application of GATT 94 Articles III(4) on national treatment and XI(1) on quantitative restrictions.[13] It does not even define a trade-related investment measure. Instead the approach taken was to include an illustrative list of measures agreed to be inconsistent with the two key paragraphs of the GATT (III.4 and XI.1).[14] This list covers measures that are mandatory or enforceable under domestic law and administrative rulings and measures for which compliance is necessary to obtain an advantage. The list includes local content schemes, foreign exchange and trade balancing, and export restrictions. There is no text specifically addressing issues related to granting national treatment to investors.

The TRIMS agreement allowed any WTO Member access to an extended transition period for bringing policies that they might have into compliance with it, if and only if the relevant measures were notified within 90 days of the commencement of the Agreement. Twenty-six Members, all developing countries but of widely varying economic characteristics, notified a variety of measures,[15] most of which were local content schemes. The second most frequently notified measure was foreign exchange balancing. Subsequent to the expiry of the transition period, 11 Members applied and were granted extensions until 2004.

The basic issue regarding the TRIMS Agreement is whether it should be extended beyond clarification of measures that might be inconsistent with GATT Articles III and XI.[16] Indeed, during the Uruguay Round negotiation of the Agreement, a number of types of 'performance requirements' placed on foreign investors by governments that might

---

[13] The TRIMS Agreement is a rather modest attempt at disciplining policies that are targeted at foreign enterprises and which came about through conflicting positions on the extent to which investment issues should be covered by the WTO. Many developing countries resisted the extent to which market access for foreign firms would be covered, and as a result the negotiations focused on policies that applied to the operations of foreign firms. Even then, negotiations proved difficult, as there was no consensus as to whether or not a specific policy instrument was indeed trade-distorting. Furthermore, some developing countries took the position that they should have access to policy instruments that could be used to offset any perceived negative effects associated with the operations of transnational corporations.

[14] There was nothing to suggest that the list was exhaustive of all the measures that could be considered to be inconsistent.

[15] B. Bora, *Foreign Direct Investment: Research Issues* (2002).

[16] An interesting aspect of the Panel decision on India is that it found the measures to be inconsistent with Arts. III:4 and XI:1 and chose not to address the claims under the TRIMS Agreement. While it is tempting to interpret this as an irrelevancy of the TRIMS Agreement the decision was based on judicial economy, as opposed to a judicial interpretation of hierarchy of agreements. See WT/DS146/R, 21 December 2001.

create trade distortions but were not necessarily inconsistent with the two GATT articles were identified and proposed for inclusion in the Agreement.[17] But, as a compromise among the negotiating parties, all of these were removed from the Agreement more or less at the last moment. (Hence, the answer to the 'mystery' noted above: had it not been for this last-minute compromise, the TRIMS Agreement might have indeed evolved into a full-blown agreement and not a 'clarification' of existing GATT obligations.)

In addition to market access for investors and potential disciplines on incentives and performance requirements there are also provisions in the TRIPS Agreement that have the potential to protect an investor's assets.[18] Some developing countries have argued that these provisions are 'overreaching' and in fact impede development. Whether or not these claims have merit is hotly disputed. However, at the present time, it does not appear that any existing provisions of the TRIPS Agreement will be subject to renegotiation during the Doha Round.

III. IS THERE ANY VALUE ADDED BY INCLUDING A NEW INVESTMENT AGREEMENT IN THE DOHA DEVELOPMENT AGENDA?

The investment-related paragraphs of the Doha Ministerial mandate recognize the case for a multilateral framework to secure transparent, stable, and predictable conditions for long-term, cross-border investment, particularly FDI that contributes to the expansion of trade:

Investment work programme in the Doha Ministerial Mandate

20. Recognizing the case for a multilateral framework to secure transparent, stable and predictable conditions for long-term cross-border investment, particularly foreign direct investment, that will contribute to the expansion of trade, and the need for enhanced technical assistance and capacity-building in this area as referred to in paragraph 21, we agree that negotiations will take place after the Fifth Session of the Ministerial Conference on the basis of a decision to be taken, by explicit consensus, at that Session on modalities of negotiations.

21. We recognize the needs of developing and least-developed countries for enhanced support for technical assistance and capacity building in this area, including policy analysis and development so that they may better evaluate the implications of closer multilateral co-operation for their development policies and objectives, and human and institutional development. To this end, we shall

---

[17] See E. M. Graham, and P. R. Krugman, 'Trade Related Investment Measures' in J. J. Schott (ed.), *Completing the Uruguay Round: A Results-Oriented Approach to the GATT Trade Negotiations* (1990).   [18] See Maskus, *supra* n. 11.

work in co-operation with other relevant intergovernmental organisations, including UNCTAD, and through appropriate regional and bilateral channels, to provide strengthened and adequately resourced assistance to respond to these needs.

22. In the period until the Fifth Session, further work in the Working Group on the Relationship Between Trade and Investment will focus on the clarification of: scope and definition; transparency; non-discrimination; modalities for pre-establishment commitments based on a GATS-type, positive list approach; development provisions; exceptions and balance-of-payments safeguards; consultation and the settlement of disputes between Members. Any framework should reflect in a balanced manner the interests of home and host countries, and take due account of the development policies and objectives of host governments as well as their right to regulate in the public interest. The special development, trade and financial needs of developing and least-developed countries should be taken into account as an integral part of any framework, which should enable Members to undertake obligations and commitments commensurate with their individual needs and circumstances. Due regard should be paid to other relevant WTO provisions. Account should be taken, as appropriate, of existing bilateral and regional arrangements on investment.

The identified issues concern both the liberalization of foreign investment and its operation once established in foreign markets. It recognizes the points made in the previous section that foreign investment in general, and FDI in particular, is seen as a way of transferring needed capital as well as other assets, such as technology, managerial skills, and improved access to export markets to host countries.

Nevertheless, potential drawbacks of foreign investment should also be noted. Of particular concern is the impact of short-term and volatile capital flows on the macro-economic and balance-of-payments stability of host countries. Other concerns include the impact of foreign investment on domestic investors, competition in host-country markets, domestic savings and consumption patterns, and the ownership of productive and financial assets. The Doha Ministerial Mandate thus places particular emphasis that any multilateral framework must reflect the special development, trade, and financial needs of developing and least-developed countries, and on allowing Members to undertake obligations and commitments commensurate with their individual needs and circumstances. This includes that any prospective investment framework in the WTO must preserve the right of Members to govern and regulate in the public interest. It is emphasized also that creating a more open and stable climate for foreign investment is itself an important development objective. Not only do developing countries have an interest in encouraging inward investment and the benefits that accrue from it; these countries also have a growing interest in creating a more secure international framework for outward investment, as they increasingly became exporters of FDI and home countries to transnational corporations.

The negotiators thus provided a mandate that could best be described as pragmatic. The pragmatism arises from the recognition that existing WTO rules already partly cover the four substantive key issues. For example, market access via FDI in the context of services (but, importantly, not industrial goods) is covered under commercial presence under the GATS. Disciplines on government subsidies towards investment as they relate to merchandise trade are not identified in the Doha Declaration because, as noted in the previous section, they potentially are covered under the ASCM and the TRIMS Agreement. These agreements might not be as fully developed as they could or even should be, but negotiations to enlarge or clarify their coverage could be argued better to fall under negotiations specific to these agreements, not to a new agreement. (On this, however, see our concluding remarks.)

Even so, the Ministers of the WTO Member states did agree to include the relevant paragraphs in the Declaration. Given the lack of consensus on the intrinsic value of investment-related rules, a plausible question is in fact why Ministers agreed to the mandate at all. Four reasons can be put forth.

A. Coherence argument

Coherence in the WTO context usually means the aligning of the policies and practices of WTO with those of the World Bank and the International Monetary Fund (IMF). However in this context, we mean coherence between trade and investment policy. The intellectual history of FDI started with a supposition that trade and FDI are substitutes. In this context, FDI was seen mostly as a means to overcome tariff barriers. Over time, however, this dichotomy has blurred substantially. Both evidence and theory provide valid reasons for trade and FDI to be complements.[19] This blurring is amplified by the fragmentation of production, which causes intermediate products to be cross-hauled among various subsidiaries of transnational corporations. A good example that trade and investment indeed are complementary is the identification of *investment* restrictions as non-tariff *trade* barriers (NTTBs) by the private sector. A recent survey found that investment measures are one of the most frequently cited NTTBs by the private sector.[20] Hence, the reduction of tariffs over the past 50 years has, in some sense, increased

---

[19] See J. Markusen, 'Foreign Direct Investment and Trade' in B. Bora (ed.), *Foreign Direct Investment: Research Issues* (2002); E. M. Graham and E. Wada, 'Is Foreign Direct Investment a Complement to Trade' in E. M. Graham *Fighting the Wrong Enemy* (2000). Appendix B.
[20] OECD, *Overview of Non-Tariff Barriers: Findings from Business Surveys* (2002).

the need to address foreign investment barriers as one type of trade barrier at the multilateral level.

B. Single undertaking

The Uruguay Round agreements expanded the scope and mandate of the WTO in an unprecedented fashion. In addition to extending the rules-based discipline to agriculture, textiles, and clothing, new agreements covering intellectual property, trade in services, and contingency measures were concluded. That these agreements all became part of a single undertaking happened because, given the diversity of trading interests of the WTO membership, some of the underlying issues are relatively more important to certain Members than others, and interests of the membership are not symmetric. Thus, concessions could be granted by one Member in exchange for concessions by other Members, enabling progress on a range of issues where such progress might not have been possible had each issue been separately negotiated. Much the same can be said for investment. Progress on investment might in fact result from progress on other issues. For example, one of the more accepted political realities of the Doha Round of negotiations is the pressure on the European Union (EU) to reform its agricultural policy. This could be done unilaterally by the EU, of course. However, this is unlikely in today's mercantilist world, and thus there is a political need for the EU to receive a 'concession' in return, even if it is most likely the EU itself that would receive the most benefit from reform of its agricultural policy. Such a 'concession' might come in the form of movement on the investment front; the EU has been the leading advocate of expansion of WTO rules to cover investment. In the words of Hoekman and Saggi, progress on investment in the WTO could be part of a 'grand bargain'.[21]

C. Changing business environment

An important element of international trade policy is that it should be relevant to the private sector. As such, it must be noted that international business today is conducted quite differently than it was as recently as 15 years ago. In particular, falling barriers to the international trade in goods and services, combined with rapidly changing technology, have caused significant changes in the organizational structure of businesses. Lower tariff and transport costs, plus improvements in information

---

[21] B. Hoekman and K. Saggi, 'Multilateral Disciplines and National Investment Policies' in B. Hoekman, A. Mattoo, and P. English (eds), *Development, Trade and the WTO: A Handbook* (2002).

technology, have made it increasingly easier to locate different stages of production in different countries, to take advantage of special characteristics of each country. As this happens, intra-firm international trade in 'intermediate goods' (e.g., components, subassemblies, and semifinished goods) rises. In order to take advantage of these opportunities there is clearly a need for a firm to make investments in many countries. The nature of these investments goes beyond the traditional view that FDI is simply 'green-field' type investments of 100 per cent ownership. In many cases, the investments are joint ventures or licensing and contracting relationships. An increasing need thus arises that the rules on international trade take into account the various forms in which international investment takes place.

D. The complicated architecture of plurilateral rules

While investment rule-making at the multilateral level has proceeded slowly, this does not mean it has not proceeded at all. Many countries have been quite active in this area over the past 15 years. The initiatives range from the comprehensive and controversial Chapter 11 of NAFTA to the many bilateral investment treaties (BITs) currently in force. These instruments differ greatly in terms of their coverage and level of discipline.

This increase in activity raises the issue of consistency and discrimination. BITs are not necessarily the same between countries and investment provisions in regional trade agreements (RTAs) such as NAFTA Chapter 11 vary considerably. Moreover, differences among various instruments can lead to inefficiencies and distortions. As a result, the proliferation of such agreements raises the issue of whether or not a multilateral approach would be superior for reasons of efficiency to a network of BITs and investment agreements within RTAs. A single multilateral instrument would also arguably create a more equitable environment for investment than would a patchwork of inconsistent agreements.

IV. STATE OF PLAY IN INVESTMENT NEGOTIATIONS[22]

Paragraph 22 of the Doha Ministerial Declaration (see p. 342) mandated the Working Group on the Relationship between Trade and Investment to focus on *clarifying* the following issues: scope and definition; transparency;

---

[22] Much of this section is based on the discussions of the Working Group on Trade and Investment in 2002. See the *Annual Report* of that Group for further details, WT/WTGTI/6.

non-discrimination modalities for pre-establishment commitments based on a GATS-type, positive list approach; development provisions exceptions and balance of payments; consultations and the settlement of disputes between Members. In addition, the Working Group also was instructed to continue work on the relationship with other WTO agreements and International Investment Agreements and on the issue of FDI and the transfer of technology.

Each of the seven issues identified in paragraph 22 are now considered in turn.

A. Scope and definition

There are two main approaches to defining investment—an intrinsically narrow approach, such as an enterprise-based or transaction-based definition, on the one hand, and a broad, asset-based approach, with different options for including or excluding various categories of investment. The US for the most part has championed the broader approach. A number of developing countries, on the other hand, propose a narrower approach, e.g. that any coverage of a future WTO agreement be limited to FDI (but see subsection on balance of payments below).

In addition to the difficulty of defining investment, there is the added difficulty of defining what exactly is an 'investor' for purposes of implementing an investment agreement. This is an important issue because implicitly any agreement involves rights and obligations of investors, as opposed to governments. For example, if a future agreement were to guarantee national treatment to investors and/or their investments, it would be of paramount importance to define precisely what entities qualified for this treatment.

B. Transparency

In describing the objectives of a multilateral investment framework, Ministers at Doha began with the concept of securing a 'transparent' framework for foreign investment. The discussion in the Working Group did not focus on the benefits of transparency, but rather on the nature and depth of transparency provisions and on the scope of their application in a possible WTO agreement on investment.

Some possible transparency obligations discussed in the Working Group are:

• publication and notification requirements;
• enquiry points;
• prior notification and comment;

- administrative and judicial procedures;
- investor and home-country obligations.

At this point in time, the positions of individual WTO members on what transparency-related obligations should be contained in any future investment agreement are not fully clear.

C. Development provisions

The main areas where developing countries are seeking flexibility in any WTO agreement on investment are in regulating the entry of foreign investment (through general screening, selective restrictions, and conditions on entry) and in using policies to enhance the contribution that foreign investment can make to their economic and social development needs and objectives (through performance requirements, investment incentives, and preferences for domestic investors). Not surprisingly, a consensus on exactly what approach is best from a development perspective does not exist. Rather, views range from it being desirable that there be widespread scope for government intervention or, alternatively, that there be strong obligations on governments not to use such intervention on a selective basis. Various broad options have been identified during the period after the Doha Ministerial during discussions in the working group. These are:

(1) That the development objectives of an agreement on investment be included in the preamble of the agreement.
(2) That the scope of an agreement be clearly delineated—e.g. that it be made explicit whether the agreement applied to FDI only or to all forms of investment, and whether it covered the pre- as well as the post-establishment phase of investment.
(3) That the agreement should allow at least some exemptions from obligations.
(4) That Member countries be allowed some flexibility in undertaking specific commitments.
(5) That any agreement allow longer transition periods for implementation for poor countries than for richer countries.
(6) That some means should be provided for technical assistance and capacity building for poorer countries.

Furthermore, it should be recognized that the seven issues listed for 'clarification' in paragraph 22 did not exhaust the scope for development provisions; rather, one could expect further discussion to reveal whether certain items should be excluded from the list, and whether new items should be added.

D. Non-discrimination

The principle of non-discrimination is at the core of most international commercial treaties, although its application is typically subject to carefully defined conditions. These conditions might allow governments to give preferential treatment to domestic products, producers, and investors, or to certain of their commercial partners but not to others, or to pursue domestic policy objectives that could not be realized without practising some degree of discriminatory treatment. The scope for the application of non-discrimination can also be limited by the definition of 'investment' in an agreement—i.e. by the range of assets to which non-discriminatory standards applied.

An important distinction can be drawn between the application of non-discrimination—and national treatment in particular—at the pre-establishment and post-establishment phases of investment. Similarly, MFN and national treatment also differ. An argument can also equally be applied to the application of the national treatment standards. National treatment, like MFN treatment, could also be extended to all stages of investment—its entry, its operation after establishment, and its liquidation. In doing so, however it will be important to take into account the need (or at least preference) on the part of some developing countries to have some flexibility to discriminate between domestic and foreign investors.

In the context of the discussion of non-discriminatory standards at both the pre- and post-establishment phase, it is important to note, once again, that scope of application depends crucially on the definition of the term 'investment', as well as on the exceptions allowed and the specific commitments made under the agreement's provisions by individual Members.

E. Modalities for pre-establishment commitments based on a GATS-type positive list approach

The GATS approach to scheduling market-access commitments has been suggested in paragraph 22 as a model of development-friendly multilateral rules. Discipline is achieved through the binding of policy, but at a pace that is consistent with the needs of each Member. At the same time, there are also valid criticisms about the degree of the liberalization that could be realized through such an approach. Bindings have policy value in the sense that they are credible commitments of policy, but under the GATS approach, different countries can put forth significantly different bindings. Moreover, it has been argued that, under the GATS approach, the degree of effective liberalization has been limited to the status quo; countries have been unwilling to date to bind themselves to any commitment that does not already exist under current law and policy.[23]

F. Exceptions and balance-of-payments safeguards

Another element for consideration is ways in which general, security, and regional integration exceptions as well as balance-of-payments safeguards might be incorporated in a prospective WTO investment agreement. An issue of great importance to some developing countries is balance-of-payments safeguards, since it touches directly on concerns about short-term capital flows and exposure to financial volatility. Indeed, such concerns are at the heart of why these countries seek that any such agreement be limited to cover FDI only. However, it is also noted that foreign direct investors do engage in short-term financial transactions, and thus it is argued that even an investment agreement that is limited to foreign direct investment must contain some balance-of-payments safeguard, perhaps one similar to that already contained in the GATT (which in turn is meant to be consistent with International Monetary Fund (IMF) rules regarding balance of payments).

G. Consultation and the settlement of disputes between Members

Although there are different models for settling investment related disputes (e.g. NAFTA Chapter 11, which allows for private parties in some circumstances to initiate dispute settlement procedures under so-called investor-to-state provisions), judging from reports of the Working Group there is a widely shared view that the existing WTO dispute settlement mechanism should apply to any future investment agreement—just as it applied to all other WTO agreements. Moreover, there seems to be a widely shared view that the WTO would not include investor-to-state dispute settlement procedures such as are found in the NAFTA. Even so, there is no doubt that the application of the existing WTO dispute settlement system to investment obligations and disciplines would raise a number of issues that would require further examination and clarification such as: the scope for non-violation actions; extending cross-retaliation and cross-compensation to the investment area; the interaction of investment rules with other substantive rules

[23] Indeed, a frequently heard complaint about GATS is that national commitments under GATS often are less than the *de facto* status quo. In other words, the extent of *de facto* liberalization actually exceeds that achieved *de jure* under GATS. Defenders of the GATS approach counter that, while this latter might be true, GATS is an unfinished work that will, with time, achieve a net liberalization. Whether this proves true, of course, only time will tell.

in existing WTO agreements; and the relationship with other dispute settlement systems in existing international investment agreements.

V. CONCLUSIONS

Much of the concern about a possible framework agreement in the WTO for FDI is the possibility that it may shift the balance of rights and obligations of foreign-controlled firms operating in a national jurisdiction. Some such concern is warranted and we would not quarrel with that, although elimination from consideration at WTO of NAFTA-like investor-to-state dispute settlement procedures takes some of the edge off of this concern. The focus of this paper, however, is on the issue of whether or not good investment policy requires a multilateral system of binding and enforceable rights and obligations. The chapter takes as a starting-point the ongoing debate on the link between FDI and development, noting in particular that FDI can make significant contributions to development but, at the same time, is not strictly necessary for development to occur.

In our view, the ground has now been prepared sufficiently to move the agenda on investment forward. Each of the proposed issues has been covered and there has yet to be a claim that technical assistance delivery has not been fulfilled. The difficulty at this stage is whether or not the differences among WTO Members that have emerged can be resolved outside a negotiation forum. For the most part, discussions on investment within the WTO so far have avoided any use of the term 'negotiation'. But, even to the casual observer, the nature of the national position papers and the report of the Working Group on Trade and Investment suggest that the Members have not been merely engaging in discussions aimed at achieving some sort of intellectual clarity but rather, they have been *de facto* preparing for an upcoming negotiation.

In this respect two matters can be identified that bear on whether a constructive negotiation is now likely to ensue. First, there does exist a group of Members who remain steadfastly opposed to investment issues in the WTO under any circumstances. Exactly which Members are in this camp is, however, not wholly clear, as many countries have maintained a stance of deliberate ambiguity on this issue. The 'anti-investment' camp might be limited to India and certain of the Association of Southeast Asian Nations (ASEAN) countries. But it could include a majority of developing countries. Since the exact numbers are not known the probability that the 'Indian position' (i.e. do nothing on the investment front) is likely to carry the day remains uncertain.

The second matter compounds the first: there is genuine concern on the part of a number of developing countries that, even if they were in the end to support investment negotiations, they do not have the power or capacity to negotiate an agreement that is in their interests. Thus, these countries might be classed as ones that believe that although an agreement that indeed is in their interests is feasible, nonetheless the actual outcome of a negotiation could very well be an agreement that is antithetical to their interests.

The existence of these two groups of developing nations must be taken into account when viewing the broader context of the negotiations. How these groups play their cards in Cancún will bear greatly on the nature and extent of any negotiation on investment. The most divisive but key issue in the upcoming round of negotiations, for example, is not investment, but agriculture. *Demandeurs* for agricultural reform could very well be willing to use investment negotiations as a 'bargaining chip' to affect the outcome in agriculture, regardless of whether or not they fundamentally support inclusion of an investment agreement in the negotiations. Thus, developing countries in the second of the two groups, and perhaps even in the first, might be quite willing for extensive negotiations on investment to proceed, if this would induce the EU to reduce its resistance to reform of its agricultural policy. Investment could prove to be a bargaining chip with respect to other issues as well, e.g. access to essential medicines. In the end, whether there is to be negotiated an investment agreement in the WTO might thus itself be a matter to be negotiated.

We conclude by noting that if negotiations to conclude an investment agreement do proceed in the WTO, there is a major issue lurking that must be resolved that we have already hinted at. This is whether the new agreement would supplant existing rules bearing on investment in the WTO. For example, provisions pertaining to market access (national treatment, MFN) for foreign investors in the services sectors are already part of the GATS, as already noted. Would parallel provisions in a new investment agreement supersede these? Some parties have already suggested that the answer should be 'no' and thus that a new investment agreement might cover only goods and not services, much as the present GATT covers trade in the former while GATS covers trade in the latter. However, some private parties have objected to this, noting in particular that many foreign-invested operations in practice deal in both goods and services and thus that it would be undesirable to have two agreements in effect that could be inconsistent with one another. It also has been pointed out that the reason why GATS covers investment in services is because, when the GATS was first negotiated, there really was no prospect for WTO rules on investment; because trade and services and investment in services are highly intertwined, the GATS negotiators realized that the new services agreement would have to cover at least some investment-related issues. In this context, the GATS agreement could be seen as provisional with respect to investment coverage, i.e. filling a lacuna that then existed. Once the lacuna is removed, arguably, the need for investment-related provisions in the GATS would expire, and the new agreement could thus be written to supersede GATS. Similar statements could be made about other investment-related issues, e.g. the unresolved issues in the ASCM could be resolved by explicit provisions pertaining to investment incentives in an agreement on investment. Likewise, the existing Agreement on TRIMS, which we have already argued is really less than a full-blown agreement, could be incorporated into an agreement on investment.

On the issues of the previous paragraph, however, we don't pretend to have the final word. Rather, we simply note that these issues of consistency and possible overlapping coverage between an agreement on investment, if one is negotiated, and existing provisions of existing WTO agreements pertaining to investment, must be dealt with.

VI. EPILOGUE

This chapter was drafted prior to the 5th WTO Ministerial Conference, which was held in Cancún in September 2003. The outcome of that Ministerial is well known to all who follow trade policy issues; there was no agreement on the 'Singapore issues', of which investment was one, and in the end investment was dropped altogether from the negotiating agenda. Media reports indicate that the Chair of the Conference, Minister Derbez of Mexico, gavelled the meeting to a close when a group of key ministers were unable to agree on the number of Singapore issues that should be included in the Doha negotiations. One group of countries argued that all four should be included, whereas other countries argued none should be included. The precise number for and against is not known.

Pascal Lamy, the Trade Commissioner of the EU, in order to obtain an agreement, offered to 'drop' competition policy and investment from the negotiating agenda. This offer set the stage for what appeared to be a battle of numbers; a bidding war, so to speak. Instead of negotiating all four issues, Commissioner Lamy was offering to negotiate only two. To this day, his reasons for deciding on which two to negotiate are not well known, but could be found in the fact that some negotiating countries considered negotiations on transparency in government procurement and trade facilitation less contentious.

The mood, atmosphere, and level of debate about what had occurred in Cancún was strange; some suggested that the trading system was headed for a complete collapse, others suggested that the failure was an example of the trading system working at its best. Whatever one's perspective, it was clear that the EU, the principal champion for expanding rules on investment policies in the WTO, had lost interest in this issue. Without such a key player, other WTO Members who championed the issue continued, but with a substantially diminished negotiating position.

In Cancún, Ministers agreed to a deadline of 15 December to move the negotiations ahead, or to do what couldn't be done during the Ministerial Conference. That deadline was not met and in recognition of the fact that two key individuals in the push for a new round of negotiations, the US Trade Representitive Robert Zoellick and Pascal Lamy were likely to be in different posts by the end of 2004, WTO Members made a concerted effort at coming to an agreement on the directions of the negotiations by July 2004. Unlike virtually every other deadline set in the negotiations, this time the deadline was met. The end result was that negotiations would commence on only Trade Facilitation. The remaining three issues would be 'dropped from the negotiating agenda'.

The purpose of this epilogue is not to lament the fact that investment has been dropped from the Doha negotiations. As indicated in section III, the final decision on whether or not to undertake negotiations would depend on the contours of a 'grand bargain'. This would not be the first time that tactics and strategies come to the forefront. Indeed, as pointed out before, the EU viewed investment as one of its 'offensive' positions. In losing investment, it will now focus on other areas of the negotiations.

The fact that an agreement was reached in July 2004 to revive the broader negotiations is a good thing. Perhaps the most important issue is the sense of *déjà vu* with regards to investment and the multilateral trading system, a parallel even to what we witnessed in Cancún more than 55 years ago in the Havana Charter. Will it be another 55 years before investment again is raised in the WTO? Who knows? Predicting whether and when investment comes back on the WTO negotiating table is the subject for another book. For now, this chapter can close by highlighting the paradox that, despite investment being dropped from the WTO's formal agenda, it continues to be one of the key negotiating issues in RTAs, which complements the growing number of BIT being signed by developing countries. Moreover, as noted in this chapter, investment continues to be a key component of a number of ongoing issues within the WTO; the decision to drop negotiations on investment rules *per se* does not change the fact that investment remains on other agendas within the WTO. Taken together, investment rule-making and policy disciplines are still a fundamental aspect of good development policy.

PART VII

CHALLENGES TO THE POLITICAL LEGITIMACY OF THE WTO SYSTEM

17

The 'Human Rights Approach' Advocated by the UN High Commissioner for Human Rights and by the International Labour Organization: Is It Relevant for WTO Law and Policy?

ERNST-ULRICH PETERSMANN

The current universal recognition of 'inalienable' human rights implies that the legitimacy and legality of all government measures, including rules and decisions of intergovernmental organizations, depend also on their respect for human rights as defined in national constitutions and international law. This contribution argues that the universal human rights obligations of every Member of the World Trade Organization (WTO) pursue objectives (like protection of personal autonomy, freedom of choice, legal security) that complement those of liberal trade and may be legally relevant context for the interpretation of WTO rules (sections I–II). The human rights approach to international trade advocated by the United Nations High Commissioner for Human Rights (section III) could, like the 1996 WTO and 1998 International Labour Organization (ILO) Declarations on core labour standards (section IV), promote synergies between human rights law and General Agreement on Tariffs and Trade (GATT)–WTO law. The 'basic rights approach' to trade liberalization in European integration (section V), as well as the GATT, WTO, and European Community (EC) dispute settlement jurisprudence (section VI) confirm that, on the level of principles, human rights and liberal trade rules do not conflict with each other. The emerging 'human right to democratic governance' requires, however, more effective parliamentary involvement, citizen participation, and 'deliberative democracy' in WTO matters (section VII). A WTO Declaration (1) confirming the commitment of WTO Members to respect their existing human rights obligations in all policy areas; (2) supporting the progressive development of human rights through the competent United Nations (UN) and other human rights bodies; and (3) welcoming the UN initiatives for harnessing the complementarity of WTO rules and human rights for welfare-increasing cooperation among free citizens, could enhance the 'input-legitimacy' as well as the 'output-legitimacy' of WTO negotiations—without creating new WTO obligations or new WTO competencies. The limited mandate of the WTO, however, and the divergent human rights concepts and diverse constitutional traditions in WTO member countries, make a consensus among WTO Members on such a declaration unlikely. Even though the WTO should leave the interpretation, monitoring, and progressive development of human rights to specialized human rights bodies outside the WTO, WTO dispute settlement bodies may be legally required to address arguments that human rights may be relevant legal context for interpreting WTO rules (section VIII).

I. SHOULD THE WTO PLEDGE RESPECT FOR THE HUMAN RIGHTS OBLIGATIONS OF WTO MEMBERS?

The current worldwide 'recognition of the inherent dignity and of the equal and inalienable rights of all members of the human family (as) foundation of freedom, justice, and peace in the world'[1] entails increasing challenges to the democratic legitimacy of multilevel market regulation by intergovernmental organizations (such as the WTO) and multinational corporations. The end of the Cold War has led to universal recognition in the Vienna Declaration of the UN World Conference on Human Rights (1993)[2] that 'all human rights are universal, indivisible, and interdependent and interrelated' (section 5); that 'democracy, development and respect for human rights and fundamental freedoms are interdependent and mutually reinforcing' (section 8); and that there is a need also for 'international organizations, in cooperation with non-governmental organizations, to create favourable conditions at the national, regional, and international levels to ensure the full and effective enjoyment of human rights' (section 13). Every WTO Member state has ratified one or more of the major worldwide UN human rights

---

[1] This quotation from the Universal Declaration of Human Rights (UDHR) was confirmed, e.g. in the 1966 UN Covenants on Civil and Political Rights and Economic, Social and Cultural Human Rights as well as in the 1989 UN Convention on the Rights of the Child ratified by more than 190 states.

[2] The Vienna Declaration was adopted by consensus and is reproduced in *The United Nations and Human Rights 1945–1995* (1995) at 450.

conventions and has obligations to respect and protect human rights also under the UN Charter and general international law.[3] Human rights activists, non-governmental organizations (NGOs) and UN institutions therefore claim that the WTO—like other worldwide organizations (e.g. the UN, ILO, Food and Agriculture Organization (FAO), World Health Organization (WHO), United Nations Educational, Scientific and Cultural Organization (UNESCO) and regional organizations (e.g. the European Union (EU), Organization of African Unity (OAU), and Organization of American States (OAS)—could enhance its democratic legitimacy by explicitly recognizing the existing human rights obligations of all WTO Members as relevant 'legal context' for the interpretation and application of WTO rules. Such an explicit recognition (e.g. in a WTO Ministerial Declaration) could—without introducing any new legal obligations or new WTO competencies—increase the input-legitimacy of WTO negotiations and of WTO dispute settlement proceedings by allaying the widespread fears that—in negotiating and applying WTO rules—WTO bodies risk 'trading away human rights' and neglecting non-economic values. As human rights and liberal trade rules aim at empowering individuals (e.g. by increasing their legal autonomy and freedom of choice) and specifying government obligations to protect general citizen interests, regional economic integration agreements increasingly refer to human rights.[4] A WTO Declaration pledging respect for the human rights obligations of WTO Members within the limited trade policy mandate of the WTO could also promote democratic participation by NGOs and help to mobilize 'cosmopolitan constituencies' supporting the welfare-increasing division of labour based on WTO rules.[5]

WTO diplomats and WTO bodies have so far avoided official positions on the proposals by the UN High Commissioner for Human Rights to

[3] In the Barcelona Traction judgment (ICJ Reports 1970, 32) and the Nicaragua judgment (ICJ Reports 1986, 114), the International Court of Justice (ICJ) has recognized that human rights constitute not only *individual rights* but also, in case of universally recognized human rights, *erga omnes* obligations of governments based on the UN Charter, human rights treaties, and general international law. The ICJ has also recognized (e.g. in its Advisory Opinion of 25 March 1951 on *WHO v Egypt*) the applicability of general international law rules to intergovernmental organizations. The European Court of Justice and the European Court of Human Rights have likewise recognized that general international law and human rights may be binding also on intergovernmental organizations.

[4] See e.g. the references to human rights in the EC and EU Treaties, in some 50 bilateral treaties concluded by the EC with third countries, the Cotonou Agreement among more than 90 countries in Europe, Africa, the Caribbean, and the Pacific, and in the 2001 Quebec Ministerial Declaration on a Free Trade Area of the Americas among 34 North, Central, and South American states.

[5] For a discussion of the proposal by EU Trade Commissioner Pascal Lamy to improve global governance—also in the WTO—by new forms of 'cosmopolitics' see S. Charnovitz, 'WTO Cosmopolitics' in 34 *New York University Journal of International Law and Politics* (2002) 299–354.

adopt a 'human rights approach' to international trade.[6] Views on the contents of human rights (such as the 'right to development') and on their relevance for intergovernmental organizations differ widely; also the 2001 Doha Declaration on the Agreement on Trade-Related Intellectual Property Rights (TRIPS) and Public Health includes no reference to human rights.[7] Trade experts fear that a 'human rights approach' will unduly complicate WTO negotiations in view of the fact that, for example, the 1966 UN Covenant on Economic, Social and Cultural Human Rights (ICESCR) has not been ratified by more than 30 WTO Member countries including the United States (US). Just as UN human rights conventions do not refer to international division of labour, 'market freedoms', and property rights as essential conditions for creating the economic resources needed for the enjoyment of human rights,[8] so WTO law does not explicitly refer to respect and protection of human rights as necessary means for realizing the WTO objectives of 'raising standards of living, ensuring full employment and a large and steadily growing volume of real income and effective demand, and expanding the production of and trade in goods and services' (WTO Preamble). Notably, less-developed WTO Members have voiced concerns that labour standards and human rights risk being abused for protectionist import restrictions that may undermine the comparative advantages of developing countries and aggravate their development problems. Less-developed WTO Members therefore insist that core labour standards and human rights should be left to specialized organizations like the ILO and UN human rights institutions, and trade policies and human rights should remain separate.

II. LEGAL RELEVANCE OF HUMAN RIGHTS FOR WTO LAW AND POLICIES

There are three major legal, political, and economic reasons why human rights are legally and politically relevant for WTO law and policies and

---

[6] The proposals by the UNHCHR are described and discussed in section III below.

[7] WTO Ministerial Conference, *Declaration on the TRIPS Agreement and Public Health*, adopted on 14 November 2001, WT/MIN(01)/DEC/2. The follow-up WTO Decision of 30 August 2003 on the implementation of para. 6 (compulsory licensing for exports of medicines to countries without manufacturing capacity for such products) of the Declaration on the TRIPS Agreement and Public Health likewise avoids references to the human right to health.

[8] It is only in the context of the right to work (Art. 6) that the ICESCR of 1966 refers to the need for government policies promoting 'development and full and productive employment under conditions safeguarding fundamental political and economic freedoms to the individual' (Art. 6:2).

why WTO Members should offer convincing answers to the UN requests to adopt a 'human rights approach' for international trade.

A. Human rights may be legally relevant context for the interpretation of WTO rules

In Article 3:2 of the Dispute Settlement Understanding (DSU) of the WTO, 'Members recognize that it serves to preserve the rights and obligations of Members under the covered agreements, and to clarify the existing provisions of those agreements in accordance with customary rules of interpretation of public international law'. The WTO Appellate Body has consistently held that international customary law and Article 3:2 require an interpretation of WTO rules 'in good faith in accordance with the ordinary meaning to be given to the terms of the treaty in their context and in the light of its object and purpose', including 'any relevant rules of international law applicable in the relations between the parties'.[9] In view of the human rights obligations of every WTO Member,[10] it seems only a matter of time that—just as the European Court of Justice (ECJ) had to construe EC Treaty rules in light of the human rights obligations of EC member states long before human rights provisions were included in the EC Treaty—WTO dispute settlement bodies will have to respond to legal claims or questions such as the following:

- Are the 'General Comments' adopted by the UN Committee on Economic, Social and Cultural Human Rights (UNCESCR) on the human rights to food and health 'relevant legal context' for interpreting the WTO Agreement on Agriculture, for example its 'green box provisions' on food security programmes, food aid, natural disaster relief programmes, and infrastructural services like water supply facilities? Following the emphasis placed by the UNCESCR on the need to 'ensure that in international agreements the right to food is given adequate consideration',[11] a recent WTO submission by Mauritius referred to the right to food as being particularly relevant for future WTO negotiations on the provisions of the Agreement on Agriculture dealing with 'non-trade concerns' (e.g. Article 20), such as the human rights obligation to take 'affirmative action' in order to deal with serious adjustment problems caused by subsidized agricultural imports for competing local subsistence farmers.[12]

---

[9] Art. 31:1 and 31:3(c) of the 1969 Vienna Convention on the Law of Treaties which, according to WTO jurisprudence, reflect customary rules of international law.

[10] See *supra* n. 3 and related text.

[11] UNCESCR, *General Comment No. 12 on the Human Right to Food*, E/C.12/1999/5.

[12] Cf. WTO document G/AG/NG/W/36/Rev.1 of 9 November 2000. Certain adverse impacts of liberalization of agricultural trade on vulnerable groups in less-developed

- Are the human rights obligations of WTO Members relevant legal context for the interpretation of the numerous 'general exceptions' in WTO agreements, and for their references to 'measures necessary to protect human life or health' and 'public morals' (GATT Article XXa, b)?
- Can WTO Members limit their GATT and General Agreement on Trade in Services (GATS) commitments on market access if the production processes of foreign goods, services, and service providers do not comply with ILO labour standards and human rights (e.g. on prohibition of child labour and discrimination of women)?
- Are trade sanctions in response to human rights violations abroad (such as the Burma sanctions adopted by the US Congress in 2003), the 'human rights conditionality' of trade preferences (e.g. by the EC and US) for developing countries, or politically motivated private demonstrations blocking freedom of transit (GATT Article V)[13] compatible with WTO law (e.g. the 'necessity' requirement in GATT Article XX), especially if trade restrictions are applied without a prior 'human rights assessment' of their possibly adverse impact on poor people?
- Are the human right to health (e.g. access to essential medicines) and 'the right of everyone to enjoy the benefits of scientific progress and its application' (ICESCR Article 15) relevant legal context for an examination of the need 'to prevent the abuse of intellectual property rights by right holders' (Article 8 of the TRIPS Agreement)? Can the requirement of the TRIPS Agreement (Article 2 in connection with Article 10bis of the Paris Convention)—that WTO Members must protect nationals from other WTO Members against false, misleading, or discrediting allegations that constitute 'unfair competition'—be examined by WTO dispute settlement bodies without regard to freedom of speech and other human rights (like freedom of information)? Why is it that human rights courts tend to interpret freedom of commercial speech in a broader sense than trade courts?[14] Why has the WTO Appellate Body construed WTO rules in a more flexible manner in favour of domestic policy autonomy (e.g. to restrict

countries are documented in: FAO, *Agriculture, Trade and Food Security: Issues and Options in the WTO Negotiations from the Perspective of Developing Countries* (2000).

[13] Cf. the recent ECJ judgment of 12 June 2003, case C-112/2000 *Schmidberger v Austria*, in which the ECJ accepted the invocation of freedom of expression (ECHR Art. 10) and freedom of assembly (ECHR Art. 11) as justification for a demonstration blocking Austrian motorways and restricting free movement of goods inside the EC (EC Art. 28).

[14] See e.g. the judgment of the European Court of Human Rights of 25 August 1998 in *Hertel v Switzerland* (published in Reports 1998-VI) which concluded that restrictions on freedom of speech imposed under the Swiss Unfair Competition Law, and upheld by Swiss courts, were in violation of ECHR Art. 10.

imports of dangerous asbestos products and of hormone-fed beef) than WTO panels?

- Do the WTO prohibitions of 'nullification or impairment' of treaty benefits also protect 'reasonable expectations' that the competitive benefits of WTO market-access commitments for goods and services shall not be impaired by prohibitions of advertising and limitations on freedom of speech? Or that the property rights of holders of 'trade quotas' and patents, or of service providers, shall not be nullified by discriminatory 'regulatory takings'? Or that GATS commitments for free movement of natural service providers should be construed in conformity with human rights to respect family life?

The increasing references to such human rights dimensions of trade rules in the jurisprudence of the ECJ suggest that—also in WTO disputes over free movements of goods, services, persons, capital and related payments—dispute settlement bodies cannot always avoid examining claims that worldwide, regional, or national human rights instruments may be 'relevant context' for the interpretation and application of WTO rules. The need to respect the 'margin of appreciation' of each country regarding the implementation of its national and international human rights obligations, and the legitimate diversity among national and international human rights rules, raises difficult questions as to how far WTO bodies should take into account the jurisprudence and 'general comments' of specialized human rights bodies, especially if not all the parties to the WTO dispute are parties to the human rights conventions invoked by a WTO Member. Are third-party WTO Members legally required to accept interpretations of WTO rules referring to international human rights conventions if they have not ratified the conventions concerned? In view of the political delicacy of setting the limit beyond which 'human rights interpretations' by WTO dispute settlement bodies risk 'adding to or diminishing the rights and obligations provided in the covered agreements' in violation of Article 3:2 of the DSU: would it be more appropriate for the 'political branch' of the WTO (e.g. its Ministerial Conference) to determine the relevant scope of general human rights obligations of WTO Members rather than to leave the controversial clarification of WTO rules, once again, to the judicial branch of the WTO?

B. Utilitarian output-legitimacy may no longer be enough for democratic approval of WTO agreements

International trade liberalization under GATT and WTO continues to be justified mainly in terms of utilitarian economics and politics. Welfare economists explain why liberalization of discriminatory market access barriers (e.g. tariffs) may enable each member country to increase its 'total welfare' through trade.[15] Yet, even though maximization of general consumer welfare (rather than of the welfare of rent-seeking producers) would require open markets and non-discriminatory competition rules, trade policies in the WTO remain 'producer-driven', subject to numerous discriminatory trade distortions, without adequate disciplines on anti-competitive practices (e.g. cartels), and are often abused for welfare-reducing protectionism. Many GATT–WTO rules serve powerful producer interests (e.g. in the agricultural, textiles, clothing, and pharmaceutical sectors in developed countries) and leave the 'just distribution' of the gains from trade, and the social adjustment problems of international competition (e.g. for subsistence farmers, poor and sick people dependent on access to cheap medicines), to the discretion of governments. Apart from GATT–WTO rules on special and differential treatment of less-developed countries, questions of 'social justice' are discussed only rarely in WTO bodies and, if so (e.g. in the Doha Ministerial Declaration on Access to Medicines), usually without reference to the benchmarks used in modern theories of justice (e.g. human rights, democratic procedures, general consumer welfare, satisfaction of basic needs enabling a life in dignity).

Human rights directly empower citizens (e.g. by legally defining their citizen interests, offering legal and judicial remedies and accountability standards) in a more effective manner than it might be possible by relying only on representative government through popularly elected bodies. In most WTO countries where the more than 25,000 pages of the Uruguay Round Agreements were discussed by national parliaments in 1994, the parliamentary debates were all too often limited to a few hours without leading to changes in the intergovernmentally agreed treaty rules. Since the US Reciprocal Trade Agreements Act of 1934 and GATT 1947, there is increasing recognition that reciprocal trade liberalization agreements—far from circumventing democracy—can be essential for protecting general citizen interests in limiting 'government failures', as in the case of the infamous Smoot–Hawley Tariff Act of 1930 when 'rent-seeking' protectionist coalitions and logrolling in the US Congress led to a dramatic increase in import protection triggering a breakdown of the international payments and trading system, ushering in widespread unemployment and World War II. Constitutional economics explains why not only mutually agreed trade transactions within given rules, but also agreements on changing the basic 'rules of

---

[15] E.g. by increasing the quantity, quality, and variety of low-priced goods and services, promoting competition, productivity, and economic efficiency.

the game' may be mutually welfare-enhancing, for instance if the rules limit 'market failures' and contribute to the provision of 'public goods' (like open markets). Compared to previous GATT Rounds, WTO negotiations have become more transparent for the general public and are widely reported and discussed in newspapers. Yet, similar to the utilitarian justification of GATT rules by welfare economics, political justifications of GATT–WTO rules by their 'domestic policy functions' for limiting 'government failures' fail to address important human rights concerns: for instance, is the broad trade policy discretion of governments (e.g. to restrict welfare-increasing trade transactions, to treat citizens as mere objects of trade policies, to avoid references to human rights in WTO rule-making and trade policies) consistent with their human rights obligations to respect, protect, and fulfil human rights and basic human needs also in the trade policy area?

C. Human rights and liberal trade rules serve complementary functions

The UN Development Programme (UNDP)[16] and modern economics[17] demonstrate that protection of human rights can make citizens not only 'better democrats' but also more effective 'economic actors', and that much of the poverty in less-developed countries is due to inadequate protection of legal security, property rights, and other human rights as incentives for savings, investments, and division of labour. They criticize that, in contrast to the 'market freedoms' recognized as 'basic individual rights' in European integration law,[18] UN human rights conventions tend to ignore the fact that liberal trade is necessary for creating the economic welfare needed for enjoying human rights.

Consumer-driven competition and trade enable producers, investors, traders, and consumers to increase their welfare through division of labour at home and abroad and to force producers to take into account consumer preferences and offer goods and services at the lowest prices. Human rights and liberal trade rules empower individuals by protecting personal autonomy (e.g. freedom of profession), equal basic rights, and satisfaction of basic needs necessary for personal self-development in dignity. Without the economic resources created through division of labour and trade, the human rights objectives of protecting personal autonomy and human dignity cannot be achieved. And without legal protection of individual rights, the legal security needed for investments, division of

[16] See UNDP, *Human Development Report 2000: Human Rights and Human Development* (2000).

[17] Cf. e.g. E. U. Petersmann, 'Constitutional Economics, Human Rights and the Future of the WTO' in *58 Aussenwirtschaft (Swiss Review of International Economic Relations)* (2003) 49–91.   [18] See section V below.

labour, and exchange in property rights in traded goods, services, and related payments cannot be realized. At national and regional levels, the welfare-increasing functions of trade law, and the rights-protecting and distributive functions of human rights, are increasingly integrated in order to enhance the incentives for savings, investments, and decentralized division of labour as well as 'social justice' in the distribution of the welfare gains and in dealing with the social adjustment problems of international competition (e.g. for poor and vulnerable people). Respect for human rights and for the basic needs of the 'losers' in market competition enable a 'social market economy' whose social cohesion and solidarity may also enhance economic growth.[19] The more than 100 less-developed WTO Members, national parliaments, and civil society may reject new WTO rules if such rules are not seen to take into account the social dimensions of worldwide competition and the basic needs of the 2 billion people living on less than 2 dollars per day.

III. THE 'HUMAN RIGHTS APPROACH' ADVOCATED BY THE UN HIGH COMMISSIONER FOR HUMAN RIGHTS

Fulfilment of most human rights (e.g. to food, health, education) depends on access to scarce goods and services (e.g. drinking water, cheap medicines, health and educational services). Also enjoyment of civil and political human rights (e.g. personal freedom, rule of law, access to justice, democratic self-government) requires economic resources (e.g. for financing democratic and law-enforcement institutions). The widespread yet unnecessary poverty, health problems, and legal insecurity (e.g. among the 1 billion people living on less than 1 dollar a day) bear witness to the fact that UN law has so far failed to realize, in many of the 191 UN Member states, the UN objective of 'universal respect for, and observance of, human rights and fundamental freedoms for all' and 'creation of conditions of stability and well-being which are necessary for peaceful and friendly relations among nations' (UN Charter Article 55). Recent UN Resolutions recognize the potential synergies of human rights, consumer-driven competition, and citizen-driven democracies for empowering citizens and forcing producers and governments to respect general citizen interests (as defined by human rights) and consumer welfare.[20] Yet, even though international trade is

---

[19] On this European concept of a 'social market economy' see e.g. W. Röpke, *A Humane Economy: The Social Framework of the Free Market* (1998).
[20] See e.g. *supra* n. 2 and *infra* nn. 22–27.

essential for increasing the availability and quality of scarce resources, UN human rights bodies, until recently, tended to ignore GATT and WTO or, as in a report for the UN Commission on Human Rights of 2001, discredited the WTO as 'a veritable nightmare' for developing countries and women[21]—without prior consultation of WTO experts and without regard to the WTO's flexible 'public interest exceptions' enabling WTO Members to meet their human rights obligations in conformity with WTO law.

In response to the widespread criticism of the anti-market bias of such 'nightmare reports', the UN High Commissioner for Human Rights (UNHCHR) has recently published more differentiated reports analysing human rights dimensions of the WTO Agreements on TRIPS,[22] the Agreement on Agriculture,[23] GATS,[24] international investment agreements,[25] non-discrimination in the context of globalization,[26] and on the impact of trade rules on the right of everyone to the enjoyment of the highest attainable standard of physical and mental health.[27] The reports call for a 'human rights approach to trade' which

1. sets the promotion and protection of human rights as objectives of trade liberalization, not exceptions;
2. examines the effect of trade liberalization on individuals and seeks to devise trade law and policy to take into account the rights of all individuals, in particular vulnerable individuals and groups;
3. emphasizes the role of the State in the process of liberalization—not only as negotiators of trade law and setters of trade policy, but also as the primary duty bearer of human rights;
4. seeks consistency between the progressive liberalization of trade and the progressive realization of human rights;
5. requires a constant examination of the impact of trade liberalization on the enjoyment of human rights;

---

[21] *Globalization and its Impact on the Full Enjoyment of Human Rights*, E/CN.4/Sub.2/2000/12 (15 June 2000) at para. 15. Apart from a reference to patents and their possibly adverse effects on pharmaceutical prices (depending on the competition, patent, and social laws of the countries concerned), the report nowhere identifies conflicts between WTO rules and human rights.

[22] *The Impact of the Agreement on Trade-Related Aspects of Intellectual Property Rights on Human Rights*, E/CN.4/Sub.2/2001/13 (27 June 2001).

[23] *Globalization and its Impact on the Full Enjoyment of Human Rights*, E/CN.4/2002/54 (15 January 2002).

[24] *Liberalization of Trade in Services and Human Rights*, E/CN.4/Sub.2/2002/9 (18 June 2002).

[25] *Human Rights, Trade and Investment*, E/CN.4/Sub.2/2003/9 (2 July 2003).

[26] *Analytical Study of the High Commissioner for Human Rights on the Fundamental Principle of Non-Discrimination in the Context of Globalization*, E/CN.4/2004/40 (15 January 2004).

[27] The right of everyone to the enjoyment of the highest attainable standard of physical and mental health: *Report by the Special Rapporteur Paul Hunt on his Mission to the WTO*, E/CN.4/2004/49/Add.1 (1 March 2004).

6. promotes international cooperation for the realization of human rights and freedoms in the context of trade liberalization.[28]

The High Commissioner differentiates between obligations to respect human rights (e.g. by refraining from interfering in the enjoyment of such rights), to protect human rights (e.g. by preventing violations of such rights by third parties), and to fulfil human rights (e.g. by taking appropriate legislative, administrative, budgetary, judicial, and other measures towards the full realization of such rights). In contrast to the often one-sided focus in the human rights literature on the use of trade sanctions for promoting respect for human rights abroad, the UNHCHR reports analyse the human rights dimensions of trade liberalization, trade protection, and other trade regulation in a broader perspective. As enjoyment of human rights depends on availability, accessibility, accept-ability, and quality of traded goods and services, the relevance of WTO rules for the collective supply of 'public goods' (like access to low-priced goods and services), for limitations of 'market failures' (e.g. in case of essential services), and for protection and fulfilment of human rights is acknowledged and discussed. The reports underline that, what are referred to—in numerous WTO provisions—as *rights* of WTO Members to regulate, may be *duties* to regulate under human rights law (e.g. so as to protect and fulfil human rights of access to water, food, essential medicines, basic health care, and education services at afford-able prices). The UNHCHR suggests the recognition of the promotion of human rights as an objective of the WTO; the encouragement of interpretations of WTO rules that are compatible with international human rights as progressively clarified, for example in the 'General Comments' adopted by UN human rights bodies; the carrying out of 'human rights assessments' of WTO rules; and the development of inter-governmental protection of human rights so as to ensure that trade rules and policies promote the human rights and basic needs of all.[29]

The reports by the UNHCHR identify potential tensions between 'existential' human rights and 'instrumental' WTO rules (e.g. on protection of intellectual property rights and investor rights). They explain potential advantages of 'human rights assessments' by human

---

[28] E/CN.4/Sub.2/2002/9, p. 2.

[29] The report on TRIPS (*supra* n. 22) notes that 'the commercial motivation of IPRs means that research is directed, first and foremost, towards "profitable" disease. Diseases that predominantly affect people in poorer countries—in particular tuberculosis and malaria—still remain relatively under-researched' . . . 'questions remain as to whether the patent system will ensure investment for medicines needed by the poor. Of the 1,223 new chemical entities developed between 1975 and 1996, only 11 were for the treatment of tropical disease' (para. 38).

rights bodies of trade rules and policies, and the need for actively promoting mutually coherent interpretations of WTO rules and human rights. Yet they do not identify concrete conflicts between human rights and WTO law. In view of the 'constitutional function' of WTO rules for limiting welfare-reducing government policies (e.g. discriminatory market restrictions), for enhancing domestic policy autonomy for non-discriminatory policy instruments,[30] and for protecting the priority of non-economic values (as reflected in the numerous 'public interest clauses' in WTO law), conflicts between the often flexible WTO rules and human rights appear unlikely at the level of international principles. Yet this general compatibility of WTO rules and human rights in no way precludes that human rights obligations are not adequately taken into account in the legislative and administrative implementation of WTO rules and in their application (or disregard) by domestic courts.

Also, the UNHCHR calls increasingly upon all 112 states parties to the ICESCR to 'ensure that the Covenant is taken into account in all of their relevant national and international policy-making processes'.[31] The UNDP[32] likewise emphasizes the complementary functions of human rights and economic markets; in a world of scarcity, competition and market prices inevitably emerge in order to meet consumer demand for private and public goods. Economic markets, like political markets (democracy), involve dialogues about values and consumer-driven information mechanisms whose proper functioning requires legal and judicial protection of liberty rights (e.g. freedom of contract, freedom of expression, freedom of information), property rights, liability rules, legal guarantees of non-discriminatory competition, individual access to courts, and protection of other human rights as incentives for welfare-increasing division of labour.[33] In order to promote general consumer welfare rather than particular producer interests, market competition requires market access rights, legal obligations of market actors, governmental correction of 'market failures', and collective supply of 'public goods'.

---

[30] National policy autonomy is safeguarded, e.g. by GATT Arts. III, XVI, and XXVIII, GATS Arts. VI and XIX, Arts. 8, 30, 31, 40 of the TRIPS Agreement and by the numerous WTO 'exceptions' and safeguard clauses.

[31] This 'fundamental principle' of human rights law is emphasized in the recent report for the UN Commission on Human Rights on *The Right of Everyone to the Enjoyment of the Highest Attainable Standard of Physical and Mental Health*, E/CN.4/2003/58 (13 February 2003) para. 8.   [32] See *supra* n. 16.

[33] For a detailed explanation of why human rights, non-discriminatory markets, and consumer-driven competition serve complementary functions, and on the differences between a 'human rights approach' focusing on 'basic needs' and a broader 'constitutional approach' protecting equal constitutional rights beyond the basic needs of citizens, see Petersmann (*supra* n. 17).

IV. THE 1998 ILO DECLARATION ON FUNDAMENTAL PRINCIPLES AND RIGHTS AT WORK: THE EXPANDING SCOPE OF AN 'INALIENABLE CORE' OF BASIC RIGHTS

Human rights are increasingly acknowledged today in national constitutions as well as in the law of worldwide organizations (like the UN, the FAO, WHO, UNESCO) and regional economic integration agreements (like the EC Treaty, the 2000 Cotonou Agreement, the 2001 Quebec Ministerial Declaration on a Free Trade Area of the Americas) as international *erga omnes* obligations of states and of intergovernmental organizations, with an 'inalienable' and 'indivisible' *ius cogens* core. The 1996 WTO Declaration on core labour standards helped to reach consensus in the ILO to adopt, on 18 June 1998, the Declaration on Fundamental Principles and Rights at Work which recognizes:

that all Members, even if they have not ratified the Conventions in question, have an obligation, arising from the very fact of membership in the Organization, to respect, to promote and to realize, in good faith and in accordance with the Constitution, the principles concerning the fundamental rights which are the subject of those Conventions, namely: (a) freedom of association and the effective recognition of the right to collective bargaining; (b) the elimination of all forms of forced or compulsory labour; (c) the effective abolition of child labour; and (d) the elimination of discrimination in respect of employment and occupation.[34]

The ILO Declaration and other modern human rights instruments[35] illustrate that—in addition to the long-standing prohibitions of, for example, genocide, slavery, and apartheid—there is an increasing core of additional human rights which must be respected even 'in time of public emergency'[36] and, since the end of the Cold War, is evolving into international *ius cogens*,[37] notwithstanding divergent views on the precise scope and definition of such 'inalienable human rights'. The 'inalienable core' and 'constitutional primacy' of human rights calls for interpreting national and international law as a functional unity for promoting and protecting human rights.

---

[34] ILO, *Declaration on Fundamental Principles and Rights at Work*, (1998) at 7.

[35] E.g. the 1989 UN Convention on the Rights of the Child (ratified by more than 190 states) and the 1993 Vienna Declaration which recognizes, in para. 1, that 'the universal nature of (human) rights and freedoms is beyond question'. Many recent studies confirm that the values underlying human rights (such as respect for human dignity, life, freedom, equality, property, rule of law, procedural justice) can be found in all major cultures and religions.

[36] Cf. e.g. Art. 4 of the International Covenant for Civil and Political Rights (ICCPR), ECHR Art. 15.

[37] For detailed references to state practice see I. Seiderman, *Hierarchy in International Law* (2001).

Human rights instruments recognize that human rights need to be mutually balanced and implemented by democratic legislation which may legitimately vary from country to country. International courts have elaborated a number of legal 'balancing principles' (like non-discrimination, necessity, and proportionality of governmental limitations of freedom and other human rights) and emphasize the need to respect the 'margin of appreciation' of parliamentary legislation implementing human rights.[38] As human rights also protect individual and democratic diversity, views on the interpretation of government obligations to respect, protect, and fulfil human rights often differ among countries. In view of the limited mandate of international organizations, there are also diverging views on whether, and to what extent, international organizations should not only *respect* human rights, but also *protect* and *fulfil* human rights.

V. THE NEED FOR HARNESSING THE COMPLEMENTARY FUNCTIONS OF HUMAN RIGHTS AND MARKET COMPETITION: LESSONS FROM THE EU?

The recent 'human rights assessments' of international trade, services, investment, and intellectual property rules by the UNHCHR offer a promising start for mutually beneficial cooperation between human rights bodies and specialized economic organizations. As indicated in the report of the Special Rapporteur P. Hunt on his 'mission to the WTO', such cooperation can help to deal more effectively with the problem of 'disconnected government',[39] i.e. the often inadequate cooperation of different branches of national and international governance in the coherent implementation of human rights obligations across all relevant policy-making processes. However, as long as more than 30 WTO Members have not ratified the ICESCR and UN bodies fail to effectively protect human rights in so many UN activities and UN member states, WTO bodies will remain reluctant to apply the 'ICESCR approach' to economic and social human rights. Until the UN specifies more precisely the general human rights obligations of all UN Member states (e.g. following the model of the 1998 ILO Declaration on core

---

[38] On the 'margin of appreciation' doctrine in the case-law of the European Court of Human Rights see e.g. H. C. Yourow, *The Margin of Appreciation Doctrine in the Dynamics of European Human Rights Jurisprudence* (1996). On the similar 'balancing principles' developed in WTO jurisprudence relating, e.g. to GATT Art. XX, see E. U. Petersmann, 'Human Rights and the Law of the WTO' in 37 *Journal of World Trade* (2003) 241–281.   [39] E/CN.4/2004/49/Add.1 (*supra* n. 27), para. 9.

labour standards), the customary law status of many economic and social human rights will remain contested, and those WTO Members with different human rights traditions (like China, the US) remain entitled to protect human rights, basic needs, and 'social justice' in different ways.[40] Due to their case-oriented focus (e.g. on the human rights to health and food), the UNHCHR reports have not yet developed a methodology for examining the manifold interrelationships between human rights and trade rules more systematically, with due regard to the 'indivisibility' of civil, political, economic, and social human rights and of their constitutive functions for consumer-driven and welfare-maximizing market competition.[41] The High Commissioner seems to be aware of this need for better mutual understanding, as his reports 'highlight the need not only to bring a human rights perspective to trade but also a trade perspective to human rights'.[42]

The explicit recognition and legal protection of 'indivisible' civil, political, economic, social, and cultural human rights in European integration law—in contrast to their legally and institutionally separate regulation in the UN human rights conventions of 1966—illustrates the potential advantages of an integrated human rights approach to economic integration. The once revolutionary human rights proclamations of the eighteenth century, for example that 'the aim of every political association is the preservation of the natural and imprescriptible rights of man' (Article II of the French Declaration of the Rights of Man and of the Citizen, 1789), and that the legitimacy of governments derives from protecting the human rights of their citizens (US Declaration of Independence, 1776) are reflected in the EU Treaty requirements to respect human rights and democratic governance not only inside the EU (cf. EU Treaty Articles 6, 7, 49), but also as objectives of the EU's common foreign and security policy (EU Treaty Article 11) and external

---

[40] On the diverse constitutional traditions protecting social welfare rights see e.g. V. C. Jackson and M. Tushnet, *Comparative Constitutional Law* (1999), ch. XII.

[41] A more systematic examination of the human rights dimensions of WTO rules and policies would have to distinguish between the different kinds of trade policy measures (e.g. import restrictions, non-discriminatory economic regulation, subsidies, trade liberalization, special and differential treatment of developing countries) and among protection of civil, political, economic, social, cultural, and 'third generation' human rights at home and abroad, at national and international levels. It would also have to clarify the UN human rights concepts of 'human dignity', 'inalienability', and 'indivisibility' of human rights and their controversial nature as *ius cogens, erga omnes* obligations, and general international legal obligations under UN law. The very limited lists of *ius cogens* human rights proposed by US authors (cf. Third Restatement of the Foreign Relations Law of the US, American Law Institute 1990, section 701) need to be updated in the light of the expanding UN consensus on 'inalienable' human rights such as the human right to health, now incorporated in over 100 national constitutions as well as in worldwide treaties like the UN Convention on the Rights of the Child, ratified by almost all states except the US.   [42] E/CN.4/Sub.2/2003/4 at para. 66.

development policy (EC Treaty Article 177). The 'market freedoms' (for free movements of goods, services, persons, capital, and related payments), 'fundamental rights' (e.g. to 'equal pay for male and female workers for equal work') and 'EU citizen rights' protected by the EC Treaty and by the ECJ complement the explicit references in the EU Treaty to the European Convention on Human Rights (cf. Article 6). The EU Charter of Fundamental Rights of December 2000[43] proceeds from 'the indivisible, universal values of human dignity, freedom, equality and solidarity' and protects specific liberty rights, equality rights, and solidarity rights in economic and social areas no less than in civil and political fields. The market freedoms, fundamental rights, EU citizen rights, and other human rights are all protected by the ECJ as constitutional rights with legal primacy, in case of conflict, over secondary EC legislation. Apart from a few conflicting judicial interpretations of human rights, the ECJ and the European Court of Human Rights have succeeded in defending the consistency of European human rights law and economic integration law.[44] Yet even though the ECJ has long since recognized the common human rights guarantees of EC Member states as general constitutional principles limiting the regulatory powers also of the EC,[45] there appears to be not a single judgment of the ECJ invalidating an EC measure on grounds of violation of human rights.

The regional integration law of the EU—even though it may be no model for worldwide organizations like the WTO—confirms the complementary functions of liberal trade law and human rights. The 'basic rights approach' to market liberalization in Europe is, however, neither applied in North America (e.g. in the North American Free Trade Agreement (NAFTA)) nor in the reports by the UNHCHR which view economic production, trade, and economic rights as mere 'instruments' for fulfilling human rights. Arguably, the rights-based EU approach to the international division of labour protects individuals and the 'indivisibility' of their human rights more effectively. Since most people spend most of their time on production and consumption of scarce ('economic') goods and services and consider their right to choose a profession as being of no less 'existential importance' for their personal

---

[43] The Charter is reproduced in *Official Journal* C 364/1 (18 December 2000).

[44] Cf. D. Spielmann, 'Human Rights Case Law in the Strasbourg and Luxembourg Courts: Conflicts, Inconsistencies and Complementarities' in P. Alston, M. Bustelo, and J. Heenan (eds), *The EU and Human Rights* (1999) 757–780.

[45] In *Internationale Handelsgesellschaft* (Case 11/70, ECR 1970, 1125, 1134), the ECJ held that respect for human rights forms an integral part of the general principles of Community law: 'the protection of such rights, whilst inspired by the constitutional traditions common to the Member States, must be ensured within the framework of the structure and objectives of the Community' (paras. 3–4).

development in dignity than their political human rights; proposals for a higher ranking of civil and political over economic and social rights involve a 'double standard' which, if 'human dignity' is defined in the Kantian sense of moral and rational individual autonomy and responsibility, should be left to individual choice rather than be imposed top–down.[46]

From a cosmopolitan perspective, recognition of 'market freedoms' as 'fundamental rights' in EC law reflects the 'indivisibility' and interdependence of personal self-development in economic and non-economic areas, without preventing government regulations balancing economic with non-economic rights and public interests. The protection of fundamental rights in EU law, and of economic liberty rights in the national constitutions of federal states (like Germany and Switzerland), further illustrates that the constitutional protection of economic rights purports to protect not only disadvantaged groups,[47] but serves broader constitutional functions for empowering individuals as legal subjects ('market citizens') rather than mere objects of integration, notably for protecting their personal self-development and equal basic rights against welfare-reducing government limitations. Given the economic interrelationships between consumption, production, and trade, EC law rightly protects freedom of production and freedom of trade no less than freedom of consumption and access to essential goods and services necessary for satisfying basic needs.

VI. HUMAN RIGHTS AND THE WTO: NO CONFLICT IN PRINCIPLE?

The 1994 Agreement establishing the WTO promotes 'human rights values' (such as individual freedom and mutually beneficial cooperation among citizens) through legal WTO guarantees of freedom,

---

[46] Cf. E. U. Petersmann, 'Human Rights, Markets and Economic Welfare: Constitutional Functions of the Emerging UN Human Rights Constitution' in C. Breining and T. Cottier (eds), *International Trade and Human Rights* (2004). All UN human rights conventions proceed, like EU human rights law, from 'recognition of the inherent dignity and of the equal and inalienable rights of all members of the human family (as) foundation of freedom, justice and peace in the world'. The text of Art. 1 of the UDHR suggests to define 'human dignity' by the moral and rational autonomy and responsibility of human beings to exercise one's freedom in a 'just' manner respecting maximum equal legal freedom of all others and treating individuals as legal subjects entitled to personal self-development in dignity. From such a Kantian perspective, freedom of profession and freedom to trade the fruits of one's labour in exchange for the goods and services needed for personal self-development are no less rooted in dignity and of 'existential importance' than personal freedoms in non-economic areas.

[47] The UNHCHR reports emphasize that 'trade liberalization will create losers even in the long run and that trade reforms could exacerbate poverty temporarily. Human rights law concerns itself in particular with the situation of the individuals and groups who might suffer during the reform process' (E/CN.4/2002/54, para. 34).

nondiscrimination, rule of law, and international division of labour across frontiers. Like the law of other international organizations, WTO law contributes to the 'constitutionalization' of modern international law, for instance by conferring a higher legal rank on the WTO Agreement over the multilateral trade agreements listed in its Annexes (cf. WTO Agreement Article XVI:3); by promoting rule of law and submitting all WTO Members to compulsory international jurisdiction by WTO dispute settlement bodies and domestic courts; and by reinforcing horizontal and vertical checks and balances among rule-making, executive, and judicial powers at national and international levels. From a human rights perspective, WTO rules should be construed as serving 'constitutional functions' for protecting freedom, non-discrimination, rule of law, economic welfare, and peaceful settlement of disputes not only among states, but also in cosmopolitan trade relations among citizens across frontiers and inside states.[48] Hence, there are not only legal, but also economic and political reasons for construing WTO rules, human rights, and domestic laws of WTO Members in a mutually consistent manner.

In the several hundred dispute settlement proceedings under GATT 1947 and the WTO during more than half a century, no conflict between GATT and WTO rules and human rights has so far been identified.[49] Although WTO law does not explicitly refer to human rights, there is so far no convincing evidence for *systemic* conflicts—at the international level of legal principles—for instance:

- between the non-discrimination requirements of human rights (which may call for 'positive discrimination') and those of WTO law (which permits, e.g. subsidies, tax benefits, and other preferential treatment in favour of poor people, vulnerable minorities, and suppliers of 'essential services');[50]
- between the human rights to liberty[51] and property[52] and the WTO guarantees of freedom of trade and protection of property rights

---

[48] Cf. e.g. E. U. Petersmann, 'The WTO Constitution and Human Rights' in 3 *Journal of International Economic Law* (2000) 19–25.

[49] For a detailed analysis see—in addition to the above-mentioned reports by the UNHCHR—Petersmann (*supra* n. 38) and G. Marceau, 'WTO Dispute Settlement and Human Rights' in 13 *European Journal of International Law* (2002) 753–813.

[50] The UNHCHR report on the interaction between the principle of non-discrimination in human rights and trade law (*supra* n. 26) identifies various common elements (e.g. no requirement to demonstrate discriminatory intention, applicability to both *de jure* and *de facto* discrimination, justifiability of differential treatment) and suggests that the 'flexibility' of WTO rules can avoid legal conflicts.

[51] Whereas human rights lawyers tend to treat the 'right to liberty' (UDHR Art. 3) and 'economic freedoms' (ICESCR Art. 6) as separate rights with separate functions, European constitutional law (e.g. in Germany, Switzerland, EC law) guarantees economic liberties more broadly in order to protect human dignity (cf. Arts. II-1, 15, 16 of the Draft Treaty Establishing a Constitution for Europe, EC 2003).

[52] The 'right to own property' is protected in Art. 17 of the UDHR and in regional human rights conventions (e.g. Protocol I to the ECHR), but omitted from UN human

(which permit, e.g. compulsory licenses and other limitations in order to prevent 'abuses' of intellectual property rights); also WTO market access commitments are subject to 'general exceptions' (e.g. in GATT Article XX, GATS Article XIV) which appear flexible enough to do whatever is necessary for protecting and promoting human rights;[53]

- among the human rights guarantees of due process of law and access to justice and the corresponding procedural guarantees in WTO law;
- between the numerous 'general exceptions' in WTO law and the human rights obligations of WTO Members.

Yet this mutual consistency of WTO rules and universal human rights at the level of international law in no way precludes that—in domestic trade laws and trade policies—the human rights obligations of WTO member countries may not be adequately taken into account. Explicit recognition (e.g. in a WTO Ministerial Declaration) of the need to respect universally recognized human rights in the trade policy area could make it easier to interpret WTO rules in conformity with universally recognized human rights. Whether universal human rights—such as the 'right to development' which has been interpreted in many UN resolutions as requiring respect for universal human rights[54]—may be relevant for the interpretation of WTO rules (such as the WTO objective of promoting 'sustainable development') may be clarified more appropriately by UN human rights bodies than by WTO bodies which, for instance in case of WTO disputes, are likely to exercise judicial self-restraint by deciding only those legal issues that are indispensable for settling a trade dispute.[55]

---

rights covenants except for the 'author rights' mentioned in ICESCR Art. 15. Intellectual property rights are based on legislation and limited in time (cf. e.g. Art. 33 of the TRIPS Agreement relating to 20 years of patent protection).

[53] The UNHCHR report on the GATS (*supra* n. 24) refers to the 'Cochabamba case' in Bolivia where 'the city's water system was liberalized to the subsidiary of a foreign service provider, leading to price increases of more than 35 per cent. This resulted in mass demonstrations and strike action that led the Government to reverse the decision to liberalize the sector and restore public ownership.' The report does not claim that the privatization was part of a WTO commitment (GATS does not mandate privatization of essential services), or that WTO law may not be flexible enough to protect essential services (cf. e.g. GATS Arts. X, XIV, and XXI).

[54] In UN practice, the 'right to development' and the corresponding government obligations have been defined in terms of realization of all human rights (cf. UN General Assembly Declaration 41/128 of 4 December 1986 on the 'Right to Development').

[55] See e.g. the numerous references to 'judicial economy' in the recently adopted WTO Panel report on *Mexico—Measures Affecting Telecommunications Services*, WT/DS204/R (2 April 2004).

VII. THE 'RIGHT TO DEMOCRATIC GOVERNANCE' AND THE WTO

Human rights instruments have for a long time recognized that human rights need to be protected and mutually balanced through democratic legislation, and that 'everyone has the right to take part in the government of his country, directly or through freely chosen representatives'. 'The will of the people shall be the basis of the authority of governments; this will shall be expressed in periodic and genuine elections which shall be by universal and equal suffrage and shall be held by secret vote or by equivalent free voting procedures' (Universal Declaration of Human Rights (UDHR) Article 21). Most states claim today to respect this 'human right to democratic governance'.[56] Yet national parliaments and civil society groups often complain of the 'democratic deficits' resulting from intergovernmental rule-making in distant international organizations, often without effective parliamentary participation and effective democratic control by public opinion and civil society (e.g. 'inclusive' decision-making with participatory and/or consultative rights of non-governmental groups that may be affected by the decisions concerned). Such democratic concerns increase if intergovernmental negotiations (e.g. in the WTO) are strongly influenced by powerful interest groups (e.g. agricultural, textiles, and steel lobbies), take place behind closed doors without adequate 'deliberative democracy', and do not refer to human rights and general consumer welfare in the international negotiations and balancing processes. This may lead to comprehensive 'package deals' (like the 1994 WTO Agreement) that can hardly be reopened once the international negotiations have been closed.

The political distance between individual citizens, national parliamentarians, and the WTO is not inevitable. The effective parliamentary oversight and control of US trade policies by the US Congress suggests that much of the alleged 'democratic deficit' is due to inadequate parliamentary involvement in trade policy-making (notably in the EU). European integration illustrates that international law and international organizations can also enlarge citizen rights, limit abuses of trade policy powers, and facilitate parliamentary accountability of foreign policies beyond what is possible through merely national rules and institutions.

---

[56] On the emerging 'human right to democratic governance' see e.g. T. M. Franck, 'The Emerging Right to Democratic Governance' in 86 *American Journal of International Law* (1992) 46–91; E. Stein, 'International Integration and Democracy: No Love at First Sight' in 95 *American Journal of International Law* (2001) 489–532. See also the UNHCHR report on the expert seminar on the interdependence between democracy and human rights (E/CN.4/2003/59).

In an increasing number of worldwide treaties (e.g. on prohibition of land mines, establishment of an International Criminal Court), NGOs, and more democratic forms of consensus-building (e.g. on a new European Treaty constitution) have usefully complemented intergovernmental treaty negotiations and parliamentary ratification.

If democracy is defined as self-government of the people, by the people and for the people, then the diverse forms of local democracy (e.g. in the Greek city–republics in the fifth century BC), national democracy (e.g. in the US), and international democracy (e.g. in the EU) have at least three complementary elements in common:

- A *liberal element* based on the instrumental function of democracy to promote the freedom, equal rights, and basic needs of citizens.[57] This democratic function tends to be enlarged by WTO guarantees of freedom across frontiers and by non-discriminatory access to foreign markets enabling mutually beneficial trade exchanges, especially if international trade liberalization takes place in the context of 'embedded liberalism' (J. Ruggie) promoting 'social justice' through national institutions.

- A *majoritarian, representative element* based on the need for majority decisions by local, national, or transnational communities and their representative institutions for the collective supply of public goods that cannot be supplied through private markets (e.g. democratic legislation, accountability of the rulers). In contrast to the effective parliamentary control by the US Congress of trade policy-making, parliaments in most WTO Members (including the European Parliament) do not appear to effectively supervise and influence the trade policies of their governments. This 'parliamentary deficit' in intergovernmental negotiations and rule-making needs to be reduced by more precise parliamentary negotiation mandates, parliamentary involvement in and surveillance of intergovernmental negotiations, and parliamentary scrutiny of international rules prior to the ratification of international agreements. There are also various means of promoting transnational democracy inside intergovernmental organizations, for example through consultative parliamentary bodies and participation or consultation of representative NGOs (as in the ILO and in the International Federation of Red Cross Societies). State-centred international law principles (such as 'sovereign equality' of states) and majority decisions among state representatives, however, are unlikely to promote individual and democratic self-government as

---

[57] On the important distinction between liberal and 'illiberal' democracy, and on the need for restraining popular majority politics by equal basic rights and by other general constitutional constraints see F. Zakaria, *The Future of Freedom. Illiberal Democracy at Home and Abroad* (2003).

long as state representatives are not fully accountable to all affected individuals.

- The horizontal and vertical constitutional constraints on abuses of public and private power constitute a third *constitutional element* of the diverse forms of local, national, and international democratic governance in order to hold the rulers accountable to citizens, parliaments, and courts. WTO rules reinforce such constitutional restraints on discretionary trade policy powers and strengthen rule-oriented (rather than 'power-oriented') policies at home and abroad based on liberal democratic values. Empowering citizens to directly invoke and enforce (e.g. through domestic courts) precise international guarantees of freedom and non-discrimination offers a decentralized, democratic method of enlisting self-interested citizens as guardians of the rule of law.

VIII. POLICY CONCLUSIONS

The more than 100 international treaties and universal UN resolutions on protection of human rights reflect today's universal recognition of an 'inalienable core' of human rights as part of general international law and international treaty law. Even though WTO law does not explicitly refer to human rights, and references to human rights in WTO decisions and WTO reports remain very rare,[58] it follows from general international law and from Article 3 of the DSU that universally recognized human rights may be 'relevant context' for legal and judicial interpretations of WTO rules.

Trade regulation (e.g. of agricultural subsidies, limitations on advertising, and freedom of commercial speech), trade liberalization (e.g. of essential services, international movements of service providers), and domestic implementation of WTO rules can create competitive pressures and social adjustment problems which, without government protection of human rights and of basic human needs, may have adverse human rights implications (e.g. for small subsistence farmers, separation of foreign service providers from their family, access of poor or vulnerable people to food, medicines, and essential services at affordable prices). The input-legitimacy of rule-making and adjudication in the WTO could be enhanced by an explicit recognition in a WTO Ministerial Declaration that all WTO Members are committed to respect for universal human rights within the limited confines of WTO law and policy. In view of the diversity of views on the interpretation and balancing

---

[58] See e.g. the recent *Waiver concerning Kimberley Process Certification Scheme for Rough Diamonds*, WT/L/518 (15 May 2003) which refers, in its Preamble, to 'gross human rights violations' in 'conflicts fuelled by the trade in conflict diamonds'.

of human rights, the WTO should remain an economic organization promoting a mutually welfare-increasing division of labour. Yet, the WTO should welcome the initiatives by UN human rights bodies to clarify the interrelationships between human rights and WTO law as well as the contribution of trade policy to fulfilment of human rights. International 'human rights assessments' and the interpretation, progressive development, and monitoring of human rights should not become the task of WTO bodies, but should be left to specialized human rights bodies and to national governments.

The WTO objectives of protecting freedom, non-discrimination, and rule of law in the worldwide division of labour, and to thereby increase economic welfare and mutually beneficial cooperation among citizens across frontiers, complement the human rights objectives of promoting personal and democratic self-development through legal protection of equal basic rights and fulfilment of basic needs necessary for a life in dignity. There is so far no evidence of conflicts between WTO rules and universal human rights at the level of international principles. Initiatives by UN bodies to promote respect for human rights and labour standards in the domestic implementation of WTO rules and trade policies are likely to promote also the WTO objectives of, for example, 'sustainable development', 'raising standards of living', and peaceful settlement of disputes.

Human rights protect individual and democratic diversity and require democratic implementing legislation which may legitimately vary from country to country and change over time, as reflected in the Charter of Fundamental Rights of the EU of December 2000. In spite of the 'General Comments' elaborated by UN human rights bodies, views on the inter-pretation of human rights, on their 'inalienability' and 'indivisibility', their legal relevance for international organizations, and their judicial protection continue to differ widely among countries. The clarification of the legal relevance of human rights for international and national trade law and policy should therefore, primarily, be left to specialized human rights bodies and to democratic legislatures and domestic courts. WTO bodies should acknowledge and support the potential contribution of universal human rights to a mutually beneficial international trading system promoting not only economic welfare but also respect for human rights and 'social justice'. Such a positive response to the human rights approach advocated by the UN could facilitate consensus on new WTO rules if they are seen to take into account also the social dimensions and adjustment problems of the world trading system in the Doha Development Round negotiations as well as in domestic implementation of WTO rules and trade policies.

18

Parliamentary Oversight of WTO Rule-Making: The Political, Normative, and Practical Contexts

GREGORY SHAFFER[1]

This chapter addresses the issue of parliamentary oversight of World Trade Organization (WTO) rule-making at the national and international levels. Parliamentarians' views of alternative mechanisms for ensuring parliamentary control of the WTO tend to vary by jurisdiction. From a positive perspective, these views reflect power structures at the national, regional, and international levels, as well as parliamentarians' experiences with supra-national governance institutions. European political representatives are more accustomed to shared supra-national governance institutions. They tend to propose expansion and adaptation of the European Union (EU) model to address global governance challenges. United States (US) Congressional representatives, in contrast, tend to be wary of how US 'sovereignty' and US power can be constrained through the WTO or any other global governance regime. They tend to oppose adding a parliamentary dimension. From a normative perspective, in order to meaningfully discuss WTO accountability we need a conceptual framework that permits us to assess the trade-offs between different mechanisms for ensuring oversight, including parliamentary oversight, of the WTO. This chapter adopts a comparative institutional one; it addresses the policy arguments for and against the addition of such a parliamentary dimension to the WTO and examines some of the many institutional challenges that would arise. The chapter maintains that the creation of a WTO

[1] Thanks go to the participants at the conference *WTO Negotiators Meet the Academics: Challenges to the Legitimacy and Efficiency of the World Trading System*, European University Institute, Florence, 26–27 June 2003, and to interviewees working for the US Congress, European Commission and Parliament, International Parliamentary Union, and WTO for their comments. Thanks also to Gregory Creer for his valuable research assistance.

parliamentary body should be judged in terms of its impact on the participation of less powerful stakeholders, and in particular of developing countries and their constituents, relative to other institutional alternatives.

Demands for greater accountability of the WTO intensify as WTO rules broaden in scope and become more binding in effect. How can WTO rule-making be subjected to greater democratic oversight and control? Most academic commentary has focused on enhancing WTO transparency and the role of organized civil society. This chapter, in contrast, focuses on parliamentary oversight of WTO rule-making at the national and international levels. The chapter makes five primary points.

First, in order to meaningfully discuss WTO accountability, we need a conceptual framework that permits us to assess the trade-offs between different mechanisms for ensuring oversight, including parliamentary oversight, of the WTO. No institutional mechanism is perfect. All proposed mechanisms should be assessed in terms of how well they permit parties to participate in decision-making that affects them in a relatively unbiased manner compared to other non-idealized institutional alternatives. This analytical framework can be termed 'comparative institutional analysis', and is set forth in section I below.

Second, ensuring parliamentary oversight of WTO rule-making can be conceptualized at two-levels: the international level (at the WTO itself) and the national/WTO member level (or in the case of the EU, regional level). The approach of almost all US congressional representatives is to focus only on the national level, examined in section II. The European Commission's Trade Commissioner, Pascal Lamy, in contrast, together with European parliamentarians, have called for interparliamentary meetings at the WTO/supra-national level, assessed in section III. These two mechanisms—domestic and supranational—can complement each other, which is Mr Lamy's view.

Third, parliamentarians' views of alternative mechanisms for ensuring parliamentary control of the WTO tend to vary by jurisdiction, as analysed in section IV. These views reflect power structures at the national, regional, and international levels, as well as parliamentarians' experiences with supra-national governance institutions. European political representatives are more accustomed to shared supra-national governance institutions in light of the development of the EU itself. European political figures tend to propose expansion and adaptation of the EU model to address global governance challenges. US Congressional representatives, in contrast, tend to be wary of how US 'sovereignty' and US power can be constrained through the WTO or any other global governance regime.

In addition, the US Congress plays a relatively powerful role in US trade policy, and the US plays a relatively powerful role in the WTO. Members of the US Congress are much less likely to consider interparliamentary meetings because such meetings could diminish their power, not enhance it. They prefer to harness the clout of the US government, over whose policies they have a significant say, to advance their constituents' interests. In contrast, the European Commission needs only consult with the European Parliament concerning EU trade policy pursuant to an informal procedure. Although the European Parliament's informal consultative role has increased over time, and although provisions of the draft constitution for Europe, if adopted, would further enhance Parliament's powers, the EU treaties have so far provided the European Parliament with no formal power over trade policy.[2] European parliamentarians thus can increase their relative prominence over trade policy through interparliamentary WTO meetings.

Fourth, these proposals should be assessed in terms of how they address a central challenge facing current WTO decision-making—that of the difficulty of most developing countries to participate effectively in the WTO, whether in its political or judicial processes. Most developing countries are at a severe disadvantage on account of their relative lack of resources (both financial and human capital), their lower aggregate stakes in the trading system (even though they may have high relative stakes), and the increasingly complex and resource-demanding nature of the WTO system. The issue of absolute compared to relative stakes is the most important explanation for developing countries' inability to participate in proportion to their needs. Because of individual developing countries' relatively smaller value, volume, and variety of exports, they obtain lower absolute benefits from participation in the WTO system. Their aggregate benefits are less likely to exceed the threshold of the cost of participation, especially in light of the uncertainty that they can realize the benefits desired.[3] Even so, many developing countries may have much higher relative stakes over trade measures in relation to their respective economies than the US and EU.

The creation of a WTO parliamentary body should be judged in terms of its impact on the participation of less powerful stakeholders

[2] See E. Mann, 'A Parliamentary Dimension to the WTO: More than Just a Vision?' in this volume (citing Art. III-217 and 227 of the draft constitution). Compare Arts. 133 and 300 of the current Treaty Establishing the European Community (EC). See also G. Shaffer, *Defending Interests: Public–Private Partnerships in WTO Litigation* (2003), comparing the roles of EC and US governmental institutions in trade policy.

[3] See G. Shaffer, *How to Make the WTO Dispute Settlement System Work for Developing Countries: Some Proactive Developing Country Strategies* (2003), online at http://www.ictsd.org/pubs/ ictsd_series/resource_papers/DSU_2003.pdf.

and, in particular of developing countries and their constituents, relative to the institutional alternatives, as examined in section V. That is, would a WTO parliamentary body further increase the costs of participation in WTO rule-making, favouring wealthy, well-organized, and well-connected parties with higher absolute stakes (i.e. US and European multinational enterprises and issue-specific non-governmental organizations (NGOs)) over parties with lower absolute stakes (i.e. developing country constituents)? Or, would a WTO parliamentary body increase the relative understanding of the perspectives of developing countries and increase their impact in the shaping of WTO debates?

Finally, the implementation of a parliamentary dimension to the WTO raises a number of practical issues that would need to be confronted. Section VI addresses the policy arguments for and against the addition of such a parliamentary dimension. Section VII examines some of the many institutional challenges that would arise.

This chapter does not assess the role of organized 'civil society' at the international level, which has been copiously promoted, criticized, and analysed in academic and policy journals. Depending on one's normative perspective, expanding the role of civil society oversight and parliamentary control of WTO rule-making at the international level can, nonetheless, operate as institutional alternatives, complements, or mirror-images. Some proponents of adding a parliamentary dimension to the WTO advance a competitive concept, arguing that parliament-arians are the true democratic representatives of civil society, not unelected leaders of non-governmental organizations. They support the creation of a parliamentary assembly within the WTO framework, in part, because they wish to capture a public space from anti-globalization 'civil society' activists.[4] In contrast, some proponents of a greater role for organized civil society in WTO decision-making may criticize proposals for a WTO parliamentary body precisely because it could provide a gloss of legitimacy and constitutionalized entrenchment of what they deem to be an illegitimate process.

Other proponents of establishing a WTO parliamentary body view the role of organized civil society and parliamentarians as complements within a modified WTO structure. Under this scenario, representatives of organized civil society would still participate in a more transparent WTO, but do so through advocacy before multiple bodies, including a WTO parliamentary body consisting of representatives from

---

[4] See e.g. M. Moore, *A World Without Walls: Freedom, Development, Free Trade and Global Governance* (2003) at 121 ('parliamentarians are the legitimate accountable representatives of civil society'). In addition, EC officials note that parliamentary involvement is important to overcome the impression that NGOs are civil society's representatives. Telephone interview with EU Commission representative, 28 May 2003.

parliaments of all WTO Members, as well as WTO delegates, the WTO Secretariat, and political representatives in national capitals. In addition, the WTO could include an analogue to the EU's Economic and Social Committee consisting of civil society representatives that periodically would be consulted.

Still other proponents maintain that a civil society cosmopolitics and a WTO parliamentary assembly are analogous or even one and the same. They argue that representatives from civil society themselves could jump-start a global parliamentary process and potentially be the global parliamentarians themselves. Richard Falk and Andrew Strauss, for example, have asserted that their proposal for a global parliamentary body 'would not be constituted by states'.[5] They have maintained that 'civil society is now capable of founding the GPA [Global Parliamentary Assembly]'.[6] These contentions should be assessed from a comparative institutional perspective, an analytic framework to which we now turn.

I. A COMPARATIVE INSTITUTIONAL CONCEPTUAL FRAMEWORK

The core concept of contemporary democracy is to hold rulers accountable through elected representatives.[7] However, in a world of increasing numbers and complexity, it is impossible for representative institutions to address all matters having a social impact. In consequence, decision-making is delegated—whether formally or informally—to non-representative institutions, such as markets, bureaucracies, courts, quasi-public bodies, private companies, and public–private networks. We differentiate the concept of governance from that of government to assess decision-making mechanisms that are not directly accountable to a popularly elected political body of a constitutional democracy.

Most scholarship addressing international institutions and regimes focuses on the concept of 'global governance' because there is no popularly elected global 'government'.[8] The fact that global institutions are not subject to control through direct popular elections or referenda

---

[5] R. Falk and A. Strauss, 'Bridging the Globalization Gap: Toward a Global Parliament' in *Foreign Affairs* (January–February 2001) 212, 216.

[6] R. Falk and A. Strauss, 'On the Creation of a Global Peoples Assembly: Legitimacy and the Power of Popular Sovereignty' in 36 *Stanford Journal of International Law* (2000) 191.   [7] See e.g. R. Dahl, *On Democracy* (1998).

[8] However, some scholarship refers to the creation of (or need for) a global democratic constitutional order. See D. Held, *Democracy and the Global Order: From the Modern State to Cosmopolitan Governance* (1995).

subjects them to frequent charges that they are 'illegitimate' because they are not 'democratic'. The WTO, for example, is a frequent target of such challenges, in particular where WTO judicial bodies find that national legislation is inconsistent with WTO rules. Although there are legitimate normative concerns about the accountability of global institutions, critics, whether from the left or the right, also can manipulate arguments over 'legitimacy' to advance their particular policy preferences.

The central normative concept for assessing the normative legitimacy of decision-making should not be whether a decision has been rendered by a popularly elected body. If that were the case, then no decision-making should be delegated to markets, bureaucracies, courts, or any other body. Rather, the legitimacy of institutions should be viewed in a broader sense as concerning the relative *accountability* of decision-making processes to those affected by them. Governance mechanisms implicitly can be democratic, in this broader sense, to the extent that decision-makers (or decision-making processes) are held accountable to the public through accountability mechanisms. As Robert Keohane writes, accountability mechanisms can operate in multiple manners, which he characterizes as hierarchical, legal, market, reputational, fiscal, supervisory, and participatory. Accountability mechanisms exist to sanction decision-makers when they fail to take account of affected interests.[9]

Comparative institutional analysis is a conceptual framework for assessing public policy in terms of the relatively unbiased participation of affected parties in alternative institutional settings.[10] From a comparative institutional perspective, normative legitimacy depends on how well parties' diverse views and interests are taken into account in an institutional context (be it a political, judicial, market, or other process) in *comparison* with alternative non-idealized institutional settings. In a world of large numbers and complexity, no institution provides for completely unbiased participation or representation of affected interests. All institutions are imperfect. Thus, single institutional critiques are necessary but insufficient.

National constitutions and global governance mechanisms conceptually have much in common in that they both address the allocation of

---

[9] See R. Keohane, 'Political Accountability', paper prepared for Conference on *Delegation to International Organizations* (on file with author). See also R. Keohane and J. Nye, 'Redefining Accountability for Global Governance' in M. Kahler and D. A. Lake (eds), *Governance in a Global Economy* (2003).

[10] See the important work of N. Komesar, including *Imperfect Alternatives: Choosing Institutions in Law, Economics and Public Policy* (1995), and *Law's Limits: The Rule of Law and the Supply and Demand of Rights* (2002).

decision-making authority to alternative institutions. The difference between national constitutional orders and (often inchoate) global governance mechanisms is one of degree and gradation along a spectrum.[11] Global governance mechanisms should not be judged, and simply dismissed, against some ideal type of national democratic constitution. Rather, global governance mechanisms should be assessed in terms of whether they allocate decision-making authority in a manner that permits for a relatively less-biased representation of affected parties compared to other institutional alternatives, whether these alternatives lie at the local, national, or global level.

Global governance mechanisms help address conflicts over foreign and national values, priorities, and interests. They allocate decision-making over conflicting goals to alternative institutions, playing roles conceptually similar to those of national constitutional orders. In a globalizing world of complex interdependence, there is an increasing amount of policy initiatives and scholarship that addresses the need for such governance mechanisms. This scholarship ranges from assessments of the appropriateness of centralized global institutions (including parliaments), decentralized epistemic and transgovernmental regimes, civil society networks, and cross-border social movements, often contrasting the respective roles of representative, deliberative, market, and expertise-dominated processes. These alternatives need be assessed from a comparative institutional perspective.

There is nothing inherent that makes global governance mechanisms more or less representative of affected parties' competing views and interests than domestic processes. We live in a world of multiple constitutional orders whose disparate decision-making processes affect one another's constituents. On the one hand, government representatives cannot control for the impact on their constituents of foreign political decisions.[12] On the other hand, government representatives make decisions that affect foreign constituents without those constituents being represented. Global governance mechanisms address the linkages between these imperfect constitutional orders. Yet, as with any institution, global governance mechanisms also involve trade-offs, in this case between the quality of participation (reduced because of distance and numbers) and the scope of representativeness (enhanced because of scale and numbers).

---

[11] See N. Walker, 'The EU and the WTO: Constitutionalism in a New Key' in G. de Burca and J. Scott (eds), *The EU and the WTO: Legal and Constitutional Issues* (2001) 33 (noting gradations of constitutionalism at the national, EU, and WTO levels).

[12] Of course, governmental representatives in powerful states retain relatively greater discretion and control over decision-making affecting their constituents than do those in weaker states.

II. PARLIAMENTARY OVERSIGHT OF THE WTO AT THE NATIONAL/WTO MEMBER LEVEL: OVERVIEW OF THE US SYSTEM

Traditionally, parliamentary oversight of the WTO lies at the national level. Under this approach, each WTO Member arranges for parliamentary oversight in conformity with its own constitutional requirements. Almost all members of the US Congress and their staffs specialized on trade matters espouse this traditional view. This section provides an overview of how Congress exercises oversight of the WTO at the US domestic level.

Under the US Constitution, Congress maintains authority over US trade policy.[13] Congress delegates authority to the executive through congressional legislation. Starting with the 1974 trade act, US administrations periodically have sought and obtained what is referred to as 'fast-track', and more recently 'trade promotion', power to engage in GATT, WTO, and bilateral and regional trade negotiations. Congress sets the mandates. Sometimes the mandate permits the executive to sign binding agreements for tariff reductions without further congressional ratification, as occurred at the time of the first GATT tariff bindings in 1947. The Agreement Establishing the WTO, in contrast, as well as the North American Free Trade Agreement (NAFTA) and recent bilateral trade agreements, were subject to ratification by a majority vote of both houses of Congress under a special procedure. In August 2002, Congress granted the Bush administration trade promotion authority by one vote, subject to numerous conditions, including an expiration date of 1 June 2005, to be extended automatically until 1 June 2007 if neither congressional chamber adopts a resolution opposing extension.[14]

Each body of Congress, the Senate and House of Representatives, has special committees on trade, known as 'watchdog committees'. They are the trade subcommittees of the Senate Finance Committee and of the House Ways and Means Committee. Members of each party are designated to these committees in proportion to the parties' representation in the House and the Senate. Since members of the Republican party currently hold a majority of the seats in the House and the Senate, a Republican currently chairs each of these committees. The Trade Act of 1974 provides that five members of the Senate Finance Committee and five members of the House Ways and Means Committee

---

[13] US Constitution, Art. I, sec. 8.
[14] See Trade Act of 2002, Public Law Number 107–210, x 2103, 116 Statute 933 (6 August 2002).

will be official 'congressional advisers on trade policy and negotiations'.[15] In each case, 'not more than three of [them can be] members of the same political party'.

The Office of the United States Trade Representative (USTR), the administrative body responsible for representing the US on WTO matters, is a creature of Congress. Congress created the Office of the USTR in 1962 (originally named the Office of the Special Representative for Trade Negotiations). Congress did so in order to shift power in executive branch deliberations from those agencies that focus on non-export goals (such as the Departments of State, Treasury, and Defense) to those more likely to defend private commercial interests. The transfer of authority to the USTR permitted congressional committees to call USTR representatives before them and press them to take action on commercial matters or explain the reason for failing to do so. If unsatisfied with USTR policy, Congress retains the power to pass legislation forcing the USTR to act, to withhold or withdraw trade negotiating authority, to block ratification of signed agreements, to limit budgetary allocations, or to hold other legislation hostage.

Each of the congressional trade subcommittees is served by Republican and Democratic staffers. Many of these staffers formerly worked at the USTR or at other US trade agencies, such as the International Trade Commission. They specialize on trade matters and work closely with the senior Republican and Democratic committee members. They informally meet with USTR negotiators a couple of times each week on trade matters. When a negotiation reaches a crucial stage, they may meet daily or multiple times per day, including by teleconference call. In this way, staffers learn about textual developments in WTO negotiations. If anything controversial arises, they can immediately call the respective congressional representatives who, in turn, can contact USTR, hold a press conference, or otherwise attempt to exercise pressure. In addition, members of Congress can request research on trade matters from the bipartisan Congressional Research Service and the International Trade Commission, as well as Congress's General Accounting Office and the Congressional Budget Office. Through these reports, they can spotlight issues that are of particular concern to them and their constituents.

When Congress granted the Bush administration 'trade promotion authority', it added a new institutional mechanism for overseeing trade

---

[15] See Trade Act of 1974, Public Law 93–618, x 161 (3 January 1975). See generally H. Shapiro and L. Brainard, 'Trade Promotion Authority Formerly Known as Fast Track: Building Common Ground on Trade Demands More than a Name Change' in 35 *The George Washington International Law Review* (2003) 1 (providing an excellent overview of congressional mechanisms for overseeing US trade policy).

policy—the Congressional Oversight Group (or COG).[16] The COG consists of members of the Senate Finance Committee, the House Ways and Means Committee, and the chairs and ranking members of other congressional committees of jurisdiction (those committees having jurisdiction over matters implicated by trade agreement negotiations). The COG is to receive 'detailed briefings', access to negotiating documents, 'the closest practicable coordination' with the USTR 'at negotiating sites', and 'consultation regarding ongoing compliance and enforcement of negotiated commitments'.

Under guidelines drawn up with the USTR, the designated congressional representatives are to receive a copy of any trade proposal before the USTR tables it. Congress would like to receive these proposals at least two weeks in advance, although, at times, they receive the proposals only the night before the proposals are tabled. In the words of one congressional staffer, this latter practice, although sometimes unavoidable in the heat of negotiations, can make 'a joke' of the process, since congressional representatives cannot provide meaningful input.[17]

Members of Congress may attend WTO ministerial meetings as members of the US delegation. They largely self-appoint themselves in practice. Congressional representatives receive 'detailed briefings' and copies of negotiating texts. The Democrats' ranking member on the Senate trade subcommittee, Senator Max Baucus, has demanded that representatives of both parties of Congress be in the negotiating room at WTO negotiations as 'observers'.[18] He so far has lost that battle.

Members of Congress have also demanded more oversight of WTO dispute settlement panels. These demands increased following a series of US losses in challenges to US trade remedy laws. A growing number of congressional representatives accuse WTO dispute settlement panels of 'legislating'. Senator Baucus, formerly chair of the Senate Finance Committee, has labelled WTO tribunals 'kangaroo courts', lambasting them for having 'attacked and weakened . . . our laws' by 'exceeding their authority'.[19] When Congress ratified the Agreement

---

[16] See Trade Act of 2002, Public Law Number 107–210, x 2107, 116 Statute 933 (6 August 2002). A democratic staffer on the House Ways and Means Committee maintains that the democratic 'fast track bill', which lost in the House by only 'three votes', would have granted Congress greater 'leverage' over trade policy so as to 'create incentives' for better USTR 'collaboration' with Congress. Telephone interview, 28 May 2003.

[17] Interview with democratic staffer on House Ways and Means Committee, 28 May 2003.

[18] See Statement of Senator Baucus to Congressional Oversight Group meeting, 19 September 2002.

[19] Congressional Record, S4308–26 (online edn, 14 May 2002). Senator Baucus also maintains that 'WTO dispute settlement panels are legislating . . . They are making up rules that the United States never negotiated.' Speech on Senate floor, 26 September 2002.

Establishing the WTO in 1994, the Senate Majority leader, Robert Dole, proposed the formation of a commission of US judges to assess whether WTO judicial decisions conform with WTO treaty obligations. Congress has considered new legislation to adopt a version of a 'WTO Dispute Settlement Review Commission'.[20] The Commission would review, in particular, WTO panels' adherence to prescribed standards of review.

USTR and congressional representatives jockey over the substance and timing of what USTR provides. Although congressional representatives, especially when they are from the opposing party, maintain that they do not receive enough information from USTR, they nonetheless consistently retain pressure on the trade agency. With the assistance of its professional staff, the US Congress is able to oversee WTO developments to a much greater extent than the legislative bodies of probably all other WTO Members.[21] According to I. M. Destler, the dean of studies of American trade politics, 'Open US trade policy had been founded, in part, on closed politics.'[22] The days of those 'closed politics' appear to be over. Given the increasing domestic regulatory implications of WTO negotiations, this development is likely positive.

III. PRACTICE OF INTERPARLIAMENTARIAN MEETINGS: CONFLICTING EUROPEAN PARLIAMENT AND US CONGRESSIONAL PERSPECTIVES

Prior to the turmoil at the 1999 WTO Ministerial Meeting in Seattle, the WTO and the General Agreement on Tariffs and Trade (GATT) paid little heed to parliamentarians. Starting with the Seattle Ministerial Meeting, parliamentarians began to meet on WTO matters in interparliamentarian sessions, and the WTO Director-General's office began to pay more attention to them. Members of the European Parliament presented a proposal at the Seattle Ministerial Meeting for 'the establishment of a Parliamentarian Assembly attached to WTO', which was unanimously adopted by those parliamentarians present.[23] However, most WTO Member governments, as well as many parliamentarians, did not support

---

[20] See World Trade Organization Dispute Settlement Review Commission Act, S. 676, 108th Cong., 1st Session (2003).

[21] For example, Brazil's Ambassador to the WTO, Mr de Seixas Correa, notes how Brazilian parliamentarians do not have the staff resources held by members of the US Congress. De Seixas Correa formerly was Brazil's Ambassador to the US, and he notes how 'impressed' he was with Congress staff. Discussion in Florence, 26 June 2003.

[22] I. M. Destler, *American Trade Politics* (3rd edn 1995) at 68.

[23] E. Mann, *The Initiative for a Parliamentary Assembly within the WTO: Background and State of Play*, 6 April 2003.

the concept of a standing WTO Parliamentary Assembly. The focus then switched to the addition of an informal 'interparliamentary dimension' to the WTO that potentially could evolve over time. An interparliamentarian meeting was held at the Doha Ministerial Meeting, and another at the Ministerial Meeting in Cancún.

European parliamentarians have been entrepreneurs in coordinating these interparliamentarian meetings. A number of the meetings were funded, in part, from the EU's budget, including to help cover the expenses of delegates from ACP countries (the African, Caribbean, Pacific Group of States with which the EU has preferential trade arrangements). The European Parliament adopted resolutions in conjunction with the WTO ministerial meetings in Seattle, Doha, and Cancún. Although its resolutions initially called for the establishment 'of a Standing Parliamentary Body of the WTO',[24] the European Parliament has become more flexible in its approach. A member of the European Parliament, Mr Carlos Westendorp y Cabeza, chaired the interparliamentarian post-Doha Steering Committee, which was delegated the task of studying and coordinating the addition of a parliamentary dimension to the WTO.[25] The European Parliament has institutionalized the selection of European parliamentarians to attend WTO Ministerial Meetings, determined in proportion to political representation within the European Parliament. Twenty members of the European Parliament attended the Doha Ministerial Meeting and 26 attended the Cancún meeting.[26] The EU's Trade Commissioner, Pascal Lamy, has supported the European Parliament's initiatives to add a parliamentary dimension.[27] The European Commission has proposed to 'hold, on a yearly basis and back to back with the annual open WTO meeting, a meeting of parliamentarians of WTO members'.[28]

---

[24] See European Parliament resolution on the communication from the Commission to the Council and the European Parliament on the EU approach to the WTO Millennium Round, COM (1999) 331 (18 November 1999) para. 74; and European Parliament resolution on the Third Ministerial Conference of the World Trade Organization, para. 4.

[25] Steering Group, Parliamentary Conference WTO, 3 July 2002.

[26] Representatives from the European Parliament were complemented by members of national European parliaments. The German and French parliaments were each represented by 11 members, and the Danish parliament by ten members. See List of Participants, Cancún Session of the Parliamentary Conference on the WTO, 9 and 12 September 2003, online at http://www.ipu.org/splz-e/cancun.htm.

[27] See e.g. P. Lamy, 'The Convention and Trade Policy: Concrete Steps to Enhance the EU's International Profile', 5 February 2002 (speech on file) ('Trade is the only common policy without any role in the Treaty for the European Parliament . . . The Commission pushed hard for a greater role for the Parliament until the very last hours of [the Treaty of] Nice, but the IGC refused. All of them. We are fighting again.'); and S. Charnovitz, 'Trans-Parliamentary Associations in Global Functional Agencies' in 2 *Transnational Associations* (2002).   [28] Commission document cited in E. Mann, *supra* n. 23.

The Inter-Parliamentary Union (IPU), the Geneva-based international organization founded in 1889 which traditionally has coordinated meetings of national parliamentarians, has also helped promote the addition of a parliamentary dimension to the WTO.[29] In June 2001, the IPU organized an interparliamentarian meeting in Geneva, with which the European Parliament was not formally associated. Then WTO Director-General Mike Moore spoke at the meeting, supporting the concept of interparliamentary meetings on international trade matters. There initially was some rivalry between the IPU and the European Parliament, with the IPU calling for a less formalized parliamentary role. The European Parliament and IPU subsequently began to work together, co-organizing an interparliamentarian meeting at the WTO's 4th Ministerial Meeting at Doha, Qatar, in November 2001. There, participating parliamentarians again adopted a declaration calling for a closer association of parliaments with the WTO. They agreed to establish the Post-Doha Steering Committee to prepare future interparliamentary conferences on trade policy.

In February 2003, the European Parliament and IPU co-organized a Parliamentary Conference on the WTO in Geneva, which over 500 delegates from around 75 national parliaments attended. The participating parliamentarians issued a declaration proclaiming that 'the days when foreign policy, and more specifically trade policy were the exclusive domain of the executive are over'.[30] The declaration called for adding a 'parliamentary dimension' to the WTO that will 'evolve around regular parliamentary meetings held initially once a year and on the occasion of WTO Ministerial Meetings'.

The European Parliament and IPU next co-organized the holding of two interparliamentarian sessions on 9 and 12 September 2003 at the WTO Ministerial Meeting in Cancún, Mexico. The first session focused on the substance of the negotiations, and the second focused on a parliamentarian declaration and an assessment of the Cancún meeting. Over 300 delegates participated, representing 70 countries, the broadest representation to date. Most parliamentarians came as members of the official national delegation to the WTO, which was the first time that many nations included parliamentary representatives at a WTO ministerial meeting. WTO Director-General Supachai Panitchpakdi, EC Trade Commissioner Pascal Lamy, and the Mexican Minister of

---

[29] See IPU website, online at http://www.ipu.org/english/home.htm. The UN General Assembly has recognized the IPU as the world organization for national parliaments. See 'Cooperation between the United Nations and the Inter-Parliamentary Union', G. A. Res. 57/47, UN Doc. A/RES/57/47 (2003).

[30] See Final Declaration, Parliamentary Conference on the WTO, 17–18 February 2003.

Foreign Affairs and chair of the ministerial meeting Luis Derbez addressed the parliamentarians. For the first time, there was significant political debate among parliamentarians that reflected a left–right political divide. Parliamentarians from the International Parliamentary Network, a leftist group founded in Porto Alegre, Brazil, passed their own declaration which was not reflected in the declaration adopted at the main interparliamentarian meeting.

The USTR and US Congress have been much less enthusiastic about adding a parliamentary dimension to the WTO than the European Parliament. Although the former Republican chair of the Senate Finance Committee, William Roth, was more active in interparliamentary affairs, helping to coordinate the interparliamentarian meeting at Seattle in November 1999,[31] current congressional leadership appears disinterested. At Doha, only one Congressman and one congressional staffer attended the ministerial meeting. No US congressional representative or staffer attended the steering meetings in Brussels in May 2002 or in Geneva in June 2003, even though a place on the Steering Committee is reserved for the US.[32] No US representative attended the interparliamentarian meeting in Geneva in February 2003, even though over 500 delegates were present.

Similarly, although over 30 congressional representatives came to the Cancún Ministerial Meeting, not one of them, or any of their congressional staff, attended either interparliamentarian session.[33] Rather, US congressional representatives were briefed by and oversaw USTR, met with trade associations, coordinated positions with USTR, and met with negotiators from other WTO Members.[34] Congressmen met or attempted to meet with WTO delegates from Brazil, India, Mexico, China, the EC, and certain WTO 'allies'. In response to the rise of the G21 group of developing countries that posed a serious challenge to traditional US and EU dominance of multilateral trade

---

[31] See Steering Group, Parliamentary Conference WTO, Strasbourg, 3 July 2002. However, although around 40–50 US congressional representatives attended the WTO Ministerial Meeting in Seattle, largely on account of its proximity, House members generally did not attend the interparliamentarian meeting. Telephone interview with congressional staffer, 4 June 2003.

[32] Interview with member of the Steering Group, 23 June 2003.

[33] Congressional representatives had yet to arrive in Cancún for the 9 September session because of votes scheduled in Congress. They missed the 12 September meeting because USTR had scheduled a briefing meeting at that time. Telephone interview with a democratic staffer of a member of the House of Representatives, 5 December 2003.

[34] I was informed that this would be the pattern well before the ministerial meeting. Telephone interview with congressional staffer, 4 June 2003. Confirmed by separate telephone interviews with two Democratic congressional staffers, 5 December 2003. In the words of one staffer, 'congressional representatives would discuss with USTR what sort of message to get across and what information to solicit' when representatives met with other WTO delegates.

negotiations, congressional representatives worked with the USTR to attempt to break up the developing-country block and isolate its leaders. Leading congressmen, such as Senator Charles Grassley, Republican chair of the Senate Finance Committee, and his Democratic counterpart Senator Max Baucus, threatened to block congressional approval of any bilateral or regional trade agreement with any country associated with the developing-country block.[35] Within weeks, Costa Rica, Colombia, Peru, and others dropped out of the G21 group in order to maintain separate trade negotiations with the US.[36]

The US government and US Congress generally are not supportive of global interparliamentarian meetings. In particular, the US Congress looks adversely upon the Inter-Parliamentary Union. Although the US was a founding member of the IPU, Senator Jessie Helms led the passage of legislation in October 1998 requiring the US to withdraw from the IPU if the IPU did not accept certain US congressional demands.[37] Then Secretary of State Madeleine Albright notified the IPU of the US's withdrawal from the IPU in September 2000, although there is some question as to whether the US has taken the proper steps procedurally.[38]

Many congressional members feel antagonistic toward the IPU, in part, because many of the IPU's members are not democracies and, in part, it appears to be left-leaning. A Libyan representative sits on the IPU Executive Committee, which, from a US perspective, undermines the IPU's interparliamentary claims. Similarly, the IPU meeting immediately preceding the one at Cancún was held in Havana, Cuba, on 3 September 2003. The mere idea that an interparliamentarian meeting could be held in Cuba delegitimizes the body in the eyes of the majority

[35] 'Grassley Threatens FTAs Post-Cancun; Aldonas Offers Softer Tone', 21(38) *Inside U.S. Trade* 1 (19 September 2003); and 'Baucus Questions CAFTA Given Lack of Concessions, G–21,' 21(38) *Inside U.S. Trade* 5 (19 September 2003). A congressional staffer noted that Senator Grassley was not present at Cancún, but that he worked, as is often the case, through issuing press releases after consulting with a congressional staffer. Telephone interview, 5 December 2003.

[36] See 'Costa Rica, Colombia, Peru Drop Out of Shrinking G–21', 21(41) *Inside U.S. Trade* 1 (10 October 2003); and D. Pruzin, 'Three More Latin American Countries Defect from G–21 Alliance on Farm Trade', 20 *International Trade Report* (BNA) 1685 (16 October 2003) (noting 'the defections bring up to six the number of Latin American countries that have left the G–21 since the WTO's Cancún ministerial meeting last month . . . in response to what is widely being viewed as pressure from the United States to break up the group').

[37] See Pub. L. 105–277, Div. G, Title XXV, x 2503(a), 21 October 1998, 112 Stat. 2681–836. For example, the Congress allegedly insisted that the IPU accept a US 'donation' in a reduced amount, as opposed to a US membership fee equal to 15 per cent of the IPU's budget. Interview with IPU representative, Geneva, 23 June 2003.

[38] Letter on file with author. According to the IPU, the letter needed to be addressed to it from the US Congress itself, since only parliaments are members of the IPU. Interview with IPU representative, Geneva, 23 June 2003.

of the US Congress. As one congressional staffer remarked in reference
to the Havana meeting, 'need one say more'.[39] The staffer pointed out
that 'the IPU was not involved' when former Senator Roth played
a supportive role at the interparliamentarian meeting at the WTO
Ministerial Meeting in Seattle.[40] In contrast, the IPU maintains that
its goal is to spur parliamentary involvement in international
and domestic governance. For example, the only reason that the IPU
meeting was held in Havana was because a United Nations (UN)
meeting on desertification and climate change was scheduled there.[41]
Many US congressional representatives, however, associate the IPU with
the UN and global governance endeavours generally, upon which they
look warily, although the IPU is not a UN subsidiary.

Congress feels antagonism or disinterest not just to interparliamentarian meetings under the IPU. In 1995, the US and EU created an
inter-parliamentarian forum to address transatlantic issues, named the
Transatlantic Legislators' Dialogue. This legislators' dialogue, however,
has been unsuccessful, largely because of the lack of US congressional
interest. When meetings are held in Brussels, allegedly no one from
Congress attends. When meetings are held in Washington, representatives from the European Parliament are ignored and generally feel
mistreated.[42] A trade specialist within the US government recalls 'no
serious [congressional] attempt to work with other parliamentarians' in
'over twenty-five years of work'.[43] As former Congressman David
Skaggs remarks, there is 'an aversion of members of Congress to get out
of the country'.[44] Politicians fear that an opponent can make an issue
out of their foreign travel 'in a thirty second TV commercial'.[45] In fact,
a number of Republican members of the House allegedly boast that they
do not even have a passport.[46]

There remains one interparliamentarian grouping with which
members of the US Congress have participated with somewhat
greater enthusiasm—the North Atlantic Treaty Organization (NATO)

[39] Telephone interview with Republican staffer to the House Ways and Means
Committee, 4 June 2003.
[40] This point was also volunteered by a Republican staffer on House International
Relations Committee, telephone interview, 2 December 2003.
[41] The meeting is organized by the Secretariat of the Convention to Combat
Desertification. See IPU website, *supra* n. 29.
[42] Telephone interview with EU Commission representative, 28 May 2003.
[43] Telephone interview with US civil servant on trade matters, 28 May 2003.
[44] Remarks at *WTO Negotiators Meet Academics* conference in Florence,
26 June 2003.   [45] *Ibid.*
[46] See A. Zitner, 'Critics Taking Aim at Bailout of IMF' in *Boston Globe* (7 October
1998) (citing comments of Republican Brent Scowcroft, as well as the remarks of former Republican House majority leader Dick Armey about not leaving the country for
over 12 years).

Parliamentary Assembly. This assembly meets about twice per year, in addition to staff-level meetings.[47] Participating congressional representatives may have shown greater interest because the assembly's representatives are limited to Western democracies (i.e. NATO members) and the assembly played an important expressive role during the Cold War by incarnating the concept of a democratic West. In addition, the assembly has addressed security policy, and, since the fall of the Berlin Wall, the incorporation of Eastern Europe into the alliance, areas having relatively greater political prominence. Yet US congressional representatives similarly showed greater support for the IPU during the Cold War years, when the US Congress typically sent the largest delegation to IPU meetings.[48] If NATO does not define a new role for itself in the post-Cold War world, congressional involvement in the NATO Parliamentary Assembly could also wane.

When I raised the issue of congressional oversight and democratic control of the WTO with the staff of Congress's trade and foreign relations committees, as well as with the heads of staff of some congressional representatives, *no one expressed much interest in interparliamentarian meetings*. Such meetings were viewed as either purely symbolic or, even worse, legitimizing an illegitimate process. As one congressional staffer remarked, 'if you try to systemize interparliamentary meetings, the danger is creating something that itself bears no legitimacy.'[49] Under this view, legitimacy should take place 'through national oversight', whereas the establishment of an interparliamentary body actually would be 'hurting legitimacy'.[50] From this US perspective, the international level simply is 'not ready' for this sort of development.

IV. EXPLAINING DIVERGENT US AND EU PARLIAMENTARIAN VIEWS

The two primary explanations for the divergent approaches of US congressional representatives and European parliamentarians are their relative power over trade policy, on the one hand, and their experience with supra-national governance mechanisms, on the other. US congressional representatives wield significant authority over trade policy and can advance their constituents' interests best through working with the USTR in intergovernmental WTO negotiations. Congressional representatives generally see 'nothing to be gained from

---

[47] Telephone interview, Democratic staffer for Senate Foreign Relations Committee, 28 May 2003.   [48] Interview with IPU representative, Geneva, 23 June 2003.
[49] Telephone interview with US congressional staffer, 27 May 2003.   [50] *Ibid.*

participation' in interparliamentary meetings.[51] They are concerned that establishing such a forum could reduce US leverage in negotiations, providing an 'opportunity for people who are losing in the big negotiation'.[52] They do not wish to create an opportunity for WTO Members without power to have a new forum to advance their positions. If congressional representatives wish to obtain WTO rule changes, they work with the USTR, sometimes playing 'good cop–bad cop' roles. Congressional representatives hold press conferences and attempt to exercise pressure on trade negotiators from other members about US demands and constraints. They see little to be gained by talking with other parliamentarians who have little to no power in determining the final negotiated WTO texts. Rather, many US congressional representatives believe that their constituents' interests are best advanced when the USTR negotiates in a closed intergovernmental context.

The US Congress's position also is explained by the relative uniqueness of Congress's institutional position compared to that of other parliamentary bodies. When congressional representatives vote against the executive's proposed policy, even though the executive is from the same political party, they do not threaten to bring down the government on a 'vote of confidence'. In contrast, there is greater party discipline in most parliamentary systems because of the risk of a call for new elections. Since the US executive and legislative branches are more likely to disagree on trade policy in the US political context, Congress's chief focus lies in overseeing and controlling the US executive branch, not in interacting with parliamentarians from other countries.

In contrast, European parliamentarians currently hold no formal power over EU trade policy. As European parliamentarian Erika Mann writes, 'the European Parliament's participation in the area of commercial policy is essentially limited, while national legislatures' competences have even been reduced in the course of the European integration'.[53] European parliamentarians thus could increase their authority through participation in WTO interparliamentarian meetings. By adding a parliamentary dimension to the WTO, the European Parliament also strengthens its bargaining position against EU Member states over the need to enhance Parliament's role in the formation and ratification of EU trade policy.

Furthermore, European parliamentarians have experienced the meshing of national constitutional orders through the creation of

---

[51] Telephone interview with US civil servant, 28 May 2003.

[52] Telephone interview with congressional staffer to House Ways and Means Committee, 4 June 2003.   [53] Mann, *supra* n. 23.

supra-national institutions. Their experience informs their views concerning the legitimacy of supra-national institutions. As a member of the European Commission states, 'because of the EU experience', European parliamentarians do not hold the 'traditional view' that 'legitimacy lies only at the national level'. Rather, they hold a 'dual view' that supra-national governance mechanisms also need to be developed that are not 'state-based'.[54]

Proponents of a WTO parliament or a Global Parliamentary Assembly often cite 'the European Parliament [as] the laboratory of international democracy'.[55] EU officials often advance this EU model. As European Commission President Romano Prodi states, 'Europe has a role to play in world "governance", a role based on replicating the European experience on a global scale.'[56] There remain obvious problems with applying the EU model to the WTO context. To mention one, the relevant analogue to WTO ministerial meetings in the EU context are EU intergovernmental conferences that negotiate changes to the underlying EU treaties. Yet EU intergovernmental conferences, as reflected in their name, remain dominated by interstate bargaining among European national governments. Nonetheless, the future prospects of a WTO interparliamentary body may result from the outcome of US–EU contention over their respective models for parliamentary oversight of the WTO and other international institutions.[57]

V. PARLIAMENTARY OVERSIGHT AND DEVELOPING COUNTRIES

Most developing countries initially resisted stronger involvement of parliaments in the WTO.[58] A 2002 interparliamentarian Steering Committee, for example, acknowledged 'massive resistance of developing countries' to the option of creating 'a parliamentary assembly as part of the institutional framework of the WTO'.[59] Developing-country

[54] Telephone interview with member of the European Commission handling trade matters, 28 May 2003.

[55] Quote from L. Levi, *World Federalist Movement, International Democracy, United Nations Reforms and the Role of Global Civil Society* (Port Alegre, World Social Forum, 4 February 2002).

[56] Quote in R. Kagan, *Of Paradise and Power* (2003) (concerning divergent US and European views toward international law and institutions).

[57] Compare Kagan, *supra* n. 56, with Levi, *supra* n. 55. Levi explicitly stresses the need 'to defeat the opposition of the United States' to 'the plan for a world democratic order:' *ibid.* at 6.

[58] Charnovitz, *supra* n. 27, citing a statement by EU Trade Commissioner, Pascal Lamy.

[59] Steering Committee, Parliamentary Conference WTO, Strasbourg, 3 July 2002. Many developing-country parliamentarians, however, may be quite interested in participating in WTO parliamentary meetings.

government concerns, of course, vary. Some countries fear that the addition of a parliamentary dimension would add to their burden, exacerbating the disadvantages that they already face in WTO negotiations on account of resource asymmetries. The addition of a parliamentary dimension, they fear, would favour large countries with larger delegations. Other developing countries fear that adding a parliamentary dimension shifts the focus toward the WTO's 'external transparency', away from their chief concern over the WTO's 'internal transparency' toward developing country members.[60] Still other developing countries fear that their parliamentarians could undermine their negotiating positions, and they want to be sure that they can 'control' the process.[61] Some fear that parliamentarians could defend vested protectionist interests, and possibly undermine a mutually beneficial trade deal.

Nonetheless, developing country governments also recognize that they could gain from the addition of some form of interparliamentarian interface at the WTO level. Many parliamentarians from developing countries favour the holding of parliamentary sessions involving the WTO precisely because it is difficult for them otherwise to obtain information about WTO developments. They find themselves being asked to ratify WTO agreements about which they know little until the deal is done.[62] Developing country executive officials, on the other hand, may find that parliamentarian attendance at WTO Ministerial Meetings could help them explain the difficulty of WTO negotiations in national capitals.[63] The holding of interparliamentarian meetings on the WTO brings parliamentarians into closer contact with their national trade officials simply to prepare for these meetings.[64] Parliamentarians come away from these preparatory sessions and the interparliamentary meetings much more informed about WTO negotiations and their context. In this way, the holding of interparliamentary meetings at the WTO level can foster the US model of domestic parliamentary oversight of WTO rule-making.

[60] Interview with IPU representative, Geneva, 23 June 2003 (relating the statement of a developing country representative from northern Africa).

[61] Interview with Asian developing country representative to the WTO, 24 June 2003. China has an additional concern about Chinese Taipei's potential participation. Interestingly, China sent seven representatives to the Post-Doha Steering Committee meeting of 17 June 2003, which, together with the European Parliament's, was the largest delegation.

[62] Interview with member of the WTO Secretariat, Geneva, 24 June 2003 (relating concerns of African parliamentarians related to him).

[63] Interview with Asian developing country representative, 24 June 2003.

[64] Confirmed in discussions with Brazil's Ambassador to the WTO, Mr de Seixas Correa, and South Africa's permanent representative to the WTO, Mr Faizel Ismail, concerning their experiences, Florence, 26 June 2003.

In addition, the potential benefits to developing countries of adding an interparliamentarian dimension are reflected in US congressional concerns about whether the process could advance the interests of the less powerful in the 'main WTO negotiations'.[65] Developing countries find themselves in weak bargaining positions in trade negotiations.[66] An interparliamentarian consultative assembly could help them advance their perspectives and agendas in global forums, including before the media, provided that they can send representatives to meaningfully participate. For example, issues of primary concern to developing countries, such as Trade-Related Aspects of Intellectual Property Rights (TRIPS) and Public Health, Agricultural Export Subsidies, and Trade in Services were the three substantive topics of debate at the Cancún interparliamentarian meeting. The Cancún interparliament-arian meeting's final declaration specifically called for 'a clear timetable for agreeing upon the phasing out of all forms of export subsidies', and the 'development of Mode 4 of service provision' for the move-ment of persons providing services, of great interest to developing countries.

Ultimately, the impact of a WTO parliamentary body on developing country participation needs to be compared with the current altern-ative of organized global 'civil society' non-governmental representatives advocating on the international stage. According to some analysts, those non-governmental groups with the greatest resources tend to consist of US and European nationals, financed by US and European constituents. In consequence, they too could predominantly reflect US and European perspectives and priorities, even when criticizing certain US and EU governmental positions.[67]

VI. COMPETING RATIONALES FOR ADDING A WTO PARLIAMENTARY DIMENSION OR RELYING ON PARLIAMENTARY OVERSIGHT ONLY AT THE NATIONAL/MEMBER LEVEL

The primary criticisms of an interparliamentary WTO body are (i) that it would provide a facade of WTO legitimacy and privilege an illegit-imate WTO process; (ii) that national parliaments, who remain the sole

---

[65] See *supra* n. 52.

[66] See e.g. R. Steinberg, 'In the Shadow of Law or Power? Consensus-Based Bargaining and Outcomes in the GATT/WTO' in 56 *International Organization* (Spring 2002) 339.

[67] See discussion in G. Shaffer, 'The World Trade Organization under Challenge: Democracy and the Law and Politics of the WTO's Treatment of Trade and Environment Matters' in 25 *Harvard Environmental Law Review* (2001) 1.

source of democratic legitimacy, should focus their attention on enhancing their oversight of national positions within their own constitutional orders; (iii) that well-organized groups, such as Western multinational corporations and single-interest non-governmental groups, would be best placed to lobby and advance their interests through an interparliamentarian body; and (iv) that adding a parliamentary dimension would add further complexity to the already difficult process of multilateral trade negotiations. These views are reflected not only within the US Congress, but also by leading US political theorists. For example, Robert Dahl, the renowned US theorist on democracy, writes, 'I see no reason to clothe international organizations in the mantle of democracy simply in order to provide them with greater legitimacy.'[68] Dahl suggests that 'we treat [international organizations] as bureaucratic bargaining systems'.[69] Similarly, Joseph Nye, Dean of the Kennedy School, writes, 'For now, the key institution for global governance is going to remain the nation state', as 'national governments . . . are the real source of democratic legitimacy'.[70] Moreover, adding a parliamentary process only to the WTO, as opposed to another international institution such as the UN, could again be viewed as privileging trade norms and rules over competing ones.

As testified by mass demonstrations at EU summits over the past years, shifting primary rule-making power away from national legislative bodies to supra-national institutions remains highly contested. Not all affected stakeholders are equally positioned to participate in supra-national legislative and negotiating forums. For example, large businesses can be particularly effective lobbyists at the EU level since the forum is too distant for most constituents to follow policy debates and developments. Not only WTO protestors are concerned about biased participation in supra-national fora.

Finally, some sceptics assert that an interparliamentarian body within the WTO would simply add further institutional complication to an already extraordinarily difficult negotiating process, raising further barriers to multilateral trade liberalization.[71] Other critics of the idea contend that such a parliamentary body would be a waste of resources

---

[68] R. Dahl, 'Can International Organizations Be Democratic? A Skeptic's View' in I. Shapiro and C. Hacker-Cordon (eds), *Democracy's Edges* (1999) at 32.

[69] *Ibid.* at 33.

[70] J. Nye, 'Parliament of Dreams' in *Worldlink* (March/April 2002) 15, 16. See also J. Nye, 'Globalization's Democratic Deficit: How to Make International Institutions More Accountable' in 80(4) *Foreign Affairs* (July/August 2001) 2. However, Nye supports the idea of interparliamentarian meetings 'associated with some organizations to hold hearings and receive information, even if not to vote': J. Nye, *The Paradox of American Power: Why the World's Only Superpower Can't Go it Alone* (2002) at 168.

[71] Telephone interview with Republican staffer on House International Relations Committee, 2 December 2003. This concern was advanced by a number of ambassadors

in light of more urgent needs. The creation of a meaningful WTO interparliamentary dimension would not be cheap. Some policy-makers question the utility of expending resources on such a body. For example, some US congressional critics question whether such a body would serve as a 'boondoggle' for a few elite representatives to travel to exotic places and stay in fancy hotels, eating fancy meals.[72]

In contrast, the primary rationales for adding a parliamentary dimension to the WTO, at this stage, are (i) to inform parliamentarians of WTO developments, thereby enhancing their ability to participate in the formation of national positions in WTO negotiations; (ii) to foster deliberation among parliamentary representatives at the international level so that they better understand the perspectives of peoples from other jurisdictions and, in particular, the implications for other constituencies of WTO and national trade-related policies; and (iii) to monitor, and thereby enhance, public support of the WTO as a multilateral forum for resolving cross-border trade disputes in a relatively neutral and peaceful manner.[73]

Since WTO rules and procedures have significant implications for domestic regulatory policy, parliamentarians see an increasing need to oversee the WTO. Yet many parliamentarians do not receive sufficient access to information on WTO developments. Adding an interparliamentarian dimension to the WTO could facilitate more informed parliamentary oversight of the WTO at the national level. As a Moroccan parliamentarian states, 'A Parliamentary forum at the WTO level could make Parliamentarians from developing countries more aware (of WTO matters), improve their understanding of the WTO system and involve them more in formulating and steering trade policy.'[74] A parliamentarian from Mauritius agrees, maintaining that '[t]he forum could stimulate parliamentary debate at the national level'.[75] The WTO Secretariat itself has organized national and regional parliamentary workshops on the WTO and WTO decision-making processes.[76]

and other high-level national representatives to the WTO present at the conference at the European University Institute in Florence.

[72] Telephone interview with US congressional staffer, 27 May 2003.

[73] The WTO's mission and impact, of course, are not limited to this aspect. As WTO trade rules have expanded in scope, and as their binding effect has increased, the organization has become more controversial.

[74] Remarks of Mr Souhail, Summary Record of the Meeting of the Steering Committee, Brussels, 18–19 May 2002.

[75] Remarks of Mr Gunness, Summary Record of the Meeting of the Steering Committee, Brussels, 18–19 May 2002.

[76] Telephone interview with Patrick Rata, member of external relations division of the WTO secretariat, 16 October 2003. Workshops have been held in South Africa and in Trinidad, respectively, for the Commonwealth Parliamentary Association, and in São Paulo, Brazil, for the Parlamento Latinoamericano (also known as Parlatino).

In addition, national political processes, by their nature, fail to account for the impact of national decisions on foreign constituents. Concomitantly, national political bodies cannot control for the impact of other jurisdictions' decisions on national constituents. One goal of establishing a WTO parliamentary dimension is to foster better understanding among parliamentarians of the perspectives of parties from other jurisdictions affected by national and international rule-making. Under this view, the creation of an interparliamentarian interface could have a socializing effect, as it has within Europe, so that parliamentarians take a broader view of the implications of policy beyond the national level on each other's constituents. It is hoped that the process of deliberation can conduce policy-makers to modify their outlooks, often unconsciously.

Finally, an interparliamentarian body could monitor and support the WTO as a multilateral body needed to resolve cross-border economic disputes in a relatively neutral and peaceful manner. We could be entering a dangerous period of rising nationalist tensions stoked by global economic stagnation or recession. Through supporting a rules-based multilateral dispute settlement system, WTO Members could help protect themselves from the threat of protectionist beggar-thy-neighbour policies that beset the world during the early 1930s. These policies not only exacerbated global economic decline, but also helped spur the rise of anti-democratic political movements. Some WTO institutional supporters wish to establish an interparliamentarian body in order to occupy a public space to offset calls among some 'civil society' critics to disband the organization. Following the Seattle ministerial debacle, WTO Director-General Mike Moore declared that 'elected representatives are the main expression of civil society'.[77] He stressed that 'parliamentarians have a special responsibility to inform their constituents of the benefits a rules based trading system can offer'.[78] Similarly, EU Trade Commissioner Pascal Lamy has argued that a parliamentary consultative assembly could 'lead to stronger public support for the multilateral trading system'.[79] Likewise, at a 2002 inter-parliamentarian steering committee meeting, an Indian parliamentarian remarked, 'the principal task of Parliamentarians [is] to convince

---

[77] Charnovitz, *supra* n. 27. See also Moore, *supra* n. 4 at 121, 235–237.

[78] 'Moore Calls for Closer Parliamentary Involvement in WTO Matters', *WTO Press Release* (21 February 2000).

[79] See S. Charnovitz, *Trans-Parliamentary Associations in Global Functional Agencies* (2002), citing a statement by EU Trade Commissioner, Pascal Lamy. Similarly, a member of the Commission confirms that debate at the international level 'currently is dominated by NGOs, whereas parliamentarians are absent from the debate'. Telephone interview, 28 May 2003.

the public at large of the opportunities which the WTO rules also offer to developing countries for their economic development'.[80]

VII. MECHANISMS FOR ESTABLISHING A WTO INTER-PARLIAMENTARIAN DIMENSION

Creating an inter-parliamentarian dimension to the WTO raises a series of practical issues. First, what should be the role of inter-parliamentarian meetings? Most proponents now agree that an inter-parliamentarian body would act only in a consultative capacity, facilitating an exchange of information about WTO developments and views among parliamentarians. In this way, parliaments could be more informed about WTO matters when interacting with domestic trade officials, and would better understand the political context in which negotiations take place.

Second, would the parliamentary assembly be a standing body within the WTO institutional structure, or would *ad hoc* annual meetings be organized, including at WTO Ministerial Meetings? Most proponents agree that the latter option is more realistic at this stage. WTO Members simply are not ready to modify the WTO's institutional structure. However, inter-parliamentarian meetings could be institutionalized over time, if a parliamentarian dimension were to evolve.

Third, creating a WTO parliamentary dimension would require important organizational decisions, including regarding the funding of meetings; whether the IPU would operate as the coordinating entity or whether an independent network of legislators would be formed; how delegates would be selected (whether by national bodies, through self-selection subject to limits per WTO Member, or otherwise); and how delegates would be apportioned among WTO Members (whether taking account of population, participation in global trade, or any other factor). Rules for the procedure of meetings, including voting rights, would need to be established. When inter-parliamentarian debate became more heated at the Cancún sessions and some left-leaning parliamentarians left unhappy with the meeting's final declaration, coordinators acknowledged the need to establish clear procedural rules for future meetings.[81] As for the designation of parliamentarians, a system eventually could be institutionalized whereby parliamentarians would come from the trade committees of national parliamentary bodies to whom they, in turn, would report.

---

[80] Remarks of Mr Swain, Summary Record of the Meeting of the Steering Committee, Brussels, 18–19 May 2002.
[81] Telephone interview with IPU representative, 7 October 2003.

Fourth, in light of the proliferation of issues addressed within the WTO, how could inter-parliamentarian meetings play more than a symbolic role? In order for inter-parliamentarian meetings to focus on substance, parliamentarians could form subcommittees and working groups with issue-specific expertise, just as in national parliaments. Again, they could assign parliamentary staffers specialized in trade matters to work with these subsidiary bodies. These committees could prepare working documents and presentations to the plenary inter-parliamentary body. To give just a few examples, working groups could address such issues as the domestic regulatory implications of various GATS negotiations, the impact of agricultural and fishery subsidies, and mechanisms for implementing the Doha Declaration on access to essential medicines. These subcommittees could reflect the committee and working group structures within the WTO. National parliaments ultimately enact laws to implement WTO requirements. Those committees responsible for initiating such legislation could monitor the relevant negotiations up front. Once again, however, implementing this strategy faces significant hurdles on account of national parliaments' constrained resources. Given developing country demands for enhancing the capacity of their own executive agencies to participate meaningfully in WTO negotiations, such resources might not be available, or even requested.

Fifth, how can new technologies be harnessed to facilitate inter-parliamentarian exchange between meetings? Entrepreneurs are developing an inter-parliamentarian internet site that could serve as a virtual forum.[82] Similarly, under an initiative of former WTO Director-General Mike Moore, the WTO Secretariat has prepared periodic electronic bulletins for parliamentarians concerning WTO developments, which Director-General Supachai Panitchpakdi has agreed to continue.[83] Parliamentarians could assign individuals from their national parliamentary staffs to attend to WTO-related matters and coordinate exchanges through the internet. Parliamentarians thereby could work with each other to gather information and further agendas that they mutually support, while remaining locally based. However, since many parliaments lack professional staff, implementing this strategy faces significant challenges.

Sixth, how would the WTO Secretariat interact with the parliamentarians? An inter-parliamentarian liaison office could be established within the WTO Secretariat, possibly in the Director-General's office or in the external relations division. Currently, the Secretariat's external

---

[82] See e.g. N. Dunlop and W. Ury, *The e-Parliament Initiative*, online at www.earthaction. org/eparl/.   [83] Interview with IPU representative, Geneva, 23 June 2003.

relations division is the primary interface, although the Director-General's office was highly involved under Mike Moore. Members of the WTO Secretariat who service existing WTO committees and working groups could also service a WTO inter-parliamentarian body on matters falling within their jurisdiction, including through provision of documents to an inter-parliamentarian internet site, coordinated through the WTO external relations division.

VIII. CONCLUSION

The establishment of a parliamentary dimension within the WTO could promote greater parliamentary oversight at the national level. However, where legislative bodies, such as the US Congress, already wield significant authority over trade matters, including through the creation of negotiating mandates, guaranteed access to trade negotiators and negotiating texts, and ratification of trade agreements, they feel less need to participate in inter-parliamentarian meetings. Time and resources are limited. The more time that parliamentarians spend in inter-parliamentarian meetings, the less that they may participate (indirectly through their own trade representatives) in the 'main' negotiations. In contrast, parliamentarians who wield less authority over national trade policy, and have less access to WTO negotiating documents, benefit more from attending WTO inter-parliamentarian meetings. Inter-parliamentarian meetings help them monitor not only WTO negotiations, but also their own government's positions.

Nonetheless, many parliamentarians may become frustrated by the slow pace and the complexities of WTO agreements and negotiations. They may find that it simply is not worth the investment of time to understand and follow WTO developments when their involvement will bring few pay-offs to their domestic constituencies. Parliamentarians are held accountable primarily through elections. They may find that their chances of re-election are better served if they attend to other issues. In contrast, NGOs, especially single-issue ones, may have much greater incentives to remain engaged with particular WTO matters. As a consequence, there is a chance that NGO oversight and pressure on the WTO will continue, while most parliamentarians' interest in WTO negotiations could wane.

A second rationale for holding inter-parliamentarian meetings is more controversial, in particular within the US—that of fostering a global forum for cosmopolitics. Under this second rationale, parliamentarians should deliberate over the impact of WTO policies and national practices that affect each others' constituents. In an idealized world, were such deliberation to take place in a relatively unbiased manner, and were it to have an impact on domestic and global policy-making, the world arguably would be more democratic and harmonious. However, in practice, such an inter-parliamentarian body would be beset by severe institutional imperfections. Its precise role and structure, were it to exist, thus needs to be subjected to comparative institutional analysis—that is, an analysis that compares the *relative* costs and benefits of institutionalizing this participatory mechanism compared to other institutional alternatives. At this stage, it appears preferable to tread lightly, organize annual meetings where parliamentarians can learn about the WTO, coordinate with their governmental representatives, and interact with each other in an inchoate cosmopolitan process of parliamentary exchange.

19

How Can Parliamentary Participation in WTO Rule-Making and Democratic Control be Made More Effective in the WTO? A United States Congressional Perspective

DAVID E. SKAGGS

More effective democratic control of the World Trade Organization (WTO)—both real and perceived—is desirable. However, this issue is not yet at the top of the list for most Members of Congress. If they worry about trade policy and democratic values, they are more likely to worry about the compromise of democratic values (or legislative authority) built into the United States (US) domestic process for considering trade bills: the no-amendment rules of the Trade Promotion Authority (TPA; formerly, 'fast track') law.

Legitimacy for the WTO arguably depends upon its being grounded in democratic authority and upon its having sufficient transparency to be subject to effective accountability to democratically elected authority. Most Americans, including most Members of Congress, feel at best vaguely uneasy about those dimensions of the WTO.

Let me offer a few observations about the political and psycho-sociological environment that obtains as a typical Member of Congress deals with trade matters.

There is a kind of schizophrenia that infects the American political scene when trade issues come up. On the one hand, a Member may have a rational sense of agreement with the macro-economic arguments for trade; on the other, there is an emotional wariness born of the much-reported micro-economic consequences for particular firms and employees in one's home district.

A Member most often *hears* about trade from angry constituents. The anger may be because of job or business losses, or it may be couched in terms of philosophical opposition: from the left usually because of lack of transparency, and from the right usually because of loss of national sovereignty.

The 'transparency' argument is often a proxy for a generalized mistrust, for concern about democratic accountability, for protectionism, for basic fairness. The 'sovereignty' argument is often a proxy for isolationist tendencies, for unilateralism, or for American exceptionalism. The left and the right can come together in a powerful way in opposition to the WTO regime, with fears about globalization and populist arguments about the increased power of multinational corporations.

That said, it is important to bear in mind that the average US Congressperson (at least those not on House Ways and Means Committee or Senate Finance Committee) is not especially concerned with trade issues except in an episodic way. The episodes occur when, as in 2002, there was a vote on TPA, or since, as specific agreements are presented under TPA for an up-or-down vote. In those instances, the rhetoric can become hot and the vote very close (e.g. the TPA debate and vote).

In each instance, the Representative or Senator also receives a somewhat jarring reminder that, unlike most issues in the US constitutional system of divided legislative–executive power, there is no real opportunity for a legislator to practice the legislative craft on trade bills. It is simply a 'yes' or 'no' vote on a bill that the executive has primarily shaped. (This entails a loss of *legislative* sovereignty, if you will.)

It often comes as a surprise to parliamentary colleagues from the rest of the democratic world to learn that many Members of Congress have mixed feelings about foreign travel. There are several reasons, including the fear that a political opponent in the next campaign will accuse you of taking 'foreign junkets', and the simple disinterest many Members have in going abroad. In any case, in assessing the way Congress approaches trade matters, it helps to understand this aspect of congressional behaviour and the general attitude it evinces about foreign policy—indeed viewed as 'foreign' by the constituencies of many Members.

This is, of course, in sharp contrast to most of the rest of the world, for which there is not such a dividing line between domestic and foreign policy. That has changed somewhat in the US, since 9/11, but not that much.

While, as Professor Shaffer suggests, most Members see their influence and leverage on the *domestic* aspects of trade policy as sufficient to fulfil their responsibilities, there is a small but growing number of Members, I believe, who take more than passing interest in WTO matters.

(On this point, a systematic survey of Members about their views and attitudes would be useful.) These Members probably would see a WTO parliamentary entity of some sort as a healthy and appropriate way to address the concerns of WTO legitimacy, transparency, and accountability, though perhaps more troubling to those upset mainly about loss of US sovereignty to international organizations.

A new entity modelled to a degree on the US Government's 'Helsinki Commission' and its relationship to the Organization for Security and Cooperation in Europe, with observer and consultative status, would be a workable approach. Participation by Members of Congress in that Helsinki process has been pretty good. With the increased attention to globalization and concern about trade, and with some encouragement from congressional leadership, we could expect a decent level of US participation in such a WTO Consultative Assembly.

There is broad concern expressed about the fragility of the international trading system and its susceptibility to attack—from the demagogic or the misinformed or the protectionists. That fragility, it seems to me, is inversely related to the degree of public understanding of the system.

In a world that honours democratic values, the legitimacy of the WTO system must ultimately be grounded in public understanding and support. The question is whether a reasonably well-informed politician or citizen can with reasonable effort hope to understand this system sufficiently to give informed support.

The WTO regime is not one that can be sustained over the long haul by professional elites, no matter how decent and well-meaning. The public must *believe* that it has a stake in liberalized trade, must understand its positive qualities and its institutional limits, and must embrace or at least accept the idea that its enlightened self-interest is well served over the *long term*.

In other words, for a democracy to buy a liberal trading system, its people need the political maturity to appreciate that the occasional short-term costs are outweighed by long-term gains, that the deferred gratification will exceed the immediate. This takes leadership from politicians and from civil society.

Any shoring-up of the fragility of the system depends on the ability of domestic politicians and civil institutions to explain what is going on to their constituents and their society and why it should be supported. (Think of a US Congressperson needing to explain WTO resolution of a pending trade dispute at a town meeting in the middle of the country.) Thus, an increased role for national parliamentarians and Congresspersons and for national and international non-governmental organizations (NGOs) should have a direct bearing on the public's sense of the WTO system's legitimacy and trustworthiness.

The existing flexible and secretive structure may be efficient and practical for those on the inside, but it appears opaque and clubby to those on the outside. Yet, it is those on the outside who must eventually give, or withhold, their consent. So, it is in the enlightened self-interest of the WTO bureaucracy and professionals to move to make their system more accessible to the people—as represented by national politicians and NGOs—on whose consent the system rests.

A 'trust us' approach is unlikely to work for long. Given the high stakes and the consequences of fragility leading to fracture, WTO elites should adopt a preventative strategy of making their work and power as understandable and accountable as possible to the publics of their member states.

WTO personnel do not have primary responsibility for public education, but they do bear responsibility for shaping a system that can be comprehensible to the public. That responsibility extends to encouraging both national-level political leadership and NGOs to help in the process by establishing an institutional structure to facilitate and encourage their consultation and observation.

20

How Can Parliamentary Participation in WTO Rule-Making and Democratic Control Be Made More Effective? The European Context

MEINHARD HILF

I. WHY ARE 'PARLIAMENTARY PARTICIPATION' AND 'DEMOCRATIC CONTROL' BY NATIONAL PARLIAMENTS AND THE EUROPEAN PARLIAMENT NECESSARY?

The concept of democratic governance which confers legitimacy is emerging as an objective principle under public international law. A subjective fundamental right for 'democratic governance' has its source in the right of human dignity and is part of the common European constitutional traditions as expressed in Articles 6 and 7 of the Treaty on European Union (TEU) as well as in Article 3 Additional Protocol of the European Convention on Human Rights (ECHR). The concept of democratic governance means that all acts of any public authority should be legitimized by a democratic process.[1]

National parliaments and the European Parliament can be considered as the predominant sources of legitimacy, which is based on common national and European identity and solidarity. Thus TEU Article 6(1)

[1] A. Beviglia Zampetti, 'Democratic Legitimacy in the World Trade Organization: The Justice Dimension' 37 in *Journal of World Trade* (2003) 1, 105 (107); T. Franck, 'The Emerging Right to Democratic Governance' 86 *American Journal of International Law* (1992) 1, 46ff; M. Hilf, 'New Economy—New Democracy? Zur demokratischen Legitimation der WTO' in C. D. Classen (ed.), *In einem vereinten Europa der Welt zu dienen . . . Liber amicorum Thomas Oppermann* (2001) 427 (431); M. Hilf, 'Ein europäisches Grundrecht auf Demokratie?' in J. A. Frowein *et al.* (eds), *Verhandeln für den Frieden—Negotiating for Peace, Liber Amicorum Tono Eitel* (2003) 745 (747).

states 'The Union is founded on the principles of liberty, democracy, respect for human rights and fundamental freedoms, and the rule of law, principles which are common to the Member States.' Likewise TEU Article 6(3) adds that the Union shall respect the 'national identity' of its Member States. And, finally, TEU Article 1(3) underlines that the relationship between the various European Union (EU) Member States and their peoples has to be built on the principles of coherence and solidarity.

The World Trade Organization (WTO) (and 'globalization') is seen as a danger for the democratic process within each Member's constitutional systems. The same applies in the case of the EU, which has to share its sources of legitimacy with those of its Member States. In a sort of ill-conceived misconception the WTO is only seen as a 'bureaucratic bargaining system' where there is no prospect for democratic legitimacy.[2]

The more the WTO is involved in the exercise of public authority by affecting regulations on the domestic level, the more that authority must be legitimized. This means that it needs a high degree of moral and normative justification for its political and social actions. Thus national regulations relating to the protection of health and environment or consumer welfare can come into conflict with the liberal import of goods and services from other WTO Members. A prime example are the European legislative acts on imports of hormone-treated beef or products containing genetically modified organisms (GMOs). Therefore the WTO and its respective agreements dealing with these conflicts need a high degree of legitimization in order to be respected. The foundation of such legitimization lies in the process of constitutionalization.

A model for this process can be found in Article 23 of the Basic Law (*Grundgesetz* = GG), the German Constitution. GG Article 23 requires that in each case of a transfer of powers there has to be a guarantee that this transfer is based on a commitment to 'democratic, rule of law, social, and federal principles as well as the principle of subsidiarity and provides a protection of fundamental rights essentially equivalent to that of this Constitution'. All these principles are interrelated. One should add the principles of external effectiveness and internal efficiency to the exercise of such powers.[3] In sum, GG Article 23 aims at stopping the tacit erosion of parliamentary influence in European and international relations.

GG Article 23 should be applied in analogy to any transfer and exercise of powers as for example in the case of the WTO.[4] Paragraphs 2–7

---

[2] R. A. Dahl, 'Can International Organizations Be Democratic? A Skeptic's View' in I. Shapiro and C. Hacker-Cordón (eds), *Democracy's Edges* (1999) 19 (33, 34).
[3] Beviglia Zampetti, *supra* n. 1, 105 (106).   [4] Hilf, *supra* n. 1, 427 (432).

of GG Article 23 require—by way of compensation for the transfer of powers—the continuous involvement of the national parliament in the decision-making process of the German and European executive branch in European and international matters.[5] Its aim is to add to the democratic legitimization of the decision-making process under the Common Commercial Policy of the EU and to preserve the residual powers of the sub-national entities such as the federal states (*Länder*) in the fields of, e.g. culture, health, education, and regional policy.

These procedures should be expanded to cover the WTO decision-making process in which the EU as well as its Member States are directly involved.

II. IS THERE A DEMOCRATIC DEFICIT IN THE WTO SYSTEM? WHAT ARE THE OPTIONS FOR PARTICIPATION AND CONTROL?

In the decision-making processes within the WTO system there are various stages at which national parliaments (or the European Parliament) may intervene and exercise their influence.

At a very basic level parliamentary participation might entail an active involvement in the internal national process of preparation of negotiation positions with respect to new agreements under the WTO or with respect to the continuing process of rule-making on a secondary level within the WTO institutions (such as the Ministerial Conference, the General Council or any other sub-institutions like committees and even working groups). However, in practice there seem to be only limited efforts on the part of the responsible executives to seek the support of national parliaments.

In addition, democratic control could refer likewise to a permanent control during negotiations as well as to an *ex post* control of final results. However, there are inherent difficulties to analyse and compromises to evaluate. The most prominent act of an *ex post* control is the parliamentary consent to the ratification of WTO agreements.

The 'democratic deficit' stems from the elaboration of General Agreement on Tariffs and Trade (GATT) rules as from 1947 onwards. These rules were agreed mainly on a provisional basis and thus by-pass the need for formal parliamentary consent. Pre-existing acts of parliaments were 'grandfathered' as being unaffected by any later-in-time GATT law.

---

[5] GG Art. 45 provides for a specific Standing Committee of the German Parliament—'*Bundestag*' (Committee on the European Union).

Rule-making during the Uruguay Round was primarily handled by trade diplomats acting on behalf of legitimated governments. National parliaments and the European Parliament were to give their formal consent to the ratification, but had practically no influence on the decisions, which had already been taken.[6] The well-known exception is the US Congress.

During the Ministerial Conferences of Seattle and Doha an increasing number of members of parliaments were present in order to obtain first-hand information rather than becoming actively involved in the actual negotiations.

The respective parliaments nowadays tend to follow more closely the continuing activities of WTO Members in the 'forum for negotiations' provided by WTO Article III:2. There, the built-in Agenda on issues like the General Agreement on Trade in Services (GATS) and trade in agricultural products as well as the accession of new members, like China, are discussed. Furthermore, matters of interpretation of and amendments to the WTO agreements could be dealt with under WTO Articles IX and X. These procedures have not been used so far.

As to the procedure on accession, it is questionable whether the act of accession may be considered as a unilateral act under public international law, which does not require parliamentary consent. At least in a case like China, the accession should have taken the form of a multilateral treaty because of its far-reaching political and economic ramifications; it should have, therefore, needed the approval of WTO Members' parliaments.[7]

Parliaments try to influence trade policy-making in many ways such as:

• by establishing a permanent dialogue with the respective executives (EC Commission/Member States' executives) on all relevant WTO issues;
• by asking for *ad hoc* or regular reports such as on the follow-ups of given processes and negotiations;
• by participating in the process of giving instructions to negotiators;
• by addressing formal questions;
• by establishing special commissions of inquiry or *enquête-commissions*;[8]

---

[6] See the various reports for different countries in J. H. Jackson and A. O. Sykes, *Implementing the Uruguay Round* (1997).
[7] M. Hilf and G. J. Göttsche, 'Chinas Beitritt zur WTO' in *Recht der Internationalen Wirtschaft* (2003) 161ff.
[8] See e.g. Schlussbericht der Enquete-Kommission 'Globalisierung der Weltwirtschaft—Herausforderungen und Antworten', *BT-Drs. 14/9200* (12 June 2002).

- by voting on resolutions—often even referring to policies beyond their respective legislative powers.[9]

Some parliaments also nominate members to the official negotiating delegation of their country.

There seem to be no formal direct links between the permanent delegations of the EU or the EU Member States at the WTO and members of their respective parliaments. It seems that instructions are given only by the respective executives.

Secondary WTO law is scarce. Anyhow, the rule of consensus (WTO Article IX:1) favours the influence of national parliaments with regard to the respective executives. However, there seems to be little or no 'input-legitimation' provided by such parliaments.

With respect to the Trade Policy Review Mechanism (WTO Article III:4) parliaments do not seem to be involved in drafting the relevant country reports. The final reports are, however, communicated to the respective parliaments with—as far as can be seen—no further attention or follow-up.

With regard to the Dispute Settlement Procedure (WTO Article III:3), national parliaments occasionally request their respective executives to open consultations under the Dispute Settlement Understanding (DSU) or to take specific positions during the ongoing procedure. However, the overall influence is practically insignificant:

- there seems to be no parliamentary influence during the formal consultations as well as in the selection of Panelists or Members of the Appellate Body;
- arguably, parliaments rarely exert influence on their country's legal position before the dispute settlement institutions;
- parliaments have not yet submitted amicus briefs;
- parliaments occasionally deal with the follow-up or the implementation of the Dispute Settlement Body (DSB) decisions (e.g. bananas, hormones);
- neither national parliaments nor the European Parliament have yet challenged the policy of not accepting the direct effect of DSB rulings or of WTO law in general.

---

[9] Thus, in the period 2000–03, the German Bundestag dealt with the Doha Agenda, the ongoing negotiations on GATS (water, education, culture including audiovisual activities, etc.), intellectual property rights, competition, environment, developing countries, social policies, and agriculture. Further the Bundestag and the relevant committees were concerned with the cases handled under the Dispute Settlement Understanding (DSU) such as bananas, shipyards, GMO, US foreign sales corporations, hormones, asbestos, steel, etc.; see also *infra* n. 16.

As an overall assessment, it can be stated that national parliaments and the European Parliament are still at a considerable distance from the decision-making process of the WTO.

III. HOW TO OVERCOME THE LACK OF PARTICIPATION AND CONTROL OF NATIONAL PARLIAMENTS AND THE EUROPEAN PARLIAMENT?

Internal and external transparency are prerequisites for more efficient participation of national parliaments and the European Parliament. The use of the internet facilitates participation and control but hardly adds to an effective interaction of weighing and balancing within the WTO rule-making process.

A WTO or world parliament is illusionary: a *demos* necessitates at least a community which is able to express a common will and communicate on common values.[10]

A WTO Consultative Parliamentary Assembly could be established. Each WTO Member could delegate a reasonable number of up to e.g. four members of their respective parliament. Various groups represented in these parliaments could thus be present on an equal footing at the global level. In composing such an assembly the share of world trade and/or the population should be taken into account. This consultative assembly has been favoured, *inter alia*, by the European Parliament.[11]

The functions of such an assembly could be:

- to receive information;
- to demand and initiate specific actions;
- to address the WTO Secretariat or other WTO organs;
- to inform and to influence and by that to educate their respective national parliaments at home thus creating a better understanding and expertise in WTO matters;
- to help civil society to channel their influence to WTO institutions and finally;
- to build up a net for reciprocal information between various parliaments.

---

[10] See the proposals made by O. Höffe, *Demokratie im Zeitalter der Globalisierung* (1999), ss. 308ff.

[11] P. Lamy, '*What Are the Options after Seattle?*', speech to European Parliament (25 January 2000), online at http://europa.eu.int/comm/commissioners/lamy/speeches_articles/spla09_en.htm; see also P. Bender, 'The European Parliament and the WTO: Positions and Initiatives' in *European Foreign Affairs Review* (2002) 193 at 206ff; M. Krajewski, 'Democratic Legitimacy and Constitutional Perspectives of WTO Law' 35 *JWT* (2001) 1, 167 (184).

It is difficult to conceive how such an assembly could directly enter into contact with the Ministerial Conference or the General Council. Arguably, an observer status could be an option.

Others prefer a consultative body like the EC Economic and Social Committee.[12] This body would be composed of specialists of various economic sectors. Members could either be delegated or even nominated by the respective organizations. Such an institution, however, would not be able to be called a parliamentary body. Experiences with such bodies in the EU as well as in some EU Member States are not very promising, at least in cases where they are merely subsidiary bodies alongside the representative parliament.

In the EU, the European Parliament could become involved in WTO matters in a more efficient way. The procedure of co-decision should be the general rule. All commercial treaties should require the consent of the European Parliament. However, the Constitutional Treaty 2004 has not addressed this question of a more effective involvement of the European Parliament in a satisfactory manner. The European Parliament was not given any new rights at the Nice summit, not even a formal right of consultation, although EC Treaty Article 133(5) in its current form provides that the European Parliament be consulted with respect to the extension of paragraphs 1 to 4 concerning the negotiation and conclusion of agreements on trade in services and trade-related intellectual property rights. The Commission's proposal to apply the co-decision procedure of EC Article 251 to internal measures that implement the core elements of an international agreement in secondary Community law, has not been supported by any delegation. Thus, the status quo remains, that is, an informal information procedure.[13]

The influence of civil society expressed by some 20,000 non-governmental organizations (NGOs) and linked by the internet has increased enormously. Some consider their political pressure to be lacking in legitimacy and destabilizing. With respect to WTO decision-making a number of specific requirements for NGOs could be established which have to be met before they can be admitted to the decision-making process.

Summing up it seems that parliaments are the best accountable representatives of civil society having the closest links to all citizens.[14]

---

[12] T. Oppermann, 'Demokratisierung der WTO?' in R. Briner *et al.* (eds), *Law of International Business and Dispute Settlement in the 21st century, Liber amicorum Karl-Heinz Böckstiegel* (2001) 579 (587ff).

[13] H. G. Krenzler and C. Pitschas 'Progress or Stagnation? The Common Commercial Policy after Nice' in *European Foreign Affairs Review* (2001) 291 (312); M. Hilf and F. Schorkopf, 'Das Europäische Parlament in den Außenbeziehungen der EU' in *Europarecht* (1999) 185 (190ff).

[14] See the corresponding statement of (former) Director-General Mike Moore, *WTO Press Release* 169 (21 February 2002).

IV. OUTLOOK

In order to gain a higher degree of democratic/social legitimacy the WTO should strive to be present more often in public debate and the media. Thus current issues such as GMOs, services negotiations, and others would be more reflected in the deliberations of national parliaments.

The WTO should show a sensitive political and judicial restraint with respect to democratically legitimated national regulations, which are and should be primarily responsible for weighing and balancing competing public interests.

There should be no admission of non-democratic states to the WTO. The EU constitution-building debate within the Convention 2004 shows that international negotiations dealing with highly political issues can be made open to the public and can be organized with active involvement of the public.

As long as individuals with their particular interests are not represented within the WTO decision-making process one cannot foresee a greater output-oriented legitimacy. A Consultative Parliamentary Assembly of the WTO would be an adequate instrument to channel the interests and aspirations of individuals into the decision-making process of the WTO.

Under any circumstances, the ongoing tacit erosion of parliamentary influences should be stopped. A greater degree of democratic legitimization leads certainly to a better respect for the rule of law, can enhance solidarity and the protection of fundamental rights, and finally may add to the effectiveness of world trade law.[15]

The WTO is acting in the limelight of world conflicts and economic interests. The process of its constitutionalization should go on.[16] Enhanced parliamentary participation remains desirable even if it may not lead to a higher degree of free trade and cooperation.

---

[15] See also Beviglia Zampetti, *supra* n. 1, 105 (120).
[16] M. Hilf, 'Die Konstitutionalisierung der Welthandelsordnung—Struktur, Instutionen und Verfahren' in M. Bothe (ed.), *Entschädigung nach bewaffneten Konflikten/Die Konstitutionalisierung der Welthandelsordnung* (2003) 257ff; W. Benedek, 'Kompetenzen und Rechtsordnung der WTO' in M. Bothe (ed.), *Entschädigung nach bewaffneten Konflikten/Die Konstitutionalisierung der Welthandelsordnung* (2003) 283ff.

21

A Parliamentary Dimension to the WTO: More than Just a Vision?

ERIKA MANN

Trade matters used to be highly technical matters, dealt with only by a few trade negotiators and experts. With the conclusion of the Uruguay Round in Marrakesh in 1994, a new era of international trade began. In contrast to the General Agreement on Tariffs and Trade (GATT), the World Trade Organization's (WTO) scope now covers more issues, extending far beyond the traditional domain of tariffs and trade in goods. Its rules reach deeply into domestic affairs affecting areas as diverse as intellectual property, services, telecommunications, or government procurement. The WTO has an increasing impact on neighbouring policy areas such as health policy, environment, food safety, and resource management. In addition, decisions of the WTO judicial bodies now have a binding character. In short, the WTO has a direct impact on the lives of citizens and their societies. At the heart of globalization, the WTO encroaches on some of the traditional prerogatives of legislators as the primary law-makers in democracies.

The days when trade policy was the exclusive domain of the executive branch of government are over.[1] The boundaries between domestic and foreign policy increasingly blur. Political parties—no matter if left or right, opposition or in office—fear that their views are not sufficiently taken into account when their governments negotiate at the international level. The partly violent demonstrations at the Ministerial Conference in Seattle in December 1999 made very clear that trade unions and public interest groups—often promoting a single issue only—also try to influence the WTO's policies. The latest Ministerial Conference in Cancún in September 2003 has demonstrated that the interest civil societies in North and South take in issues such as trade

---

[1] Cf. para. 7, Final Declaration of the Geneva Session of the Parliamentary Conference on the WTO, adopted on 18 February 2003, in Inter-Parliamentary Union and European Parliament (ed.), *Parliamentary Conference on the WTO*, 17–18 February 2003, Geneva, 19–20.

and development, trade and environment, or trade and labour standards has not been some kind of ephemeral *en vogue* phenomenon.

This important shift in WTO competencies and societies' concerns about it should be acknowledged by formally adding a 'parliamentary dimension to the WTO'. This does not prejudge the form, function, and structure parliamentary involvement may take. Since Seattle, several parliamentary meetings on international trade policy have been organized, partly alongside WTO Ministerial Conferences albeit outside the institutional framework of the organization. Now, the time has come to officially recognize and institutionalize the parliamentary dimension to the WTO in order to further enhance transparency and democratic legitimacy of WTO activities.

One may envisage different institutional designs on a continuum ranging from a permanent Parliamentary Assembly to occasional meetings of parliamentarians. Whatever outcome might finally emerge, the most important issue is to institutionalize the process.

I. THE NEED FOR A PARLIAMENTARY DIMENSION TO THE WTO

Globalization of politics may lead to a deficit of transparency, democracy, and accountability if it is not compensated by substantive and procedural mechanisms of checks and balances similar to those that are usually applied to domestic policy-making. This is because the current process of globalization shifts decision-making to the international level and thereby transfers power from legislators to the executive.

However, the traditional legalistic approach holds that international organizations are sufficiently authorized if national governments are scrutinized and overseen by their respective parliaments. Many decision-makers in governments still adhere to this thinking, thereby putting some real constraints on any more ambitious role parliamentarians could play at the international level.

Whatever side one takes, I would argue that parliamentarians must 'go international': to understand the global political process, legislators must have their own network of information sharing and be closely involved in the process. Government officials, enterprises, and non-governmental organizations (NGOs) should all build up global networks, share information, and gain some common understanding of the issues at stake. If trade specialists in national and regional parliaments do not keep pace, they will not obtain the first-hand information, insights, and expertise which are necessary to influence their governments and to shape trade policy on the domestic level.

In democracies, parliaments are usually consulted before international negotiations are kicked off, and they must ratify trade agreements once they have been signed. The United States (US) Congress even wields total control of trade policy, which would allow it to amend international agreements once they are before the Congress for approval. The Congress may, however, decide to transfer authority to the US Trade Representative under an act, which used to be called fast-track procedure and is now known as the Trade Promotion Authority.

At the European level, the present situation is more complex. For certain trade agreements which have, for instance, budgetary implications or set up new institutions (such as the WTO), the European Parliament has to give its assent.[2] If the conditions of EC Article 300, paragraph 3 are not met, the European Parliament plays no formal role. However, the European Commissioner for Trade, Pascal Lamy, has made great efforts to build up informal channels of communication with the European Parliament, which have acquired quasi-formal character. The draft Treaty establishing a Constitution for Europe as adopted by the heads of State and Government on 25 June 2004 considerably strengthens the role of the Parliament in trade policy. When the Constitution is ratified and comes into effect, the Parliament will play a role comparable to the one of the US Congress under fast-track procedure. As far as autonomous trade policy is concerned, the Parliament will become a co-legislator.[3] It will also have to approve all international trade agreements.[4] Furthermore, it formally has to be informed about the state of play of negotiations on a regular basis, on an equal footing with the so-called Article 133 Committee which is following trade policy on behalf of the Council of Ministers.[5]

A great benefit of legislators discussing trade issues internationally is the chance to gain knowledge about challenges other countries are facing, and to develop a shared understanding of issues of mutual interest. Scholars of international relations increasingly value the benefits of communication and arguing as opposed to a pure interest-based approach to negotiations.[6] Looking beyond one's own constituency may thus be a first step to finding a mutually acceptable solution. While it is true that legislators are primarily accountable to their constituencies and will therefore represent their interests, political assessment may nevertheless change over time. A good example of this process is how the European

---

[2] EC Treaty Art. 300, para. 3.
[3] Draft Treaty establishing a Constitution for Europe as of 25 June 2004, Art. III-217, para. 2. [4] *Ibid.*, Art. III-227, para. 7 in conjunction with Art. III-217, para. 2.
[5] *Ibid.*, Art. III-217, para. 3.
[6] T. Risse, ' "Let's Argue!": Communicative Action in World Politics' in 54(1) *International Organization* (2000) 1–39.

Parliament discussed the reform of European agricultural policy during the last few years. In my opinion, it is hard though to change domestic policies independently from general (global) trends. Politicians networking on trade are therefore more likely to contribute to policy change. Furthermore, the global picture is important to explain the need for change back home.

Interparliamentarian communication will also help to overcome the 'clash of cultures' one could witness at the last Ministerial Conference and which contributed to its failure. In Cancún, a very rationalistic approach of 'give and take' bargaining of Northern countries met a moral approach to trade negotiations promoted by developing countries, especially by the so-called 'Group of 90' (African, the African, Caribbean, Pacific group (ACP), and least-developed countries). No doubt, this clash was partly due to problems of communication and misperceptions between negotiators. Geopolitical considerations and ethical arguments were not sufficiently taken into account, especially by the European Union (EU) and US. In contrast, the 'Parliamentary Conference' managed to adopt by consensus, after a long and lively debate, a final declaration including political content on some of the most controversial issues such as agriculture (including cotton). The final statement which was agreed in Cancún, and which arguably strikes a fine balance between interest-based and moral-based arguments, could help to foster common ground for a compromise acceptable to all negotiators in the future.

II. FLASHBACK: WHAT HAS BEEN DONE SO FAR?

The first formal meeting of parliamentarians dates back to the Ministerial Conference in Seattle in December 1999. US Senator Bill Roth and Mr Carlos Westendorp y Cabeza (who was then the head of the European Parliament's Commission for Industry, External Trade, Research and Energy) led the efforts to organize a parliamentary meeting alongside the WTO Ministerial.

This initiative has been strongly supported by the European Parliament. In November 1999, it had adopted a resolution calling on 'the Council and the Commission to examine the possibility of setting up a WTO Parliamentary Assembly to achieve greater democratic accountability'.[7] The proposal was then taken up and unanimously approved by the parliamentarians from WTO Member states present at

---

[7] Cf. para. 74, European Parliament resolution on the communication from the Commission to the Council and the European Parliament on the EU approach to the WTO Millennium Round (COM(1999) 331—C5–0155/1999—1999/2149(COS)), A5–0062/1999.

the Seattle Ministerial, calling for the 'establishment of a Standing Body of Parliamentarians whereby members of parliament can exchange views, be informed and monitor WTO negotiations and activities'.[8]

The year 2001 saw a speeding up of parliamentary commitment towards trade issues. In April 2001, the European Parliament organized a seminar to discuss issues of internal and external transparency and democracy in the world trading system. A parliamentary meeting on International Trade was then organized by the Inter-Parliamentary Union (IPU) in June 2001, which brought together members of parliaments from over 70 countries. Two sessions of a working group have been held in Strasbourg and Geneva in September and October, respectively organized by the European Parliament and the IPU. Both organizations also hosted a one-day parliamentary meeting in Doha, Qatar, on 11 November, which was attended by over 100 members of parliaments. The WTO Director-General, Mike Moore, addressed the meeting. The Final Resolution called for setting up a 'parliamentary dimension to the WTO'.

After Doha, a formal Steering Committee between the European Parliament and the IPU was established. The Committee was composed of parliamentarians from 22 countries and representatives of four international organizations.[9] The two seats reserved for the United States are still vacant. I do hope that colleagues from the US Congress will join the Steering Committee in the future.

The European Parliament created its own Steering Committee. Five members were chosen to manage the process on behalf of the Parliament. At this stage, the European Parliament and the IPU co-finance the meetings and publications to a certain degree.

After Doha, the Steering Committee met twice in 2002 to prepare the Parliamentary Conference in February 2003 in Geneva. The latter was attended by around 300 parliamentarians from 76 countries and by representatives of five multinational parliaments. It was decided to meet regularly and during Ministerial Conferences.

Alongside the 5th Ministerial Conference, a Parliamentary Conference was held in Cancún in September 2003, which was jointly organized by the European Parliament and the IPU in co-operation with the Mexican Congress. For the first time, the final declaration included substantial statements on several key topics of the Doha negotiating round, including

---

[8] Call for establishment of Standing Body of Parliamentarians Representing All Member Countries by the Parliamentarians attending the Third Ministerial Conference of the World Trade Organization, 2 December 1999, Seattle.

[9] Representatives came from the following countries and organizations: Belgium, Canada, China, Egypt, Finland, France, Germany, India, Iran (Islamic Republic of), Japan, Kenya, Mauritius, Mexico, Morocco, Namibia, Netherlands, Niger, Nigeria, South Africa, Thailand, Uruguay, United States of America, Inter-Parliamentary Union, European Parliament, Parliamentary Assembly of the Council of Europe, World Trade Organization. See http://www.ipu.org/splz-e/trade03.htm#postdoha.

agriculture, intellectual property rights, and access to medicines, as well as the General Agreement on Trade in Services (GATS) negotiations. These topics had been prepared by rapporteurs, who presented their conclusions and also summed up the following debate.[10] Just like in the actual WTO negotiations, the debate among the 350 parliamentarians present was very controversial. Due to the requirement to approve the final declaration by consensus, it proved to be difficult to find compromise language on some of these issues. The final declaration was presented by myself since I had written the draft text in cooperation with members of the Mexican Congress, the IPU Secretariat, as well as one of the vice-presidents of the European Parliament.

The most recent parliamentary conference took place in Brussels in November 2004 on the premises of the European Parliament. Parliamentarians held sessions to discuss the developments in agriculture and services negotiations as well as practical aspects of trade-related capacity-building. Speakers included Mr Supachai Panitchpakdi, Director-General of the WTO, Mr Peter Mandelson, the new European Commissioner for trade policy, Mr Oshima, permanent representative of Japan to the WTO and chairman of the WTO General Council, as well as Mr de Seixas Corréa, permanent representative of Brazil to the WTO.

The European Parliament and the IPU are the main drivers of parliamentary involvement. Considering the different histories, functions, structures, and decision-making procedures of the two organizations, it is more than understandable that the cooperation has not always been without difficulties. Political problems occasionally also arose from the lack of congruence between the respective memberships of the IPU and the WTO. Most prominently, Taiwan is a member of the WTO as a Separate Custom Territory without being a member of the IPU. By contrast, Iran is a member of the IPU but not of the WTO. Some WTO Members even lack a parliament or have one that is suspended.

I would suggest that as long as the parliamentary dimension to the WTO is not formally established, one should strive to achieve pragmatic solutions to the non-congruence problems.

III. WHAT CAN BE DONE TO IMPROVE PARLIAMENTARY INVOLVEMENT IN THE WTO?

The 'Parliamentary Conference' has repeatedly called on the respective governments to add the following paragraph to the respective final

---

[10] The rapporteurs were Mr Kharabela Swain, MP (India) on trade in agriculture, Mr Jean Bizet, MP (France) on intellectual property rights and public health, and Mr Kimmo Kiljunen, MP (Finland) on trade in services.

declaration of the Ministerial Conference: 'Transparency of the WTO should be enhanced by associating parliaments more closely with the activities of the WTO.'[11]

Two main schools of thought have emerged in the debate.[12] One approach is to establish, in the long term, an assembly called a 'standing body of parliamentarians', which would be formally linked to the WTO. The second approach is to establish a network-like forum and to work with the WTO through existing structures such as the European Parliament and the IPU. This would avoid creating yet another inter-parliamentary structure needing substantial financial resources.

There are undoubtedly many other possible scenarios. One certainly should look at options for parliamentary involvement with a sense of realism. I believe that at this stage, it is less important to know the exact and precise character of the parliamentary dimensions to the WTO. Institutions tend to evolve over time. There are many examples—the European Parliament is one of them—where parliamentary assemblies initially dubbed as just another 'talk shop' have developed into important political players. The political priority at present should therefore be to establish an inter-parliamentary forum on a permanent basis which is as close as possible to the WTO.

One should keep in mind that a formal assembly linked to the WTO would require consent of all 147 WTO Members, which is clearly lacking. For this reason, it appears that a consensus is now emerging to continue walking down the road that the process is already taking. The inter-parliamentary process for the WTO should evolve around regular meetings held initially once a year and on the occasion of WTO Ministerial Conferences. These meetings would be open to all parliamentarians involved in activities dealing with international trade. No formal membership in terms of countries or individual MPs is necessary. The task of inter-session political administration should be assured by a Steering Committee composed of parliamentary representatives according to a geographical caucus.

There are, however, some issues calling for clarification and improvement in the short run. As a priority, formal channels of communication

---

[11] E.g. para. 13, Final Declaration of the Cancún Session of the Parliamentary Conference on the WTO, adopted 12 September 2003.

[12] See K. Chutikul, 'Options for a Parliamentary Dimension of the WTO' in Inter-Parliamentary Union and European Parliament (ed.), *Parliamentary Conference on the WTO*, 17–18 February 2003, Geneva, 85f.; See also S. Charnovitz, 'Trans-Parliamentary Associations in Global Functional Agencies' in 2 *Transnational Associations* (2002) 88–91; P. Lamy, 'Global Policy without Democracy?,' paper presented at the Conference on the *Participation and Interface of Parliamentarians and Civil Societies for Global Policy*, 26 November 2001, Berlin; G. Shaffer, 'Parliamentary Oversight of WTO Rule-Making: The Political, Normative, and Practical Contexts' in this volume.

and forms of cooperation with the WTO should be developed. Moreover, the function and modalities of the parliamentary meetings could be reviewed and specified, taking also into account the institutional evolution of the WTO.

To improve scrutiny over national trade policies, the Parliamentary Conference to the WTO could craft minimum standards for the information and consultation of national parliaments in trade policy. A comparison of best practices should inform these recommendations. Another useful suggestion aiming at the same objective has been made at the Cancún meeting. An 'international trade day' could be held once a year in all national parliaments in order to increase awareness of trade issues. Sadly, this proposition was not accepted by the plenary at the Cancún meeting.

IV. CONCLUSION

The process of creating a transnational network of parliamentarians specializing in trade issues is well on its way. Of course, obstacles remain on the road and will have to be overcome. A fundamental legal problem is to clarify the question of how to maintain the principle of separation of powers between WTO Members' executive and legislative branches. What actually happens if parliamentarians from a given country say exactly the opposite of what their government's position is? In countries where parliaments retain far-reaching competences in the field of trade policy, this may leave government negotiators in an awkward situation. The US is a case in point. With the extension of its competences in the draft Constitution for Europe, the European Parliament may soon have the same problem.

With the compromise on the Doha Work Programme reached at the WTO General Council in Geneva on 1 August 2004, the WTO process is back on track. Spotlights are now turned on the next Ministerial Conference in Hong Kong on 11–12 December 2005. Parliamentarians will hold their next meeting at this occasion. A strong participation of colleagues from all over the world will certainly help to contribute to a positive climate for the negotiations, although I personally do not expect that the round will be concluded in Hong Kong.

22

A Few Thoughts on Legitimacy, Democracy, and the WTO

JAMES BACCHUS[1]

I am fortunate in having the benefit of a unique combination of experience. I am the only person who has had the privilege of serving as a trade negotiator in the Office of the United States Trade Representative, as a Member of the Congress of the United States, and also as a Member of the Appellate Body of the World Trade Organization.

This unique combination of experience gives me the benefit also of a unique perspective. I have shared at different times in my life the different points of view of, first, those trying to conclude international trade agreements in the executive branches of states; then, later, those trying to affect international trade agreements in the legislative branches of states; and now, most recently, those trying to help uphold international trade agreements in the quasi-judicial branch of an international institution comprised of states. So I am able to see, uniquely, from the differing perspectives of them all.

What does this unique personal perspective tell me about the 'legitimacy' of the World Trade Organization (WTO)? What does it tell me about the 'democratic governance' of the WTO? And what does it all tell me in answer to these questions about how much the world understands the role of the WTO as an international institution?

Above all, the unique vantage point of my unique perspective shows me that there is too little understanding in the world of the essential 'legitimacy' of the WTO, and of the extent of the 'democratic governance' that already prevails in the WTO. It shows me that there is too little understanding in the world about what the WTO really is, and about how it really works. Regrettably, this is so even among many of those who are in important positions of responsibility in the world, and who thus might be expected not only to know better, but also to help

---

[1] These are his personal views, and are not the views of his colleagues on the Appellate Body or the official views of the WTO.

encourage a better understanding in the world of the reality of the WTO.

There are many examples of this lack of understanding. Perhaps foremost among them is the mistaken, but widespread, notion that the WTO is some 'illegitimate' global entity that is somehow separate and apart from the various individual 'nation states' of the world, and that aspires in some vague way to an overarching global dominance. A corollary of this mistaken notion is the equally widespread view that the WTO can attain global 'legitimacy' only by eliminating a perceived 'democratic deficit'. From this basic misunderstanding about the basic nature of the WTO have emerged many of the concerns about the WTO that have been heard from protesters, from pontificators, and even from quite a few legislators in the ongoing debate about the 'globalization' of the world.

The truth is, the WTO is not some 'illegitimate', self-aggrandizing global suzerain that seeks in some sinister and mysterious fashion to impose its arbitrary will on the sovereign nations of the world. Far from it. The truth is not nearly so melodramatic. The truth is simply this: the WTO is only a label. The WTO is only the name that the vast majority of the sovereign nations of the world have chosen to use to describe their shared efforts to work together to lower barriers to world trade and to increase the flow of world trade. The WTO is nothing more nor less than—at last count—147 sovereign countries and other customs territories working together as something they themselves have chosen to call '*the WTO*'.

Yes, there is a place called 'the WTO'. There is a worldwide head-quarters for 'the WTO' in a lakeside building in Geneva, Switzerland. There are several hundred people from all over the world who work there. About half are translators. About half of the rest are clerical workers. The remainder are lawyers or economists or international civil servants of some other technical sort who work for 'the WTO'. I am one among them.

Altogether, the entire administrative endeavour of the WTO costs the 147 Members of the WTO a total of about US$80 million annually. Of this sum, about US$15 million is paid in annual dues by one WTO Member, the largest trading nation in the world, the United States of America. This amount reflects an annual calculation of the American share of overall world trade. This is a lot of money. But, in global terms, and in terms of the American federal budget, it is a pittance. In my own experience, I used to obtain, on a good day, more than US$15 million for a federal appropriation for a new road or a new bridge in my Congressional district in Florida when I was a Member of the Congress of the United States.

If numbers of personnel and amounts of financial resources are any measure, then the WTO is hardly the global juggernaut that appears so ominously in the heated speeches of 'anti-global' activists. The entire annual budget of the WTO is less than the annual travel budget of the International Monetary Fund, and it is considerably less than the annual budgets of a number of the well-funded global non-governmental organizations that sometimes seem so apprehensive of the WTO. Even so, apprehension remains in much of the world about the global role of the WTO, and about who and what those of us who work for the WTO are truly working for.

There is no need for such apprehension. The several hundred of us who work for 'the WTO' do not work for ourselves, or for some expansive global entity that is accountable and answerable only to itself. In all we do every day, we work *exclusively* for the 147 Members of the WTO. We work *only* for what they work for. We do *only* what they *agree* we should do. We are simply the agents of their shared will as expressed by consensus in the 'Member-driven' institution that is 'the WTO'.

The source of the 'legitimacy' of the WTO is the Members of the WTO. The 'legitimacy' of the WTO is a 'legitimacy' that derives from, and is inseparable from, the *individual legitimacy* of each of the individual 'nation states' that, together, comprise 'the WTO'. Far from being an effort to subvert the sovereignty of individual states, the WTO is, rather, a mutual effort by individual states to assert and to sustain their sovereignty in an effective way in confronting the many challenges that face individual states in an increasingly 'globalized' economy.

There is, therefore, 'democratic governance' of the WTO to the extent that the individual states that comprise the WTO are democracies. And, the fact is, the vast majority of the Members of the WTO are democracies. They have representative governments that are chosen by their citizens in free and democratic elections. The delegates to the WTO who assemble in Geneva and elsewhere in the world to make decisions as 'the WTO' have been appointed by the elected leaders of those governments in accordance with their own domestic traditions and their own democratic institutions.

I would be the last to contend that the 'nation states' of the world are as democratic as they should be. I know of no one involved with the WTO who would. But this should not obscure the fact that gains for democracy have been made throughout the world in recent years. Nor should it blind us to the reality that many of those recent gains for democracy are reflected in the membership of the WTO, even as they are reflected in the membership of the United Nations and other international institutions.

I, for one, would argue that, in part, the recent gains for democracy are a consequence of the recent gains from trade. And I, for one, would argue also that still more gains for democracy can be made if we make still more gains from trade. This is an important part of what must be understood more fully about the WTO.

Unquestionably, there is more that can and should be done to help ensure 'democratic governance' of the WTO. Unquestionably, for example, there are additional gains for democracy that can be made in how the Members of the WTO deliberate on trade issues and in how they decide on trade agreements in their ongoing work *within the WTO*. There are numerous additional improvements that can and should be made in the ways the Members of the WTO work together toward building a worldwide consensus as 'the WTO'. On this, the Members of the WTO agree. Indeed, the Members of the WTO are busy trying their best right now to make some of those needed improvements.

But, from my perspective, the most pressing issues of 'democratic governance' relating to the WTO are not in the day-to-day work within the WTO. From my perspective, the 'democratic deficit' relating to the WTO that demands the most attention is, instead, the shortfall from the fullest measure of representative democracy that persists within some of the individual states that comprise the WTO. To the extent that the individual states that are the Members of the WTO become more truly democratic, and to the extent that those individual states are more democratic in the making of their own domestic trade policies, the combined efforts of those individual states in their combined capacity as the WTO will be more truly democratic as well.

Despite all the misplaced apprehensions about the WTO, the reality is that the WTO is not in any way a threat to sovereign, individual democratic states. Quite the contrary. The WTO is a shared effort by sovereign states to assert their continued sovereignty. The very idea of individual states is premised on a world in which there can be *independence*. In contrast, our increasingly 'globalized' economy is a consequence of a world in which there is, increasingly, *interdependence*. The WTO is a shared effort by the sovereign Members of the WTO to make continued political *independence* meaningful within the context of increased economic *interdependence*. The success of the WTO, thus far, is encouraging evidence of their shared success in doing so.

From my perspective, derived from my varied experience, the notion that there has been a marked decline in the significance of individual 'nation states' in the world has, like the rumored death of Mark Twain, been greatly exaggerated. The noted American theorist of international political economy, Robert Gilpin, has made this same point, and has concluded that, 'For better or worse, this is still a state-dominated world.'[2] The WTO is one example that supports this conclusion. In the face of 'globalization', the WTO is an international assertion by individual states that individual states remain the most significant political actors in the world. As I see it, the success of the WTO makes sovereign states stronger, not weaker. It proves that independence is still possible for sovereign states in an increasingly interdependent world.

If this is so, then how best can the continued significance of individual states be asserted in their combined efforts as 'the WTO' in a way that is consistent with 'democratic governance'? One obvious way is by doing more to ensure that the actions of Members of the WTO *as the WTO* reflect the democratic will of the world's peoples as manifested not only in the executive branches, but also in the *legislative* branches, of the many democratic governments of WTO Members. And one important way of doing this is by involving more individual legislators within individual states in a more effective way in the making of the national trade policies that are ultimately transformed by international trade negotiations into international trade agreements.

How best can individual legislators within individual states, as the elected representatives of the citizens of those states, be given such a say? Here, I confess, the American in me shows through in my personal perspective. For it seems to me that the best way of assuring legislators around the world of more say in shaping the WTO-based world trading system is the way that has long been followed by the United States of America. The 'American model' of ensuring that the legislative voice is heard and is reflected in the national executive expression of trade policy has long given American legislators a strong and effective voice in the making of America's trade policy, and, in my view, is well worth emulating in other parts of the world.

The American model is a logical consequence of the Constitution of the United States of America. Under the US Constitution, the executive branch of the US government has certain treaty-making and other constitutional authority to conduct foreign policy.[3] Likewise, under the Constitution, the legislative branch of the US government has constitutional authority 'to regulate commerce with foreign nations'.[4] These constitutional authorities overlap, and, over time, the executive and the legislative branches of the US government have succeeded in working out ways to work together effectively in the shared exercise of their respective constitutional authorities.

---

[2] R. Gilpin, *Global Political Economy: Understanding the International Economic Order* (2001) at 363.   [3] Constitution of the United States of America Art. II.
[4] *Ibid.* Art. I, sec. 8.

These American ways of working together enable the Members of the Congress of the US to have their necessary constitutional say in the making of international trade policy, and in the concluding of international trade agreements. They are consistent with American democratic traditions, and with the basic constitutional integrity of American institutions. They are also, for the most past, highly effective in asserting America's interests in international trade. Not least, they are effective in asserting those interests in a democratic way that helps ensure 'democratic governance'.

Specifically, there are a number of statutory and other mechanisms in the US that make this possible on a continuing basis. The Office of the US Trade Representative (USTR) is one important example. By statute, the USTR answers to both the President and the Congress. The statutory delegation by the Congress of 'trade promotion authority' to the President is another example. The ability of the President to negotiate international trade agreements is constrained by the extent of the authority the Congress delegates to the President to do so. The recent creation of the new Congressional Oversight Group by the Congress in the Trade Act of 2002 is the latest example.[5] The new Congressional Oversight Group is the newest of many statutorily mandated means of ensuring ongoing executive consultation with the legislative branch of the US government on issues relating to international trade.

Admittedly, the American model of legislative involvement in the ongoing efforts of the executive branch to conclude specific trade agreements and to implement overall trade policy is precisely that—an 'American' model. It is uniquely American. This model has emerged from the uniquely national circumstances of national institutions in the US. Moreover, Americans are not alone in such democratic endeavors. Many other Members of the WTO have domestic practices that are equally democratic. Nevertheless, these American practices are, from my perspective, proven examples of effective ways for legislators to help ensure 'democratic governance' in the making of national and, ultimately, international trade policy-making, and, as such, are worthy of consideration by other Members of the WTO when making their own sovereign choices about how best to govern their own democratic participation in the WTO.

Other suggestions have been made by others. Some of these suggestions may also be worthy of consideration. Should the elected national legislators of the Members of the WTO spend more time in Geneva and elsewhere learning about what the WTO really is, and about how it

---

[5] Trade Act of 2002, Public Law Number 107–210, Section 2107, 116 Statutes 933 (6 August 2002).

really works? Certainly. Should elected national legislators from different Members of the WTO get together more often to get better acquainted, and to talk about better ways their countries can work together as Members of the WTO? Of course. Should the Members of the WTO continue to try to enhance 'democratic governance' and to ensure the effectiveness of 'democratic governance' within the elected councils of the WTO? Surely they must.

However, to my mind, the principal focus of efforts to improve the 'legitimacy' of the WTO-based trading system by increasing the 'democracy' in international trade policy-making should *not* be on creating any new international mechanisms to supplement those means that already exist, and that are already in the process of being improved within the WTO. Rather, the principal focus of those efforts should be on ensuring more 'democratic governance' of national trade policy-making through more effective domestic mechanisms of 'democratic governance' within the national governments of the individual states that are the Members of the WTO.

Such efforts will vary with the varying uniqueness of national circumstances and national institutions. But common to them all, in my perspective, can be some of the basic aspects of the American model of ensuring national legislators a larger say in the making of trade policy at the *national* level. This larger say *nationally* can then be reflected *internationally* in the expression of national trade policies by national delegates of WTO Members in their international deliberations as the shared international enterprise known as 'the WTO'.

23

The WTO and Cosmopolitics

STEVE CHARNOVITZ[1]

In early 2001, European Commissioner for Trade Pascal Lamy gave a noted lecture at the London School of Economics entitled, 'Harnessing Globalization: Do We Need Cosmopolitics?'[2] Lamy explained that better global governance requires a system which provides for interconnections between governments, markets, and civil society. He further suggested that non-governmental organizations (NGOs) and civil society can contribute to legitimization by fulfilling a demand for new social intermediaries which is not provided elsewhere. Reflecting on the globalization debate, pre-September 11, Lamy opines that the term 'governance' connotes too much control, and instead offers the term 'cosmopolitics'. With reference to the short-term challenges for the World Trade Organization (WTO), he points to the idea of pulling on cosmopolitical constituencies for support.

Lamy's lecture inspired new thinking about the role of cosmopolitics generally and in the WTO. In the article 'WTO Cosmopolitics', I sought to build on Lamy's speech by tracing the history of the cosmopolitan idea in international law, by identifying the eight ways in which cosmopolitics is manifested, and by advocating a thicker cosmopolitics in the WTO in order to make that body more effective in liberalizing trade.[3] What follows in this report are my own views, and should not be attributed to Commissioner Lamy.

[1] Thanks to H. E. Ambassador Julio A. Lacarte for being the commentator on this paper, and to Merit Janow for helpful suggestions which predate her appointment to the Appellate Body.
[2] Online at http://www.lse.ac.uk/collections/globalDimensions/lectures/harnessing GlobalisationDoWeNeedCosmopolitics/transcript.htm.
[3] S. Charnovitz, 'WTO Cosmopolitics' in 34 *New York University Journal of International Law and Politics* (2002) at 299, online at http://www.nyu.edu/pubs/jilp/main/issues/34/h.html. One way in which cosmopolitics is practiced is issue alliances among governments. See E. Taylor, 'Brazil, India, South Africa Join to Foster Trade, Possible WTO Bargaining Positions' in *BNA Daily Report for Executives* (11 June 2003) at A-5.

I. OUR COSMOPOLITICAL WTO

If conventional politics is the idea that unitary states each speak with one voice, and that the only relevant players in the trading system are the voices of the 147 WTO Members, then surely conventional politics in that pure form no longer exists in the WTO. Today, more than ever before, the governmental delegates to the WTO are looking outward, to situate negotiations about trade within a world constitutive process. For example, in June 2003, the WTO Secretariat held a three-day public symposium to examine the challenges on the road to Cancún. At the symposium, WTO Director-General Supachai Panitchpakdi announced that he had set up an informal Business Advisory Body and an NGO Advisory Body.[4]

In 1969, Professor John Jackson could write that even though the General Agreement on Tariffs and Trade (GATT) has 'an immense impact on the individual citizen, there is presently no *direct* relationship between GATT and such private persons'.[5] The same point could have been made in 1979, and in 1989.

But during the 1990s, the traditional insularity of the GATT/WTO ended. Cosmopolitics came to the WTO—most painfully at Seattle in 1999. Cosmopolitics came to the WTO because the public and NGOs began to see how emerging trade law affected numerous social, environmental, development, cultural, and ethical concerns. NGOs were not willing to leave these matters to trade technocrats, and were not willing to assume that the representatives of the Members could find the optimal solutions on their own.

The discussion here focuses on the WTO rather than its constituents. That is, to what extent does the WTO currently embrace cosmopolitics, and what more should be done? Let me briefly highlight some of the most important developments since 1995:

- Using its authority in Article V:1 of the Marrakesh Agreement, the WTO General Council has pursued and accepted cooperation with other intergovernmental organizations, such as the United Nations Food and Agriculture Organization (which has observer status).
- Using authority in Article V:2 of the Marrakesh Agreement, the WTO has increased consultation and cooperation with NGOs. For example, the WTO Secretariat posts new NGO position papers periodically on the WTO website.[6] In April 2001, the WTO joined the World Health

---

[4] D. Pruzin, 'WTO Chief Sets up Advisory Bodies with Business, NGOs to Boost Dialogue' in *BNA International Trade Reporter* (19 June 2003) at 1044.

[5] J. H. Jackson, *World Trade and the Law of GATT* (1969) at 187.

[6] Online at http://www.wto.org/english/forums_e/ngo_e/pospap_e.htm.

Organization, the Norwegian Foreign Ministry, and Global Health Council (an NGO) to hold a workshop on affordable drugs.[7] In September 2003, NGOs around the world received accreditation to be observers at the forthcoming Ministerial Conference in Cancún.

- In 2001, WTO Member governments agreed at Doha to express a commitment 'to making the WTO's operations more transparent, including through more effective and prompt dissemination of information, and to improve dialogue with the public' (para. 10).

- The WTO has achieved a great deal of transparency in its own operations, particularly through its website. For instance, many documents are downloadable on a timely basis, including now the *Trade Policy Reviews*. A current calendar of WTO meetings is provided. The value of this free public access is enormous. Just to give one example, anyone with internet access in any part of the planet can read and download freely the Agreement on Trade-Related Aspects of Intellectual Property Rights (TRIPS) from the WTO website in at least three languages. We have become so used to such access that it may sound trivial. But I would invite the reader to go to the website of the International Civil Aviation Organization and try to download a copy of its founding Convention.[8]

- The WTO Secretariat works hard at improving public understanding of the WTO and its processes. Everyone from the trade neophyte to the trade expert can learn a lot by spending 30 minutes periodically perusing the WTO website and looking at 'WTO News', 'Trade Topics,' the 'Community/Forums', etc. The availability of such information not only better informs interested individuals, but also enhances the accountability of the WTO to governments and to the market. Recently, the new *Global Accountability Report* gave the WTO high marks for its website and overall accountability.[9]

- WTO Director-General Mike Moore established a public advisory committee reporting to him, and recently Director-General Supachai Panitchpakdi has set up a private committee to prepare a report on the challenges and opportunities facing the WTO.[10]

- The WTO Appellate Body has ruled that panels and the Appellate Body may consider amicus curiae briefs.[11] In that one respect, the WTO is ahead of most other international tribunals.

---

[7] Online at http://www.wto.org/english/tratop_e/trips_e/tn_hosbjor_e.htm.

[8] Online at http://www.icao.int.

[9] Online at http://www.oneworldtrust.org/Ch99/htmlGAP/report/report.htm.

[10] WTO, 'WTO Director-General Establishes a Consultative Board on the Future of the Multilateral Trading System' in *WTO Presse/345* (June 2003).

[11] See P. -M. Dupuy, 'Sur les Rapports Entre Sujets et "Acteurs" en Droit International Contemporain' in L.C. Vohrah *et al.* (eds), *Man's Inhumanity to Man: Essays on International Law in Honour of Antonio Cassese* (2003), 261, 274.

- In at least two instances, WTO dispute panels have sought information from the World Intellectual Property Organization, which has responded.[12]

This report intentionally starts with the goods news in the hope of orienting the conversation toward the future and making it pragmatic. Let us take as a baseline the current openness of the WTO, and the trends in other organizations, and ask whether greater transparency and non-governmental participation would be good for the trading system.[13] The emphasis here on transparency and the non-governmental role, as two important dimensions of cosmopolitics, reflects the Kantian tradition in international law.

II. IMPROVING WTO TRANSPARENCY

The WTO needs to do much more to improve transparency. Let me begin with transparency at the national level before discussing the WTO level.[14]

One of the least known and most positive features of WTO law is the rule requiring national governments to manifest transparency through procedures for notice and comment.[15] In the years since the Uruguay Round, the value of such 'good governance' provisions has become better understood as a driver of development and equity. Issues of transparency are again on the agenda in the Services negotiations of the Doha Round.

The WTO could strengthen requirements on Member governments to provide more information to the public and to the WTO. Let me give one example on a substantive topic of WTO law that loomed important in the past ten years—that is, Article XX of the GATT which provides General Exceptions. In 1969, Professor Jackson made the interesting suggestion that governments be required to report all instances where regulations are utilized when those restrictions are consistent with GATT only by virtue of Article XX.[16] Recognizing as we do today the delicacy of litigating the Article III and XX interface, we would probably not want to phrase the notification requirement in that exact way. Nevertheless, Professor Jackson was surely right in contending that

---

[12] This occurred in United States—Omnibus Appropriations Act of 1998 and United States—Section 110(5) of the US Copyright Act.
[13] Certainly, greater governmental participation would also be good for the WTO.
[14] This chapter does not discuss the vital issue of internal WTO transparency, that is, the transparency of WTO decision-making to the governmental members.
[15] These provisions build on GATT Art. X which requires publication of trade regulations. [16] Jackson, *supra* n. 5 at 744.

more information about such measures would help governments bring order to international trade.

Although the WTO imposes many rules for reporting and transparency by WTO Members, the WTO treaty does not reflexively impose similar requirements on the WTO itself. The WTO constitution does not posit openness and transparency as a fundamental value of trade law nor does it state that individuals have any *right* to information. The one semi-exception occurs in Annex 3 of the Understanding on Rules and Procedures Governing the Settlement of Disputes (DSU), which states an obligation of a Member (upon request by another Member) to provide a non-confidential summary of its submission that could be disclosed to the public. So far, the experience under this rule has been disappointing. It has not led to significantly greater disclosure of submissions to panels.

Even without a constitutional commitment to transparency, the WTO can and should take legislative action to open up more to civic society. The two main reasons for doing so are that openness enhances legitimacy and that openness can help to build public support for the WTO's mission. Social and economic actors need information in real time about what the WTO is doing if these private actors are going to be able to influence governments. Here is one possible programme to enhance openness:

- Rules are needed to strengthen protection for business confidential information.
- Other categories of WTO secrecy should be defined and instituted as needed.
- Aside from that, all other WTO documents should be publicly available. Recently, I read that the Chairman of the Special Session of the Dispute Settlement Body had prepared a Chairman's Text, denoted 'JOB(03)91'. That document is not available on the WTO website, however, and an email I sent to the WTO Enquiries Office asking for a copy went unanswered.[17] A similar problem occurred at the Doha Ministerial Conference where none of the negotiating documents was made public until the negotiations had ended. The only logic to such a policy would be to keep the public from knowing what law-making is going on until it is too late to influence it.
- Written submissions to panels should be posted on the WTO website by the Secretariat.
- Observers should be permitted to watch proceedings of the WTO General Council and the Dispute Settlement Body.

---

[17] Of course, the document was immediately available to subscribers of *World Trade Online*, to which I have access both at my law firm and at the law school where I teach.

The above current list does not include opening sessions of WTO panels to the public. The United States (US) government has made this proposal, but it has drawn little support from other governments. The proposal of the European Communities (EC) of March 2002 was a bit more cautious; it would allow the parties to decide whether certain parts of a panel or Appellate Body proceeding should be open to the public. Such a change would reverse the rule in DSU Appendix 3 which states that the panel shall meet in 'closed session'. The EC proposal would have been an interesting experiment. While on this subject, let me note that the US–Singapore Free Trade Agreement provides that unless the parties otherwise agree, a dispute panel will hold at least one public hearing (Article 20.4(4d)). (This is an example of the way in which bilateral trade agreements can offer opportunities for policy experiments not possible in Geneva.)

III. ENHANCING PARTICIPATION IN THE WTO

The Marrakesh Agreement provides for consultation and cooperation with NGOs. This provision mirrors a similar provision in the 1948 Charter of the International Trade Organization. The designers of the post-war trading system anticipated that there would be space for NGO participation, and yet that vision of a competition culture has not been fulfilled.

The advocates of NGO participation sometimes undermine their cause by claiming that NGOs can boost the representativeness of the WTO. Many of the WTO ambassadors have found that baffling because they do not see how NGOs can improve on the official representatives of governments. Instead, the NGO community should not promise more than they can deliver. The value added from NGOs is not really enhanced representation in Geneva.[18] Rather, it is that NGOs can inject new energy, ideas, and values that may help to improve deliberating in the WTO. NGOs' proposals can improve the market of ideas that undergirds the WTO. NGOs also provide a mechanism for an individual to influence other governments beyond her own. Such transnational politics is especially important in the WTO given its consensus decision-making rule in which one foot-dragging government can impede the entire Organization.

Thus, in terms of the analytical framework employed for this Conference, the value of NGOs for the WTO is not so much that they

---

[18] The WTO Secretariat has stated that 'Citizens are expected to be represented at the WTO through their governments.' WTO, *WTO Policy Issues for Parliamentarians* (May 2001) at 14, online at https://secure.vtx.ch/shop/boutiques/wto_index_boutique.html.

may enhance the 'input legitimacy' of the WTO, but instead that NGOs can enhance 'output legitimacy' by leading to better, more effective intergovernmental decisions. By de-emphasizing the issue of whom NGO spokespersons represent, we can avoid the fruitless (yet currently popular[19]) efforts to vet NGOs so as to examine who their members are and where their funding comes from. International organizations should not care whether an NGO has 100 members or 1 million. Counting is for votes. Ideas are weighed not by how many people hold them, but rather by their scientific or philosophical merit.

The three major entities in the international system are: (A) intergovernmental organizations, (B) parliamentarians, and (C) NGOs. All three should gain a greater participatory role in the WTO.

A. Intergovernmental organizations

Functional international organizations make progress through specialization, but are vulnerable to tunnel vision. That's why it is important for international organizations to work closely with each other. The WTO is much better at this than was the GATT, but more cooperation would be beneficial.[20]

Let me give one example. In April 2003, the WTO Secretariat released a Special Study titled 'Adjusting to Trade Liberalization'.[21] One chapter of the report was about how 'Government can facilitate the adjustment process', and this chapter contained several pages of interesting information about social safety-nets, labour markets, education and training, export promotion, etc. WTO attention to the difficult challenges of adjustment is certainly appropriate. Yet one wonders why the Secretariat sought to reinvent the wheel rather than work with the functional international organization with expertise in worker adjustment, the International Labour Organization (ILO)? Did the WTO Secretariat not know that the ILO has a comparative advantage on worker issues?

B. Parliamentarians

Elected parliamentarians are a growing and important part of cosmopolitics. This volume contains a number of papers on that issue.[22]

---

[19] Recently, three new publications have been launched to report on NGOs. They are: *NGO Monitor*, *NGO Watch*, and *NGO Watch Digest*.

[20] See G. P. Sampson, 'Is There a Need for Restructuring the Collaboration among the WTO and UN Specialized Agencies so as to Harness their Complementarities?' in this volume.   [21] WTO, *Adjusting to Trade Liberalization*, Special Study No. 7 (2003).

[22] See Chapters 19–22.

C. NGOs

Greater NGO participation could help make the WTO more effective and would, at the very least, enhance the voices of developing countries at the WTO. A full implementation of Article V:2 would provide for accreditation of NGOs and for observer status in some of the WTO committees, bodies, and councils. Many models exist for how this could be done in United Nations practices, and in the 80-plus years of experience of NGO participation in intergovernmental organizations in Geneva. One possibility is an Advisory Economic and Social Committee, as proposed in the International Law Association.[23] Another possibility would be to convert the new advisory committees appointed by the Director-General into official advisory committees to the WTO.

My own preference is that international NGOs be mainstreamed into the WTO's functional committees and bodies. For example, development NGOs might be invited to observe the Committee on Trade and Development; food safety and agriculture NGOs might be invited to the Committee on Sanitary and Phytosanitary Measures; transparency and consumer NGOs might be invited to the Working Party on Domestic Regulation. For the first two-year cycle, the role of the NGOs might be purely observational, but once governments gain more confidence, opportunities could be provided for NGOs to make presentations.

IV. CONCLUSION

This author wishes that he could be more optimistic that the WTO would act soon to improve external transparency and participation. Unfortunately, two barriers exist: one is the *de facto* consensus decision-making rule. The other is that many WTO Member governments are not democratic, and therefore may not share the values of transparency and participation.

At the Conference in Florence in June 2003, one of the senior ambassadors present cautioned the participants to avoid 'wishful thinking'. Injecting a dose of realism into a policy discussion is always a good idea, and led me to reflect on whether it is merely wishful thinking that NGOs participation will promote free trade and increase public support for the WTO. Perhaps it is. Even so, such an effort seems worth trying because the advocates of free trade have the more intellectually honest case to make.

---

[23] E. U. Petersmann, 'Constitutionalism and WTO Law: From a State-Centered Approach Towards A Human Rights Approach in International Economic Law' in D. L. M. Kennedy and J. D. Southwick (eds), *The Political Economy of International Trade Law* (2002) 32, 62–63.

Two trends of the past few decades point to a need to refine our understanding of transgovernmental organizations. One is the ever-expanding need for international cooperation. The other is the deeper rooting of democratic expectations throughout the world. As a result, the challenge for all international organizations will be to better connect the decision-making of the organizations to the democratic processes in each country. In an era where cosmopolitics will be ascendant, the WTO cannot be aloof. It should continue down the path of expanding transparency and public participation.

24

Transparency, Public Debate, and Participation by NGOs in the WTO: a WTO Perspective

JULIO A. LACARTE

Diplomacy and international negotiations have traditionally thrived on discretion and secrecy; indeed, they could not exist if they were deprived of them. Habits became deeply ingrained for career diplomats, and successive generations of negotiators throughout the world became accustomed to carrying on their business far from prying eyes. Indeed, there was little demand outside the governing sphere to know more of these activities, and public opinion as we know it today had little interest in becoming better acquainted with foreign affairs.

In historical terms, it was but yesterday that the proposal for open agreements openly arrived at threatened to shake old and cherished practices to their foundations. All this has changed. Today, we all want to know all about these things, in greater detail the better.

Partly due to the conditions surrounding its establishment—a small membership with a substantial number of influential countries pursuing essentially parallel objectives, delegates who in the main knew each other intimately, and the fact that it was a trade agreement being provisionally applied with the ensuing uncertainty as to its permanence—the General Agreement on Tariffs and Trade (GATT) functioned for many years sheltered from the public gaze. It was essentially run by trade mandarins who were experienced in diplomacy and economic relations. Ministerial meetings were few and far between. All in all, closeness was the rule.

For lengthy periods, minutes of meetings were undecipherable for the uninitiated, since they did not identify the speakers; and other times there were no adequate minutes, for example as recently in the Uruguay Round. A good bit of dispute settlement today in the WTO would be simpler if only negotiators had set out clearly their intentions, in the black and white of agreed minutes, during the Round.

This is the negotiating culture inherited by the WTO, whose extent and importance today it would be both rash and difficult to underestimate. Procedures and habits built up over more than half a century do not disappear overnight; and they tend to perpetuate themselves, specially when change often calls for approval by a consensus of the membership.

Let us endeavour to put the question of openness in the WTO in a reasonable perspective. Recently, citizens of the world were able to follow on live television and radio United Nations Security Council discussions and a number of national parliamentary debates on the issue of Iraq. Here, the question was of war and peace, of life or death, of possible material destruction and social suffering. Nobody seems to have objected to the publicity surrounding differing and even confrontational governmental positions and policies. And rightly so.

Responsible people want to know, they need to know, what is happening in the world and how their governments are behaving. This is part—a big part—of the spread of democracy. As globalization brings us closer together, so information on international relations increases in importance. Educational levels advance, access to information is made massively available, and larger and larger numbers of citizens feel they should participate in some way in events which, they increasingly realize, shape their lives.

This growing awareness is something new because of the widening scale in which it occurs. Needless to say, the extraordinary increase in the number and significance of non-government organizations (NGOs) is one way in which these demands for information are being met.

So, should the WTO—and other intergovernmental organizations—stick to existing practices, or should they respond to a seeming evolution in the way in which international relations are looked upon by people in general? The reply should be clearly affirmative, within the bounds set by practicalities and realism.

A great deal can be done along these lines in the WTO, without impinging on the unavoidable and necessary confidential side of diplomacy. Reverting to my earlier example, does any one doubt that the public debates on Iraq were accompanied by intense, secret diplomatic contacts? If public discussion and private negotiations can take place simultaneously in the Security Council, they certainly can do so in the trade field.

Television and radio coverage of meetings when there is a demand for it, public access to meetings of WTO Councils, open hearings of panels and the Appellate Body, and a substantially enlarged availability of documentation, spring to mind. None of this would really run counter to the need for confidentiality in trade negotiations, since Members could at any time go into private session when they considered it advisable, or decide to restrict sensitive documents.

Going on to the role of NGOs, this has to be seen from at least three basic angles: each one of these organizations very often represents a particular interest which may be at odds with the position taken by other NGOs; there is a very large number of NGOs, to the point that the WTO expectation was that more than 1,000 of them would seek registration at the Cancún Ministerial Conference; and I believe there is a widespread view among developing countries that since the most powerful and resource-rich NGOs are based in developed countries, anything that enhances their role in the WTO is likely to operate to their detriment.

NGOs are an important segment of civil society and should be able to contribute fresh ideas and innovative responses to trade issues. Indeed, governments routinely maintain close contacts with national NGOs and this is not seen as anything that should be objectionable. On the contrary, the lack of such intercommunication would seem out of place.

However, because of the factors mentioned earlier, there are practical and political obstacles that need to be surmounted properly if NGOs are to occupy a more significant place in WTO affairs. I do not think that ways suggested up to now fulfil completely the essential requirement of acceptability by the full membership.

One formula which has been proposed, and which appeals to me, is an Advisory Economic and Social Committee which would have a suitable link to the WTO. I can visualize in broad perspective some of the elements that could lead to a reasonable scheme which, while fully respecting governmental prerogatives, would allow civil society to contribute to the furtherance of world trade and to its links with other areas of endeavour, which are of interest to the world community.

Clearly, such a scheme would keep discrepancies among NGOs far from the WTO: they would have to be worked out by the NGOs themselves and any suggestions or recommendations they made would come at the end, and as a result, of those internal discussions. NGOs would have to determine their own mechanism for taking account of each others' views; if over 1,000 NGOs were to attend the Cancún Ministerial Conference, it is not adventurous to speculate that on a number of given WTO subjects as many as 100 or 200 NGOs might wish to express their views. I do not see how this could be determined by the WTO Membership without embroiling the governments in lengthy and almost certainly futile discussions. This would have to be settled by the NGOs themselves.

Whatever proposals came out of any new NGO advisory body would certainly have to be just that: proposals that Members would take up if and when they saw fit. At this stage in political thinking it would be optimistic to hope for much more. Indeed, this would already signify a significant change in GATT–WTO traditional procedures which governments may or may not wish to accept.

The WTO has been the subject of large and sometimes violent public demonstrations on the part of those who attribute to it some of the evils they see in the accelerating globalization process underway. Witness the farmers in the Uruguay Round, and more recently the Seattle and Evian episodes.

Very often the demonstrators respond to slogans which are based on distorted information. If they do not have access to reliable sources of information, they will believe the contents of these slogans. If they perceive the WTO as being shrouded in secrecy, they will inevitably distrust it.

As things stand today, whatever its merits may be, the image of the WTO tends to worsen in many sectors of society. Transparency will contribute heavily to rectifying this state of affairs.

If governments feel the WTO is working well, they should be desirous of proclaiming its success to public opinion. If the opposite is the case, then we should all know about it.

This being so, transparency should be reinforced by closer involvement of parliamentarians who have a strong and particular approach to the welfare of their electors. Their daily contact with public opinion and their constantly renewed contribution to national legislation make them ideal actors in these broad-ranging issues. There is considerable lack of knowledge of the WTO in many parliaments, and this works to the detriment of the Organization.

It has been said that legitimate trade agreements should not be driven exclusively by export interests. Obviously, trade is and will remain the *raison d'être* of the WTO. That is what it is all about.

However, the definition of what and whose export interests are being effectively served, lends itself to considerable debate and leads to taking into account other factors which have not been at the foreground of the GATT–WTO system.

Behind practically any WTO decision lie economic and social interests. A simple example: when a customs tariff is modified, consumers frequently gain or lose, producers in one place gain and those somewhere else lose. Jobs are gained and jobs are put at jeopardy.

These consumers and producers are people, individuals who strive to lead a good life and be useful members of their community. Very often, they are unaware of WTO decisions that make them prosper or fail, have a gainful occupation, or join the ranks of the unemployed.

Behind the terminology of the Preamble to the WTO Agreement and the many provisions agreed during the Uruguay Round, there is a living reality that affects untold millions of people. This is a crucial facet of trade that is imperfectly conveyed and understood.

Increased worldwide public awareness of the full import of WTO decisions would almost certainly generate new pressures and demands on governments; this could very well complicate an already complex panorama for them, but it would certainly put the Organization in closer touch with the real world.

PART VIII

WTO DECISION-MAKING PROCEDURES, 'MEMBER-DRIVEN' RULE-MAKING, AND WTO CONSENSUS PRACTICES: ARE THEY ADEQUATE?

25

Improving the Capacity of WTO Institutions to Fulfil their Mandate

RICHARD BLACKHURST AND DAVID HARTRIDGE

The first part of this chapter briefly reviews the increasingly serious shortcomings of the World Trade Organization's (WTO) 'Green Room process', and then proceeds to develop the case for creating a formal 'WTO Consultative Board'. As with Green Room meetings, a WTO Consultative Board would not be empowered to take decisions that bind the general membership. It would consult, discuss, debate, and negotiate, but its output would be limited to recommendations put forward to the entire membership for approval/acceptance. The second part of the chapter deals mainly with practicalities and previous experience. There is a long history of tension between formal and informal processes of consultation and negotiation in the General Agreement on Tariffs and Trade (GATT) and the WTO, which throws useful light on the issues raised in the first part. That history is presented with reference to the Green Room and the Consultative Group of Eighteen.

I. REFORMING WTO DECISION-MAKING[1]

The December 1996 Singapore Ministerial Declaration was based on a draft prepared in Geneva containing agreed text on all but certain sensitive issues. In Singapore, an 'inner circle' composed of Ministers from 34 of the WTO's then 128 Members took responsibility for arriving at an agreed text on the remaining issues. At the late evening session devoted to getting a consensus on the draft declaration, most of the other 90 or so WTO Members with delegations in Singapore took the

[1] This first part of our brief chapter was prepared by Richard Blackhurst. It is based almost entirely on, and draws heavily from, the author's paper 'Reforming WTO Decision Making: Lessons from Singapore and Seattle' in K. G. Deutsch and B. Speyer (eds), *The World Trade Organization Millennium Round: Freer Trade in the Twenty-First Century* (2001).

floor in turn, each making virtually identical interventions consisting of three points: first they thanked the 34 members of the inner circle for their hard work; second, that although they had some reservations on certain points, they could join the consensus in favour of the draft declaration; and third, that the way in which the draft declaration had been prepared was undemocratic, unfair, and disgraceful, that they were no longer willing to accept decision-making processes that always presented them with *faits accomplis*, and that they attached the highest priority to fundamentally revising the way important decisions are arrived at in the WTO.

Three years later, almost to the day, the venue shifted to Seattle. WTO Ministers arrived with no agreed text for a Ministerial Declaration launching a new round of multilateral negotiations. Near the end of the conference, the usual way of arriving at decisions—as exemplified by the 34-member inner circle at Singapore—broke down completely. This time comments by countries excluded from the Green Room meetings—the name frequently given to inner circle meetings—found their way into the popular press.[2] It was abundantly clear from those comments not only that there had been no improvements in this area of WTO decision-making since Singapore, but that the situation had become notably worse.

Apparently this *ad hoc* and informal approach to decision-making worked better in Doha. It is difficult, however, to avoid the conclusion that this outcome can be traced to a combination of the particular personalities and personal relationships involved, plus a dose of luck. None of the growing, very fundamental weaknesses of the Green Room process identified below has been dealt with.

A. Two points to keep in mind

First, the processes by which WTO Members discuss, debate, and negotiate issues is distinct from the organization's reliance on consensus to *adopt* decisions (the Members have made it very clear they plan to keep the emphasis on consensus decision-making). Any organization with a large membership, and in which all groups, committees, and councils are open to all its members, is going to have a problem functioning, regardless of whether it takes decisions by consensus or by simple majority. It is that particular problem—the debate and negotiation process by which the WTO Members arrive at the point where the entire membership is asked to adopt a particular decision—that is the subject of this paper.

---

[2] See Blackhurst, *supra* n. 1, for 15 quotations from the international press covering the period 5 December 1999 to 29 March 2000.

Second, the question of reform of the WTO's decision-making process is not a North–South issue. Large and influential developing countries are regular participants in the Green Room meetings. It is, instead, a classic 'insider/outsider' issue, with the industrial countries and 'important' developing countries on the inside, and the other 110 or so WTO Members on the outside.

B. Green Rooms

The Green Room or inner circle model was the organization's *de facto* way of dealing with the fact that while membership in virtually every GATT and now WTO body is open to all GATT–WTO members, once the active participation in a group/committee exceeds a certain number (say 25 or 30), discussion, debate, and negotiation become increasingly cumbersome, inefficient, and ultimately impossible. Organizations with a large membership traditionally deal with this problem by having a steering body with a limited membership. For example, the International Monetary Fund (IMF) and the World Bank have 24-member executive boards, and the United Nations (UN) has the Security Council. There is no corresponding limited-membership *formal* body in the WTO.

The growing criticism of the Green Room process is the result of an increasing number of situations in which the number of countries wanting to participate in the process exceeds the number that can be accommodated. The reasons behind the growing demands to participate suggest very strongly that this trend can only intensify:

- The membership is growing.
- Over the past 15 years a large number of developing countries—and virtually all the transition economies—have come to accept the view that a more liberal trade regime and fuller integration into the global economy must be a key part of their development strategies. And they understand that active participation in the WTO not only contributes importantly to both goals, but also allows them to have a say in the evolution of the multilateral trading system.[3]
- In the Tokyo Round, the GATT began to write rules for policies applied 'inside the border' (e.g. technical barriers); that process continued in the Uruguay Round (e.g. services, Trade-Related Aspects

---

[3] Although the vast majority of WTO Members account for only a tiny proportion of world trade, a very large number of these 'tiny traders' have ratios of trade to GDP that are higher than the corresponding ratios of the big traders. For such countries, trade and the fair and efficient functioning of the multilateral trading system are crucial to their economic futures.

of Intellectual Property Rights (TRIPS)), and it continues today (e.g. investment, competition rules). Virtually all of these 'inside the border' issues are far more politically sensitive than tariffs and quotas. As the GATT–WTO takes on these issues, countries are less and less willing to sit on the sidelines and let other countries do the work.

- Under the GATT, many of the rules governing trade-related policies were—officially or *de facto*—optional for developing countries. Another reason for no longer being willing to sit on the sidelines is that under the WTO's 'single undertaking' every Member is subject to all the rules.

- In a similar vein, whereas under the GATT any Member had the power to block a dispute settlement case—that is, to block the application of a rule it objected to—that option no longer exists.

C. Two interim conclusions

First, in those instances in which interest among WTO Members in the issue at hand is sufficiently narrow that a Green Room group can be constituted without excluding any member desiring to participate, this model functions well and should continue to be used.

Second, in those instances in which it is impossible to organize a Green Room meeting without excluding one or more WTO Members wishing to be included, continued reliance on this model can only progressively damage the WTO's ability to function and erode its internal and external credibility (Ministerial Green Rooms come immediately to mind). Clearly the WTO needs an efficient-size sub-group of members for the purpose of discussing, debating, and negotiating draft decisions that can be put to the entire membership for adoption. What needs changing is the basis for putting together such a sub-group, for deciding which delegations will be in the room and which delegations are excluded. The new basis needs to be one that is fully transparent, predictable, equitable, and legitimate in the eyes of all WTO Members.

D. A 'WTO Consultative Board'

The option developed in this chapter for a new sub-group of WTO Member countries involves creating what might be called a 'WTO Consultative Board'. It would not be necessary to have predetermined, regularly scheduled meetings since the Board normally would meet only when a Green Room meeting could not accommodate all WTO Members wishing to participate.

As with Green Room meetings, the WTO Consultative Board would not be empowered to take decisions that bind the general membership.[4] It would consult, discuss, debate, and negotiate, but its output would be limited to recommendations put forward to the entire membership for approval/acceptance. And, as with the IMF and World Bank Executive Boards, the Board would be a formal part of the WTO organization chart, and the Board's composition—which Members have a seat at the table and when—would be fixed (that is, *predictable*), presumably with the largest traders having individual seats and the remaining WTO Members divided into groups, each with one seat that is shared among the members of the group on a rotating basis.

1. Minimizing the exclusivity of a WTO Consultative Board

A major challenge would be to minimize the exclusivity of the Board in the eyes of Members which would have a seat at the table only on a rotating basis. The fact that the Board could not take decisions would be vitally important from this perspective. Surely the other major factor would be transparency. It would be crucial, as regards both substance and political acceptability, to make the work of the Board *fully* transparent and accessible to all the members. Along with increasing the political acceptability of such a Consultative Board, a high degree of transparency would facilitate subsequent efforts to get a consensus because countries which were not members of the Board would be aware of the nature of the 'give and take' involved in arriving at a decision to recommend to the entire membership.[5]

2. Size of a WTO Consultative Board and the allocation of seats

The question of how many seats the Board should have would be very contentious. One option for getting around this politically charged issue would be to follow the practice of the IMF and the World Bank, whose sub-groups for discussion, debate, and negotiation—that is, their respective Boards—each have 24 members.

As in the IMF and World Bank Boards, the groupings could be self-selected and could have the option of 'self-changing' their composition, say once every two years. The countries in each group could also

---

[4] See Blackhurst, *supra* n. 1, for a discussion of the GATT's experience with the CG.18, and of the IMF and World Bank Executive Boards.

[5] Another way to minimize the exclusivity of the Board, or at least the perceived downside to the exclusivity, would be to use broad similarities in interests and viewpoints on trade-related issues as the basis for composing the groups of WTO Members which share seats. In that way, the members of any particular group—when it was not their turn to be at the table—would feel that at least their group's seat was occupied by a country that shared many of their concerns and priorities in the trade area.

be given the freedom to decide how often to rotate the occupancy of the group's seat at the table. In general, the principle could be to allow as much flexibility as possible, in order to accommodate a variety of situations that can change over time.

Cooperation among the self-selected group members to support the member currently occupying the seat would help compensate for the shortage of experienced professionals—in Geneva and in support units back home—that plague so many of the middle- and lower-income WTO Members. It would be an important learning process—and morale builder—for the officials involved, both in Geneva and in capital. Domestically, the much more active involvement in important WTO activities of the 110 or so countries routinely excluded from Green Room meetings would raise the profile of the WTO, and trade policy in general, in government circles and in the private sector. Governments that have been slow to recognize that commercial diplomacy has replaced political diplomacy as the critical priority for countries pursuing economic development would be encouraged to reallocate scarce human resources away from activities, abroad and at home, that contribute little or nothing to the country's economic development, and put those resources to work on the WTO.

The latter point calls attention to one of the most damaging aspects of the Green Room model, with its opaque basis for deciding which delegations are allowed into the room, and its *de facto* permanent exclusion of more than three-quarters of the WTO Membership. It is only human nature that if a country's senior trade officials—the Geneva ambassador and the cabinet minister responsible for trade—feel marginalized by the WTO, they will be inclined to marginalize the WTO at home. A new kind of sub-group of WTO Members along the lines of a WTO Consultative Board could go a long way toward solving this problem.

3. Where will the opposition come from?

The strongest and most vocal opposition will come from the 20 to 30 Members that are big enough to demand entry to any Green Room, but not big enough to demand an individual seat on the new Board. (The delegations in this category can be obtained by subtracting the United States (US), the European Union (EU), and Japan from either the 25 countries reportedly invited to the Green Room meetings in Seattle, or from the 34 countries that drafted the Singapore Ministerial communiqué.)

4. Predictability, transparency, and—above all—legitimacy

The predictability, transparency, and legitimacy of any new 'sub-group process' would be critically important. From this perspective, the IMF and World Bank Boards have two very important characteristics: the Board is a formal part of the organization's structure, and *every* Member country's 'participation rights' in the Board are fully transparent and predictable. This contrasts with the Green Room model—or for that matter, with any informal, *ad hoc* WTO sub-group—which lacks predictability, typically suffers from serious transparency problems, and has none of the legitimacy that comes from being a *formal* part of the institution's organizational structure. Any informal group or forum risks collapsing in acrimony and distrust at the first serious confrontation because it would have no 'structural strength' and would suffer from a 'deficit of legitimacy'. The new group must be a formal part of the Organization—on the WTO organization chart and connected by a solid line, not a broken line, to the rest of the chart.

E. A brief summing-up

It is now widely accepted that the WTO's 'legislative' bodies are working, if at all, very poorly. The risk facing the WTO is that the political challenge of getting a consensus on a fundamental reform of the decision-making process along the lines proposed in this paper, coupled with the GATT–WTO's traditional pragmatism, will create a nearly irresistible momentum to attempt to 'muddle through'. If the Member countries and the Director-General give in to this temptation, the prospects for the WTO realizing its full potential will be very bleak indeed.

What is not easy to understand is why the 110 or so WTO Members routinely excluded from Green Room meetings continue to accept being *de facto* disenfranchised by the current system—by the selfishness and short-sightedness of the '34 minus 3' countries (Singapore) or the '25 minus 3' countries (Seattle) who readily admit to the need for a limited membership steering body, but can focus only on the 'feasibility' of creating one (that is, on their own unwillingness to change).

If the medium- and smaller-size countries want to see the creation of a formal and fully representative sub-group of WTO countries along the lines of a WTO Consultative Board, where (i) each of them would have the opportunity to periodically occupy a seat at the table, and (ii) when they were not in the seat, they would know it is occupied by a fellow group member which shares their views on many issues, and which would listen to them when they want to make an input, they will have to fight for the change. The countries that have grown accustomed to 'running the show' at the GATT and now the WTO are not going to hand it to them on a silver platter.

II. LESSONS FROM HISTORY[6]

The WTO, and the GATT before it, have always needed, and for the past 17 years have lacked, a steering committee or management body. This need grows more urgent as the membership and the difficulty of managing the daily business of the Organization increase. So a formal consultative body should be established. This second part, written by the second co-author of this chapter, deals mainly with practicalities and previous experience. There is a long history of tension between formal and informal processes of consultation and negotiation in the GATT and the WTO, which throws useful light on these issues. Much of this history can most easily be presented with reference to the Green Room and the Consultative Group of Eighteen.

A. The Green Room

In talking of the 'Green Room', a distinction must be made between the informal meetings of restricted groups of Ministers which take place at Ministerial Conferences of the WTO, as at Singapore, Seattle, and Doha; and the informal restricted meetings held at ambassadorial level in the WTO, at the initiative of the Director-General—less frequently in recent than in earlier years—in the process of managing the regular business of the Organization.

Ministerial Green Rooms are mercifully rare and always controversial. Richard Blackhurst describes the discontent of those excluded from the restricted meetings at the successful Singapore Conference of 1996 and the disastrous Seattle conference of 1999. But I do not think one can draw the conclusion that Seattle was a turning-point, demonstrating conclusively the non-viability of the long-standing practice whereby the critical issues at Ministerial Conferences have been negotiated in informal, non-transparent meetings of about 25 key countries, and are then presented to the full membership for adoption. The experience of Seattle—a uniquely under-prepared and ill-managed Ministerial—is a bad basis for any conclusions about the handling of business in the WTO. Since then we have had the Doha Conference of 2001, at which the same processes—a Green Room of the same size and largely identical membership, together with Ministers invited as 'Friends of the Chair' to conduct open consultations on subjects of particular importance—produced agreement with very little acrimony on virtually the same agenda. The great difference between Doha and Seattle was the submission to the former of a well-prepared and largely complete

---

[6] This second part was drafted by David Hartridge.

draft declaration: no process yet invented could have produced agreement on the basis of the draft sent to Seattle (the strongest protests about the Doha process, oddly enough, came from countries that had been in the Green Room throughout). The Doha experience is the more typical, though it no doubt benefited from the determination of governments, less than three months after September 11, to demonstrate commitment to international cooperation.

At Punta del Este in 1986 a similar restricted group of Ministers, in a 12-hour overnight meeting, agreed the Declaration which launched the Uruguay Round—on the basis, it is true, of a very highly developed draft—with little complaint from those excluded. At the premature Geneva Ministerial of 1982, on the other hand, which came close to disaster but produced a respectable Declaration and work programme, the embarrassingly protracted Green Room did cause resentment; manifest failure of the meeting would have called forth recriminations about the process to rival Seattle.

Restricted meetings are in principle indefensible, and they are always understandably resented by those excluded. But experience shows that they are tolerated, because they are recognized as necessary, so long as they produce results. Since much of the resentment is caused by the apparently arbitrary selection of Green Room participants (I say 'apparently' because the basis of selection is well understood in fact), a major benefit of a formally constituted consultative body would be to do away with selection by providing an objective qualification for inclusion. The difficulty of obtaining agreement on the principle of such a body would of course be increased by the knowledge that its members would automatically qualify for Ministerial Green Rooms, but that is inescapable. Such initial difficulty would be greatly outweighed by the escape from invidious selection processes at future Ministerials.

But since Ministerial Green Rooms are exceptional events, the case for reform needs also to be made in terms of the handling of regular WTO business at the level of ambassadors in Geneva. Successive Directors-General have always used informal consultations with key delegations (meaning those crucial for the issue in question) as a means of resolving problems and preparing decisions by the full membership. The more formal of such meetings used to be called 'Seven plus Sevens', meaning seven developed plus seven developing countries, though the actual number and the composition varied with the subject: it would never make sense to discuss agriculture in the absence of Argentina, or textiles in the absence of Hong Kong, but the major powers would almost always be there, whatever the subject. That too made sense, since they accounted for well over 60 per cent of world trade.

The name 'Green Room' came into use when Arthur Dunkel was Director-General, to designate his conference room; I claim to have originated it while Dunkel's *chef de cabinet*—a dubious distinction considering the obloquy into which it has fallen. In Dunkel's hands, the Green Room was for several years a highly efficient tool of management. Discussions between the countries primarily concerned would take place in any case, outside the GATT, but in the Green Room the Director-General could act as a facilitator and as a spokesman for the multilateral system and the interests of the membership as a whole. The process broke down in the crisis of 1986, when disagreement over the launching of the Uruguay Round paralysed the Preparatory Committee, forced the negotiation of the draft declaration outside the GATT building, and made it impossible to convene Green Room meetings on the subject. It has been used less regularly by Dunkel's successors, but it remains a vital instrument for any Director-General, since in normal times these are the only meetings whose convocation and handling are entirely in his hands. (We should not forget the effective use made by Peter Sutherland and Renato Ruggiero of a 'Committee of the Whole' in concluding the Uruguay Round and preparing the Singapore Ministerial.) It is to be hoped that the insistence of Members in recent years on the 'Member-driven' nature of the Organization does not translate into a curb on the initiative of the Director-General in such matters.

The creation of a formal consultative body would not make such meetings unnecessary. For many of the issues brought to the Green Room it would be too large and transparent to serve the negotiating purpose. Negotiators can rarely explore the limits of their partners' flexibility, or expose their own difficulties, in big on-the-record meetings. Nor could a formal body be convened at a few hours' notice to deal with an immediate problem, which is the great value of the Green Room. It seems to me that the real functions of a consultative body should be to provide strategic direction, debate major policy issues, and anticipate problems. These were the functions performed by the Consultative Group of Eighteen (CG. 18) between 1975 and 1985.

B. The Consultative Group of Eighteen

The CG.18, temporarily established in 1975 and on a permanent basis in 1979, was a conscious attempt to mirror in the GATT the development in the IMF of a management group in the form of the Interim Committee. Consultations by the Director-General, Olivier Long, in 1973–74 revealed strong support for a restricted group of high officials from capitals which would not infringe on the authority of the Contracting Parties but would discuss trade problems from a political viewpoint, anticipate developments, and facilitate the 'concertation of policies in the trade field'. It was certainly Long's hope that the CG.18 would develop over time a more explicit role in steering policy and managing the system. His original proposals were however toned down in deference to the caution of the GATT Council. Contracting parties insisted that the CG.18 must not take any binding decisions; its advisory function was made clear in the change of its title by the Council from 'Management Group' as originally proposed to 'Consultative Group'. But it did bring officials at Deputy Minister level to Geneva two, three, or four times a year and it did make recommendations, which were often important and effective—for example the recommendation that a Ministerial meeting should be held in 1982.

Negotiating the composition of the Group had been very difficult. In addition to 18 full members, each with a second seat for an 'adviser', there were nine alternate members, with the right to speak but only one seat. The member states of the EC were present as full members, each with two seats, though only the European Commission spoke for the Community. (Their presence often irritated the US—perhaps unreasonably, since they constituted a captive audience of high officials, usually full members of the 113 Committee.) There was provision in the Group's mandate for 'rotation of membership as appropriate', and there was regular rotation between Finland, Norway, and Sweden, between Czechoslovakia, Hungary, and Poland and between the Association of Southeast Asian Nations (ASEAN) countries (Indonesia, Malaysia, Philippines, Singapore, Thailand).

Blackhurst is right in criticizing the lack of transparency in the CG.18. There seems no reason now why papers prepared for it by the Secretariat should not have been circulated to the entire membership; it is in any case nonsense to suppose that papers given to over 40 delegations are in any sense confidential. However, very detailed reports of the Group's meetings were made to the GATT Council. They reveal that it made a major contribution to the development of the negotiating agenda and to the emergence of the WTO as it now exists. In the absence of an Agriculture Committee, it was the only forum in which agricultural policy could be discussed, and this was done in a sequence of seven meetings in 1981–82. New subjects such as Services, Trade-Related Investment Measures (TRIMS), and Intellectual Property were first discussed in the CG.18 on the basis of papers by the Secretariat, along with many other subjects which subsequently figured in the Uruguay Round agenda. In 1985 all three of its meetings were entirely devoted to the question of the launching of a new round of trade negotiations. The Group thus made a major contribution to the transition from the GATT to the WTO.

It ceased to function after 1985, for two reasons. The first was difficulty over its composition. The accession of Mexico to the GATT had made difficult the allocation of the third seat allotted to Latin American countries, and Hong Kong was insisting on its claim to membership, as the 13th largest trader in the world. Under heavy pressure Dunkel proposed the enlargement of the Group to 22 full members, and this was agreed in November 1985. The Group never met again: some members had found the original membership too large to be efficient, and were even less enthused by the enlarged membership. In addition the crisis of 1986, referred to above, made it as difficult to convene the CG.18 as the Green Room.

The second reason advanced for the failure of the Group to meet after 1985 was that it would be 'inappropriate' for it to do so while the Uruguay Round negotiations were in progress. But this is hard to take seriously; there were many occasions during the Uruguay Round when a policy discussion among top officials—as in Arthur Dunkel's working dinners for the heads of CG.18 delegations—would have been invaluable. Since 1995 the need for such a group has been underlined by the informal and infrequent *ad hoc* meetings of high officials from capitals—essentially from the same countries as in the CG.18 and all informal groupings—sometimes known as the 'Invisibles'. These have taken place in Geneva or other cities, but always outside the WTO, to discuss the same strategic issues as the CG.18, but with no written input by the Secretariat, no continuity in the Chair or reporting to WTO Members, and of course no power to make recommendations. Restricted meetings of Ministers, known as 'mini-Ministerials', convened *ad hoc* by host countries, have also become a regular feature of trade policy discourse, and they have sometimes been valuable. But they suffer from the same lack of legitimacy (in the eyes of the excluded) and of transparency. There is no mechanism for transmitting the product of such meetings to the wider Membership. It would be healthier and more efficient if they could take place in the WTO. Meetings that cannot take place inside the WTO will happen elsewhere. To exclude restricted meetings on transparency grounds produces less transparency.

No decision to discontinue the CG.18 was ever taken, but it was a creation of the GATT and expired with it. Some thought was given to the possibility of reviving it at the time of the constitution of the WTO, but the conclusion was that this would be one step too far, given the great number of structural changes which had to be negotiated. To maintain it after 1986 would have been vastly easier than to recreate it now, but that is essentially what is involved in setting up a formal consultative body. There are important differences between the CG.18 and the board proposed by Richard Blackhurst, the most significant of them being that the CG.18 had no 'constituencies' permitting representation of all Members, and very limited provision for rotation. I believe it would have developed in those directions and that it would now be very difficult, perhaps impossible, to set up any group of restricted membership without such provisions. But in most other respects—the inability to make binding decisions in particular—a new body would be much like the CG.18, though somewhat larger. In my view it too should be chaired by the Director-General, and it should meet both at official and Ministerial level, performing the functions of the 'Invisibles' and 'mini-Ministerials', though of course not depriving any country of the right to convene what meetings it likes.

In one respect I believe the mechanism proposed by Blackhurst could not work. This is the idea that the Consultative Board would not meet regularly but would be convened *ad hoc* when it became impossible to accommodate in the Green Room all countries wanting to be present. It will never be possible to accommodate all countries expressing the wish to be present, if the question is put to them. It is easier for an ambassador to suffer arbitrary exclusion, and retain the right to complain about it, than to justify self-exclusion to his capital, and this would apply *a fortiori* at Ministerial Conferences. For these it would be better to start from the premise that the Consultative Board will be the Green Room participants, and to add countries representing particular interests if necessary. In the normal course of business in Geneva the Consultative Board should have regular scheduled meetings which can be properly prepared. It could of course be convened *ad hoc* if smaller-scale consultations on some issue became impossible, but the danger of presenting it as an ever-present on-demand alternative to small meetings is that it may make the latter impossible—or rather, force them outside. It should not delegitimize the informal small-scale process, which will continue to be needed.

The great difficulty in constituting such a body would of course be the opposition of countries which would be excluded from it. The inclusion of a representative or 'constituency' function might well be insufficient to overcome such opposition. The failure of the recent Ministerial Conference at Cancún, which was caused by breakdown in negotiations rather than the intrinsic difficulty of the decisions to be taken, underlined the necessity for new thinking about the management and decision-making procedures of the WTO. Unfortunately it also made very clear how serious would be the obstacles to any change which might be proposed.

Nevertheless, I believe a Consultative Board would perform vital functions, as a legitimate negotiating group at Ministerial Conferences and as a steering committee in normal times. It would be worth the inevitable pain of negotiating its membership.

26

Chairing a WTO Negotiation

JOHN S. ODELL

Efforts by Member states of the World Trade Organization (WTO) to negotiate multilateral decisions have been less efficient and less legitimate since 1997 than many would prefer.[1] The most powerful and the least powerful Members alike have complained about the WTO process of negotiating. The last effort to decide upon a new Director-General in 1999 produced a remarkably nasty and prolonged fight that damaged the Organization's credibility and the Members' ability to reach consensus on substantive issues. Two of the three most recent Ministerial Conferences have ended in frustrating impasses. Although these were not the first deadlocks in history, conditions today are likely to make impasses more frequent and more difficult to break than before. And when WTO Members fail to agree on improvements to their rules, conflicts tend to be driven into the legal dispute settlement process. Thus there has been some concern, as well, that potentially explosive conflicts that ought to have been settled by political negotiation will damage the dispute settlement institution.

Multilateral deadlocks are a problem for developing countries at least as much as for industrial countries. Stalemate may seem like a good thing, at first glance, to business leaders or politicians in a poor country who fear external pressure to open the home market to greater competition or absorb new regulatory burdens. But multilateral stalemate equally means no improvements to WTO rules that many of these citizens feel are imbalanced or inadequate and yet may well be enforced. When deadlocks drive problems into the realm of adjudication, the developing countries' larger numbers make no difference to the outcome.

[1] This chapter draws from J. S. Odell, 'Mediating Multilateral Trade Negotiations', paper presented at the *Annual Meeting of the International Studies Association* (2004). I am grateful for comments by Oran Young on that paper, to Stuart Harbinson and Sheila Page for comments on an earlier draft of this paper, and for the support of the University of Southern California College of Letters, Arts, and Sciences and its School of International Relations while conducting this research. None of these friends nor any official who spoke to me confidentially is responsible for my claims or conclusions.

Members and their Director-General have made modest changes to their negotiation processes since 1999, and these changes helped them fashion an agreement to launch the Doha Round in 2001. But in 2003 they ran aground again in Geneva and Cancún. In 2004 they hammered out some partial deals that they hoped would move the talks ahead once again. Farther-reaching institutional changes have been proposed. Some would strengthen the centre while others would limit leaders' discretion.[2] But stalemate reigns regarding these more ambitious ideas as well.

It is a truism that ultimate responsibility for future WTO outcomes will rest with the Member states. If trade ministers want future conferences to be more productive under present rules, for instance, they could instruct their ambassadors to close more gaps in Geneva prior to the conference, giving authority to make concessions earlier rather than holding back as many concessions until the last moment. This truism is only part of the story, however. Each minister and diplomat is surrounded by an international reality, and his or her future decisions will also depend on the collective reality in view. This chapter addresses one means by which this collective reality can be managed or mismanaged. I assume for the moment that there will be no formal changes to WTO institutions for negotiation and decision-making.

Member states of the General Agreement on Tariffs and Trade (GATT) and WTO have given their Director-General the role of overall chair of the Uruguay and Doha Round negotiations. Members also give special influence to ministers and ambassadors who temporarily chair ministerial conferences and subsidiary negotiating bodies. Casual observation suggests that these chairpersons' decisions can make a difference to the collective outcomes. Yet little has been published analysing or even describing how they play this role or what determines the results.[3] Part of what chairs do is a type of mediation, but most research on

[2] R. Blackhurst, 'Reforming WTO Decision-Making: Lessons From Singapore and Seattle' in K. G. Deutsch and B. Speyer (eds), *Freer Trade in the Next Decade: Issues in the Millennium Round in the World Trade Organization* (2000) 295–310; J. J. Schott and J. Watal, 'Decision Making in the WTO' in J. J. Schott (ed.), *The WTO After Seattle* (2000) 283–292; Oxfam GB, *Institutional Reform of the WTO* (2000), online at http://www.oxfam.org.uk/what_we_do/issues/trade/wto_reform.htm; Sampson, G. P. (ed.), *The Role of the World Trade Organization in Global Governance* (2001); T. Cottier and S. Takenoshita, 'The Balance of Power in WTO Decision-Making: Towards Weighted Voting in Legislative Response' in 58 *Swiss Review of International Economic Relations* (2003) 171–214; Kenya and 10 other African states, WT/GC/W/510 (14 August 2003); Commission of the European Communities, *Reviving the DDA Negotiations—the EU Perspective* (2003).

[3] The pioneering article by Winham (G. R. Winham, 'The Mediation of Multilateral Negotiations' in 13 *Journal of World Trade Law* (1979) 193–208) has not been followed up, to my knowledge. The present piece takes a step toward describing recent practice. More rigorous analysis will have to await the accumulation of more thorough description.

international mediation has concentrated on wars and military–political disputes. I have found nothing that a future WTO chair or others could read to learn about the informal essence of the process of mediating multilateral trade impasses. It is more like a folk art at this stage. I have interviewed a number of individuals who have played the role and others who have observed them closely. This chapter reports provisional findings from research still in progress.

The main emerging points are that WTO chairs have limited but significant capacity to influence the efficiency of consensus-building and the resulting distribution of gains and losses and its legitimacy. Chairs can consider three types of mediation tactics for helping members overcome deadlocks. But chairs face challenges and dilemmas in deciding how to use this influence, which sometimes open them to controversy. Experience suggests positive and negative lessons for future practice.

I. INCENTIVES TO DELEGATE INFLUENCE TO A MEDIATOR

Three types of obstacle stand in the way of negotiated agreements that would advance the common interest, in any international negotiation involving dozens of states. Still other impediments arise from the special features of the WTO. These recurring problems give governments that seek agreements incentives to delegate influence to a mediator and consensus builder on behalf of the whole.[4]

First, the information obstacle to achieving complex multilateral agreements is huge. To discover whether any package deal would satisfy more than 100 governments from extremely heterogeneous countries on highly technical issues poses a mind-boggling challenge. The needed information in the WTO includes not only economic forecasts but also political information such as Member governments' true minima, and whether a coalition defending a common position is likely to hold together or fragment.

Furthermore, each player has a tactical incentive to conceal or exaggerate its true reservation value, worsening the information problem for a consensus-builder. When all do so, they can shrink or eliminate the

---

[4] J. Tallberg, 'The Power of the Chair in International Bargaining', paper presented at the *Annual Meeting of the International Studies Association* (2002) provides valuable insights on this subject. See J. S. Odell, *Negotiating the World Economy* (2000) 400–429 for a survey of negotiation analysis and new contributions regarding trade and monetary negotiations. Also see the *Economic Negotiation Network,* online at http://www.usc.edu/enn, for information about more research on the process of negotiating over international trade and finance.

perceived zone of agreement. If no one can identify a deal that would satisfy all the exaggerated minima, they walk away even when some deals would have satisfied their genuine but unknown minima.

Exacerbating the effects of deliberate tactics is less conscious partisan bias in interpreting information. Experimental subjects playing partisan roles genuinely tend to overvalue their own alternatives to agreement, compared with judgements by non-partisan observers given exactly the same information.[5] Partisans tend to recall more information favourable to their own position[6] and to use a self-serving conception of fairness.[7] These biases encourage firm refusals to concede, which intensify impasses.

A second obstacle in any large group is the familiar free-rider problem. In the WTO, the Organization's credibility as an enforcer of rights and a forum for negotiating future agreements is a public good for the members. One cost of supplying this good is taking the initiative to propose a compromise that would strengthen the Organization. Taking the initiative is costly in negotiation terms since a proposal for a compromise undermines the credibility of the speaker's commitment to his or her preferred position and hence the ability to claim the largest possible share of the gain. Only the very largest traders conceivably stand to gain enough individually to pay, individually, this cost of taking the initiative toward compromise in the WTO.

Third, vast inequalities in power and wealth across Member states can be a source of suspicion and resistance to multilateral agreement. Naturally weaker Members worry about exploitation and try to use the Organization to compensate for their weakness, and naturally stronger Members resist agreements that would cost them. In all realms of world politics negotiating is partly a struggle over the distribution of gains and losses. Today poor small traders such as those in the African Group are better organized and prepared than earlier, and many are drawing support from non-governmental organizations (NGOs). Developing countries are showing greater willingness to stand firm and block the whole in order to defend against losses and claim greater gains.

On top of these general obstacles to agreement, the WTO in particular makes decisions not by majority vote but by consensus, theoretically giving the smallest member the authority to block the whole. One

[5] D. A. Lax and J. K. Sebenius, *The Manager as Negotiator: Bargaining for Cooperation and Competitive Gain* (1986) at 58.

[6] L. Thompson and G. Loewenstein, 'Egocentric Interpretations of Fairness and Negotiation' in 51 *Organizational Behavior and Human Decision Processes* (1992) 176–197.

[7] L. Babcock and G. Loewenstein, 'Explaining Bargaining Impasse: The Role of Self-Serving Biases' in 11 *Journal of Economic Perspectives* (1997) 109–126 at 111–113.

reason is that the stakes are often higher than in many organizations, since negotiated WTO rules become binding legal obligations that can be enforced through dispute settlement. At the same time, the WTO lacks formal devices for promoting consensus that are available in other organizations. The Director-General lacks explicit authority to advance original proposals. This Organization has no small representative executive body that could function as a site for more private efforts to change negotiating positions and build consensus. All formal meetings are open to the whole membership.

These structural obstacles give rational Members who seek agreements an incentive to delegate to a mediator the function of helping them break impasses in the common interest. Formally the WTO gives its chair only limited authority. The shared understanding is that the WTO is to be a Member-led organization. The only rules pertaining to this post are general and sketchy. Chairs are selected by the Member states by consensus. 'Chairpersons should continue the tradition of being impartial and objective; ensuring transparency and inclusiveness in decision-making and consultative processes; and aiming to facilitate consensus.'[8] Chairs are not permanent civil servants; they are national delegates except for the Director-General as chair of the Trade Negotiations Committee. The term of office is short—one or two years for subsidiary bodies and only a week for the ministerial chair. They have no authority to make policy decisions for any other member or to originate substantive proposals. They have no budget or staff independent of their own governments and the Secretariat. Thus chairs from most states, which have small or tiny missions in Geneva, rely heavily on the Secretariat. Secretariat officials typically collect evidence for and suggest ideas to chairs and facilitators including ministers, and sometimes draft possible language for the chair's summation of a meeting's outcome.[9] Individual chairs vary in the degree to which they follow or reject Secretariat advice.[10]

Informal convention gives the chair's office greater influence than the sketchy rules provide. Chairs have the capacities to consult privately with Members, convey information and ideas to them, schedule formal and informal meetings, set meetings' agendas, preside over sessions, assemble texts based on delegations' proposals as possible vehicles for consensus, decide when to adjourn meetings, and make statements to the mass media as chair of the conference or council.

---

[8] Para. 2.2, WT/L/510, rules for selecting officers to standing WTO bodies, December 2002. Also see minutes of the WTO Trade Negotiations Committee, 28 January 2002, TN/C/M/1, 3–4.
[9] Telephone interview with a veteran chair, 13 July 2004. Interviewees spoke on condition of anonymity.
[10] Interviews with Secretariat leaders, Geneva, 2002 and 2003.

Mediation has been defined as a form of assisted negotiation.[11] The mediator is a helper who intervenes with the consent of the parties and with the mission of attempting to help them find an agreement. A mediator does not have authority to make a decision for the parties.[12] The function has been partly institutionalized in many international organizations.

Mediation becomes relevant when there is a deadlock, and deadlocks often form early in multilateral trade negotiations. As a rough generalization, WTO diplomats typically open with what are called distributive tactics—high demands, resistance to discussing the demands of others, and interpreting and manipulating information to their advantage and the disadvantage of adversaries. Governments link their concessions on some issues to gains on other issues. If there is an announced deadline, they tend to delay integrative proposals and concessions until weeks and hours prior to that deadline. Delegates meet in small groups without necessarily reporting to the chair all they are doing.

Another basic property of these situations opens space for chairs' influence. Governments' reservation values, as theorists call them, or bottom lines as negotiators call them, are not always as clear and firm as theorists assume. The reality, one veteran GATT and WTO negotiator declares flatly, is that 'Most delegations don't know their own bottom lines.'[13] One reason is that some WTO delegates and most trade ministers know little of many technical legal and economic WTO issues they must manage, until they have to begin negotiating over them. In addition, while a vocal constituency might pose a clear limit on some issues, many WTO delegations hear little or nothing from constituents back home about many issues under negotiation. (The shortage of expertise and attention in many capitals also means that the Geneva process among professional negotiators and mediators has scope to operate with greater autonomy from political leaders than a simple model of state-to-state international relations would suggest.) Even experienced trade policy-makers from the richest countries have at most an approximate feel for what might be negotiable abroad, before

---

[11] M. D. Bennett and M. S. G. Hermann, *The Art of Mediation* (1996).

[12] Some understandings of mediation are narrower than what I have in mind. Here mediation is not restricted to bilateral conflicts or *ad hoc* interventions. Mediation is not restricted to the activities of outsiders or strictly neutral helpers. The partiality or impartiality of the mediator is a variable to be observed rather than a matter of definition. Scholars have engaged in lengthy debates over the distinctions between negotiation, mediation, facilitation, and arbitration. See for reviews see J. Bercovitch (ed.), *Studies in International Mediation* (2002) 4–8 and H. Raiffa, J. Richardson, and D. Metcalfe, *Negotiation Analysis: The Science and Art of Collaborative Decision Making* (2002) at 311–312.

[13] Interview, Florence, 3 July 2004.

talks begin. The difficulties in identifying a clear reservation value at the outset multiply in a complex round of talks encompassing a dozen or more technical issue areas simultaneously. There, a final deal will link special deals on most of these areas, and trade-offs between areas probably will pose choices later that can be foreseen only dimly. Another experienced chair adds that even when they begin with clear instructions and limits, negotiators often find with experience that their instructions need adjusting.[14] Instructions from capitals as a set are mutually inconsistent at the outset, and some diplomats begin exploring for ways to make a gain on one issue by trading a concession on another, and sometimes for ways to reframe the issue space itself. Thus in practice rationality is bounded and reservation values, if they exist, are unavoidably partly subjective and partly endogenous to the international process.[15] As a result, the chair has a capacity to facilitate or impede this informal exploration and adjustment.

The WTO chair, facing these general and special obstacles to agreement, has a menu of three types of mediation tactics from which to choose. The types increase in strength from the more passive to the more interventionist or manipulative.[16] Available space permits only selected illustrations.

II. TYPE 1: OBSERVATION, DIAGNOSIS, AND COMMUNICATION TACTICS

The most passive WTO mediation tactics consist of observation, diagnosis, and communication. The chair is given a privileged central position for collecting information about the sources of impasses and is expected to use this capacity to help governments find a balanced consensus. Thus as a deadline approaches, the effective mediator speaks privately with delegations, trying to separate bluffs from true reservation values and to form a diagnosis of specific blockages. One negotiator

[14] Telephone interview, 13 July 2004.

[15] J. S. Odell, 'Bounded Rationality and the World Political Economy' in D. Andrews, R. Henning, and L. Pauly (eds), *Governing the World's Money* (2002) 168–193 develops this theoretical point and its long-term implications for political economy and constructivist scholarship.

[16] Scholarship on mediation of other international conflicts suggests a typology for organizing our thinking about this role, adapted from J. Bercovitch, 'Mediation in International Conflict: An Overview of Theory, a Review of Practice' in I. W. Zartman and J. L. Rasmussen (eds), *Peacemaking in International Conflict: Methods and Techniques* (1997) 125–153 which built on S. Touval and I. W. Zartman, *International Mediation in Theory and Practice*, SAIS Papers in International Affairs No. 6 (1985).

described such tactics used during the drafting of the Uruguay Round dispute settlement understanding:

Ambassador [Julio] Lacarte [of Uruguay] was a great chair. He listened very carefully. He went to great lengths to give everyone a sense of being included. Then he also called in each delegation, or spokesman for several delegations, for what he called 'confessionals.' He also traveled to some capitals. Essentially he said, 'Trust me. Show me your cards.' I'm not sure how many really did. But he tried to test, to feel, to probe for where you had flexibility and where you really had none. And once he found something where you really had no flexibility, he took that on board as something you were going to have to have. On other issues, he expected you to sit silently and cooperate when it was something the other guy had to have.[17]

The effective chair also communicates information back to delegates and groups to attempt to offset partisan biases, for instance reporting confidential evidence from other 'confessionals' indicating that the delegation's position is not winning support. In addition, sometimes when a chair has felt the debate is not well enough informed technically, the chair has recommended to delegates that they ask the Secretariat to prepare a technical background paper for the negotiating group. During the Uruguay Round talks on dispute settlement rules, for instance, such neutral papers, stimulated indirectly by the chair's initiative, may have helped move discussions beyond the reiteration of initial partially informed positions.[18]

Even this passive level of activity raises some dilemmas and pitfalls:

- The most obvious pitfall would be failing to ask and listen carefully. Critics of the chair of the 1999 Ministerial, United States (US) Trade Representative Charlene Barshefsky, complain that she devoted too little effort to consensus-building. She spent little time coordinating with the Director-General or the other ministers who were to act as facilitators, she arrived in Seattle at the last moment, and in Seattle she seemed to spend less effort consulting privately with ministers than veterans expected.[19]

- Giving an impression of bias would undermine confidence that the chair can be trusted not to exploit confidential information, and low trust would choke off the flow of information. This constraint is likely to bind any prospective chair from a country that has significant trade stakes in the issue to be negotiated. Participants report that

---

[17] Interview, Washington, 19 June 2000.

[18] Interview with a participant in those talks, Florence, 3 July 2004.

[19] Interviews, Geneva, June 2000. See J. S. Odell, 'The Seattle Impasse and its Implications for the World Trade Organization' in D. L. M. Kennedy and J. D. Southwick (eds), *The Political Economy of International Trade Law* (2002).

Barshefsky deepened this predictable scepticism about the US as chair with her actions in Seattle. In one session she even acted personally as the chief US negotiator, claiming value from others while also occupying the post of the conference's top mediator.[20] A European GATT veteran summed up the conclusion of many by saying, 'The American in the chair was one of the reasons for failure. She gave the impression she would not do anything that was contrary to US national interests.'[21]

- Operating without thorough personal knowledge of the issues would be another pitfall. The currency of these negotiations consists of highly technical commercial and legal language and facts. One experienced mediator, thinking of Directors-General, could have been referring to any chairperson: 'The DG has to know the inner detail of the subject, the small print. The delegations are well aware of the small print and will use it for their own purposes whenever possible. The DG must know more than they do, or at least as much.'[22]
- A related pitfall would be to accept a fake bottom line as genuine. Doing so would narrow possibilities for agreement unnecessarily and perhaps fatally. During the Uruguay Round, one chair spotted what he, given his knowledge of the issues and the interests, regarded as an obviously fake minimum: 'In a consultation with the European Community, I remember the delegate told me he had to have something. I said, "Forget it. We are not even going to discuss that." He protested and I said, "Tell your ambassador that the chair would not even talk about that." And sure enough, when they heard this, they dropped it.'[23]

III. TYPE 2: FORMULATION TACTICS

WTO chairs regularly go beyond minimal tactics and reach for moderately interventionist ones. First, at the earliest stages the Director General, other chairs, and Members create an organization for the talks. Multilateral trade negotiations are far too complex for any single individual to perform the mediation function effectively alone. Thus if this form of leadership is to be provided, an organization of individual mediators must be constructed and managed to oversee the process and unify it at the end. Thus they establish specialized negotiating groups by issue area, select chairs for these groups, set interim deadlines, coordinate

---

[20] Interviews, Geneva, June 2000 and July 2004.
[21] Interview, Geneva, 19 November 2002.   [22] Interview, 5 December 2002.
[23] Ibid.

the agendas, schedule meetings, and preside over them. The Secretariat provides organizational support.

Supplementing the formal organization, the informal gathering is a standard conflict resolution technique in nearly every realm of social life. In the GATT, the informal 'Green Room' meeting became a regular feature. During the Uruguay Round Director-General and Chairman Arthur Dunkel invited chief negotiators from the states representing three-quarters of world trade to meet off the record, first in a small conference room in the Director-General's office suite. Other members were not notified that a meeting would occur, no written summary of remarks was prepared, and each participant was free to speak personally. After complaints from the excluded, Dunkel shifted to hosting private dinners in his home. The table accommodated up to 24 chairs and no deputies— only chief negotiators as he called them—were welcome. The country list was the same each time except for perhaps 20 per cent. It regularly included developing countries such as Brazil, Argentina, Chile, Mexico, Egypt, Morocco, India, and others. The Association of Southeast Asian Nations (ASEAN) and the Nordics each chose to send one member to attend for their group. Dunkel might add an ambassador from a small country who could be counted on to inject the right joke when arguments became heated. Sometimes Dunkel tested an idea for a settlement and heard franker statements about what capitals could and would not accept. The EC ambassador sometimes explained which EC member states were the main opponents or *demandeurs* of a particular idea, cueing others to talk to them. Some participants also served as chairs of negotiating groups and thus potential mediators. Dunkel hoped these dinners would help create a core of individuals who would identify personally, in their hearts, with the success of the Uruguay Round as a common enterprise, while also defending their national positions. Assembling them regularly as a team contributed to *esprit de corps*.[24]

WTO Directors-General continued this tradition of off-the-record meetings of leading states occasionally in Geneva and during Ministerial Conferences as a device for breaking deadlocks. But 1999 and especially the chaotic Seattle Ministerial brought an explosion of angry complaints. Some smaller members and NGOs publicly denounced the WTO for being non-transparent, undemocratic, and unfair to the weak. Immediately after Seattle, the Organization was chaotic, clearly lacking consensus on how they could organize their work. US and European Union (EU) leaders acknowledged that the traditional negotiation process had to change. Yet through what process were the Members to negotiate such a change if the inherited GATT process was no longer legitimate?

---

[24] Interview with a regular participant in these meetings, Geneva, 19 November 2002.

This situation generated an example of how chairs handle dilemmas at this level. In 2000 Director-General Mike Moore proposed some confidence-building measures, including special meetings to give attention to the developing countries' demands concerning implementation of the last round. Moore also met with coalitions in Geneva and travelled to capitals to meet ministers of countries that felt excluded. The first Director-General to visit Africa, Moore made seven trips there. Between visits he telephoned two or three ministers a week to keep them informed and strengthen relationships for the next ministerial conference.[25]

Meanwhile Kåre Bryn, Norway's Ambassador and chair of the WTO General Council, held more frequent Council meetings, held private consultations, and attempted to propose a set of procedures that would permit some work to be done privately in small groups while still respecting the authority of the plenary meeting. This issue (labelled 'internal transparency') remained sensitive and some refused to agree. Then he attempted to propose some principles to guide such procedures; again no agreement. Yet Bryn realized eventually that no one had been complaining about the way Members had actually been operating that year so far. In mid-year he wondered, 'What about just writing down a description of what we have been doing?' Bryn published his understanding of a possible consensus, in his own name, making two main points. It is important, first, that Members are advised of the chair's intention to hold a small meeting and 'members with an interest in the specific issue under consideration are given the opportunity to make their views known'.[26] Second, small groups never make decisions for the whole; all their results must be reported back to the full membership for their consideration. He was not certain even this statement would survive, but although the statement was not agreed, members continued to cooperate on this basis. The next year his successor as chair, Stuart Harbinson, followed this understanding during preparations for the Doha Ministerial. That year there were no official complaints about exclusion from Geneva consultations and the WTO reached agreement on an agenda for a new round. In 2002 the Trade Negotiations Committee (TNC) agreed to work on the basis of its best practices of the past and cited the 2000 Bryn statement.[27]

During the period up to 2004, chairs also relied increasingly on selected members to represent coalitions of states during private

[25] Interview, Geneva, 9 November 2002.
[26] 'General Council, Monday 17 July 2000, Internal Transparency and the Effective Participation of Members, Chairman's Statement', provided by Ambassador Kåre Bryn, Norway's Mission to the WTO, Geneva.
[27] Interview, Geneva, 28 November 2002.

consultations. One state would represent the African Union, another the Caribbean Community, and so on. Some coalitions, like the Least Developed Countries, were defined functionally rather than geographically. In agriculture talks in 2004 the chair invited Indonesia to represent the Group of 33, formed to protect special products of developing countries. Initially chairs decided which state to invite, but practice trended toward inviting whichever state had been selected by the group's members.[28] Delegates were becoming accustomed to operating as members of coalitions, and it was expected that the delegated representative would confer with fellow coalition members before and after the restricted meeting. It was also understood that a delegation that disagreed with its coalition partners would still have a chance to speak on its own behalf in plenary sessions. Complaints from delegations about inadequate representation in informal consultations declined sharply relative to 1999 and before. (NGOs continued to voice complaints.) Although proposals to formally establish a representative executive body failed to achieve consensus, an approximation reportedly became normal informally.

Recent Directors-General have also organized informal meetings of selected ministers prior to full Ministerial Conferences. In 2001 Moore invited 22 ministers to meet in Mexico City in August and in Singapore in October, prior to the November Doha meeting. Moore added selected African ministers to the inner circle for the first time. An ambassador from a developed country described what occurred in these 'mini-Ministerials':

These were not decision-making sessions and were not meant to be. They were important, first, for building relationships between people. This way you didn't show up in Doha and shake hands for the very first time. There were lunches where no one was present except ministers. So they could relax and begin to get to know each other. And second, they were important for putting things in a political context. Pascal Lamy would say things like, 'You've got to understand that I have *got* to have something on environment.' These were all politicians and they all understand political demands. And so I heard some say, 'Well, I don't like what you are doing and don't agree, but I hadn't quite thought of it that way.' These meetings were very very useful. I don't think Doha would have been a success without them.[29]

Going beyond organization, another consequential formulation tactic is to introduce an informal single negotiating text (SNT) in the chair's name. This familiar move normally occurs after delegates have made

---

[28] Interviews with a senior Secretariat leader and a delegate to several Ministerial Conferences including Seattle and Cancún, August 2004.
[29] Interview, Geneva, 1 November 2002.

conflicting substantive proposals and attempted to generate support yet no consensus has been reached. The chair normally decides what to include in the text after considering Secretariat proposals and conducting extensive 'confessionals' with delegations. The SNT is meant as a vehicle for moving the large group toward agreement. It is informal in the sense that no delegation has approved it; it is an intermediate starting-point for more talks if the parties accept it as such. A cautious variant presents two or three alternative positions on each issue in square brackets. This move can help reduce a plethora of options to a few, excluding proposals that are not generating support, without taking a position between the few, but is not a true 'single' text. A moderately risky variant suggests a particular resolution for each issue and introduces a package of multiple issues meant as a single balanced compromise. The bolder variant can be conceived as attempting to inject a focal point into the process or pull the parties toward one.[30]

This bolder procedure subtly changes the negotiators' incentives in talks among themselves. Before there is any mediator's text, as each delegation attempts to conceal the space it may have for falling back, they all make it difficult to coordinate their expectations about how each would behave regarding a potential compromise settlement. But once they expect that a chair is going to introduce a package deal, parties have a greater incentive to initiate compromises among themselves since otherwise the chair will take the matter out of their hands.[31] Furthermore, if the chair presents a revised SNT and reports that it represents the closest these parties can come to consensus, judging from his or her private soundings, the chair uses that information advantage to persuade the parties that the cost of rejecting it will be high. His or her text will be the most prominent focal point. The chair with Secretariat advice frames their alternatives in a new way that is more favourable to agreement than if there were no focal point.[32] Intervening more boldly always runs a risk of rejection, but 'your need to take risks increases the closer you get to the deadline', as one veteran puts it.[33] Even the fairest and most public-spirited chair can expect criticisms of a compromise text from delegates seeking to defend their preferred positions strongly. One sign of an effective mediation will be that few delegations reject the SNT as a basis for further talks.

---

[30] T. C. Schelling, *The Strategy of Conflict* (1960) ch. 3.

[31] B. Buzan, 'Negotiating by Consensus: Developments in Technique at the United Nations Conference on the Law of the Sea' in 75: *American Journal of International Law* (1981) 324–348.

[32] See M. H. Bazerman and M. A. Neale, *Negotiating Rationally* (1992) ch. 5, for general insights about framing in negotiations.

[33] Interview, Geneva, 23 September 2002.

Some of the best-known examples of chairs formulating texts appeared in the so-called Dunkel draft of 1991. The 1990 Brussels Ministerial Conference, the scheduled end point of the round, ended in disarray. The next year Dunkel managed to get the talks restarted with the hope that a comprehensive deal could be hammered out by November 1991. In some negotiating groups, delegates and chairs worked out agreements, but by mid-December, after an intense period of essentially non-stop negotiations, divisions still remained on other key issues:

On 18 and 19 December, each of the chairmen . . . made their own decisions on all the questions still unsettled. The GATT Secretariat gave advice, but these final decisions were those of the individual chairmen. . . . Dunkel pointed out that [this Draft Final Act] was the outcome of both 'negotiation among you, the participants, and arbitration and conciliation by the chairmen when it became clear that, on some outstanding points, this was the only way to put before you the global package of results of this Round'.[34]

He told the members they could either accept this draft in its entirety or reject it, and to add to the pressure to settle, he announced that he would be leaving as Director-General. Dunkel personally took responsibility for proposing a settlement for the most explosive issue, agriculture. To help refine the terms of that deal he staged a private simulated negotiation.[35] The EC soon rejected that section as too demanding. But this GATT text, along with credible bilateral threats from the US, may have helped EC commissioners build support for an internal reform of the Common Agricultural Policy in 1992, which paved the way for a GATT agreement late in 1993.

The tactics used in Geneva to prepare for Ministerial Conferences in 1999 and 2001 offer contrasts between the two variants.[36] In both years many governments sought a declaration launching a new round while others sought to prevent or delay negotiations on many issues. In 1999 the members were divided on many issues and many circulated proposals. General Council chair Ali Mchumo of Tanzania then issued a draft ministerial declaration in October. Rather than an integrated compromise text, this 34-page document presented rival texts advanced by contending groups in square brackets. Under the implementation issue, he listed three alternative paragraphs and under

[34] J. Croome, *Reshaping the World Trading System: A History of the Uruguay Round*, (2nd and revised edn 1999) at 254–255.
[35] Interview with a participating GATT Secretariat leader, 19 November 2002.
[36] Developed further in J. S. Odell, 'Making and Breaking Impasses in International Regimes: The WTO, Seattle, and Doha', paper presented at the 2002 meeting of the British International Studies Association and the University of Southern California Center for International Studies (2003).

agriculture, four. The chair even accepted provocative language that criticized Members whose ministers would have to sign it. No mediator can make governments resolve their differences. But once delegations saw their positions in this official WTO document, the process amounted to convincing them to lose things they seemed to have won, making it more difficult to move them toward consensus.[37] The cautious variant (resulting from a process which had been favoured by many besides Mchumo) runs an unintended risk of making the deadlock more difficult to dissolve.

In 2001, after this experience and Bryn's consultations, General Council chair Harbinson eventually followed the bolder variant. In April after consultations he proposed a bare checklist of topics that would need to be included in a declaration, without any text. Members accepted this list, formed coalitions, wrote proposals, and negotiated among themselves over these issues. Harbinson held informal meetings open to any interested delegation to try to explore solutions for particular issues. By July most gaps remained substantial and firm. He announced that in September he would issue an informal compromise draft declaration and he did so, a package deal with few square brackets, meant to be seen as balanced. Many delegations predictably criticized it for the ways in which it diverged from their positions. But many said it could serve as a basis for further talks. Some in fact said off the record that it was probably as close to a consensus as could be achieved before ministers gathered.[38] In addition Harbinson issued two special draft declarations, concerned with implementation and health and property rights. After a revision to the main text in October, Harbinson sent his SNT to the minister who was to chair the conference. He did not characterize the text as agreed, though this procedure naturally made it more difficult for dissenters to prevail. Pakistan and India denounced Harbinson for excluding some of their positions and for exceeding his authority. But much of the negotiating work of 2001 had been completed. By the time the ministers left Doha, they had adopted a main declaration whose language was the same in many respects, and whose structure was identical to Harbinson's October draft. It had functioned as a focal point.

Attempts in 2003 to use the same formulation tactic fell short and illustrate the hazards of boldness when parties are far apart. On 24 August General Council chair Carlos Perez del Castillo, in close cooperation with Director-General Supachai Panitchpakdi, proposed a

[37] Interviews, Geneva, June 2000. This insight is consistent with psychology's prospect theory, i.e. the laboratory finding that people hate losses more than they value gains of the same magnitude, and hence will take greater risks (e.g. of no agreement) to avoid losses.
[38] *World Trade Agenda* (15 October 2001) 1.

largely integrated draft declaration for ministers in Cancún.[39] Their agriculture text was based mostly on a joint proposal from the EU and the US with some nods to the new G20 group of developing countries. Regarding the proposed 'Singapore issues'—which the EU and its allies Japan and Korea wanted added to the agenda and which 90 developing countries repeatedly opposed—this text cautiously presented two alternative texts in square brackets. Perez del Castillo and Panitchpakdi did, however, append annexes specifying modalities for negotiations on the two most controversial Singapore issues, as drafted by the EU coalition but not approved by others. This text as a whole was disappointing to those developing countries that had been demanding improvements in special and differential treatment and implementation and an end to cotton subsidies, citing promises in 2001 that this would be the 'development round'.

In Cancún the conference chair, Mexico's Minister Luis Ernesto Derbez, introduced a bolder revised draft declaration on Saturday 13 September. Derbez had selected several other ministers to join his team of mediators, including Singapore's George Yeo to specialize in agriculture and Canada's Pierre Pettigrew for the Singapore issues. Derbez largely delegated mediation of each issue to the respective 'facilitator' aided by Secretariat leaders.[40] The Pettigrew–Derbez draft had ministers commencing negotiations on two Singapore issues and setting a future date for talks on investment, the most controversial issue—that is, moving beyond the Geneva draft in the EU direction despite public warnings from 90 other members. At the same time the larger declaration continued to reject Africa's proposal on cotton subsidies[41] and other developing country demands on Special and Differential Treatment (SDT) and implementation. On cotton the mediators inserted diversionary language from the US, the leading subsidizer. This formulation did include some new nods to developing countries on agriculture[42] and one option to continue protection of industrial sectors.[43]

Many developing countries denounced the Derbez text angrily and bitterly, especially its tilt in favour of EU demands they had repeatedly rejected, during a Saturday evening Heads of Delegations meeting.

---

[39] WTO document JOB(03)/150/Rev.1. This was a revision of an earlier first draft. Other accounts of the Cancún process include L. E. Bernal, R. S. Kaukab, S. F. Musungu, and V. P. B. Yu III, *South–South Cooperation in the Multilateral Trading System: Cancún and Beyond*, T.R.A.D.E. Working Paper No. 21 (2004) and A. Narlikar and R. Wilkinson, 'Collapse at the WTO: A Cancún Post-Mortem' in 25 *Third World Quarterly* (2004) 447–460.   [40] Interview with a member of the Mexican team, 3 July 2004.
[41] A proposal from Benin, Burkina Faso, Chad, and Mali, WT/GC/W511 (22 August 2003).   [42] *Inside US Trade* (15 September 2003) 9.
[43] *Ibid.* 1–2.

Africans expressed outrage at finding US language on cotton subsidies in place of their own.[44] Some suspected the giants had again cooked up a deal in private and were planning to twist arms to ram it through.[45] WTO spokesman Keith Rockwell said the only consensus seemed to be that all disliked this chair's formulation.[46] After the session, India's minister met privately with the Director-General to make his anger about the Singapore issues even more credible.[47] Many participants report that the mood among negotiators that night was unusually ugly. Delegations did not converge around this single text as a focal point. Indeed judging from the reaction, the decision to introduce this particular formulation might have unintentionally made the task of settling in Cancún more difficult.

This intermediate level of mediation, then, raises its own dilemmas and risks.

1. The dilemma of timing

Two veteran chairs warn newcomers not to offer their own formulations too early.[48] It is important to keep the heat on delegates to suggest their own integrative formulations and convince their capitals of the need for compromise. Otherwise they might not be ready to accept the mediator's suggestion. After Cancún in spring 2004, WTO mediators made a point of trying to stay out of the action until parties had begun to move off their positions. But waiting too long can also make a chair ineffectual.

2. The dilemma of the square brackets

The cautious approach of listing major alternatives in square brackets is safer but runs the risk of reinforcing an impasse. One veteran chair believes that presenting no chair's text at all will be better for the organization than one with many square brackets.[49] The bolder approach has a better chance of spurring movement toward consensus but runs a greater risk of rejection by the dissatisfied.

---

[44] *Bridges Daily Update* (15 September 2003). Kenya expressed its deep disappointment in WT/MIN(03)/W/21 (13 September 2003). Brazil detailed its objections to the agriculture annex (talking points used by Minister Amorim, 13 September), online at http://www.ictsd.org/ministerial/cancun/documents_and_links.htm.

[45] Interview with a participating developing country ambassador, Geneva, 5 November 2003.   [46] *Inside US Trade* (15 September 2003) 8.

[47] Interview with a Secretariat official, 13 August 2004.

[48] Interviews, Geneva, 19 November and 28 November 2002.

[49] Interview, Geneva, 19 November 2002. This resistance to compromise positions laid on the table might have increased in recent years as more governments began to publicize their WTO negotiating positions at home during the process for the first time.

3. The related dilemma of determining whether stated reservation values are bluffs or genuine

Confessionals may help resolve this dilemma, if they allow confident identification of true bottom lines different from stated ones. But when the chair hears the same firm positions in private as in public, he or she, always lacking complete information, may on the one hand bet that a stated position is a bluff and issue a compromise formulation. The danger on this side is illustrated by the 2003 case, when Pettigrew and Derbez may have bet that African and Least Developed Countries' ministers would accept some Singapore issues despite their public rejections. The opposite risk is to bet that inconsistent stated positions are final when in fact players still can be convinced they have room for flexibility, offer no compromise formulations, and fail to realize an available opportunity for agreement.

4. The dilemma of the weights

If Members work out their own provisional compromises, the chair can incorporate those. Otherwise how much weight should the chair assign to the positions of the respective Members and coalitions? The chair is in the midst of a struggle among Members with vastly unequal power despite their legal equality. A chair's compromise deal will be the most prominent focal point and thus may well influence the distribution of gains in the final deal. One scholar maintains that actually the WTO decides with invisible weighted voting; no small trader has anything approaching the effective clout of the US or the EU.[50] A vocal minority of WTO governments complains that informal practice is systematically biased against their preferences.[51] Proposals that are not generating support tend to be dropped unless they are from the EU or the US. One past chair acknowledges that shares of world trade are taken into account when deciding what elements to add to or exclude from a package.[52] But today the small are better organized in groups and more willing to use their authority to block the whole as a means of shifting the distribution of gain in their direction. The chair's obvious dilemma

---

[50] R. H. Steinberg, 'In the Shadow of Law or Power? Consensus-Based Bargaining and Outcomes in the GATT/WTO' in 56 *International Organization* (2002) 339–374.

[51] The Like Minded Group of 15 developing countries, led by India, has proposed rules that would curtail chairs' informal discretion to take initiatives and make decisions without approval by the full membership: WT/GC/W/471 (24 April 2001). F. Jawara and A. Kwa, *Behind the Scenes at the WTO: The Real World of International Trade Negotiations* (2003) report evidence of tactics used by the strong to coerce the weak into acquiescence. Also see A. Narlikar and J. S. Odell, 'The Strict Distributive Strategy for a Bargaining Coalition: The Like Minded Group in the World Trade Organization' in Odell, J. S. (ed.), *Developing Countries and the Trade Negotiation Process* under review.

[52] Interview, Geneva, 28 November 2002.

is that leaning too far in any direction may lead other members to reject the formulation.

IV. TYPE 3: MANIPULATION TACTICS

Occasionally GATT and WTO chairs, like mediators in other conflicts, go still further, resorting to more decisive or manipulative tactics that attempt to give the process or individuals a push in a particular direction.[53] In the WTO evidently most of these pushes come just prior to a deadline and after parts of a consensus have already been accepted informally. A GATT veteran recalls a time when the first Director-General, Eric Windham-White, intervened after a long and fractious discussion that had failed to generate consensus:

Windham-White came into a meeting and said, 'I've got the answer in my pocket.' Everyone said, 'Great!' Then he said, 'But I won't reveal it unless you agree to accept it first.' Eventually they said okay, they would. And that was the end of it.

A participant in the 1986 conference that launched the Uruguay Round reports how the chair, Minister Enrique Iglesias of Uruguay, orchestrated that process in the face of strong opposition from a minority, especially the ministers of Brazil, Argentina, and India:

On Wednesday we were still stuck on which of three texts to work on. He took 30 ministers off to the nearby town hall, and basically wouldn't let them go until we settled at least which text to work from. This was not the final outcome but at least a way forward.

He was a master in knowing when to push and when not to push. I'll never forget we were working on investment. The US had come down a great deal from what they wanted, yet Argentina would not give. Finally he looked over at the Argentine, just like this, and said, 'Please minister, surely this is something you can give.' If the minister had replied, 'absolutely not,' it would have been a mistake. But he said, 'Oh, well, if you insist . . .'[54]

Later during the Uruguay Round, Ambassador Julio Lacarte chaired the negotiating group working on a dispute settlement understanding. According to a participant in that group, Lacarte

would come to us and say, 'You can get what you want on A and on B but you are not going to get C also. You need to decide what you want most.' He went to all the important parties this way.

---

[53] Mediators in this institutionalized setting of course lack the wherewithal to manipulate parties as strongly as mediators who have attempted to end wars—for example, Lord Carrington at Lancaster House 1978, or President Carter at Camp David 1979.

[54] Interview, Geneva, 7 June 2000.

He tried to get groups [of delegates] to meet; he worked deals. I remember that the US, India and Brazil worked out one secret agreement with only Lacarte, outside room F [the official meeting room], then carefully scripted how we would act in the meeting. 'You say you can compromise on X, then I'll say I can compromise on Y.' This was all Julio's work.

By 1993 the Uruguay Round had dragged on for seven years, much had been agreed provisionally, yet a few major issues still blocked a package deal. With half a year remaining before the extended deadline, the Members turned to Peter Sutherland as a new Director-General and chair of the TNC. Sutherland banged heads together, according to many accounts. He threatened Geneva ambassadors that he would telephone their capitals if they did not make greater concessions. He did call ministers and even heads of state—US President Bill Clinton personally took one of his calls—to make the case for flexibility to save the round. Sutherland also used the public platform and the media to generate maximum pressure on governments. At the negotiating table in some instances he gaveled deals through, declaring them accepted, when he knew some members were not satisfied. He believed a failure after all those years would be catastrophic for the world trading system. Three weeks before the final deadline he told the ambassador of a major country that if the ambassador blocked the deal in a coming meeting, he would declare the Uruguay round over. The time remaining was too short to allow further work on this area.[55] In the meeting the ambassador did not raise his hand to object. These tactics might not have been insignificant in the outcome. In January 2004 as the Doha Round was frozen and only a year remained before its deadline, Director-General Supachai Panitchpakdi also began making public threats to go over the heads of ambassadors.[56]

Among the strongest moves available to a WTO chair is the threat to abandon mediation, as a means of stimulating concessions. With a Uruguay Round deadline extremely close, major gaps still divided the group on dispute settlement and future institutions. Lacarte decided that all participants had had ample opportunity to make all possible arguments. He personally drafted four short paragraphs that settled the outstanding issues and that he regarded as a fair resolution (a formulation tactic). During a lunch recess he invited four delegates—from the EC, the US, India, and Brazil—to his office. He selected these because they represented the extremes that had to be convinced. He presented his proposal to them, and although they had been at loggerheads, they told him after some discussion that they would support the compromise.

---

[55] Interview with a participant who was present, 6 December 2004.
[56] *Bridges* (January 2004).

After lunch, back in the plenary meeting Lacarte, saying nothing about the private meeting, announced that he had a proposal to make. He left a strong implication that if this proposal were not accepted, there would be no more efforts from this chair toward compromise (a manipulation tactic). The document was distributed and a long silence ensued. Lacarte said nothing to relieve the pressure. Eventually Canada gently said it could endorse the proposal. After another silence Japan followed, and eventually so did the rest.[57] The risk paid off in this case.

An even stronger move, though in the opposite direction, would be to end a negotiation when members prefer to keep talking. Chairman Derbez's decision to pull the plug in Cancún proved to be one of the most controversial acts by a WTO chair to date. After the crisis Saturday evening, Derbez met with five key ministers to decide what to do, then called the first Green Room meeting for Sunday morning. He decided the most urgent priority was to try to resolve the crisis over the Singapore issues. On Sunday morning, the last scheduled day, the EU's Pascal Lamy fell back from his demand to add four, eventually offering to settle for two, the least controversial two. After a break for representatives to consult their coalitions, the African Union held firm on its position refusing to add even one. Other developing countries concurred at that time, saying, 'There was not enough on the table.'[58] Arrangements had been made to stay another night, since these meetings are normally extended beyond the official closing date.

But Derbez, hearing this African position, announced he was closing the conference, before a plenary had been able to discuss agriculture or any other issue.[59] Saying it was pointless to continue, he perceived that harsh rhetoric by critics had fatally poisoned the atmosphere.[60] The Director-General agreed with the decision to end the conference at that time.[61] On the other hand Patricia Hewitt, the United Kingdom Trade Minister, complained that this decision was 'premature' and 'utterly unexpected.'[62] The EU delegation had expected the talks to shift to agriculture and allow a 'cooling-off period'. Some US team members also appeared surprised and frustrated.[63] All year many delegations had said they were holding back concessions on several issues until they saw more on the table for agriculture. Mediator George Yeo had offered a compromise text and felt there was a 2/3 chance of consensus

---

[57] Interview with a participant in these meetings, 5 December 2002.
[58] *Inside US Trade* (15 September 2003) 6.
[59] *Ibid.* at 1. Reportedly Derbez had told the facilitators or others in advance that he would end the conference if the parties remained divided (two interviews, July 2004).
[60] Interview with a Mexican participant, 24 September 2003.
[61] Interview with a Secretariat participant, 13 August 2004.
[62] *Bridges Daily Update* (15 September 2003).
[63] Interview with a participating US official, Mexico City, 4 May 2004.

around it.[64] The EU, the US, and other delegations later said they were working on a deal on farm trade and had not used all their flexibility.[65] The G20 had spent seven hours working on a new joint position moving somewhat from their previous position.[66] Brazil, leader of the G20, said it was equally surprised and did not prefer to stop talking.[67] Some African delegates, told that Derbez had decided to close the conference, were described as first doubting it could be true and were not happy.[68] Bangladesh's Minister and chair of the Least Developed Countries later said they could have shown more flexibility on the Singapore issues if they had been offered more on cotton.[69]

For some future chairs, then, an additional challenge in a stalemated negotiation will be to judge how long to wait before pulling the plug. A possible pitfall would be to intervene in this manner too early. But again to be fair, no chair will have complete information for forecasting delegations' true scope for concessions. More generally, if Members delay many difficult problems until one short conference, as in 2003, they will increase the odds of breakdown there. For instance, had the EU fallen back on the Singapore issues two weeks or even two days earlier, it would have made a major difference to this process. And politicians who fail to win their stated objectives will also have an incentive in domestic politics to find someone else to blame.

V. CONCLUSION

Deadlocks in multilateral WTO negotiations are more likely and more difficult to resolve today than prior to 1994. Numerous obstacles to agreement that are common in all multilateral negotiations are compounded by special features of this organization. Its Members depend in part on the efforts of chairpersons of its negotiating bodies, including the Director-General, to help them overcome these impasses, given its present institutions.

WTO chairs seem to have limited but significant influence on the efficiency and legitimacy of negotiations and the resulting distribution

---

[64] *Straits Times* (15 September 2003).

[65] Interviews, Geneva 2003 and August 2004.

[66] *Inside US Trade* (15 September 2003) 11.

[67] Interview, Geneva, November 2003.

[68] Correspondence with a delegate who was inside the delegates' area of the building, 26 June 2004.

[69] *Bridges Daily Update* (15 September 2003). My research casts doubt on the press report (*New York Times*, 16 September 2003), quoted many times thereafter, that this conference ended because developing countries 'walked out'. Also note that the following summer, developing countries agreed to add one Singapore issue (trade facilitation) to the Round's agenda, when there was more on the table in the agriculture area.

of gains and losses. Mediators in the WTO, like those working elsewhere in international relations, can choose from a menu of tactics. The options range from the more passive—observation, diagnosis, and communication—to formulation tactics, to the most decisive manipulation tactics.

Carrying out the function of chair–mediator raises several tricky challenges and dilemmas. They include diagnosing impasses, separating bluffs from true reservation values, imagining integrative multi-issue deals, deciding when to offer a single negotiating text, how cautious or bold to make it, how to weight the demands of diverse Members to satisfy the expectation of perceived balance, when if ever to push particular members in certain directions, and how long to wait before ending a stalemated negotiation. It is easy to go wrong or become sidelined. Experience nevertheless suggests positive lessons as well as pitfalls to avoid.

While this preliminary effort has scratched the surface, deeper research would improve our understanding of this phenomenon. Fuller and more case-studies of mediation attempts might tease out better generalizations about the conditions and tactics that favour success. Scholars could consider the analytical value of the concept of the 'batma,' the mediator's best alternative to a mediated agreement,[70] for understanding and influencing mediator behaviour. Comparisons of attempts at different stages of the process and in organizations with different rules and cultures might be instructive.

What a future chair–mediator will be able to do will also depend on the state of the institution. The WTO during its formative first decade experienced an unanticipated clash of two diplomatic cultures. Trade diplomats with experience in the GATT naturally expected to continue the special informal decision-making practices of their experience. But the membership expanded dramatically, by the formal accession of non-members and also effectively, as developing and transition GATT Members that had been largely passive became much more active in negotiations. Many WTO diplomats from newly active Members had never worked in the GATT but did bring experience in the United Nations (UN) and other multilateral organizations. These delegates too naturally expected the new WTO to operate according to their experience. For UN veterans, the normal way to produce a written agreement was to appoint a formal drafting committee of national delegates, which decided which text to include and exclude. These delegates from small states felt disenfranchised by the less transparent GATT practice,

---

[70] P. Steenhausen, *Negotiating among Mediators: Multiparty Mediation in International Politics*, Dissertation, University of Southern California (2003). Other research suggestions are found in Odell, *supra* n. 1.

whereby a small group of the most powerful traders and the Secretariat met privately without notice to the majority, rejected many proposals without notice, hammered out important deals, and reported them to the many. Chairs during that time found themselves with the task of helping to discover what modes would be acceptable in this old–new organization.

At the time this is written, the GATT mode seems to have largely prevailed over any alternative. Most fundamentally, new members joined the old in deciding after Seattle to reaffirm the GATT norm that WTO decisions should normally be made by consensus rather than majority voting, especially regarding obligations that will be legally binding on each Member state.[71] Nor are facilitators for ministerial conferences elected by the majority. Virtually all governments acknowledged that informal consultations in smaller groups are essential steps in building multilateral consensus. No major formal changes in decision-making institutions were adopted. But leaders have made the process more inclusive and somewhat more transparent than before 1994, through an informal representative system based on coalitions and by adding African ministers to 'mini-Ministerials'. The legitimacy of this adjusted GATT mode in 2003 and 2004 among governments seemed higher than in 1999, at least judging from a decline in official complaints about internal transparency.

To make this mode as efficient and legitimate as possible, the organization could consider widening and institutionalizing the process of drawing lessons for chairs and passing them along. Members could ask the Director-General to host a private one-day retreat each year to help prepare chairs of Geneva bodies due to take office the next year. Veterans could be invited to join the new team, and all could share ideas and ask questions about the recurring functions and dilemmas of the chair that are not spelled out in rules but on which experience can be brought to bear. Such a meeting would no doubt also discuss the issues of the day and how the work of the several bodies might be coordinated. The Director-General and the chair of each ministerial conference could consider hosting an analogous private session a month prior to the conference, bringing together ministers who have been asked to function as a team of facilitators. They could receive briefings on the state of play on the outstanding issues, receive training, establish

---

[71] 'The View of the African Group on Enhancing the Internal Transparency and the Effective Participation of all Members of the World Trade Organization', March 2000, provided by the Geneva office of the Organization of African Unity; and 'General Council, Monday 17 July 2000, Internal Transparency and the Effective Participation of Members, Chairman's Statement', provided by Ambassador Kåre Bryn, Norway's Mission to the WTO, Geneva.

working relationships among themselves, and plan how they will coordinate during the conference. Regular retreats at both levels might help increase *esprit de corps* and personal identification with the Organization and the common interest as well as efficiency.

In even the best case, no team of mediators will have the power to solve all the WTO's problems of efficiency and legitimacy. To that end the future could bring more attempts to change this institution formally. But in that case too, members seeking and resisting such changes will depend in part on their chairpersons to mediate and seek a consensus result.

ANNEX: PARTIAL LIST OF PERSONS INTERVIEWED

Abbott, Roderick, Ambassador of the EU to the WTO, 1996–2000; Deputy Director-General, WTO, 2002 to present

Amorim, Celso, Ambassador of Brazil to the WTO, 1998–2000; Foreign Minister 2003 to present

Bradley, A. Jane, US Trade Representative's office, 1982–2003

Bryn, Kåre, Ambassador of Norway to the WTO, 1999 to present; chair of Dispute Settlement Body and of General Council, 2000

Castillo, Dacio, Ambassador of Honduras to the WTO, 1998 to present

Chandrasekhar, K. M., Ambassador of India to the WTO, 2001 to present

Chidyausiku, Boniface G., Ambassador of Zimbabwe to the WTO, 2000–02; chair of Council on TRIPS special session, 2001; chair of Committee on Regional Trade Agreements, 2002

Deily, Linnet, Ambassador of the US to the WTO, 2001 to present

Dunkel, Arthur, Director-General, GATT, 1980–93

Girard, Pierre-Louis, Ambassador of Switzerland to the GATT 1984–88 and to WTO 2000 to present; chair of Working Group on China's Accession; chair of negotiating group on Non-Agricultural Market Access, 2001–03

Harbinson, Stuart, Ambassador of Hong Kong to the WTO, 1998–2001; chair of General Council, 2001; *chef de cabinet* to Supachai Panitchpakdi, 2002 to present

Hartridge, David, *chef de cabinet* to Arthur Dunkel, 1980–85; Director, Office of Multilateral Trade Negotiations, GATT Secretariat, 1986–93; Director, Trade and Services Division, WTO Secretariat, 1993–2001

Hayes, Rita, Ambassador of the US to the WTO, 1997–2001

Lacarte Muró, Julio, Ambassador of Uruguay to the GATT, 1961–66 and 1982–92; chair of GATT Council, the Contracting Parties, and the negotiating group on dispute settlement and institutional questions; member of the WTO Appellate Body, 1995–2000

Low, Patrick, Counsellor, GATT Secretariat 1980–88; *chef de cabinet* to Mike Moore, 1999–2002, Director, Economic and Development Research, WTO Secretariat, 1997–99 and 2002 to present

Moore, Mike, Prime Minister, New Zealand; Director-General, WTO, 1999–2002

Otten, Adrian, Director, Intellectual Property Division, WTO Secretariat, 1995 to present

Ouedraogo, Ablassé, Foreign Minister, Burkina Faso, 1994–99; Deputy Director-General, WTO, 1999–2002

Perez del Castillo, Carlos, Ambassador of Uruguay to the WTO, 1998 to present; chair of several WTO bodies including the General Council in 2003

Rana, Kipkorir Aly, Ambassador of Kenya to the WTO, 1998–2001, Deputy Director-General, 2002 to present

Ricupero, Rubens, Ambassador of Brazil to the GATT, Chair of the GATT Council and Contracting Parties, 1987–91; Secretary-General of UNCTAD 1995–2004

Rodriguez Mendoza, Miguel, Minister of Trade, Venezuela, 1991–94; Deputy Director-General, WTO, 1999–2002

Seixas Corrêa, Luiz Felipe, Ambassador of Brazil to the WTO, 2002 to present

Smith, Ransford, Ambassador of Jamaica to WTO, 1999 to present; Chair of the Negotiating Group on Trade and Development, 2001–03

Stoler, Andrew, US Trade Representative's Office 1982–99; Deputy Director-General, WTO, 1999–2002

Sutherland, Peter. Director General, GATT and WTO, 1993–95

Weekes, John M., Ambassador of Canada to the GATT, Chair of the GATT Council and Contracting Parties, 1989–90; Ambassador of Canada to WTO, 1995–99; Chair of the General Council, 1998

Zain Dom, Mohammed, Malaysia's Mission to the GATT during the Uruguay Round, and Deputy Permanent Representative to the WTO, 1999 to present

27

Are WTO Decision-Making Procedures Adequate for Making, Revising, and Implementing Worldwide and 'Plurilateral' Rules?

CLAUS-DIETER EHLERMANN AND LOTHAR EHRING[1]

I. INTRODUCTION

The World Trade Organization (WTO) currently has a membership of 148 sovereign States and independent customs territories. Its agreements cover some 95 per cent of international trade and regulate the trade of goods and services as well as the protection of intellectual property rights. Its membership comes close to that of a universal organization, even more so if one considers that a significant proportion of the remaining non-Members are currently negotiating their accession to the WTO. The reason why the WTO is important and unique, however, is also that it has been and continues to be *the* forum in which trade negotiations take place at the worldwide level in subsequent rounds. These negotiations result in binding international agreements that can be enforced in a highly effective, compulsory and exclusive quasi-judiciary.

Together with other factors, the strong increase of international trade (significantly faster than the growth of world gross domestic product (GDP)) and of other aspects of economic interaction (e.g. investment) has resulted in an increased international economic interdependence. In view of this interdependence, nation state governments cannot regulate

[1] We are most grateful to Christoph Bail, Karl Friedrich Falkenberg, Julio Lacarte Muró, Andy Stoler, Peter Witt, and Rufus Yerxa for sharing with us their historic insights on various aspects developed in this paper, to Tomer Broude, Ignacio García Bercero, Julio Lacarte Muró, and Andy Stoler for commenting on an earlier draft, and to Denchu Georgiev, Stuart Harbinson, David Shark, Faizel Ismail, Carlo Trojan, and John Weekes for commenting on the paper presented in Florence on 2 July 2004 at the 3rd *Annual Conference on Preparing the Doha Development Round: WTO Negotiators Meet the Academics*. This paper expresses only the authors' personal views.

effectively any more in many areas,[2] which is why effective international governance is needed in order to manage globalization. At a time when global governance is more necessary than ever before,[3] the WTO is a forum in which the international community can achieve many important things, given its rule-making vocation, its broad membership, and its effective enforcement mechanism.

Yet the WTO has not always presented itself as an organization that pursues its agenda effectively and easily. Sometimes, or even regularly, it goes through periods of crisis and perceived or threatening paralysis. The Ministerial Conferences at Seattle and Cancún are two recent examples. Signs of inefficiency regularly also appear in Geneva, be it in the context of negotiating new agreements or in the context of the revision or even just application of the existing trade rules. A recent high profile example is the Agreement on Trade-Related Aspects of Intellectual Property Rights (TRIPS) and public health issues.[4] Arguably, the pressure imposed by the upcoming Cancún Ministerial Conference was essential in achieving a provisional solution in late August 2003, whereas the post-Cancún talks on a long-term solution have again been deadlocked. The big failures of course attract even more attention and also generate more reflection and criticism regarding the WTO's effectiveness. The recent Cancún collapse certainly has aroused doubts about the organization's effectiveness[5] and has prompted people to see the WTO as being at a 'crossroads'[6] or even in a 'constitutional moment which parallels the creation of the GATT 1947 and the WTO.'[7]

Of course, the failure of Cancún, and previously that of Seattle, was rooted in the divide that exists between Members of the WTO on many issues of substance (agriculture, trade and investment, trade and competition, market access, etc.).[8] In that sense, it has been said that the

---

[2] J. H. Jackson, 'The WTO "Constitution" and Proposed Reforms: Seven "Mantras" Revisited' in 67 *Journal of International Economic Law* (2001) at 69.

[3] One may even say that there is not enough international governance. See e.g. P. Lamy, 'Mondialisation: Pascal Lamy dénonce un déficit de gouvernance internationale', interview in *Les Echos* (22 May 2000), online at http://europa.eu.int/comm/commissioners/lamy/speeches_articles/intla01_fr.htm.

[4] Where the WTO was not able to meet the December 2002 deadline imposed in para. 6 of the Doha Declaration on the TRIPS Agreement and Public Health, and where one single Member prevented consensus for a protracted period of time.

[5] S. Cho, 'A Bridge too Far: The Fall of the Fifth WTO Ministerial Conference in Cancún and the Future of Trade Constitution' in 7 *Journal of International Economic Law* (2004) 219 at 220.

[6] S. J. Evenett, *Systemic Research Questions Raised by the Failure of the WTO Ministerial Meeting in Cancún*, 1 *Legal Issues of European Integration* 2004 at 2. The 2004 Symposium of the WTO, held in Geneva to foster dialogue with civil society, has also been named 'Multilateralism at a Crossroads'.

[7] Cho, *supra* n. 5 at 221 and 244.

[8] For a perspective on the chronology of events, see Cho, *supra* n. 5 at 221–235.

failures were programmed. It is obvious that if all Members were in agreement over the substance, the world trading system would work smoothly and there would be no crises. However, substantive divergences are to some extent a normal phenomenon (even though it is at times difficult to understand the existing divergence on particular topics). The fact that conflicting interests are a frequent reality in just about every polity or other organization is precisely the reason why it is so important to have in place institutions that can balance these diverging interests. The situation of conflict is thus the situation in which an effective decision-making mechanism is most needed to resolve contentious issues. This is what has not worked well enough in the recent past.

In this sense, the European Commissioner for Trade, Pascal Lamy, has ascribed the collapse of Seattle and Cancún to the WTO's 'medieval' decision-making process. After Cancún, discussions have taken place on the need and possibility of reforming the WTO. Given the prominence of the outstanding substantive issues, the post-Cancún discussions, however, soon returned to the specifics of the Doha Mandate. Therefore, it seems worthwhile and important to continue to devote attention to the question of whether the WTO shows institutional deficiencies and how they could be addressed with a view to improvement. In terms of how to measure improvement, effectiveness and efficiency are of course not the sole considerations. The importance of transparency, participation, and accountability, as well as other aspects of democratic legitimacy, should in no way be discounted. Yet it is submitted that promoting these higher values will be difficult or at least insufficient if the decision-making system is not effective.

A reform of the current system can mean two basically different things: on the one hand, one can think of changing the rules on decision-making in the WTO Agreement (along with changing the practice). On the other hand, reform can mean exploring the scope for improvement within the framework of the existing rules, i.e. changing the practice, but not the rules. We believe that, for both dogmatic and pragmatic reasons, the latter exercise should receive priority over the former. First, it would be extremely difficult to achieve a modification of the rules on decision-making in the present context where the adoption of new multilateral trade rules is in general rather difficult.[9] Second, before resorting to proposing legislative change, one should explore the existing rules and the extent to which improvements are possible within their limits without formal change, as only such an exercise can reveal the need, if any, for legislative change.

---

[9] One might prefer not to imagine the kind of institutional crisis that would probably be necessary for convincing the WTO Members of the necessity to modify the rules on decision-making.

With this in mind, we propose to take a closer look at the rules on decision-making and rule-making in the WTO Agreement. Of course, there are other levels on which, more in the sense of fine-tuning, improvements can and should be explored, e.g. how Ministerial Conferences are organized, the role of the chair, etc. This chapter, however, undertakes a more fundamental critique, also with the intention of keeping the debate on the WTO's institutional reform alive, even when negotiations are currently gaining momentum again. There is also hope that the institutional debate will be revitalised when the Consultative Board set up by Director-General Supachai Panitchpakdi in June 2003 and chaired by former Director-General Peter Sutherland publishes its report.

II. PROCEDURES FOR MAKING, REVISING, AND IMPLEMENTING TRADE RULES IN THE WTO

One needs to distinguish between rule-making and decision-making, as these exercises are different in nature from a constitutional point of view. The formal rules of the WTO reflect this distinction, even though it largely disappears in the Organization's practice.

A. The rules as they currently exist

1. Procedures for implementing trade rules

As is well known, the process of decision-making in the WTO is dominated by the practice of consensus. As is also well known, consensus means that 'no Member, present at the meeting when the decision is taken, formally objects to the proposed decision'.[10] Often, at least one Member objects to a proposal, and in those circumstances, the next step is typically a protracted effort to reach consensus by overcoming the existing resistance, e.g. by finding a compromise. If this does not work, no decision is taken.

This contrasts with Article IX:1 of the WTO Agreement, which does not require consensus for all cases. While the first sentence states that '[t]he WTO shall continue the practice of decision-making by consensus followed under GATT 1947', the second sentence allows votes: 'except as otherwise provided, where a decision cannot be arrived at by consensus, the matter at issue shall be decided by voting'. Those decisions are reached with a (simple) majority of the votes cast. An exception is Article 2.4 of the Dispute Settlement Understanding (DSU),

---

[10] Footnote 1 to the WTO Agreement.

according to which the Dispute Settlement Body (DSB) decides by consensus, with the notable exception of the reverse consensus mechanism for the key steps of a dispute settlement procedure.[11] Hence, except for the DSB, the bodies of the WTO would normally decide according to a two-step approach: consensus if possible, otherwise vote.

The Rules of Procedure contain quite detailed rules on how votes would take place. Rule 16 of the Rules of Procedure for Sessions of the Ministerial Conference and of the Rules of Procedure for Meetings of the General Council provides that a majority of Members must be present for votes to take place (quorum). Rules 29 and 34 specify that when decisions are required to be taken by vote, such votes be taken by ballot but that the representative of any Member may request, or the chairperson suggest, that a vote be taken by raising cards or roll-call. Where the WTO Agreement requires a vote by a qualified majority of all Members, the Ministerial Conference/General Council may decide that the vote be taken by airmail ballots or ballots transmitted by telegraph or telefacsimile. The respective Annex 1 of these Rules of Procedure contains further details for such airmail/telex/telefax ballots, *inter alia* a notice to be sent to each Member and a time limit of a maximum of 30 days.[12] The Councils, Committees, and other subordinate bodies of the WTO, however, are required by Rule 33 of their respective Rules of Procedure to refer a matter to the General Council whenever they are unable to reach a decision by consensus.[13]

2. Procedures for making trade rules

When rules are made from scratch, i.e. new international agreements adopted, it is no wonder that consensus generally governs the procedure. After all, the signatories of the agreement are to ratify the text ('express their consent to be bound'), which is even more than consensus because a subject of international law becomes party to the agreement only by express (and typically written) consent.

Nevertheless, it is worth pointing out that Article 9(2) of the Vienna Convention on the Law of Treaties foresees that the 'adoption of the text of a treaty at an international conference takes place by the vote of two-thirds of the States present and voting, unless by the same majority they shall decide to apply a different rule'. Yet this only goes for the adoption of the text which does not yet result in the States being bound.

---

[11] Arts. 6.1 (panel establishment), 16.4 (panel report adoption), 17.14 (Appellate Body report adoption), 22.6/22.7 of the DSU (authorization of the suspension of obligations).

[12] WTO, *Rules of Procedure for Sessions of the Ministerial Conference and for Meetings of the General Council*, WT/L/161 (25 July 1996).

[13] See e.g. WTO, *Rules of Procedure for Meetings of the Council for Trade in Goods*, WT/L/79 (7 August 1995).

A majority vote in which up to one-third of the negotiation participants are outvoted therefore risks reducing the number of States that will later sign up (and ratify). Even if there are in many cases other reasons for non-signing or non-ratification, it is interesting to point out that the number of signatories of many United Nations (UN)-sponsored conventions is far below the number of conference participants; in fact this is the fate of the Vienna Convention itself.

In international trade, it is desirable that the number of countries that sign up to the agreements be as large as possible for economic[14] and legal[15] reasons. It is therefore productive if trade agreements are shaped in such a manner that, if possible, all become a party. This involves a search for compromises, persuasion, and sometimes a certain degree of pressure on other States. Sometimes, an agreement with partial reach is better than no agreement, and in those cases plurilateral agreements are the best choice. However, Article X:9 of the WTO Agreement requires consensus of the Ministerial Conference for adding a plurilateral agreement to Annex 4.[16]

The required consent of every single State for that State to be bound by an international agreement constitutes an inbuilt preference for the status quo in international law (by default, this status quo amounts to a lack of legal disciplines, otherwise the status quo comprises those legal disciplines that have emerged so far). This contrasts with domestic democracies (representative or direct) where simple majority votes are formally neutral on making or not making, unmaking or changing rules. Obviously, in comparison, international rule-making is highly cumbersome and less effective, possibly more cumbersome and less efficient than it should be in the light of today's demand for international governance in a world of increased international interdependence and eroding independence of single States as regulators.

3. Procedures for revising/modifying trade rules

(a) Amendment

The default rule on amendments in public international law is Article 40 of the Vienna Convention, according to which an amendment does not

---

[14] Raising prosperity of all, protecting comparative advantage rather than creating distortions in the form of trade diversion.

[15] Homogenous rights and obligations, most-favoured-nation clause.

[16] Which may seem somewhat counter-intuitive because the parties to the plurilateral agreement could also enter into this agreement outside of the WTO. Such an approach would, however, subject the advantages granted under the agreement to the obligation of most-favoured-nation treatment under Art. I:1 of GATT 1994. For plurilateral agreements, Art. II:3, second sentence, of the WTO Agreement precludes obligations or rights for non-parties. Art. II:3 supersedes the GATT according to Art. XVI:3 of the WTO Agreement.

require the consent of all parties, but obviously no party is bound by the amendment unless it gives its consent. With one exception, Article X of the WTO Agreement is stricter. It first provides that the Ministerial Conference must approve an amendment proposal with a two-thirds majority of the Members, if it cannot reach consensus. Then, two-thirds of the Members must accept the amendment for it to become effective: for all Members, where the amendment does not alter substantive rights and obligations; for those who accept the amendment, where it does alter substantive rights and obligations.[17] The former procedure, however, requires a three-quarters majority decision by the Ministerial Conference. Amendments to the DSU are possible only through consensus. Modifications of Articles IX and X of the WTO Agreement, of the most-favoured-nation (MFN) treatment rules and of Article II of GATT 1994 (on bindings) require every Member's consent.

(b) Accession

A special form of amendment is the accession of a new Member to the WTO. Such accession is an amendment of the WTO Agreement because this Agreement is modified so as to cover an additional subject of international law. Legally, the standard WTO Accession Protocol amends the WTO Agreement by becoming an integral part of the WTO Agreement.[18] Nevertheless, the Accession Protocol is an agreement between the new Member and the WTO (Article XII:1 of the WTO Agreement), not an (amendment) agreement between the new and the old Members. In terms of decision-making, Article XII:2 stipulates that the Ministerial Conference approves the accession agreement by a two-thirds majority of the Members. Yet when a new Member accedes, Article XIII permits Members to exclude the application of the WTO Agreement in relation to the new Member by so notifying the Ministerial Conference.

(c) Renegotiation of commitments

In the WTO Agreement, rights and obligations are also set out in each Member's schedule of commitments. As is known, this part of the Agreement accounts for the majority of the famous 25,000 pages. If a Member intends to modify or withdraw a concession under the General Agreement on Tariffs and Trade (GATT) (typically a tariff concession), Article XXVIII of the GATT 1994 provides for the possibility to do so

---

[17] In the latter case, the Ministerial Conference can decide with a three-quarters majority of the Members that Members who do not accept the amendment must withdraw from the WTO or can remain a Member with the consent of the Ministerial Conference.

[18] E.g. para. 1.2 of China's Accession Protocol states: 'This Protocol, which shall include the commitments referred to in paragraph 342 of the Working Party Report, shall be an integral part of the WTO Agreement.'

according to a procedure that is considerably lighter than the amendment procedure under Article X of the WTO Agreement. Preferably, that Member should reach agreement with the other Members primarily concerned (principal supplier(s) and Members holding an initial negotiation right) and with those having a substantial interest, i.e. only a subset of WTO Members. If no agreement is reached, the Member in question can nevertheless proceed (unilaterally) with the modification or withdrawal of its concession and the other Members with rights under Article XXVIII may then withdraw substantially equivalent concessions initially negotiated with that Member.

Article XXI of the General Agreement on Trade in Services (GATS) provides for a similar, but slightly stricter procedure for a Member that wishes to modify a commitment it has made in its services schedule.

(d) Waiver

In exceptional circumstances, the Ministerial Conference and the General Council may waive particular WTO obligations of any given WTO Member by a three-quarters vote.[19] Waivers are exemptions for certain Members from specific WTO obligations. They must be temporary (although they can be extended) and reviewed annually.

(e) Authoritative interpretation

A special instrument foreseen in the WTO Agreement that can be used to refine or revise multilateral trade rules is the interpretation provided for in Article IX:2. This instrument is an invention of the Uruguay Round; it did not exist under the GATT 1947. In Article 3.9 of the DSU, it is referred to as the 'authoritative interpretation', which allows it to be distinguished from the kind of interpretation performed by panels and the Appellate Body in clarifying the provisions of the WTO Agreement.[20] Article IX:2 attributes the responsibility for adopting such interpretations to the Ministerial Conference and the General Council and stipulates a decision by three-quarters majority of the Members and—for interpretations of the GATT, multilateral agreements on trade in goods, the GATS and the TRIPS Agreement—that there has been a recommendation by the respective Council (for Trade in Goods/Services/Intellectual Property). Article IX:2 also states that it must not be used in a manner that would undermine the amendment provisions in Article X.

Although the legal effect of an authoritative interpretation is not spelt out in Article IX:2 of the WTO Agreement, it is relatively clear that such

---

[19] Art. IX:3 of the WTO Agreement. Footnote 4 of the WTO Agreement requires consensus for decisions to grant a waiver with respect to implementation periods.

[20] See Arts. 3.2 and 17.6 of the DSU.

an interpretation would bind all Members.[21] It has also been suggested that, unlike panel and Appellate Body reports and DSB rulings and recommendations,[22] an authoritative interpretation may add to or diminish rights and obligations of Members under the WTO Agreement.[23] This latter aspect is somewhat contested, also on the basis of the last sentence of Article IX:2, which prohibits undermining the amendment provisions. Yet if an authoritative interpretation were not able to modify the law, it could only clarify existing obligations in accordance with the Vienna Convention interpretation rules. This does not make much sense for a decision emanating from a political organ and it would excessively narrow the purpose for which an authoritative interpretation could be used. Also, it would arguably mean that the Appellate Body could revise any such interpretation as regards whether it constitutes a 'permissible' interpretation of the relevant provisions under the customary rules of interpretation (in order to be valid). Otherwise, if an *ultra vires* interpretation were nevertheless to be binding on (i.e. non-reviewable by) the Appellate Body, the whole question would be academic. Thus, the General Council arguably need not apply the rules of treaty interpretation in formulating an 'authoritative interpretation', in other words it may modify WTO law. The attribute 'authoritative' would seem to further support this thesis. The prohibition on undermining the amendment provisions in Article IX:2, last sentence, certainly imposes a limit on the extent to which the authoritative interpretation can serve for the purpose of revising trade rules. However, the verb 'undermine' is relatively strong, which permits reading that proviso somewhat restrictively, also to avoid making Article IX:2 redundant and void of effect. According to such reading, not every fine-tuning of a provision of the WTO Agreement would immediately 'undermine' the amendment provisions.

Theoretically speaking, the authoritative interpretation under Article IX:2 of the WTO Agreement is of high potential relevance. It gives the political bodies of the WTO an opportunity to refine existing trade rules. This can serve to determine the scope of rules in a prospective manner, but also to correct an interpretation given by a panel or the Appellate Body, whose rulings can no longer easily be blocked.[24]

---

[21] See the inferences in Appellate Body Report, *Japan—Alcohol II*, p. 12; and, more explicitly, Appellate Body Report, *US—FSC*, paras. 112–113, including footnote 127.

[22] Arts. 3.2 and 19.2 of the DSU.

[23] The Appellate Body has implicitly endorsed this position; see Appellate Body Report, *US—FSC*, para. 112, footnote 127.

[24] Arguably, even if Members were exceptionally to succeed in preventing the adoption of a panel (and Appellate Body) report, by building a negative consensus, the relevant piece of jurisprudence would not disappear. A subsequent panel, or the Appellate Body in a subsequent appeal, may well adhere to the interpretation of the earlier panel (or Appellate Body) report, if they find it convincing. See Panel Report, *Japan—Alcoholic Beverages II*, para. 6.10; Appellate Body Report, *Japan—Alcoholic Beverages II*, p. 14.

The quasi-automaticity of the adoption of dispute settlement reports makes the authoritative interpretation a necessary instrument of checks and balance vis-à-vis the WTO's quasi-judiciary. If, unlike under the GATT 1947, individual WTO Members can no longer veto the adoption of a report, in fact even an overwhelming majority of WTO Members could not do so as long as one Member (presumably the winner, but in fact any Member) insists on adoption, corrections of jurisprudential developments should be possible to allow for a legislative response. The authoritative interpretation should perhaps not be viewed exclusively through the lens of dispute settlement, but for the reasons mentioned, such a strong correlation exists, as Article 3.9 of the DSU corroborates.

Whether an authoritative interpretation that is adopted during a pending dispute (i.e. after the panel has been established and before the Appellate Body issues its report) has legal effect on the outcome of this dispute depends on the relevant point in time for the legal evaluation of the matter in dispute. Although the WTO jurisprudence is somewhat unclear and arguably also inconsistent on this point, the tendency is to focus on the facts (the challenged measure) as they existed at the time of the establishment of the panel. This would theoretically preclude taking account of subsequent legal modifications, as far as substantive obligations are concerned. Nevertheless, at the stage of implementation, a losing Member would arguably have to (and be entitled to) be guided by the authoritative interpretation adopted in the intervening period. It might therefore be worthwhile to clarify this issue so as to prevent interference with pending disputes (and resistance from the party fearing a disadvantage for its litigation) by limiting any effect of an authoritative interpretation to other (future) cases.

B. How the WTO rules came about and how they were intended to operate

If one compares the WTO rules on decision-making, in particular Article IX, with the consensus-dominated practice of the WTO, one may wonder why such rules were incorporated that foresee votes when consensus cannot be achieved. When the WTO Agreement was drafted in the Uruguay Round, was there a belief that this would remain dead letter? In the search for a response, it is worth exploring the historical background. This is, on the one hand, the law and the practice under the GATT 1947. On the other hand, it is worthwhile to explore, to an unavoidably limited extent, the intentions and expectations of the negotiators during the Uruguay Round when they formulated the WTO Agreement, notably Article IX.

1. *The GATT 1947 and evolving practice*

When one reviews the institutional provisions of the GATT 1947, it becomes clear that Article XXX of the GATT 1947 inspired Article X of the WTO Agreement on amendments, and Article XXXIII of the GATT 1947 inspired Article XII of the WTO Agreement on accessions. Article XXV:4 of the GATT 1947 states that: 'Except as otherwise provided for in this Agreement, decisions of the Contracting Parties shall be taken by a majority of the votes cast.'[25] Article XXV:3 gave each contracting party one vote. Special majorities were called for in Articles XXIV:10, XXV:5, and XXXIII. Article XXIV:10 provided for a two-thirds majority for approving a regional trade agreement that does not fully comply with the requirements of Article XXIV:5–9. Article XXV:5 provided for waivers of obligations but required that 'any such decision shall be approved by a two-thirds majority of the votes cast and that such majority shall comprise more than half of the contracting parties'.

Voting did take place, but routinely only in decisions on waivers under Article XXV:5 and on accessions under Article XXXIII of the GATT 1947. In relation to other business, the Contracting Parties did not usually proceed to a formal vote in reaching decisions, but the chairperson took the sense of the meeting.[26] Even on waivers, a consensus in the GATT Council very often preceded the votes. Notable exceptions prove this rule, and one such situation occurred in 1990 at the annual session of the Contracting Parties when the European Economic Community (EEC) requested a vote by roll-call on a waiver for the German Democratic Republic's trade preferences to former Soviet bloc countries. Despite the surprise and confusion this caused to many delegated who did not even have time to seek instructions, the unperturbed chairman applied the existing procedures and immediately proceeded to the vote by roll-call.

In the early days of the GATT, the chairman of the Contracting Parties often resolved questions of interpretation through rulings that were tacitly or expressly accepted or put to a roll-call vote.[27] Over the years, decision-making by consensus became increasingly prevalent with the number of developing countries entering the international system in the wave of decolonization and their accumulation of large voting majorities, although this is not a sufficient explanation if one looks at the early days of the GATT.[28] The GATT Analytical Index stated in

---

[25] Which included the possibility of postal voting, See GATT, *Analytical Index: Guide to GATT Law and Practice* (6th edn 1995), at 881.
[26] *Ibid.*, note 24, pp. 1098–1099.   [27] *Ibid.*, p. 875.
[28] M. E. Footer, 'The Role of Consensus in GATT/WTO Decision-Making' in 17 *Northwestern Journal of International Law and Business* (1996–97) 653 at 663–664.

1995 that the most recent recorded decision of the Contracting Parties adopted by vote, other than decisions on waivers or accession, was in 1959.[29] However, the United States (US) called for and obtained a vote in 1985 on whether to hold a special session of the Contracting Parties for the purpose of launching a new round of negotiations (the Uruguay Round).

The GATT 1947 is thus a partial answer to the question of where the rules on voting in the WTO Agreement come from. When the WTO Agreement was drafted, the evolution from votes to consensus (a term that did not even appear in the GATT 1947) was reflected in Article IX:1 of the WTO Agreement by making consensus the first choice. Article XVI:1 reinforced this by stipulating that the WTO be 'guided by the decisions, procedures and customary practices followed by the Contracting Parties to GATT 1947'. Yet it is important to note that voting was not abandoned in the text of the new Agreement and one can also say that the text gives it a more prominent role (vote when no consensus) than the GATT practice had given (outside the area of waivers and accessions). This justifies posing the question about the intentions and expectations of Uruguay Round negotiators.

2. *Uruguay Round negotiations on the establishment of a World Trade Organization*

One must recall that the negotiations on the Multilateral Trade Organization (MTO, later in the negotiations to become the WTO) as an institution and international organization had started between the EEC (later becoming the EC) and Canada, subsequently they also involved Mexico. This resulted in the 'Dunkel Draft' version of the Agreement Establishing the MTO. The US joined in only at a later stage when it became interested in the MTO as a vehicle for the single undertaking. The US disliked the draft text because it perceived the decision-making rules to be stronger than those in the existing GATT and considered these to be a threat to its sovereignty. It was already clear that there would be a strong majority of developing countries in the MTO/WTO. Some countries therefore intended to avoid the risk of frequent votes which, if taken along developed versus developing lines, could have resulted in majorities adverse to their interests. Thus, in the autumn of 1993, some major players worked hard on previous drafts in order to constrain the decision-making process.[30]

---

[29] *Analytical Index, supra* n. 25, p. 1099. The object of the vote was the Recommendation on Freedom of Contract in Transport Insurance of 27 May 1959, *BISD* 8S/26; adoption by 22–7 vote with 4 abstentions, SR.14/9 p. 115.

[30] Jackson, *supra* n. 2 at 74.

One of the main objectives of the US was to change the MTO text and to make it as difficult as possible to take decisions. The main concerns were (i) that developing countries would try to use the decision-making voting rules to get out of their obligations later on (note that Footnote 4 to Article IX:3 of the WTO Agreement exceptionally requires consensus for waivers of transition periods) and (ii) that US sovereignty would be undermined by amendments forced through by quickly formed majorities. The latter was ultimately protected by a return to the GATT approach for amendments with an impact on rights and obligations. Also, the US successfully fought for the combination of the three-quarters majority rule and the prohibition to undermine the amendment procedure in the context of authoritative interpretations (Article IX:2).

On other types of decisions, the ultimate compromise consisted in laying down a two-step approach: first consensus, and if necessary, as a second step, voting. In a way, this codified 'consensus' which had previously not been part of the GATT text, but had been the practice. At the same time, one must note that the two-step approach does not reflect a practice in which practically no votes took place other than on accessions and waivers (that are regulated elsewhere than in Article IX:2). Thus, the fact that voting was not eliminated from the MTO draft and that qualified majorities were introduced (for interpretations) and increased (for waivers) where qualified majorities had existed in the GATT, can be taken as a sign that the Members involved, notably the US, at the time accepted the idea that votes on such matters would take place.

C. Comparison with other international organizations

It is interesting to compare the situation in the GATT–WTO with that of other international organizations. It would seem that only international organizations operating at the universal level would be relevant for this comparison. The fact that organizations of regional integration sometimes have more advanced decision-making mechanisms is due to their higher level of ambition in terms of integration. Therefore, and also because of the more limited diversity in their membership, these organizations do not lend themselves to a comparison with the WTO.

For reasons of space and brevity, this chapter will not set out in detail the decision-making process of multilateral or (nearly) universal organizations other than the WTO. For present purposes, it should merely be pointed out that voting is an inbuilt mechanism in the UN both in the General Assembly and in the Security Council. Every State has one vote. In the General Assembly, however, a trend towards consensus rather than formal votes has emerged over the past decades. In the Security

Council, the body that adopts decisions that are binding for all UN members including decisions on war and peace, votes are standard practice. In addition, only a fraction of the UN members, 15 States, are represented in the Security Council. This fact, however, may be precisely the reason why voting does not seem to be an issue. With its 15 members, the Security Council automatically is a representative body acting on behalf of the entire membership. This may make it more acceptable that decisions be taken by a majority, since the authority is a representative one anyway.

The Bretton Woods organizations have voting mechanisms but, unlike in most other organizations, not every member has the same number of votes. Instead, weighted voting applies. The principle is the same in the other development banks for Asia, Africa, and America. Nevertheless, in these financial institutions also, many decisions are adopted by consensus, not through formal votes.

III. SUBSEQUENT PRACTICE

A. Decision-making practice of the WTO (as compared to the GATT)

The WTO did not only continue the practice of decision-making by consensus as it had emerged under the GATT 1947. Soon, the WTO even replaced votes with consensus where votes had existed in the GATT, such as in relation to accessions and waivers. Practice differed only in 1995, the first year of the WTO when the General Council submitted the draft decisions on the accession of Ecuador and on certain draft waivers to a vote by postal ballot (after reaching consensus on the contents of these decisions).[31] Thereafter, the General Council agreed on a statement by the Chair that waivers and accessions would be decided by consensus. Nevertheless, the statement makes clear that where consensus is not achieved, the matter shall be decided by voting and that the agreed procedure does not preclude a Member from requesting a vote.[32]

The systemically important tool of authoritative interpretations has remained completely unused. Only once did a Member, the European Communities, attempt to obtain an interpretation in order to resolve the so-called 'sequencing' issue regarding the relationship between

[31] General Council, *Minutes of Meeting held on 31 July 1995*, WT/GC/M/6 (20 September 1995), pp. 2–5.

[32] General Council, *Minutes of Meeting held on 15 November 1995*, WT/GC/M/8 (13 December 1994), pp. 6 and 7, subsequently circulated in WTO, *Decision-Making Procedures under Articles IX and XII of the WTO Agreement*, Statement by the Chairman as agreed by the General Council on 15 November 1995, WT/L/93 (24 November 1995).

Articles 21.5 and 22.2 of the DSU. The European Communities specifically suggested that the decision-making procedure foreseen in Article IX:2 of the WTO Agreement could be used without delay if consensus could not be achieved.[33] It might also be noted that there has been only one proposal to use Article X to amend the WTO Agreement, on the same issue.[34]

Thus, no legislative response came from the Membership in the famous amicus curiae row, in which an overwhelming majority of the Members fiercely criticized the Appellate Body for transgressing its competences by stating that panels and the Appellate Body itself could accept unsolicited briefs.[35]

In the TRIPS and public health saga, the implementation of paragraph 6 of the Doha Declaration was not achieved within the December 2002 deadline. Up until August 2003,[36] consensus could not be reached because one single Member felt unable to abandon its resistance against the proposed draft waiver. The question at issue was presented by some to be one of life or death for thousands of people in Africa. Yet no Member considered requesting a vote.

Recently, towards the beginning of the Cotton dispute, Brazil requested the DSB to appoint a facilitator pursuant to Annex V of the Agreement on Subsidies and Countervailing Measures, an appointment which the US opposed. At some point, the question was put to the chair whether consensus was truly necessary for that appointment. One would think that Article 2.4 of the DSU, which generally requires consensus (and rules out votes) for DSB decisions *under the DSU* does not apply to a decision under a different agreement, so that Article IX:1 of the WTO Agreement applies. The Secretariat (Legal Affairs Division) nevertheless took and maintained the position that the appointment was only possible through affirmative consensus.[37] In the end, the DSB did

---

[33] See General Council, *Request for an Authoritative Interpretation Pursuant to Article IX:2 of the Marrakesh Agreement Establishing the World Trade Organization— Communication from the European Communities*, WT/GC/W/133 (25 January 1999); and General Council, *Request for an Authoritative Interpretation Pursuant to Article IX:2 of the Marrakesh Agreement Establishing the World Trade Organization— Communication from the European Communities*, WT/GC/W/143 (5 February 1999).

[34] See the *Proposal to Amend Certain Provisions of the Understanding on Rules and Procedures Governing the Settlement of Disputes (DSU) Pursuant to Article X of the Marrakesh Agreement Establishing the World Trade Organization—Submission by Bolivia, Canada, Chile, Colombia, Costa Rica, Ecuador, Japan, Korea, New Zealand, Norway, Peru, Switzerland, Uruguay and Venezuela for Examination and Further Consideration by the General Council*, WT/GC/W/410/Rev.1 (26 October 2001).

[35] See General Council, *Minutes of Meeting*, WT/GC/M/60 (22 November 2000).

[36] General Council, *Decision of 30 August 2003, Implementation of Paragraph 6 of the Doha Declaration on the TRIPS Agreement and Public Health*, WT/L/540 (2 September 2003).

[37] DSB, *Minutes of the Meeting of 15 April 2003*, WT/DSB/M/147, paras. 68–72.

not appoint any facilitator and thus failed to fulfil its obligation under the Agreement on Subsidies and Countervailing Measures.

The daily practice of the WTO offers quite a few other examples where the consensus requirement has resulted in a deadlock. As examples one could adduce the rules on derestriction of documents, the observership of other internal organizations, Iran's accession request and the consistent inability of the Committee on Regional Trade Agreements to reach a conclusion on the free trade or customs union agreements it reviews. The extent to which that deadlock is protracted and whether a breakthrough is possible at some point obviously depends on such factors as the political context of the question at issue and whether tradeoffs are made.

B. Effects

The result is that it is in theory possible for any Member to block any decision. If consensus cannot be achieved, no vote takes place, contrary to what Article IX:1 of the WTO Agreement suggests. The flip side is that even an overwhelming majority of Members is not able to achieve what they want to decide if at least one Member maintains a veto.

Such a decision-making structure contains an inbuilt preference for the status quo. It is much easier to maintain the current legal situation than to achieve change.[38]

The practical impossibility of a vote means that the negotiations in search of a consensus do not even take place *in the shadow* of a threatening vote. The only shadow that exists is the shadow of public exposure for the Member(s) opposing the consensus and the shadow of a crisis for the organization. In purely mathematical terms, one has to recognize that the likelihood of at least one Member opposing a decision increases with the number of Members. This creates a real danger of paralysis.[39]

Whom does this situation favour? Sometimes it is said that the consensus requirement favours the small Members, sometimes it is said that the developed countries benefit most, since they are a minority.[40] Yet each of these propositions makes the assumption that the respective group would typically find itself in a minority in which it could be outvoted. Formally speaking, consensus protects every single Member, whoever may be in a minority.

[38] In this context, one should remember that, in many instances, no decision is also a decision.

[39] J. H. Jackson, 'Sovereignty-Modern: A New Approach to an Outdated Concept' in 97 *American Journal of International Law* (2003) 782 at 782.

[40] A. Narlikar, 'The Politics of Participation: Decision-Making Process and Developing Countries in the WTO' in *The Round Table, The Commonwealth Journal of International Affairs* (2002) 171, at 177.

Does consensus provide for equality? In theory yes, because any single Member can block any decision. Where all must (at least tacitly) agree, it does not even matter whether or not all Members have the same amount of votes, given that a single opposing Member is sufficient for blocking a decision. Thus, consensus also operates as a way to avoid dealing with the respective weights of different Members' votes.[41] The proposition that consensus provides for equality among Members, however, is flawed in that it wrongly assumes that any Member is equally able to sustain a veto.[42] Where a Member is alone in opposing a decision, it can find itself in quite some isolation and exposed to quite some pressure which arguably only robust, big Members can sustain for an extended period of time.

Accordingly, it seems unavoidable that the proposed texts that emerge in a negotiation process reflect the views of different Members to very different degrees. These texts arguably give more weight to the positions of Members who are less likely to give up their veto than to the views of Members with weaker consensus resistance capacity. This capacity tends to be linked to their size and importance in international trade.[43] In a way, therefore, consensus is a partial substitute for weighted voting.[44]

It has been said that the negotiation process which is overshadowed by the danger of any Member's veto tends to be less transparent because negotiations take place in informal mode and are often not recorded. Yet it would seem that this is not inherent in this type of negotiations and can equally be the case where a formal majority vote marks the end of the procedure.

IV. POTENTIAL AND DESIRABILITY OF IMPROVEMENTS

A. Advantage of the current system

The advantages of consensus are obvious and should in no way be downplayed. Where a decision is taken on the basis of consensus, it will tend to enjoy broad support; at least no one expressly opposed it. The decision achieved through negotiations resulting in a mutually satisfactory compromise also means that no one loses face.[45] There is often no

---

[41] Jackson, *supra* n. 39 at 782.
[42] See also T. Cottier and S. Takenoshita, 'The Balance of Power in WTO Decision-Making: Towards Weighted Voting in Legislative Response' in *Aussenwirtschaft* (2003) 171 at 176. [43] *Ibid.*
[44] John H. Jackson, referred to by Footer, *supra* n. 28 at 668.
[45] C. Tietje, in G. M. Berrisch and H. J. Priess (eds), *WTO-Handbuch, Die institutionelle Ordnung der WTO* (2003) para. 51.

open battle, at least no open tensions emerge from the situation, and implementation is secured. One could say that the consensus require-ment protects the delicate balance between international regulation and national sovereignty.[46]

Consensus is powerful and effective if the majority wishes to secure the cooperation of the minority in the implementation of the decision. In that sense, majority voting can be ineffective and damaging if it risks alienating powerful or disaffected minorities.[47] Consensus is built on a broader and often stronger basis. One must note, however, that this is likely to affect the substance because the search for consensus regularly involves the search for a compromise solution that is somehow accept-able to all. The outcome will in this way also reflect the stake that various Members have in what is at issue, and their influence.[48]

One can thus consider as an advantage the fact that no decisions are likely to be taken against the opposition of the big and mighty, who generally need to implement the decision for it to have practical value. One could perhaps further argue that (due to the need to actively object) the consensus system is sometimes easier for reaching a decision than voting where a certain threshold of affirmative votes must be reached (due to the possibility of passive abstention). In addition, the WTO practice disregards the quorum requirements of the Rules of Procedure when decision-making is by consensus, which is convenient where meet-ings have a level of attendance below the quorum. Accordingly, the supermajorities required for certain votes are even more difficult to reach in the meeting room, and recourse to postal ballot or telefax does not necessarily yield a high response rate within the deadline. Thus, an important reason for the replacement of votes by consensus on acces-sions and waivers after Ecuador's accession was the fact that the postal ballot votes regarding that accession arrived in small numbers and late.

It has also been said that consensus is not necessarily popular, but that for both developed and developing WTO Members it is the least bad alternative. Developed countries fear being outvoted, while developing countries fear being presented with *faits accomplis*.[49]

Even if not all Members' interests are protected under the consensus system, because not every Member can oppose any disliked decision, vital interests are. One would have to qualify this, however, by saying that this is true only if these interests are threatened by a *modification*

---

[46] T. Broude, *International Governance in the WTO: Judicial Boundaries and Political Capitulation* (2004) 289.   [47] Footer, *supra* n. 28 at 664.

[48] Cottier and Takenoshita, *supra* n. 42 at 178.

[49] Narlikar, *supra* n. 40 at 177. See also R. H. Steinberg, 'In the Shadow of Law or Power? Consensus-Based Bargaining and Outcomes in the GATT/WTO' in 56 *International Organization* (2002) 339.

of rules (a decision to be adopted), not if vital interests create the *need for* some decision. In the latter case, the consensus requirement makes it extremely difficult to pursue those vital interests. Consensus therefore creates a trade-off between the ability of easily objecting and the difficulty of achieving desired decisions.

In its public relations, the WTO also lauds consensus as being more democratic than majority rule.[50] We do not intend to enter into a political theory debate at this point. However, there are some doubts about this beautiful-sounding democracy argument, if one thinks of the situation in which a decision supported by an overwhelming majority of Members is blocked by one or several governments, and possibly by governments that lack democratic legitimacy at the domestic level.

B. The problems with the current system

The current practice appears to threaten the effectiveness of the political decision-making process of the WTO—not in all cases, but sufficiently often. It seems that the GATT decision-making system worked well because there were far fewer countries and the issues were less complex.[51] Also, the membership was less diverse than it is nowadays.

The problematic flip side of the mentioned advantages of consensus are the known and unknown decisions that are not adopted. Even where the decision-making mechanism works, the outcomes are bound to be the lowest common denominator and the process can take an excessively long time. Although this ineffectiveness has its roots in a voluntary choice by the Members of the WTO, it can become a real problem in certain circumstances. First, the WTO does not deliver where there are real demands for rule-making in the face of today's economic interdependence.[52] The dispute settlement system is neither able nor authorized to meet all these demands by way of dynamic interpretation of the provisions at issue. Second, there is an inherent danger of crisis and paralysis,[53] and of the WTO losing its importance when it does not deliver.

Thus, if Members' efforts to find compromises do not take place in the shadow of a possible vote, the existing shadow of institutional crisis is not an appropriate substitute, as such a crisis is remote from single issues. This is even more the case for the shadow of a WTO that

[50] WTO, *10 Misunderstandings*, p. 11, online at http://www.wto.org/english/res_e/doload_e/10mis_e.pdf.
[51] S. Ostry, 'WTO: Institutional Design for Better Governance', paper presented in June 2000 at Harvard University, online at http://www.ksg.harvard.edu/cbg/trade/ostry.htm.   [52] See also Broude, *supra* n. 46 at 279.
[53] Jackson, *supra* n. 2 at 74.

loses its importance,[54] a shadow that might have worked in Doha. Also, both these shadows of crisis and reduced relevance are too negative in nature for the day-to-day operation of an organization—perhaps similarly to the shadow of divorce not being a good tool for living a successful marriage day to day.

One can also say that under-use of the political/legislative decision-making systems, albeit voluntary, is not strengthening the legitimacy of the WTO.[55] Thus, the inability of the political organs to reach difficult decisions is important already of itself. This inability is of course due to a lower level of convergence among Members on matters of trade policy than existed at earlier periods of time and also during the Uruguay Round. Nevertheless, it is submitted that these substantive differences could be less visible and less detrimental if the decision-making process were more effective.

In addition, the political paralysis becomes problematic when seen in the context of the active and effective dispute settlement system that has been created in the Uruguay Round. Indeed, the contrast between the very burdensome political decision-making process and the highly effective, (quasi-)automatic dispute settlement system appears like an institutional paradox,[56] when previously, under the GATT, both areas were dominated by the consensus rule. Of course, there are inherent differences between these two kinds of processes, that make it impossible to simply transfer the mechanism used in dispute settlement (where a small and odd number of independent adjudicators *must* decide on the basis of the law) to the political/legislative area (where a large number of government officials bound by instructions are free to adopt decisions of open content or not to adopt them). Nevertheless, the imbalance is problematic and in the long run also dangerous for the WTO.[57]

An independent (quasi-)judicial system, in which norms are clarified and thereby developed, should not be left without a (democratically more directly legitimized) counterweight. If legislative response to judicial developments is not available or not working, the independent (quasi-) judiciary becomes an uncontrolled decision-maker and is weakened in its legitimacy. In domestic systems, such mechanisms of legislative response are usually available and important from a democratic point of view. Although legislative reversals of judgments remain the exception, they

---

[54] Because major players could turn to other fora, such as regional or bilateral agreements, or even unilateral measures to solve their problems.

[55] Broude, *supra* n. 46 at 306, 311, 312, 313.

[56] I. García Bercero, 'Functioning of the WTO System: Elements for Possible Institutional Reform', in 6 *International Trade Law and Regulation* (2000) 103, at 105.

[57] C. D. Ehlermann, 'Tensions between the Dispute Settlement Process and the Diplomatic and Treaty-Making Activities of the WTO', in 1 *World Trade Review* (2002) 301.

do occur once in a while and are important in terms of determining who has the final say on what the law is.[58] In the WTO, legislative response is theoretically available, mainly in the form of amendments and authoritative interpretations. Yet the mechanism does not actually work.[59] A good example is the amicus curiae issue, where one might have expected a legislative response, given the vehemence of the reactions of an overwhelming majority of the Members.[60] This example also demonstrates the detrimental tensions that can arise between the different 'branches' of the WTO, if such disagreements are not resolved, but instead remain a contentious issue.

In a way, it is puzzling that legislative response does not seem to work in the WTO, where the dispute settlement system formally depends on the political institutions. The consensus rule is probably not a sufficient explanation for this phenomenon, especially if one explains the strong adherence to consensus with the concern to protect national sovereignty and to avoid supra-national decision-making authority. This does not sufficiently explain the dysfunction of legislative response because the resulting loss of Member control is even greater when the questions at issue are surrendered to dispute settlement panels and the Appellate Body,[61] which, if asked and unable to avoid the issue, can be forced even to address the most sensitive questions.[62]

In that sense, one can observe that Members voluntarily surrender their decision-making powers in the interest of avoiding divisive votes. It has also been suggested that Members may have a (possibly partly unconscious) preference for deferring decisions to the judiciary because: (i) this allows Members to take less clear positions on issues that are contentious also at the national level; (ii) lowest-common-denominator compromises result in ambiguity and give the possibility to later blame the dispute settlement system; (iii) linkages can be avoided; (iv) Members prefer to focus on specific cases rather than on rule-making for the future; and (v) dispute settlement can be used for domestic political ends, both by the complainant and the respondent.[63] This

---

[58] An entertaining recent example from Germany was the very fast modification of the social security legislation after an administrative court had found against the government in a lawsuit brought by a German social security recipient who demanded that the government pay him the rent for an apartment in beach proximity in Florida.

[59] Cottier and Takenoshita, *supra* n. 42 at 171.

[60] See General Council, *Minutes of Meeting*, WT/GC/M/60 (22 November 2000).

[61] See Broude, *supra* n. 46 at 287, 289, 290, 291, who also makes the point that if sovereignty were the real issue, one would have seen (more) amendments of the WTO Agreement that do not alter rights or obligations and amendments where the outvoted minority does not become bound by the modification.

[62] L. Bartels, 'The Separation of Powers in the WTO: How to Avoid Judicial Activism' in 53 *International and Comparative Law Quarterly* (2004) 861 at 865.

[63] Broude, *supra* n. 46 at 293–300.

explanation is of course not complete, but it does contain plausible elements. Also, it does not apply to all potential questions, because not all of them are, for legal reasons, candidates for adjudication in dispute settlement. Conversely, not all questions dealt with in dispute settlement would lend themselves to legislative rule-making instead of the dispute, since Members often bring disputes when there is simply a breach of obligations (e.g. national treatment), which as such are not problematic or contentious, and when a waiver is merely a theoretical option.

As the example of the sequencing issue demonstrates, it also seems that Members are sometimes reluctant to resolve a single issue (by way of amendment or interpretation), but prefer to include this issue within larger negotiations where a concession might be obtained from those who propose the modification.

A further, also incomplete, explanation for the strong adherence to consensus can probably be found in the human tendency of inertia. By this we mean the widespread preference for continuing to do things the way they have always been done, rather than trying out something new and foreign, especially when it is unclear what might be the consequences. For this and other reasons, one is likely to encounter this degree of risk-aversion among many of the WTO Members' delegates in Geneva, many of whom have become acquainted with the WTO by observing its practice and have a strong sense of upholding institutional traditions. If one does not read the WTO Agreement, the Rules of Procedure, or the few existing official documents on decision-making, one cannot be certain to come across the fact that the WTO Agreement mentions votes.[64]

In reference to a long-standing mantra and the title of the part of the conference for which this paper was initially written,[65] one might provocatively state that the WTO can claim to be a 'Member-driven' organization only if the Members actually sit in the driver's seat and actually drive (forward), not if they merely press down the brake. Otherwise 'Member-driven' is reduced to an indirect claim regarding who should *not* be driving the organization.

Be it as it may, the under-use of the political decision-making mechanisms results in a dispute settlement system that is even stronger than according to the WTO's formal design.[66] In the long run, this imbalance is unhealthy for the WTO as a whole and uncomfortable even for the dispute settlement system, notably the Appellate Body (due to an awareness that mistakes or disapproved legal interpretations will not be corrected). In addition to the lack of legislative response, there is a danger that issues

---

[64] Conversely, one might be surprised about the fact that the text of the GATT 1947 did not mention the term 'consensus'.

[65] *WTO Decision-Making Procedures, 'Member-Driven' Rule-Making and WTO Consensus Practices: Are They Adequate?*   [66] Broude, *supra* n. 46 at 309.

best left to rule-making are handed over to the dispute settlement process,[67] a problem known also from domestic settings. Such deferral involves an inherent legitimacy problem.

C. Possible ways for improvements

As already explained in the introduction, it appears that the exploration of possible improvements should first and foremost take place within the framework of existing rules on decision-making. Indeed, it is rather unlikely that WTO Members are willing to revisit the basic rules on decision-making,[68] also against the background of how these rules came about in the Uruguay Round.[69]

If one takes the existing rules as a given framework, improvements are nevertheless possible at various levels. In order to increase the effectiveness of the decision-making system, it is worth exploring possibilities to mitigate the potential pitfalls of the consensus system as we know it. It is submitted that this should include the question of the role that the *availability* of voting, not necessarily holding that many actual votes, could play. Despite all the advantages of the consensus mechanism, it has been seen that it also brings about many downsides and periodically also the danger of paralysis. In some of these circumstances, voting may even appear as the lesser evil,[70] given its ability to resolve a contentious issue.

However, given the one-Member-one-vote principle, decisions on substantive matters that are based on simple majorities would not be representative of the realities of international trade, measured in terms of actual participation and weight of different WTO Members in international trade.[71] Also, the imbalance between the US (one vote) and the European Communities (25 votes)[72] would make it difficult to move to the acceptance of simple majority votes as seemingly foreseen by Article IX:1, second sentence, of the WTO Agreement.[73] This however, essentially argues against narrow simple majorities to serve as the basis for decisions. The arguments are not equally valid if one thinks of

---

[67] Jackson, *supra* n. 2 at 73.   [68] García Bercero, *supra* n. 56 at 105, 107.

[69] And, of course, the fact that any reform would involve winners and losers, see Ostry, *supra* n. 51.   [70] Ehlermann, *supra* n. 57 at 304.

[71] García Bercero, *supra* n. 56 at 107. It has even been argued that the one-state-one-vote principle creates inequalities that would be dangerous to apply against the large trading nations and, on that basis, proposed that majority voting with weighted votes similar to the IMF be introduced; see Cottier and Takenoshita, *supra* n. 42 at 171 and 184–186.

[72] And, in addition, the stronger alliances with other Members which, so far, the European Communities were able to build, as compared with the US.

[73] Although one can argue that this allocation of votes is clearly set out in the WTO text agreed in the Uruguay Round, which must have given satisfaction to the negotiating parties, at a time when the US also expected votes to continue on waivers and accessions.

qualified majorities as they are foreseen in the WTO Agreement for certain questions, or even overwhelming majorities as they are likely to often exist in practice.

Also, it may not be at all necessary to actually hold votes on important substantive issues in order to achieve an improvement. One would normally consider that the fact that voting is *available* under the existing rules alone should limit the risk of consensus leading to a paralysis of the WTO.[74] This however can only work if the possibility of a vote is a *shadow* under which the quest for consensus takes place. This 'shadow of a vote' must be visible and not absent as it presently is, which leaves only the 'shadow of isolation', if only one or extremely few Members prevent consensus, and the 'shadow of crisis' for the WTO as a whole.

In this sense, a possible proposition would not be that of abolishing the rule of consensus, but of abolishing the taboo of majority decision-making.[75] Also, it should be recalled that voting or consensus is not a binary choice and that there may be many variants between the two that are worth exploring.[76] A possibility could be the distinction between decisions that can only be adopted by consensus from decisions that may be adopted by majority voting, as a matter of course or under certain qualifying conditions.[77] A plausible suggestion of this kind would be the introduction, in the practice of decision-making, of a distinction between procedural aspects and real substance.[78] This could facilitate overcoming the currently existing problem that even procedural issues of minor importance can get stuck in a deadlock or become the object of protracted consultations until consensus is reached. As a remedy, it has been proposed to use a written procedure for such decisions or to resort to voting when consensus cannot be reached within a certain deadline.[79] The value of such a modest step in the context of procedural issues should not be underestimated in terms of gradually revitalizing the underlying dynamics of decision-making.

In a different way, improvements could be explored by aiming at reducing the likelihood of individual Members interjecting their veto and thereby blocking consensus. For this, one would have to find tools that would encourage Members not to block consensus or to do so only in defence of vital interests. The possibility of a vote, albeit distant, could be such an instrument. Increasing the implicit costs of the veto would be another, e.g. by resorting to Rule 33 of the Rules of Procedure (see below) or by finding other means of exposing the blocking Member

---

[74] García Bercero, *supra* n. 56 at 107.   [75] Broude, *supra* n. 46 at 321.
[76] Jackson, *supra* n. 2 at 71.   [77] Broude, *supra* n. 46 at 321.
[78] A similar distinction already exists in Art. X of the WTO Agreement on amendments; see also Jackson, *supra* n. 2 at 74.   [79] García Bercero, *supra* n. 56 at 107.

to internal and external criticism, etc. The objective could be a system in which individual Members refrain from blocking consensus if an overwhelming majority supports a decision.[80]

As a more radical tool, *actual* votes can of course have the effect of discouraging those in the minority from upholding their resistance. Formalizing the decision-making procedure may at times also make it more difficult for individual Members to hide behind a lacking consensus when they would not openly vote against a proposal in the decisive situation of a vote.[81] Indeed, the fact that blocking consensus at times merely results in delay and further consultations/negotiations where a negative vote would result in final failure of the proposal reduces the cost of blocking consensus. If it is felt that individual Members are reluctant to join a majority because they do not want to openly forsake a special national interest, one could think of using secret ballots,[82] although this would obviously involve a problematic tension with the objective of transparency. In any event, a system in which it is more difficult for individual Members to block decisions would also make it easier to overcome the resistance of domestic special interest groups.

In any event, one should think of more extensive use of Rule 33 of the respective Rules of Procedure of the subordinate Councils, Committees and other bodies of the WTO. This rule prescribes that they refer a matter to the General Council whenever they are unable to reach a decision by consensus. At present, this referral often does not take place when consensus cannot be reached.[83] Such referral could expose the contentious issue to higher visibility and politicize the debate, rather than leaving it at the lower, more technical level where consensus cannot be reached. This would increase the costs of blocking the proposal for the opposing Members and thus in certain cases encourage them to abandon their opposition.

Because of the reasons already mentioned, it would seem particularly valuable if the decision-making mechanism could be reinforced in a way that would reduce the gap in effectiveness between the WTO's political bodies and its dispute settlement system. For this purpose, the so far unused authoritative interpretation pursuant to Article IX:2 of the WTO Agreement would seem to be an ideal tool for giving Members normative guidance in the context of ambiguous rules, instead of

---

[80] Jackson, *supra* n. 2 at 74–75.

[81] A difference that reportedly played a role at the vote on the German reunification waiver mentioned above in text following n. 26.   [82] Broude, *supra* n. 46 at 322.

[83] See e.g. the long stand-off in the TRIPS Council before it reached consensus on the *Implementation of Paragraph 6 of the Doha Declaration on the TRIPS Agreement and Public Health* in the form of a consensus recommendation to the General Council, IP/C/W/405 (28 August 2003). See also *supra* text accompanying n. 36.

resorting to dispute settlement. The three-quarters majority requirement foreseen in Article IX:2 is already quite demanding such that it would be neither helpful nor justified to assume that authoritative interpretations can only be developed on the basis of consensus.[84]

In any event, it is likely that the most realistic options for procedural improvement would be those that could be introduced through small, seamless steps that gradually have an impact on the practice of the WTO. If these steps are less noticeable, they are more likely to be accepted by those Members who would otherwise resist formal institutional reforms. For achieving such improvements, courageous and visionary chairpersons of various WTO bodies could play a pivotal role, and so could the Secretariat, by fulfilling its duty of impartially advising the chairs on procedural matters. In this context, it is worth recalling the *Cotton* incident in the DSB where several Members seemed ready to consider the applicability of voting, but the Secretariat was not.[85]

Further, in terms of the making of new trade rules, where not all Members are ready to sign up for new rules, but a critical mass is, those Members could resort to techniques such as those used for the telecommunications reference paper, financial services, the Information Technology Agreement, or plurilateral agreements,[86] and the non-participating Members should allow this to happen.

Although this has not been the focus of this chapter, it should finally be pointed out that at a less formal level, the decision-making processes at the WTO could be facilitated through the reintroduction of a high-level steering group of senior capital-based trade officials.[87] Such a group, the Consultative Group of Eighteen, existed in the GATT between 1975 and 1988. It would of course not be easy to make such a body acceptable to all Members by finding a balance between inclusiveness, flexibility, and efficiency. Nevertheless, it may well be worth another effort if a system can be found that ensures rough representation of the various regions and interests in a system of rotation that gives even small Members a chance to be part of that group at some point in time.[88]

---

[84] García Bercero, *supra* n. 56 at 109. See also Cottier and Takenoshita, *supra* n. 42 at 177, who propose votes on interpretations and amendments in order to strengthen the much-needed legislative response.

[85] See *supra*, text accompanying n. 37.

[86] García Bercero, *supra* n. 56 at 109; Jackson, *supra* n. 2 at 75; J. H. Jackson, 'Perceptions about the WTO trade institutions' in *World Trade Review* (2002) 101, at 107.

[87] García Bercero, *supra* n. 56 at 108; Jackson, *supra* n. 2 at 75.

[88] See further R. Blackhurst and D. Hartridge, 'Improving the Capacity of WTO Institutions to Fulfil their Mandate', 7 *Journal of International Economic Law* (2004) 705 at 708–710 and 713–716.

28

Is There a Need for Restructuring the Collaboration among the WTO and UN Agencies so as to Harness their Complementarities?

GARY P. SAMPSON

The objectives of the General Agreement on Tariffs and Trade (GATT) were far-reaching: to raise standards of living, achieve full employment along with a large and steadily growing volume of real income, and develop the full use of the world's resources while expanding the production and exchange of goods. These are also the goals of the World Trade Organization (WTO), with the important addition being the optimal use of the world's resources 'in accordance with the objective of sustainable development'.

At the most general level, these objectives provide an example of the WTO and the United Nations (UN) Agencies pursuing common goals, and therefore the need for 'collaboration among the WTO and the United Nations Agencies to harness their complementarities'. One specific example relates to sustainable development. Not only does it now appear as an objective of the WTO; at the meeting in Doha, Qatar, in November 2001, the trade ministers strongly reaffirmed their 'commitment to the objective of sustainable development'. They expressed their conviction that 'the aims of upholding and safeguarding an open and non-discriminatory multilateral trading system, and acting for the protection of the environment and the promotion of sustainable development can and must be mutually supportive'. At the UN World Summit on Sustainable Development in September 2002 in Johannesburg, ministers committed themselves to continue 'to promote open, equitable, rules-based, predictable and non-discriminatory multilateral trading and financial systems that benefit all countries in the pursuit of sustainable development and . . . support the successful completion of the work programme contained in the Doha Ministerial

Declaration'. They recognized 'the major role that trade can play in achieving sustainable development and in eradicating poverty'; 'we encourage WTO members to pursue the work programme agreed at the Fourth WTO Ministerial Conference'.

Such political declarations are very much 'top–down' in nature, frequently stating the desirability of consistency and mutual supportiveness between institutions pursuing common goals. Notwithstanding such declarations, there appears to be a widespread view that there is scope for greater cooperation between the WTO and the UN Agencies. It is argued in this chapter that useful as such declarations may be, what is important for there to be effective cooperation is to identify the specific areas where complementarities and overlaps exist in the work of the WTO and the UN Agencies. Knowing what the substantive areas are would facilitate the identification of any areas where restructuring the collaboration could lead to a harnessing of the complementarities of these institutions.

While space does not permit all such areas to be identified—and indeed it is a considerable task—a selection of areas are presented on the basis that they are all quite different in nature but do provide examples of specific areas of potential collaboration. The argument made in this chapter is that identifying such areas would permit a 'bottom–up' approach to collaboration to be pursued. It could play a potentially important role in complementing political declarations of good intent.

I. AREAS OF COMPLEMENTARITY

The agreements reached in the Uruguay Round greatly expanded the responsibilities of the original GATT. Rules relating to intellectual property rights and trade in services became part of the agenda, and competition policy, investment, government procurement, and trade facilitation have emerged as prime candidates for new WTO agreements. The declaration launching the Doha Development Round not only calls for modalities for negotiations in all these areas but also launched negotiations in the very controversial area of trade and environment. Of the new agreements that are now part of the WTO agenda, the nature of the rules they contain has become far more important from a domestic regulatory perspective than the earlier focus on border protection. They relate to sensitive areas such as financial and telecommunication services, patents and copyright, environmental subsidies, and support measures for agriculture. These rules extend well beyond border measures and reach deep into regulatory structures of the member countries.

Given the ambitious objectives of the WTO and the extension of the subject-matter covered by the WTO Agreements, it is not surprising that there is considerable overlap between the very specific subject matter dealt with by the WTO and that dealt with by the UN Agencies. There are many examples.

The Trade-Related Intellectual Property Rights (TRIPS) Agreement and its relationship to the Convention on Biological Diversity (CBD) is regularly singled out. The linkage comes from the fact that the CBD recognizes the sovereign rights of States over their natural resources and their authority to determine access to their genetic resources. The objective of the Convention is 'the conservation of biological diversity, the sustainable use of its components, and the fair and equitable sharing of the benefits arising out of the utilization of their genetic resources'. The TRIPS Agreement makes no reference to the CBD or access and benefits sharing, or to traditional knowledge. As the CBD recognizes that access, where granted, shall be on mutually agreed terms and subject to prior informed consent of the provider party, intellectual property rights are clearly important. In this respect the question is raised as to whether instruments contained in the TRIPS Agreement promote the equitable sharing of benefits between commercial users of genetic resources and indigenous communities. Not surprisingly, ministers in Doha instructed the Council for TRIPS to examine the relationship between the TRIPS Agreement and the UNCBD.[1]

Another example of the interface between WTO rules and UN treaties comes from recent dispute settlement cases at the WTO dealing with the environment and public health. Unlike the GATT process, it moves forward automatically with Panel and Appellate Body reports adopted unless there is a consensus against them. The rule of negative consensus backed up by a mechanism providing for compensation and sanctions in the case of non-compliance has greatly increased the attractiveness of the process for some looking for a more effective compliance mechanism than that found in—for example—multilateral environment agreements negotiated under the auspices of the UN. The result is that:

Purists want environmental regulations left to specialised agencies, whereas many environmentalists want them enforced by the WTO. The argument for using the WTO is simple, for unlike most other international organisations, the WTO has a mechanism for enforcing its rulings: trade sanctions. The WTO convenes panels of experts to rule on trade disputes among member

---

[1] See WTO, *Ministerial Declaration*, Ministerial Conference (4 Session, Doha, 9–14 November 2001), WT/MIN(01)/DEC/W/1 para. 19.

governments. If the losing government refuses to comply with the ruling, the panel authorises the winning government to impose trade sanctions.[2]

The result is that the WTO dispute settlement process finds itself dealing with cases relating to non-traditional trade areas such as the environment and public health.

The so-called Shrimp–Turtle dispute provides a good example of the complementarities between WTO rules and UN Agreements. In this case, the Appellate Body was required to determine if a trade measure that had been invoked related to the conservation of an exhaustible natural resource and therefore qualified for provisional justification under the GATT 1994 exceptions article. At issue was whether a living creature should be considered to be an exhaustible natural resource. The Appellate Body ruled that in the light of contemporary international law, living species, which are in principle renewable, 'are in certain circumstances indeed susceptible of depletion, exhaustion and extinction, frequently because of human activities'. In taking this decision, the existence of a Multilateral Environmental Agreement (MEA) was critical. As 'all of the seven recognised species of sea turtles are listed in Appendix 1 of the Convention on International Trade in Endangered Species of Wild Fauna and Flora (CITES)', the Appellate Body concluded that the five species of sea turtles involved in the dispute constitute 'exhaustible natural resources' within the meaning of Article XX(g) of the GATT 1994.[3] The UN Convention on International Trade in Endangered Species had an important complementary role to play.

There are other cases where complementarities are potentially very important. In another case the Appellate Body noted that the more 'vital and important' the policy pursued by a national government, the easier it would be to prove that a non-conforming WTO measure was 'necessary' in the context of Article XX of GATT 1994 to meet the objectives of the policy concerned. In this case, the public health objective being pursued was characterized as 'vital and important in the highest degree'.[4] This then begs the question as to whose responsibility is it to decide whether the objective pursued is vital and important in the highest degree. The World Health Organization (WHO) of the United Nations is certainly one candidate for providing an input.

---

[2] M. M. Weinstein and S. Charnovoitz, 'The Greening of the WTO' in *Foreign Affairs* (November–December 2001).

[3] See WTO, *United States—Import Prohibition of Certain Shrimp and Shrimp Products*, Appellate Body Report, WT/DS58/AB/R (12 October 1998) para. 128.

[4] *European Communities—Measures Affecting Asbestos and Asbestos-Containing Products*, Appellate Body Report and Panel Report, WT/DS135, adopted on 5 April 2001.

The European Commission has also proposed a role for the WHO in settling questions surrounding compulsory licensing, access to essential medicines, and the TRIPS Agreement.

Quite apart from specific WTO agreements and the dispute settlement mechanism, it is the view of many that the everyday work of the WTO impacts on matters dealt with by UN Agencies. Human rights is one example. In reporting to the 55th session of the General Assembly, the UN Secretary-General stated that:

the goals and principles of the WTO Agreements and those of human rights do share much in common. Goals of economic growth, increasing living standards, full employment and the optimal use of the world's resources are conducive to the promotion of human rights, in particular the right to development. Parallels can also be drawn between the principles of fair competition and non-discrimination under trade law and equality and non-discrimination under human rights law. Further, the special and differential treatment offered to developing countries under the WTO rules reflects notions of affirmative action under human rights law.[5]

Some areas dealt with by UN bodies have been proposed as candidates for collaboration with the WTO. Here an example is core labour standards and the appropriate relationship between the WTO and the International Labour Organization (ILO). In Singapore in December 1996, trade ministers renewed their commitment to the observance of internationally recognized core labour standards. They affirmed both that the ILO is the competent body to set and deal with these standards, as well as their support for its work in promoting them. They stated their belief that economic growth and development fostered by increased trade and further trade liberalization contribute to the promotion of these standards and rejected the use of labour standards for protectionist purposes, agreeing that the comparative advantage of countries, particularly low-wage developing countries, must in no way be put into question. In this regard, they noted that the WTO and ILO Secretariats will continue their existing collaboration.

That collaboration is required to increase the complementarities of the WTO and the UN and its specialized agencies and is formally recognized by the WTO. Article V of the Agreement Establishing the WTO requires 'the General Council [to] make appropriate arrangements for effective cooperation with other intergovernmental organizations that have responsibilities related to those of the WTO' (paragraph 1).

---

[5] UN, *Globalization and its Impact on the Full Enjoyment of all Human Rights*, Preliminary Report of the Secretary-General, 55th session of the General Assembly, Document A/55/342 at 4.

II. WHAT ROLE FOR THE WTO?

While there is political recognition of the need for collaboration between the WTO and UN bodies, controversy surrounds whether the WTO is the appropriate body to deal with a number of matters that have gravitated towards it. The WTO is fiercely criticized by public interest groups who argue that its rules constitute an unwanted intrusion into the domestic affairs of sovereign states; that they impede the proper workings of democratically elected governments by denying them, for example, the possibility to restrict imports of goods produced in an environmentally unfriendly manner or without respecting core labour standards. A common cry is that there should be an acceptance on the part of the trade community that those responsible for trade policy should recognize that social norms are inextricably linked with the international economic system, and provide the common moral and legal underpinnings for the global economy. It is argued that integrating social norms into all aspects of economic policy-making—including trade policy—would ensure that markets are not only open and efficient, but also fair and just.

Desirable though this goal may be, the question to address is in what way could WTO concepts, principles, rules, and processes be adjusted to enable the integration of such norms into the WTO. From a practical policy perspective, many of the proposals involve changing fundamentally the manner in which the WTO operates. There is frequently a call, for example, for the WTO to modify the interpretation of non-discrimination.

As things stand, and very loosely put, non-discrimination means that products that compete in the same market and are physically similar can not be discriminated against in the trading system because of the manner in which they were produced. It is argued that the role of the WTO be rendered more 'useful' by permitting discrimination in trade in order to enforce standards that achieve objectives addressed by the UN and its specialized agencies: human rights (High Commission for Human Rights), public health (WHO), labour standards (ILO) and the environment (UN Environment Programme, UNEP). For many—and particularly developing countries—discrimination in trade is an option only available to powerful countries; considered an encroachment on national sovereignty; nothing more than thinly disguised protectionism; and therefore staunchly opposed.

There is, however, clearly a gap to be filled. The thought of consuming imported products that have degraded the environment or been produced without respect for core labour standards is anathema to public interest groups concerned about environment and social conditions beyond their borders. If the WTO is to find itself in the position of legitimizing trade discrimination for the implementation of social and other norms *that are not universally held*—and that is what is being asked of the WTO by some today—the reach of WTO rules would increase dramatically.

In very practical terms, this interpretation of non-discrimination means that from a *trade policy* perspective, goods produced in an environmentally unfriendly manner, or without respecting core labour standards, are like any other. With this understanding, it is not the role of trade officials to judge the appropriateness or otherwise of national standards adopted to meet national goals in non-trade areas. From an *international relations* perspective, this interpretation serves to minimize any unwanted encroachment on national sovereignty, with powerful countries riding roughshod over less powerful ones, by forcing them to produce goods according to the preferred environmental or other standards of the importing country. From a *multilateral agreement* perspective, this interpretation leaves the necessary space for existing treaties to be enforced and new ones negotiated to deal with the establishment and enforcement of commitments relating to the environment, labour standards, human rights, and other social norms.

A strong argument can be made that a trade policy organization such as the WTO should not be responsible for the non-trade issues that are gravitating towards it. The UN and its specialized agencies are charged with advancing the causes of development, the environment, human rights, and labour. A complementary case can be made that they should be strengthened—and given the resources they need to successfully carry out their tasks—in order for the WTO to go ahead and deal with a narrower agenda than what it is now acquiring. Not surprisingly, this view has been expressed on a number of occasions by Kofi Annan, the Secretary-General of the UN, as well as a number of Heads of specialized UN agencies.[6]

However, it seems there is not the same willingness to forgo national sovereignty and accept strong compliance mechanisms in those treaties negotiated under the auspices of the UN and its specialized agencies as in the WTO. As Peter Sutherland *et al.* recently remarked:

The weakness of other multilateral institutions, and the inadequacy of existing decision-making fora, *has increased* the demands on the WTO to deal with issues not heretofore within its mandate. Labour and environmental issues are the two most notable cases. . . . These pressures have been brought to bear on the WTO not only because of the attraction of its unique enforcement power,

---

[6] See the chapters by Mary Robinson and Kofi Annan in G. P. Sampson (ed.), *The Role of the WTO in Global Governance* (2000).

but also because the institutions that might be expected to deal with labour and environment issues either do not exist or are weak.[7]

III. MULTILATERAL ENVIRONMENT AGREEMENTS AND THE WTO

Against this backdrop, an important question is how to proceed in practice. One interesting case study is the relationship between the WTO and the trade provisions in the United Nations Multilateral Environment Agreements (MEAs). With the coming of the WTO, the Committee on Trade and Environment (CTE) was created with broad terms of reference. Through intensive discussion in the ensuing years it has in my view been particularly effective in 'harnessing complementarities'. It has promoted a greater understanding on the part of trade and environment officials of their respective concerns and the policy tools available to deal with them. This has been achieved through practical initiatives including the WTO organizing 'trade and environment' symposia attended by national government officials, academics, representatives of the UN and specialized agencies, etc; joint technical cooperation missions involving both WTO and UNEP staff; observer status for MEAs in the Committee on Trade and the Environment (CTE); and regular presentations by representatives of MEAs to the CTE on the trade-related aspects of their agreements. This has certainly contributed to the fact that there has never been a dispute brought to the WTO relating to a WTO-inconsistent measure provided for in an MEA.

These exchanges have arguably led to a better understanding of the goals of trade and environment policy and the respective roles of the MEA Treaties and Secretariats as well as that of UNEP.[8] At the Doha Ministerial Meeting, trade ministers welcomed 'the WTO's continued cooperation with UNEP and other inter-governmental environmental organizations'. . . and . . . encouraged 'efforts to promote cooperation

---

[7] See the chapter by P. Sutherland, J. Sewell and D. Weiner in G. Sampson (note 6), at p. 81 *et seq.*

[8] Mutually supportive statements have been a feature of both the Doha Ministerial and the World Summit on Sustainable Development. In November 2001, trade ministers in Qatar told the world that 'We strongly reaffirm our commitment to the objective of sustainable development. . . . We are convinced that the aims of upholding and safeguarding an open and non-discriminatory multilateral trading system, and acting for the protection of the environment and the promotion of sustainable development can and must be mutually supportive.' Shortly after the meeting in Doha, environment ministers called for 'urgent action at all levels to continue to promote open, equitable, rules-based, predictable and non-discriminatory multilateral trading and financial systems that benefit all countries in the pursuit of sustainable development. We support the successful completion of the work program in the Doha Ministerial Declaration. . . .'

between the WTO and relevant international environmental and developmental organizations, especially in the lead-up to the World Summit on Sustainable Development'. In concrete terms, pursuant to discussion in the CTE, ministers agreed at the Doha Ministerial to clarify and improve WTO disciplines on fisheries subsidies, taking into account the importance of this sector to developing countries.

As far as 'restructuring' is concerned, there have been proposals for changes in WTO rules and procedures to accommodate MEAs. One aspect of the debate has centred on the possibility of a conflict arising over trade-related measures contained in MEAs: namely, their potential inconsistency with WTO rules, and how conflict in these rules could be avoided or dealt with. Given the importance of the global trade and environment regimes, any clash over the application of rules agreed to among nations would have unfortunate ramifications for both regimes. Given the importance of the issue, trade ministers agreed in Doha to negotiations on the relationship between existing WTO rules and specific trade obligations set out in multilateral environmental agreements.

It has been suggested that an 'environmental window' be created through providing for exceptions to WTO-inconsistent measures being taken in light of the provisions of environment agreements. This has not met with the unanimous approval of WTO Members. Nevertheless, it can be argued that it is very much in the interests of the WTO to have effective multilateral environment agreements to ensure that trade-related disputes do not gravitate towards the WTO. To achieve this, any WTO-inconsistent measures should be clearly identified and agreed to by the parties to the MEA. The environment agreements would set the standards for environmental protection and enforce them. If this means that if WTO Members forgo their WTO rights not to be discriminated against if certain environmental standards are not met, then so be it. This course of action however requires 'effective' (from a WTO perspective) MEAs, characterized by clearly specified trade measures taken for environmental purposes, broad-based support in terms of country membership, and a robust dispute settlement system.[9] Unfortunately this is not the case today.

While there has been clear evidence of collaboration to harness complementarities in trade and environment, it is difficult to envisage similar processes being established in the WTO for other areas where the UN has responsibilities. It is hard to imagine the creation of a

---

[9] Further, with a view to enhancing the mutual supportiveness of trade and environment, Ministers agreed 'to negotiations on the relationship between existing WTO rules and specific trade obligations set out in multilateral environmental agreements (MEAs), procedures for regular information exchange between MEA Secretariats and the relevant WTO committees . . .'

Committee on Trade and Human Rights or Labour Standards within the WTO. Developing countries are far too suspicious of hidden protectionist intentions behind any such initiatives, believing that these issues should be dealt with in the UN and the specialized agencies with the mandate and expertise to deal with them.

IV. CONCLUSION

In a perfect world, meeting the challenges facing the global economy requires a coherent approach and institutional structure at the global level. This means the existence of institutions that determine the substantive policies and public processes with a clear delineation of the responsibilities of the various actors involved. The goals of the institutions should be to facilitate the attainment of agreed policy objectives through cooperation, while providing for the avoidance and resolution of any disputes that may arise in the pursuance of these objectives. Good governance requires a set of such institutions that are coherent, mutually consistent, and supportive, and which operate in an effective, accountable, and legitimate manner. At the international level, these are the characteristics of an effective global governance structure characterized by collaboration among the WTO and UN Agencies in order to harness their complementarities.

I would like to make two proposals as to how to proceed. One is 'bottom–up' in nature and the other 'top–down'. Both are potentially far reaching, but far from radical in the sense that both have been experienced as past GATT initiatives. One relates to the clarification of WTO rules. It has been remarked that WTO jurisprudence has not yet been clarified with respect to the relationship between WTO rules and a number of areas of concern to the UN Agencies. Examples given include the impact of human rights obligations and the interpretation of the TRIPS Agreement, as well as the numerous WTO exceptions protecting national policy for non-trade concerns. In this respect, 'Closer co-operation between the WTO and UN Specialized Agencies could facilitate clarification of the extent to which human rights (e.g. those recognized in the law of the International Labour Organization (ILO) and of the World Health Organization) are relevant also for the interpretation and application of WTO rules.'[10]

The first proposal is based on the fact that in the Uruguay Round, the Articles of the GATT were reviewed. It is perhaps time to address

---

[10] E. U. Petersmann, 'Human Rights and the Law of the World Trade Organization' in 37(2) *Journal of World Trade* (2003) 241–281.

once again the question of whether an Understanding or an interpretation is required to clarify the grounds for deviating from—or seeking an exception from—the non-discrimination obligation of the WTO. The optimal manner to deal with the solution to the problems confronting the WTO in this do not lie with *de facto* rule-making through litigation.

The second proposal is 'top–down' and relates to the fact that there is no world government to determine the appropriate division of labour among existing multilateral institutions, or to decide when new organizations need to be created or existing ones closed down. In this context, attention has been drawn to a need for a global process with concerted, broad, and high-level political leadership that could review, *inter alia*, the appropriate distribution of tasks between the WTO and the UN Agencies. A summit meeting of heads of state—a 'globalization summit'—has been proposed by Peter Sutherland, another former Director-General of the WTO, to strengthen the UN institutions and address global problems that require global solutions. The current Director-General, Dr Supachai, has proposed a high-level panel to resolve some of the threatened divisions over the pending trade and non-trade issues facing the WTO at present.[11]

In the Uruguay Round, a group was created to examine ways in which the WTO and the Bretton Woods institutions could bring greater coherence to global economic policy-making. The 'so called' FOGS (Functioning of the GATT System) Group produced a Ministerial Declaration which recognized that 'difficulties, the origins of which lie outside the trade field, can not be redressed through measures taken in the trade field alone'. The policy prescriptions of the FOGS Group look remarkably relevant for the problems confronting the global economy of today. For example, ministers declared that the 'inter-linkages between the different aspects of economic policy require that the international institutions with responsibilities in each of these areas follow consistent and mutually supportive policies'. The outcome of the Declaration was the negotiation of formal agreements between the WTO and the Bretton Woods institutions on how to ensure consistent and mutually supportive policies in their own operations.

My second proposal, then, is that a FOWTOS (Functioning of the World Trade Organization System) Group be formed to make recommendations on how to bring greater coherence to policy-making at the global level—as the FOGS Group successfully did—but extending its mandate to review and make proposals on collaboration among the WTO and UN Agencies with a view to a possible restructuring of the relationship.

---

[11] See chapters by Peter Sutherland *et al.* and Dr Supachai in Sampson (ed.), *supra* n. 6.

29

Can the WTO Dispute Settlement System Deal with Competition Disputes?[1]

CLAUS-DIETER EHLERMANN AND LOTHAR EHRING[2]

The current discussions on a future framework for competition policy within the World Trade Organization (WTO) have revealed strong reservations against the full application of the WTO dispute settlement system to such a framework.

The possibility of enforcing the legal obligations resulting from the agreements negotiated within the WTO and the stronger force that these agreements thus have is one of the key reasons why the proponents of a WTO competition agreement favour the WTO as a negotiation forum. Nevertheless, these proponents now contemplate at most a limited future role for the WTO dispute settlement system to play within a future competition agreement.

In order to address some of the objections voiced against the full application of the dispute settlement system in this area, this paper explores the extent to which the dispute settlement system of the WTO would be suitable to apply to competition-related cases. It first recalls that already under existing trade rules, national competition law and practice are not exempt from, but rather subject to, the application of the dispute settlement system. Both competition laws as such and their application in individual cases must comply with the current substantive standards of the WTO Agreement, and complaints can be brought against both. Extending the application of the dispute settlement system

[1] This chapter draws from the analysis contained in Claus-Dieter Ehlermann and Lothar Ehring, 'WTO Dispute Settlement and Competition Law—Views from the Perspective of the Appellate Body's Experience', EUI-RSCAS Policy Paper No. 2002/12 and 26 *Fordham International Law Journal* (2003) 1505. This chapter expresses only personal views.

[2] We thank Terry Collins-Williams, Deputy Permanent Representative of Canada to the WTO, for commenting on this paper at the conference in Florence.

to a new agreement to be negotiated in the area of competition would therefore be no *qualitative* innovation.

Drawing a parallel to the area of trade remedies, this chapter further argues that the standard of review applied in WTO dispute settlement would also be appropriate for competition cases. This standard of review excludes *de novo* review, but sets rather high standards for the national authorities' duties of investigation and explanation.

The system, however, shows significant weaknesses in connection with the fact-finding conducted by panels. Competition-related cases are very fact-intensive and they frequently involve confidential business information, for which no generally applicable rules of procedure exist to date. For the dispute settlement system to be able to apply effectively to a review of individual decisions under a future WTO competition agreement, it would be important to overcome this impediment, which already today regularly creates significant practical problems. Another weakness is rooted in the non-permanent character of panels. A body composed of *ad hoc* selected members cannot be expected to conduct fact-finding with the same determination as a permanent body. It would therefore be beneficial to increase the structural independence of panel members.

I. COMMITMENTS PROPOSED FOR A FUTURE WTO COMPETITION AGREEMENT

Even if, in principle, the start of negotiations on a competition agreement has been agreed at Doha, this says nothing so far about the outcome and the content. Paragraph 25 of the Doha Ministerial Declaration indicates that negotiations will probably deal with the topics clarified in the Working Group on the Interaction between Trade and Competition Policy (WGTCP), headed by Professor F. Jenny. These topics are:

[C]ore principles, including transparency, non-discrimination and procedural fairness, and provisions on hardcore cartels; modalities for voluntary co-operation; and support for progressive reinforcement of competition institutions in developing countries through capacity building.

According to the proposals of the supporters of a multilateral competition framework, such a future agreement should include the following elements: a commitment to a set of core principles, including transparency, non-discrimination and procedural fairness; a commitment to take measures against hard-core cartels; modalities for cooperation between Members; a commitment to technical assistance to developing countries; and the establishment of a standing WTO Committee on Competition Policy.

For the Members who will sign the agreement, several of these commitments will have a two-fold meaning. First, they will have to *adapt* their national laws to the requirements of the agreement, where the required rules (e.g. on hard-core cartels or procedural fairness) have up to now been absent or the existing rules insufficient. Second, these Members will have to ensure that their national rules are *applied* in accordance with the agreement.

II. THE ROLE FORESEEN FOR THE DISPUTE SETTLEMENT SYSTEM

Normally, the WTO dispute settlement system is available to enforce both of these two types of obligations, i.e. to review whether the laws of a Member conform to the obligations of the agreement, but also whether there is compliance in individual cases. However, for a future multilateral competition framework, several Members propose a narrower role, if any, for the dispute settlement system.

The European Commission's initial position was that the dispute settlement system is useful both for disputes about the legislative implementation of a competition agreement and for disputes about its application in individual cases.[3] This was met with strong scepticism if not rejection from the United States (US), particularly regarding the review of individual national decisions in competition cases, as this could interfere with national sovereignty concerning prosecutorial discretion[4] and involve panels in 'inappropriate reviews of case specific, highly confidential business information'.[5] Possibly influenced by the negative attitude of the US and others, the European Community (EC) modified its position by exempting the review of individual decisions from the scope of dispute settlement under a future competition agreement.[6] To be

---

[3] COM (96) 284 final, 18 June 1996, online at: http://www.europa.eu.int/comm/competition/international/com284.html.

[4] For a demonstration that the exercise of such prosecutorial discretion already today is bound by GATT rules, see *infra* text accompanying n. 22.

[5] J. I. Klein, 'A Note of Caution with Respect to a WTO Agenda on Competition Policy', address to the Royal Institute of International Affairs (Chatham House) London (18 November 1996), online at: http://www.usdoj.gov/atr/public/speeches/jikspch.htm. J. I. Klein, 'A Reality Check on Antitrust Rules in the World Trade Organisation, and a Practical Way Forward on International Antitrust', address before the OECD Conference on Trade and Competition (30 June 1999) in *OECD, Trade and Competition Policies: Exploring the Ways Forward* (1999).

[6] *Communication from the European Community and its Member States to the WTO Working Group on the Interaction Between Trade and Competition Policy of 14 March 2001*, WT/WGTCP/W/160, page 3; *Communication from the Commission to the Council and to the European Parliament, The EU Approach to the Millennium Round*, COM (99) 0331 Final. See also I. García Bercero and S. D. Amarasinha, 'Moving the

precise, this exemption of the review of individual cases has also been framed as a limitation of e.g. the national treatment obligation of a future competition agreement to outlawing *de jure* discrimination and as not banning *de facto* discrimination.[7] To avoid a possible misunderstanding, it must be emphasized that, according to a different, but common usage of this terminology, *de facto* discrimination can also be found in a piece of competition legislation itself, not only in its application, and *de jure* discrimination arguably also in the manner the administrative authority applies the law, not only in the law itself. *De jure* versus *de facto* therefore matches the distinction between law versus application in individual cases only if one uses these terms in such a sense (as the submissions of the EC do to some extent).

The annual reports of the WGTCP reflect that several proponents of a WTO competition agreement foresee at most a limited role for the dispute settlement system in this field and that this system should, in any case, not apply to individual decisions.[8] The WGTCP has not discussed these questions in great detail during the past few years. In 2003, it devoted specific attention to the nature and scope of compliance mechanisms that might be applicable under a multilateral framework on competition policy. Some delegations have suggested that a system of voluntary peer review might provide a less adversarial compliance mechanism better suited to competition law enforcement.[9]

III. THE SITUATION *DE LEGE LATA*

In order to answer the question of the appropriateness of WTO dispute settlement in a multilateral competition framework it is worthwhile to explore the current legal situation. This examination will show that it is already now possible to invoke the dispute settlement system in order

Trade and Competition Debate Forward', 4 in *Journal of International Economic Law* (2001) 481, 494.

[7] *Communication from the European Communities and its Member States, A Multilateral Framework Agreement on Competition Policy*, WT/WGTCP/W/152 (25 September 2000) at 6; *Report (2002) of the WTO Working Group on the Interaction between Trade and Competition Policy to the General Council*, WT/WGTCP/6 (9 December 2002), para. 20; *Report of the Meeting of 26–27 September 2002*, WT/WGTCP/M/19, para. 63; *Report of the Meeting of 20 November 2002*, WT/WGTCP/M/20, para. 5.

[8] WTO, *Report (2002)*, *supra* n. 7, para. 20; *Report (2001)*, WT/WGTCP/5 (8 October 2001), para. 87; see also *Report (1999)*, WT/WGTCP/3 (11 October 1999), para. 79.

[9] See *Contribution of Canada*, WT/WGTCP/W/226 at 6–7. On dispute settlement and peer review, see also the *Communication from the European Communities and its Member States, Dispute Settlement and Peer Review*, WT/WGTCP/W/229 (14 May 2003).

to review the compatibility of national competition laws and their application in individual cases with existing WTO law.

This analysis will focus on the so-called violation complaint under Article XXIII:1(a) of the General Agreement on Tariffs and Trade (GATT) 1994, given the high statistical prevalence of this type of disputes, several of which had links to competition related issues.[10] Nevertheless, most of the issues discussed in relation to dispute settlement are also valid for non-violation and situation complaints, which present a particular interest in the area of competition. For that reason, these two types of complaints will be addressed separately towards the end of the article. The *Kodak— Fuji* dispute has also demonstrated the potential role of the non-violation complaint in the area of competition law.[11]

A. The review of competition laws as such

National competition legislation must comply with the substantive requirements of the WTO Agreement. Of particular relevance are the rules of non-discrimination contained in the GATT 1994, the General Agreement on Trade in Services (GATS) and the Trade-Related Aspects of Intellectual Property Rights (TRIPS), i.e. the obligations of most-favoured-nation (MFN) and national treatment. For the sake of simplicity and brevity, but also because this principle is likely to have the greatest practical relevance, this paper focuses on the principle of national treatment of the GATT 1994.

As regards the scope of application of Article III:4 of the GATT 1994, a national competition act falls within the category of 'laws, regulations and requirements affecting the internal sale, offering for sale, purchase, transportation, distribution or use' of goods. The verb 'affecting' has correctly been interpreted broadly as covering 'any laws or regulations which might adversely modify the conditions of competition' of imports.[12] However, since Article III:4 of the GATT 1994 expressly applies only to governmental treatment accorded in respect of 'laws, regulations and requirements', it would not seem to be a possible yardstick of legal scrutiny wherever competition rules are totally non-existent.

---

[10] See, for example, the violation claims in the Panel Report, *Japan—Measures Affecting Consumer Photographic Film and Paper (Japan—Film)*, WT/DS44/R, adopted 22 April 1998, DSR 1998:IV, 1179; or the Panel Report, WT/DS161/R, WT/DS169/R, and the Appellate Body Report, WT/DS161/AB/R, WT/DS169/AB/R, in *Korea— Measures affecting Imports of Fresh, Chilled and Frozen Beef*, adopted 10 January 2001.

[11] Panel Report, *Japan—Film, supra* n. 10.

[12] Panel Report, *Italian Discrimination Against Imported Agricultural Machinery*, adopted 23 October 1958, BISD 7S/60, para. 12. See also Appellate Body Report, *United States—Tax Treatment for 'Foreign Sales Corporations'—Recourse to Article 21.5 of the DSU by the European Communities*, WT/DS108/AB/RW, adopted 29 January 2002, paras. 209 and 210, with further references.

It is not overly likely,[13] yet certainly not excluded, that competition laws as such (*per se*) violate Article III:4. Competition laws as such (*per se*) will seldom treat imports less favourably than like domestic goods, be it *de jure* or *de facto*. This is especially true if the competition law at issue applies to all products irrespective of their nature and origin. Such a law could only violate Article III:4 of the GATT 1994 where imports have to be treated differently from like domestic goods in order to afford both equally favourable treatment.[14] The situation is different, however, where there are special laws or sub-legislative regulations, which apply only to a certain category of products, for instance (block) exemptions. If there is a divergence in the treatment of some imports (not falling under the exemption) and some different, but like domestic goods (covered by the exemption) and this divergence is simultaneously a competitive disadvantage for the excluded imports, there may be a breach of Article III:4 of the GATT 1994. Whether such a regime violates the national treatment obligation will depend on whether the mere differentiation is sufficient or whether there has to be a disadvantage for like imports, those covered and those not covered by the block exemption, taken together, compared with like domestic goods, taken together. This question is yet to be resolved with final clarity in the WTO jurisprudence.[15]

Where a piece of competition legislation exceptionally affords like imports less favourable treatment, this treatment might not be mandatory, but be left to the discretion of the competent authorities. In such a case, the traditional GATT doctrine would apply and allow only mandatory legislation to be challenged as GATT-inconsistent as such.[16] In contrast, in the case of non-mandatory (discretionary) legislation, the complainant must wait for an instance of GATT-inconsistent application.[17] In this sense, the proposed limitation of dispute settlement in a future competition agreement to laws as such might become problematic. It would prevent panels from avoiding addressing laws as such, and the mandatory/discretionary distinction might even come under pressure, as it would

[13] See also García Bercero and Amarasinha, *supra*, n. 6 at 494.

[14] See Panel Report, *United States—Section 337 of the Tariff Act of 1930*, adopted 7 November 1989, *BISD* 36S/345, para. 5.11.

[15] See L. Ehring, 'De Facto Discrimination in WTO Law: National and Most-Favoured-Nation Treatment—or Equal Treatment?' in 36 *Journal of World Trade* (2002) 921–948.

[16] Ultimately, it depends on the WTO provision in question, whether it precludes only mandatory inconsistent laws or also discretionary ones. See Panel Report, *United States—Sections 301–310 of the Trade Act of 1974*, WT/DS152/R, adopted 27 January 2000, DSR 2000:II, 815, paras. 7.53–7.54.

[17] Appellate Body Report, *United States—Anti-Dumping Act of 1916* (US—1916 Act), WT/DS136/AB/R, WT/DS162/AB/R, adopted 26 September 2000, paras. 88 and 89, with references to past jurisprudence.

give no recourse under that agreement against the WTO-inconsistent application of discretionary legislation.

A competition agreement to be negotiated within the WTO would increase the number of legal requirements to which national competition laws are subject. Such an agreement would probably also contain express obligations as to the introduction of competition laws, for instance those addressing hard-core cartels. These obligations would go beyond those that can already now be derived from isolated provisions of the WTO agreements, for instance, Article VIII of the GATS. In addition to Article VIII of the GATS, the Telecommunications Annex to the GATS requires that service providers in other Members be given access to public telecommunications networks on reasonable and non-discriminatory terms. The Telecommunications Reference Paper on Regulatory Principles further provides for certain 'competitive safeguards'. Under the terms of the Reference Paper, the WTO Members who signed it are obliged to maintain '[a]ppropriate measures . . . for the purpose of preventing . . . major suppliers from engaging in or continuing anti-competitive practices' (paragraph 1.1). Members must also ensure interconnection with major suppliers under non-discriminatory terms, in a timely manner, on transparent, reasonable, cost-oriented, and unbundled terms (paragraph 2). The 'appropriate measures' that Members must maintain arguably include both the enactment of competition laws and their enforcement in individual cases. In 2000, the US brought against Mexico the first complaint under the Reference Paper,[18] for which the Panel Report is expected soon.

Beyond Article VIII and the Reference Paper, the GATS also addresses restrictive business practices of non-monopoly service suppliers in Article IX. In Article 40, the TRIPS Agreement does not only allow Members to enact laws against the anti-competitive abuse of licences on intellectual property rights. It also obliges Members to enter into consultations with another Member which believes that its competition laws are being infringed by the licensing practices of a foreign intellectual property right owner. The thesis that trade policy chiefly deals with (negative) prohibitions directed at Members and not with positive obligations to take action is no longer tenable.[19] The TRIPS Agreement is the best example of a host of far-reaching positive obligations to take action, that are likely to exceed by far what can be expected from a competition agreement even under a best-case scenario.

---

[18] *Mexico—Measures Affecting Telecommunications Services*, Request for Consultations by the United States of 17 August 2000, WT/DS204/1.

[19] D. K. Tarullo, 'Norms and Institutions in Global Competition Policy' in 94 *American Journal of International Law* (2000) 478–504 at 489.

B. The review of individual competition decisions

More interesting and complicated than the question of the review of competition laws as such is the issue of reviewing individual cases in which competition authorities apply competition laws. Taking again Article III:4 of the GATT 1994 as a prime example, this provision expressly applies to 'laws, regulations and requirements'. Individual decisions of competition authorities can fall under the concept of 'requirements'. At least one panel report clearly expressed itself in favour of understanding individual decisions as falling within that category.[20] In addition, Article III:4 does not prohibit less favourable treatment '*through* laws, regulations and requirements', but '*in respect of* all laws regulations and requirements'. It would seem plausible to hold that the application of a law qualifies as 'treatment . . . in respect of' that law.

Individual competition decisions can be made by the executive or by courts. Decisions by administrative authorities are typical in Europe, whereas in the US such decisions are left to the courts. For the application of Article III:4 this distinction is irrelevant as States are responsible for the acts of their courts as they are responsible for the actions taken by their administrative authorities. There is also no prerequisite of the exhaustion of domestic remedies before a Member can turn to the WTO dispute settlement system.

Article III:4 can even apply to instances where a competition authority or a court has *failed* to act, unless there is complete inaction which would appear not to qualify as 'treatment' in the sense of Article III:4. There certainly *can* be less favourable governmental treatment, where the competition authorities have taken no action in one case but have acted in another, similar case relating to like products. An example would be that where a competition authority refrains from intervening against a buying cartel which refuses to purchase imports, and this non-intervention departs from that authority's practice with regard to buying cartels harming like domestic products.[21]

A different example of a violation of Article III:4 would be the situation in which a competition authority authorizes an exclusive retail system to the benefit of a domestic producer, whilst prohibiting a similar exclusive retail system for like imported goods. Such challenges will probably remain the exception and, where individual decisions by

---

[20] Panel Report, *Canada—Administration of the Foreign Investment Review Act* (FIRA), adopted 7 February 1984, *BISD* 30S/140. In the same direction: Panel Report, *EEC—Regulations of Imports of Parts and Components*, adopted 16 May 1990, *BISD* 37/132.

[21] M. Matsushita, 'Restrictive Business Practices and the WTO/GATT Dispute Settlement Process' in E. U. Petersmann (ed.), *International Trade Law and the GATT/ WTO Dispute Settlement System* (1997) 357, 370.

competition authorities contravene Article III:4, the Member concerned may invoke Article XX(d) as a justification. Although in practice it may well be difficult to prove that there has been a violation of the national treatment obligation, these examples make clear that, already today, the national treatment obligation limits the prosecutorial discretion, which some competition authorities enjoy.[22] Accordingly, the WTO dispute settlement system applies to individual decisions in the area of competition.

In addition to Article III:4 of the GATT 1994, other existing provisions of WTO law may be relevant to the conduct of national competition authorities in individual cases. For example, Article 11.3 of the Agreement on Safeguards prohibits Members from encouraging or supporting non-governmental measures equivalent to a voluntary import or export restraint. Article 11.3 thus prohibits governmental encouragement and support of import or export cartels. It has been suggested in the literature that the terms 'encourage or support' could be interpreted broadly so as to cover the non-application of existing anti-cartel legislation,[23] and that Article 11.3 could be the basis for building a jurisprudence relating to restrictive business practices.[24] From a textual point of view, 'support' seems to mean more than just 'tolerate'.[25] On the other hand, one may argue that the intentional non-application of competition laws that would normally (have to) be applied can be a strong form of support. It has also been suggested that the *authorization* of import or export cartels as it exists in some national competition laws could qualify as a positive contribution to a restrictive business practice because it brings that practice about.[26] It is again a question of whether a legislative exemption (possibly coupled with an approval requirement) suffices for satisfying the condition 'encourage or support'.[27] This question does not arise in the event of (informal) governmental guidance or suggestion, as this is precisely the kind of governmental contribution that the words 'encourage or support' envisage.[28]

---

[22] R. Anderson and P. Holmes, 'Competition Policy and the Future of the Multilateral Trading System' in 5 *Journal of International Economic Law* (2002) 531, 533. See *supra* text accompanying n. 4.

[23] F. Roessler, 'The Concept of Nullification and Impairment in the Legal System of the World Trade Organization' in E.-U. Petersmann (ed.), *International Trade Law and the GATT/WTO Dispute Settlement System* (1997) 123, 140.

[24] F. Roessler, 'Should Principles of Competition Policy be Incorporated into WTO Law Through Non-Violation Complaints?' in 2 *Journal of International Economic Law* (1999) 413, 421.

[25] See also Matsushita, *supra* n. 21 at 369: 'too remote a linkage with any governmental action'.   [26] *Ibid.* at 368.

[27] One may argue that a legislative exemption is no more a positive contribution ('encourage or support' arguably require a positive contribution) than an administrative inaction where the law does prohibit the cartel. See, however, Matsushita, *supra* n. 21 at 368–369.   [28] *Ibid.*

The result is clear: not only competition laws of WTO Members but also their application in individual cases already today are subject to the dispute settlement system. Extending this system to a binding competition agreement to be negotiated within the WTO would therefore be no qualitative *novum*. However, in quantitative terms, such an agreement would of course extend the obligations of WTO Members in the area of competition policy and the scope of the WTO dispute settlement system.

It is clear that where the government's role has a different quality than supervising private competitors, additional WTO obligations can become relevant. For instance, a government's positive contribution to anti-competitive behaviour amounts to a violation of Article XI:1 of the GATT 1994 and possibly of Article 11 of the Agreement on Safeguards, where this behaviour has the effect of restricting imports or exports.[29] In other cases, such a contribution can violate the national treatment obligation. Pursuant to Article 3.4 of the Agreement on Technical Barriers to Trade, Members must not encourage private testing and certification organizations to discriminate against foreign products. Where the government itself becomes the economic operator having exclusive import or export rights, Article XVII of the GATT 1994 mandates the respect of the GATT's non-discrimination disciplines and transactions to be made 'solely in accordance with commercial considerations'. Finally, the grant of monopoly rights can contravene the national treatment obligation where the monopoly is bestowed on a domestic operator for reasons of nationality.

IV. STANDARD OF REVIEW

A. General remarks

An important question of a procedural nature is whether the WTO dispute settlement system allows for an appropriate international review of national decisions in the field of competition. At least in developed legal systems, such administrative and/or judicial proceedings ensure not only an optimal clarification of the facts and the law, but also procedural fairness. These proceedings demand not only special legal expertise, but also a good understanding of the economic context and of economics itself. The WTO dispute settlement system is able to meet these demands, given that in competition disputes panels could be composed of experts who are familiar with the

---

[29] Mitsuo Matsushita, *supra* n. 21 at 368, uses the term 'precipitation'.

questions arising in competition law.[30] The current panel system may well be problematic in many regards,[31] but flexibility in the selection of panellists allows for a tailor-made composition of panels of experts in the particular area of the dispute. A future WTO competition agreement could also expressly provide for the selection of panellists to ensure that panels have the relevant specific expertise. Finally, it should be recalled that panels can resort to experts, who could also be experts on economic, competition related questions. All of this should be able to counter the perceived risk of 'contamination' by trade policy considerations.

As regards the actual conduct of the panel's review, the dispute settlement system applies a standard of review that would be appropriate for competition related disputes. National competition proceedings are not the only instances in which an optimal exploration of the facts must be reconciled with procedural fairness. Similar problems arise in procedures about safeguard measures or anti-dumping and counter-vailing duties. In all these procedures, it would be inept to repeat the entire investigation that has been conducted by the national authorities and/or courts. A WTO panel would not even be in the position to do so. On the other hand, it would be highly unsatisfactory if a WTO panel were to review only compliance with purely formal, procedural aspects in the national investigation procedure. The optimal standard of review therefore has to be positioned between these two extremes.

The panel's standard of review is generally stipulated by Article 11 of the Dispute Settlement Understanding (DSU).[32] In *EC—Hormones*, the Appellate Body defined this standard as neither *de novo* review as such, nor 'total deference', but rather the 'objective assessment of the facts'.[33] The Appellate Body Report in *Argentina—Footwear* stated with regard to the investigative obligations of national authorities under Article 4 of the Agreement on Safeguards that a panel must assess whether the national authorities have examined all the relevant facts and provided a reasoned explanation of how the facts support their determination.[34] In *US—Wheat Gluten*, the Appellate Body refined the national authorities' investigative obligations in safeguard cases and thereby further clarified the panels' standard of review. According to the Appellate Body, Articles 3 and 4 of the Agreement on Safeguards require national authorities to look for and evaluate relevant information *ex officio*, irrespective of

---

[30] Article 8 of the DSU.   [31] See *infra*, section V. C.

[32] Appellate Body Report, *EC—Measures concerning Meat and Meat Products (Hormones)*, WT/DS26/AB/R, WT/DS48/AB/R, adopted 13 February 1998, paras. 115–117.

[33] *Ibid.*, para. 117, with references to previous panel reports.

[34] Appellate Body Report, *Argentina—Safeguard Measures on Imports of Footwear (EC)*, WT/DS121/AB/R, adopted 12 January 2000, para. 121.

whether any interested party involved in the national proceedings has relied upon it.[35]

In *US—Lamb Meat*, the Appellate Body acknowledged that 'panels are not entitled to conduct a *de novo* review of the evidence, nor to *substitute* their own conclusions for those of the competent authorities', but that 'this does *not* mean that panels must simply *accept* the conclusions of the competent authorities'. Instead, they must critically examine the competent authorities' explanation as to whether it fully addresses the nature, and the complexities, of the data, and responds to other plausible interpretations of that data.[36] The most recent Appellate Body Report about the standard of review under Article 11 of the DSU relates to a special safeguard measure imposed under the Agreement on Textiles and Clothing. In this Report, the Appellate Body starts out by stating that the duties of competent authorities simultaneously define the duties of panels in reviewing the investigations and determinations carried out by competent authorities. The Appellate Body further reasons that the panel must put itself in the place of that Member at the time it makes its determination and consequently not consider facts (data) which did not exist at that point in time.[37]

In the absence of a divergent special provision, the standard of review set out for panels in Article 11 of the DSU also applies to the review of actions taken by national authorities or courts in the area of competition—to the extent that these actions (or inactions) are covered by existing WTO law. The clarifications derived from the Agreement on Safeguards do not directly apply to individual decisions in the area of competition. They do, however, correspond to the internal logic of investigations in this area and are therefore suitable for an application by analogy.

B. The special standard of review in Article 17.6 of the Anti-Dumping Agreement

Only one of the WTO agreements, namely the Anti-Dumping Agreement in Article 17.6, sets out a special standard of review that departs from Article 11 of the DSU. This special provision was meant to give Members

---

[35] Appellate Body Report, *United States—Definitive Safeguard Measures on Imports of Wheat Gluten from the European Communities (US—Wheat Gluten)*, WT/DS166/AB/R, adopted 19 January 2001, para. 55.

[36] Appellate Body Report, *United States—Safeguard Measures on Imports of Fresh, Chilled or Frozen Lamb Meat from New Zealand and Australia*, WT/DS177/AB/R, WT/DS178/AB/R, adopted 16 May 2001, paras. 103 and 106.

[37] Appellate Body Report, *United States—Transitional Safeguard Measure on Combed Cotton Yarn from Pakistan*, WT/DS192/AB/R, adopted 5 November 2001, paras. 73 and 78.

a greater margin of manoeuvre than Article 11 of the DSU when they apply the Anti-Dumping Agreement. In the academic literature, it has been suggested that the margin given by Article 17.6(i) should also be allowed within a competition agreement to be negotiated within the WTO.[38]

However, according to the findings of the Appellate Body, Article 17.6(i) ultimately does not differ from Article 11 of the DSU with regard to the standard applying to the *assessment* of facts. In *US—Hot-Rolled Steel*, the Appellate Body stated that it would be inconceivable for the 'assessment of the facts' required from panels under Article 17.6(i) to be anything other than 'objective'.[39] With regard to *evaluating* facts, Article 17.6(i) respects a certain margin of appreciation of national authorities that is not subject to review by requiring no more than that this evaluation be 'unbiased and objective'.

It seems that no one has so far recommended using the special (legal) standard of review of Article 17.6(ii) of the Anti-Dumping Agreement for a future competition agreement. It may be argued that subparagraph (ii) indeed provides for a departure from the general standard of legal review applicable under Article 11 of the DSU. As regards the extent of this departure, one must first ask whether the application of the rules of treaty interpretation can truly result in more than one permissible interpretation.[40] If or where this is the case, the next question would be to what extent Article 17.6(ii) produces different outcomes from the generally applicable principle *in dubio mitius*. The rules of a future WTO competition agreement will presumably be formulated in a much more general and open manner and therefore accord a greater margin of manoeuvre than the detailed and precise provisions of the Anti-Dumping Agreement, to which Article 17.6(ii) applies. Consequently, there will be less need for a provision such as Article 17.6(ii).

Competition laws and individual decisions in the field of competition law are thus to be reviewed—to the extent that they fall under existing WTO obligations—in accordance with the standard of review set out in Article 11 of the DSU. Provided that one agrees with the proposition that the described jurisprudence on Article 11 can be transferred to the area of competition, this standard excludes *de novo* review when applied to measures adopted following a national investigation. However, it

---

[38] M.-C. Malaguti, 'Restrictive Business Practices in International Trade and the Role of the World Trade Organization' in 32(3) *Journal of World Trade* (1998) 117, 145.

[39] Appellate Body Report, *United States—Anti-Dumping Measures on Certain Hot-Rolled Steel Products from Japan* (*US—Hot-Rolled Steel*), WT/DS184/AB/R, adopted 23 August 2001, para. 55.

[40] One should not be excessively dogmatic and sceptical about such a possibility. In many legal orders, there are principles of interpretation requiring that laws be interpreted, wherever possible, in accordance with, for instance, superior law. These principles of interpretation are far from being inoperative in practice.

specifies relatively demanding requirements with regard to the duties of investigation and justification of competent national authorities or courts.

V. FACT-FINDING: A WEAK SPOT IN THE WTO DISPUTE SETTLEMENT SYSTEM

A. The panels' right to seek information, the Members' duty to surrender information, and the panels' right to draw negative inferences

By nature, decisions in the area of competition are fact intensive, but this is similar to investigations about safeguards and anti-dumping or countervailing duties. Resistance against the application of the GATT–WTO dispute settlement system to restrictive business practices also stems from the belief that the powers of investigation of panels are inadequate.[41] It is therefore worth examining whether the investigation powers offered by the current dispute settlement system are adequate.

Fact-finding is reserved to the panels because the Appellate Body's action is limited to a review of legal questions (Article 17.6 of the DSU). Article 13 of the DSU entitles panels to seek information from any appropriate source for the exploration and establishment of the facts necessary to adjudicate on a dispute. This right is broad and comprehensive,[42] and has been understood as an unconditional right, which also covers as a source the Members that are parties to the dispute.[43]

That a Member 'should respond promptly and fully' to any such request for information appears to weaken the panels' right, but it has nevertheless been understood as embodying a full legal duty of parties to surrender requested information.[44] If a Member violates this obligation under Article 13 of the DSU (as happened in *Canada—Aircraft*), the panel may draw negative inferences from the attitude of the non-cooperating Member. The Appellate Body derived this right—the

---

[41] See the majority opinion of the 1958 GATT expert group, *BISD* 9S/176.

[42] Appellate Body Report, *United States—Import Prohibition of Certain Shrimp and Shrimp Products*, WT/DS58/AB/R, adopted 6 November 1998, DSR 1998:VII, 2755, paras. 104 and 106.

[43] Appellate Body Report, *Canada—Measures affecting the Export of Civilian Aircraft (Canada—Aircraft)*, WT/DS70/AB/R, adopted 20 August 1999, DSR 1999:III, 1377, para. 185.

[44] *Ibid.* paras. 188 and 189. This interpretation is one of the very few cases in which the Appellate Body went beyond the ordinary meaning of the text and based its interpretation on the object and purpose of the provision.

use of which is to the discretion of the panel—from the normal function of panels as confirmed by Annex V of the Agreement on Subsidies and Countervailing Measures,[45] which specifically provides for adverse inferences against non-cooperating parties. The Appellate Body did not hesitate to apply the right to also draw negative inferences with respect to the Agreement on Safeguards. However, in this case also, the Appellate Body came to the conclusion that the panel did not overstep the boundaries of its discretion by refraining from drawing negative inferences.[46]

B. The absence of standard rules of procedure for panels and the problem of confidential information

Despite the general obligation of Members to share information and the right of panels to draw negative inferences, there are serious weaknesses in the panel procedure related to the investigation of facts. In contrast to the Appellate Body's own Working Procedures (Article 17.9 of the DSU), there are no such standard procedural rules for panel proceedings, although their existence would be desirable.[47] The Working Procedures set out for panels in Appendix 3 to the DSU are very rudimentary, which is why Article 12.1 authorizes panels to adopt additional or different rules after consulting the parties. Standard working procedures would contribute to the investigation of facts only if it were possible to solve the structural problem of the surrender of confidential information.

The structural problem of confidential information is well known in the area of competition law or anti-dumping. On the one hand, there is the interest of ensuring an optimal clarification of the facts, which militates in favour of using confidential information. On the other hand, principles of 'due process' require that the principle of equality between the parties be respected. It is therefore necessary to make confidential information that one party uses available to the other party. How can this fundamental procedural right be reconciled with the legitimate interest of protecting confidentiality, an interest that is particularly relevant with regard to commercial secrets?

All the WTO agreements that are relevant in the present context require that confidential information be treated as such and not be

---

[45] Appellate Body Report, *Canada—Aircraft, supra* n. 43, paras. 198–203.
[46] Appellate Body Report, *US—Wheat Gluten, supra* n. 35, paras. 170–176.
[47] Appellate Body Report, *Argentina—Measures affecting Imports of Footwear, Textiles, Apparel and Other Items*, WT/DS56/AB/R and Corr. 1, adopted 22 April 1998, DSR 1998:III, 1003, footnote 68 to para. 79, with references to previous reports.

disclosed. Article 6.5 of the Anti-Dumping Agreement, for instance, also provides for an obligation to furnish a non-confidential summary, unless it is exceptionally not possible to give such a summary. In Article 6.2, the Anti-Dumping Agreement attempts to live up to the principle of due process by requiring that all interested parties have a full opportunity to defend their interests. Article 6.9 obliges the authorities to inform all interested parties of the essential facts under consideration before making a final determination. Ultimately, however, the tension between the establishment of the truth and the protection of confidentiality remains unresolved, as Article 12.2.2 requires a public notice of an affirmative conclusion of an investigation to contain all relevant information, 'due regard being paid to the requirement for the protection of confidential information'.

In *Thailand—H-Beams* the panel attempted to derive from Article 3.1 in conjunction with the already mentioned Article 17.6 of the Anti-Dumping Agreement that it is prohibited to rely on confidential considerations that have not been made available to the parties for the determination of the definitive anti-dumping duty. The Appellate Body disagreed and reasoned that neither Article 3.1 nor Article 17.6 prevents the competent national authority from relying on confidential information, as these issues were comprehensively dealt with in other provisions, notably Articles 6 and 12.[48]

In Articles 12.2, 12.3, 12.4, and 12.8, the Agreement on Subsidies and Countervailing Measures contains partly identical, partly similar provisions. The Agreement on Safeguards is less detailed, but Article 3.2 also guarantees the protection of confidential information. *Mutatis mutandis*, the conclusions of the Appellate Body in *Thailand—H-Beams* may probably also be applied here.

The protection of confidential information is not limited to investigations before national authorities, but extends to panel proceedings. Article 13 of the DSU stipulates that confidential information not be revealed without formal authorization. Under Article 18.2 of the DSU, Members must treat as confidential information submitted by another Member which that Member has designated as confidential, and paragraph 3 of the Working Procedures for panels in Appendix 3 to the DSU repeats this obligation. Consequently, the conflict between the clarification of the facts, the protection of confidential information and the principle of due process also arises at the level of WTO dispute settlement. None of the existing procedural rules resolves this conflict either way. Individual panels tried to defuse it by adopting *ad hoc*

---

[48] Appellate Body Report, *Thailand—Anti-Dumping Duties on Angles, Shapes and Sections of Iron or Non-Alloy Steel and H-Beams from Poland*, WT/DS122/AB/R, adopted 5 April 2001, paras. 117 and 118.

procedural rules. In the relationship between the US and the EC, all these attempts failed. The US then refused to make confidential information available. Communicating it only to the panel was not possible due to the prohibition of *ex parte* communications (Article 18.1 of the DSU).

Where no procedural rules for the protection of confidential information can be adopted, a fall-back option for the panel is to persuade parties to submit information that is aggregated, indexed and/or partly blacked out. Such information can be useful to show the development of individual factors over a set period of time, without exposing firm-specific details. This fall-back option, however, is not a sufficient solution in each and every case, especially where information about only one or two commercial actors is involved.

Even if a panel adopts *ad hoc* procedural rules for the communication of confidential information, this is not yet any guarantee that a party will actually make such information available. This is apparent from the already mentioned case *Canada—Aircraft*, in which Canada refused to communicate confidential information, although the *ad hoc* procedural rules that the panel had adopted essentially corresponded to those proposed by Canada itself.[49] Without the cooperation of the parties, the currently practised procedure for sharing and protecting information does not work.

In such a case it may well be appropriate that a panel draws negative inferences from the behaviour of the non-cooperating party. This, however, demands quite a bit of courage from panellists who have been selected for an individual case.[50] In addition, negative inferences are not always the right answer, for instance, where a panel does not succeed in adopting *ad hoc* procedures for the communication of confidential information. In contrast, where the refusal to transmit confidential information appears to be unjustified or even ill-minded, a panel should, in discharging its fact-finding duty, take this into account as an element weighing against the party concerned. The weight to be attributed to this element is the panel's decision and obviously depends on all the other factual elements before that panel.[51] In making this decision, the panel as the sole trier of facts enjoys a degree of 'discretion', since the appellate review is limited to compliance with legal standards.

The Anti-Dumping Agreement, as well as the Agreement on Subsidies and Countervailing Measures, expressly provide that in certain situations the competent national authority may decide on the basis of

---

[49] Appellate Body Report, *Canada—Aircraft*, *supra* n. 43, para. 195.
[50] On structural weaknesses of the panel system, see further section V.C, infra.
[51] See also Appellate Body Report, *US—Wheat Gluten*, *supra* n. 35, para. 174.

'available information'.[52] Those rules practically allow national authorities to do the same as panels under the principle of negative inferences. One could think about generalizing these rules and about extending them to all cases of refused transmission of confidential information. As long as the resort to such rules remains the decision of the body to which the confidential information has not been made available, there should be no fundamental objection. A systematic and automatic resort to negative inferences that would set aside the other factual elements before the panel, however, would be highly questionable. The problem of confidential information can, therefore, not be solved alone through the instrument of negative inferences or the decision on the basis of best information available.

Decisions in the area of competition, by nature, are not only fact-intensive. They also require knowledge and evaluation of confidential information. In competition law, confidential information is even more important than in the areas covered by the Agreement on Safeguards, the Anti-Dumping Agreement, and the Agreement on Subsidies and Countervailing Measures. The problem of the treatment of confidential information has correctly been labelled a 'serious systemic issue'.[53] Already today, its resolution is urgent. In the long run, the WTO dispute settlement system can only be applied satisfactorily to the three areas mentioned, if the conflict between clarification of facts, protection of confidentiality, and the principle of due process can be resolved in a sound manner. For a future WTO competition agreement, the solution of the tension between the establishment of the truth, the protection of confidential information, and procedural fairness is even more import-ant. This dilemma is perhaps the most significant obstacle that would have to be overcome for a satisfactory arrangement for the settlement of disputes in individual competition cases.

In addition to the quasi-judicial settlement of disputes by panels and the Appellate Body, WTO agreements normally provide for discussions in special committees that are responsible for the application and super-vision of the implementation of the respective agreements. A future competition agreement should establish a similar committee for ques-tions related to competition. A sort of peer review of individual decisions in the area of competition would be highly desirable. According to some of the current proposals, a peer review mechanism is to play an import-ant role in a future WTO competition agreement, to some extent, as an

---

[52] Art. 6.8 and Annex II of the Anti-Dumping Agreement and para. 8 of Appendix V of the Agreement on Subsidies and Countervailing Duties. On the interpretation and application of Art. 6.8 and of Annex II of the Anti-Dumping Agreement, see Appellate Body Report, *US—Hot-Rolled Steel, supra* n. 39, paras. 77–110.

[53] Appellate Body Report, *US—Wheat Gluten, supra* n. 35, para. 170.

alternative to dispute settlement.[54] The absence of a satisfactory solution to the problem of confidential information would, however, also stand in the way of such a peer review, given that a competent peer review depends on the knowledge of all relevant facts on which the scrutinized decision has been based. It can be presumed that the agreement on a procedure for the protection of confidential information raises at least as important problems for a system of peer review as it does for the quasi-judicial dispute settlement system.[55]

C. The problem of the panel structure

In contrast to the Appellate Body, which is a permanent institution, panels are established and composed *ad hoc* for each dispute. Panel members are independent and Article 8.2 of the DSU requires explicitly that they be selected with a view to ensuring their independence. For the same reasons, Article 8.3 of the DSU excludes citizens of Members whose governments are parties or third parties in the dispute from serving as panellists, unless the parties to the dispute agree otherwise. Many panellists exercise this function only once, whereas others are reappointed. Serving on a panel is an honour and a personal distinction. It is therefore not surprising if a panel member is interested in being appointed to another panel in the future. Panel members are generally highly qualified persons and there is no doubt about their personal independence. The rules of the WTO dispute settlement system, however, do little to guarantee this independence in an institutional sense. There are only some safeguards based on the obligations contained in the Rules of Conduct.

In contrast to the Appellate Body members who are appointed for several years, one cannot expect that the *ad hoc* appointed panel members act as resolutely as the members of a permanent institution with regard to the outlined problems of fact-finding. This is particularly true of the problems related to confidential information and negative inferences. An additional facet of the weak institutional independence of panellists arises from the main profession of the individuals concerned. Many panellists are Geneva-based diplomats or capital-based trade officials, which means that they already have a full-time job and meet in Geneva for only a couple of weeks. Outside of the dispute, they may often deal with the diplomats or officials of the

---

[54] WTO, *Report (2001)*, *supra* n. 8, paras. 88–90.

[55] The information transmitted to a committee responsible for this peer review would become available to officials of as many as (currently) 146 Members (plus perhaps observers), compared to the much lower number of officials of the (few) Members involved in a dispute governed by rules of confidentiality.

parties to the dispute on other trade matters. The very people participating in the oral hearing of the panel, i.e. the representatives of the parties and panellists, may find themselves around the negotiating table the next day.

In the current reform negotiations on the DSU, the EC has made the case for modifying the structure of panels and for guaranteeing the independence of panel members in an institutional manner.[56] Two means appear to be available to achieve that objective. One possibility and proposal in the current DSU reform negotiations is the establishment of a permanent panel body with fixed membership, which could include the creation of chambers for different subject-matters (agreements).[57] This solution would probably increase the administrative cost of panel proceedings, and concerns in that regard have accordingly been expressed in the negotiations.[58] A different, less radical possibility would be the establishment of a closed list of potential panel members. Such a list would also have to be of limited length. There are also possible combinations of the mentioned suggestions: for instance, the panel chairperson could be part of a standing panel body and the other members be drawn from a list or selected according to the specific expertise required.

Reforming the panel structure would significantly enhance the institutional independence of panellists. If the Members of the WTO wish to move in that direction, the panel structure would again have to receive priority in the current negotiations on the revision of the DSU, which resumed after the Doha Ministerial Conference and for which the General Council has extended the initial May 2003 deadline to 31 May 2004. After the start of the negotiations, when the EC presented and defended their proposal, the panel structure was at the centre of the discussion, but it has lost prominence since, perhaps because it involves a structural and fundamental reform. Accordingly, the last (May 2003) version of the chairman's text does not include any aspect of the proposal to establish a permanent panel body, but the continuation of negotiations is not limited to that text for its basis; it also includes the proposals submitted by Members. The reform of the panel structure would become even more important than it already is now if the WTO dispute settlement system were to be extended to a new competition agreement.

---

[56] *Contribution of the European Communities and its Member States to the Improvement of the WTO Dispute Settlement Understanding, Communication to the DSB Special Session*, TN/DS/W/1 (13 March 2002), p. 2.   [57] *Ibid.*

[58] See *India's Questions to the European Communities and its Member States on their Proposal Relating to Improvements of the DSU, Communication to the DSB Special Session*, TN/DS/W/5 (7 May 2002), p. 3.

VI. THE NON-VIOLATION COMPLAINT

This chapter so far has focused on the most common form of complaint under the WTO dispute settlement system, the so-called violation complaint. The chapter would, however, be incomplete if it did not even briefly mention the much less frequent non-violation complaint. A successful GATT complaint depends on the nullification or impairment of benefits accruing to a Member directly or indirectly under one of the agreements, or the impediment of the attainment of any objective of an agreement. According to Article XXIII:1(b) of the GATT 1994, this condition can also be satisfied by the application by another Member of any measure that does not conflict with the agreement.

Not many non-violation complaints have so far been brought before panels and it has been stated that this remedy 'should be approached with caution and should remain . . . exceptional'.[59] In this vein, it has been suggested in the literature that the non-violation complaint should not be used as a remedy against restrictive business practices without prior normative guidance from the membership of the WTO.[60] Another argument is the historic evolution of the multilateral trading system from a consultation and negotiation forum to binding third-party adjudication which must not 'add to or diminish the rights and obligations' provided in the WTO Agreement (Article 3.2 of the DSU).[61]

Non-violation complaints accordingly may appear not to be the intuitive remedy to be taken wherever restrictive business practices impede imports. Yet, the potential, and practically difficult,[62] role of the non-violation complaint in this field has not only been demonstrated by the *Kodak—Fuji* dispute, but had already been discussed many years earlier. The GATT expert group assessing restrictive business practices under Article XXIII of the GATT 1947 specifically dealt with the question of whether non-violation complaints against restrictive business practices should be possible.[63] There is no doubt that restrictive business practices can obstruct market access in a similar way to a governmental import restriction and they therefore can impede the value of a trade concession. Accordingly, Jagdish Bhagwati argued in 1994 that, through non-violation complaints, competition policy related questions could be brought before the GATT.[64] Finally, the above argument that dispute settlement must not 'add to or diminish the rights and obligations'

---

[59] Appellate Body Report, *European Communities—Measures affecting Asbestos and Asbestos-Containing Products*, WT/DS135/AB/R, adopted 5 April 2001, para. 186; Panel Report, *Japan—Film*, *supra* n. 10, para. 10.37.
[60] Roessler, *supra* n. 24 at 420.   [61] *Ibid.*
[62] Anderson and Holmes, *supra* n. 22 at 551.   [63] *BISD* 9S/176.
[64] Quoted in Roessler, *supra* n. 24 at 414.

under the WTO Agreement can easily be turned on its head: panels and the Appellate Body must not disregard what the non-violation complaint already covers.

A non-violation complaint is successful only if three cumulative conditions are satisfied: (i) the application of a measure by a Member; (ii) the existence of a concession or an advantage resulting in a benefit accruing to another Member directly or indirectly under the agreement in question; and (iii) the nullification or impairment of this benefit as a consequence of the measure of the other Member.[65] Anti-competitive behaviour of private actors without governmental link does not satisfy the first condition. Competition related norms—such as a formal competition act—certainly fall within the concept of a Member's measure. The same should be true about individual decisions in the area of competition. The text and purpose of Article XXIII:1(b) of the GATT 1994 militate in favour of a broad interpretation of the concept 'measure'.[66] It would be more difficult to qualify inaction of a competition authority as a measure. Complete inaction is not the application of a measure,[67] but a measure might be seen in a positive decision not to intervene in a particular case of anti-competitive private behaviour,[68] in an abrogation of a piece of competition legislation, in an exemption, or in the combination of instances of intervention and of non-intervention. The limits imposed on the application of Article XXIII:1(b) of the GATT 1994 therefore seem to be similar to those relevant for Article XXIII:1(a) combined with Article III:4 of the GATT 1994. In other words, the non-violation complaint also depends on the existence of some competition related norms and/or their application. In contrast, it does not cover the case where market access concessions are nullified or impaired by nothing more than private agreements.[69]

The two other conditions of a valid non-violation complaint do not give rise to any particularity that would have to be discussed in the present context. For the sake of brevity, these conditions will not be discussed here. Instead, one may refer to the thorough reasoning in the panel report in *Kodak—Fuji*.[70]

---

[65] Panel Report, *Japan—Film*, *supra* n. 10, para. 10.41.

[66] *Ibid.*, paras. 10.42–10.60.

[67] P. C. Mavroidis and S. J. Van Siclen, 'The Application of the GATT/WTO Dispute Resolution System to Competition Issues' in 31 (5) *Journal of World Trade* (1997) 5 at 11.

[68] On the other hand, such non-intervention can be seen as toleration and hence passivity. See, however, B. M. Hoekman and P. Mavroidis, 'Competition, Competition Policy, and the GATT' in 17 *World Economy* (1994) 121, 141 and 145.

[69] The situation is different, of course, where a Member's government in some way contributes to the anti-competitive private behaviour or to its effects.

[70] Panel Report, *Japan—Film*, *supra* n. 10, paras. 10.61–10.81 and 10.82–10.89, respectively.

VII. THE SITUATION COMPLAINT

The preceding analysis has shown that competition related actions of Members already *de lege lata* must comply with important WTO obligations and that, in addition, non-violation complaints may be filed with regard to a Member's measures taken in the area of competition. It has also been established, however, that such obligations, and equally a non-violating measure—unusual circumstances aside—require the existence of competition laws or other positive action by a Member. Purely private conduct combined with the absence of competition laws or their non-application can most probably be caught only by the so-called situation complaint.[71] For such a situation complaint, however, there is no precedent in the history of the GATT–WTO dispute settlement system so far. Situation complaints have already been raised in a number of cases,[72] but none of them resulted in a panel or Appellate Body report with findings based on Article XXIII:1(c) of the GATT 1994.

Should such a complaint on the basis of governmental inaction against private anti-competitive behaviour be brought in the future, one may expect the objection that the obligation to adopt or enforce competition laws must not be introduced into WTO law through the back door of the rather extraordinary situation complaint. However, even if it has remained largely unused to date, the situation complaint is an established and confirmed part of WTO law.[73] Therefore, what this complaint covers is already part of the world trading system and would not be introduced as a new dimension. In the literature, it has specifically been suggested that (legislative or administrative) governmental inaction against privately erected market barriers may be a case of application of the situation complaint.[74] The fear that the situation complaint could give rise to an obligation to adopt or enforce competition laws is also exaggerated in that the quasi-judicial rules and procedures of the DSU apply only up to the circulation of the panel report:[75] Regarding the adoption and the surveillance and implementation of recommendations and rulings, the old dispute settlement rules and procedures contained in the Decision of 12 April 1989 continue to apply.[76] It remains that the solution, which is adopted at the conclusion of a

---

[71] Except in the case where inaction in one case is coupled with positive action in another, similar case.

[72] See GATT, *Analytical Index: Guide to GATT Law and Practice, Vol. I* (6th edn 1995), II.A.2.(5)(b).

[73] See Art. 26.2 of the DSU. See also Roessler, *supra* n. 23 at 140.

[74] Roessler, *supra* n. 23 at 139–140; Mavroidis and Van Siclen, *supra* n. 67 at 12, note 10; Matsushita, *supra* n. 21 at 370–371.

[75] Art. 26.2 of the DSU. This also excludes an appeal against the panel report.

[76] *BISD* 36S/61–67.

situation dispute (and accepted by the respondent), may provide for the responding government's intervention against the anti-competitive private behaviour. Certainly, given the role of situation complaints in practice, it is not the most likely scenario that a situation complaint of the kind described will emerge in the current dispute settlement system,[77] and others have questioned whether this would provide an appropriate forum,[78] or even argued that such a course of action would be 'risky' and 'premature'.[79]

Should such a situation complaint nevertheless be brought, the panel concerned would have to develop the legal standards to be employed for the decision about its merits. In the literature, it has been suggested that, similarly to non-violation complaints, the complainant would have to establish that it had a reasonable expectation that the situation would not occur and, in addition, a reasonable expectation that the government would intervene to correct this measure.[80] It cannot be ruled out that the conditions of Article XXIII:1(c) would be easier to satisfy than just suggested, given that a cartel can erect barriers to the market access of foreign competitors that are equivalent to a governmental import restriction (as regards the effect on importers). Clearly, the difficulties of the fact-finding process in a situation dispute arising from restrictive business practices are likely to be significant,[81] which reaffirms the statements made in this chapter in that connection.[82]

VIII. CONCLUSIONS AND SUMMARY

The conclusion is simple: to the extent that existing WTO law imposes standards for the design and application of competition laws, the dispute settlement system of the WTO applies. Already today, it therefore potentially has to deal with competition disputes. The dispute settlement system also can deal with such disputes and with disputes under a future competition agreement, as it provides for an appropriate standard of review. Its (partial) non-application to new and additional rules to be negotiated within a future WTO competition agreement (possibly the price to pay to achieve such an agreement) would be a step back—not in a formal sense, but in a substantive sense. In addition, the full application of the dispute settlement system should not present huge problems if the scope of the substantive rules in a future competition agreement is limited to very general obligations.

---

[77] Mavroidis and Van Siclen, *supra* n. 67 at 12, note. 10.
[78] Hoekman and Mavroidis, *supra* n. 68 at 139.
[79] Matsushita, *supra* n. 21 at 370–371.   [80] Roessler, *supra* n. 23 at 139–140.
[81] Roessler, *supra* n. 23 at 140.   [82] In section V.C, *supra*.

The WTO dispute settlement system, however, shows a number of weaknesses in the area of fact-finding, which should become particularly noticeable in the examination of competition-related individual decisions by domestic competition authorities, be it under existing WTO law or under a new competition agreement. These weaknesses are present in the procedure followed by panels, and the most serious weakness relates to the problem of the communication of confidential information. There has not been a satisfactory solution to this problem so far, although the need for a solution is pressing already today. The current reform of the WTO dispute settlement system should provide an opportunity to find such a solution. The current DSU reform should also be used in order to improve the panel structure. It should guarantee greater institutional independence.

If dispute settlement in a future competition agreement were restricted to laws as such, of course, several of the problems related to fact-finding in individual cases are not likely to come up in such disputes. They can, however, still come up in disputes involving individual competition cases under other relevant WTO agreements discussed in this chapter. Similarly, a limitation of the prohibition of discrimination to *de jure* discrimination could encourage Members to challenge (the more frequent) *de facto* discriminatory measures under these other existing agreements, namely the GATT 1994.

Index